Waves
of
Wisdom

Grace, Guts, and Gators
on the Lower Mississippi

Written and Illustrated by

Nancy Scheibe

Raven Productions, Inc.
Ely, Minnesota

Text, illustrations, and photos
© 2012 by Nancy Scheibe
www.RipplesOfWisdom.com

Published December, 2012 by
Raven Productions, Inc.
P.O. Box 188, Ely, MN 55731
218-365-3375
www.RavenWords.com

Cover photo by Cis Hager
Back cover photos by Sara Jo Dickens

Printed in Minnesota
United States of America
10 9 8 7 6 5 4 3 2 1

Library of Congress Cataloging-in-Publication Data

Scheibe, Nancy, 1954-
 Waves of wisdom : grace, guts, and gators on the lower
Mississippi / written and illustrated by Nancy Scheibe.
    pages cm
 Includes bibliographical references and index.
 ISBN 978-0-9835189-6-9 (trade pbk. : alk. paper) --
1. Women--Mississippi River Valley--Social conditions.
2. Women canoeists--Mississippi River Valley--Social
conditions. 3. Canoes and canoeing--Mississippi River.
I. Title.
 HQ1421.S35 2012
 305.40977--dc23   2012046509

Excerpts from *The Language of Letting Go* by Melody Beatty
are used with permission from Hazelden Publishing.

TABLE OF CONTENTS

DEDICATION

This book is dedicated to my sister, Diane, who experienced many hardships in her short life of fifty years; but her big heart, robust laugh, and faith in people sprinkled joy everywhere she went.

Diane was the seventh of eight children. When Mom died, Diane and my other siblings became like my own children. When Diane died two weeks after I got home from this part of the journey, I was devastated.

Diane had a tough life. Things never seemed to come easily to her. She experienced many physical issues, including debilitating migraine headaches and bouts of depression. Her relationships with men were challenging. But through it all she showed the world her smile and unbounded love.

Diane was most proud of raising two incredible, strong sons, Jason and Jonathan. "She was the best mom anyone could ever ask for. She never stopped showing how much she loved us—hugs and kisses whenever we saw her," said Jonathan. The boys are close and pull together during difficult times because of Diane's influence.

She had a unique laugh. When people heard it they would say, "Yep, Diane's here." Her son Jonathan said of her, "If laughter is the best medicine, our mom OD'd on it." Diane was always laughing. She made light of the situations in which she found herself, regardless of how bad they were.

I will remember the goofy things she did. At a Christmas family gathering—in Ely, in August—she attached a wreath to the front of her car and drove it that way for two weeks. She drove her junker cars fearlessly. She broke down on the Mendota Bridge, a major bridge crossing the Mississippi River in the Twin Cities, and told a highway patrolman that one of her brothers would be by any time. She hadn't called any of them. Sure enough, Bruce drove by—and he happened to be in a tow truck. Magical things like that happened for her.

Perhaps it was because Diane had experienced so much pain that she was good at comforting people. It was her real job in life, and she did it well. I miss her.

Acknowledgments

Donna Gehl - Our web mistress, who worked tirelessly behind the scenes for the last two sections of the trip and has attended Gatherings. Donna's beautiful spirit, sense of humor, and can-do attitude made the difference.

Meg Heiman - My editor, who asked probing questions, connected fully with the mission, and made the challenging parts of writing a joy. She brought out the best in me as a writer and gave us all a gift.

Ann Bambas and Sue Cherne - Silent Auction Chairs and Reconnaissance Team who brought creativity and enthusiasm to the successful Silent Auction. Their job during the reconnaissance trip was to assist me in acquiring the knowledge I needed and to make sure I played along the way. We played. Ann and Sue are a joyful dynamic force.

Thea Sheldon, CPCC, The True-Voice Coach for Women - My personal coach, who created an environment where I discovered core beliefs that lurked in the recesses of my brain and were the driving forces behind my behaviors and goals.

Priceless Volunteers

Annette McBride, Alanna Dore, Barbara Cary Hall, Barb Henning, Becky Stigen, Brian & Jayne Grout, Britney Hendrickson, Carol Orban, Cid Rode, Cis Hager, Dan Crealy Jr., Doug Scheibe, Gwyn McKee, Heidi, Sam & Matt Favet, Joette Nuyen, Jonas Perry, Kate Henehan, Kathy Ernst, Kitty Kennedy, Kimberly Bielawski, Nancy Scheibe, Naomi & Nick Lepore, Mike Haney, Mitch Bockman, Pat & Dave Gillett, Patti Zupancich, Sarah Hanson, Sarah & Andy Guy-Levar, Sherry Leveille, Wade Jeske Pharr, White Buffalo Man, Winnie Renner and the many nameless folks who helped during our travels.

Nancy's husband, Doug, working at the Silent Auction

Individual Donors

Adrianne, Ann Bambas, Barbara Cary Hall, Bev Schillenger, Bill and Missy Collins, Carol Orban, Consie Powell, Dave Hunsche, Dick Zahn, Don Sovil, Doug & Nancy Scheibe, Edna Smetana, Gloria Erickson, Gwyn & Mark McKee, Heidi Breaker, Heidi Mae Niska, Heidi, Matt and Sam Favet, Irene Hartfield, Jan & Phil Hogan, Jeanne Bourquin & Peter Pestalozzi, Jen Gubrud, John Buccovich, Judy & John Viken, Kate Henehan, Kay & Bob Tomsich, Kitty Kennedy, Larry Favet, Laura Donovan, Linda Ganister, Lisa Maas, Mary Lax, Megan Divine, Melinda Miller, Mike Haney, Nancy Powers, Pat & Dave Gillett, Peggy & Dale Humphrey, Peg Greenside, Polly Carlson-Voiles, Sandy Scheibe, Sarah Hanson, Sarah Kingston, Susan Chernak, Susan Cherne, Vince O'Connor, Winnie Renner

Business Donors

Thunderbird Wildlife Consulting, Inc., Current Designs/Wenonah Canoe, NRS, Creative Journeys, Inc., Front Porch Coffee and Tea Co., Stokes Bay Resort & Pokorny's Resort, Blue Moon Thrift Store, Brandenburg Gallery, Hand Done T-Shirts, Deborah Sussex Photography, Greenstone Landscaping & Nursery, Jackpine Bob Cary Enterprises, Jim Orcutt Guide Service, Studio North, The Original Bug Shirt Company, White Wilderness Sled Dog Adventures, Wintergreen Dog Sled Adventures, Camp Van Vac, Dorothy Molter Museum, Ely Club House, Ely Steak House, Evergreen Spa & Wellness, Highstone Glassworks, Lady Bug Lodge, Looney's Gift and Rock Shop, Mealey's Gift & Sauna, Mike's Liquor, Pebble Spa, Piragis Northwoods Company, Raven Productions, Inc., Secret Sisters, Sharee Design, Spiritwood Music, Starkman Oil, The Bike Shop, Wolfland Computers, Wolftrack Classic Sled Dog Race

Reconnaissance Trip Assistance

Leonard Naquin for key information about Louisiana and Bayou Lafourche; Carol Stone and Rachell Anderson – Unitarian Church of the River; Barataria-Terrebonne Estuary Program team members; Debbie Hudson – Natchez Chamber of Commerce; Kerry - Millington, Tennessee, Chamber of Commerce; Sally Durkin – Natchez Visitor Center; Stacy Simon – Baton Rouge Area Convention and Visitors Bureau; Sarah Vickery– Cape Girardeau Convention and Visitors Bureau; Steve Shell – Trail Of Tears; Tiffany Parker – Southeastern Missouri University

WAVES OF
WISDOM
JOURNEY
SEPTEMBER 21 TO
OCTOBER 31
2011

THE DREAM
AN INTRODUCTION

*I think it an invaluable advantage to be born and brought up
in the neighborhood of some grand and noble object in nature:
a river, a lake, or a mountain. We make a friendship with it;
we in a manner ally ourselves with it for life.* from *River-Horse:
A Voyage Across America* by William Least Heat-Moon.

Have you ever had a recurring dream and wondered how amazing
it would be to wake up one day and find yourself living it? As an
eight-year-old girl I had dreams about paddling from the headwaters of the Mississippi at Itasca State Park, which I'd seen on a family
vacation, to Minneapolis, where I played on the river's banks almost
every day. With my feet in the water I watched boats pass and imagined
that I'd traveled the whole way on one of them, seeing how a creek just
ten steps across turned into the big river in my backyard.

That eight-year-old's dream resurfaced when I was turning fifty and
wanted to prove to myself that life is just as vital at fifty as at any other
age. I wanted not only to paddle the river, but also to meet the women
who lived along the river's banks. This idea evolved into a mission that
made my fiftieth-birthday adventure trip into a much deeper experience—one that eventually involved spending seven years of my life
raising thousands of dollars, traveling thousands of miles, coordinating
events in which more than 350 women participated, and writing three
books!

As planning progressed, the mission of the trip evolved toward gathering the wisdom of extraordinary women. But I soon discovered that all
women are extraordinary, which made the task at hand formidable. God
or fate or my unrelenting imagination took over, and the dream developed a life of its own. Originally I planned to paddle from the

headwaters at Itasca 595 miles to Red Wing, Minnesota, but after I made it to Red Wing the rest of the dream was revealed: I would paddle to the Gulf of Mexico, another 1,716 miles.

The mission of my dream became clearer: The Ripples of Wisdom quest, as it came to be called, would celebrate the value, power, and sacred abilities of women by providing opportunities for Grandmothers to share their voices, by collecting their truths, and by sowing the seeds of these truths far and wide. Grandmother is a title of great respect borrowed from the Native American culture. This term recognizes wisdom born out of time and experience, embracing women age fifty and older whether or not they have had children or grandchildren.

The core belief behind this project is that women over fifty come from a generation that tends to be silent or unheard. Our culture hasn't placed value on their perspectives, and their valuable stories and healing wisdoms are being lost. I was determined to create an environment where the Grandmothers' words would be heard, valued, documented, and shared.

My dream began to materialize in 2004 when I paddled 570 of the 595 miles from the headwaters of the Mississippi to Red Wing. It continued in 2007 when I paddled 634 of the 683 miles from Red Wing to St. Louis, and again in 2011 when I paddled 523 miles of the remaining 1033 miles from St. Louis to the Gulf of Mexico.

My books *Water Women Wisdom: Voices From the Upper Mississippi* and *Ripples of Wisdom: A Journey Through Mud and Truth* portray the wisdom and adventure from the first and second parts of the trip. This book holds the wisdom of the last part. It tells my story of paddling the lower Mississippi and the stories of the extraordinary women I met along the way.

A dream doesn't develop in isolation. It develops within the arena of relationships, an arena where we learn about our inner selves—our boundaries, values, and truths—and about other people's boundaries, values, and truths. My dream fell like a pebble in a pool of water, creating ripples that touched the lives of those around me. As a child, I had no idea my connection to the Mississippi River would mean so much to so many.

My dream became a shared vision for the main planning team—Kitty, Gwyn, and Heidi. We worked together for eighteen months fund-raising, promoting, creating policies and procedures, inventorying equipment, and doing all the to-dos that are part of any trip.

Kitty, age fifty-six, lives in Ely, Minnesota. This trip was her second of the three. She has a daughter, Aryn, who is married to Chris. Kitty enjoys swimming, skiing, hiking, paddling, snowshoeing, and gardening. She works for the University of Minnesota doing water research, at times in a laboratory and at times on the Great Lakes aboard a research vessel. Kitty has a deep connection with water.

Gwyn, age fifty-one, lives in Gillette, a town in northeast Wyoming. This trip was also her second. She has been married to Mark for fifteen years and has three dogs she considers her children. Gwyn enjoys any activity that takes her into nature. She works as a wildlife biologist and operates Thunderbird Wildlife Consulting, Inc., her business that helps a wide variety of energy-related companies meet their goals in an ecologically responsible way with the least possible impact on wildlife and their habitats.

Heidi, age forty, lives in Ely, Minnesota. She offered a great deal of support during the first two trips—paddling during the first one. She has been married to Matt for fifteen years, and they have an adorable five-year-old son, Sam. Heidi is committed to living purposefully. She enjoys paddling, gathering wild rice, skiing, quilting, basket weaving, gardening, and exploring with her family. She has worked as a guide for Outward Bound wilderness courses and sled dog trips, and she is currently the executive director of the Ely Area Community Health Council.

The interpersonal adventure began during the planning stages. The planning team Grandmothers—Kitty, Gwyn, and myself—shared an unspoken assumption about how planning would go based on the experience and rhythm we shared from the previous trip. We had developed a comfortable joint leadership and quietly moved forward with no need for an assigned leader. We didn't verbalize this to Heidi, who functioned from a more traditional mode of leadership and organization. As the inevitable conflicts arose, the Grandmothers found themselves confused and fell back on the very behavior our mission spoke to: we grew quiet, creating an environment for Heidi that was even more confusing and frustrating. Awareness of what was happening came slowly and painfully. Some of the tension was still present when the journey downriver began, but our love for each other triumphed.

The women who served as van support shared the dream by providing off-water care: making meals, setting up camp, doing laundry, getting groceries, handling vehicle issues, and driving the van to drop off and pick up the paddlers.

Pat, age sixty, lives in Villa Ridge, Missouri. She served briefly as van support during the second trip and was primary van support on this one. She has been married to Dave for thirty-seven years. Pat is devoted to her family of five siblings, seventeen nieces and nephews, four great nieces, and one great nephew. Her passions are quilting, gardening, birds, dogs, traveling, sharing ideas, and music. She worked for twenty-two years with raptors at the Raptor Rehabilitation and Propagation Project (now the World Bird Sanctuary).

Barb, age sixty-three, lives in Ely, Minnesota. She paddled for a few days with us on the second trip and was van support on this one. She has been married to Steve for thirty-seven years and has a daughter, Jessica. Music is her life. Barb is committed to community and enjoys being on several volunteer boards. She had a twenty-five-year career as a professional musician, and she still performs locally. She is currently writing and directing a local musical.

Cis, age fifty-eight, recently moved to Bozeman, Montana, from St. Louis. She paddled with us on the second trip and was a paddler and van support on this one. Cis has been married to Charlie for thirty-seven years and has two children. She and Charlie care for her ninety-two-year-old dad. Cis worked for twenty-two years at the Raptor Rehabilitation and Propagation Project and teaches Taiji and Qigong. She's a Taoist, falconer, paddler, skier, hiker, hermit, and animal lover who is knowledgeable about many things.

Even on a great adventure such as this, people become accustomed to their surroundings and accept as routine occurrences that are far from normal in their daily lives. Paddlers who joined us along the way added to my ability to see the river through fresh eyes and reminded me of the greatness and beauty of the Mississippi River and the natural world surrounding her.

Kit, age fifty-four, lives in Florissant, Missouri. She paddled with us on the second and final trip. As a woman who rose above breast cancer to paddle the Mississippi River, she was an inspiration. She has been married to Bob for twenty-six years and has a daughter, Adrienne, and son, Zach. Kit is still a Girl Scout at heart who enjoys camping and paddling a kayak. Her passion is playing her Native American flute near water and trees. She is a computer geek who chases worms and viruses.

Laurel, age fifty, lives in Hermann, Missouri. She has been married to Keith for twenty-nine years and is a mother of seven. Laurel's passion is her family, and she's devoted to raising her children to be whole, caring, and confident individuals. She is a part-time emergency room physician who honors the birthing process and is working to reform the way women are treated in the medical system.

Sara Jo, age thirty-five, lives in Riverside, California. She is my daughter and was a paddler for several days on each part of this adventure. She has been married to Doug for twelve years. Sara Jo's passions are the environment, climbing, biking, and camping. She has a doctorate in soil and plant ecology and is doing postdoctoral work at the University of California Berkeley.

And I'm Nancy. I'm fifty-seven years old and live in Ely, Minnesota. I have been married to Doug for twenty-nine years, and I have three children–Wade, Sara Jo, and Naomi—and a grandson, Antonio. My career has been eclectic: dishwasher, burger flipper, public speaker, artist, author, school administrator, youth worker, counselor, intuitive-development workshop teacher, and currently owner of a coffee house, The Front Porch, which means I'm back to being a dishwasher.

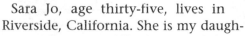

At the end of the second part of the journey, I received a stuffed alligator as a gift from Cis. When she gave it to me she laughed and said, "This is your future." Cis meant the gift as a joke. As I made plans to paddle from St. Louis to the Gulf, many people warned me about the alligators I'd encounter along the way. Alligators are silent lurkers, I heard. They have the most forceful bite ever recorded. They submerge with their prey and spin, behavior referred to as a death roll, drowning their prey and tearing it to pieces. They eat snakes, fish, turtles, birds, and mammals as large as deer. Alligators tend to shy away from people, but attack if they feel threatened. If fed by people, alligators become dangerous because they see people as a source of food.

While paddling on the lower Mississippi I discovered Cis's prediction had a double meaning. Alligators became a metaphor for those things within us that lurk below the surface– those beliefs, fears, and insecurities that, unless allowed to surface where we can contend with them, wait in the darkness and cause havoc in our lives. Those alligators warrant acknowledgment and respect, for they provide opportunities for growth and they unlock our personal power and serenity.

Cis was right: alligators were in my future.

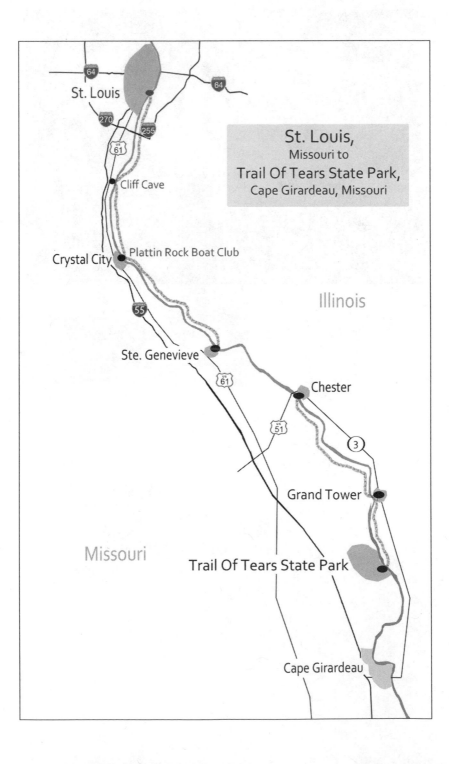

St. Louis,
Missouri to
Trail Of Tears State Park,
Cape Girardeau, Missouri

1

Trail of Tears

This must be what a dog feels like when it finally catches the car it has chased its whole life. After years of planning, my teammate, Kitty, and I were on the road to the third and final part of paddling the Mississippi to gather women's wisdom. We grinned broadly and giggled spontaneously. I was experiencing a strange sense of openness and a feeling of "Now what do I do?"

Woven into the giddiness were heavy threads of stress. Loose ends needed to be tied up, the route at the end of the journey was unclear, and promotional materials needed to be distributed. On the first two parts of this journey I'd learned that nothing was predictable, which added to the sense of adventure. Letting go and trusting things would work out had become the team's mode of operation. As we drove south on Interstate 35, I took a deep breath and attempted to let go of expectations so the trip could unfold on its own.

Compared to the first two parts of the journey, the final section had many unknowns: the speed of the river; whether the longer daily paddling mileage was realistic; if our budget was accurate given the economy; if we could manage the complex strategic details; how cultural differences would play a role; and how turbulent the river was below the confluence with the Missouri River, where we planned to put in. Kitty and I drove through the Twin Cities collecting equipment—walkie-talkies, audio recorders, a GPS, sleeping bag, tent, and life jacket—like squirrels gathering nuts in the fall. We enjoyed dinner in Rosedale with friends, and I had a chance to spend a couple of hours with my grandson, Tony. Then we were on to Red Wing, Minnesota.

We arrived at Sherry's after dark. When she greeted us, her smile lit up the night. Sherry had provided van support on the previous trip. Her sense of adventure was a gift that opened many doors and hearts. Ironically, heart and health issues prevented her from joining us this time. She was in the process of selling her home and very excited about her yet-to-be-determined next adventure. Sherry talked about how she was entering a new phase of her life and welcomed the changes that were coming.

The next morning Katie and her daughter, Constance, joined us for breakfast at Sherry's. We'd met them at the Lake City Gathering in 2007. Eighty-five-year-old Katie had difficulty containing her exuberance. She and Constance had recently taken a trip to Anchorage, Alaska, and she told us about the majestic scenery and the highlight of the trip—big-game fishing, a first for her.

"There's nothing like being there," Katie said with a dreamy look. "You don't get the same feeling watching it on TV. We were fishing for halibut. My line was only out there for two minutes when I caught the first fish. It was exciting! I got to do the greater share of reeling the fish in. You have a minute to decide if you're going to keep it or not. The deck hand said mine was a keeper. It was twenty-five pounds and better than twenty-four inches in length." She held her hands apart showing us the fish's size. "While we were in Alaska we saw sea lions, otters, and a huge bear that was fishing along shore. The trip was a great experience."

"I had a great experience once volunteering on a tall ship," said Constance. "I lived in a three-and-a-half by six-foot space. All I took with me for the entire two months had to fit in a backpack. When I came home after that marvelous trip, I had a difficult time dealing with the vastness of my space and all the stuff I had. That experience moved me to make some decisions that I'd been pondering. One was to sell my house and donate, sell, or give away most of my possessions. Doing that allowed me to share a house with Katie. I'm in Lake City full time now, and I'm so happy. I wake up every morning and look out at Lake Pepin or walk over to my boat. I can easily get out on the water in my kayak."

"I need to tell you what Constance did with the majority of her things," said Katie. "My son was the head of the flood relief in the Zumbro Valley. He needed a lot of things. And Constance practically outfitted a home for someone in Hammond. She brought very few things to my house. It was difficult for her to let go of some of her things."

"I bet you feel lighter now," said Kitty.

"Indeed, and I still have more stuff to get rid of," said Constance. "I'll feel even lighter after that. The gentleman in Hammond whose home I helped furnish said, 'Why would you give me new stuff–stuff that's so nice?' I said, 'Because it's what I have to give and you deserve it. Why would I not give you the best that I have to give?' It felt right to me."

Constance and Katie walked us out to the van. Katie asked what the names of our kayaks were. Kitty had named hers Monarch. I hadn't thought of naming my new white kayak. Katie took one look at it and said, "I think yours should be called Hope."

"I like the meaning behind that," I said. "I think I'll call her Hope Floats."

Kitty and I drove toward Winona, Minnesota. We traveled Highway 61, which parallels the Mississippi River, and I saw a great blue heron flying along the opposite shore. I pointed her out to Kitty. We smiled and said, "Good morning, Kee." Kee is Keewaydinoquay, our friend Dan's treasured Native Grandmother. During her lifetime Kee was dedicated to bringing peace and balance back to all people. After her passing, many believed her spirit had returned in the form of a great blue heron. Great blue herons were with us every day of the journey from the headwaters on down. When we needed to choose a direction they often guided us by flying along one of the routes we were considering.

In Winona we stopped at the shop of one of our sponsors to pick up some paddles and my mango-colored kayak. I'd paddled that one since this adventure started in 2004. The folks at Wenonah Canoe had generously given her a tune up. After twelve hundred miles and seven years, she needed some tender loving care. On this last trip we'd be enjoying a rainbow of Current Design Squall kayaks: white, mango, green, and red.

Owner Mike Chichanowski sent us to tour the factory while Scott, one of the Wenonah Canoe crew, took a short break from building canoes to fix a minor problem on our trailer.

Our tour guide, Dave, explained how they made kayaks. For a roto-molded polyethylene (poly) kayak, the poly powder is poured into a metal mold. There's one mold for each kayak design. In the oven the mold is continuously rotated and moved back and forth so the poly melts evenly, coating the surface of the mold. The poly is removed from the mold, cooled, and sent to the finishing department. The process takes seven hours to complete. Making a composite kayak involves more steps and takes thirty-four hours to complete. Our forty-minute tour of the factory helped us appreciate the technology that had gone into making our kayaks. We thanked Dave for the tour and got back on the road.

I continued working on planning details while Kitty drove. Our mobile modem proved invaluable as it provided Internet access anywhere our phones had service. With so many people participating in the journey, planning was in constant flux. I preferred to have everything tied up in a neat package before I headed out, but life likes to tinker with me. Not having the promotions in place for Gatherings downriver gnawed at me.

We were not even to St. Louis when I got a call about a gap in our van-support schedule due to a family emergency. Having faced the issue on the previous trip, I trusted the solution would be revealed. We sent emails and made phone calls, getting the word out that we needed help, and I let the issue go.

On an open stretch of freeway, I looked up from my computer to enjoy the scenery. I glanced at the rear view mirror in time to see our bright yellow and red five-gallon water jug fly off the trailer, bounce a few times on the side of the highway, and skip out of sight. Kitty pulled to the shoulder and slowed the van to a stop as I put on my running shoes. I didn't get far before a man pulled over to assist me. He thought our van had broken down and I was running to town. About a quarter mile back, I spotted the water jug deep in the weeds. I grabbed it and ran back to the van.

A few hours later as we neared St. Louis we drove over the Missouri River and saw churning water, huge whirlpools, and floating trees. I felt my heart skip a beat; my anxiety rose. The Missouri dumped into the Mississippi a few miles north of where we'd be putting in the next day. I felt unnerved looking at the Missouri River, knowing how crowded with industry and barges the first five miles would be for us. The unseasonably high water in the Missouri River could make the Mississippi even more dangerous than usual at our starting point. Kitty and I agreed to decide in the morning where we'd start, based on the conditions. By not putting in at the St. Louis Gateway Arch as planned and instead starting at Cliff Cave County Park, we could bypass the first five miles of dangerous congested water.

Late in the afternoon we arrived at Dave and Pat's in Villa Ridge, a suburb of St. Louis. We were joined by Cis, who would paddle with us the next week, and Kit, who would start with us the next day. Barb also joined us. She would be van support with Pat. We repacked the trailer and van with their additional gear.

Repacking became a creative challenge that involved getting six kayaks and everybody's gear on board with enough room left for us. Every inch had to be utilized. While we packed, women arrived to join us for a send-off celebration dinner. Becky, Mallika, Liz, Jody, Jo, Celia, and Connie filtered in, watched, and assisted where they could.

We enjoyed a delightful potluck dinner with new and old friends. Barb played guitar and sang folk songs, and we chatted about our journeys, past and present. The evening flew by quickly, and before Cis and Kit headed home, we convened to discuss details of what to expect on the river. After reviewing what the first five miles had in store for us, we decided Kit would join us at Cliff Cave County Park. We planned to be on the water by ten o'clock the next morning.

September 21, Day One

Kitty, Pat, Barb, and I said goodbye to Dave and headed to the river. Cis and Kit would meet us at the river. As we drove down the freeway, talking and listening to Barb sing "Lazy River" by Louis Armstrong. "Up a lazy river by the old mill stream. That lazy, hazy river where we both can dream. Linger in the shade of an old oak tree. Throw away your troubles, dream a dream with me."

I saw in the rear view mirror the trailer doors flapping in the wind. Visions of gear scattered across the freeway and our dodging traffic to retrieve the gear sent a wave of fear through me. We pulled over quickly and ran to the trailer. The doors stood open with the locks precariously hanging on the latches. A quick scan inside revealed everything was miraculously in place with the exception of Barb's pink backpack with her clothes in it. The hunt was on.

We climbed into the van and backtracked. Pat called Dave to ask him to join our quest from the other direction. All the while Barb was a great sport. Jokes about sharing underwear and finding great outfits at the local thrift store flew around the van. In a few minutes, Dave called. He had found the backpack undamaged by the side of the road near their home at the first sharp left turn. Its bright color made the backpack easy for him to spot.

Our eagerness to start our adventure had made us careless. We had been lucky this time. We made a rule to keep the padlocks in place and to check them each time we got in the van.

Gear secured, we got back on the road, and our excitement again rose quickly. My heart pounded when the Gateway Arch came into view. I wasn't sure if my heart's pounding was caused from excitement for the start of the trip or fear of the turbulent water I'd seen yesterday.

We pulled onto the cobblestone landing where Kit, Cis, Laurel, Anna, and Anna's daughter and grandson gathered to see us off. Although I was happy and touched to see them, my attention was on the river and our safety. I got out of the van and headed straight to the shoreline. As I scanned her surface, I put my sandaled feet in the river. The Mississippi

River had effortlessly absorbed the bulging Missouri River and was not turbulent. I felt as if I'd come home to my partner. I was calmed.

Kitty met me by the shore and I smiled. "Let's do it," I said.

We got our kayaks and gear to the river's edge and took a few moments to conduct a ritual that we had performed every morning of the journey. We sang a sacred Anishinabe song taught to me by a friend, Dan Creely, when he first heard about my quest. The song calls us to stand together to fulfill our obligations to nature, the spirit world, the Creator, and future generations. Dan introduced me to kinnikinnick, an evergreen ground cover used by some Native Americans as an offering to the Great Spirit. I'd been instructed to say a prayer of gratitude to Spirit and drop an offering of kinnikinnick into the water for safe travel. "I thank you for keeping us safe on the water and on land. I thank you for the women's hearts you touch and making them a part of this amazing journey. I thank you for the honor of doing this work and experiencing your great beauty."

The Gateway Arch loomed over our heads as Kitty and I paddled into the river with well wishes shouted from our friends.

"See you at Cliff Cave County Park!" Pat shouted. She, Barb, and Kit would meet us there for lunch.

The first strokes felt reminiscent and right, allowing the remainder of fear I held about turbulent waters to subside. Not far from shore, floating in the main current, I paused to place into the water

Photo by Barb Hall

each of the aspiration sticks from the Gathering we'd held in Ely last June.

Traditionally we end Gatherings with a closing ritual in which each woman is given two pieces of yarn. The women are instructed to wrap the yarn around the first stick, the "releasing stick," while they visualize tying the struggles and pains of their life onto it. The first stick is respect-fully placed in the fire, and the women are encouraged to say a prayer. While wrapping the second stick, the "aspiration stick," the women visu-alize their hopes and dreams. The women are given a choice: they can send the aspiration sticks with us to be placed into the river at the begin-ning of the trip, or they can place the sticks into the fire. Many women choose to send the aspiration sticks to the river. As I placed the sticks in the water, I said a simple prayer of gratitude to Spirit, "Thank you for this woman's contributions to our world." The sticks representing the women made a colorful flotilla on the surface.

That first day paddling was exhilarating. I looked over at Kitty and saw the excitement bubbling up. She started with a smile that grew larger. Then her eyebrows and shoulders went up, then the excitement peaked and she yelled, "This is so cool!" The current tugged at us, pushed us forward, and periodically spun us a little as it made its way down the channel. We remained on high alert for signs of danger, keeping a look-out for objects up and down the river. We knew we had to be vigilant concerning what was behind us. The current could quickly push some-thing from that direction, and we wouldn't necessarily hear it before it was on top of us. Anything coming at us from downriver moved more slowly, so we'd be more likely to see it.

For the first seven miles the river was relatively narrow. Forty-one industrial facilities were located along that stretch including oil tanks, warehouses, cement plants, harbor services, chemical plants, coal facili-ties, and riverboat cruise docks. Their barges were parked alongshore. When a tug pushing barges passed, the movement created three- to five-foot waves that we rode as we shouted for joy.

I was thoroughly enjoying the perfect weather–temperature in the seventies with a light breeze–when my phone rang. My friend Bill called to be sure the SPOT, a satellite GPS messenger he'd loaned us, worked. We had the SPOT with us for two reasons. First, it had an SOS feature so that in the event of a life-threatening emergency, we could press a red button and the device would send an SOS message to notify emergency services of our GPS location so they could send assistance. Second, the device's track-progress feature allowed us to regularly send and save our location to a Google Maps page that allowed people to track our progress downriver.

Bill called because we hadn't showed up yet on the Google Map. Equipment is only as good as the operator: I hadn't used the SPOT cor-rectly. Paddling got a bit tricky as I tried to talk on the cell phone in the middle of the river with barges going by. I floated while listening to his directions, put the phone and the SPOT onto my lap when I needed to paddle past a barge or keep the bow of my kayak pointed downriver, and then quickly picked the phone up for more directions. I repeated the process a couple of times and had us laughing at the awkward situation. Bill's patience and instructions paid off. At last he said, "It looks like you're going under the Highway 255 bridge." That was exactly where we were.

Expectantly, I scanned the shores for Kee. Even in the most industrial areas, a great blue heron sends us off. Today was no exception. She rose from her perch in a tree and flew downriver, calling to us. I said, "Good morning, Kee. Thank you for joining us again."

Approaching Cliff Cave County Park, we passed a dredge near our landing. The Army Corps of Engineers regularly dredges the river channel to maintain its depth. We got close to the dredge when we landed, and I was captivated by the enormous amounts of water that poured from it. What resembled a substantial waterfall poured back into the river from two sides.

Our first landing proved to be challenging, and I sensed that would be the norm. Rocks and mud formed a steep bank. We secured our kayaks and met Pat, Barb, and Kit under the picnic shelter where Pat had a variety of cold-cut sandwiches, fruit, and chips waiting for us.

"Twelve miles down. Seventeen to go!" I said.

Kit smiled and said, "Let's do it." Her tone was a combination of excitement and psyching herself to override her fear.

Heading back to our kayaks I walked to the other side of a ravine where I had a clear view of the river. I saw barges parked alongshore and traveling on the river. Wing dikes rose at the edges of the river, and lush vegetation grew along the banks. I watched the team effort required to get Kit's kayak and gear to the water. Kit, Kitty, Pat, and Barb made their way through tall grass to get to the edge of the embankment. Two carried the kayak across the mud, over driftwood, over the rocks, and into the water, while the others carried her paddle and deck bag. As we soon discovered, this was a typical embankment for the water conditions.

Pat smiled quietly while Barb gave us an exuberant farewell. Kit, Kitty, and I headed downriver. I pointed out the wing dikes that reached four feet above the water level. North of St. Louis, the same rock structures were called wing dams. I'd been concerned that the wing dikes would be under the surface due to the influx of water from the Missouri River. In high water conditions we could paddle over them. In other conditions, they became waterfalls that we'd have difficulty seeing in time. Even though we could see the wing dikes, we had to depend on our sense of hearing to alert us to danger. Due to our low profile on the water we could be on top of danger before we saw it, so we listened intently for the sound of rushing water to warn us.

For safety reasons we paddled close to each other. Whenever the distance between kayaks became more than about forty feet, we closed our ranks. We wanted to be close enough that if someone got in trouble, the others could get to her quickly.

On the Missouri side of the river we passed a large, stylish home set back from the twenty-foot river embankment; its enclosed porch along two sides was inviting. People watched us from a deck built out over the water. Nearby was a marina with small personal watercraft.

We took a break on a large sandy beach nestled between two wing dikes. Anytime anyone needed a break we pulled off, hopefully onto a sand bar and not onto rocks. We made a point to stop every couple of hours to stretch our legs. Riding in a kayak for long periods of time caused our legs to get stiff and our backs to ache. Regular intervals of walking or even standing on shore helped keep us limber.

Staying hydrated was essential. We carried water bottles that we drank from often, and regular breaks also allowed for needed restroom stops. For restrooms, we found whatever shrubbery or piles of driftwood were available for privacy.

We carried easy-to-eat snacks—cheese sticks, energy bars, and gorp (a mixture of peanuts, raisins, M&Ms, almonds, and cashews)—that we munched in our kayaks and during our breaks. Our goal was to eat small portions often, before we got hungry, to keep our energy level even. Lunches on the river were often hard-boiled eggs, cheese, and sandwiches. I usually had an electrolyte replacement drink too.

Shortly after lunch we passed the confluence of the Meramec River and moved into a long stretch of river with no industry. Even though we were still in highly populated areas, we were surrounded by wilderness.

Fatigue from paddling twenty-nine miles was setting in when we arrived at Plattin Rock Boat Club, where Pat and Barb waited on the dock for us. Our plans changed from staying in a motel to camping at the boat club after Pat and Barb contacted Roger, the president of the boat club, to confirm our use of their boat ramp. He suggested we camp right there at the landing.

After camp was set, Pat made dinner. She loved the creative challenge of finding things in our cooler or food box and putting them together for a meal. She found zucchini, tomatoes, onions, and carrots, stir fried them, and served it over quinoa. She added her own blend of delicious spices she had brought from home. She enlisted one of us to help her with the chopping. I had brought a big bag of tomatoes from my garden at home; some were green. They ripened in a timely fashion and lasted until the end of the trip.

We had a great view of the river. Roger came by to make sure we had everything we needed. He leaned his tall body against his truck and told us that the spring before, the boat club's property was under two feet of water, and every year they got another layer of silt. The majority of the silt comes from the Missouri River and the Plains states. Their new clubhouse had to be built one foot higher than the crest of the flood in '93.

Roger and two other club members who came to visit with us warned about the bendway weirs, known as ben weirs, near Ste. Genevieve. Ben weirs are a series of underwater upstream-angled stone sills designed to control and redirect currents throughout a bend of a river. They're located in the navigation channel low enough to allow normal river traffic to pass over unimpeded. Weirs are designed to reduce erosion on the outer bank of the bend.

"That water can spin a big boat around," Roger said. "I can't imagine what it'll do to your tiny boats. Whatever you do, don't meet a barge in there."

This was the third time that warning had been offered. We took notice.

The sun dropped quickly, and mosquitoes drove us to our tents. I stayed up posting information and photos on our Facebook page, downloading photos, making sure everything that needed charging was getting charged, and journaling—a routine I would repeat each evening. I drifted off to sleep while a barred owl called in the distance.

September 22, Day Two

Threatening rain motivated us to move quickly in the morning. Headed to the water, I came over the top of the embankment, saw our three colorful kayaks lined up on the boat ramp, and experienced a wave of joy. The journey was underway. As with any venture when several people traveled together, we allowed ourselves time to find a rhythm. We experienced some stumbles, but the group melded quickly into a team.

At breakfast Kitty pulled out one of the bottles of water she'd collected from the headwaters of the Mississippi. "On my way back from a visit with family in North Dakota, I stopped at the headwaters to gather water from the river. I wanted to carry the water from the headwaters down to the Gulf and share it with others as we travel," she said, "but I realized on the way to the headwaters that I didn't have any tobacco to offer to the river. So I decided to watch at the gift shop area in the park for someone smoking and offer to buy a cigarette.

"A man pulled out a cigarette, and I walked over and asked to buy one. He smiled and said I could have one. I thanked him for the cigarette and started down the path that leads to the headwaters. It was a generous gesture for this gentleman to give me the cigarette, so I walked back to where he sat to thank him again. I explained that I stopped smoking eleven years ago and that I needed the tobacco to make an offering to the river so that I might carry water away on our journey down the Mississippi River. He looked at me and said, 'Thank you for honoring our traditional ways.' I hadn't noticed until that moment that he was a Native American."

Kitty had made a tiny bottle for each of the paddlers and van support helpers. She had labeled each bottle: "This bottle was collected at the Mississippi River headwaters. As this river moves us, may we remember CLARITY – of water, of ROW mission, our thoughts and actions." We marveled at the crystal clear water she had collected, a stark contrast from the muddy water we paddled.

We'd been hearing a loud cicada serenade since we arrived in camp. Pat and Kitty pointed out cicada skins that hung on the bark of a cottonwood. A cicada sheds its skin like a snake and leaves behind a prehistoric-looking replica of itself. Dozens of cicada skins hung all around the tree.

A gentle steady rain started shortly after we launched and accompanied us for several miles. Occasionally the rain poured heavily. The sound of raindrops on the rain gear, kayak, and water created a soothing solitude accented by the rhythm of paddling. I experienced an altered state of mind that left me feeling one with the river and the rain.

The banks of the river were distinctive. The Illinois side was flat, and we were unable to see past the trees that lined the shore. Sandstone bluffs thick with tree cover towered above us on the Missouri side. Caves sat twenty feet above the water and reached deep into the bluff. We passed rock quarries that astoundingly cut into the earth, removing entire bluffs.

Watching my paddle move in and out of the water, I felt grateful that I *could* paddle. A year after the second part of this adventure, I experienced discomfort in my right arm. The pain grew and decreased my ability to use that arm until it became useless. A simple movement of my wrist was excruciating.

My ailment was diagnosed as a frozen shoulder. The prognosis of only gaining 75 percent use of my arm was devastating. With that diagnosis, I couldn't safely paddle the Mississippi, and the restricted movement would limit what I could do as an artist. I asked my physical therapist why I should anticipate only 75 percent range of motion, and he said people typically stop therapy because it's too painful. I couldn't imagine compromising my physical abilities for the rest of my life because therapy was too hard, and I decided to give therapy all I had, no matter how painful.

Two or three times a week for nine months I experienced some of the worst pain I could imagine and understood why people quit. I wanted to quit too. Eventually I regained 95 percent use of my arm, and since then I've continued to push that shoulder.

From the start of the shoulder issue, I learned many lessons. For one, I had to let people do things for me, which was almost as agonizing as the pain in my arm. While I healed, I had bonding time with my son-in-law Doug, who was recovering from knee surgery. When we sat on the couch and watched everyone else go outside to play in the snow, I gained a small sense of what it must be like for people with permanent disabilities–another lesson. In therapy, I learned lessons about how the nervous system is interconnected as pain radiated into other parts of my body, and I experienced an increase in pain tolerance. And I learned humility. I was lucky, I realized. Some people in therapy had conditions that wouldn't get much better.

Through it all, humor was my best friend. Some people said, "You'll laugh about this later." I decided not to wait until later and found ways to laugh sooner. In between screams at therapy, I joked. All I had to do was state something obvious, like what wounded animal I sounded like that day. I learned my endurance was intimately connected to perceived gain. Now, on the river, each paddle stroke came with a sense of accomplishment and deep gratitude.

A tugboat shuffled barges on the opposite side of the river and brought my thoughts back to the present. The tugboat's erratic movements made it difficult to tell if the tug would come across to our side. Kit focused on the tug and forgot to look ahead. A red buoy came fast, and she was headed right into it. An encounter with a buoy can be dangerous. If the current catches the kayak it could be pulled into the buoy and flipped over or pulled under by the water rushing around the buoy.

"Kit, paddle!" I was concerned she might not hear me because she can't wear her hearing aids on the water, but she looked up, grabbed her paddle, and paddled hard and fast, barely clearing the buoy. Watching her left me breathless. A look of relief crossed her face, then one of guilt, as if she had done something wrong and let us down.

"Wow! That was a close one," I said.

"I was only watching the tug," she said apologetically.

"That's understandable," said Kitty. "He was really moving around."

"That's a good lesson for all of us to keep checking everywhere," I said. Then I started laughing "You sure can move when you have to."

Immediately after the buoy encounter, we approached the curve of ben weirs with trepidation. We slowed our pace while earnestly scrutinizing the surface of the water ahead. A knot in my stomach grew as we neared the curve, but I didn't see anything. A large sand bar stretched into the distance on our right. We stayed close to it to avoid the faster current on the outside of the bend. We found little turbulence or whirlpools. Across the river were vigorous ripples. The curve stretched three miles with the bulk of the ben weirs on the downriver end. Heavy rain made the distant shore's pale shadows difficult to use to judge distance. After paddling awhile, I looked down at my charts and realized we'd passed the curve without incident.

The rain continued. The dampness wicked up my shirtsleeves under the raincoat and seeped down my neck. I began to feel damp and chilled. With some paddle strokes I reached down so my hands were under the surface of the water for a few moments to warm them. The water was warmer than the air. We packed neoprene gloves to wear on colder days, but I didn't have the gloves with me.

We reached Ste. Genevieve where Barb was on shore watching for us. As we neared, Pat joined her. The rain continued as we loaded the kayaks onto the van and trailer. Driving into Ste. Genevieve we saw one of several flood markers located along the river. The marker at Ste. Genevieve had ten floods listed between 1943 and1995. The worst was in 1995 when the river crested at forty-four feet.

Later, warm and dry, we enjoyed dinner at the Old Brick House, which boasts being the first brick building west of the Mississippi, built in1788. Ste. Genevieve was settled in the 1740s. Its earliest residents were French Canadian, and the Old Brick House retained its French character.

While talking about our day over a salad and fried chicken Kit said, "There were two parked barges that we paddled through not too long after another barge had gone through that part of the channel. We had nice rolling waves. I cut the corner too quickly when I went around the second of the parked barges and was surprised by lateral waves. I had rollers coming in front and got hit by another wave broadside. I won't say that I was afraid, but I was surprised. I switched from using my core muscles to using my arm muscles and dug the paddle in hard." She rubbed her left shoulder. "I was exhausted and sore by the time we reached our takeout point.

"Something I need to pay attention to is not getting so close to stationary objects and buoys. The thing that's hard to remember is even though it looks like you're standing still, you aren't. When you stop paddling, you're still moving with the river. That's hard for me to get used to because I paddle on lakes. All in all, it was a great day."

Kitty and I shared our concerns regarding the river's not moving as fast as we had anticipated. We had been traveling six miles per hour, but our itinerary was based on the river's moving ten to twelve miles an hour. Everyone offered solutions, but we didn't have the charts or maps we needed to make decisions. We needed to reconsider the length of our paddling days. I realized we might not be able to do the planned distances within the timelines I had set.

Back at Hawn State Park, Pat arranged things in the cook tent while we relaxed and enjoyed the forest of pine and oak. Our tents were near Pickle Creek, which was fed by Pickle Springs. Eventually we retreated to our tents. My exhausted body was soothed to sleep by the creek babbling a few feet from my head.

September 23, Day Three

Fellow camper Charlie Wilson visited our camp. In his introduction he compared himself to the original Charlie Wilson of *Charlie Wilson's War* fame. He took one look at our kayaks and called them "squirts." He

thought we were "a little touched" to be out on that river in them. He had a dog with him that he and his wife had recently rescued. The dog had been attacked once by pit bulls, and he warned us it was unpredictable. It was not the first dog they'd rescued with a similar background.

After we broke camp, we traveled back roads to find the Kaskaskia State Memorial to see The Liberty Bell of the West. The bell has a crack in it just like the one in Philadelphia, and it's housed in a bell shrine, a red brick building bearing the date 1737. From a plaque on the building we read: "This bell was given by King Louis XV of France to the Catholic Church of the Illinois Country in 1741." For many years, we learned, the bell rang on the Fourth of July. To view the bell, we walked to a double door that had an iron gate across the front of it. We pressed a button and the inside door opened, allowing us to view the bell but not to enter the building. Next to the bell shrine stood the Church of the Immaculate Conception, a beautiful red brick structure built in 1675.

We crossed the river on the Chester Bridge, which was built in 1942, the only bridge crossing the Mississippi between St. Louis and Cape Girardeau. Then we stopped at the Chester Illinois Welcome Center. Chester is the hometown of Elzie Segar, the man who created the character Popeye the Sailor. A bronze statue of Popeye stands in front of the welcome center, and other Popeye characters, such as Bluto and Olive Oyl, are located around town. Chester even has a Spinach Can Museum.

I began to notice a change in weather and directed my attention to the sky. Downriver was a picture-perfect sunny day. Upriver, however, the Chester Bridge was a ghost against a darkening blue-gray sky. Threatening billowy clouds hung low while lower wispy clouds raced ahead of the rain that poured in the distance. We hurriedly prepared to leave Chester. Kitty, Kit, and I got on the water with the same intention as those lower wispy clouds–to stay ahead of the rain.

The landscape south of Chester, called Turkey Bluffs, was lush green and speckled with hints of fall's reds and oranges. I felt a longing for the fall colors of home. Six miles into our twenty-eight mile paddle, we lost our race against the rain. We gathered together and floated, assisting each other with rain gear so no one would roll over while putting it on.

Barge traffic was heavy. Many barges carried heavy loads of rock from the quarries. The barges moving downriver created big waves, which were exciting to ride. Our kayaks rose to the crests where we briefly felt thrust forward before the nose of the kayak dove into the oncoming wave. The waves continued for several minutes.

"What do you think?" I asked Kit as we bobbed about. "Do you like the waves?"

"Yes," she replied, grinning, "after the first one."

The rain eventually subsided. With fatigue setting in, we headed to Rockwood Island for lunch. We picked out a spot to land and paddled directly for it, but the strong current had a different plan. No matter how hard we paddled, we couldn't get closer to shore. A buoy a good half mile downriver came at us fast. The current was unnerving. Using diversionary tactics, we got around the buoy, hit calmer water, and landed.

"The buoy came up fast and got my heart pumping," said Kitty. "I kept paddling harder and harder, and the buoy kept coming closer and closer."

"I felt like a buoy magnet," said Kit "I thought the buoy was coming to get me."

"I have a theory to explain why the buoys come after us," I said as I secured my kayak on shore. "Those buoys have been out here for years, and they only get to see ugly old men traveling the river. Now they have a rare opportunity with three hot, gorgeous women paddling by, and they're furiously pulling us in for a closer look." We laughed. "Kit, maybe it's just you they're after." She blushed.

Paddling the Mississippi takes a different kind of paying attention than paddling the lakes in Minnesota. There's little time to make decisions about the best way to handle danger. We needed to listen constantly and carefully for the sound of rushing water, often our only warning sign. Windy days concerned me because the sound of the wind had the potential to drown out the sound of rushing water.

Waiting for barges to pass made our lunch break longer than we'd intended, but the time ashore gave us a needed rest. We watched the barges, and I studied the driftwood nestled in the sand. I checked my watch. It was four thirty. I studied the charts and determined we'd need to paddle hard to reach our destination before dark, which would hit about six thirty. Our fatigue concerned me, particularly Kit's, which was evident in her inconsistent paddle strokes.

Even though I couldn't find another takeout location on the charts, I called Pat to arrange an early pick up. She conferred with local folks at the campground for options. With concern in her voice she told us there were none. With fourteen miles to go, we pressed on. Realizing we needed motivation, I called out the remaining miles as we passed them. Kit cheered each time.

Fatigue tends to create long periods of silent paddling, which offer time for reflection. I realized I wasn't in the mindset I wanted for the trip. I was too stressed over details not yet finalized, and I had a sense of hypervigilance regarding others on the water. My head was like a pinball machine as my thoughts bounced from my surroundings—the reflections and subtle color changes on the surface of the water—to my concerns—emails to the media in Vicksburg, Grosse Tete, Baton Rouge, and Natchez that I needed to get out that night—back to my surroundings—the vast, changing landscape the river had carved out of rock—and again to my concerns—the call I needed to make to a woman who worked for the newspaper in Grand Isle and another call to follow up on possible van support replacements.

The long periods of silent paddling also offered time for doubt. "Why am I doing this again?" I wondered as I reached, dipped, and pulled my paddle. "It's too hard," I thought with every reach, dip, and pull. When that whiny voice surfaced and my back ached, I searched for something beautiful to focus on; on the river something beautiful is never far away.

On a curve four miles out from our destination, with the sun beginning to set, we cautiously approached another series of ben weirs. We waited for Kit so we could close our ranks before paddling through. Hugging the inside curve next to the sand bar, we hit turbulent water. On the downriver side of the curve we could see whirlpools and funky water to our left with current moving in every direction. Fortunately we were able to stay safely on the edge of the funky water.

A little further down, the landscape became strangely juxtaposed. On our right, the stunning clouds were brilliant shades of purple and orange as the sun set. The scene was serene and comforting. On our left, wild turbulent water rushed against itself. One large whirlpool had a wave that could easily mean disaster.

Kitty and I were tired and increasingly concerned about Kit. She was lagging behind, and fatigue was evident on her face. As we reached Tucker Point I was relieved that we only had a quarter mile to go. We floated to wait for a barge to pass and soon realized it had parked. Assuming the barge was waiting for another barge to pass, we paddled back into the current to get to camp before it caught up to us.

Low water, wing dikes, and sand bars caused the river to narrow considerably at Tucker Point. Narrow waterways mean fast, turbulent water. We rounded the curve and were met with upriver waves, many of them more than three feet high, that broke over the tops of our kayaks. Kitty and I called to Kit. "Keep padding hard!" At this point in the day, our desire to stop paddling for a moment's rest was intense, but we knew the result could be disastrous. We passed through that set of waves and spotted our destination, Devil's Backbone Park Campground.

"Yes!" I hollered, pointing ahead with my hand. Then we hit a second set of waves with lateral waves crashing in on us. We were again bounced around, and we struggled to aim our kayaks into the oncoming waves.

Barb was on the shore, waving her arms. "Over here!" Her lime green jacket glowed in the remaining light like a welcome beacon. A third round of big waves lay between us and shore.

"Paddle hard!" Kitty yelled.

"You can do it, Kit!" I cheered as we bounced through the last set of waves, occasionally getting a face full of water. The delightful relief we felt when we landed our kayaks was followed by intense exhaustion and acute hunger. Barb was insistent about the best place for us to stow our kayaks, and I didn't take it well. I glared at her and didn't reply. I needed a moment to get my land legs and scope out the terrain. Feeling the tension Barb headed back to camp as Pat arrived to help us. Even stowing the kayaks was physically challenging.

Arriving at our campsite I felt deep gratitude to see our tents set up and dinner cooking. I caught a whiff of something burning and saw the camp stove was black. Barb followed my eyes and explained. "I came down to greet you guys, and then I went to get the soup heated up so it'd be hot when you got up here. I got the stove started and put the pot on it when all of a sudden–swoosh!–a big circle of flames shot up around the pot. My immediate thought was to get the pot off the flame to save supper. Then the flame started coming at me. I yelled, 'Help!' Doug, the guy who's camped next door to us—a great guy, ran over and threw his beer on the fire to put it out."

"What a sacrifice," said Pat.

Undaunted by her fire episode, Barb had the minestrone soup hot and ready for us.

At dinner I asked Kit how she was doing. "I feel like I let you guys down," she said sadly.

"Really? Why?"

"I was nervous starting out. I was worried I wouldn't be able to keep up with you. Things went well for a while, even with the rain and strong wind. I kept a steady pace with my paddle, and strains of 'They Call the Wind Mariah' echoed in my mind. I kept hoping the wind would change direction.

"After lunch, as fatigue set in, I kept you both in sight, but I couldn't catch up. I lost my rhythm, so I focused instead on trying to catch up to you. I was worried my slower pace would keep us on the river past dark. At last, the shore was in sight and you were waiting for me to catch you. Then we hit the surprise challenging chop between us and the shore. Time seemed to stand still.

"Then, at last, the choppy water was over and Barb was there to help me out of my kayak. 'What a story to tell your grandchildren,' Barb said as she helped me up. As we secured our kayaks and headed up to camp, I felt I'd let the team down. I was trembling and exhausted."

We told her she did great and that we were struggling too, and concerned about how soon it would be dark. We decided we wouldn't paddle that late in the day again, particularly if we were that tired.

After dinner the rain began again, so we hung our wet clothes inside the screen cook tent. Barb sang "Goodnight, Sweetheart, Goodnight" for us as we prepared for bed. "Goodnight, sweetheart, well it's time to go."

I was dead tired. Sleep came quickly.

September 24, Day Four

We slept in, a necessary luxury after the previous day. The rain turned the campground into puddles and mud. Even though the sky was threatening I went for a short run around Devil's Backbone, a large rock point paralleling the river, and into town. While on my run I read a sign that said the Devil's Backbone and Tower Rock served as a landmark for river pilots. The Lewis and Clark expedition camped across the river in 1803.

In town I peeked into the windows of the Mississippi River Museum and Interpretive Center, wishing it were open. On the way back to camp it began to thunder and rain. I was soaked by the time I got to my tent.

The cookstove fire put an end to the cookstove, so Pat set out cold granola, yogurt, and fruit for us to eat while she put our lunches together, paying careful attention to each of our food preferences. At breakfast I presented Barb with a van support appreciation gift. A tradition had begun on the first trip of bringing found objects to our van support team members. Usually the objects were found along the river. I found Barb's gift next to my tent. I smiled when I found it, knowing exactly who should have the tiny plastic cartoon character, Smurfette. Barb received her gift in regal form and declared that she wanted to be called Smurfette from then on.

Sitting at the picnic table I watched barge traffic pass camp all morning. Passing barges often create waffle waves, which are difficult to paddle. Waffle waves are waves that cross each other, making a pattern in the water much like the surface of a waffle. There's no consistent direction in which to point a kayaks to mitigate their effect. Also if the waffle waves are high, our paddles tend to hit air rather than water, which can throw the paddler off balance. I knew we might need to pull off the water for a while if we hit a patch of waffle waves, and that would extend our day. The heavy barge traffic could last all day, and I wasn't looking forward to it

Eventually the rain eased, and we quickly packed our gear into the van. The plan was that Barb and Pat would head down the road while we got on the water. Barb and Pat didn't get far. We learned that when we use the van to charge cell phones, cameras, and lap tops, the battery gets run down. Ours was dead. Fortunately Doug came to the rescue again. After a jump, Barb and Pat headed down the road. Kit, who had been quiet all morning, Kitty, and I headed for our kayaks.

The sky remained overcast. The boats we encountered on the river were small. As a sail boat, mast down, motored downriver, its driver waved and shouted, "Got any cigarettes?" The woman with him laughed and said, "I'm making him quit, so he's jonesing for a cigarette."

I felt the effects of the previous day's push, and I was sure Kitty and Kit did too. My back aches when I'm fatigued, and my posture deteriorates. I made frequent futile attempts to readjust my position to ease my discomfort.

Our slow progress was a growing concern. We had a sixty-four-mile distance to cover in three days. The pace we'd need to keep was unrealistic; we had to find a solution.

The rain was light and sporadic. We passed two men fishing from a small boat on the downstream side of a wing dike. Trains hugged the Missouri bluff on a rock ledge that seemed to have been created just for them. We maintained a steady pace to ensure an early arrival.

We landed at Trail of Tears State Park at two o'clock, which gave us time to relax. Pat and Barb had spent a frustrating day trying to locate a new cookstove. Pat was irritated with the useless mileage they put on driving in circles. They ended up buying a single burner stove that none of us could figure out how to work. Kitty took the new stove, placed it on the blacktop pavement to light it, and—poof!—the stove and blacktop around it burst into flames. "Holy smokes!" She kicked the stove over, shut it off, and let the fire burn out. After that, no one wanted to touch the stove let alone put a light to it. I called Becky in St. Louis, and she agreed to get a stove for us and bring it down when she came to the Gathering. We were grateful for electricity at the campsite and the use of Pat's electric skillet and kettle.

Pat created a beans and rice dinner. While she cooked she separated the meal into corners of the electric skillet based on our food preferences. Kit was a vegetarian, so her corner had no meat. As Pat added things like onions, peppers, and spices, she asked each of us what we wanted in our portion. The end result was a personalized delicacy. We sat beside a smoky fire that struggled to stay lit. "Last night it was the stove," said Barb. "Tonight it's the stove and the campfire. When we got here, there was cardboard and boxes around so I threw them on the fire. We were sitting at the table and all of a sudden—whoosh!—ashes were floating everywhere."

Even though we all tried not to show it, tension was building within the team. I saw moments of tension in our faces, and there were moments of uncomfortable silence. A simple thing, like not stating preferences, had grown into a bigger issue. In our group, decisions were based on meeting the needs or wants of the majority of the team members. An I-don't-care or no-preference silence following a request for preferences created awkwardness and led to quiet resentment.

I proposed a rule that each team member must state her preference when asked anything, but some women in our group felt uncomfortable with that because not everyone was used to stating what she wanted. Some felt it wasn't their place to make a request. "I've not had to put my preferences out there like that before, and it's a little uncomfortable," Kitty admitted as we all tried to talk the issue through. "This will be good practice for me."

I knew the new rule would challenge me too. I was just as guilty as the rest of them at passing the responsibility of decision making on to someone else by remaining silent.

Betty, the lively campground host who shared the job with her husband, Jerry, checked in with us after her shift at the Trail of Tears Visitor

Center. With concern in her eyes she told us about a young man paddling the river who'd recently stopped at the campground for the night. He was a Desert Storm vet. The mosquitoes were particularly bad that night, she said, but he insisted on stringing a hammock in the trees down by the water, where the bugs were the worst, and he refused any help she offered him.

"He said he thought that by being on the river by himself he could get back to earth 'cause he wasn't fit for man nor beast. I thought, 'Please don't let something happen to him on the way.' I gave him my phone number, but he never called. I was wishin' he would've because it would've been interesting to know that he made it. He was such a nice young man. He said he went home after serving in the war, but he couldn't stay home. Nobody understood. He thought he could get himself straightened out by floating down the Mississippi. I told him to be careful because the Mississippi takes people.

She shook her head and with a loving motherly expression she said, "Y'all be very, very careful and get down there safe. That durn river. When the weather's nasty like this, the river really stirs up. A whole lot of people don't realize how dangerous it is.

"You know, I'm glad for you that you decided to do this. I wouldn't have done it at fifty, forty, or nothing. Any other kind of thing like hiking in the woods and camping out I'll do. But my idea about water is it's to drink and to bath in. Period." We laughed.

"Jerry said that you were high school sweethearts and that you've been married over fifty years," said Barb.

"Fifty-nine in March," said Betty proudly. "Yeah, we're both in our eighties."

"Really?" I said. "I wouldn't have guessed eighties."

"Me either," said Kitty.

"I've been very lucky," said Betty. "I've had surgeries out of this world, but I've been very healthy. Jerry's slowing up a little bit because his health is going downhill. When we leave here, we're going to our son's house and babysit a twenty-one-year-old, an eighteen-year-old, and a thirteen-year-old."

"That's a handful," Barb said.

"And two dogs," laughed Betty. "The first thing out of their mouths when we hit there is, 'We love you, Grandma.' Second is, 'Are we having chicken and dumplins?' I roll out the dumplins and drop them, and they think that's something you just gotta do. I better go. You girls take care."

Everyone headed to bed, but Kitty and I stopped to talk to Kit because she had been quieter than usual.

"How are you doing?"

"I lost my mental balance the other day when it was such a long, hard paddle," Kit said. "I'm still feeling a bit down, like I was letting you down and holding you back."

"That's not how we saw it," said Kitty.

"Really?"

"Really," I said. "In fact, we were impressed with how you kept pushing on even though you were tired. And then to get hit at the end of that long hard day of paddling with challenging choppy water . . . That last quarter mile was grueling. To continue to paddle and face challenging obstacles when you're that exhausted requires an ability to dig deep within. That was impressive paddling."

"Yes, it was," said Kitty.

"I'd been feeling discouraged, but paddling today it all clicked," said Kit with a proud smile. "At times I felt tired, but my tiredness wasn't overwhelming, and it didn't affect my mental attitude. I think that's what made the difference. Today was a great day, and sharing dinner tonight and having time together helped. What makes this trip special to me is spending time with women because I work with men, and the experience is different. Very different.

"Learning to recognize a personal success has always been a struggle for me. In school and at work, I always felt I had to work twice as hard to keep up. I'm learning to slow down and enjoy life's journey. Like many things, my life is still a work in progress. Usually paddling keeps me in the moment. I'm mindful of each stroke as my paddle pulls me along. The movement becomes a soft meditation. It's one of the things I love about paddling. Thank you for asking about me."

"You're welcome," I said. "Sleep well."

"I don't think I'll have any trouble."

We laughed.

Kitty and I stayed in the cook tent and took care of business. One of Kitty's duties was to manage the finances. Money was something we took very seriously because our funds were limited and came from hard-earned and donated money. In the previous year and a half, we had held a number of rummage sales and a silent auction; sold chocolates; contacted potential sponsors; sold gift items such as T-shirts, hats, and mugs; taken donations; and contributed our own funds. Along the route we were selling gift items and books whenever the opportunity presented itself.

At this point we had $8,800 in cash and a credit card should we go over budget. We divided our available funds by the number of days we'd be traveling, which gave us a budget of $214 per day to cover lodging, food, and gas. Tracking the financial details were complicated and time consuming. We believed with diligence we could make it to the end of the journey with what we had, so each evening we tracked our expenditures to stay on top of our finances. Kitty was meticulous about making sure everything was entered correctly.

While I was working on a logo, I had a conversation with my son-in-law Doug, and he said that he thought of the Ripples of Wisdom project as representing a woman unleashed and celebrating in her kayak. That inspired me to create this image as the graphic for our logo.

September 25, Day Five

The thunder cracked and boomed so loudly during the night I felt the ground vibrate. The rain was relentless. Streams ran through our cook tent and seeped into sleeping tents, creating puddles and soaking sleeping bags—and the women in them. The high humidity inside the tents formed water beads that created mini rainstorms of their own. While Pat and Barb prepared breakfast, a thick fog hung in the cook tent. Everything was wet. We were chilled to the bone.

We piled into the van to drive to the river overlook. We stopped at the restroom to pick up Kitty and found her playfully dancing and splashing in the deep puddles. "This is my no-more-rain dance," she called out, laughing.

At the Bushyhead Memorial, a tribute to the Cherokee people who died on the Trail of Tears, we stopped next to the road. Legend says that Nancy Bushyhead Walker Hildebrand was buried within the Park's boundaries. She was the sister of Rev. Jesse Bushyhead, a Cherokee religious and political leader who led one of the detachments during the tragic Federal Indian Removal, and the wife of Lewis Hildebrand, who led another. Her two children traveled on and made it to Indian Territory. Our curiosity about the Trail of Tears was piqued, and we added a trip to the visitor center to our agenda.

A triathlon was scheduled in the park that day. Driving to the overlook, we came upon an area where the event organizers had set up tents for registration and a first aid station. A few yards further we encountered a roadblock. Moans of disappointment echoed through the van, but Pat was undaunted. She drove around the roadblock and kept going. We sat in stunned silence. "The triathlon doesn't have the right to stop us from seeing something that is part of a state park," Pat said.

"Well, that road block would've been enough to stop me," said Kitty. "I follow the rules and do what I'm supposed to."

"I do too," I said.

"Really, what's the worst that's going to happen to us?" said Kitty. "Is somebody going to tell us to turn around and go back? How many times are we going to be to this overlook again? Probably never. Are we going to let a little used-car-lot string of flags stop us from experiencing something?"

"No!" we cheered. Pat grinned.

"This trip allows me to consider stretching in ways I never would have otherwise," said Kit. "I'd never have crossed the cones either. I'd have stopped and turned around. This was an opportunity to grow. I've had lots of opportunities to grow on this trip."

"Thanks, Pat, for going around the barriers," cheered Kitty.

"You're welcome."

"We all appreciate it," said Barb.

"Makes me wonder how many more rules I'm following that I don't want to," I said.

"That's a good awareness I'm taking to heart," said Kitty.

"Look out, lower Mississippi. Kitty has been set free," I kidded. We laughed.

"Those southern belles won't know what to think of us," said Pat.

We drove through the forest of white oak, black oak, tulip poplar, and hickory. The humidity hung thick in the air. Bundled in rain gear from head to toe, we started down the wooden boardwalk that stretched into the treetops to the overlook and moved through a lacework of greens splashed with autumn reds and yellows. The viewing platform was perched out past the edge of the bluff. We scanned the muted-gray horizon. Visibility was less than a mile, making it difficult to discern details of the landscape before us, yet the river was still impressive from that vantage point.

When we were back in the van, Kitty noted we hadn't seen anybody since we crossed the barrier. Pat honked as we drove over the triathlon's finish line, declaring us winners.

On our way to the visitor center, the battery light on the van's dashboard repeatedly came on. Realizing that further downriver the options to take care of a potentially bad battery or alternator would be limited, we headed into Cape Girardeau. On the way Barb sang a few lines from the James Taylor folk song "Fire and Rain," taking liberty with one of the words, "I've seen fire and I've seen rain. I've seen rainy days that I thought would never end." (Original lyrics say sunny days) She had us laughing.

Cape Girardeau had been home to many peoples, including the Ozark Bluff Dwellers and the Mississippian Tribe that lived in the Mississippi Valley between 900 and 1200 AD. Around 1733, a Frenchman named Jean Baptiste de Girardot, whom the city was named after, established a trading post. At the time of the Lewis and Clark expedition, more than eleven hundred people lived there.

At the Walmart auto department we learned, sure enough, the battery was the issue. While waiting for the repairman to replace the battery, we split up and wandered the aisles, not quite how we wanted to spend the layover day. Some of us bought stylish rubber boots to keep our feet dry at our soggy campsite. I bought a scarf to adorn my straw hat. We bought tarps to put over our tents to reduce saturation and condensation. On the way back to the park we heard on the radio that four and a half inches of rain had fallen so far. And the rain continued.

We stopped at the visitor center on our way to camp and watched a video about the tragic Federal Indian Removal. "Between 1830 and 1850, about 100,000 American Indians living between Michigan, Louisiana, and Florida were moved West after the U.S. government coerced the leaders to sign treaties and used the U.S. Army against those resisting. Many were treated brutally. Some were transported in chains...

"The Cherokee, Creek, Choctaw, Chickasaw, and Seminole were considered civilized tribes because they had accepted Christianity and adopted many European customs. Some had successful businesses, but even they were not spared.

"The Cherokees protested. They didn't believe that they'd be forced to move. In May 1883, federal troops and state militia began the round up of the Cherokees into stockades. Three groups left in the summer traveling from present-day Chattanooga by rail, boat, and wagon, primarily on the Water Route... One group traveling overland in Arkansas suffered three to five deaths each day due to illness and drought...15,000 captives still awaited removal... The Cherokees asked to postpone removal until the fall and to voluntarily remove themselves... The delay was granted... By November, twelve groups of 1000 each were trudging 800 miles overland to the West. Two thirds of the ill-equipped Cherokees were trapped between the icebound Ohio and Mississippi rivers during January...

"By March 1839, all survivors had arrived in the West. No one knows how many died throughout the ordeal, but the trip was especially hard on infants, children, and the elderly. Missionary Dr. Elizur Butler, who accompanied the Cherokee, estimated that over 4000 died, nearly a fifth of the Cherokee population ... In 1987, Congress acknowledged the significance of the trail by establishing the Trail of Tears national historic trail. The park itself was located where nine of thirteen groups of Cherokee Indians crossed the Mississippi River during the winter." (Quoted from the Trail of Tears brochure supplied by National Trails Intermountain Region National Park Service, supplied by the Trail of Tears State

Park Visitor Center.)

When the video was over Pat sat and stared at the blank screen for several moments with tears running down her cheeks. We left the auditorium teary-eyed and quiet. The documentary was heartbreaking and left us feeling deep sadness, anger, and less than proud of that part of our country's history. On the ride back to camp we were silent. A collective sense of shame surfaced from our being descendants of a people who could inflict such injustice and pain onto other people.

Back at camp the rain and wet gear brought our focus closer to home. Barb and Kit volunteered to get our laundry going. There were a lot of clothes and sleeping bags to dry before nightfall, and the Gathering was to start soon. As Kitty and I headed to the Greens Ferry Shelter to set up for the Gathering, we were surprised by the amount of water that gushed down the gullies. I was concerned about what all that water was doing to the river.

Normally, the first thing put into place for the Gathering was the Peace Fire, but the rain had saturated everything, so we opted for lighting a candle and putting one of the Peace Fire coals into it.

The Peace Fire coals were given to me to carry down the river. They came from the Peace Fire started at an international conference at Lake Geneva, Wisconsin, in 1995 by Bruce Hardwick, a Fire Keeper in his home area of Rapid River, Michigan. More than 1,500 people from all over the world, including Arun Gandhi, Mahatma Gandhi's grandson, attended the Peace Fire. Later Peace Fires were started by others to awaken our consciousness about peace, love, sisterhood, and brotherhood. At the end of the conference, which became an annual tradition, participants made coal bundles, which have since been distributed around the world and used to start other Peace Fires. Since our journey started in 2004, I've collected coals from the fire of each Gathering and carried them downriver to the next fire.

Becky and Jo arrived first. Becky strutted up to the picnic shelter like a force to be reckoned with. Jo followed her, grinning. They had the new cook stove for us. Becky brought her best canine friend, Rusty. Generally we don't let males join us at a Gathering, but Rusty was considered one of the girls.

Laurel, who'd be paddling with us for the next few days, also arrived. Her sister, Donna, drove her down from St. Louis along with Laurel's two daughters, Anna and Audrey. Undaunted by the cold and rain, thirteen women gathered around our candle. Most drove down from St. Louis. I was disappointed that no local women attended. We heard later that due to the intensity of the rain, they assumed the Gathering had been canceled.

At the Gatherings only the Grandmothers were asked to speak. It was a time for younger women to listen. Five questions were created as a

guide or conversation starter. Participants were encouraged to share what was in their hearts or answer one of the questions. The questions for this trip were:

1. What makes your life rich?
2. How has courage affected your life?
3. What brings out compassion in you?
4. How have you persevered in times of adversity?
5. What life experiences or choices generated the most wisdom for you?

We used a special fan made of heron and raven feathers as a "talking stick." Only the person holding the fan was to talk; everyone else was to listen.

We began the Gatherings by honoring the oldest woman in attendance. We gave her a purple ceramic mug with our logo on it and then handed her the fan and a basket with a tape recorder in it. This elder was the first one to speak. The fan and tape recorder were passed around the circle until every Grandmother had spoken, and then to whomever wanted to speak.

Donna, at age seventy, was our honored elder for the evening. She wore a brightly colored sweater and a gray and white plaid hat with earflaps that didn't quite match.

"I was born in Bonne Terre, Missouri, which is not far from here, and it's good earth. That was a good sign.

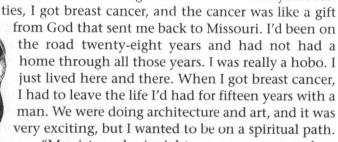

"I've had a fortunate life filled with grace. When I was in my late forties, I got breast cancer, and the cancer was like a gift from God that sent me back to Missouri. I'd been on the road twenty-eight years and had not had a home through all those years. I was really a hobo. I just lived here and there. When I got breast cancer, I had to leave the life I'd had for fifteen years with a man. We were doing architecture and art, and it was very exciting, but I wanted to be on a spiritual path.

"My sister, who is eighteen years younger than me, wanted me to help raise her kids. Laurel has five kids, and I just adore them—and her and her husband. So twenty years ago I came to Missouri, and I was so grateful because I love Missouri. I love the Missouri River. This weekend we cleaned the Missouri River, me and my buddies. Missouri River Relief it's called. I've lived on ocean and seas, but I always missed rivers.

"I've been on a spiritual path all of my life, my dad being a Christian minister. Then I met a Tunisian man in college, and I became a Muslim in North Africa. I lived there for five years. I was in Tripoli when Gaddafi took over. That was quite exciting, but after five years, I came back and went to seminary.

"I thought that love would solve all of the world's problems, but then architecture took over. And when I got the breast cancer, I was able to come to Missouri and to pursue Native American studies, Buddhist studies, Hindu studies, and Christian, Jewish, and Sufi—all are good things that I do. There's singing and dancing. You get with the Sufis, and they break into song and dancing. The Buddhist study really entices me because it's a philosophy or psychology rather than a worship of anything.

"The architect bought me a little house about five years ago, so I'm sort of set up. I don't need very much money, but I get some from Social Security – that ol' Ponzi scheme." We laughed. "I'm so grateful for that.

"I think the country needs to stop going to war. It's really disturbing. When the Gulf War happened, I had connections with the Muslims. I just have to ignore that we are over there doing that to those people for their oil or whatever. It's not my reality. Neither is the government of this country my reality because it doesn't follow a real path.

"I live my simple life on the river. I sing in the church choir. I just love choir. I have two dogs that I adore, and I have a cat. I just love my animals. Enough about me. What you think about me?" She laughed robustly.

"The girls think I'm kind of crazy until their friends come over and they say,

'Whoa, your Aunt Donna is really cool!' Okay, so one friend did anyway, once.

"Two people said they didn't like having their pictures taken. If you look at the camera and the person taking the picture with love, you will always be beautiful in the picture. It seems to work for me."

Donna sat tall and said, "I'm loud and I'm proud. I love my body. I think it's beautiful. It's only because I think so. If I look in the mirror or I look at pictures, I'm not that pretty. I'm fat and I'm old, but so what? I learned to live alone twenty years ago and love it. Not bad for a seventy-year-old."

Donna handed the fan and basket to her sister, Laurel. "I'm honored to be part of this age group and to have discovered a group of women who value this passage in life. Vacationing in Ely, I happened into a coffeehouse and saw the amazing books about this adventure. I thought that's the way to turn fifty—to celebrate, to look forward, and to ask what next, what now?

"Over the last four or five years, I've been contemplating what turning fifty might mean. For me, it coincides with our youngest child entering kindergarten while our oldest is in college in Minnesota. That allows me open space that I'm very excited to fill.

"My work is in the area of empowering women through their birth experiences, to help them live their lives reflecting earth-based power and experience, even women who have not ever given birth themselves. I help them embrace that role, that unique place. For seven years that meant creating a birth center where women could honor the spiritual in an individual way and could safely birth. Through the four to five hundred births that we did there, I learned that part of the life cycle prepares you for the next. Now, in the grandmother role, I want to try to make sure that's held sacred for my daughters and my sons. I'm realizing I may only have thirty to fifty more years to do it, so I better get busy. We all laughed with her.

"I feel very blessed that I was raised in a family of very strong and vocal women, possibly to a fault. We all speak with a loud voice. I love it when women can speak and encourage it in each other. I think it holds healing for our culture and our world. The time has come.

"The idea of floating down the river appeals to me as a time to reflect on where the river of life will take me from here. It turns out that I'm now living maybe a hundred yards from the Missouri River in a community where my husband's family has lived for six generations. It's a very rich, fertile soil and a nice place to grow children, to grow ideas, and to grow closer to the wisdom that will carry me on."

Alynn hesitated before accepting the fan and basket from Laurel and said, "I'm honored and a little daunted by this.

"I'm a psychotherapist in St. Louis. I've come to know and be a part of this circle through Becky. She met my daughter Celia, who is sitting next to me and who is my oldest daughter, at a yoga class in St. Louis. The connection I witnessed that day was almost electric. It was amazing to see two women separated by a generational line connect so strongly. It was really inspiring to me. That connection brought Celia an opportunity to paddle the Boundary Waters with Nancy and Becky and another young woman from Ely, Jen, who is closer to Celia's age. It struck me as amazing for women to have this kind of opportunity, not just because I'm a therapist or because of the work I do, but because I think about how the opportunities for women have shifted and changed through the centuries."

Alynn paused and looked around at the women in the circle. "I love the presence of sisters here. I have no sisters of my own. I have three brothers. I don't know what it's like having a sister, in terms of growing up with another woman. I'm thinking of all of the women in my life. I, too, come from a lineage of very strong but very quiet, almost meek and humble, women. They would have probably melted into the background

in a situation like this where they would be challenged to speak or con-
tribute in some way. Their presence was known through their humility.
My maternal grandmother, in particular—who was my primary caregiver
for the first nine years of my life—and her sister are who I'm thinking
about.

"For these women, their strength was in their humility and their
quietness. They are the ones I draw the greatest strength from as I look
back over their lives. Even in my day-to-day living, I think about how
they would handle situations. My mother, I know, will become that
model for me as time goes on. My mother is eighty-six and still living in
the Florida Keys, which is where I'm from, born and raised near the
ocean.

"I don't know a lot about rivers. I lived near the Missouri River for
twenty-five years. My husband is a native of St. Louis and loves the rivers
and the out-of-doors. He is part of the Missouri Stream Team, and he also
helps clean rivers. Water is very powerful. I'm grateful to be part of this
connection and the opportunity to be a part of it."

She put her arm around her daughter and looked at her fondly. "I'm
grateful for my daughter to have this opportunity because it's not something I'd have ever known about. Celia is wise beyond her years. When
Celia was born, I remember my mother stayed with me and helped me.
She was very instrumental in Celia's and her younger sister's and
brother's development when they were infants. I will never forget when
my mother took Celia to the store when she was about two years old.
While Celia was sitting in the cart, my mother opened a bottle of shampoo to see if Celia would like the smell. Celia became immediately and
urgently concerned that my mother had to buy the shampoo. We call
my mother Bushi from the Polish word for grandmother, babcha. Bushi
is how it got mangled by my kids. 'Bushi,' Celia said, 'you got to buy that
now that you opened it.' It was priceless.

"I see a lineage of much more strong and verbal women to come."

The rain continued to pour and it grew colder. Laurel and her daughters wrapped themselves in a blanket while Jo began to speak. "Yesterday
I was paddling in my new inflatable kayak on a little lake that's near our
house that I've not been out on before. I saw two cranes. One was white
and the other one was blue. I saw hawks fishing, and I watched one of
them catch a fish. I wasn't even sure he had it. Then he did a victory lap,
and he came right over my head. I could see the fish in his talons. It was
very amazing. My husband was on the shore, and I asked him if he saw
the hawks fishing, but he said no. He was sitting back a little bit, and he
couldn't see from the land what I saw on the water.

"I think women's visions are getting clearer. Earlier, you were talking
about a childbirth center. I, too, had a child at home and went through
that process. I'm a nurse, and the births that I saw way back when were

not very lovely. They were all where women were knocked out completely and the babies were pulled out with forceps. It was a long journey for me to come full circle to this.

"I think it's more possible for women to be open and honest now than it has been in the past. Sometimes we have these moments when we are on the water and we can really see what is happening, but someone on the shore can't really see.

"I believe the things I've heard about this being the time for women. It's going to be a painful shift in our country, as we can see now with so many people suffering from the economic disturbances caused by greed. I don't know how long this will take or how it will play out. I'm from the era of the Dawning of Aquarius." We laughed. "So maybe it's going to be like that.

"It's so wonderful to hear these heartfelt stories. It makes me in awe. I'm in awe of the paddlers too."

Kit, who generally spoke softly, spoke with confidence and conviction. "This is my second opportunity to paddle with Nancy. It all came in a very roundabout way. Until 2005, I was very typical—wife, mother, caregiver, Girl Scout leader, school volunteer. And then I found a lump. A week later, I started chemotherapy and a good eight months of treatment and tests and a lot of trials and tribulations until they decided I'd be okay after all.

"Cancer turned out to be a blessing in disguise. It gave me the opportunity to figure out that where I was wasn't where I wanted to be. Cancer forced me to accept help—something I still have trouble with, but I'm getting better at. While I was trying to figure out what was next, I heard about a retreat in Ely. I knew that I needed to do something different. The retreat gave me the opportunity to reconnect with nature and water.

"My dad was in the Air Force. Girl Scouts was probably the only thread that went from base to base with me. There was always a Girl Scout troop around and the opportunity to camp and swim and be in the woods. When I got married, I left that all behind as being kids' stuff.

"In Ely, I discovered it's not kids' stuff. It's part of who I am and what I want to be. In Ely, I met Nancy and learned about her incredible journey, and my involvement has brought me on an incredible journey too." Tears came to her eyes. "I swore I wasn't going to cry, but I don't think I'm going to be able to do it." She laughed and shed some tears. "This week has been probably the most fun and the hardest I've ever had. It's really easy to say 'paddling the Mississippi,' but it's actually a lot different when you are on the water in a kayak. Twelve miles was a breeze, I thought. Twenty-eight miles? Well, that was a little harder. Thirty miles? I hit my limit." She laughed again.

"Water." She shook her head. "I've tried many times to explain it to my husband because he is not a water person and not much of a camper.

The first time my paddle hits the water, I feel complete. I'm very centered. I'm very in the moment. I don't worry about the latest worm we have just detected at work. I don't care if my cell phone is off or not—or anything else. It's the water, the kayak, and me. Sharing that experience with Nancy and Kitty makes me glad I'm alive. It makes me grateful that I'm here.

"It has been a real gift to meet women and be around women. I work in a field that's mostly men. We get along fine. It's just different being with women and laughing with women. It's a connection I didn't know I missed until I found it here in these circles and in the time I've spent with Nancy and Kitty on the river.

"Last time, I had the fortune to bring my daughter to a Gathering. She is at college now. The last thing she said to me when I headed out on the trip was, 'Mom, have fun. You are going to be great. I will be thinking about you.' I know she really supports what is happening here and that she was really awed when she read the book from the second leg, *Ripples of Wisdom, A Journey through Mud and Truth*.

"I think that what is happening here—sharing our stories with all women and younger women—is important work. I'm so very grateful to be here with all of you right now.

"I have a little book of wisdom for kayakers that my husband gave me. I was flipping through it last night, hoping for some inspiration, and found a quote that seems very appropriate: 'Just because you stop paddling doesn't mean the river stops moving.'" We all laughed. "It has a double meaning. I had a too-close encounter with a red buoy on the river. I stopped paddling because I was watching a tugboat, and I thought, 'I'm going to wait for the tug to get out of the way, and then I'm going to take a picture of the buoy.' The buoy, at that time, didn't look like it was moving—and I forgot I was. Nancy loudly reminded me that the buoy was coming up very rapidly.

"There's a lot of wisdom in that quote for life in general. Life doesn't stop just because we do. The journey continues. I think that what I am finally learning to do is—when the water gets rough—paddle harder. Sometimes it bothers me that it took so long for me to figure that out, but then I'm grateful I figured it out."

Pat took the fan and gazed at it for a few minutes before speaking. "I worked in van support on the last leg of this journey. I came for just a day to meet a dear friend of mine from Wyoming who was going to do van support, and I couldn't leave." She became tearful. "It's going to be really hard to leave again.

"We saw a movie today at the visitor center about the Trail of Tears, and I just can't get the movie out of my head." Her voice trembled. "I feel like something happened within me. The Trail of Tears was such a tragedy. I don't know how to explain it. The movie really touched me.

The thought of what we did to the Cherokee—well, to all of the Indians, not just with the Trail of Tears—makes me feel like I'm shedding tears for the people who died along the way.

"I shed tears for my mom, who I never got to really know very well. She died very young. We have a history of that happening in our family. My dad died very young. I have three beautiful sisters, and I cherish every moment I can spend with them. I love getting new sisters, so thank you for allowing me to join you on this journey. I'm enjoying every moment of it.

"The most important thing for me when I do these Gatherings with women—especially with women—is there's a very different feel to the conversations. I feel like I can express myself and say anything that comes to mind. It's very refreshing. I crave that in my life.

"I'm not a water person. I must admit I'm somewhat terrified of water. That's why I've not wanted to paddle. That's why I choose to be van support and have the opportunity to have conversations, even if it's just a few moments. The opportunities to share thoughts with other women are the moments I will cherish. It has just been very special." Pat was choked up, she smiled and passed the fan and basket to Kitty.

"I paddled the last section of the Mississippi with Nancy from Redwing to St. Louis," said Kitty, "and I'm honored to be here again and to get on the water again in St. Louis.

"Watching the film this afternoon in the center reminded me how little respect there is in the world today, not just here and not just us, but all over the world. I go to a place of being really sad and angry. I wonder what there is to do about the injustices that seem so much bigger than me. There's something to the saying that speaking is the first part of healing."

She paused collecting her thoughts. "When I look around, I see how fortunate my life has been and how all the people around me enrich my life too. Thank you for being here tonight. To sit in a circle of women is not something I thought I'd be doing much in my life. I so appreciate all of the wisdom I get from everybody.

"As long as I am up and breathing, I know there's more life to live. There are moments on the river when I feel alive. There are lessons everywhere. That's why I'm here." There was laughter at that.

With a Cheshire grin, Barb said, "My name is Smurfette." The others laughed. "This is a name I gave to myself when I received this gift." She held up the toy Smurfette. "It's a tradition with this group that you give a found item to support crew members. Smurfette is kind of me in a way.

"I've known Nancy for a while. We live in the same town, and I've followed her journey and love what she is doing. I got to paddle with her last year and spilled my guts at a Gathering, so buy the book.

"Being part of the support crew has been a different experience than paddling and much more enriching for me. My van support partner, Pat, and I got to know each other very well. That's been really enriching as well. It's been an honor for me to be here. I will miss you when I leave in two days."

"I'm going to make an exception to the fifty rule," I said, "because I have a friend here who's been nagging at me that I needed to wait six more years to finish this trip so she'd be fifty." Everyone laughed. "Becky, I'd like to hear from you."

Hesitantly, Becky took the fan and tried to give it back. I insisted she talk. She laughed nervously and began. "On the way down, Jo and I talked about courage and compassion. I've been thinking about what that means to me in my life. I think I have compassion more than I thought I did, which is a cool thing.

"What makes my life rich is belonging to a couple of Twelve Step groups. Happiness being what makes your life rich has been a topic of conversation. I went through my life not really feeling anything but anger and apathy. I call it apathy. I felt a lot of anger and confusion. Through the help of these programs, friends, counseling, and all of this, I've discovered what makes me feel rich right now is to experience a variety of emotions, to laugh and to really mean it, not just to laugh because I'm nervous or because everyone else is laughing, but to really feel it and to agree to have this wide range of emotions."

She leaned in towards the group resting her elbows on her legs. "I've been really feeling lately, and it's hard, but it's . . . well, I hesitate to say . . . good. It makes me feel alive, richer, deeper, more connected to myself, to the world, and to other people. I feel rich now because I can use a rainbow of emotions—sad, glad, mad— rather than use them as a weapon or hide in my anger.

"I used to think I needed a companion or this job or that house to have a more enriched life. Now I've come to understand that being enriched comes through feelings.

"Rusty, do you have any words to say? He's a good listener, don't you think?" We laughed.

The Gathering concluded, and we improvised our closing ritual. With no fire to put the releasing sticks into, we decided to put both the releasing sticks and the aspiration sticks into the river.

We ended each of the Gatherings with this blessing:

> May the gifts you have offered by your presence here circle back around to reward you.
> May your head bless you with clear thinking.
> May your heart bless you with love, compassion, and joy.
> May your feet always walk in honor.
> May your hands always do good work and respect the things the Creator has made.

May your ears be sharp to hear the Creator's voice.

May you be safe from inner and outer harm.

And may you be healthy and strong.

When the ritual was over, the ladies talked until the cold and rain drove them to their cars. We packed everything and headed to camp for piping hot drinks and a planning meeting.

Streams of water ran through our cook tent. "We need to talk about tomorrow," I said. "There's a change of plans. The reason for the change is the amount of rain that's fallen and the amount of water that's currently surging into the river. We'll be crossing one of the more challenging parts of the river on this next section. Remember those waves as we approached Devil's Backbone the other day? We have another spot like that, only it has the potential to be worse because of the water pouring into the river. For safety reasons Kitty and I've decided we aren't going to paddle tomorrow. It's disappointing because I was hoping that Kit and Laurel would get to paddle together, but we'd rather we all survive."

"Having paddled that section at Devil's Backbone, the thought of repeating that experience doesn't thrill me very much," said Kit. "Big waves are okay, but when they start coming at me from different directions, that's a little different. When I can ride them, it's okay. When I don't know which way to point the bow, that's a problem."

"The change in plans makes for a relaxing day tomorrow," I said. "I'm giving a presentation about the trip at Southeastern Missouri University in Cape Girardeau at ten o'clock. We'd have had to be on the water by seven in order to get there in time if we paddled. The change in plans gives us time for breakfast. Loading the kayaks might take a little extra time. The decision to store them on the mud embankment during all this rain wasn't the best choice because they're disgustingly muddy now and they will need to be cleaned."

"Our primary concern is safety," said Kitty. "With so much water going into the river and the potential for floating logs, the risk is higher. Nancy and I checked the charts, and there's nowhere on the river we could get off until we got to the next town down, Cape Girardeau. Van support couldn't reach us if we needed to get out before that."

"I, for one, am looking forward to the motel and a warm dry bed," I added. Everyone smiled and nodded in agreement.

"If anyone needs a dry sleeping bag, we have a couple more," said Pat. "It's important that you're warm and dry tonight."

"Let's get Laurel up to speed on the river and what to expect," I said.

Kit jumped right in. "What was hard for me was realizing that when you stop paddling, you're still moving, and the current moves quickly. The buoys are like magnets. They come out of nowhere, and they come right after you."

"We think they're really attracted to you, Kit," teased Kitty.

After going over details and securing tarps, we went into our tents. I felt a myriad of emotions from needing to take care of my evening responsibilities: updating the website, checking email, journaling, and reviewing plans for the next couple of days. I hadn't been sleeping well, which caused fatigue to vibrate throughout my body. My mind was stressed by details, and I was tired of the vigilance I couldn't let go of. I wanted to let go. I needed to let go. But I struggled with how things were being done, how much work I'd put into things, how plans needed to be changed, and a thousand other details. I hadn't counted on trouble with the van; in fact, I'd had it in the shop before we left for a complete check. I felt the weight of each day's plans and issues.

Yet, after the Gathering, I had a sense of having emotionally arrived on the trip, of being connected to its purpose. Listening to the stories and the impact that the journey has had on others gave me a sense of warmth, pride, and amazement.

September 26th through 29th

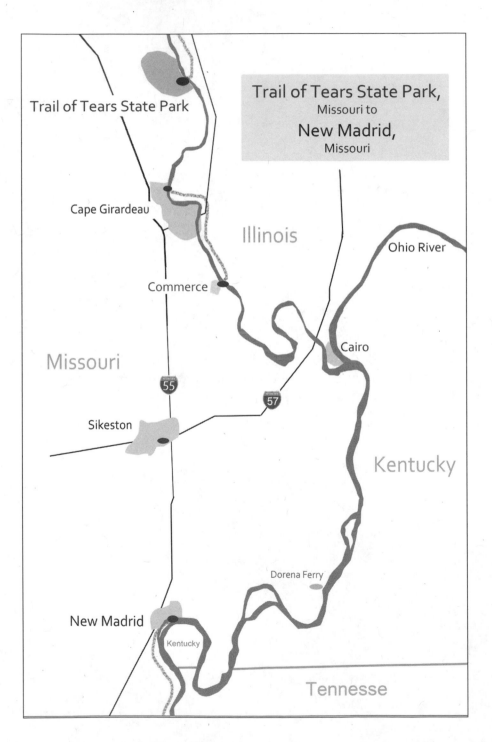

Trail of Tears State Park

Trail of Tears State Park,
Missouri to
New Madrid,
Missouri

Cape Girardeau

Illinois

Ohio River

Commerce

Cairo

Missouri

55

57

Sikeston

Kentucky

New Madrid

Kentucky

Dorena Ferry

Tennesse

2

NEW MADRID

September 26, Day Six

A screech owl woke me before sunrise. I pulled my sleeping bag up to my neck and relished the warm, cozy feeling. I felt no desire to get up. As an introvert, being with people for long periods of time requires that I have moments to myself. My tent provided respite and security while I processed my thoughts.

It was day six. I was feeling grateful for the women who traveled with me, overwhelmed by the details to be managed and revised on a daily basis, fatigued from a lack of sleep, frustrated that the planning book wasn't being used, and delighted with the experiences we'd had.

At the Gathering, Becky had talked about feeling a variety of emotions and how that made her life rich. Her words made me wonder what I had lost by trying to temper my emotions. I've often run from my true feelings or tucked them away to protect myself. Exposing my feelings left me feeling vulnerable and fragile. So I learned to temper feelings, even good feelings like joy. What if I let myself feel joy and then it was taken away?

Hiding my feelings became a habit that disconnected me from others and myself. I kept love at a distance. I thought if I let people in, I'd be devastated if they left or, worse yet, died. I grew to mistrust—and fear—my feelings. Sadness became my constant companion, which led to depression, but even sadness was tempered. Could I handle the depth of my pain? It has taken time to turn those thoughts around, to believe not only that I can handle my feelings, but also that fully experiencing them benefits me. As Becky said, "Allowing feelings makes me feel alive, richer, deeper, more connected to myself, to the world, and to other people."

The attitude Donna shared at the Gathering was enticing. "I'm loud and I'm proud! I love my body. I think it's beautiful. I'm beautiful because I think so." I was getting there. Each year I'd let go of some unrealistic expectation of perfection or some cultural norm that I'd adopted and used to judge myself harshly. I looked outside of myself for validation less, and I felt the freedom that comes with not needing outside approval. I was better at standing up for myself. I became less afraid to speak my truth.

As I lay in my tent, I realized I'd forgotten a book at home that would be helpful in keeping me grounded and focused. For years I'd read daily meditations to help process my emotions, set boundaries, and trust my internal validation. I decided to get a copy of *The Language of Letting Go* by Melody Beattie to read on the trip.

I looked over at the plastic tub in which I stored my clothes and noticed it sat in a big puddle. It isn't often I'm grateful for sleeping on an incline, but this time it kept me dry. I got up and soaked up the puddle with the clothes from my laundry bag while the tent was warmed by the sunshine that danced on it. Herons called *roh-roh-roh* in the distance and drew me outside. I took in the sun's warmth on my face like a welcome friend. Pelicans spiraled in the sky above, slowly moving southward.

photo by Kathy Ernst

I was lured to the river by flute music. Kit stood at the bottom of the boat ramp with her feet in the murky water, serenading the sun with her lovely song. The sweet notes seemed to float on the mist that rose off the water. The sun's golden light transformed the sky and water into a magical auburn and ginger-colored wonderland.

Betty, also drawn to the water's edge by the flute music, joined us. We stood quietly gazing out over the water, and Betty said, "She's a beauty, isn't she?" On the walk back to camp, Betty told us her family used to raise horses. Jerry was the breeder and Betty broke them. Their kids trained the horses and entered them in shows, where the horses did well. "It was a family adventure," she said with pride.

Back at camp we spread tents, sleeping bags, tarps, and anything that was absorbent in the sun to dry. Barb told me she'd heard me singing the Anishinabe song in my sleep. "I listened to you sing two verses, and then a screech owl chimed in and sang with you. I think you have owl energy with you." Owls in many cultures are a symbol of wisdom. I took the owl's singing as a sign to trust myself more.

Kitty sat thoughtfully for a few moments at the breakfast table and then said, "Do you realize that we've had nearly five inches of rain, all in the Trail of Tears Park? What does that tell us?" Her hands hugged her coffee mug as she slowly raised it to her mouth, but then she stopped midair, saying softly, "I think the rain shows us the profound sadness that the Trail of Tears story still carries with it. All that rain feels like nature is still shedding tears over the injustice that took place a hundred years ago, and we are here to witness it. This experience is profound to me since the trip is about witnessing the lives and stories of others." We nodded in agreement.

Kitty, Kit, Laurel, and I headed to the river to take a picture and to haul up the kayaks. When we got back to camp, we laughed at the sight of our things overflowing into several campsites. The humidity was high, and our things didn't dry quickly. Our leisurely morning slipped past, and we found ourselves scrambling to pack and head to Cape Girardeau for the presentation at Southeastern Missouri University.

While we strapped the last kayak down, Kitty went to say goodbye to Betty. Kitty told her we wouldn't be paddling that day. Betty took Kitty's face in her hands and said, "Good. I don't have to worry about you today. I don't want that durn river to take you."

Later Kitty said, "I felt like one of her children she was sending off. There was such a sense of relief on her face." Kitty had promised we'd let her know when we got to the Gulf.

Southeastern Missouri University is in the heart of town on a beautiful campus. Tiffany Parker, who'd helped set up the presentation, got us situated. At ten o'clock I spoke to thirty-five social work and nursing students and community members. I talked about our journey, focusing on the women's stories that we'd heard along the way.

When a photo of Kit appeared on the screen, I shared how her story made an impact on me. She'd gone from thinking her life was over when she was diagnosed with breast cancer to paddling with us for a second time. Kit was surprised that we saw her as courageous and inspirational for having walked from death's door to an adventure such as Ripples of Wisdom. She received a well-deserved applause and smiled broadly, shifting nervously in her seat.

Barb announced that her husband, Steve, had told her that lunch was his treat. We ate at the Port of Girardeau Café, which is housed in a red brick building built in 1836. The building, one of the oldest structures west of the Mississippi River, stands directly across from the levee. Inside, the walls are covered with historic photographs and memorabilia. The restaurant is known for its hickory-smoked barbecue dinners. The adjoining bar made us feel as if we had stepped back into the 1800s with its metal tile ceiling, long wooden bar with a brass railing, and a mirror behind it extending to the ceiling and reflecting a long line of liquor bottles. The kind long-haired bartender looked as if he'd been slinging beers there since it opened.

After a delicious lunch of hickory-smoked barbecue chicken, we left the restaurant and crossed the street to walk along the levee. On the levee wall, murals entitled *Mississippi River Tales* run the length of the downtown shopping district. Twenty-four panels, each with an explanatory marker, portray Cape Girardeau's rich history and heritage. Reading the first panel, I was surprised to learn that the Carolina parakeet was once prevalent in the Cape Girardeau area. The bird had vanished by 1900. One panel portrays St. Vincent's Young Ladies Academy, founded in 1839, the first school for women west of the Mississippi.

Kitty, Barb, Laurel, Kit, Pat, and I stood onshore and studied the water. Turbulence and whirlpools made the water churn. I wondered if the churning was normal for that part of the river or if the rain had increased the turbulence and whirlpools. The river's bottom constantly changes and moves with the current. The surface doesn't reveal the river's mood or capabilities; untold stories lie beneath her surface. The river claims things that fall into her, holding some in their watery grave for eternity while releasing others. Our charts noted sunken boats deep under the main channel. Creatures lurk in her depths, growing to monstrous size. My respect for the river grew greater with each encounter.

We checked into our motel. For the rest of the day we did laundry and relaxed. It's our tradition that those who travel the river with us write in our journal before they depart.

Barb's journal entry read:

Where you travel with friends, no beginnings, no ends.
A ribbon in the sky, over the River of your lives.
This journey goes on even after we are gone.
"Listening and learning and turning, run, River, run."
   Barb (Smurfette)

Kit's journal entry read:

This morning I said goodbye to the River and, with my new boots planted firmly in the Mississippi mud, I said a prayer. The water lapped gently around my ankles as the mist reached for the sun, not quite visible.

I did it! I paddled the Mississippi River for four days with friends. I was part of an incredible journey that celebrates life and women, and I felt alive and exhausted. I sent a prayer for safe travel for all continuing the journey—Nancy, Kitty, Gwyn, Pat, and Laurel. Barb and I leave tomorrow, but our thoughts and prayers are with you. It was good to be on the River with you again. The anxiety I'd felt fell away when my paddle hit the water.

Spending time with other women on and around the River has opened my heart and eyes. I've learned much about wisdom and myself this week through the Ripples of Wisdom journey. There was a time when I avoided other women because we had nothing in common. I've since learned we're all the same, but different. I'll take home memories of laugh-

ter, big waves, rainy days, fast-moving buoys that seemed to be drawn to us like a magnet, and meals shared with special friends. Water has always had a special place in my life, and it's always where I go to de-stress.

This trip reminded me how easy it is to get distracted and out of sorts. The real challenge is recognizing how success looks and feels for me. Certainly, having a good story to tell future grandchildren counts as a success today.

It took time to recognize this as an accomplishment. Success and reassurance from Kitty and Nancy helped the process along. Realizing they had a different perception of the days' events surprised me and gave me pause. Perhaps the expectations I had for myself were unrealistic. Thank you for allowing me to share a part of your journey. I shall miss you all. Safe travels until our paths cross again!

Love, Kit

P.S. When the paddling gets tough, be grateful, laugh out loud, and enjoy your time with the water!

September 27, Day Seven

Gwyn arrived from Wyoming during the night and joined me in my motel room. After breakfast we prepared to leave from Cape Girardeau for our twenty-seven mile paddle. We said goodbye to Barb, who had worked hard to assist us in many ways. We'd miss her singing and sense of humor. Kit was leaving too. Her can-do attitude had been an inspiration. She shared this poem about her experience:

The Clarity of Water
The Mississippi swirls around my feet;
a soft gurgling echoes
as the waves gently chase each other up the bank.
My eyes close as my ears open
to the first notes of the Morning Prayer.
My breath slows.
My thoughts center.
I'm here.

Anxious thoughts invade.
The boat is ready. Am I?
My paddle touches the water.
My breath slows.
My thoughts center.
I'm here.

Leaving Cape Girardeau, Kitty, Laurel, and I paddled under a cloudy sky. The weather prediction was for clear skies and temperatures in the low seventies. I watched along shore for a heron and saw her standing in the water. I felt the warmth of being watched over lovingly each time I saw her. "Good morning, Kee," I said softly.

We headed into a curve where Laurel would get an introduction to the ben weirs that stretched a mile downriver. The water was slightly turbulent, and we passed without issue. Early on, heavy barge and boat traffic created large waves. The water was murky, and my paddle blade disappeared only an inch below the surface.

Calm air with an occasional breeze allowed the sound of water rushing past a buoy to be heard from a great distance. Each time I heard rushing water my ears perked up, and I strained to determine if the sound was from a buoy or a wing dike. We came a little too close to a green buoy and feared it would pull us in; instead, the current tossed us aside.

"The buoys must only want Kit," Kitty said, and we laughed, remembering how the buoys seemed to target Kit.

While floating, we'd attempted to adjust Laurel's paddle to a better feathered position, but the button wouldn't release. The term "feathered" refers to the position of the blade. An unfeathered paddle lies flat with both blades on the same plane. A feathered paddle has one blade angled differently from the other. This makes them more efficient because the angle is set to allow the blade that's out of the water to slice through the air rather than acting as a wind block. It may seem insignificant for one paddle stroke, but the extra effort adds up with the thousands of strokes made in a day of paddling. Before we continued I gave Laurel my extra paddle, and we attached hers to the side of her kayak.

Laurel paddled as if she had been with us from the start. Kitty and I had an easy transition from paddling with Kit to paddling with Laurel.

We took a break on the shore and waited for barges to pass. I felt constrained by my drypants. I needed a laugh, so I hiked them as far above my waist as they'd go. Because the pants were designed to ride high to keep water out, the waist of the pants easily reached my armpits. Walking comically, I turned to Kitty and Laurel and in a high-pitched voice said, "Look. I'm Pee Wee Herman."

As they laughed, I grabbed Laurel's paddle, determined to adjust the blade. I took the paddle to a huge downed tree, aimed the rusted button down, and pounded it on the trunk. The bark was loose and bounced, so I peeled it off and pounded the paddle again, this time on the bare wood. It left divots in the wood where the button hit, but the rust wouldn't break loose no matter how hard I hit. "It's not working," I said, turning around, and I saw Kitty and Laurel laughing even harder. I carried the paddle back to Laurel and said, "You're not using that one again."

Through laughter, she replied, "It wasn't a good paddle to start with. The guy I rented it from said I could easily take it apart. I didn't even look at it."

"Obviously he didn't look at it either," I said.

The sun came out while we got in our kayaks. We had the river to ourselves. All was quiet and peaceful. The swirling water kept us alert, yet the scenery was calm and soothing. At times we drifted, soaking in the sun and appreciating the lush green landscape along the shorelines. Ahead, the surface of the water reflected myriad shades of blues, whirling and blending into each other. Pausing, I looked straight down into the water, a muddled mixture of browns and greens.

While we floated, Laurel pulled her legs out of her kayak and rested them on top. Kitty and I looked at each other wide-eyed. "What the hell is she doing?" I thought to myself. I wouldn't do that on this river for fear of putting myself at greater risk. I knew her kayak was wider and more stable than our sea kayaks, and her cockpit was larger so it was easier to get her legs in and out. Still, seeing her prop her legs up on the kayak made me uneasy. I felt I needed to be a bit more watchful because I worried she did not have the same respect for the river as I did or an understanding of how quickly danger can appear.

A white plastic baseball floated past, and I paddled over to it, snatched it from the water, and tucked it into my kayak. The baseball would become our traveling mascot. I looked downriver and wondered how different the river would be when we paddled next, after the Ohio River changed her. The confluence of the Ohio makes the Mississippi faster, wider, and more turbulent.

Hunger crept in as we ended an eleven-mile paddle and approached Commerce, Missouri, where we were to meet Gwyn and Pat for lunch. I

scanned the shoreline for the boat ramp, grateful I'd been to Commerce during the reconnaissance trip and was familiar with the terrain. The boat ramp was difficult to spot, and I didn't want to miss it and have to paddle upstream.

The flood had created mounds of mud over the boat ramp. A narrow passage, wide enough for a vehicle, was cleared. We pulled in and saw a sign indicating it was a private ramp. I walked the road to a house and was greeted by a barking dog. A thin man wearing cowboy boots and blue jeans came out and reassured me the dog was his harmless alarm. The man was standoffish at first. After introductions, Darriel told me it cost five dollars a kayak to use his landing. He was surprised we were a group of women kayakers, something he'd never seen on the river before. He warmed up quickly as I told him about our journey. I headed back to the ramp to pull our kayaks out of the way while we waited for Gwyn and Pat and lunch.

As we started hauling our kayaks up the ramp, Darriel drove down and offered to help with his truck. I looked at the short box. "We have seventeen-foot kayaks," I said. "I don't think your truck is going to work." So he helped us carry them up the ramp instead.

While we moved the kayaks out of the way, we received a phone call from Gwyn, who said the drive shaft had broken on the van and it wouldn't be ready until the following day. She and Pat were still working on a way to pick us up. They wouldn't be meeting us for lunch. Darriel's eyebrows went up when he overheard me say we had a bagel and an apple between us. Kayaks secured, he headed back to the house. Moments later his wife, who'd been sitting in the garage in a pink bathrobe, headed out in the truck. Darriel came back and invited us to hang out in his garage with him. By the time we finished putting our gear in our kayaks and heading up to the house, his wife had returned from her errand.

Nearing the house, we were greeted by two dogs that quieted down once we entered the attached garage. We took a seat at a patio table near the door. One wall was lined with a collection of cast iron skillets hung by large nails. A propane deep-fryer was warming up next to the table. Darriel offered us sweet tea and said he was fixing catfish and hushpuppies. "A bagel and an apple isn't enough. I told Annie we had to feed you, and she ran to the store for more French fries."

For three hours we enjoyed Darriel and Annie's company. Darriel didn't stop cooking. "This is the best catfish I've ever had," said Kitty. "The French fries and hushpuppies are incredible!" Each time we reached for more, Darriel smiled, which made us reach for more yet, and we overate. We asked about the batter on the fish, and he said it was his secret recipe of cornmeal, salt, and pepper.

Frankie, a small, friendly dog that slept in a plush padded chair near the front door, was a family pet they'd had for ten years. Darriel said that chair was just for him. The other dog, Dingo, had wandered up to the house two years earlier, and they'd been taking care of him ever since. Dingo wouldn't come in the house or let them pet him. In two years, they'd been able to touch his nose a few times. He slept in the garage next to the back door, his coloring blending in with the brown rug he lay on.

Darriel lit a cigarette, tilted his head back, and blew a quick puff of smoke. "I love it here in Commerce," he said. He'd been born on the Mississippi and remembered when they couldn't eat fish from the river because the fish tasted like diesel. The river had been cleaned up over the years. Darriel was a retired heavy-equipment operator, and he'd built his own boat ramp. While we listened to him, a truck revved its engine down on the ramp. The truck had gotten stuck in the mud. Over the noise of the truck spinning its wheels, Darriel told us that the spring flood had come up to his house, and he'd used a backhoe to build a levee around it. In town a few homes got flooded, he said, and fortunately the owners of the homes were insured.

The aroma of frying catfish filled the air. Darriel and Annie called each other "Baby" as they continued to focus on feeding us. Darrel asked if we had ever eaten squirrel. "Friends would come by, and we'd fry squirrel, eggs, and gravy, and it was real good," he said. "If it wasn't for squirrel, rabbit, and coon, I'd have starved as a kid."

Darriel and Annie were married when she was fifteen and he was nineteen and in the service. They'd lived in Commerce for thirty-six years. They had two children of their own, an adopted son, a grandchild, and two great-grandchildren.

Barges passed, pushed by two tugs. We'd seen that combination before and wondered why the two tugs. Darriel said that one of the tugs was deadheading, that is, hitching a ride to save fuel. He told us about pictographs on a rock face under the water north of him. "The water has to be mighty low to see them," he said.

Annie pulled a strand of her long dark hair away from her face and got after Darriel. "You need to quit talking. You're neglecting your cooking. Put a step on it." We laughed.

Earlier, Darriel had been boasting about being highlighted in *River-Horse: A Voyage Across America* by William Least Heat-Moon. The author had been traveling the river to write about his experience and spent the night at Darriel's. I'd been taking notes from the time we sat down with him, but he hadn't noticed. Laurel pointed at me and said, "She's an author, too, and writing about this trip."

Darriel got flustered, and his face grew as red as his hair. "Oh, my. Am I going to be in another book?" He lit another cigarette, and a few moments passed before he could focus on cooking again.

When Annie went inside for more sweet tea, we asked Darriel about the cast iron skillets hanging on the garage wall. Annie collected them, he explained, and the large variety of sizes and shapes we saw was the overflow from the house. Darriel said she bought them anywhere she could find them and had collected them for years.

Darriel bragged about the catfish he'd caught. The biggest was sixty pounds. He was stocked with enough for the winter. And he told us about hoggin'. Laurel said other people called it noodlin', a way to catch fish where you put your hand into a hole under the water and reach around until you catch something. Darriel said, "When you catch a snake, you simply throw it aside and put your hand back in." We laughed.

A picture of a man hung on the wall with a plaque next to it. The plaque read, "Good friends will bail you out of jail. The best of friends will be sitting next to you saying 'Damn that was fun.'" Darriel said the man was his best friend. Tears welled up in his eyes as he said, "We'd been drinking. He was killed in a car crash on the way home from here."

Needing to stretch our legs, we walked around town. We explored the outside of the historic Anderson Guest House, built in 1847, that sat overlooking the river on a hill behind Darriel's home. It was a red brick structure with white trim that had been closed for some time. Remnants of gardens were in the front and back yards. We were told shackles still hung on the basement walls, left over from the days of slavery.

Commerce was established in 1790 and was considered a real river town. There used to be a ferry in town, and Commerce had been the county seat. Laurel was intrigued by the town's history and read a historical marker that spoke of Tywappity Bottoms—a village of fifteen families that was settled in 1788. The plaque read, "[The bottom] was then covered with great forest, interspersed with small prairie, numerous lakes . . . and many sluggish streams called bayous . . . Part of this bottom produced rushes also known as scouring rush or horsetail eight feet high, so large and thick that it was difficult for a man to make his way among them." (From Louis Houck's description of Tywappity Bottom in his 1908 history of Missouri.)

A magnolia tree caught our attention, and Laurel went over to touch its leaves. We hadn't seen one that towered above a three-story house before. Many of the trees in town were sizable. Back at Darriel's we asked about the trees, and he said that one of the huge cottonwoods in the town's park was where people had been hung. We wondered which one.

Darriel said the '93 flood was bad for town, but the '95 flood was the worst. A lot of people had been bought out after that, and many houses were moved to Blodgett, ten miles from Commerce.

Annie came out with the third round of sweet tea while Darriel made a fresh batch of fish. Shortly afterward, Gwyn and Pat arrived in a rented jeep. As they walked up to the table of food Pat said, "Well, it's clear we didn't need to worry about you." Gwyn's eyes lit up when she saw the hushpuppies—her favorite, and not something she can get in Wyoming. Gwyn and Pat sat with Annie and Darriel and enjoyed the food while the three of us went to secure the kayaks for the night.

I told Darriel we'd settle up with him in the morning when we came for the kayaks, and he said, "I don't know about that." I thanked him for letting us leave them there.

In the jeep, Pat told us what had happened. "This morning after you got going on the water, we pulled out of the levee parking area with Kit and Barb behind us. When we turned the first corner, we heard *click, click, click*. Gwyn got out of the van and said—"

"—just roll forward slowly," Gwyn continued. "We couldn't hear the clicking sound anymore, so we kept rolling forward. We wanted to check on it, so I got out of the van and ran beside it to watch it as Pat drove."

"We went slowly down the street with Gwyn walking beside the van," said Pat. "Two gentlemen on the right were watching us, and one on the left."

"You could tell they wondered, 'What are those women doing?'" laughed Gwyn. "I'm running down the middle of the street beside the van, not in the van. Kit and Barb were still behind us."

"They didn't get out and try to find out what we were doing," said Pat. "We made a left, they made a left. Then we made a right into Schnucks grocery store and never saw them again."

"In the parking lot, we lay down on the ground, rolling around trying to see what was going on," said Gwyn.

"Gwyn got back in the van and started driving slowly, and we heard *clickety-click, clickety-click*," said Pat. "At that point we decided to get ourselves to a tire store, which was nearby. We pulled in and took up the entire parking lot. While Gwyn worked on her computer, I told our story. Within a matter of minutes, a rather large man came out to look at the van. He barely fit in the seat, but he was the kindest man. In moments, he had the trailer unhitched and the van in the shop.

"Gwyn said, 'I think I'll go find a post office,' and right after the words got out of her mouth, a post office truck pulls up and the postman tells her where the post office is—right up the street. The bookstore, where we wanted to get a copy of *The Language of Letting Go*, was right across the street, so Gwyn headed out.

"When Gwyn came back, she started working on her computer

again. It wasn't long and the gentleman came out and told us there wasn't anything wrong with the tires. He thought something was wrong with the drive shaft and that we needed take it to a Chevy repair place."

"We asked him how much, and he said nothing because it was diagnostic," said Gwyn. "Pat gave him a tip, which he reluctantly accepted. We headed out, and with each right turn the *clickety-click, clickety-click* got louder. We pulled into the Doad Chevy dealership and found the service department. One of the servicemen, Shawn—bless his heart— totally helped us.

"As soon as Shawn heard what we were doing, the crew squeezed us in. The issue was the drive shaft. The dealership didn't have the parts we needed, so Shawn sent the shaft to a machinist and got it rebuilt the same day. Then he called Enterprise and got a car rental arranged. The car rental guy gave us a cool jeep with lots of room in it for our gear. They wanted to rent us a full-size pickup so we could put the kayaks in the back, but then we explained how long our kayaks were."

"Shawn was a gentleman and opened the doors for us where the service area was. We got our sandwiches out and had lunch. Gwyn worked, and I read a book."

"We were thinking, 'Oh, my gosh, they don't have anything to eat,'" said Gwyn. "Meanwhile you guys were feasting on catfish and hushpuppies. From now on, paddlers are going to have to take lunch with them, even if we plan to meet up with the van."

We arrived at the dealership in time to gather what we needed for the night. Shawn greeted us and said the crew was able to get things done quickly and we'd have the van back by nine o'clock the next morning. John, the mechanic, already had the shaft and was preparing to put it in.

We went to the hotel to quickly clean up and then headed to dinner.

Kitty, Laurel, and I weren't hungry and shared an appetizer while Gwyn and Pat enjoyed their dinners. "Getting stranded made for a pretty rich day," I said. "While we were at Darriel's, I couldn't figure out how to get a message to you that we were fine. I knew you two would have a good time because you were together."

"How do you two know each other?" asked Laurel.

"Gwyn is one of my long-time, absolutely fabulous friends," answered Pat.

"We've known each other since Earth Day 1980," said Gwyn.

"We worked together," said Pat. "There were rough times, as I recall. She's the reason I started with Nancy on the second leg of this journey. Our friend Cis said, 'Pat, you have to come with me to the Gathering because Gwyn is going to be there.' Gwyn didn't know I was going. My being there was a total surprise. I'd only planned to stay the weekend, but I was there for ten days."

"Pat and her skillet . . ." said Gwyn shaking her head and grinning.

"She brought her electric skillet along last time, and it proved to be invaluable at campsites. She created some of the best meals in that thing."

"I made fried peaches at camp night before last," said Pat.

"On Sunday?" said Kitty. "I haven't caught up with the days yet, they're going by too fast."

"They're going by faster than I expected too," I said. "That's because there's always something going wrong." We all laughed.

"Where do you normally paddle?" Gwyn asked Laurel.

"As a kid, we floated the rivers," answered Laurel. "My dad used to take the whole family on the river every fall. When we went to Colorado, I went whitewater rafting and that was fun. I took classes around Columbia, Missouri. I'd never done a big river."

"What did you think?" asked Gwyn.

"I love it," answered Laurel, adjusting her glasses. "I've lived in Missouri my whole life, and I live a hundred yards from the Missouri River. It seems silly not to be on it. I'd been on it in little boats, but I'd never paddled. There's a race from Kansas City to St. Louis that's getting real popular with kayakers. My family provided support with sandwiches and stuff the last three or four years.

"I told my kids I wanted us to float part of the Missouri together. We haven't done that yet. When we vacationed in Ely and I saw Nancy's books I thought, 'Oh my gosh, I've got to do this when I turn fifty.' That was five or six years ago, and I didn't think it would really happen. This summer I started thinking about turning fifty and looked up Nancy's website. I thought, 'Oh my gosh. They're going to do it again. This is too good to be true.'"

"I think we should keep a running tab of all the people who are helping us," said Pat. "Nearly every day somebody does something. There's been no hesitation. You know how some people might say, 'Oh, here we go again with another sob story.' There hasn't been any of that."

"I think it has to do with our attitudes," I said. "We don't come in whining and complaining. We didn't say anything to Darriel. He overheard the phone call and went back and told Annie they had to feed us."

We couldn't help overhearing the conversation at the next table regarding emails and text messaging. The people at the table spoke with the abbreviations people use while texting, like LOL. We felt as if we were listening to people speak a foreign language. We couldn't follow what they were saying.

"LOL is a written expression of that uncomfortableness that can happen before or after conversations," said Laurel, "that little giggle-thing that girls often do. I have five teenagers who hang out at our house. We have two staying with us who are eleven and fourteen, so I'm learning all of that."

"Foster kids?" asked Gwyn.

"Not exactly," replied Laurel. "The youngest is my daughter's best friend, and the older one is in the same classroom as my other daughter. We've known them for six years. They were about to lose their trailer. The floor started to fall out of it, and it leaked. So the mother and her two kids moved in with us about a year ago. The situation works out because the mother works split shifts as a waitress and struggles to make a living. The kids are great."

Laurel paused for a moment while our water glasses were refilled and then asked, "Have y'all thought about whether you're floating tomorrow?"

"We need to look at the charts," I said. "We have a couple of ideas about where we could put in, but it'd mean a thirty-mile day with no options for getting off."

"We can't guarantee we can arrange a catfish lunch for tomorrow," kidded Gwyn.

"If the van hadn't broke down, we'd have paid him the fifteen dollars and that would've been it," I said. "We wouldn't have been invited into the garage."

"It's a unique place," said Laurel. "How else would we have learned about Commerce, Missouri, Lewis and Clark, the shackles, the slaves, and the hanging tree. Today we got a whole chapter of history that we'd never have known to seek out. So," she said, shifting back to the topic of paddling, "the options for tomorrow are no paddling or thirty miles?"

"I have to look at the charts," I said.

"That's a wilderness area we are headed into downriver," said Pat.

"We might be able to alter where we start," said Gwyn.

"You won't get to ride the Dorena Ferry," I said.

"That's what I was thinking," said Pat.

"We could ride it for fun," said Gwyn, teasing. "We could ride it and then turn around and come right back."

"Forty-five minutes till cookies back at the hotel," announced Laurel. "We could run around the building three or four times beforehand."

"This girl is really into sugar," I said.

"My kids are underweight, so I do everything I can to get calories into them," said Laurel. "At my house, we have cookies and milk at bedtime."

We headed to our hotel. Over chocolate chip cookies, our conversation grew serious.

"I lost custody of my children for four years when I was first divorced," I said. "Shortly after I got them back, I sensed something wasn't right and suspected the girls had experienced some sexual abuse. I didn't have a way to talk to them about it. Then when Sara Jo got into junior high, she started acting out.

"I was painting at the time, something I called *The Emotion Series*, pieces that helped me recover from abuse I'd experienced. The kids

watched me express deep emotions in a safe way. Sara Jo began drawing pictures. One day she left a picture on the kitchen table of an empty bed, and underneath it was written "The Biggest Witness." My suspicions were confirmed and I felt helpless. 'What do I do with this? How do I fix this?'

"A couple mornings later, after she'd gone to school, I found a note from her on the table. It explained what had happened when she was seven and how her father and his girlfriend, the mother of the abuser, hadn't believed her. She was called a liar. I had just read her note and was overwhelmed with emotion when Sara Jo popped back in the door—she'd forgotten her flute. She saw the note in my hand, and her eyes widened like an animal caught in a trap. She bolted past me, grabbed her flute, and dashed for the door. I grabbed her and said, 'I believe you, and we're going to do something about this. I don't know what right now. I love you.' She pulled away and ran out the door."

With a lump in my throat I continued. "I never understood the difference between rage and anger until then. In that moment, I was capable of killing the thirteen-year-old kid who'd abused Sara Jo, and maiming her father and his ex-girlfriend.

"The girls got counseling, and Sara Jo connected with her rage, which she aimed at me for a while. I was a safe target. I also felt I deserved some of it. I felt guilty. I should have protected her, but I didn't know. The experience was painful, but I knew where her rage was coming from. Eventually she wanted to prosecute the perpetrator. We were unable to locate him because her father couldn't provide the kid's last name. It was frustrating because the statute of limitations ran out while we searched for him. It tore Sara Jo apart that she couldn't stop him from abusing other girls. To turn her experience into something positive, she told her story to her classmates at the junior high."

"That's courageous," remarked Pat.

"I know!" I said. "She took verbal abuse from her classmates at first, but the more she told her story, the more respect she gained. She continued telling her story into high school, and many kids who were being abused came forward.

"I hadn't heard the details of what happened, and one day she asked me to come and hear her story. The kids in the class were nervous about my being there. In her talk she shared some of the details of what he had done, how he had threatened her to keep her quiet, how scared she was, and how she felt like she was bad. As the students listened to Sara Jo talk, they spun around to see what kind of reaction I had. I tried to buffer the emotions on my face, but rage surfaced again.

"I had the kids when I left my ex-husband, but I couldn't make a go of it and asked him to take them for a couple of weeks while I found a job and figured things out. During those two weeks, our divorce proceedings went to court. I lost the kids because back then, in the state of Minnesota, whoever had physical custody of the children at the time of the divorce retained custody. That technicality was one of many things my lawyer didn't inform me about. The day we went to court, I heard my lawyer say to my ex-husband's lawyer on the way out of the courthouse, 'There's another man who didn't get railroaded by a woman.' I was devastated and felt completely alone. My connection to the kids was reduced to two weekends a month, and I was ordered to pay child support.

"I took that opportunity to do whatever I could to get my head on straight. If I was going to help the kids, or have a chance at getting them back, I had a lot of healing to do. I did a lot of counseling and started college to be a counselor. Getting them back was a long, difficult dance that got ugly."

"Before each medical exam," Laurel said, "we doctors ask our patients the same question: Is there anything in your past, be it physical abuse or other trauma, that'll make this exam difficult? What I've found after seven years of practice is that very few women would tell me the truth until the third or fourth year that I asked that same question. After the third or fourth year, they'd say, 'Yeah, that happened to me when I was five.' It's been documented that 30 percent of women have been abused. I have to say the percentage is actually closer to 50."

"Does it take that long to trust someone?" asked Kitty.

"Yes," said Laurel emphatically. "It's good that doctors ask that question every time now. I think every time patients hear the question, they think about it. I have a good friend who, when we were twelve, called me and said, 'I think I'm pregnant because my dad's been abusing me for many years, and I've never had a period. You're into all of the science stuff, so maybe you can tell me.' I said, 'I don't think so. I think you're too young.' We were only twelve at the time! I didn't know what to do, so I didn't do anything. I have regrets about that. She was twenty-seven the next time she brought the abuse up. She said, 'Did I ever say anything to you about that?' I said, 'Yes, we were twelve, and you asked if I thought you were pregnant. You don't remember that?'"

"It's amazing what we can block out," I said.

"What brought the abuse forward for her when she was twenty-seven?" asked Kitty.

"She was going to have a baby," replied Laurel. "The abusive experience gets stored, and having a baby releases it. Being pregnant forces you to deal with your body. You have to look at your physical being."

"That reminds me of a question that has been on my mind," said Kitty. "There are a rising number of Caesarean sections. Why?"

"I believe the modern obstetric system is one of the most abusive systems for women that there is," answered Laurel. "I believe the men who go into obstetrics are driven there by the need to have power and control over women. I wouldn't tolerate the kind of treatment most women receive at the hands of obstetric physicians. I think women need to stand up and say, 'You can't treat me that way.' When are you more vulnerable? When are you more exposed? Unfortunately that field doesn't draw many people who are compassionate, tuned in, and caring. Maybe 20 percent are. I wouldn't let the people who went into that field from my medical school touch my dog."

"I've never gone to a male gynecologist," said Gwyn.

"It's not just the men," Laurel said. "In order to succeed, women have to play the game, although they're better. It's a surgical field. People who go into it want to cut."

"All three of my children were born by Caesarean," I said. "My doctor told me, 'Once a Caesarean, always a Caesarean.' I was told the option of having a child normally was never on the table for me because the incision would burst and I could die if I tried. I walked away from the first one feeling like I'd done something wrong."

"The hierarchy is set up to make you feel that way," said Laurel, sitting up straighter and leaning toward us. "Who do we want to blame if things don't go well? The victim. We're certainly not going to blame the hospital or the obstetrician. Everything is set up to blame the woman, who wasn't supported or cared for during the process. I look at my sister, Donna, who was a big bra burner in the '60s. She fought for equality and birth control, which is phenomenal because women could then choose. But women who chose natural childbirth had few resources. Gaining control of how women are treated by doctors, particularly in obstetrics, is the last frontier where women are systematically devalued and victimized, and their moms stand behind quietly."

"They don't know anything different," I responded.

"The moms are a generation older. They should have figured it out," Laurel said.

"No . . ." said Pat, Kitty, and I in unison.

"We're talking about women who didn't feel they had any say and believed they must be wrong in the face of authority," I said. "It's going to be our generation that's going to change things."

"It's not going to be our parents," pleaded Pat.

"Here's what young women are faced with," Laurel continued. "A woman is in the middle of labor, and somebody comes in and says, 'Your baby is going to die unless you do what I say.' What is she going to say? What would any woman who loves her child say? 'I don't care what you do to me—save my baby.' And that's the way these things are approached. In fact, there's a book called *How to Get Women to Agree to Your Treatment* that's circulated among obstetricians. The book lists fifteen steps on how to take somebody you think is being difficult and convince her to do what you want her to do. The last of the big guns you pull out is 'Your baby is going to die unless you do what I say.' Who on earth is going to argue with that in the middle of labor?"

"Nobody," said Kitty.

"Who wrote the book?" asked Pat, disgusted.

"A male obstetrician," said Laurel.

September 28, Day Eight

Staying in a hotel gave me a chance to catch up on planning details: studying charts to locate new boat ramps, reviewing road maps to determine routes for the van, getting press releases out, and emailing contacts downriver. I got a lot done and felt lighter even though the daily reworking of plans due to the van's breaking down and our not making daily paddling mileage was frustrating. Each evening the planning chores ensued. I scoured the charts and maps and considered mileage. How far could we realistically paddle given the skill levels of those paddling any given day? How long would the day's paddling take? How would we work in the day's commitments? I considered the speed of the river, how much daylight we'd have, van support, and the ripple effect a change in plans would have on future days' plans, including the transportation of participants to and from airports for arrivals and departures.

I struggled to keep the details in my head, but with so many I often lost track of them. Each day I was repeatedly asked by the other team members about the following day or the day after that. I couldn't answer their questions because I hadn't reworked that day's schedule yet. It was tiresome to keep explaining that I only had a day at a time clearly figured out. I understood the need for that information—I had the same need. There just wasn't enough time to get ahead of the game.

I was feeling particularly frustrated when Pat asked me about where we were staying the following evening. "Look in the book," I said curtly.

"I haven't had time to look in the book," she said sharply.

To answer her question I'd have to look in the book, which was kept out so it was readily available to everyone. Why was I supposed to have time to look?

Fuming, I picked up *The Language of Letting Go*, which I often referred to as "the meditation book," and randomly opened it. The words I turned to were about temporary setbacks. I laughed. The passage reminded me that setbacks were a part of life and only temporary, and it helped me keep my feelings in perspective.

We picked up the van from Doad Chevrolet as soon as it opened in the morning, and then we headed to Darriel's for the kayaks.

I wanted to settle up with Darriel and he resisted, but we insisted. I gave him copies of the books about the previous two trips. He was

photo by Kitty Kennedy

excited to receive them and said he'd start reading them right away.

Kayaks loaded, we drove to New Madrid, Missouri, where we would put in for the day's paddle. We appreciated the trailer modifications my son, Wade, had made for us. Four kayaks fit and were easy to load. The interior design of the trailer accommodated much of our gear, so less had to go in the van. The Hullavator, one borrowed from our friend Mitch and the other donated by our friend Donna, made loading the other two kayaks on top of the van effortless. The Hullavator is a kayak lift system that brings the loading brackets down alongside the van. Then the system's gas-assist shocks raise the kayak onto the van and do the heavy lifting. On the previous trips, we had lifted the sixty-pound kayaks up to the top of the van each time we loaded.

While we prepared our kayaks, Gwyn was double checking her gear and everything on her kayak. A barge moved opposite the boat ramp and parked in the channel. A van pulled up and a woman got out and waited at the bottom of the ramp. Kitty struck up a conversation with her and learned she was a tugboat cook and was there to begin her shift. Like most tugboat crew members, she worked thirty days on and thirty days off, with a daily schedule of six hours on, six hours off. She traveled the Mississippi, Ohio, and Missouri rivers. A small boat pulled away from the barge and headed in our direction. On board was the cook she was to replace.

The river was wider here than back at Commerce. I felt anxious preparing to paddle, not knowing the effects of the Ohio River. I expected faster water and possible turbulence. Slightly downriver, turbulent waves bounced off the north end of New Madrid Island where the current collided with it. Paddling our side of the island wasn't an option because the New Madrid Bend Dike stretched from the island to shore, making it impassable. Watching the rolling waves, I thought that Gwyn's first day of paddling and Laurel's last day of paddling could be exciting.

Gwyn's excitement about paddling was evident in her wide eyes, quick speech, and determined smile. We said goodbye to Kitty and Pat and headed directly across the river toward the channel, but the current pushed us quickly downriver toward the island and into the choppy water. A barge approached that we hadn't seen from the landing and I watched it intently. The barge traveled the far side of the river, and I concluded it wouldn't be a problem. As waves beat against my kayak I called back to Gwyn and Laurel to paddle hard. They were close behind. We cleared the island, and finding the channel calmer, I breathed more easily.

The day was rich with bird sightings: blue herons, pelicans, cormorants, egrets, and turkey vultures. We enjoyed riding the wake of an upstream barge for the longest time. The weather was good and offered a breeze, which gave us relief from the smell of cotton crop defoliant that was so thick I could taste it.

Searching for a lunch spot, I saw a heron that led us to a perfect place. I plopped down in the sand. Laurel and Gwyn flanked me and took a seat. Before digging into her lunch Gwyn stared at the river. I could see the tensions of her life melting away as she said, "This is truly amazing."

Laurel looked up at the expanse. "It sure is. It's amazing to be out here."

We let our imaginations play and identified shapes, including Snoopy on a skateboard, in the drifting clouds.

The sand was fine and the beach had shallow ridges carved into it from varying water levels. Small bits of shells were scattered about. Behind us the landscape was thick with willows. Around us lay driftwood of all sizes. Pieces half buried in the sand showed signs of heavy water wear and were stripped of their branches. Others had branches intact, which created perfect places for spiders to spin webs. Tire tracks from a four-wheeler swooped out of the trees, looped around, and returned. Delicate bird tracks ran in several directions.

I looked at the river charts and checked the time. It was later in the afternoon than I had imagined. I was disappointed that our mileage hadn't changed. The Ohio River wasn't having an effect on how far we traveled in a day.

With four miles of our thirteen miles to go, we reluctantly left our secluded beach. We followed a narrow waterway the river had carved out between the mainland and the sandbar. Three hours later we cut along the inside of the last curve and headed to the opposite shore to Linda Boat Landing where Kitty and Pat waited. A headwind created waves as we aimed for a spot an eighth mile north of the boat ramp in an attempt to adjust for the current. The current was stronger than we anticipated, and the closer we got to shore, the harder we had to paddle to stay on course for the ramp. The- push was exhausting.

At the end of a paddling day we appreciated the eager, smiling faces waiting for us. Kitty and Pat helped us land and get our gear loaded. Linda Boat Ramp was particularly challenging. The ramp was longer than we were used to and covered in loose gravel that made walking precarious.

Kitty reported that the motel where we had a reservation was seedy, so she and Pat had made new reservations in Sikeston, which meant we'd be doing more miles of driving. The added driving time detracted from our being on the river and ate into the time I needed to take care of planning details. My mood slipped downward.

The wind on the highway was stronger than we'd experienced paddling, and it shook the van every time a semi blew past us, adding to my irritation. Laurel got her iPhone out and began giving directions to the motel. I attempted to let go of the idea of traveling the river the way I'd held it in my mind for the past few years. Things were not going according to my plans.

For dinner we went to Lambert's, the home of the "throwed rolls." We laughed from the time we got to the parking lot until we returned to the hotel. Lambert's entryway is rustic and lined with arcade games. The dining room has dozens of long tables with bench seats. Car license plates from all over the country cover the walls. Servers walked between tables offering the pass-arounds: fried okra, fried potatoes and onions, macaroni and tomatoes, black-eyed peas, and sorghum for the hot rolls.

Shortly after being seated at our table we were offered samples of fried okra. In the spirit of trying new things, we each sampled the hog jowls that Laurel bravely ordered. They looked like short strips of thick bacon but didn't taste like bacon. A jowl is a cheek muscle. The piece I tried was slightly salty and chewy like a rubber band.

While we waited for our food, we watched a young man throw fresh hot rolls to customers. Our food arrived, and it was our turn to have rolls thrown at us. I waited until he was across the room to put my hand up for a second roll so he'd have farther to throw it. His aim was often better than a customer's ability to catch. One staff person was assigned to pick up the rolls that landed on the floor.

September 29, Day Nine

I headed to the lobby to work on my laptop knowing Gwyn would be there working on hers too. Soon Kitty, Pat, and Laurel joined us. During breakfast we watched a pair of fledgling mourning doves who'd outgrown their nest. Puffs of fluffy down stuck out from among the mature feathers, making them look unkempt. They made repeated trips to the end of the branch and back to the nest while fluttering their wings. We laughed as they nearly fell trying to get around each other. One of the birds took its first flight and landed on the ledge above the window to the cheers of our group. The second one enjoyed having the nest to itself, but it eventually took flight and landed on the ground.

Laurel told us about a friend of hers who had found a dove after its mother was killed. She took it home as a pet. It sat on her shoulder and came when she called it. She took it to work at her flower shop, where it flew around the store.

My mind wandered to the list of things I needed to do, and I thought about the plastic baseball we had found in the water. "We haven't put a face on the ball I found yet. We need to do that if we're going to give her a personality like the balls that traveled with us on the last two trips," I said. "She doesn't have a name either."

"What were the names of the balls from the other trips?" asked Gwyn.

"Penelope, a standard-size football, was the first one," said Kitty. "The second one was Penny, a smaller football."

"So we need another P name," said Gwyn. "How about Pricilla or Polly?"

"Pansy?" I asked, at a loss for any other names that started with P. The others laughed.

"Polly seems the best so far, so Polly it is," said Gwyn emphatically.

I retrieved the ball and markers from the van, and we each claimed a characteristic of the face to draw. Polly acquired a personality as Gwyn hesitantly drew her chin, making it look like a canoe crossing big waves; Laurel gave her wide eyes with long eyelashes; Pat drew her eyebrows with an expression of excitement; Kitty gave her a Roman nose; and I drew a mouth that could either be singing or screaming. We cut a plastic cup in half for her body and used the hot pink duct tape to secure her to it.

While the others put the finishing touches on Polly, I called my Auntie Joyce, who's ninety-five. Before I left for the trip, she'd sent me a letter saying if she were younger she'd be paddling with me, or at least riding along in the van. Now she told me to pay attention to the small things because they helped shape the major events of her life. She told me to have a wonderful trip. "Do you feel me with you?" she asked. "I've been visualizing myself standing with you each morning when you sing that lovely song at the shore."

"I do," I said. "I feel you with me always." I told her I appreciated the undying support she'd offered me through the years. I felt teary and grateful for her when we hung up. Joyce and her sister Jean had been like mothers to me, which filled a void left by my mother's death.

In the hotel conference room Pat used the electric skillet to cook a lunch of all the leftovers from the cooler, and she covered them in cheese. Carroll, a hotel staff person, helped us set up. Carroll's name had the same unique spelling as Gwyn's mother's name. Carroll said her name meant love in Apache.

Gwyn had a persistent headache, and Laurel showed her how to use acupressure points, which gave her some relief. I was still feeling frustrated and down. The vigilance I kept and planning I needed to do left me feeling separate from the group. I talked about how I felt, and Gwyn declared the following day would be a no paddle day. She, too, was overwhelmed with the work she needed to finish. A day off would give us a chance to catch up and relax.

Later that afternoon in New Madrid we split up to get things done before the Gathering. We dropped Gwyn off at the park where the Gathering would be held. Kitty and Pat ran errands around town. Laurel and I went to the New Madrid Historical Museum.

In the museum we learned that the town of New Madrid was founded in 1789 and named for Madrid, Spain. More than 160 Indian mounds have been discovered in the county. New Madrid is located on a fault line of the same name. In 1811 people in town experienced the most severe earthquakes on record in the area, with aftershocks that continued for a year. Shocks were felt as far as 1,100 miles away.

According to details we found in a pamphlet produced by the New Madrid Historical Museum, survivors said the ground rose and fell like waves on the water. Waves on the Mississippi swamped many boats and washed others ashore. For a time the river ran upstream. Islands disappeared and new ones appeared. Small tremors continue to be felt in the area but are considered routine.

During the Civil War a Confederate leader chose a huge bend located near New Madrid to set up defenses, which included a stronghold on Island No.10. The Union forces, led by General John Pope, cut a canal through the forest to a bayou and bypassed the stronghold. Then Pope's men used armor-plated gunboats and attacked with a long-range bombardment, gaining control of the river.

Laurel and I spoke with eighty-six-year-old Dorothy, who worked at the museum. When we asked about her life, Dorothy freely shared details with us. She was Woman of the Year for the local sorority in 2011, she began. She told us she'd lived in St. Louis, New Orleans, Birmingham, and New Madrid. "Everybody's nice here. It's a small town, and you have to get used to that." One of her fondest memories was playing softball between the ages of fifteen and twenty-two. The most important thing to her was getting married and having her girls. "I was married at twenty-one, and I've had a good life." Dorothy told us she has four daughters and thirty-three grandchildren and great-grandchildren, and then she stopped abruptly. "That's all about me. I need to let y'all go. Y'all enjoy looking around."

Laurel went through the museum to quench her appetite for information while I went out for a walk. As I headed out the door Dorothy called out to me. "Just have fun. That's my motto."

Walking the levee, I met Claire, a tall dark-haired woman. I asked her about the building on Main Street with a metal cage-like structure around it.

"That's the telephone company building," said Claire with a melodic southern accent. "That stuff around it is called retrofitting—for earthquakes. The Catholic school has been retrofitted too. Do you know about the New Madrid fault?"

"Yes, I learned about it in the museum," I said.

"We have earthquakes all the time," said Claire. "Small ones we can feel. You hear them first, a rumble that sounds like a truck going down the street. Things in the house shake for a little bit. We had one about two weeks ago that was felt over in Poplar Bluff.

"In 1990 Iben Browning from Colorado predicted a sizable earthquake on the New Madrid fault. We had a mass media influx, thirty satellite trucks, all kinds of reporters from Minnesota and Michigan. I asked one of them, 'What are you going to do if we do have a big one?' He said, 'My company will come and get me out.' I said, 'Well, buddy, they won't be able to get you out, and you probably won't be here to get out.'

"Browning's prediction was for a size eight earthquake that would have struck from Memphis to St. Louis. The whole infrastructure of the United States would be gone. This reporter thought his company would send a helicopter to get him." She scrunched her eyebrows, looked me in the eye, and said, "Can you imagine if they did send a helicopter and there were survivors? They'd all be trying to get on that helicopter."

"I can't imagine the panic."

"I've seen all kinds of vessels going up and down the river," said Claire, looking out over the water. "I've actually seen a raft made out of fifty-gallon drums. I've seen replicas of old ships that stopped in here. About four years ago, there was a man in a kayak who'd started in St. Louis. It was in April and the water was high. He said to me, 'I have these maps, and they show all these dikes, but I haven't seen any.' And I said, 'Well, honey, you're going over them.' "

"He didn't realize that?"

"Guess not," Claire said laughing, and then she grew somber. "Two years ago, a young man from Minnesota came through. He was all by himself. His father had passed away in February, and three months after that his girlfriend died from a heart attack."

"That's so sad."

"She was diabetic," said Claire. "He was paddling and raising money for the Diabetes Association. This guy was doing his trip to clear his mind. I don't know what ever happened to him. That's the deal. You meet these people and then you wonder, 'Did he make it?' I gave him my address."

We finished talking, and I invited her to our Gathering. Just as I returned to the museum, Laura was coming out and Kitty and Pat pulled up to get us. Then we headed to the park. When we arrived the park was buzzing with people, and the pavilion was full. Gwyn informed us the school athletic team photos were being taken there and that a football game would be starting across the street the same time as our Gathering. We moved our things away from the pavilion and set up in the shade of a tree.

While waiting for us Gwyn had a conversation with Arlene, an older woman who'd lived in New Madrid her whole life and had a great affinity for the river. She said she really wished she'd known that we were coming through because she would have liked to paddle with us. Since she was born Arlene had been a member of the First United Methodist Church, the oldest Methodist church west of the Mississippi, and her family members were some of the church's oldest members. She wanted to stay for the Gathering, but she was headed to church for a bereavement dinner.

We sat in a circle and Donna, Laurel's sister, joined us. Donna's comfortable bright patterned clothes reflected the '60s era. Kids played around us. People rode golf carts in the park and walked past us. Some greeted us, asking if we were the people paddling the river. Many said, "Godspeed to you." They said our trip sounded exciting and dangerous, and they wished us luck. Each time a woman headed our way my hopes were raised, but each time she walked past, declining our invitation, I felt let down.

An older man pulled up on his golf cart. Walter introduced himself first and then his Shih Tzu, Baby Beebe. Walter had been a sheriff for twenty-five years. He liked being sheriff, he said, but he got voted out because he didn't play the game. He flirted and teased us a bit and then mentioned his wife was kind of jealous. "I don't know why. My gosh, I'm eighty-two years old."

"You're still a catch," said Kitty with a wink.

"Well, it looks like you got everything under control here, so I guess I will be moving along," said Walter. "I better go before I step on my toes."

The park continued to fill with people as families and fans arrived for the high school football game. "It's impressive to see how many people turn out for football night," said Gwyn. People continued to greet us as they walked past, yet no one joined our circle.

The fire was burning and a cool breeze blew as Donna, Laurel, Gwyn,

Pat, Kitty, and I began talking.

"Jenny Morgan says I have the spiritual mentality of a seven-year-old," said Donna laughing. "I didn't know if that was a compliment or a criticism.

"I lived a thousand miles south of the California border in Baja, where the beaches are free and you can live right on them." A look of sweet nostalgia crossed her face. "We carried water and pooped in the desert and had a little solar electricity. The dolphins would go by in the morning. People were building houses on the beach. We built a house using a lot of Mexican labor. The roof was pitched inward. It was a total concrete house. You could open up all of the doors in three separate sections under this monolithic roof that was like a stingray. It pitched inward and had a concrete beam in the center, so it was a hyperbolic paraboloid.

"A hurricane came and put holes in it, so we tore it down. It didn't fit in the neighborhood anyway. None of our houses fit in the neighborhood. They were weird.

"The first house we built was the snail house, and it was made with laminated barn rafters. It started small and went up and around a central concrete post made of manhole risers stacked on top of each other to make a tower. The floor was like a spider web. It was cool.

"Then we built a silo house made out of spruce-green silos for a couple who had just come back from Tanzania and wanted something resembling African huts. The house was one silo inside the other to allow space for insulation and wiring. It had a conical roof with a huge solar collector on the top. This was in the '70s.

"In '76, I met some guys south of San Francisco building a house with a sod roof. It was one of highest spots in the Bay area, and it followed the curve of the hill and had a tram wall. A tram wall is a concrete wall that has glazing in front and airspace behind it. The cold air falls down behind the walls and rises up by the windows. The tram wall can either bring the heat into the house or send the heat out.

"A few years later, I lived on a thousand-acre ranch. A millionaire had sent me from New York to live with his ranch manager. That was pretty cool. He wanted me to get married to the ranch manager and have kids. He loved his ranch manager, and I was a little present for him." She laughed and shook her head. "I didn't marry the ranch manager. I'm not the marrying type.

"Once I had a pretend marriage to a Tunisian guy when I lived in Tripoli. I had to become a Muslim first, so I became a Muslim in the court. When I went in to get married, the judges asked, 'Who is your father? You have to have a father to get married.' So they went and got the janitor to be my father. The judges were so happy because they had gotten points in heaven because I had become a convert to Islam.

"Every time we would get in a fight, the Tunisian guy and I, we would say it was time to get the divorce. We would go to the court, but it wouldn't be open. It would be in the middle of the night or it would be the wrong day. After a year of this, the court was open one day, and we went in to get the divorce. Boy, were those judges upset. They lost their comp points in heaven because they lost their convert. When you divorce, you just say it three times, but a woman has to prove she is not having her period first. So I told the judges I had just had my period and I wasn't pregnant."

"In Missouri, you can't get divorced if you are pregnant," said Laurel. "It's the law."

"Really?" asked Donna. "I think that's something to know."

"Wow," Kitty said, furrowing her brow. "Are there other states like that?"

"I don't know." Laurel replied. "My friend Louise went to a lawyer to get a divorce, and he said, 'Nope, not while you are pregnant.'"

"Well, isn't that something," said Donna. "In Maryland, if you walk into your house and find your wife in bed with someone, you can commit murder and get away with it. Isn't that insane?"

"Tell us the camel milk story," I requested of Laurel.

"The Bedouins have drunk camel milk for years," Laurel said. "But I'm going to try to tell my story like a Native American."

"You're not going to tell the camel milk story?" I asked.

"Oh, I will get that in there," Laurel replied mischievously. Then she began. "I realize that my mother was very strong because my father had weaknesses. Even though I've spent a lot of time in my mind beating him up for those weaknesses, I realized just yesterday that she wouldn't have been so strong if he hadn't had those weaknesses. She raised her daughters to be very strong, and that was a good thing. That was her gift to us.

"I remember an important event that happened when we took my favorite cat to the vet. I was eight or nine years old. The vet said, 'She has distemper, and she's not going to make it. You ought to put her down.' I said, 'Can't you just try?' And she said, 'Well, all right. If you drop-feed her and try this medicine, maybe there's a chance she'll live.' So we bottle fed her for a week, and she lived. I remember thinking, 'I want to be a healer.' It's pretty cool to see things that you were going to give up on come back and be healed.

"I thought medical school would teach me to be a healer, but it really didn't. It taught me about drugs and surgery, so I had to look other places. Fortunately, while in medical school at one of the conferences, I met a midwife, Ina May Gaskins, America's most illustrious midwife. She would go to medical conferences and teach classes on natural childbirth and water birth, and she would show videos of the hippies on the communes having their babies in a really wonderful way. The midwife taught me more about healing than medical school.

"What ties into my experiences with the Mississippi is the healing power of water. When women are in labor, water provides them with warmth, support, and a sense of security and safety. If you are in a pool of water, it keeps everybody at an arm's distance. I think the reason I was really drawn to be on the Mississippi is that healing power of water and the transformative power. I'm going to go back and share that along with the idea that the grandmothers and grandfathers really need to speak their truths and share their wisdom and make a difference.

"The camel milk is one of those ways of healing that you wouldn't expect. If you look at the diversity and harshness of the conditions the camels live in, it makes sense. In the desert, the camels eat scrub brush and thorns and go days without water. Their offspring would never survive if they didn't develop resilience. The camels have immunoglobulin in their milk. It has ten times the vitamin C of cow's milk plus naturally occurring insulin.

"Researchers found that autistic children do incredibly well when they are ingesting something that rich. Who knows what's in it that's really doing it. They haven't quite figured it out. The Mennonites and the Amish milk camels and share the milk with families of children who have any kind of neurologic problem, and they're getting some good results. A naturopathic lady in North Carolina is trying to get FDA approval so it can be more widely available."

"What does the camel's diet have to do with it?" asked Pat. "Over in the desert, people are eating something completely different than they are here in the United States. Does the desert diet affect the camel's milk?"

"Yes, researchers found that if the camels are fed too well, their milk becomes diluted," replied Laurel. "You have to keep the camels on a desert-type diet. You can have them in the States and have them just eat brush in the woods. You don't want them on a grassy field of clover. If you feed them well, their milk becomes more like cow's milk and doesn't have all the good stuff."

"So maybe if we fed the desert-type diet to cows, their milk would get better," added Donna.

"One of the newest drugs for diabetes comes from the Gila monster," said Laurel. "The salivary secretions of the Gila monsters has an insulin-like substance in it which allows them to maintain their blood sugar even if they don't eat for a long time. I don't know who figured that out, but it's commercially available now. Somebody will probably come out with a drug that has camel's milk in it. All that was available when my son Matt was young was camel's milk."

"Do you feel the medical community is holding back information that could be helpful?" asked Pat. "Maybe there's research that may have been done and it's not moving forward because the pharmaceutical companies aren't going to make their money."

"I think a lot of good ideas don't go anywhere because there's no profit to be made from them," replied Laurel. "We know broccoli prevents colon cancer, but who's going to make money off broccoli? The things being promoted in our country are the things that feed that greed machine. Gila monster saliva could make a fortune because there's so much diabetes. I don't think the medical community is deliberately holding back. I think if everybody in power is greed driven, all of our policies and developments in the future are going to be greed driven."

"Don't you think we are already there, though?" Pat said more as a statement than a question.

"We are about as bad as you can get in that direction," said Laurel. "What I love seeing are people my son's age—the twenty-year-olds—who don't want to have a big house and a car. They don't aspire to wanting a bunch of money. It turns their stomachs. I think they're starting to figure out that we're way off course.

"Medicine is huge money, and it's driven by greed. The insurance industry has exploited the daylights out of this country for thirty years now, and it doesn't want to give up its control. The pharmaceutical industry has exploited us for maybe twenty years. The hospitals for the last fifteen to twenty years are purely profit driven. There's no service component at all.

"Insurance used to be this idea that we were going to take care of our community. When you take huge amounts of profit off it, I don't know . . ." her voice trailed. "But there's hope because the younger people are seeing it for what it is. *Rolling Stone* is exposing all kinds of greed-based decisions that we wouldn't know about otherwise. When the press becomes independent again, it can expose greed, and the next generation will see it for what it is and make a change. That's my idea.

"Health care is not about health. It used to be—it could be—but people are going to have to vote with their feet and refuse to buy health insurance. They'll have to refuse to undergo surgery unless it's life saving. Life-saving surgery is great, but all this other stuff that we do isn't."

"So how do we do that?" asked Kitty with a heavy heart. "It's like people have given their power away. How do you convince people to take that back? How do you convince people that respect is something that we are lacking in our culture?"

"I think it has to do with taking responsibility for yourself," said Pat. "There are so many people out there who say, 'Okay, you take care of me.' I think that's part of it. We each have to figure out what we can do to make our lives more fulfilled. It has to come from the individual."

"With the current lack of respect in our country, how do we build that?" asked Kitty. "I know it can be done on an individual basis, but that seems like such a small answer."

"You live your truth and teach it when you can," said Laurel confidently. "I decided that the personal was very political. I decided, even though I was in medicine, I wouldn't birth my children in a hospital."

"That's what I meant about it coming from the individual," said Pat. "Taking charge of your personal life and voting with your dollars."

"And voting with your feet," said Laurel. "Beyond that, know what your truth is and teach it. I love Oprah's magazine because in the back there's a section called 'What I Know for Sure.' This is something that I know so deep in my heart that I can stand on solid rock and share it. That teaches other people. It's a personal thing. For me, what I know for sure is raising good kids.

"I've decided that what I do as a doctor is really insignificant compared to what I do with my kids. I'm willing to work one or two days a week, but I want a lot of time with my kids. They are learning to make choices, and if they see the greed structure for what it is, then they won't be sucked into it.

"When my oldest was deciding to go to college he said, 'I think I'm going to go to Roland to become an airplane pilot.' I asked him, 'Why do you want to do that?' He said, 'Well, I know I can do it. And then I will have enough money to play music on the weekends and have a recording studio in the back of my house.' I said, 'Isn't that what you really want to do?' And he said, 'Yeah, that's what I really want to do.' I said, 'Are you willing to live simply?' He said, 'Oh, yeah. All I need is a room and a cot. I could share a room with somebody. I can live simply.' I said, 'Well, then why do you want to get this degree, to have this job, to get this money, so you can then do what you really want to do?'

"Turns out, he didn't go that route. I don't know about the rest of my kids yet. I think if you are young, you can learn from your aunts, uncles, and grandparents. Even through the most awful things, you can learn.

"Well, I love you guys, but I think I better go."

"I was really energized by this—and the other night at the Gathering," said Donna as she hugged us all.

After Laurel departed with Donna, Kitty commented how refreshing it was to hear someone in her profession speak honestly about issues within the medical community, particularly when it came to women's issues.

Laurel's journal entry:

To all paddling friends,

Thank you for the opportunity to share in your remarkable journey! As I turned fifty and contemplate the next fifty years, I needed a time to reflect and return to the basics of life . . . food, water, sleep . . . What I found on this adventure has been so much more!

Thank you for the laughter, the tears, the great stories, the wisdom on kids, bugs, barges, waffle waves, and River ways, and on young doves taking flight for the first time from the nest.

Thank you for a chance to pause from taking care of everyone . . .

the seven children at home, the four chickens in the yard, the sick and injured at work . . . What a gift to float with such an able team of planners and guides sharing the beauty of your years of planning. It's a real gift to only have to worry about getting my own stuff in the van! Thanks, moms! And grand-moms!

Most of all, I'm thankful for the chance to reconnect with the power of women's stories. Even though they're often full of pain and hardship, they hold the power to heal, teach, and ultimately save our species. Your work to empower women to share their wisdom and encourage others to hear that wisdom is nothing short of revolutionary . . . in a time where we need a grassroots, earthshaking, feminine-led revolution, not just for our daughters, but for our sons and partners, and grandchildren . . . and, of course, for ourselves. Surely there's no greater joy or meaning in life than to know and claim your personal power . . . and to support others to do the same.

Thank you again for sharing your stories and these few days of your life with me. A stranger the River washed up on your shores. Thank you for hearing my story in its evolving versions of clarity.

I return home with a new energy for my work as a storyteller. The family will want to hear about our adventure in great detail, as they're all young adventure-seekers themselves.

My husband will be glad to have his soul mate back, refreshed and energized, to help tend the gardens we have sown together for twenty-eight years. He'll be glad I found some clarity on how to celebrate our fiftieth birthdays with passion and meaning next month.

I'll return home with cherished memories of the Great Mother River and renewed respect for the healing and earth-moving power of water. Whether we're in it, on it, or near it, water is the ultimate healing medium . . . with the power to nourish, cleanse, protect, refresh, and propel us forward. I've seen the power of water in the birth process to soothe, support, protect, and invoke strong instincts for the birthing woman. Now I see the power of water to guide and encourage throughout a woman's life. The River has so much more to teach . . . Thank you for this lesson! May there be many more.

So on you go, girls! I send you love and prayers and light to carry downstream. I'll be with you in spirit and on iPhone. Keep making those ripples, and I'll see them on distant shores.

With love, Laurel

When we got back to our hotel, we felt rowdy and playful. We jumped into the pool with our life jackets on for a little synchronized swimming, at least that's what we called it. Darriel had called us mermaids, so we dubbed ourselves the PFD (personal flotation device) Mermaids. Jessica, the hotel receptionist, was accommodating when we asked her to take our picture. She shook her head and left laughing. After a brief soak in the hot tub, we headed to our rooms feeling giddy.

September 30th through October 2nd

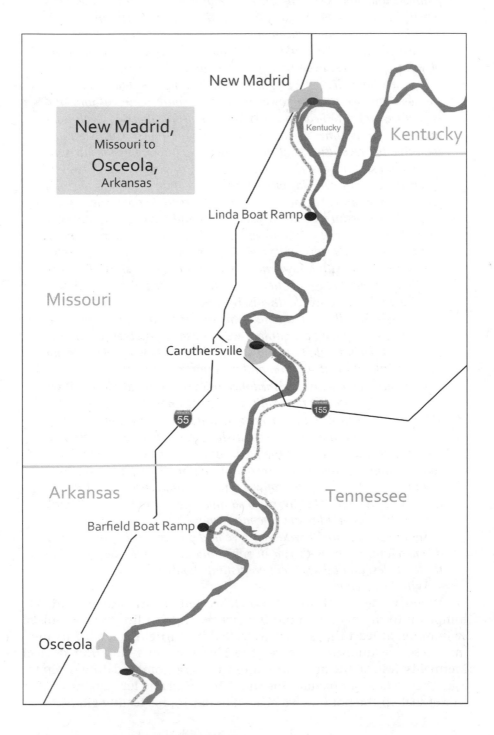

New Madrid

New Madrid,
Missouri to
Osceola,
Arkansas

Kentucky

Kentucky

Linda Boat Ramp

Missouri

Caruthersville

55

155

Arkansas

Tennessee

Barfield Boat Ramp

Osceola

3

OSCEOLA

September 30, Day Ten

I rolled out of bed, looked at myself in the mirror, and wanted to put a bag over my head. I had let my hairdresser talk me into putting a temporary red rinse in my hair, believing it would wash out I enjoyed it for a while, but I had tried everything to get it out, including vinegar and Dawn dish soap. The roots showed. I thought they glowed. I worried about first impressions every time we met someone. With unkempt hair, I didn't feel professional while talking with people about the Gatherings.

Other things were bothering me too. I was in a position of being the leader, yet decisions were often made and acted on without me. I knew van support should be making decisions too, and I didn't need to be included in every one, but if I was present and wasn't consulted, I felt invisible. I joked about how I felt because I wasn't willing to say my feelings in a straightforward manner. A typical scenario went like this: We would be traveling in the van to a location I had already checked out on the reconnaissance trip in the spring. The two women in the front seats, generally Kitty and Pat, would discuss the best way to get there. I would tell them what I knew, but their conversation would continue as if I hadn't said anything. I took their behavior personally, and I felt dismissed.

The Language of Letting Go talks about victim mentality. I realized my issue with role confusion pushed old victim buttons. I felt the front-seat folks were doing something to me, but in reality they were doing the best they could. I was determined to let go of my need to be heard about how we got to a given location.

At breakfast Gwyn said, "I was thinking about my conversation with Arlene. She said she was comfortable in one-on-one settings because she's a private person. She didn't want her neighbors and community to know her private stuff. That may be part of what we're facing as we head south. Northern women, in general, seem more open than southern women."

"Is there that much distinction between the North and South?" asked Kitty, surprised.

"In the South there are a lot of things you don't talk about," said Gwyn. "If you think about the history of the South, that makes sense. Things went on in the South that never happened in the North, like slavery."

"I'm thinking about what Laurel said about the grandmother not speaking up," said Kitty. "I see the issue as two layers—a generational layer and a location layer. I understood the generational layer, but I never thought about 'not speaking up' as being a northern or southern trait."

"Dave's mom is like Arlene," said Pat. "She is such a private person when it comes to her body. She finally told Dave and his siblings two years ago that she took a drug when she was pregnant with them. It was a drug of choice for pregnancy then and has since been banned because it caused birth defects. That's become a running joke in his family—that's why they're goofy. I don't remember my mom taking anything like that."

"There's an ethnic layer as well," I said.

"Religion is another one," said Pat.

"There's experience, family, culture," I said, "and when those elements collide, it leaves some women unsure of themselves and they grow silent."

"That sounds like a good synopsis for Kitty," said Kitty, pointing to herself. "It does! It's hard for me to mesh those different perspectives and make sense of how they come together to find my truth."

"It's a huge challenge," I said. "It can take a lifetime to separate out your own beliefs and ideas from those you picked up from all of those influences." I took a sip of my tea and continued. "Maybe we need to be ready with the tape recorders all of the time, in case we meet a woman and can get her to open up."

"When you go in places, you don't expect to strike up a conversation like that with someone, do you?" asked Pat.

"I do," I said. "Why not?"

As we pulled out of Sikeston, I pointed out a sign for the AG-Mart that caught my attention. The store was having a 50-percent-off sale on toys and ammo. We laughed.

Along the road cotton fields were green and snow white while others, after being defoliated, were brown and white. The defoliant chemical lingered in the air. The bales of cotton came in two shapes: large round yellow bales similar to the hay bales often seen up north, or enormous white and blue rectangles.

"They're spraying over there," said Pat.

"Wow," said Kitty. "Look at it blow."

"Flying east out of Denver for this trip," said Gwyn, "I looked out the window and saw agricultural fields as far as I could see. I was thousands of feet in the air, and all I saw were circle plots of agriculture. At first I thought, there's not a piece of natural vegetation as far as I can see. Then I realized we have to have areas like that so we have food in our grocery stores. I don't like the idea of defoliation, but I'm wearing cotton clothes right now. The cotton has to come from somewhere. I tend to be strident in my opinions, but I need to remember that the choices I make affect the environment too, though I try to minimize any negative damage I might cause."

"I remember when I first moved to Ely. I'd never been around logging before, and people in the community had strong opinions about it," said Kitty. "Then I remembered, oh yeah, trees are where toilet paper comes from."

"That's right," said Gwyn. "Every piece of paper you write or type on comes from trees. My friend Rochelle's husband is a forester, and she and her family use paper bags at the grocery store because he says he can grow more trees, but plastic is going to last forever."

"I had to make the transition from an agricultural tradition, where the crops are rotated every year, to forestry," said Kitty. "Trees are a crop that takes a generation or two to grow and cycle through."

"Apparently I hadn't given it much thought," said Gwyn. "That's how they train foresters—lumber is a crop. A forester looks at trees completely differently than a wildlife person. Foresters see board length and whether a tree is growing straight. As a wildlife person, I see wildlife habitat and whether a tree is dead or alive. I was interested in Rochelle's explanation about how she changed her opinion through her husband. I changed mine too, after she shared her story with me."

We were checked into the motel in Caruthersville, Missouri, by the owners, Soniya and her husband, Om. They were friendly and talkative. Om was humorous, and his grin appeared permanent. Once we were settled in we enjoyed a nap, and then I reviewed the charts. Kitty and Pat joined me, sitting on my bed.

"There's a northwest breeze coming down," said Pat.

"I hope it lasts a couple of days so we get pushed tomorrow," I said.

"All sixty-one miles," kidded Kitty.

"I broke our options down," I said. "We'll paddle thirty-seven or seventeen miles. If we have a tailwind, we could do thirty-seven miles. I'm interested to see how fast we go with just two of us paddling. I realize now that it would've been good to put the others in front for a while to help them learn the river better. When Laurel was in front, I noticed her turning her head to hear better. When she was in the back she, like others, relied on us and didn't have to pay attention to the water that closely."

"I can see how giving them a sense of leadership might have made a big difference in how the team functioned on the water," said Kitty.

I noticed Pat had a faraway look on her face. "Are you okay?" I asked.

"Yes. I was just thinking about a friend of mine, Grace, who's struggling with big issues in her life," said Pat sadly. "I think what drives her is how she wants to be perceived by other people."

"Aunt Charlotte was like that," I said. "She was dignified and proper. When she came down with bone cancer, life became challenging for her. She could no longer maintain her appearance or her home the way she wanted. Curiously, Alzheimer's set in not long after, and she didn't care as much anymore."

"I think Grace feels as if she carries the world on her shoulders and it's her responsibility to take care of the world," said Pat. "I can't understand why she feels people can't take care of themselves."

"It makes sense if you consider she might feel guilty about something," said Kitty. "I don't know, but that might be why a person feels responsible all the time."

"I don't agree with that," I said. "I've struggled with the same belief system, but not as much as I used to."

"Really?" said Pat.

"Yes," I responded. "As a kid, huge responsibilities were handed to me, and there was no one to help me see that at age eleven I shouldn't be able to do them. I was told that I should be able to handle the responsibilities, that I needed to and I was expected to. I acquired that message as a child. You grow and your family expands until the world becomes your family, and you come to believe you need to take care of the world too. It's like your brain gets rewired, and you blindly begin to caretake everyone. You don't even realize you're doing it or the degree of stress it puts on you. You simply can't stop."

"Because it's what you know how to do?" asked Kitty.

"I didn't know I had a choice," I said. "It was what I had to do, and eventually it became a piece of my identity and what I equated with my value."

"I think Grace knows that she has a choice," said Pat.

"Intellectually she may know, but I bet she doesn't know deep within," I said. "It's like when you're told something and you understand what you're told, but to actually live what you're told is a different story. I had to change things a little at a time. Being a part of Co-Dependents Anonymous helped me a great deal, and the meditation book we've been reading helps me make bite-sized changes. In that way I can internalize how I think about and do things."

"Does that book have meditations for a whole year?" asked Pat.

"Yes," I said. "I sent a copy to a friend of mine recently, and she started reading it from cover to cover. She apologized because she hadn't finished it yet. I said, 'Have you noticed there are dates on each page?'"

We all laughed.

"I fear for Grace," said Pat.

"It is easy to burn out trying to save the world," I said. "If she's like I was and still have a tendency to be, she doesn't take vacations, or much time off either."

"For vacation, Dave and I'd go to either New York or Florida," said Pat. "People we hang around with would say, 'It's strange. Whenever you go on vacation, you're always going to visit relatives. Why do you do that?' They could never understand it because their families were in St. Louis. They could go do the family thing whenever they wanted to. They traveled to places we could never go to because we had X amount of time for the year to take off, and that time was to see family.

"Growing up, I had many cousins—cousins coming out my ears there were so many. We had a big extended family. Dave never had that. Then he married me and said, 'Holy cow, there are a lot of people here!' He enjoyed getting to know the family. Sometimes he says he feels closer to my brother in Florida than his brother."

"It's a different relationship base," said Kitty.

"Because we're such a large group," I said, "every time a new person is introduced to the family, the process is like an initiation. My daughter Naomi had three tests for her boyfriends. One was the annual family get-together; one was her sister's, brother's, and brother-in-law's interrogations, and the other was our annual Jay Cooke State Park camping weekend. If a guy could get through all three tests, then he was a keeper."

"That speaks to how family is integrated into her life and how much family means to her," said Kitty. "Naomi's message is, 'If you can't get along with my family, then I'm not going to get along with you.' Think about the amount of control that people put into everything in their lives. All of that energy could get used for something positive. There are many ways to walk through this life, aren't there?" She looked out the window toward the river. "I feel like we dishonored the River by not paddling today. Wait. I can word my feelings better than that: the River feels like a sister we aren't acknowledging today."

"Let's walk down to the boat launch and pay her a visit," I said. "It's a couple blocks from here."

"Great idea," said Kitty. "I need to move."

After our walk, Gwyn and I headed to the restaurant attached to the casino to go over a few things before dinner. I showed her the display of St. Louis gooey butter cake I'd been craving for five months—ever since I was here during the reconnaissance trip. Cis said the cake recipe was created as the result of an accident in the kitchen. Some ingredient had fallen into a batch of cake batter, but the cake turned out to be so delicious the recipe took off.

We settled into a booth and ordered hush puppies, Gwyn's favorite, and fried pickles, my favorite and a new experience for Gwyn. I asked Gwyn about her recent Mexico adventure.

"This past spring I had a chance to go to Mexico to help a friend, Mickey, figure out what to do about an osprey nest that was on top of a seventy-foot-tall support leg for a floating platform that needed to be moved," said Gwyn, using her hands to express herself. "She was helping the local folks learn how to open and operate a new mine, and she taught them environmentally responsible methods to use when they took over the operation themselves. When the ospreys built their nest on this structure and began incubating eggs, she called me for help. She knew I do that sort of work for the mines in Wyoming. She wanted me to teach her crew to livetrap mice and small mammals so they could move the critters out of the way before they mined through the habitat.

"I made four trips to Santa Rosalia, which is halfway down the east coast of the Baja Peninsula, to help. The first part of the osprey project went well. We gradually floated the platform thirty feet along the dock to remove equipment for maintenance, and we moved it back without the ospreys abandoning the nest. That gave the birds a few weeks to hatch their eggs before the platform had to be moved a couple miles down the coast.

"But eventually the mine couldn't wait anymore, so the next step was to move the whole nest to a solid platform that we'd built seventy-five feet away. We went up in a crane and put the eggs in a warm padded container. The eggs were replaced with hard-boiled chicken eggs to keep the ospreys interested in the nest while we moved it to the new platform. That kept us from accidentally breaking the osprey eggs when we pulled the nest material from its platform to the new platform. We put the osprey eggs in an incubator in the mine's guest house near the waterfront. After we moved the nest to the new platform, we put the real eggs back and watched to see what would happen.

"The ospreys accepted the eggs in the new location for a short time, but eventually they abandoned their eggs. They'd already been sitting on them longer than the normal incubation period. The pair continued to hang out in the nest area, which was a good sign. I felt bad for them and for the mine crew because I couldn't make the situation work the way we'd wanted it to. The mine planned to leave the new platform in place to help the osprey pair maintain that territory so the pair might be successful down the line. None of the other pairs in the area hatched young either, which made me wonder. I'd change a couple of things if I did it again, but we got close to succeeding.

"The crazy thing was that we had Kee, a great blue heron, land on the floating platform the morning before we tried moving it the first time, and again the morning we moved the whole nest. I took it as a good sign because blue herons were your guides on the first two legs of the river trip. It was encouraging to have a blue heron show up.

"In between the osprey work, I went to the mine site a few times and worked with a couple of their guys to teach them how to trap live rodents. I showed them how to bait and lay out the traps, and we checked them in the early mornings to see what we caught. We didn't move the rodents while I was there; we practiced catching and identifying them and let them go.

"The trip was funny because I don't speak Spanish, and most of Mickey's crew didn't speak English. When she wasn't around to translate, I tried to explain why I needed hard-boiled eggs for the osprey nest and why I didn't want to eat the bacon I'd asked the cooks to make. I wanted the grease for the small-mammal bait. They thought I was crazy a few times, and for a few minutes they were shocked because they were certain that I was going to eat the osprey eggs.

"I didn't have time to learn Spanish before I went down there. I had one of my husband's bilingual students write out basic phrases that I'd need like, 'We need to move the nest from the barge to the platform.' Then I'd tell the crew, 'Uno momento por favor' and would read what I wanted them to do. I kept a little notebook with me, and every time I learned a new phrase I wrote it down. They teased me about it. Their teasing was good-natured even though I had no idea what they were actually saying to me. They talked to me so fast and with such serious expressions on their faces. I'd look at them, shrug my shoulders, hold up my hands in defeat, and smile. I definitely made new friends down there.

"The thing that struck me, aside from how friendly everyone was, was how poor the entire town is. Going to areas like that reminds me how truly rich we are in the U.S., even if we're not financially rich by U.S. standards. I left my extra pesos there because it was a ten-to-one ratio of U.S. dollars to their pesos. Three hundred of our dollars was the same as three thousand of their pesos. It was the least I could do to help the local folks when I have much more than they do.

"The fishermen at the dock each morning used fishing line wrapped around a stick because they didn't have fishing poles. Someone said that a pole would cost fifteen pesos. I tried to figure out how to buy a bunch of fishing poles for the community. Honestly, the fishermen were unbelievably good at catching fish without my help. Seeing them fish was a great reminder that we don't need all of the things we accumulate to be successful and happy. My trip to Mexico was an amazing experience for a lot of reasons, and I'm looking forward to going back if I can."

Kitty and Pat joined us for dinner, although Gwyn and I had already enjoyed our hushpuppies and fried pickles in addition to an order of jalapeno bottle caps. A musician set up in the corner and began singing hit songs from the '60s, '70s, and '80s. We had just started eating when

Ginger, a woman we'd met earlier when we walked to the boat launch, joined us. She had a beautiful smile and a rich southern Missouri accent.

"Would you like to share my dinner?" Gwyn asked.

"You're probably pretty hungry," said Ginger politely.

"Nancy and I had appetizers before you joined us, and it turns out I like fried pickles—a lot," replied Gwyn. "I'm not that hungry."

"There are a lot of foods in this part of Missouri and farther south that you've never had," said Ginger.

"I was born in North Carolina. I grew up eating some things," said Gwyn. "I love grits, for example."

"I love grits too," said Ginger. "So y'all from Minnesota?"

"I lived in St. Louis from '71 until I went to college, and again when I did that old boomerang thing that kids are prone to do," said Gwyn. "In '85 I went to Oklahoma and worked for a while and migrated north and ended up in Wyoming, which is where I wanted to be the whole time anyway. It took me a long time to get there, but I never gave up. That's the key. Never give up!"

"What attracted you to Wyoming?" asked Ginger.

"I can't say for sure," replied Gwyn. "Ever since I was a little girl, I loved the way the name of the state sounded. I love the idea of the West where your word means something—and the open spaces and cowboys, of course. I knew I should be in the West. But I never wanted to be in Colorado or Montana. I've always wanted Wyoming. I've been there for eighteen years. I moved there in '94 on Valentine's Day, as a matter of fact. That's what I celebrate on Valentine's Day: I moved to Wyoming, finally!"

"Have you traveled far on the river?" Kitty asked.

"No, mainly recreational travel right around here," responded Ginger, pushing her long blonde hair behind her ear. "I spent lots of summers on the sandbars, or we'd go up the river a ways and cut the motor and float down. I love to fish the river 'cause you never know what's going to be on the other end of the line. It could be an eel, a turtle, or a bass. You never know.

"I lived near the river all my life. I'd swim in the river, play in the river, and, of course, boat on the river. I played in the river when I shouldn't have. My parents had no idea that I was doing it. My friends and I'd go to the river and push logs upstream, and then we'd get on the logs and float them down."

"Your parents wouldn't have been happy," Gwyn said.

Ginger looked at Gwyn mischievously and grinned. "I know. I would've been grounded for sure, but I lived to tell about it. I love the river, and as a kid I wanted to go down it like Huck Finn and Tom Sawyer on a raft."

"Do you always remember the levee being there?" asked Kitty.

"It's been there my entire life," said Ginger, nodding. "I think it was built after the flood of 1937. Back in the spring of this year, when the Army Corps blew up our levees in three places, they flooded 130,000 acres of fertile farm land. We experienced record-high water levels that hadn't been seen since 1937. My dad was nine years old in 1937. They blew the levees then too, and my grandpa was with them when they did. Once, the Army Corps set the explosives when the men were changing shifts. Too many men got on the barge and it sank. My grandfather jumped from the barge to the boat. I think seventeen men drowned.

"Last spring the Army Corps closed down the barge traffic. Y'all are familiar with barge waves and how they roll and roll, I imagine."

"Those are fun to ride," I added.

Ginger raised her eyebrows skeptically and looked at me. "Yeah?" We laughed.

Ginger continued. "When they blew the levees, those waves were rolling on levees that had never experienced such waves before. Every spring the rains will flood that bottom land, but it's a slow rise and a slow fall. No waves. Well, when they blew the levee, water started rushing in a million gallons a minute. It scoured the land. The water was eight feet deep and twenty to forty feet wide. The first explosion that they did was twenty-five miles from my home, and it shook the house."

"Holy cow!" exclaimed Kitty.

"They even felt it twenty miles further down," said Ginger. "I was watching the blasts on television. They did it at night when it was raining and dark. We knew it was coming. It took a while for the sound and shock waves to travel. There were eleven explosives. Big flashes.

"We had two more explosions to go and didn't know when they'd come. I went that night to the levee in New Madrid with my dog, Maggie, but the National Guard was in town and they wouldn't let us near the levee. I thought if that first explosion was that big and the other one was right next door, what would it be like to be so close?" She paused, letting us imagine. "But that explosion wasn't like the first one. I learned later they'd used more explosives than they needed because they had one shot to get it right. Then they had to wait for the Corps to bring more of that stuff in."

"Because they used it up on the first one?" I asked.

"Yeah," said Ginger, disgusted. "The water was up to the eaves of my friend's house. We all say if they would've waited a little bit longer, the water level would've breached naturally and the situation would've been better. The rain stopped the day after they blew the levee. They were telling us the explosions weren't done just to protect Cairo [Illinois]; they were done to protect towns below. All you know is what they tell you."

"Weren't they afraid the levees were going to break?" asked Gwyn.

"Yes, there was some that was," said Ginger. "The Army Corps is building the levee back, but not as high as it was. The level they're building it back to—it's apt to flood every other year on its own."

"Nobody's going to want to live in that area," I said.

"Well, we have a lot of people who think we shouldn't be farming in a flood plain or livin' in a flood plain," said Ginger. "I guess they want us to be livin' in tree houses or something. I don't know where they want us to grow their food. My one friend got a crop in after the flood. He's back in his house now; I'm glad to see that. He had used an excavator to build a five-foot levee around his house and shop building, but even that didn't stop the floodin'."

"How do you start over after something like that?" asked Kitty emphatically.

"You go in and start," said Ginger matter-of-factly. "The flood moved his house off the foundation. He had to have special people come in and get the sand out from underneath it and anchor it back down. You rip up your carpeting and subfloor and rip out your drywall. He'd moved all of his stuff out before the flood.

"I hope I never ever have to experience that. My eighty-year-old dad left the area after the first explosion. I didn't blame him. I'm fifty-five, and I was on edge. Truthfully, not knowing if the levees are going to hold is hard. Levees aren't made for that volume of water to be rushing in and through. I took precautions and put things up in my attic. I didn't want to leave because when people evacuate, they can't get back in. There needed to be somebody around to shut the gas off if nothing else."

"Didn't you tell me that you go out and signal your friend on the river?" asked Gwyn.

A big grin spread across Ginger's face. "I have a friend who's a tugboat captain, and he texted me that he'd be coming by in forty-five minutes. He'd been in Memphis and was coming upriver. I live alone, and I'm a night owl, so I put my clothes on, grabbed Maggie, and went down to the levee. He texted me and said, 'I got my deck lights on.' I texted, 'I see you.' Then he did his spotlights and I flashed my car lights."

"River talk," chuckled Gwyn.

"Yeah," said Ginger. "His dad was a pilot. He started out as a deck hand, most of them do. You start out at the bottom and work your way up."

"What powers the tugboats?" asked Gwyn. "The engine?"

"It's a diesel," said Ginger. "I think the engine's more like jet propelled. The water runs through and pushes out the back and makes those big waves you said you liked to ride." With one eyebrow up, she threw me a look of disbelief. I laughed. "You never know what's out there," she lectured. "My dad made me promise I'd wear a life jacket when I went on the river. I'd be the only one in the group with a life jacket on 'cause I promised my daddy. I thought, Lord forbid if I get thrown out of the boat and I don't have my life jacket on and I hit my head on a log and I'd be gone. He'd ask if I had my life jacket on. I'd be floating if I did."

"We wear ours all of the time out there," said Gwyn.

"My daddy'd be proud," said Ginger.

It was getting late. We ordered three pieces of St. Louis gooey gutter cake to share before we left.

"I'm going to take these leftovers to my dog," Ginger said. "My pets are my children. I have a cat too. Her name is Zena. She was a stray kitten my neighbor found. I brought her home. It was like she was saying, 'I'm here, deal with it.' She wasn't takin' no crap off nobody. That's why I named her Zena Warrior Princess.

"Well, I gotta go. I sure am proud and excited for what y'all are doing. Life sure takes different turns, like that crooked Mississippi."

October 1, Day Eleven

The day off allowed me to decompress, and my mood lifted. My fatigue, however, persisted.

During breakfast in the lobby we visited with Soniya, who was attentive and eager to make sure we had everything we needed. Soniya is from  India, and she became excited when I turned down the standard tea she served to brew instead the chai I'd brought with me. We traded samples of chai. She and Om were delightful storytellers. While we talked I experienced a cultural difference; even though she was shorter than I, when she moved in close—nearly nose-to-nose—to speak with me, I was uncomfortable. When I took a step back, she took a step closer.

Om was an electrical engineer with several patents. They lived in Germany before moving to Caruthersville. Soniya took great pride in offering customers full service, doing their laundry, and going out of her way for them. The motel, the Casino Inn Resort, was her business, which her husband supported. "He's a nice husband," she said warmly.

I told her we were collecting wisdom from women as we traveled and asked, "What would you have liked to know when you were a little girl that would have helped you in life?"

A serious, thoughtful look crossed Soniya's face. She moved in closer, looked me in the eye, and said, "Girls need to be brave and independent, not to depend on anybody. They have inside strength and strong power. She's the good mother, the good sister. She needs to be strong. She's the source. She should always remind herself that she's a good mother, and she's a good sister, and she's the family."

When we left, Soniya came around the desk to give me a big hug and wished us well. As we drove to the boat ramp, Kitty suggested we read from the meditation book each day. Opening the book, I read an entry titled "Be Who You Are." It discusses how frightening it can be to own who you are. "What would happen if we let go of our camouflage of adaptation? ... We discover that who we are had always been good enough. It's who we are intended to be."

For me it is easy to accept my flaws but difficult to accept my greatness. Early on, self-pride and boasting about what I could do was equated with being vain and self-centered. I know how important self-love is, yet standing up and admitting what I'm good at is tough. Many times my inability to acknowledge my strengths has gotten in the way of my accomplishing things I care about.

Gwyn and I would be paddling thirty-eight miles today. Every time we prepared to paddle Gwyn reminded me of a determined little kid who took play seriously—a combination of excitement and a focus on getting all the toys in the right place.

After saying goodbyes to Kitty and Pat, we slipped from the boat landing into the water. A quarter-mile downriver we decided to pull over because sizable waves from the barges and wind warranted putting on our spray skirts. We approached shore upriver of a barge that had been parked there all night. Suddenly the barge got too close for comfort. Its nearness surprised me, and I was concerned that the current was pushing us so fast. After we landed on shore safely, we realized the barge was no longer parked; it had been moving. Cutting any closer in front of it could have had serious consequences. We looked at each other knowingly. "Wow," Gwyn said.

Throughout the day, wind came at us from every direction because the river snaked back and forth. For long stretches the wind pushed us from behind and, thankfully, cleared the air of the irritating defoliant smell.

Gwyn had an issue with her rudder pedals, so I paddled over to help her adjust them. As we put her spray skirt back on, we heard rushing water. A few yards ahead, the water dropped away. From our vantage point, we caught a peek of the white roiling water below.

"What's that?" Gwyn asked.

"It's a wing dike," I said, clutching my paddle, "and I'm afraid we're going over."

"Where did it come from?" Gwyn asked, bracing herself for the challenge ahead.

There was no time to answer. I tried quickly to help her get the spray skirt on but abandoned that idea because the swift current carried us toward the drop-off. We darted away from each other to paddle.

"I'll go first," I yelled. I had never been over a drop that big in my kayak before. I paddled ahead anxiously, assessing the situation. Then I saw a V in the current going over the dike and aimed for it. "Shoot for the V," I hollered back to Gwyn. A V-shape indicates current with no underwater obstacles. "This would be a good time to know how to do an Eskimo roll," I said aloud as I pressed my legs against the sides of my kayak for more stability.

The closer I got to the V, the more energized and nervous I became. I started coaching myself. "Oh boy. You can do this, Nancy. It's going to be great." I could hear Gwyn telling herself she'd be fine too. The drop opened up as I moved closer, and the nose of my kayak pointed straight for the drop. "Oh, God!" The whitewater raced and tumbled over itself in a series of waves. The front of my kayak crested the top and suddenly I was airborne. "Oh, shit. I'm diving in!"

I screamed the whole way down as the nose of my kayak disappeared into the white churn for what felt like much longer than the few seconds it took to drop and level out. Momentarily I'd lose my balance when the paddle hit swirling water with no resistance. When my paddle hit water, I paddled hard. The splashing, churning water was so loud I couldn't hear my paddle moving in and out of it. I focused ahead on the calmer water downriver, and I thought of Gwyn, hoping she wasn't taking on water because her spray skirt was off.

I couldn't turn around, but I could hear Gwyn's voice behind me, surprisingly calm at first. "It's going to be okay. It's going to be okay." Then her voice grew louder and her chant faster. "It's going to be okay. It's going to be okay," and I knew she must be pulling closer to the V when her voice grew demanding, "Stay calm, damn it. It's going to be okay. Damn it! It's going to be okay," I cringed for her. Then she yelled, "Oh, f---!" and I knew.

She was going over the top.

I couldn't turn around to see how she fared, but knew she was over the top and upright when I heard her reassuring herself. "I'm good. It's okay. I'm good." Strokes later, when we were both out of the whitewater, I finally turned to look at Gwyn.

"Woohoo!" I yelled.

"That was awesome!" she shouted, nearly jumping out of her kayak with excitement.

We had cleared the wing dike.

The adrenaline surged through our systems for a quarter mile of paddling and then crashed, so we pulled over to a sandbar. Tiny silver fish jumped out of the water around us as we neared the shore, and Gwyn said, "Hey, they're jumping to congratulate us for making it over that wing dike." She leapt out of her kayak and struck a victory pose.

"That sure came up on us," said Gwyn.

"I liked the thrill and kind of want to do more," I said, "but we don't know what we're getting into."

Gwyn's victory pose

"By the time we'd get to them, it'd be too late to change our minds," said Gwyn. "Somehow I managed to make it through that wild water bone dry."

"I've figured out that when there's a big wing dike, there could be an extension of it under the water," I said. "I thought we were far enough away from the main wing dike to be safe."

We sprawled out on the sandbar and watched a heron and an egret feed along the shore while a large gray fuel tanker passed headed upriver. We watched two adult bald eagles soaring in the sky. Then another eagle swooped by the pair and chased one off. A swallowtail butterfly flitted past close enough that I could see a splash of iridescent blue at the bottom of each of its midnight-black wings.

Gwyn and I talked about the difficulties of balancing work and play. Our work ethics were a driving force that, at times, had created hardship for us and the people around us. We shared the mindset that being needed equaled being invaluable. We believed that if we weren't productive or helping others, we had no value, so we kept busy and wrapped perceived value around ourselves like a cozy blanket that kept our egos snug and protected. It required raw vulnerability to turn our thoughts and behaviors around. Small steps in that direction warranted major celebration.

Gwyn and I realized we're like many women. So often we think, "If I do this one more thing, I'll be caught up and then I can relax." But that one more thing leads to another and to another until the things line up like dominos. We find ourselves buried in commitments until we're out of control, but often we don't realize this until something causes one domino to fall, and the domino effect causes the others to fall, and before we know it we're knocked as flat as the domino tiles.

We discussed that one of the hooks in our mindset that kept us from changing was the comfort we derived from being needed. When we thought we were saving the world, we felt an enormous high, a sense of accomplishment that stroked our egos. Saving the world was a big task that kept us busy. We didn't have to wonder what we were going to do with our day—the list was long. Our choice was where to start or which fire to put out first. It's not a fulfilling way to live, but once you start to function that way, it's difficult to stop. The amount of commitment, determination, and self-discipline required to change is like that needed to recover from any addiction. Before leaving the sandbar, Gwyn and I promised to support each other in gaining our balance back.

At the twenty-three mile mark we came to the Wrights Bend Dikes, a seven-mile bend shaped like a U that began with the river flowing south and ended with it flowing north. On the map it looked as if we could cut across the top of the U and save four miles of paddling. The water where we might cut across was calm and beckoning. As great as saving four miles sounded, and as pristine as the water looked in that direction, I knew we could find ourselves going over another dangerous wing dike. So we paddled on, passing the mouth of the Onion River.

Hugging the inside curve we were not in the fast current, which slowed our progress. Gwyn dubbed it the never-ending curve. Coming around the end of the curve to our right, we saw the dikes we would have had to go over for the shortcut; they were formidable. Water wasn't running over the dikes as we anticipated, but dragging our kayaks over them would have been strenuous. "Good call," Gwyn said, giving me a thumbs up.

As we paddled on I thought about the Gathering in New Madrid and felt sobered by Laurel's comments about the medical profession. What she had said about the gynecological field was in line with my experiences. In the doctor's office, my opinion was dismissed even though I live in my body 24/7. I remember being shown photos of worst-case scenarios of what an infection could develop into, and in my thirties being told that if I wasn't careful and didn't make my regular appointments something fatal could develop.

At one appointment, a doctor chose to do a uterine biopsy and didn't tell me what he was about to do; I screamed at the unexpected pain. I thought I was there for a pap. When I left the office, the nurses wouldn't make eye contact with me. The gynecologist's disregard for me as a person left me feeling violated—sobbing and terrified to return.

The fears doctors planted in my head, combined with years of being taught that doctors were an undisputed authority, left me thinking I didn't have a choice.

I remember the anguish I felt taking my teenage daughters to the gynecologist for the first time and the helplessness that I couldn't protect them. I was angry that I should even need to protect them from a medical professional.

I once had a serious case of adenomyosis—a condition that occurs when endometrial tissue, which normally lines the uterus, grows into the muscular wall of the uterus—that went undiagnosed for years. The doctors didn't take my symptoms seriously—heavy bleeding to the point of chronic anemia and bouts of pain. Because I was so afraid of the testing they might do, I was unable to be completely honest. My dishonesty was not intentional. I went into the doctors' offices with every intention of telling them everything, but then my heart would race and the words wouldn't come out of my mouth. Since then I have become more assertive with doctors, and I often find they get angry about it. When I find one who will talk to me as an equal, I feel I've found a treasure.

Fatigue in my arms and shoulders and an ache in my back, combined with a substantial headwind and slower current, made the last curve of the day grueling. We crossed to the far shore for a bathroom break and found respite from the wind. "Without the rudders, we wouldn't have gotten across that last open stretch," Gwyn said as we climbed out of our kayaks. "The wind would've kept blowing us. I felt like we were on a treadmill. The water was moving underneath us, but we weren't going anywhere."

The rocky bank was covered in poison ivy that reached to the water. Rocky banks made me nervous because they were snake terrain. I was most concerned about the poisonous cottonmouth, which gets its name from the cotton-white lining of its mouth. Its olive-brown color allows it to blend into the landscape. Cottonmouths can also be found underwater. I gingerly stepped across the rocks, avoiding the poison ivy, but I was unable to find privacy and bared my backside to the river as I squatted down to pee. Then I tiptoed over the rocks and returned to my kayak without incident.

Side by side we paddled the fast current of the outside curve just above our landing. We searched the shore for the green pylons at Barfield Boat Ramp where Kitty and Pat waited. Then movement in the water directly in front of Gwyn caught my attention. A large whirlpool developed out of nowhere. "Damn." I had been warned that in fast currents whirlpools can develop suddenly and are capable of pulling large objects under. The center of this whirlpool quickly sank deeper as it grew in size and speed. Gwyn hadn't seen it.

"You're going toward a whirlpool!" I yelled, hoping my voice would cut across the sound of the water.

She paddled faster, not understanding what I said but comprehending the concern in my voice. Somehow she rode the edge of the swirling water and passed the whirlpool safely.

"My God, Gwyn. You rode right over the edge of that whirlpool."

"That's why the water on one side of the kayak felt odd," she said. "It didn't feel like water was beside me there when I paddled."

In swirly water we couldn't paddle too close to each other because when whirlpools developed they spun our kayaks, and we would end up on top of each other.

In patches of calm water, though, we moved closer. All around us bugs hovered a foot above the water. They hurled their bodies down onto the water, but no matter how hard they slammed the surface, they bounced off. We'd never seen bouncing bugs, and we laughed as we watched them, thankful for a pleasant distraction from our fatigue.

We paddled to the landing using the last of our energy. Two empty lawn chairs greeted us onshore. We wondered where Kitty and Pat were. It turned out that bugs had driven them into the van, parked further up the hill.

While we loaded gear, Pat told us that some teenage boys had been shooting nearby, but had warned them first. And they'd had trouble finding the landing. We told them about our endless curve, and they said it took a group of barges an hour to get around the curve as they watched from the landing. The group was the largest we'd seen so far, seven barges deep and four across. "They were riding high and looked empty," said Kitty. "We couldn't figure out how they got all of that around the curve. Amazing."

On the drive to our motel, Pat said, "We didn't have time to go to the motel. We thought you'd be in at one thirty. We've been sitting there four hours."

"Sorry about that," said Gwyn.

"Oh, no," I said good-humoredly. "Am I going to have to hit you again?" Gwyn laughed. "She's been saying sorry all day," I explained. "I did playfully hit her once for saying it so often."

Kitty turned around and teased Gwyn, "Damn it, why didn't you paddle a little harder?"

"If you would have worked out more at the gym back home, we would have been here earlier," I added to the fun.

"You selfish bitches," said Gwyn, feigning anger. "I did work out. That's the reason I could still paddle at the end of the day."

We all laughed.

"At one point I said, 'Oh, man, I'm getting tired,' and Gwyn sighed, 'Oh, good,'" I told the others.

"I trail her no matter how hard I paddle," said Gwyn emphatically. "The whole time I'm thinking, 'Damn, that girl can paddle.'"

"Toward the end of the day when I'm tired, I get into a groove, and I hold it," I said. "I get into a kind of altered state of mind. That's how I work through the fatigue. The river sure isn't moving any faster down here."

As we passed cotton bales in the fields on the side of the road, Kitty said, "We stopped at the welcome center where there's a cotton exhibit."

"That's a big bale," said Gwyn, looking out the window.

"There's a compressor that puts the cotton into the bale," said Pat, pointing to a large piece of machinery out in the field.

"Farmers put two crops on the same ground here," said Kitty. "A spring and a fall crop."

"That takes a lot of nutrients out of the ground," said Pat.

"We aren't used to two crops up north," I said.

"I'm sure they do something to get the nitrogen back in," said Gwyn. "I believe the nitrogen is fixed in the roots. Tilling the plant back in would restore nitrogen. I know they rotate corn and soybeans a lot to get the nitrogen back into the soil."

"I talked with a farmer back in North Dakota who works with combines," said Kitty. "A combine costs $300,000—for one machine. That is phenomenal. His combine was nicer than my car and had air conditioning. Growing up on the farm we were out in the open. Maybe we had an umbrella propped up to keep the sun off."

"I've read from a couple of sources about the Missouri Bootheel," I said. "What's that?"

"It's the southeastern-most part of the state that drops below the rest of the border," said Gwyn. "Its name refers to its shape, sort of like the place in northeastern Minnesota named Arrowhead. The Bootheel is a true swamp, and it's called Mingo National Wildlife Refuge. It has cypress trees. No alligators. But otherwise it's a completely different chunk of habitat that's stuck in Missouri. There's a wetland management area nearby where flat areas are drained to create muddy bogs for birds to feed on insects. It's a neat swamp. I released young bald eagles down there at one time as part of a reintroduction program before they were removed from the endangered species list. That was a lifetime ago. Oh, I just remembered..."

She dug around in her deck bag. "We found another ball today," Gwyn said, presenting it to Kitty. "It's a Wiffle ball. What do you think her name should be?"

"Other than Airhead, I don't know," responded Kitty. We laughed.

"How about Ariel?" I said.

"Ariel was the Little Mermaid. How fitting is that?" said Kitty. "Ariel meet Polly, your big sister."

"I can hear her complaining," I said. "'How come she gets a body, and I don't?'"

"We can fix that," said Pat. "We have hot-pink duct tape. Did you know that all Wiffle balls are made in the United States? I can't remember what town. Boy, I never thought that information would ever be valuable." We chuckled.

"Where did you find pink duct tape?" asked Gwyn.

"Heidi's husband, Matt, said we had to have it because this is a girls' trip," I said. "How are we going to put a face on a Wiffle ball?"

"That will be challenging, won't it?" Kitty said. "On the maps it looks as if there are a lot of little lakes down here alongside of the Mississippi that used to be an old river oxbow. I'd like to see one if we can. I imagine they supply migrating birds with food."

Seeing our confusion, Kitty explained, "An oxbow lake is created over time as erosion and sediment change the river's course and a curve of the river is cut off from the river."

"I'd like to see one too," I said.

We arrived in Osceola at the motel, which was adjacent to a cotton field. Gwyn and I went out to the field to take a closer look. Gwyn studied each part of the cotton plant as if she were conducting a research project. Our curiosity satisfied, we brought back a couple of cotton balls to share.

Rest and a shower made a world of difference for all of us. We headed into town for dinner and ordered fried green tomatoes, crab cakes, and hushpuppies. The tomatoes were crisp and tasty, and the giant hushpuppies were lightly spiced so the flavor of the breading came through, which pleased Gwyn. I was disappointed that the crab cakes were deep fried. Everything was deep fried.

We overheard a customer describe someone. "She talked so fast she had corn growing out of her shoes." We laughed and Gwyn said, "I'm not getting the connection. Does corn grow fast?"

"Down south it does," said Kitty.

The hostess, Janet, walked to our table to promote the restaurant's homemade pies. While we pondered our options, she let us know we could buy a whole pie to take with us. Instead of a whole pie, we ordered slices of blackberry, coconut cream, lemon meringue, and lemon tart.

"Are you busy tomorrow night?" Kitty asked Janet.

"What do you got?" asked Janet, sticking a pencil behind her ear and tilting her head.

"We're kayaking down the Mississippi River," said Kitty.

"Oh, are you?" said Janet looking at us like we were crazy. She swept back her short brown hair. "Well, you're braver than I am. I don't get around that water. You've got to be kidding me."

"We aren't kidding," said Kitty. "Part of what we're doing is stopping along the way and inviting women to Gatherings to come together around a fire to share stories."

"I wish I wasn't busy," said Janet, disappointed. "I could tell the ladies, especially the ladies at church. How neat. I'll see what I can do for you."

"Do you own this place?" I asked.

"Yes, me and my husband run it," said Janet. "We tried being open on Sundays for a while, but it didn't work. One time I had to miss the cantata at church because something happened to all of my waitstaff that day. It's not worth it."

Janet headed back to the kitchen. We started talking about the challenges of raising children, and I was asked about a challenge I found funny now that maybe wasn't then.

"Naomi went to Australia as a student teacher for three months," I said. "It was time for her to come home, but she had a hard time with it. She asked me to come over and help her move. I was excited to go to Australia. I left Minneapolis on Christmas Eve and, because of the time change, arrived in Melbourne the day after Christmas."

"That would be weird to miss a day," said Gwyn.

"It was weird," I said. "Naomi called three days before I left and told me there was something I needed to know about her boyfriend, Malcolm. 'You need to know that he's forty years old.' Then she hung up before I could say anything."

"What?" said Pat. "She hung up?"

"Yes," I said. "I was shocked. Forty? She was twenty-one. I had a lot of time to think about it before I got there. I realized that because she'd be moving back home, their relationship would become long distance, and long-distance relationships rarely work. I decided discussing their age difference wasn't worth an argument, and I let it go.

"Malcolm came to the airport with Naomi to meet me, but he wasn't standing with her when I came down the hall from customs. I asked where he was, and Naomi said, 'He had to go find something. I think he's nervous about meeting you.'"

"I'll bet he was," laughed Gwyn.

"A man walked up to us wearing skin-tight black leather pants and a matching leather vest. His hair was bleached blonde and spiked. He looked like a poster child for male midlife crisis. He hesitantly handed me a big box of dark-chocolate macadamia nuts, and I thought, 'You can't buy me off that easy.' But because I'd already resolved the issue, I thought, 'You can keep giving me macadamias anyway.'"

"He knew their relationship wasn't okay," said Pat.

"I'd been there for four days," I continued. "We were walking on the beach, and Naomi suddenly said, 'Will you just yell at me!' 'For what?' I asked sincerely. 'I know you don't like my relationship with Malcolm,' she said. 'It's up to you if you want this relationship,' I said, 'but there's one thing I can't wrap my head around.' 'What's that?' 'He's older than my youngest sibling—your Uncle David.' A look of horror and disgust crossed her face."

We laughed.

Janet brought desserts, timed perfectly with the ending of my story. "Ooohhh," we sang.

"Those are impressive," Gwyn said. "Lemon meringue is hard to make. Hey, my fork is chilled."

We tasted each other's desserts and couldn't decide which one we liked the best. Janet returned to check on us, and Kitty said, "Janet, do you win all the county fair pie contests?"

"I don't enter contests," said Janet. "All I hope is that my customers like them."

"They're amazing," I said.

"Well, thank you," said Janet.

We silently savored the what was left of our desserts.

October 2, Day Twelve

I stared in the mirror, looking at my hair. I couldn't hide the roots no matter how I combed or tried to style it. When I pulled it back, it created a halo around my face. I didn't know how to let go of my feelings about my hair yet. I opened the meditation book randomly to the entry "Letting Go of Perfection" and read, "Sometimes, the flaws and imperfections in ourselves determine our uniqueness, the way they do in a piece of art. Relish them. Laugh at them. Embrace them, and ourselves." All I could do was laugh at the irony of opening the book to that page.

At breakfast in the lobby of the motel we met Jimmie and Peggy, who'd been married for eleven years and lived in Michigan. Jimmie was a tall older man with a sweet sense of humor. He had grown up in the Osceola area. He came from a family of twelve. Peggy was younger than Jimmie and an only child. His family reunions were held in Osceola because his oldest sister, Mildred, lived there. Tears welled up in Jimmie's eyes when Peggy told us Mildred had recently died; Mildred had been a second mother to Jimmie. Now other family members were planning to move future reunions somewhere else.

"Do you feel like you're coming home when you come here?" asked Kitty.

Jimmie teared up again and quietly answered, "Yes. They're sayin' they don't want to have the reunion in the middle of a cotton field."

He asked why we were in the area, and after we told him he said, "I thought you ladies looked like adventurers. You don't have any men telling you what to do."

"Wouldn't do any good anyway," said Pat. We laughed.

"What can you tell us about the cotton crops?" asked Gwyn.

"By this time last year the cotton was harvested," said Jimmie.

"Everything is late this year due to the drought. It takes three thousand acres to make a living on a farm. Each one of those cotton bales weighs eighteen hundred pounds. Trucks take them to the cotton gin where the seeds are cleaned out. There are eight to ten seeds in each cotton ball. They sell the seeds for cottonseed oil."

"We saw them burning the stubble in the fields," Gwyn said.

"It's the rice you see burnin'," answered Jimmie. "The cotton fields are tilled under after harvest. Tilling the cotton plant stalks under prevents the boll weevil from infesting the fields."

In the motel room, Pat and Kitty were focused on the itinerary for the next few days and worked through making adjustments in the schedule, which included changing reservations. Boat ramps were few and far between; from here on we had to plan carefully.

After Gwyn and I figured out the paddling route, we all headed down the road to find the Sans Souci boat launch for the following day. Pat and Kitty were in the front of the van and focused on where to go. They discussed the highway options to get to our destination. We neared a turn that I knew would be a shorter route to our destination, but I knew if I said something, they would ignore me.

I looked over at Gwyn. "When the van support gets in that mode," I said, gesturing to Pat and Kitty, "the people riding in back can't be heard." Gwyn looked at me, puzzled. "Watch this," I said. I leaned toward Pat and Kitty in front. "If we turn left at the next road, it'll take us there." Pat and Kitty continued to discuss options as if I had not spoken. Gwyn giggled in disbelief. I tried again with the same result. We laughed and sat back to let them figure it out. I told Gwyn that that "mode" had been happening the whole way, and the situation was worse when someone in the van had an iPhone with Internet capabilities. Technology reigned supreme, even when it didn't provide the needed information.

"What about the maps we have?" Gwyn asked.

"They're a last resort," I said. "I felt dismissed and hurt by their disregard of me at first."

"I bet, especially after the work you did putting those books together and getting maps," said Gwyn.

"Most of the time now I find it funny," I said. "We get where we're going, and I get to see different things than when I drove through here the first time."

A plaque at the landing stated that sans souci meant without care or no worries in French. The landing location had been a ten-thousand-acre plantation established in 1854 that served as a Civil War hospital when the Union fleet docked across from it.

Osceola was named for a Native American chief who led his tribe in the Second Seminole War in Florida and visited the area in the 1800s.

Osceola was the site of the Civil War battle of Plum Run Bend. During that war, a company of one hundred men called the Osceola Hornets fought in the battles of Belmont and Shiloh. Only seven of those men returned home.

Over lunch I posed a question to the group that I had been struggling with. "How do you deal with the physical changes of aging? I look in the mirror and see that it isn't me looking back."

"What?" said Pat, dumbfounded. "I don't understand the question. That's me in the mirror."

"You mean the transition has been effortless for you?" I asked.

"Yes," said Pat. "Absolutely."

"Why?"

"I don't know why that is. My feelings about my hair stem back to childhood," said Pat, who had long beautiful graying hair. "Ever since I can remember I was doted on for my red hair. Every time someone met me I heard, 'Oh, how beautiful your hair is.' I got tired of hearing that throughout my childhood and into adulthood. When my hair started turning gray I thought, no big deal. It's just the way it was. I didn't think of coloring it even once."

"I have no problem with my hair going gray," said Gwyn. "It's the rest of the changes that bother me. I'm going to the gym and doing everything I can to undo what's happening, especially because of the way my body is. Until I was forty-three, I never had to worry about my weight. I know this," she squeezed her middle, "doesn't seem like much, but for me, I'm so little, it might as well be a hundred pounds instead of ten. I'm repulsed by the way I look."

"Really?" said Pat.

"It's funny because except for this last year, I've handled all kinds of different things really well," said Gwyn. "I'm not handling weight gain well at all. I got on hormones largely to get rid of my little kangaroo pouch and because of something Nancy and I talked about yesterday regarding internal changes that make things that used to be fun not fun anymore and even painful. I've been trying to reverse that as well."

"You're on hormone therapy?" asked Kitty.

"I started two weeks ago," said Gwyn. "I'm not taking the estrogen pills doctors gave our moms. The medication is weird because it's self-regulating. I use two drops of an estrogen progesterone mix and one drop of testosterone. I mix it up and apply it to my skin. The doctors say that if you put the testosterone in the same place every day, you'll grow hair there. That's creepy. I'm trying to go to the recreation center, change my diet, and take natural hormones. I can live with the gray hair; my mom and sister had beautiful gray hair. I don't care about that. The rest of this stuff is like looking at somebody else. It's foreign to see my body look like that.

"I'm having a really hard time accepting that this is happening to me, and I have a little resentment about it, partly because everybody keeps telling me that stress is part of it. I get resentful that what other individuals are demanding of me causes the weight."

"You're literally carrying them around," I said.

"Yes," said Gwyn. "I'm not handling aging as gracefully as you are Pat."

"I'm not saying that's not part of it," said Pat. "I don't let it affect me like you do. I gain a few and lose a few and that repeats itself. It's like a teeter-totter."

"If it were only a few," I said. "I gained thirty, and it's taken me two years to drop twenty. I'd like to drop weight until I get to a point where the body I see in the mirror isn't disgusting. In my head I carry the picture of what I looked like when I graduated from high school. I weighed 105 pounds—not that that weight is healthy either. I ate like a horse then trying to put weight on.

"The struggle started for me when my girls were teenagers and running around in swimming suits. That drove my changes home. Oh my, did that drive my changes home. I recently wrote an essay called "Who Are You and What Have You Done with My Face?" I thought if I could make the experience dealing with bodily changes funny, it would help. It did for a while, but then things got worse.

"I didn't have trouble with my gray hair. Actually, I kind of liked it. Peer pressure was great and I buckled. I deeply regret coloring it."

"Maybe having children would've changed me," said Pat.

"Maybe our mothers are a factor," I said. "I didn't have a mother to watch age. I didn't see the progression happen naturally, so I don't know where I'm going. I think of one of my grandmothers and I gasp. These," I said, pointing at my breasts, "fell down to here." I ran my hand across my waist. "Last time I looked, I saw mine are on their way."

"The rest of my family is endowed totally differently than I am," said Gwyn. "When you're younger, you really want a big chest because everybody puts such value on it. My little gals are sagging a little bit, but I'm glad I don't look like my mom or my sisters because this makes me mad enough. I don't understand," she said, looking down at her chest. "If there's nothing there, how can it be sagging?"

"I remember thinking I won't have to worry about sagging," said Kitty. "There isn't enough there to sag."

"Maya Angelou was on Oprah Winfrey once and she was talking about aging," I said. "She said, 'It's a race to see which one is going to get to my lap first.'" We cracked up. "I keep trying to take the attitude that you have, Pat. I can hold that attitude for a day or two, and then it's gone."

"What changes it?" asks Pat.

"I look in the mirror again," I said. "I'm fine if I don't look in the mirror. Photographs really set me off. I look at a photograph and I only see what I don't like. There's a long history with me regarding that response. That's how I see my paintings too. I only see what I want to fix. I do the same thing at the coffee shop. I vigilantly look for what can be better when I walk in. When I apply that mindset to myself, the result is painful."

"The other day I got that call at breakfast from one of my clients, and I had to call back and tell him the project wasn't done yet," said Gwyn. "I know I'm really jamming those guys up badly. There was that mirror in that hotel room in front of the desk. I looked up and I said, 'I don't even know who you are anymore, physically, emotionally, or work-ethic wise.'" She sighed. "I hate getting my picture taken unless it's taken from far away. Up close, all I see is ugly."

"Wow," said Pat.

"It's a lack of self-acceptance," said Kitty. "In the poem "Imagine a Woman" there's a line 'The woman who looks at her changing body and accepts who she is.'"

"Mark and I go to the recreation center," said Gwyn. "He starts looking better quickly. I think, 'What's this about? I've been trying for months to lose a few pounds.'"

"There's such a difference between men and women and their hormones," said Kitty. "We don't lose weight the way that men do."

"I think what I'm hearing Gwyn say is that she doesn't care what the reasons are, the difference in results is right in your face," I said. "You work harder and get nowhere. Doug pisses me off because he thinks he's fat. He's far from fat. He doesn't have to work out and can eat everything on the table, including sugar, and he still stays thin. He becomes another reminder."

"It's like wanting to go backwards to something that we had before," said Kitty. "There's no other area in my life that I want to go backwards to. Why do I want to go backwards to a physical place? Maybe because I can do things more readily? I want to have this mind in a different body. They aren't congruent."

"That's a good point," said Gwyn.

"I went to the doctor to talk about it," said Kitty. "I told her I'd like to lose thirty pounds, and she said, 'Really? According to the charts, you should lose ten pounds. Women gain weight as they get older.' I don't see going back to being 110 pounds again. I'm shooting for 140. It's been years since I've been 140. When I go hiking or swimming, I'm grateful that my body still moves. I make comparisons to others, but it's not really good comparing myself to other people. There are people who aren't able to get out and hike the Bass Lake Trail or go swimming."

"Yesterday I was thinking Kitty looks healthy, energized, and full of life," said Gwyn. "It's interesting to hear you say that."

"Because the charts say we gain weight when we get older, do we have to?" I asked. "Maybe part of why we gain weight is because we've slowed down and are out of shape or because the charts tell us we can't help it."

"Yesterday, paddling, I'm thinking you're in shape because you were kicking my butt," laughed Gwyn.

"She kicks my butt too," said Kitty. "We will be going along and soon it's a slow easing ahead."

"I know," said Gwyn. "I catch up, and I cruise again, and the next thing I know she's pulling away again."

"I think my longer paddles give me more leverage," I said.

"I decided that's what it was," said Gwyn. "I wasn't over-exerting to keep up with you. I put power in every stroke, and you're still half a kayak ahead. Unless you stop paddling, I can't catch up."

"I've switched from wanting my body to look like it did years ago to maintaining good health," said Kitty. "That means I'm not necessarily going to look perfect in my eyes anymore."

"I don't expect perfection anymore," I said. "I've become okay with a lot of the changes, but there are some that I can't embrace, like stray hairs. I'm amazed at how fast they can grow. I swear they grow overnight."

"Stray hairs feel like they take away my femininity," said Kitty.

"That's what I was going to say," said Gwyn.

"The loss of femininity is at the core of it for me," I said. "It goes back to growing up with six brothers and watching them look at *Playboy* and *Penthouse*. Those comparisons, whether I liked them or not, started at an early age. I never measured up. I didn't get breasts until I was pregnant with my third kid, and by then I didn't really want them anymore."

"I know," said Gwyn. "They're just going to fall down."

"And they get in the way," I said, laughing.

"I was a tomboy as a kid, and I'm still a tomboy," said Gwyn. "I never looked like a girl. I don't dress like a girl, but I have no identity crisis. I'm a girl, damn it. It's never been a question in my mind whether I'm something other than what I am. When I look like this, I wonder why any guy would find me attractive, even my own husband. At least I had a figure, such that it was."

"I've worked most of my life in the guy realm," said Kitty. "That in itself is a side-step from being feminine. Driving trucks and forklifts and stuff like that, you don't find many girls who do that. Even though I like doing those things, I still want to maintain some sort of femininity. I felt like I was more of a tomboy, and I could be feminine, but I'm slowly being robbed of that too, as I go through the aging process."

"I need a new definition for what feminine is in the older years," I said. "I've been under pressure to cut my hair short. There's a belief out there that long hair on older women is not attractive. I don't understand that one."

"Your hairdresser has short hair, doesn't she?" said Gwyn.

"Yes," I said. "I grew up with six brothers, and my hair was kept short because it was easier to take care of, but I became one of the boys. Having long hair is an important piece of my getting back in touch with my femininity. My hairdresser talked me into coloring it, but she can't get me to cut it off. It'd be tragic for me if I had to cut it to get rid of the color. I'm going to see if this color I have in it can be stripped out."

"The weird thing is you can color your hair blue or green or magenta, but you can't color your hair gray," said Gwyn. "I get mad about my kangaroo pouch, and I eat like a horse because eating is my stress release. I know I shouldn't be doing it, but I do it anyway. It's a vicious cycle."

"Can you cut yourself some slack for a while?" I asked.

"Apparently not," Gwyn laughed.

"I guess I'm odd because I don't feel like you do," said Pat, who had been looking at us quizzically.

"You have something rare," said Kitty, "We don't see your perspective as being a problem."

"It's healthy," I added.

"I didn't have many role models for what old looks like or how to do old," said Pat.

"So you don't have a preconceived notion about how it should be," I said.

"Right," said Pat. "I'm definitely making it up as I go."

"That's interesting," I said. "You and I didn't have role models, but you took the healthier positive track with it. You make your future up as you go and are okay with it, while I struggle to figure out my future and I judge myself harshly. I assume that I'm doing something wrong or there's something wrong with me. That goes back to me being told I was broken to start with."

"I was never told that," said Pat.

"It's fascinating how we take similar information and do so many different things with it," I said.

"And how the messages or lack of messages still shape us," added Gwyn. "That's one of the reasons I never wanted kids. I'd never forgive myself if I made a little kid feel the way I felt when I was a kid. Plus, I never felt that I really wanted to have a kid. I think that desire should be there if you're going to have a kid."

"I'm not sure I felt that either," I said. "I was a good Catholic girl and being a mother was my role."

"I'm grateful to my mom for letting me be who I was as a kid," said Gwyn. "She bought me the tomboy things and taught me how to play ball. She let me be who I was and told me that if I didn't want to have kids that was fine, possibly because she never really wanted to have kids either."

The weather was perfect for a Gathering, and I hoped the beautiful afternoon was a sign that attendance would be better than it had been. I hoped that Janet from the restaurant was able to get the word out. For unknown reasons our ads in the paper had not. At Florida Park, a birthday party was in full swing at the pavilion we'd hoped to use. We went to the other side of the park and set up in the shade near the road to be easily visible. And we waited.

Our sadness grew as time passed. No one joined us. The smoke from the fire swirled around us, riding a gentle breeze. This Gathering began to feel reminiscent of the New Madrid Gathering. People walked by, and some stopped to chat with us briefly; women waved politely to our invitations to join us, but all continued walking.

Then a car parked near us. Bonnie and her daughter, Debbie D., had driven more than four hours from Grafton, Illinois, to join us. We had met Bonnie on the last leg of the second journey at a Gathering in Grafton. Bonnie was short compared to her tall daughter. Debbie D.'s body language indicated she was uncomfortable joining our group. Bonnie laughed, saying she had told Debbie D. that she was going with or without her. "And I know you couldn't come all this way without me," Debbie D. chided her. They bantered back and forth playfully.

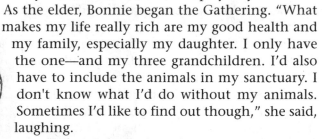

As the elder, Bonnie began the Gathering. "What makes my life really rich are my good health and my family, especially my daughter. I only have the one—and my three grandchildren. I'd also have to include the animals in my sanctuary. I don't know what I'd do without my animals. Sometimes I'd like to find out though," she said, laughing.

"When I think about how I've persevered in times of adversity," her voice trailed off. "In 2003, Debbie had a brain aneurysm. She was in the hospital in intensive care for twenty-four days and in the hospital for a total of three months, with physical therapy after that. Can you believe I let her drive me down here?" We laughed.

"In that time, she had thirteen things that could have killed her. She had a heart attack, respiratory failure, and blood clots in her arms, kidneys, and in her lungs. She had meningitis and a staph infection. The medical staff never had anyone with such complications from a brain aneurysm live that long. I'm overwhelmed every time I think of it and how lucky we have been." She stopped and looked at Debbie D. "Now it's your turn."

"I didn't come here to talk," said Debbie D.

"Well, that's how it works," Bonnie said, "so say something."

After giving Bonnie a defiant glare Debbie D. said, "I'd like to offer something that my mom taught me about persevering in times of adversity. When you get into those tough spots in life, where everything looks so difficult and upside down, you really have to look for the seed of an equivalent benefit, you have to see how you can add some creative idea or some responsive action to the adverse event to turn it to an advantage. That's my biggest winning insight from Mom."

"Listening to you talk about how adversity impacts life reminded me of the times I was hurting inside and I didn't let anybody know about it," said Kitty. "I stuffed things back inside and then they came out sideways in different ways toward people that I didn't mean to affect. To know that I have the ability to cry—and that it's okay to cry—is big. To know that if tears come up, stopping them means I'm stuffing them inside again instead of just letting them come out. I've learned to feel my way through whatever is going on.

"I thought that by the time I got to this age life was going to be pretty easy and I'd sail right along. It really isn't that way. Life is happy and sad and goes in all different directions. I'd do well to accept that's what it's going to be like for as long as I'm part of this life."

"One of the life experiences that generated the most wisdom for me happened before my husband died," said Bonnie. "The night before he died he said, 'You're going to wake up and find me dead. You're going to do something. I don't know what it is—it might be helping save a child who is going to do something special for the whole world. Taking care of me has helped prepare you for it.' I was quite shocked when I woke up the next morning and he was dead.

"What he said was quite interesting to me because I had just started taking classes on reflexology and had become a Reiki treatment person to help him. In the past year, I've helped eight or nine babies. Two were twins. The twins' mother was twenty-nine weeks pregnant when I met the twins' grandmother, who told me about her. The grandmother asked me to send distant Reiki treatments because the twins' mother was aborting and they couldn't stop it. Later the grandmother said, 'Within a few hours after I told you that, the twins were okay, and she carried them to within ten days of her due date.'

"It's been four years since my husband died, but this year is the first time I've had anything to do with babies. I love babies. They have some serious things going on.

"There's so much we don't know in this world. We think we know everything, but we haven't scratched the surface. We just don't know what's out there. There are a lot of things that can be done that we're just finding out, like sending treatments and helping people."

Pat took the fan next and quietly said, "I'm so excited to be on this trip because I turn sixty this year. It's so amazing to be spending it on the river meeting new people and experiencing what they say. I love being with friends and talking to people we meet along the way. That's so special. I'm having the time of my life.

"It doesn't matter what you're doing with friends: When you get back with them, you're right there—you haven't skipped a beat. Maybe it's been ten years since you've seen that person. It's wonderful to have friends like that—men friends as well. It doesn't matter what you are doing. It could be sitting with them while they're talking on the telephone or writing a letter. It doesn't have to be a grandiose celebration—just knowing that you're with that person is all that's really important."

Pat paused for a moment, smiling at us, and then passed the fan to Gwyn, who stared into the fire as she spoke, "Right now what's making my life very rich are the amazing friends that I have here with me this evening and spread out throughout the country. They've been so unfailingly loyal, supportive, and nonjudgmental. There have been a lot of challenges that I've been going through lately, and they've been offering me all of the love and support any person could ask for. I'm grateful for that. That's definitely making me feel very wealthy and rich right now."

"I'd like to talk about courage," I said, when Gwyn handed me the fan. "Courage has been redefined many times in my life. When I was little, courage was the cowboys in the movies going to fight the bad guys or men going to war. When I left my first husband, I didn't see it as courage. It was what I had to do to survive. I look back and realize it took a lot of courage to leave and to fight him for custody. It took courage to help my daughters recover from what had happened to them.

"People say, 'Wow, it's brave of you to be on the river.' Being on the river doesn't take as much courage as it did to do those things. Some of the day-to-day things take way more courage than getting in a kayak and going with the flow.

"We define courage too narrowly and look at it through male eyes when we think it's about conquering. If you look at courage through female eyes, it is subtler. Courage is the choices you make for the kids. It's the sacrifices made out of commitment and responsibility. It takes courage to get up in the morning when you know that today won't look any better than yesterday. You hang on to a belief that somewhere out there it's going to get better.

"Courage will continue to evolve for me. Courage means being vulnerable and speaking your truth in front of people and getting to the point where you really don't care what they think. I'm not there yet, but I'm close. I'm looking forward to the day when I'm one of those feisty old ladies who tells everybody off.

"Just before we began tonight, I was on the phone and heard about my sister-in-law, whom I care a great deal about, who'd had a stroke this summer and chose not to tell everyone about it. She lives four and a half hours away from me, but that doesn't mean I wouldn't have come to help. She had to relearn basics like walking, writing, and reading. My first reaction was hurt. Why didn't she tell me? I know she didn't want to be a bother, and I'm sure she had a list of reasons. And then I thought, 'Wait a minute. I do the same thing. I don't tell people when I need help.' I realized that by keeping secrets like that I'm unintentionally hurting people who care about me. Not allowing others to show that they love me hurts them.

"I was fascinated at how many mixed emotions I had in just that one moment when I was on the phone. Mostly I was thinking about her. The last few years have been very hard for her. To be so far away and so busy is difficult for me."

At this point the fan began to jump from woman to woman, depending on who had something they wanted to add. "I never remember how much it means to other people to be able to help the ones they care about," said Gwyn. "I'm right there to help someone, but like many people, I'm much more reluctant to let other people know that I need a hand or would even be willing to accept a hand. That's a really good reminder that part of being a friend is letting your friends help you when you need somebody."

"On the way here, my mom and I listened to one of my all-time favorite motivational tapes," Debbie D. offered readily. "One of the things the speaker suggests you do is identify yourself however you find most meaningful. You might say, 'I'm a mom.' One of the key points was about identifying yourself to yourself. I turned off the tape and said, 'Let's try this.' It's interesting how our roles change over the years. Her identification now is as a healer, a Reiki Master, and doing all of these healing kinds of things. That's a lot different than it would've been ten or twenty years ago when it might have been as a grandmother or mother. Now she sees herself more as a healer. It's fun that we get to change and discover new parts of ourselves."

"I will be eighty in February," said Bonnie proudly. "There's not a single age I'd go back to. I really am having a ball. I enjoy life.

"That reminds me of a favorite saying of mine. 'No now is forever. We can learn from the past, but we can't live in the past. You can't change the past, but you can learn from it.' There's also a saying that 'Past is history. The future is a mystery. The gift is now—and that's why they call it the present.' That's why we have to enjoy what is happening right now. Some of the best things go on unexpectedly."

"I've never really factored play into life much," said Kitty. "When I think of play, I think of children. I don't think of what it means to play as I get older. A lot factors in—time, money, the ability to travel, and filling life up with so much other stuff that I don't leave room for play. I've been guilty of that over the last year and a half. I don't see myself out of it for a while because of the commitments I've made that I want to honor—but I see the light.

"I tell my friends, 'If you see me going for something I can get involved in—even if I say I have time now—just pinch me or say, 'Kitty, do you really want to do that?' It's really easy for me to fill the void with stuff instead of picking and choosing what I want to do.

"This right here is play. It's a huge learning experience and puts me in different parts of the country that I've not been in before. I'm seeing lifestyles that I'm not familiar with. I'm going along being open to the experience and not making judgments about it. I have a tendency to compare or judge. My wish for this trip was to leave that behind and not go there. It's like putting on a pair of glasses and not having them color my experience. It's about being open and looking at people or their situations for what they are. It doesn't help anyone if I try to figure everything out or to get in there and fix it. I was reminded this morning about fixing. I need those reminders.

"I'm learning about being open to experiences and remembering that there's a lot of joy in life. I don't need to trudge through my days. I want to set aside a piece of each day to enjoy something other than going to work or going to the grocery store. It might be reading a book or going for a walk or listening to music. It doesn't have to be big and grand. I want to be in the moment, with almost nothing big going on, and still find joy in that moment. I don't want to lose play. Play can happen in a lot of ways, if I remain open.

"I enjoy seeing new places. Making big, grand plans that take me someplace else doesn't simplify life for me. I need to remember that life is as simple or as complex as I want it to be. Looking back over the past couple of years, I see my life has been pretty full. I want to have more time to myself. It's a choice I've made not to let life be so complicated, like choosing to go for a walk around the block instead of going for a five-mile hike. It's amazing how I make life hard. I found a T-shirt in the bottom of my bin that says Simplify. I have to be that tangible about it. I need to wear that T-shirt or make it into a pillow to put on my couch to remind me that's how I want to walk through my days."

"About a year ago, I told a friend that I wanted to get a lot of stuff done because I didn't want to be that busy anymore," I said. "She looked at me and said, 'You love being this busy. You will always be this busy.' I said, 'No, I don't. I've always been this busy because it made me feel like I was important or contributing something.' I've always had to be contributing to feel I had a right to exist. I don't want to play that game anymore. I don't want to be that busy. The challenge is that I'm so overcommitted. I can't stop being like that yet.

"I was fascinated that she'd put me in a box based on what I've always done since she's known me. She never realized I never liked it at all. It struck me as odd that she couldn't see that. Being that busy is stressful and exhausting. It became who I was to her, and she still thinks that is what I want.

"I used to define myself by the roles I perceived I had. Whatever that role was, I believed that was all I was. I let those roles define the box that I would function in. That dramatically limited my life. It wasn't until I realized I was all of those roles at the same time that the boxes fell away. Then the roles played nicely with each other rather than in conflict with each other. That was a turning point. I realized all those roles had a place and I could put them down, pick them up, and even let them go."

"Family definitely makes my life rich," said Debbie D. with a sweet smile. "I have the type of work that I really enjoy. It's really fulfilling, and I feel like it does good things for the world. Not too many people have that, so I feel fortunate. I sell businesses for business owners who want to retire and do something else. My firm sells those companies.

"I've been doing it for twenty years. I feel like we nurture the people who make the economy strong, who make better jobs for people and make better goods and services. We make sure the ultimate reward is there for them at the end of the rainbow. It's really satisfying.

"I travel mostly in the United States. We did sell a company in China a couple of years ago. We won't do that again," she said, laughing. "That's a long way. For a four-hour meeting, you travel eighteen hours each way and you say, 'Why did I do this?' Most of our work is in the U.S. and Canada."

"She has sold 90 percent of the businesses she accepts to sell," boasted Bonnie. "If you know anything about sales, the ratio is one out of three, not nine out of ten. That has amazed me." She looked with mock criticism at Debbie D. "I wonder why you goofed off on the last ten percent."

"You are helping people's dreams come true," commented Gwyn.

"Yeah, it's really satisfying," said Debbie D. "And meanwhile new owners take the company sold from a retiree and grow it more, so the exchange gives new, younger owners better jobs."

"And gives them a chance to chase their dreams," added Gwyn.

"Right," said Debbie D. pulling her blonde hair away from her face. "Our business comes mostly from the recommendations of other people we've worked for. I have a couple of books out, and that helps too. My work is really absorbing and time consuming. I couldn't take the time to enjoy studying life and people like you do—or to go down the river like you are."

"She does a nice amount of play, though," added Bonnie. "I'm proud of her for that. You've got to remember to play."

"I find it so fascinating how many stories are out there," said Pat. "On the other hand, there are stories we aren't hearing because they get buried with a person who has died or a person who gets sick and can't tell her story. It's pretty special to be a part of this experience and to listen to these stories. I regret the loss of the stories we will not get to hear."

"When we saw you last, you had all your animals," I said to Bonnie. "Have things slowed down for you?"

"I still have thirty-three animals in my sanctuary," said Bonnie. "I have just about everything I had when you were there. I almost didn't get to come on this trip. I have a horse that's twenty-nine, and he couldn't get up on Wednesday. I trimmed his hooves on Monday . . . maybe that's why he couldn't get up." She laughed. "I didn't hurt him. He has trouble with his feet. I have one dog that's fourteen and one that's fifteen. My USDA inspector asked me, 'How old is the cougar?' and I said, 'She's fifteen.' She said, 'I thought she was. You've just had her forever.' I asked, 'Well, how long do they normally live?' She said, 'She should have been dead at least two years ago.' I have a sloth, and they never live as old as that sloth is. I'll keep them until they die—if I don't die first.

"The cougar has gotten so lovable. Of course, if a man comes by, she snarls. I don't plan on taking in any more animals, but I won't turn anything away if it's injured. They stay there, and then they keep living. I'm just really surprised at their ages. I like them very much.

"I do Reiki on my animals. They enjoy it, and they expect it every day. They'll turn and show me where they want it. It's so cute. It does so much for them.

"I had a llama that got a disease that llamas get from deer. He couldn't get up. The disease goes directly to their spine. My llama couldn't get up. My vets say that when hoofed stock goes down, you can count them dead if they aren't up in three days. Other vets say that if you can keep them alive for four months, maybe they'll get on their feet again. Mine went down in December, and I finally had him put down at the end of May because I knew he wasn't going to make it. I'd do Reiki on him and his little guts would growl. They say they can't digest if they aren't on their feet. Reiki made him digest. We got him up in a sling and pulley. It took three men and me. They finally got it rigged so I could do it by myself, and I got him up every day. He was just never going to make it.

"In February I had a new USDA inspector come by, and she said the agency changed its mission from education to enforcement. It didn't sound good to me, and it wasn't. She was looking for trouble, and she found it. I had the sanctuary for twenty-two years. Now all my cages had to be redone.

"I have some friends who live about sixty miles from me. They have monkeys too, so they aren't too bright either," she smiled. "They asked what was going on, and I said my USDA inspector said I had to redo everything. I called them at eleven o'clock in the morning, and by two thirty that afternoon that couple was at my place to make a list of everything we had to do. He was sixty-five, just retired. They came out for 38 days in a row, 130 miles round trip each time. They redid everything, and then they decided my upstairs needed to be redone. They painted it and put new tile in the kitchen and the bedroom. They put up new light fixtures and fixed everything that was broken—which was everything on the place. We just finished up Memorial Day weekend.

"Then the inspector said I had to extend the perimeter fence. It used to be six feet and now it had to be eight feet around the cougar pen. I went ahead and started doing that because we had seventy-degree weather.

"Last July, Bram, the gentleman who had helped me, had a massive heart attack. In August his wife had surgery for cancer. They found out that she had cancer after his heart attack. She goes for her first day of chemo next week. I'm going to be there an awful lot to help them. They're really nice people.

"They had a monkey that they took in that had been in a basement apartment. He was so tame they used to turn him loose. He climbed up a pole and touched a wire, and it burned his leg so badly it had to be amputated above the knee, as well as one of the fingers on the hand on the same side. He had the longest canines I've ever seen. They called and asked me to help them load him to take him to the vet because they knew if anybody could load an animal, it would be me. We have had more fun with that monkey. He did get his canines out—and Reiki just did it all. He didn't get sick one time or have a bit of trouble. Reiki is exceptionally good with animals. They'll only accept it for about twenty minutes, and they'll move away.

"I enjoy my animals a lot."

Bonnie and Debbie D. left for their long drive home as it grew dark. Gatherings had become bittersweet: bitter because women from the areas we were in didn't attend, and I felt the mission of the trip wasn't being served; and sweet because the women present offered heartfelt wisdom.

That night, I came across a copy of the *Osceola Times* dated September 8, 2011, with a cover story about Osceola resident Sirbonnie Stanley who celebrated her 102nd birthday. The article stated she'd worked every day from six in the morning until evening, cooking, cleaning, and washing clothes for white families. When she got home, she cooked, cleaned, and washed clothes again for her own family. She had more than 220 grandchildren and great-grandchildren.

October 3rd through 5th

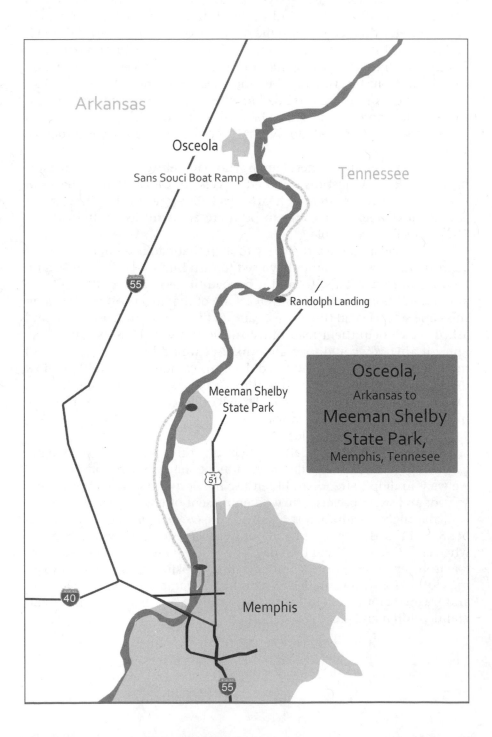

4

MEMPHIS

October 3, Day Thirteen

Alarge Asian carp lay dead on a log at the landing. Large silver scales covered its body. Asian carp are known for being easily frightened by the motion of a boat. This fear can cause the fish to leap up to eight feet above the water surface. People in boats have sustained broken noses and other injuries from collisions with the fish. Unfortunately Asian carp, an invasive species, are well established in parts of the Mississippi River. They're detrimental to the environment because they compete with native species for food. We hadn't had issues with them so far during this trip, but in 2007 we'd had several encounters with them. If one jumped up and hit a paddler, the impact could injure her or tip her kayak.

The weather had been amazing since we left Trail of Tears—warm days perfect for paddling and cool evenings perfect for sleeping. Gwyn and I departed from the San Suchi ramp on calm water under clear skies. The whole morning and into the afternoon we had the river to ourselves. The peaceful water lulled me into a meditative state. Gwyn pointed out a heron flying parallel to the shore. "There's Kee," she said with a big smile. The heron's reflection on the water mimicked her graceful movements in the sky.

"Do you hear the sandhill cranes flying over?" Gwyn asked. They were barely audible to me. "About five thousand sandhill cranes flew over me once," she said. "I got a picture of them. They were flying low late in the day, looking for someplace to spend the night. It was awesome.

"I don't understand how we can hear them, but we rarely see them," I said. "I know they make more than one sound, but the only thing I've heard is the cackle they make when they're disturbed."

"They make that cackling call when they're migrating so they can keep track of each other," said Gwyn. "You'd think they'd be big enough to see each other. They're kind of like geese. They fly in a group and can clearly see each other, but they still call."

"The birds in the front can't see the others," I said.

"That's true," said Gwyn. "I guess the birds in front are making sure all the others are still behind them."

We paddled in silence, lost in the beauty around us. Gwyn rescued a bee from the water and put it on her kayak to dry out. The bee rode there for a couple of hours and then flew away.

We spent lunch sitting on an enormous log half buried in the sand. Gwyn contemplated returning home the next day while a bee crawled on her shoulder. "This one must be thanking me for saving its buddy," she said. In a couple of weeks she'd return to paddle with us again, but leaving wasn't easy. A hawk caught her attention. "Once you leave the Mississippi River, you don't see red-shouldered hawks again until you get to California," Gwyn said. "Their territory skips the whole West."

We explored the beach and back into the trees looking for treasures to bring to Kitty and Pat, but the beach didn't offer anything. Bird tracks of many sizes were stamped in the sand in every direction. Farther back in the trees, we heard the high-pitched chirps of spring peepers and the vibrating shrill of tree frogs.

"We only have five kinds of frogs in Wyoming," said Gwyn.

"I wonder how many different species inhabit the Mississippi from top to bottom," I said. "I imagine the species vary as much as the weather and terrain do."

Back in our kayaks we squinted to discern a strange shape downriver. "Hey, do you see that?"

"It looks like the cartoon house from the movie *Up*," said Gwyn. "You know, the one that has balloons on the it."

The river had claimed half of a house; the rest was precariously

perched on the edge of the bluff. In *Life on the Mississippi* Mark Twain spoke about the pre-levee era when the topography of the river was constantly changing. When the river changed course, a town in Tennessee might end up in Arkansas or on an island in the middle of the river. Twain wrote, "The town of Delta used to be three miles below Vicksburg: a recent cut-off has radically changed the position, and Delta is now *two miles above* Vicksburg." Even homes that sat a safe distance from the river might suddenly have their foundations undercut and end up somewhere else. At times the shifting of the river resulted in huge upheavals in political and economic power. A few miles north of the crumbling house was a five-mile stretch where the river had changed course and left a half-moon piece of land on the Arkansas side that belonged to Tennessee. On our charts we saw many examples of such changes all along the river.

For the first time all day, the river's smooth surface was disturbed as a heavily loaded barge passed. The scene around the next bend was breathtaking. Towering rolling bluffs were vibrant green in the late afternoon sun. Vines cascaded down the rocky shoreline. Sheer rock cliffs rose from the lush foliage. Trees, like strands of a thick shag carpet, covered the bluff. The sky was a brilliant blue backdrop while the water reflected a myriad of intense blues and greens. I imagined the hills of Ireland looking this way.

We ended our seventeen-mile day at Randolph Landing. Locating the landing from the water proved to be challenging once again. The shoreline looked disturbed, not how I remembered the area from the reconnaissance trip. But we paddled closer to shore and soon were safely on land.

We had arrived at the landing early, so we left our kayaks secured onshore and walked to the road. Dust billowed across a field where several large bulldozers and trucks were removing sand. A truck slowed as it drove by, and we asked the burly driver what the bulldozers and trucks were doing. He said the river had breached the levee and taken out the road. Water washed tons of sand onto the farmer's field. The farmer was paying them to remove it, and the levee was being rebuilt with the sand. They had already been removing sand for thirty days, he said, and he estimated they'd be there about two more weeks.

A deep crater more than 150 yards wide split the road. They'd spent ten days filling it, the man explained, and the crater was still more than fifteen feet deep. The rest was up to the county, he said.

We went back to the ramp to get our kayaks, and a muscular man in a white Chevy pickup pulled in next to us. He was part of the levee cleanup crew. He drove over to the ramp for a look at the water and told us he loved to play on the river. As a kid he swam in it, and he still camped on the shore directly across from the landing. He spent as much time on the water as he could. We saw envy in his eyes as he said repeatedly, "That's so cool you gals are kayaking it." He looked at our kayaks and said he'd need something bigger to paddle in because he weighed three hundred pounds. He pointed to the wing dike and said, "When the water receded last spring, we found a stolen Jeep that had been driven into the river over there. That happens often here." He enthusiastically wished us well and went back to work.

We hauled one of the kayaks up the ramp and across the parking lot to a shady spot by the road. A woman pulled in at the top of the ramp and parked. When we walked by for the second kayak she rolled down her window and asked, alarmed, "What are you doing out here?" When we told her she said, "I can't believe you're out there. Don't you know you're going to die? Everybody dies out there." Other than her prediction of doom, she was pleasant. She told us that she sometimes drove to the boat ramp to sit and look at the water, but she never got out of the car. She and her husband believed the boat ramp was dangerous for women, and she told us he'd be mad if he knew she was there. She warned us to be careful because the people who came to the boat ramp were not to be trusted.

After she drove away I turned to Gwyn. "Isn't it remarkable the different ways people see the river?"

"They either love the water or are scared to death of it," said Gwyn.

"And they want to persuade us to believe what they believe."

With the kayaks situated we attempted to call Kitty and Pat, but we couldn't get through, so we made ourselves comfortable on our kayaks.

"Looking at the trees and lush green vegetation makes me appreciate Minnesota," I said. "This is beautiful, but I can't go hiking in there and not worry about snakes, spiders, and poison ivy. In Minnesota I can interact with nature and not have to be on guard."

"I was thinking the same thing about Wyoming," said Gwyn. "I enjoy being able to walk through the vegetation and see what's there, see the landscape, and see the contours of the land. I like being able to see what hazards are there without being all decked out. All I have to do to avoid potential harm is to watch where I put my feet beside sagebrush. Here you have danger coming at you from every direction," she said, indicating the woods thick with underbrush and vines engulfing everything. "I was thinking what a hassle it would be to try to break through that. You wouldn't be able to enjoy a walk because you'd be busy cutting your way through. It's kind of a neat little archway over there, though." She pointed to vine-covered trees twenty feet behind us. "I definitely belong in the open spaces."

"That vine going up that tree is poison ivy," I said, astonished by its size. Its circumference was as big as one of our water bottles.

"With its woody vine, it looks more like a tree than ivy," said Gwyn.

About ten minutes later we connected by phone with Pat and Kitty, who were an hour away. So we watched the men moving the earth on the field for a while and then fell asleep on top of our kayaks. Pat woke us up when she called to say they were having trouble finding the ramp. She said they thought they were still forty-five minutes away. Even though we knew they weren't coming yet, we kept looking down the road for them.

Heavy equipment and engines resonated in the background. Gwyn said, "It's amazing to me that I'm sitting on the Mississippi River today, and I'll be on the Wyoming-Idaho border on Friday. On Saturday, I'm going through Yellowstone on the way to my parents'. I'm looking forward to driving through there by myself. I've never done that. Usually I'm with my parents or Ed, and Ed drives too fast. He's too busy being a race car driver to stop and look around."

"It takes me a while to get places because I want to stop and look," I said. "I need to get out of the car."

"That's right," said Gwyn, enthusiastically, "to listen to the quiet and take it in."

"Doug likes to travel the same way I do," I said. "That's nice. He likes to experience the drive. If I've driven the route a million times, I drive faster, but if I've never seen the area before, I like to take my time."

While we talked we ran out of shade, and so we moved the kayaks. A couple pulled up and talked with us. The man told us that the last time the levee broke the boat launch parking lot was a sink hole. They chatted for a while and then drove off.

I kicked off my neoprene booties and sandals, and Gwyn slipped off her water boots. "What doesn't make sense to me is using the sand to build a levee that's already broken more than once," I said to Gwyn, "Actually, using sand doesn't make sense to me period, because sand is moved too easily by water."

"Maybe it's the base to put riprap on," said Gwyn. Riprap is rock or other material used to secure shorelines.

"The washout explains why the bank of the river didn't look right to me when we paddled in," I said. "No wonder the bank was just sand without trees. What a dirty job they have."

"Imagine what it costs," said Gwyn. "All those guys and equipment, twelve hours a day."

After checking down the road to see if Pat and Kitty were coming we moved the kayaks again to stay in the shade, and I lay back on the top of my kayak. "When I was a kid," I said, dreamily, "I used to like to lie on the ground and look at the leaves in the tree branches. I'm still fascinated by the different patterns, colors, and layers. I remember the sky and clouds came alive while I lay there."

"I used to look at the clouds and try to make shapes out of them, like we were doing with Laurel the other day," said Gwyn.

"From your tone I gather you failed at that," I said.

"I totally sucked," Gwyn admitted, laughing.

The day grew warm during the two hours we waited. When Pat and Kitty arrived we quickly loaded the gear and headed to Meeman Shelby State Park in Tennessee.

"We were looking for a grocery store, and the first one we saw looked like a little liquor store with bars over the windows," Pat said, speaking quickly and a bit out of breath. "We decided not to stop there and went a little farther and saw a place called Salvage Groceries." We laughed.

"Its name made you want to stop and get food there, I'm sure," I said.

"Then we saw a place that sold prehistoric pets," said Kitty. "We couldn't figure out what the prehistoric pets were. Rocks maybe?"

"And we passed a church with a sign in front that said 'Walmart is not the only saving place,'" said Pat, laughing.

"We may have had a hard time finding you guys," said Kitty, "but we were entertained along the way."

Pat joined her husband, Dave, at the park. She'd be camping with him, but joining us for meals. We were setting up camp when Cis arrived. I went to the van to get my raincoat to put away, but my raincoat wasn't there. Neither were my favorite straw hat, scarf, neoprene booties, or water bottle. Gwyn noticed her jacket and neoprene socks were missing as well. We realized we had put them on the box on the front of the trailer while loading the kayaks and forgot to put them in the van before we drove off.

Cis and Gwyn drove twenty-five miles back to Randolph Landing and returned with one of my booties and Gwyn's jacket, but nothing else. My water bottle had traveled the entire river with me and had stickers on it from points along the way. My raincoat was new, as was the scarf I used to wrapped around my straw hat. I wasn't worried about the booties; the water was warmer than anticipated. I had lost only stuff, but I was still upset. Pat said she'd loan me her extra raincoat.

The park we camped at was named for Edward J. Meeman, a conservation editor who helped establish this park and the Great Smoky Mountains National Park. The idea behind the creation of Meeman Shelby Park was to create a preserve in the Memphis area where people could enjoy the wilderness.

Cis found a music stand in her campsite next to the picnic table. The music stand looked regal standing in the woods under the light of a single ray of sun, and I expected to hear orchestra music strike up as if we were in a movie scene. Finding locations for our tents proved a bit of a challenge because of the prevalence of poison ivy.

With the sound of crickets as background music, Cis treated us to a dinner of authentic homemade tamales that she had brought from home. The drone of a barge came from a distance. Our headlamps and flashlights tied together created a chandelier hung from the top of the cook tent.

A jet black cat tried to sneak into our cook tent. A softy for animals, Gwyn let the cat in to hold it. The cat snuggled into Gwyn's lap and began purring. Pat, who has severe reactions to poison ivy, didn't want to get near the cat because the cat had walked through it.

Later in my tent updating Facebook, I stopped to listen to squirrels jumping through crackling dry leaves and to the distant echo of woodpeckers knocking on trees. The birds' chirping and chattering slowly diminished as the sun began to set.

Since Pat would be leaving soon, she wrote her journal entry that night:

> *To wonderful friends and fellow adventurers,*
> *I was asked to join this leg of the trip by Nancy. I didn't hesitate to say yes, and I couldn't wait to start! What a wonderful way to welcome the next decade of my life. I turn sixty this November. I'm embracing it and can't wait to welcome and cherish the things I've learned and continue to learn about myself.*

The most changing experience so far has been learning about what happened on the Trail of Tears in the 1800s when the U.S. government forced the Indian nation off the land. Many, many tears were shed that day. Kathy made the analogy of the Holocaust to the Indian displacement. Wow! I'll be thinking of this for the rest of my life.

The hardships of the trip changed the way I see myself dealing with negative things that happen to me. After the day—the rain, cold, muddy feet, wet tent, raining in the cooking tent—none of that was hard to deal with.

I'm glad to be a part of this world. Nothing to complain about— keeping this close to my heart will be a special thing for me to work on.

Every day brings joy and laughter. How can we other be!

I love it. Pat

October 4, Day Fourteen

I woke to the sound of pileated and red-headed woodpeckers pounding away as they searched for breakfast. Calling back and forth with a fluty tone, song birds sent their tunes out like musical alarms.

I enjoyed the forest's concert and had an insight into some of my frustrations. Traveling with women challenged me because I experienced more caretaking than I was comfortable with. Generally the caretaking felt nurturing and caring, but then there came a point where it crossed a line, and I felt controlled and smothered. I was aware I had reached that point when I got irritated each time anyone offered to do something for me, or help me with what I was doing that I was capable of doing by myself. It could be as simple as making myself a cup of tea. I had yet to learn where the line was until I began to feel frustration, and this caused inconsistency in my behavior. Something that bothered me one day I could let go of another. I knew it was confusing for the others. It didn't help that even when I knew a line was crossed I was inconsistent in telling them. I decided to try to be better about speaking up.

The black cat was back and wanted to come into the tent. She cried during breakfast and landed in Gwyn's lap again. The cat purred and rubbed against Gwyn, tempting her to take it home. While Gwyn petted the cat, Cis demonstrated pressure points to help Gwyn with her headaches. "When teaching this, I come from a place of self-empowerment," said Cis. "There isn't always someone that you trust around to help you, so you have to be able to do this for yourselves. Energywise, it's better if someone does it for you."

"Why is that?" I said. "When I give myself a foot rub it doesn't feel as good, or when I do pressure points on my feet it doesn't have the same impact as when Doug does it."

"It could be because we're our own circuitry and someone else's touch adds an outside energy to ours," said Cis.

"Nurturing comes to mind," said Kitty.

"Nurturing does come into it," said Cis, nodding.

Pat, who'd been focused on making breakfast, said, "This is flaxseed, if you would like to sprinkle it on your yogurt."

"I've been using Stevia to sweeten my yogurt if you would like to use it," I said, setting it out on the table. I looked around. "This is a big park with lots of hiking trails. We should explore it and check out the General Store."

"When I think of a general store, I think of the one in St. Thomas, North Dakota, where my friend Marlys's mom worked," said Kitty. "It had farm equipment, gardening equipment, dungarees, overalls, and T-shirts in the middle and food on one side. The store had everything. When you'd walk in, a little ninety-year-old man would ask what you needed."

"In Eureka we had that man," said Cis.

"He gets around," I joked.

"That kind of helping is a lost art," said Cis. "Used to be you'd go into such a store and say, 'My toilet is doing this.' Someone would go in the back and get the part you needed, and then he'd tell you how to fix your problem toilet. When you got home, if you needed help, you'd call him and he'd talk you through the repair."

"These days, few people work at the same place their whole life and gain that knowledge," said Kitty. "That kind of service will be a lost art because nobody is going to know what's in a store or what the items are used for."

"The store in Eureka has five billion bins of little bitty parts," said Cis. "He knew them all. He was the neatest guy."

Our conversation turned to the 2011 Pagami Creek Fire that burned in the Boundary Waters Canoe Area Wilderness thirty miles from Kitty's and my homes. Containment operations had worked until heavy wind rekindled the fire and it moved eighteen miles in one day. The forest in that area had become dense with fuel. Doug and I saw the fire's smoke from town billowing thousands of feet into the air. It was the largest fire Minnesota had seen since 1918. Although we know forest fires are necessary to keep the forest healthy and the forest will regenerate, we were sad to temporarily lose a few of our favorite campsites.

"Part of what my daughter, Sara Jo, is studying is the invasion of grasses in California and how grasses are related to fire," I said. "There are more grasslands in California now than there used to be, and the grasses are pushing native shrubs out. That's one of the reasons California is having those major fires. Grass burns readily. The native shrubs don't burn as fast."

"Once cheatgrass comes in, it changes the fire regime for the area," said Gwyn. "Decades can go by before sagebrush burns. Cheatgrass changes a fire cycle to an annual cycle, and the sagebrush can't get tall enough to support life like pronghorn, sage grouse, and other fauna."

"You and Sara Jo need to talk," I said. "The research she's doing at Berkley is on grass and soil composition, and she's studying what organisms are in the soil that make the grass grow and inhibit the native plants."

"A friend of mine does grazing management," said Gwyn. "He can get rid of cheatgrass in two years by controlling grazing with goats at the right time of year. Cheatgrass is native in Mongolia."

"Is cheatgrass an introduced species?" asked Pat.

"Yes," said Gwyn. "It greens up fast in the spring, but when the seed head comes in, the cows don't want to eat it—it's poky. Most people are using chemicals to get rid of it."

"It would be interesting to find out what they use to defoliate the cotton," said Kitty.

"It would be interesting to look at birth-defect rates in this area," said Gwyn.

"That's what I was wondering," I said. "You can smell the defoliant in the air. Remember Jimmie back in Osceola talked about the defoliant getting on his windshield? The houses next to the cotton field had children's toys in the yards. The defoliant must get on them too."

"I thought there was something leaking in the van because of the nasty smell," said Pat, pausing from cleaning up after breakfast. "Then we found out they had sprayed the fields we were driving past."

"We've had so much trouble with the van, we automatically assume the smell is from the van," I laughed. "Now that the van has so many new parts, she's happy."

We went to the river to sing and to make an offering for the evening's Gathering. There we met L.C., who wore a straw cowboy hat and a broad smile, comfortably seated at the bottom of the boat ramp. We watched as a boat took off from shore with a man and a woman aboard.

"I saw fish jumping out there," said Gwyn, pointing to a spot on the water between the river's edge and the wake of the waves from the boat.

"Oh, there's a lot of them," said L.C. with a thick southern accent that made him hard for us to understand at times. "They done broke my line twice. See what they do is, those fish, they take it out on the rocks and they break your line. The fish are smart here. I caught one catfish here one time and he had three fish hooks in 'im. He knew what he was doin'. Something's gonna bite when you throw that line out there. It might take a little while, but it's gonna bite."

"What do you use for bait?" asked Gwyn.

"I use them big night crawlers," said L.C. "They don't care about crickets and things like that."

"I met a guy who was fishing the river with corn," I said.

"You know, those old buffaloes like that," said L.C., jigging his line. "Then you've got crappies and things. Everything is out there. With buffaloes, you can take dough balls. Oh, they love that. You take that dough ball and put a little garlic in there. Some fish out there's so big the average reel ain't goin' to hold 'em no way. Problem is when they're big, you can't eat 'em. They too tough. You might as well turn 'em loose. If they don't look right, I throw 'em back. You can never tell what he been eatin'."

"My buddy that went in that boat, if he was here, he'd keep you laughin' all day. He's terrible. He's gonna aggravate the daylights outta his new wife out there." We all laughed.

"You mean he waited until after he married her to introduce her to the water?" asked Cis.

"Half the time when a man is trying to get a woman, he's lying anyway," said L.C. "You got to lie. If you tell the truth, she ain't gonna fool with you—when you look at how it goes down through the years. She looks at you and you says, 'This is my momma and daddy's car.' Girls love to hear that stuff. I have to say, 'I'm so sweet.' When you tell the truth, a girl's gonna think you're lyin'. That's what he done to her. I can tell you that right now. I've known that rascal all my life."

"Are you married?" asked Kitty.

"Yeah," said L.C., and we laughed with him. "Didn't I tell you, you got to be a good liar? I told my wife one time, 'When I first met you, I had to lie to get you to listen to me. Then I had to lie to get you to go with me. Then I had to lie to get you to marry me. And then I had to lie you into two daughters.' Don't you think I'm responsible for some of this stuff?"

"How long have you been married?" asked Kitty.

"November first will be forty years," L.C. said proudly. "I'm an over-the-road truck driver for the U.S. mail. I retired and then went back to work. Too many family folk 'round worry you to death. When I come off that road, I had nephews that dropped outta school. They got superglue in one hand 'n Elmer's in the other, and they can't turn nothin' loose that they touch. I'd rather go back to work than be 'round a bunch of them folks.

"I had a horse ranch over there in Quito and I sold it. My daughters are out of college and they is gone. My wife is still teachin' in school. I'm goin' to retire for good in 'bout another year or two. Then I'll have all day to come here. The river don't argue with you. Every woman I know wants to argue with you. The Ol' Miss, she don't argue with you.

"When you a truck driver, you don't get home-cooked food. You don't get all of that stuff. You got to stop wherever you can, but you get to see a lot. I run through Kansans City to Denver and come back twice a week. That's five thousand miles a week but don't seem like it in those trucks. You see tornadoes. You learn to see which way it's goin' and sometimes you got to hold back and let it go on past. Sometimes you got to try to outrun it. There's a lot of excitement in it—as long as you ain't too close.

"There's gonna be excitement in that boat that left here. That lady would rather be with a tornado than be with him." L.C. shook his head and laughed. "He was feelin' too good. He's liable to come back with ten or twenty knots on his head. He's a showman. He's gonna show off that he's a good boatsman. She got curious when I wouldn't go with 'em.

"Sometimes I come here and I sit and watch the boats go by. I got here at daybreak this morning. Under the Memphis Bridge it's a hundred feet deep. They got catfish that hang out underneath that bridge 'cause they eat the garbage. They got some as big as a human being down there. It's dangerous 'cause there's big suction, and if anything goes through there, it will hold it under. We was down there one day, and there was this oak tree, and it got pulled right down under. It never did come back up. It ain't no good place to play out there. Water makes its own highway. I remember when the banks was way out there, but thanks to the Army Corps of Engineers they kinda help channel this stuff. You got to know what you're doin' if you're goin' to be out there."

"Are you saying that close to the bank under the Memphis Bridge, the bridge sucks things under?" I asked.

"Yeah," said L.C. "We was there fishin' one day 'n this big ol' oak tree was floatin' down. The tree hit the spot and was goin' around a little bit." He made a whirlpool motion with his hand. "We kept watchin' it, and she pulled that tree under. There's a lot of suction in the holes in this river in different places. This is the only river you'll find that people don't play in it. Those jet skiers and all—they don't. The city don't allow it 'cause many people got drownded. The Mississippi River is a danger-ous river. If they find you out there messin' around, you can go to jail. There's something else that can kill you in this river. If you look on the *National Geographic*, sharks have done got immune to this type of water 'cause it dumped into the ocean."

"Bull sharks?" asked Cis.

"Yeah. They come all the way up this river."

"How big are bull sharks?" asked Pat.

"Oh, they big all right, and they mean."

"Eight to ten feet," said Cis.

"This is a deadly river," said L.C. "It's got everything in it. I was down there one day and we was fishin' and a deer come out of the woods runnin' and hit that river. It swam all the way across. The current was takin' 'em downriver a bit, but that rascal went across and came out on that other side."

"He must've been tired when he got over there," I said.

"I know he was," said L.C. "The old buck deer are the only things I seen in this river. If you're huntin' 'em, they jump in that river and swim to the other side. They can handle it."

"We've got to be moving on," I said.

"Well, y'all ladies enjoy yourself today," said L.C. "I'm gonna wait and see how that boat ride comes out." We laughed.

On the ride back to camp, Kitty said, "I wonder if his wife thinks she knows him other than he lies a lot. What is the truth in all of this?"

"That's his truth, isn't it?" asked Cis.

"Apparently she's accepted it as part of her truth too," said Kitty. "She's been with him for forty years."

"He has a lot of respect for the river," I said. "The river is a living entity to him. My ears perked up when he talked about the oak tree disappearing. He had no idea that tomorrow we're going to get on the river right there at his boat ramp. If he's there when we put in, he's going to think we are nuts, and he'll ask if we were paying any attention to him." We all laughed.

Cis and Gwyn headed to the Memphis International Airport. Saying goodbye to Gwyn was easy because she'd be coming back in a couple of weeks. Cis would drop off Gwyn and bring back Heidi, who was flying in from Minnesota.

Kitty, Pat, and I relaxed at camp, where the Tennessee crickets made Minnesota crickets look like ants. On the exterior wall of the bathroom we found a walking stick bug. It was five inches long, motionless, and a brown color that matched the wall. We cleaned and reorganized the trailer and van, and shortly afterward Cis and Heidi arrived and we got ready to head to the Gathering.

The five of us drove narrow roads under a canopy of green branches. A red fox crossed our path. A fox, it's believed, symbolizes adaptability and the ability to become unseen, like the wind.

We set up for the Gathering, and visualizing women arriving, we left room in our circle around the fire for their chairs. Then we sat down to wait. We felt frustrated about the lack of women at the previous Gatherings, but held tightly to the hope that this night would be different. It was a delightful evening, sunny and warm with a pleasant breeze, perfect for a Gathering. With some difficulty we lit our fire. Gwyn had done such a good job dousing the fire the night before that the coals were dripping wet. Each time I put a few coals from the Peace Fire on, the fire nearly went out.

With each passing car our excitement rose—and fell. Time passed and we realized no one from the area would join us. We pulled our chairs close together, closing the gaps we had created for other women. Trying to stay cheerful, we commented on the brightly colored sarong with a fish print that Cis wore as a skirt. Kitty and I were also wearing skirts. In many traditions it is customary for the women in a talking circle to wear a skirt.

Inevitably our conversation turned to ways to increase participation in our Gatherings, but no answers surfaced. Our group's energy was low as Kitty held the fan first and began the dialogue.

"In the journal I kept on the last leg of the Mississippi River, I wrote words I'm going to live by," she said. She read her list, three and a half pages, which included words such as compassion, spiritual, quiet, solace, worthy, integrity, intuitive, and balanced. "When I looked at how many pages of words there were, I was amazed. The words all seem so big. There's so much wrapped up in each word, and I could write a dictionary for each of them. When I get home, I'm going to find a ribbon or a piece of fabric to write the words on and hang them up where I can see them each day."

Kitty handed Cis the fan. Cis looked thoughtfully at our small fire and then said, "I'm looking forward to the routine of purpose on this trip. We do this, and go there, and come back from our duties every day. I'll need to fold back into my dad's pace when I get home, which is glacial. No," she said, reconsidering, "it's even slower than that." We laughed sympathetically. "On the occasions I have to hop to it, I think, 'Oh, my gosh, I've forgotten how to rush around.' My dad's been a great teacher of stillness and patience. I'm looking forward to finding balance on this trip with its lively, chaotic organization. I'm looking forward to just dealing with whatever comes before us because my life is absolutely routine and rhythm, and that's fine. But I'm excited to be here with you all again."

"I like what you said about your dad living at a glacial pace," said Kitty. "I thought, 'What's wrong with that?' There isn't anything wrong with that. It's about finding balance and knowing that life does move at a faster pace sometimes. There is something about being comfortable in and embracing either pace. When you said, 'I'm looking forward to it being a little more lively,' I thought, '*That's* why she's driving that way.'" We laughed again.

"I don't want to be too comfortable or complacent," said Cis. "I'm comfortable at any age, but I don't want to become complacent about anything. I want to be present. I can feel myself solidifying at Dad's glacial pace, and I think, 'Okay, I've got to get out of this. I've got to go find something to balance that out here.'"

The sound of starlings and grackles burst from the woods behind us and caught our attention. We turned and watched a large flock flit from tree to tree.

"Whether we like it or not, we all have preconceived notions that get in the way of seeing things accurately," I said. "We try not to, but we have them."

"One of the things I value about our group is the communication that it takes to do this," added Kitty. "Being in this group and planning for this trip helped improve my communication skills. At times it doesn't feel like it, and yet I know I've grown.

"As I grow older, it's important for me to communicate. Sometimes communicating is hard for me because I'm not a confrontational person. Even when I'm not comfortable, I've learned to say what I need to say, and I've realized I don't have control over another person's reaction. The Gatherings are about speaking and feeling safe doing that. This group has helped me grow in that realm. Today there is a deeper level of meaning to the importance of communication, and I will continue to say what I need to say.

"Pat and I were talking about *The Four Agreements* [by Don Miguel Ruiz] when we went to Millington. I love the agreements. They describe how I want to walk through my days. The four agreements are always do your best; speak with integrity; don't make assumptions, which I do so easily; and don't take things personally, which I also do easily. It's kind of a trick to remember them these days. When I remember that issues are not always about me, I don't take things personally. I can see an issue might be about what's going on with the other person.

"When I take things personally while talking with another person, things come out sideways. My feelings are not because of anybody out there," she said, moving her hand from her left to her right in a half circle. "They're about what is going on inside me. It's important for me to remember that and to apologize when I need to, especially if what happened affected someone in a hurtful manner. I brought *The Four Agreements* with me. I want the book with me or near me on this trip. Maybe I'll absorb it by osmosis. In the book *The Yamas and Niyamas: Exploring Yoga's Ethical Practice* [by Deborah Adele] those four agreements are expanded."

"Communication is often a challenge for me because the message I am trying to convey is often delivered at the end," I responded. "It took me a long time to understand that I tend to speak backwards. In writing, I often have to flip the entire paragraph."

"Wow, you go backwards in your thought process to find the beginning," said Kitty. "I jump in the middle, and I have to go backwards to explain myself."

"When I'm talking with people, what I am saying is perfectly clear to me," I said. "I can't understand why others don't get my point. This can be frustrating even though now I understand what I do. My communication method seems to be hardwired.

"Another factor is my intuition and my belief that people already know what I'm talking about. I think, 'What's your problem? Catch up here.' People make assumptions about what I'm saying and run with it. Sometimes I stop them, and other times I let the assumptions go because it takes too much energy to rein them back in or I don't have the words to bring them to what I am saying. I grow quiet. Then I hear people say, 'Why didn't you tell me?' I did—but it wasn't in your language." I chuckled and shrugged. "A great example is the woman we overheard the other day talking on the phone. She was speaking English, but we only understood every third word because of her dialect."

"We all speak our own language," said Kitty. "We know what we're trying to get across, but we almost have to explain it four different ways so everybody understands. We all hear differently, and words have different meanings. It takes a lot of words to explain a little message. We each have our own way of looking at things."

"We have friends who come to visit," said Cis, "lovely, lovely people, friends of my mom and dad. When one of the ladies is at our house, she breaks things and says, 'Oh, I don't know. I just break everything all the time.' I said to her, 'I wonder what that means?'"

"Isn't there something about putting a belief out there that will keep it happening?" asked Kitty.

"Absolutely," said Cis. "But my friend resisted acknowledging this."

"It's easier to be resigned than to try to do something about it," said Kitty.

"I think it has to do with being disconnected from your spirit so your timing is off," said Cis, adjusting her skirt. "Heidi, you mentioned that you feel like your spirit hasn't caught up with you after flying here from Minnesota. When you're not following your path and you're forcing things, they get disconnected and accidents happen."

"I worked with a lady who rubbed people the wrong way," added Kitty. "I don't know that she even knew it. She'd come in and say 'I need to vent,' and she'd say her piece and follow it with, 'I can't help it. It's just the way I am.' This is what we're talking about: moving responsibility for self out there. Saying 'I can't help it' explains her behavior all away for her rather than holding that behavior up, looking at it, and saying, 'Maybe that's a behavior I want to change because it isn't working.'"

"I think there's balance to be found with that too," I added. "For years I kept trying to change things that were core pieces of who I am because other people didn't like them. No matter what I did, those core pieces wouldn't change. When I said, 'This is who I am, even if you don't like it,' I found peace."

"I see a difference in that she was using the 'I can't help it' to not be responsible for her behavior, whether it was hurtful to others or not," said Kitty. "She wasn't even accepting herself as who she was."

"I bet she doesn't feel good when she says 'I can't help it,'" I added.

"There is a difference between accepting yourself and feeling the need to defend yourself," said Heidi. "She hasn't figured out how to accept and love who she is enough to be able to just be accepting of her behavior."

"That sounds like her," said Kitty. "I hadn't thought of it that way. She feels the need to explain herself every time, instead of just accepting who she is."

"In the accepting comes the ability to change," I added. "When you accept it, you can release it. But I still talk backwards. You can't change the wiring . . . "

"Part of that whole package is knowing that about yourself," said Kitty.

"I know people often don't understand me," I responded. "Maybe that's why I hesitate to share things verbally. I think Doug is the only one I've ever had a conversation with about this. One of my frustrations is people jump in and try to fix, change, or alter what I'm saying to make sense out of it. Ultimately what I'm saying gets lost, and I want to say, 'I don't need this. I'm going to leave you in your confusion. I know what I wanted to say, so you're just going to have to get over it.'" We laughed. "When I write, I can put my thoughts down and then put it in an order everybody understands."

"Losing words is a very Taoist concept," said Cis, smiling. "You just give up the need to know and go on."

"At dinner the other night, I told Nancy, Gwyn, and Kitty that I don't see aging the way they do," said Pat. "Getting older is just part of life. So my hair is going gray. So I'm sagging. So I gained a little weight. It doesn't bother me. I'm looking forward to turning sixty. Sixty is so exciting. My family is short-lived, but I'm still healthy, and I'm going to be sixty. I'm celebrating it. Why should I worry about my hair going gray?"

"Sixty is a cycle of completion," added Cis. "Your astrological signs have come back around full circle. All the things you were born under are back again in Chinese astrology. In Taoism, you're going back to zero, so next year you will be fifty-nine and then fifty-eight."

"I get how turning sixty is exciting," I said. "My mom died when she was thirty-nine. As a kid, I believed that I'd die at thirty-nine. When I turned forty, I threw a party. My friends, who were devastated by turning forty, wanted to know what was wrong with me. I wanted to celebrate because I was forty—and I was still here."

"That's right," agreed Pat. "Our culture teaches us that when you turn sixty, you're in the grave. I never bought into that, but many people do—both women and men as well."

Our fire had gone out. We glanced toward the road as if somehow, magically, a woman might appear to join us.

No one did.

We quietly packed up and headed back to camp.

Pat joined us in the cook tent for dinner and gave us each a pale-green ceramic turtle as a token of her appreciation. Pat was teary-eyed leaving us even though she'd be back at the end of the trip. Kitty and I lamented that we'd miss her cooking. She headed back to her campsite with Dave.

"I've always wanted to be part of a big expedition," said Heidi, "but to be honest I thought it would be to someplace remote—not the Mississippi River. I had a hard time leaving Sam. He just started kindergarten this year. The day you started paddling under the St. Louis Arch, Gwyn and I were experiencing a regular day back home. The day felt strange, so I called her so we could be connected. Then I followed your progress on Facebook. It feels odd to be here. I got to see the Mississippi from the plane as we approached Memphis. I love being back among the big maples and oaks. I'm less thrilled by the poison ivy."

"We're glad you're here," I said.

We began focusing on cleaning up after dinner when Cis saw the Windex in Heidi's hand. "Did you know that Windex has been outlawed in Canada to use as moose bait?" she asked.

"People were using it for moose bait?" I looked at Cis and smiled. "This sounds like a good story."

"In the process of building our house, mud splashed on the windows," said Cis. "The mud streaks were terrible, and my friend Carole was coming, so I tiptoed around the house and washed the bedroom window and the patio door. In the morning, I asked 'How did you sleep, Carole?' She said, 'I think I heard things all night.' Turns out, a moose had been licking her window." We laughed.

"Are you serious?" I asked.

"I am," said Cis. "You know what a dog smear looks like on a window? Moose tongue is like this." She held her hands sixteen inches apart. "We didn't know that at the moment. We thought she was hearing things. She was a city girl, after all. What does she know? Later that day we went into town to the farmers' market, but my daughter Alexis stayed home. We came back and Alexis said, 'I was in the kitchen making breakfast, and I look out and a moose is in the window staring at me.' We went downstairs and there, with the sun shining on it, was a big snotty moose smear on the window. I love telling that story. A few years later a guest who had been visiting said, 'Oh, yeah, Windex is outlawed in Canada because moose love it.'"

"Does it hurt them, like antifreeze?" asked Heidi. "Antifreeze will kill moose."

"Windex is a little safer," said Cis.

Heidi was visibly tired, and she kept blowing her nose. She said, "I was sick the last three days before I left. I had better not paddle tomorrow and restore my energy."

We finished tidying the cook tent, and we were heading to our tents when Cis calmly called us to her campsite. She was getting things out of the trunk of her car when she felt what she thought was the black cat move across her sandaled foot. Her flashlight revealed a foot-long juvenile black rat snake. The snake curled up beside the car and made itself look bigger than it was as we admired it.

I walked the road to the bathroom under a full moon. I turned off my flashlight and stood with my eyes closed to gain better night vision. When I opened them, I was transported into a magical forest. Stunning moonlight filtered through the towering trees and cast shadows on the road. A wispy cloud passed in front of the moon, its edges glowing silver. It seemed as if someone had taken a salt shaker and sprinkled bright sparkling stars across the night sky. The hoot of a barred owl drifted through the trees. I was mesmerized and had to force myself into my tent.

As my head rested on my pillow, my thoughts were with Doug. I missed him more than I had on other trips. I ached for a few moments in his arms.

October 5, Day Fifteen

Because I had heard so much about dangers on the river, I felt nervous about Cis's and Heidi's paddling. I didn't like being on edge, but appreciated that it would keep me from becoming complacent. As it turned out, Heidi decided not to paddle; her energy was not back after being sick. While Cis and I prepared our kayaks she sat near a fisherman named Patrick, who was relaxing on a boat cushion with his bare feet resting on the cool mud. Patrick was sixty-seven years old and had grown up on the Mississippi. He said that his wife, whom he called Mama, told him he shouldn't use his pants to wipe the knife he used to cut bait, but

he does anyway. His bait was chicken blood mixed with catfish blood, and it smelled terrible. Heidi said, "I bet your wife loves that because the stink stays on your hands."

"It's one of the reasons she left me," Patrick responded. "She didn't take kindly to that—and apparently a lot of things. It's best if you surround yourself with people who love you for who you are and what you do. I'm well loved, and God loves me unconditionally. There's nothing more important than being loved." His wife wanted different things than he did, he said as he watched his fishing line. He loved people more than things. Reflecting on their early years he thought they had shared a truly loving relationship together.

He pulled in a white catfish and talked to it while he took out the hook. The catfish clicked at him. His deep, gravely voice became soothing. "I know . . . You hold real still there, honey. I'm going to make this as gentle as I can. We're going to get this out together." Then he let it go.

Tossing his line out again, he said that we inspired him because he had a dream of taking his fishing boat from Memphis to the Gulf. "I bet a lot of people think you're crazy for being out there, but it's water, and you got to love it." He knew there was a God, he said, because everything around him was beautiful.

Cis and I paddled silently, and I pondered the reading from the meditation book: "Learn to let yourself be guided into truth. We will know what we need to know, when we need to know that. We don't have to feel badly about taking our own time to reach our insights. We don't have to force insight or awareness before its time." I thought of how often I tried to force answers. They popped out of my mouth before I allowed myself time for reflection. I didn't want to burden people by making them wait for me to process things. Then I would think, "Oh, that's how I feel about that?"

Movement to my right caught my attention. It was a heron taking off from the top of a tall cottonwood. I smiled. "Good morning, Kee."

The best ways for me to find my truth are when I'm taking in the serenity of the wilderness—paddling on a river or lake, hiking in a forest, walking a trail behind my house, or quietly sitting under a tree. Insight isn't difficult, I realized; I just needed to step away from commitments and distractions and take the time. I needed more practice.

We stopped and sat in the shade of scruffy willow trees. A coyote pranced out of the brush and took a drink from the river, paying no attention to the barge passing by. I clearly saw her thick tawny-gray fur, the black tip on her tail, and her white throat and buff-colored belly. She trotted leisurely alongshore and then back toward the brush. Her eyes focused downriver searching for something. Her ears went to attention and she paused a few yards away. We sat motionless. Then she spotted us and dashed into the brush.

Alongshore, vines covered everything. My imagination played with the shapes they created, making a tree engulfed in the vines look like an elephant. Paddling closer I imagined the elephant shape morphing into a rhino, and then a cow, and then just vines hanging on a tree.

At the Gathering, Kitty had talked about *The Four Agreements* and how powerful its message was for her. The agreements were simple, yet applying them to life challenged me. The agreements are about communicating clearly. When I was in college one of my professors had handed out a photograph, and we were to use it as a story prompt. Thirty-seven students wrote thirty-seven different stories, each one reflecting the student's view of the world, none of them accurately telling the real story behind the photo.

I have difficulty communicating clearly sometimes because I can't find the right word to explain what I mean. I say what I think is the right word, but confusion on the listener's face indicates to me that it wasn't. Cis said losing words is a Taoist concept and I needed to give up the need to know and go on. Sometimes, out of exasperation, I do give up. But the more important the message, the more flustered I become. I wondered if the ability to give up the need to know would increase with age. I doubted it because ultimately the right words are key to communicating clearly.

The Memphis skyline came into view. Memphis was the one-third mark for this trip. After padding eighteen miles, Cis and I landed on Mud Island near downtown. Mud Island is a small peninsula with the Mississippi River on the west and Wolf River Harbor on the east. Its park has a

photo by Cis Hagar

museum and amphitheater. Beautiful expensive homes line the green-way overlooking the river.

At the top of the ramp, a sign from the Tennessee Department of Environment and Conservation warned: "ALL FISH . . . from this body of water contain contaminants at levels thought to increase the risk of cancer or serious illness in humans. These fish should not be eaten." I wondered what chemicals the warning referred to and how much of the contaminants I was absorbing by having my hands and feet in the water several times each day.

On the way to the First Unitarian Church of the River, where we'd be staying for the evening, we passed the Memphis Pyramid Arena. Its architecture contrasts with the traditional buildings around it. The sparkling stainless-steel exterior reaches thirty-two stories high, making it the third largest pyramid in the world. An impressive statue of Ramses the Great, an Egyptian pharaoh, stands at the entrance. The pyramid was built as a connection to Memphis's namesake in Egypt, which is known for pyramids. Driving through downtown Memphis, I thought it looked like a healthy, thriving town. People were walking the streets, and the traffic was heavy.

I remembered driving through Memphis during the reconnaissance trip. I had become lost and inadvertently exited the freeway in the wrong place. What I saw then was a contrast to the affluence apparent from the houses along the river and the buildings downtown. I'd seen poor neighborhoods with houses in need of repair, bars on the windows of the homes and businesses, and tall fences around the yards. Some yards had large dogs in them that barked at anyone who passed by.

We were warmly welcomed and given a tour of the church, which stands at the top of a high bluff. The sanctuary has stadium-style seating, giving each parishioner a clear view of the Mississippi River. The entire two-story front wall is a glass window with an unbelievable view. Originally designed so that no man-made structures were visible from the sanctuary, the view now includes a bridge to the north. Moving from one part of the church to another, we walked through outdoor patios that connected the building to nature.

We settled in and were delighted to take a shower. Heidi's ride on the plane had made her sinus infection excruciating. "I'm trying not to feel disappointed about not being able to paddle and participate," she said. "But after all these years of planning, not being able to participate because I'm sick is hard." She was in tears. After several phone calls to the clinic back home and to local pharmacies, we acquired medication for her. We made her as comfortable as possible in a dark room, and she attempted to sleep.

We prepared for the evening. Women arrived with their arms full of food. Rachell and Carol S., leaders of two of the church's women's groups, had assisted in arranging our stay and in coordinating a mouth-watering potluck dinner. While the potluck was being set up we spoke with Sue W. "We have parks that were created for the African American community—Douglas Park and T. O. Fuller Park," she said. "Fuller was a doctor and educator. I lead river walks along the bluff for people. One of the things I talk about is how our rivers are polluted with heptachlor and chlordane." Heptachlor and chlordane are pesticides that were used on crops and household gardens.

"Chlordane was produced here by Velsicol Chemical Corporation for a number of years," she continued. "I worked with the Sierra Club on getting it banned, but it was still produced to export to the Third World. Recently my friend Donna, head of the toxic committee for the Chickasaw Group and the Tennessee Chapter of the Sierra Club, got a letter thanking her for the letter she'd written that helped convince the UN to ban that chemical entirely.

"It was in the newspaper that Memphis is now the poorest major city in the country. We're poorer than New Orleans. We have a lot of subsistence fishing. Signs for the toxic fish are supposed to be posted, but you don't see them where people fish off the banks. Virtually all of the waterways and rivers are closed to subsistence and commercial fishing. It's closed from the Loosahatchie River, which flows into the Mississippi, nineteen miles down to the state line."

"At the state line the fish are good?" I asked.

"Well, that's the Mississippi Department of Environment's responsibility," said Sue W.

"And Arkansas?" I asked, amazed. "The fish on the other side are okay, too?"

"That's what I understand," said Sue W. "I haven't investigated that, but a friend of mine told me that was true. We burn coal. As you well know, there's mercury released when burning coal, and coal-fired power plants are right next to the river with an airflow pattern that goes across and up the other side."

"This is not the only place burning coal," I said. "We've seen several along the river."

"Air quality is my personal issue," said Sue W., "but air and water are interrelated. You can't talk about one without the other. Velsicol Chemical took bankruptcy, but bankruptcy set aside dollars for the places that they've contaminated. There's no real money to clean up north of us. The Tennessee Department of Environment did testing on one of the lakes off the Wolf River north of Memphis because people were fishing there. It's contaminated, and now it's fenced off, but there are still many places that are open."

"People would rather eat now and worry about the mercury later," I said.

"Yeah," said Sue W.

We all got our plates of food and took a seat around a large table. Before she sat, Carol S. announced we were invited to a private concert with the church choir later in the evening.

"I was asked to leave the choir in second grade," Cis said. "The music teacher said it was because I was sick a lot."

"In the second grade?" said Carol S. "That's criminal."

"Oh, I don't know . . ." said Cis. "Once when my young son, who's a musician and singer now, was strapped into his car seat and we were driving down the road, he begged me not to sing." We laughed with her. "I think it truly is the voice."

"What do people say to you about being on the river?" asked one of the women.

"People's reactions range from thinking we're crazy to being envious," I answered.

"There are deaths here on the river," she replied. "A guy was kayaking with someone—I don't think he had a life preserver on. It took three or four months to find his body."

"How do you get back in if you fall out?" asked another woman.

"We have paddle floats," I said. "The hardest part of getting back in is keeping the kayak right side up. The paddle float is like a pillow that we blow up and put on the end of our paddle. We extend that end of the paddle away from the kayak. We lean on the extended paddle and the kayak at the same time to climb in. It's kind of tricky, but without it, if there is no one to help you get back in, it's almost impossible."

"Kayaking is a dry sport," said Cis. "We don't intend to go out of the kayaks."

"Should someone fall out of her kayak," I added, "she would make noise to get our attention by yelling, pounding on the kayak, blowing a whistle, or sounding an air horn. We'd get to her quickly to help. In a worst-case scenario, we would help her swim to shore and hope we could recover her kayak, which would float downriver faster than she would."

"What's the difference between a kayak and canoe?" a lady asked.

"In a kayak the paddler is closer to the water than in a canoe," I said.

"I like kayaks because I feel as if I'm part of the water. Our kayaks have rudders, so they're easier to steer. Paddling a kayak is a constant, even stroke with a double-blade paddle. Paddling a canoe is an alternating side-to-side stroke with a single-blade paddle. I find steering a canoe more challenging. Canoes are open, and kayaks have a cockpit—the opening where you sit—and the rest is closed. The kayaks we're using are the same length as many canoes—sixteen feet. In a kayak, I can investigate wherever I want. I don't have to convince the other person in the canoe to go with me."

The women gathered for our presentation in a room adjacent to where we shared our meal. At the conclusion of the presentation, the entire group went to the sanctuary. Their small choir had a rich full-size sound. They sang three songs that brought tears to my eyes. I sang along when they performed the traditional Appalachian song "Down in the River to Pray." Cherry, a former professional singer who was tall and slender with beautiful white hair, glowed during the performance. She was having the time of her life.

A few women stayed for a Gathering. As the elder of the group, Shirley R., age seventy-three, began. "I was thinking about what I treasure the most in my life, and I thought about my two daughters," she said. "Why do I treasure them so much? I raised them to be independent. I knew the divorce rate was going up, and they needed to be able to survive on their own. I wanted them to go to college, and I wanted them to be able to speak their own minds. Not only do they speak their own minds, but they also encourage others to do so as well. One is an elementary school teacher; the other is a college professor. I'm very proud of them.

"I consider education a treasure in people's lives. I grew up with two brothers knowing that we were all going to college, but that if money ran out, as the female I wouldn't be able to attend. I accepted that view and the idea that marriage was the expected option. Therefore I majored in home economics in college, married, had two children, and along with my wonderful husband, provided a loving home. I returned to school and had a career as an elementary school counselor. Family and love are also treasures.

"I'm a compassionate person. This week in church and at home, I thought of the military situation. I thought of the shameful way that the lives of young women and men are lost and the pain their families endure." Shirley R. passed the fan and tape recorder to Carol S.

"I used to think that my life was rich just having a family—two sons and a husband," said Carol S. "I resented having to go out to women's club meetings and being away from my nest. As time has passed, I've realized that I needed to get out. Now my children are grown and gone, and my husband is content with the television. I can be out guilt-free with my women friends. I gain so much richness from that.

"You've heard the sayings 'new souls' and 'old souls'? I feel like I'm a new soul. I feel totally ignorant about so many relationship issues. I feel very humble, preferring to stay behind the scenes, not making a big deal about what I'm doing. I do a lot of that.

"The companionship and love I receive from women has made me realize that it's better to give than to receive. The rewards far outreach what I give. I want to grow old with grace. I want to grow old feeling that others look up to me as a role model or as a companion or as somebody who will get something done. I'm my own worst critic and whip myself faster than anybody if I don't get something done properly.

"My life is absolutely wonderful in its balance, with women friends being my crown jewels." Carol S. exchanged a warm look with Sue W. as she handed the fan to her.

"One of the most important things we need to learn to do is to forgive ourselves," said Sue W. "I don't think we ever do as much as we should. There is a phrase in one of the songs the choir sang about truth. I'm a member of another Unitarian Fellowship, not this church. We've had arguments on our mission statement about whether something should be a plural. That's one of the ways wisdom can come: when you finally decide that there are a lot of different truths for different people.

"I have the same trouble with my husband as you have with yours," she said, looking at Carol S. "He's a TV addict. I'm happy to have all the activities that I have to get out of the house. Now that he is retired, we have home alone time.

"Friends make my life rich—and cats. I don't have any kids, by choice. I'm active on environmental issues, but I have to balance that with making myself get out and enjoy things—sunsets, nature, and hiking. I need to do more of that enjoyment than I've been doing."

Rachell took the fan and smiled fondly. "Listening to y'all, I took a trip back in time. The world is very different for me than how I remember it being when I was seven or ten or twelve or fifteen. I'm the fifth girl in my family. I grew up fifth of seven, six girls and one boy. I'm used to being around women; in fact, sometimes I used to like to get away from women who had a lot more power than I did. I was the different kid. I was the one who hid under the bed and read while other people were doing other things. Like Shirley's, my undergraduate degree was in home economics, and I'm so glad I did that. Even though I eventually went on and got a degree in clinical psychology, I can sew my own stuff. When I get bored, I make something.

"The way I deal with adversity is to keep on keeping on. Just put one foot in front of the other and keep moving. One of the things I learned about myself is that I don't get discouraged very easily. I do get discouraged, but it doesn't last very long. You can always find a way to keep moving.

"I've had a wonderful life because I don't take shit from nobody." Everyone laughed. "I can remember the day when I decided I'd had enough of that, enough shit, you know? I'm not unkind to anyone, but I'm very clear about where my boundaries are. That's how I deal with adversity—keep moving.

"I love life, and I've learned that I can do just about anything I want to do. What I get from my women friends and my sisters and my nieces are ideas and motivation. 'Hey, let's try this,' someone will say. There's a lot of give and take, doing things and enjoying each other. We have a lovely family. There are about 150 of us who hang out at my house at Thanksgiving. Last year we had eighty-seven, but it was very rainy. The weather was bad so some people couldn't get there. It's fun being in my life."

"I've always had a large number of people around me as well," I said, looking at Rachell. "Not as many as Rachell. I come from a family of eight kids. I'm number three with twin boys ahead of me. There were six boys and two girls. My sister was much younger. With no mother, there were no women around me. Recently the elders of our family have all been dying. Some of them suddenly, which is a mixed blessing, but not always good for the people left behind who didn't get to say goodbye to them.

"Seventeen years ago, my husband's father died two days before Christmas, and mine died three days after Christmas. It changed Christmas for us. Now that I have a grandson, I am hoping I can turn it around. We came home from the funerals and realized that we were now elders in the family. I thought, 'This is not how I pictured this going.' It was very sobering. I had an overwhelming sense of responsibility that I needed to somehow do something different with the family. I still haven't figured out what that is. It's surreal when the people who are your base leave."

I gave the fan to Betty T., who studied it for a few moments before speaking. "The thing that's been very emotional for me is that now *I'm* the grandmother. In the past few months, I had to put my mother in a nursing home. I'm from a very small family. My brother died a few years ago, so I've been the primary caregiver. My father has been dead for years. I put myself in this position, and I feel it's very important.

"After thirty years of being a social worker, I find that I'm used to giving all the time—giving and helping and doing. I'm realizing that I really need to take care of myself. I have lots of women friends and a wonderful daughter. My husband gets on my last nerve all the time, but I just love him. He's at home a lot too. I think, 'Oh, go on a fishing trip,' you know?" We all laughed along with her.

Betty T. continued, "I like my alone time now. I've found that I like to be home alone in the garden. I have two cats. I'm retired. I'm relishing this time to do things with people. I love getting to know new people. This group has been really special to me. Now knowing y'all and this journey you're taking is very awakening for me and helping me understand myself better. I'm realizing that what I'm doing is very important, not because I do like to give to others, but it's very important that I take care of myself."

When Betty T. finished talking, the discussion continued without the fan moving around the room. "I'm like Betty," Rachell said. "I'm in the position of taking care of my mother. I'm not the only child, thank God. I think if you live to be ninety-nine, like my mother, you need to have lots of children because it takes a lot of people to take care of you. We decided not to put her in a nursing home, so I take care of her. I have another sister who lives on the farm, and she does her part. I have another sister who left her husband in Chicago and moved in with my mom. She's the primary caretaker. I have a brother who lives on the farm. We all pitch in and do what we can.

"I also have loved being a mom and grandmother. I have four grandkids. Two grandkids are in college. The others are just little ones. Maybe there will be more? I don't know. My kids are middle aged now, so we'll see."

"I just want to say how much I appreciate my grandmother," said Sue W. "She was one of the stubbornest people you ever met. I think I've inherited that trait.

"Both of my parents had Alzheimer's, so I've seen all of that in ways I don't ever want to see again, although my mother-in-law is starting to show signs of it. You just have to say to yourself that you're doing the very best you can."

"We're talking about husbands, so I thought I'd talk about mine," said Shirley R. "I found my husband to be less restrictive than any of my family members were. He's the type of person who, well, I think he really knows how to love a person and let her be free. He tells me things like 'Don't be so hard on yourself' and 'Don't let me stop you from what you want to do.' I've never felt restricted by him. I've always felt that I could do what I wanted to do and be happy.

"He doesn't appreciate my quilts as much as I think he should," she continued, laughing, "or my blue ribbon. I'll make a quilt, and he'll say, 'What are you going to do with that? Are you going to keep it or give it away?' He doesn't stop me from doing anything I want to do. I appreciate that. I feel like he's the reason that I could let loose of some of the barriers that I've had.

"I've had a good life. I'm a great-grandmother to a little five-year-old who is just so much fun. She likes to sew, paint, stamp, and do all of the things I like to do. Anything I show her, she is ready to do, and it's really exciting."

"I have a daughter who's married and lives about four and a half hours away from me," said Kitty. "She and I have a very different relationship than my mother and I have. All the time she was growing up, I knew our relationship was very close. I'm so grateful for that in my life.

"My mother came to visit me this summer. She was with me for about two weeks, and then I left for about three weeks, and she stayed at my house. When I came home, she was there for another two weeks. She turned seventy-nine during her stay with me. This is the longest I've ever spent with her since I was five. My dad died two years ago.

"The time we spent together was different because we're both at different places than we've ever been. She's trying to figure out what she wants do with the rest her life, and she's seventy-nine years old. I never thought of her, my mother, being seventy-nine years old and trying to figure out what she wants to do with the rest of her life. She was in a caregiver role with my dad for years, which was the focus of her life. It took a lot of energy and impacted her health. For the last two years, she's been picking up her own pieces and learning how to take care of herself again. Our relationship had been contentious at times in the past. Visiting with her now, I think she seems so open and full of good humor. She's fun to be around. I'm trying to convince her to come back at the beginning of July to visit me. She's in Arizona.

"What strikes me about the relationships with my mother and my daughter is how they've changed over the years. I've changed, watched my daughter change, and watched my mother watch both of us change. I see how we perceive each other as we grow. To recognize that is such a gift for me. I didn't think we'd be in this place. As I get older, I find the things to be grateful for are very close to me, and I don't have to reach too far. It's that attitude that I want to carry into situations. Five years ago, I don't know that I even had those thoughts. I like those life changes."

"I spend a lot of time being grateful," added Rachell. "My mother prays, my sisters pray, everybody spends a lot of time praying to God for this or that. I feel like I have enough, so I spend a lot of time just being grateful. When I speak to God, I speak words of gratitude. I thank God for the mosquitoes sometimes as they run me in the house when I should've been in there anyways." We all laughed with her.

"I haven't gotten that far yet," added Carol S.

"Me neither," I said.

"Well, we do what we can," said Rachell.

"They feed some of the important critters," added Sue W.

"Yes, they do," I replied.

"Dragonflies eat more mosquitoes than any other insect," said Sue W.

"I love dragonflies," said Kitty.

The Gathering concluded and the women went to clean up the kitchen before heading home. They gave us the leftovers and showed us the juice, pastries, and yogurt they had provided for our breakfast.

Heidi was fast asleep in a room down the hall. Kitty, Cis, and I set up our sleeping bags on couches and the floor in the Gathering room so we wouldn't disturb Heidi. After turning out the lights, we gazed out the large windows facing the river at the bridge that glowed in the night, and then we climbed into our sleeping bags.

October 6th through 7th

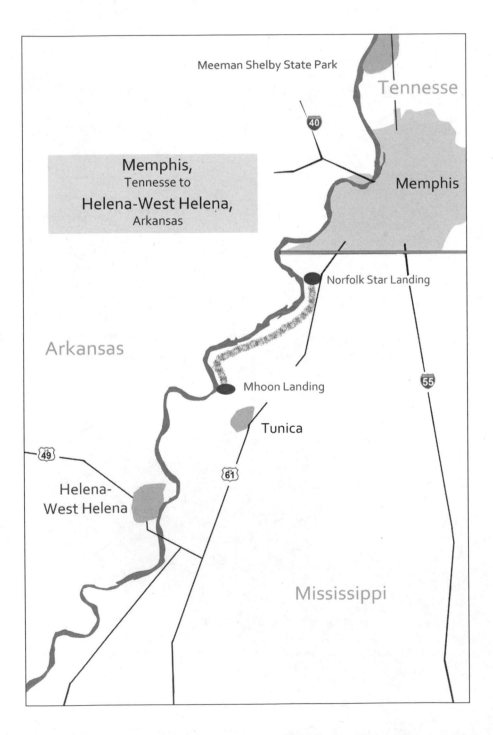

5

HELENA–WEST HELENA

October 6, Day Sixteen

I ran along the bluff in downtown Memphis. For a few moments I wished I lived in a climate where running was this easy in October. At home the snow would soon be falling. I ran past a tall sculpture dedicated to men and women who stayed to help people during the yellow fever epidemic in 1878. It has two square cream-colored concrete pillars holding up another concrete slab about twenty feet in the air. Under the slab, and between the pillars, are abstract metal cutouts of people. The cutouts decrease in size the higher up on the sculpture they are, and they overlap each other. They appear to be ascending into the heavens. I ran through a park dedicated to an African American man named Tom Lee, who saved thirty-two people after a boat capsized on the river. Lee witnessed the *M.E. Norman* capsize in a swift current downriver from Memphis. Even though he couldn't swim, he repeatedly rowed out to rescue survivors until well after dark. A remarkable dramatic sculpture depicts Lee reaching over the side of his tiny rowboat to pull in a terrified man dressed in a suit coat and clinging to a piece of wood.

Back at the church, I was glad to see Heidi moving around. She felt better, but not up to paddling yet.

Cis and I put in at Norfolk Star boat ramp a few miles south of Memphis. The first curve we paddled around was Cat Island. Several islands were indicated on the charts along the river. Like Cat Island, they were islands only during high water. The dikes caused sediment and sand to collect and connect them to the mainland in low water.

Cis saw egrets playing along shore on the backside of a sandbar, and we headed in their direction for our break. We paddled around a dike toward the egrets and into a strong current. Nearing the birds, we realized their lightweight bodies allowed them to walk on top of the soft mud. I poked my paddle in the mud, and the blade disappeared without resistance. We went back around to the river side of the sandbar for firmer ground. Across the river, the Fitzgerald Casino towered above the trees. It resembles a medieval castle, reminding me of Camelot. The casino is part of a large group of casinos in Tunica, Mississippi, which boasts being the third largest casino area in the United States.

The day grew warm with a soft breeze. The wispy clouds drifting across the sky offered no shade. We sat under a willow as we ate our lunch. A black butterfly flitted around. Cis said it was a Mourning Cloak.

"I'm blown away by monarchs migrating all the way to Mexico," said Cis.

"I was told that it takes several generations of monarchs to migrate," I said. "I've since learned there are four generations each year. The first three generations live for two to six weeks. The fourth generation is the one that migrates to a warmer climate and lives for six to eight months. Doug and I saw clusters of migrating monarchs in the trees in California. It's mind boggling that such a small creature could travel that far and know where it's going."

We wandered the sandbar and saw bobcat prints. The tracks followed a smaller set of mammal prints. They came from the mainland, went across the sandbar, and disappeared into the scruffy willow.

The heat and fatigue made me want to curl up in the shade and sleep, but we pushed on. I wasn't enjoying the beauty around me like I wanted to. I hadn't taken care of myself, which was the subject of the day's meditation book entry. "We can be concerned; we can be loving, when possible; but we can place value on our own needs and feelings too . . . We don't have to feel responsible for others." A sense of responsibility was driving me. We were all adults on this trip, yet I focused on the needs of the others in the group first, wanting to be sure they were happy, and then gave myself the leftover energy. My patience was growing thin, but it was my own doing.

With six miles left, we rounded the bend toward Rabbit Island and paddled straight into a headwind. We paddled hard. Eventually we saw our landing three miles downstream, and I pulled into a little cove on Rabbit Island for a break. Cis followed. I used my cell phone to call Kitty, who'd seen us pull over, and assured her we were okay. Cis and I started again. Each paddle stroke took effort. I was grateful to get to Mhoon Landing.

Exhausted, I moved slowly once we were onshore. Kitty and Heidi met us and helped stow our gear. Their afternoon at Mhoon Landing Park was action packed, and they excitedly began to fill us in. A five-foot-long black rat snake that Kitty had seen near the top of the boat ramp had her blood pumping. Heidi's medicine had kicked in, and she was feeling much better. Just coming off the water and being as tired as I was, I found Kitty's and Heidi's high energy and excitement level hard to handle. But they reported interesting interactions from their time at the boat ramp.

They had met Mister Bobby and quizzed him because he was an officer with Levee Enforcement. He told them the river is over one hundred feet deep and stays that way because of the current. Levee Enforcement has two busy seasons—one in the spring during flooding and another during hunting season, which runs from October through the end of January. Heidi asked if they used shotguns or rifles for deer, and he said, "Rifles, of course."

They watched thirteen campers pull in and set up. Kitty told Mister Bobby that we'd been informed that camping wasn't allowed at that park, and he said, "Oh, you can camp anywhere along the levee. You can drive on top of the levee, but not up and down the sides." Then Kitty asked about a place further down the river, wanting to know if it would be safe.

"Oh, sure it is," he said and paused for a moment. "Y'all got guns, right?"

Kitty figured he was messing with her and said, "We only carry our guns at home when we're hunting."

"When aren't you hunting?" asked Mister Bobby.

"I'm not hunting when I'm down south," replied Kitty, smirking.

Mister Bobby became serious and said the park wasn't a safe place for women to camp. When Kitty and Heidi had seen Cis and me still far upriver, Mister Bobby pulled out a pair of high-tech binoculars and said, "I'll use this here because I don't want to freak you out by using the scope on my hunting rifle." But when Cis and I disappeared behind Rabbit Island, he pulled out the rifle. "This scope has a higher power on it," he explained. Heidi and Kitty were disconcerted to see a man aiming a rifle at us.

Cis interrupted the story to say, "I'm particularly creeped out by someone scoping us with the scope still attached to the rifle."

"I would've been concerned had he not been law enforcement," said Kitty.

"Wow, we actually had a rifle pointed at us," I said.

"Absolutely," said Heidi. "He didn't eject a shell or have a gun lock or visible safety device. He removed and replaced his rifle handily from right behind the seat of his truck, which was a work vehicle. I wanted to ask him what the range was on that rifle, but I didn't want to prompt a demonstration. His binoculars had a feature to determine distance. It's a good thing you didn't pull up on Rabbit Island and bare your behinds to the world because he could have seen that in the scope of his rifle." We all laughed.

Heidi and Kitty continued relating the events of their afternoon. A group with people from Oklahoma, Arkansas, and Mississippi had pulled in and started setting up camp. They had met on the Internet and now get together once a year to fish. There were two women in the group, one a professional seamstress. The group had boats, trailers, tents, and lots of stuff. Kitty and Heidi's favorites were the teepee-style tents with big blue tarps over them and window air conditioners that blew into them. A couple people put refrigerators on top of picnic tables and plugged them in. There were generators, a chainsaw, and a lot of wood.

One member of the group, an FBI agent, had to buy a new tent because the rats at his home had eaten the bungees on his poles while the tent was in storage. His front license plate read, "You just can't fix stupid."

"I had to ask him about the plate," said Kitty. "He said, 'I'm a police officer.' That was his whole explanation."

Kitty had talked to a guy in a red shirt who kept calling himself Rodney Dangerfield. He said it was in regard to not getting respect. When another vehicle pulled up, Rodney said, "I know you have a misconception about us down here, and I'm going to prove that it's wrong." A black man got out of the pickup and sat at the picnic table by his truck. Rodney said to him, "Well, shouldn't we pull out our white robes and burn a cross out here now?" The man stared at him, and Rodney said, "Well, don't you have a handshake for me? It's been two years since you've seen me last." Kitty just sat there with her mouth open realizing Rodney was putting on a show for her.

Recalling this incident Heidi added, "When we first talked to Rodney and told him about the trip, he said, 'You must be women libbers—like it was a dirty word. We said we were a lot of things. After today, we decided we discovered a whole new book idea: *Wisdom from Mississippi River Boat Ramps.*"

Our plan was to spend the night with Rachell, whom we'd met the night before. She had volunteered her home when she realized we didn't have lodging. On the road to her home, outcroppings of trees along the edges of fields broke the flatness of the landscape. A faded red barn with a rusty metal roof was nearly engulfed in deep-green vines. They snaked into the structure and back out through every opening in the roof and walls. An abandoned tractor parked half under the roof looked like it would soon be choked out of existence.

Rachell's home was one of four homes on the family farm. She had built her house a couple of years earlier when she moved home from Chicago. Her welcoming entryway was an outdoor brick foyer with a vine-covered walkway leading to the door. A loveseat sat beside the door. Her home was open, bright, and fun. The walls were covered in artwork by artists she knew. Two of the pieces, which depicted African women, were made with butterfly wings. The colors, shapes, and lines on the wings were carefully placed to create the image of a woman. Family photos lined the staircase. Hanging on the wall near the ceiling was Rachell's rolling pin collection. National Public Radio played the entire time we were with her.

Rachell's sister, Marilyn, joined us for a dinner of catfish and a divine carrot-ginger-Craisin salad. "How did you get involved in this?" Rachell asked us.

"I sat across the desk from Nancy when we worked together," said Heidi. "I've always been an outdoors person, so I helped with the planning side. I told her I was going to be with her when she paddled into the Gulf, and here we are."

"How many miles is the river?" asked Marilyn.

"Two thousand three hundred and twenty," I said.

"What a goal! We set one once. We set out to camp in every state for at least two weeks," said Rachell. "We did thirty-one before we quit. I remember the Grand Canyon being breathtaking. And those trips through the Tetons—beautiful! I remember thinking afterwards that the things I see in my daily life are insignificant."

"It's lovely to have fish this evening," said Heidi.

"We have fish farms around us," said Rachell.

"They're four to six feet deep," said Marilyn. "The farmers raise catfish one year and grow a rice crop the next year. Long-grain rice, like Uncle Ben's."

"We harvest wild rice out of the lakes back home," said Heidi. "There's a big taste difference between hand-harvested and commercial wild rice. I think it has to do with the processing."

"I'll bet it has to do with the nutrients in the water and land," said Rachell.

"We saw a farmers' market on the way here," said Kitty. "What types of things would you find at a farmers' market here?"

"Sweet potatoes, collard greens, cantaloupe, cucumbers, okra," said Rachell. "The farmers' market had a hard time this year because of the drought."

"With the flooding this year, it's hard to believe there was a drought," said Kitty.

"Yeah, too much water in the spring and then no more," said Rachell. "We get a lot of wind here on the farm. It's open. The wind actually takes roofs off."

"Are you in a tornado belt here?" asked Kitty.

"Yes," said Marilyn, pausing for a moment and looking out the window. "Mississippi has tornadoes. This year we had some that wiped out whole little towns, like Smithville in April. One year we had fifty-one tornadoes going on at the same time. When there's a tornado, you go to the bathroom and get in the bathtub or in the hallway away from flying glass."

"There are people who are building storm shelters in the ground or set in the side of the hill," said Rachell. "The shelters are made from great big concrete slabs."

"Because of the milder weather, are there more homeless people here?" asked Heidi.

"In '82-'83, we had people living in cars," said Rachell. "It's not because they don't have jobs that some people are homeless. They can't live in an apartment or in confinement. They don't like being organized, paying rent, or dealing with utilities."

"We have a cousin who chooses to be on the street," said Marilyn.

"How many children do you have?" asked Kitty.

"I have one daughter who had four sons," said Marilyn. "I helped her raise her boys. The oldest one got killed last year. The city renamed the road out there after him. Private William Dawson. He got killed in Afghanistan the 24th of September last year. It has been hard, but it's getting better.

"My daughter's boys lived with me most of the time. Billy signed me up as his parent in the Army. He was driving and leading the convoy. You can see him on the Internet in what he was driving. On Friday morning, he told us he was going on a mission. It was a missile that hit—I think the impact killed him. One of the persons who was in the Humvee with him talked with my daughter afterwards. He said when they crawled to Billy, he was still breathing. They took him out on the stretcher. We were able to view his body. His navigator, the little girl that was with him, was from Guam. We met her parents in July. Her parents couldn't view her body.

"We were always attending things. The old veterans tell us that it's better now—volunteers and therapists, they give the guys and their families more recognition and support than when they first went in. We've gone to grief camps and different meetings; we've been to Fort Lee, Virginia. Billy has a brother that's in college that's nineteen. My grandson that got killed would be twenty-one if he'd lived. He went straight to the Army from high school.

"The military has a group called TAP strategies for survival. It's made up of military persons, and we're included in the group. You find people from the Pentagon, the World Trade Center and all around in that group. This is a war that's ten years old, so you got a lot of people and they're from the Navy, Air Force, and Marines. In Fort Lee they inducted Billy in the National Hall of Fame for Transportation. We went there for that recognition. Billy was in the Transportation Division. It's sad. We cry together."

Marilyn abruptly changed the subject. "When I'm with the kids, I go exploring." She raised her fork slightly and moved it from left to right as if pointing it across a large expanse. "The kids say, 'Grandma got us out here and we lost.' I say, 'Y'all lost, but I'm not. We're on an adventure.' I won't tell them where we're going. We went to the Petrified Forest.

They felt sure I didn't know where I was going. I knew where I was. I was going east, in the right direction. You don't get lost until you get scared. As long as you aren't scared, you aren't lost. That's the way I feel. This is what I learned—if there's electric light poles on the highway, you are going somewhere."

"Marilyn has all these things," said Rachell. "Like she doesn't ever take left turns."

"I drive to the right," said Marilyn. "I will take a left, but mostly I drive to the right, and I get where I'm going."

"Which is why she lives on the right side of the road," said Rachell.

"I have to turn left to get to my house," said Marilyn. "Living in the country you have to figure this out because you can take a country road and get lost."

Our conversation continued while we cleared the table and stacked the dishes in the kitchen.

"Nancy, is the river different here from the beginning of the river?" asked Rachell.

"The first part of the river from the headwaters down to Minneapolis is intimate. It's shallow enough to walk in at places," I said. "The river is narrower, and there are designated campsites with picnic tables along the way. They're scattered is such a way that you have a nice day of paddling and can camp easily.

"From Minneapolis to St. Louis, the river gets wider, and there are campgrounds along the way. From St. Louis to the Gulf, campgrounds are scarce on the water. People don't interact with the water down here like they do up north.

"The water in the river doesn't stay clear for long. The banks and the bottom affect how it looks. There's a lot of mud and industry along this river that affects it too. Northern Minnesota has a lot of dams."

"The water is interesting," said Kitty. "You can see the silt floating in the water, changing it different colors. The silt would settle out if it had the chance. Traveling the Great Lakes on a research vessel, I learned that those lakes each have different colors. I had no idea the lakes would be different."

"When I went to Key West," said Rachell, "on one side of a little two-lane road the water was green, and the other side was blue. It's clear as day. The Gulf is one color and the Atlantic Ocean is another."

"On Google Earth, you can see the confluence of the rivers, like the Mississippi and the Ohio," I said. "There's a distinct line where they come together."

"I got to go do Mama's medication now," said Marilyn. "I do it every day. I try to catch her before she gets into bed. Ladies, have a good trip." She left. Marilyn and Rachell's elderly mother, Emma, lived in the house next to Rachell's. Emma's daughters each had a role in her care. We settled back into our chairs at the table with coffee and tea.

"One of the problems is Mama goes places in her mind," said Rachell. "You never know where she's coming back from in her mind. I got there this morning and she said, 'How did you find me?' I said, 'You'll never know.'" We laughed.

Shortly after Marilyn left, two of Rachell's friends, Jennifer and Gloria, arrived and joined us at the table. Jennifer's and Gloria's energy made the pace of our conversation pick up dramatically. The subject turned to relationships. "I do want to fall in love," said Jennifer. "Maybe even marry. I have a certain amount of freedom and independence, and I'd have to think about givin' them up. I remember relationships take a lot of compromise."

"I've been single twenty-seven years now," said Rachell. "After I got divorced, I had partners and a long-term relationship—seven years. I could never get ready to get married. Most of them left because I didn't get married to them. Then I finally figured out I don't want to be married anymore. I already had a good enough husband, and I didn't keep him. I don't want anybody calling me all the time and expecting me to call him, showing up with expectations. I did that, and I'm done."

"I've been single twenty years," said Jennifer, whose hands and facial expressions were animated. Whatever her words didn't say was written on her face with raised eyebrows, a tilt of the head, or a playful grin. "I had a very long-term relationship—ten years. I knew from the beginning that he was never going to be my husband. I was never going to marry him. I liked him. And I loved him. But not that much."

"I find that most men are good men," said Rachell. "They want more from me than I want from them. They want more involvement, more commitment. Actually, I'd be perfectly happy if we went out and did something once a week, maybe on a Saturday night, and then he goes away and comes back the next Saturday night." We all laughed.

"More like a companion?" asked Kitty.

"I'd also like it if he is available when I see something really cool goin' on," said Rachell. "I can say, 'Hey, let's go to the Dixie Museum and see this.' Even more than on a Saturday night."

"Ooo," teased Jennifer. "You mean you might give him two days a week?"

"I don't like to wait for people," said Rachell. "I don't like to make extra trips for them."

"The waiting I don't have a problem, within reason," said Jennifer. "The running the errands thing is hard. It's been such a long while. I got to think of some of the negative things.

"When I first left St. Louis, I went to Rock Island, Illinois. Then we moved to Milwaukee, Wisconsin, and that was a little too far north, so we came back to St. Louis."

"I'm still adjusting to moving back south," said Rachell. "People think very differently here."

"Ooo," said Jennifer, raising her eyebrows. "Very differently. And they behave differently."

"I'm actually used to people following the law," said Rachell, chuckling. "Here they drive any way they want to."

"That's the most horrible thing I found down here," said Gloria. "They will run you over if you're attempting to pull out of a parking area. They are coming, and they see that you are probably gonna come out, but they aren't going to slow down."

"It depends on where you are in the South," said Jennifer. "My daughter goes to school in Oxford, and they are very polite. Is your husband from here?"

"No, he's from Louisiana," said Gloria. "My husband was a security guard at Angola Prison. Any prison you work in, as far as I'm concerned, is bad. Not all prisons have death row."

"Does Angola have that?" I asked.

"You better know it," answered Gloria emphatically. "Big time. A lot of prisoners when they go to Angola, nine times out of ten they aren't comin' out. They're going to come out in a body bag. That's the kind of prison it is.

"We used to ride up there with my husband when he went to pick up his check. My daughter asked him one time, 'Why don't you get fired from this place so you don't have to come to work up here anymore?' She was only seven years old. He said some of the prisoners had been on death row for years and years and years."

"Death row is aging," said Rachell. "They have geriatric treatment on death row."

"They need to cut that down," said Gloria, shaking her head. "Why be on death row twenty-five years?"

"Some of them might live better in prison than they did when they were out in life," said Rachell.

"I think that might be true for some of them," said Gloria. "That's so sad. It wasn't pretty stories. My husband didn't tell too many of them to us." She held up her hand as if to hold the stories or memories of them away from her.

"We lived in Baton Rouge," said Gloria. "It was a fifty-mile drive one way. He drove a hundred miles every day going up to the prison. As you can see, we got those mean sharp curves and ravines. At night you don't know what you are going to go off into. A couple of times prisoners escaped. He had to go out on a man hunt."

The heaviness of the subject matter caused us to grow quiet for a few moments. Jennifer broke the silence. "I want to understand this thing," said Jennifer. "You first start talking to people, and they go, 'How old are you?' They got to know how old you are to have a conversation with you. I don't understand that. Whether it's male or female, they tend to ask you how old you are. Nobody ever asked that question in the city."

"I've an answer for you," said Rachell. "Old enough to know the score and young enough to play the game."

"Oh, I don't want to encourage them," said Jennifer over our laughter.

"I'd like to tell you how old I feel," said Rachell. "I feel younger than I did when I was thirty-nine."

"Say it again," said Gloria with disbelief.

"Is it 'cause you're in the country?" asked Jennifer. "Is it 'cause of your lifestyle change?"

"It's 'cause I learned a thing or two," said Rachell. "I know my limits, and I don't have a man weighin' me down. When people ask me to do things I don't want to do, I just say no. I can do that."

"She learned the magic word," said Gloria, pointing her finger at Rachell and bringing her hand down on the table with a bang. "The magic word is 'no.' That's the catch to a lot of things that a lot of people need to learn."

"I can also tell people who create conflict, and I stay away from those folks," said Rachell.

"You don't look your age," said Gloria. "You know those burdens show on you. They weigh on you, you start breakin' down, and you look old."

"If it's my issue, I'm going to deal with it," said Rachell.

"My sister has a saying," said Gloria. "'You aren't going to make your problems be mine.' When you learn that magic word—no—you learn to live. When you learn things along the way, it comes easier to say 'No' or 'I don't think so.' It really shouldn't bother you to be able to say 'No, I can't do that.'"

"It used to be torture," said Jennifer, shaking her head.

"I do a lot of things for a lot of people," said Rachell. "It's manageable, and I'm willing to do it, but I'm not going to let anybody else determine my schedule."

"It feels good if you rest and you are content with yourself and your life," said Gloria. "Like I told you about the breast cancer. When you see your life flash before your eyes, you don't have time for nobody else's problems. You don't. You think 'I'm done. Finished. See you.'"

"I'm having this problem," said Jennifer, leaning in closer to the table. "I've been here for three years, and my house is what they call 'back out in the field.' I got a guy down the road to the left, and one to the right, and the guy that's workin' on plowin' the field in the back of me. I got these three guys, and they're watchin' me. They ask, 'When you going to get a boyfriend?' I say, 'How do you know I don't already got one?' They say, 'Oh, I know. Nobody come over here. I see you leave.' I say, 'How do you know I'm not going to visit him?' They say, 'Well, you know you are making me begin to wonder because you ain't got nobody in this amount of time. Maybe something is wrong with you.' I say, 'You go on and keep on wondering. You ain't going to be him.' After the three of them said that, I thought about it. I'm pretty happy, and I'm pretty cool with myself, but I just keep thinking, 'Am I supposed to have somebody?'"

"I just wouldn't have that conversation," said Rachell.

"Yeah, you would chew them up," said Jennifer, and we laughed.

"If he said, 'When you going to get a man?'" said Rachell, "I'd say, 'Real soon' and just leave it at that. I've learned diplomacy."

"Oh, you would be tactful about it, but he would still be chewed up," said Jennifer, laughing.

"You have to have a man to not be okay," said Rachell.

"Better yet," said Gloria forcefully, "you are a whole person already. A lot of women don't think that they are with or without a man."

"I'm getting ready to get into quilting," said Jennifer, leaning back in her chair. "I read my books, and I was in a course. I was gathering material. I got a notebook this tall," she said, hands spread eight inches apart, "of free patterns and the how-tos. I'm learning the terminology. I have a brand new sewing machine, and it's precious to me. I can't wait to get into those different stitches.

"When I got the opportunity, I came here because this is where I wanted to be. They said, 'You really going south? Why you want to go down there? Why you moving to Mississippi? Are you crazy?' I can't change the way people are."

"When I was getting ready to come," said Rachell, "I decided I'd take three years to get my head ready to come back down here. I wrote stories, and one of the stories I wrote was about the transition of coming back and how difficult that is."

"Then once you get here, they go, 'Do you have any regrets?'" said Jennifer. "How do you ask a question like that? Of course I got regrets, but to them I will say, 'No, I have no regrets. This was my decision. This is what I wanted to do.' When you live up north, I know we had some difficulties, but it's a little subtler, people having cultural differences with each other. It's on an intellectual level to me, but not down here."

"I'll tell you the biggest revelation that I've experienced is getting to know who my family really is," said Rachell. "Getting to know them as they really are. There's a big difference between coming and hanging out over a weekend and being here every day."

"I'm still an outsider," said Jennifer. There was a hint of sadness behind her diminishing smile. "They don't include me. They are in a little clique, and they don't do anything outside of that. I'm involved with politics. I'm involved with a writers' workshop. I'm getting ready to join the NAACP [National Association for the Advancement of Colored People]. This white lady from Florida introduced me to the NAACP here. I didn't even know there was one here. I said, 'This is not the way this is supposed to be. This is kind of weird. They let you join?' I'm looking at her real serious and she said, 'Well, did you think they were going to be prejudiced?' When she said that I just fell out laughing. I don't really have regrets, but sometimes I go, 'What the hell was I thinking?' I know I want to be here.

"My daughter went through the same thing. She was born and raised in St. Louis. She had to go to college away from me and St. Louis, so she transitioned herself to the South at eighteen. She is at Ole Miss. She can recover a lot faster. She doesn't even tell people that she is from Tunica."

"The kids at Ole Miss experience it differently because they are in a more educated setting," said Rachell. "They are with different groups of folks on campus than what you see at the post office."

"So it's easier there than here?" I asked.

"Yes," said Rachell. "For them in a college town, there's a lot more diversity, which tends to upgrade the thinking of everybody. They all got different ideas than what they say Jesus said."

"Or what has been implanted in their minds from their parents and grandparents," said Jennifer.

"We were talking before about how we handle adversity," said Rachell, "and about how it helps to laugh about it a lot."

"To think back to all the roads of life . . . ," said Gloria. She shook her head with a faraway look on her face that became somber. "You've been on so many different levels with problems that you have as a teenager, or a young adult, first marriage, children, divorce, remarry, more children, illnesses, problems, more problems. With each individual situation, you are just going to handle it differently. Who is this problem involving? Sometime it's your children. Sometime it's your husband. How you going to react?

"Some things get too overwhelming, and you just have to stop and say to life, 'What am I going to do?' Sometimes you just don't know. A lot of those years, to be honest with you, I just didn't have any answers. Now that I look back, I guess I thought that at the time, but I just didn't know that I had answers. When you think about your life, it's really kind of frightening when you think about all of the things that you've been through—love, deaths. The love that you've had is gone along with someone. How do you define what to do when you lose the most precious person in the world to you?"

"You just go on," said Rachell.

"In all of this adversity is *deal*," said Jennifer. "Just *deal*."

"You don't have no other choice," said Gloria, leaning back in her chair for the first time. "I always thought, 'What if my mother was to die? What am I going to do?' Well, that came to pass, so when she died it was just keep putting one foot in front of the other. You don't ever get over it, but you learn to live with it. What else are you going to do about it?

"There was a lot of anger, of course. I was angry because my mother was gone, and I loved her so much. It's a lot of emotions. The emotions control a lot of what you say and how you deal with a lot of situations. It's really difficult. I've had hardship, just like the rest of you. I've had hardships—husbands, marriages that fail, family members on drugs. Then you got a mother that's sick. Then you got this. Then you got that. Sometimes it gets to be too overwhelming, so I didn't even try to find an answer. It is like, 'What can I do about it?' Some things you can do something about and some things you can't."

"One of the issues that I have the most trouble with is betrayal from another person," said Rachell. "I think I can deal with death because I know that's out of our hands. I don't know how I'll deal with illness or pain, but betrayal is the hardest thing I've ever had to deal with. To have somebody betray me after making me believe."

"Me too," I said. "It's hard to get past."

"I'm such a loyal person," said Rachell. "If I say I'm gonna do something, I do."

"See, I am too, but everybody is not like you," said Jennifer, looking directly at Rachell.

"We see the world as we are, not as the world is," said Rachell.

"I've betrayed a couple of times in my time," said Gloria. "I didn't mean to hurt anybody."

"I've done that too," said Rachell. "That was when I was off on the other rail."

"Betrayal is hard especially if I've put a lot of love and energy into a relationship and it's been betrayed," said Kitty, jumping in. "The trust is gone, and I've not found how to get it back."

"On that level," said Gloria, "that has never really happened to me."

"That's the kind that I'm struggling with," I said. "It's harder when it's someone in the family you still have to have a good relationship with."

"Or you have to tolerate them," said Rachell.

"I feel like I have to pretend that everything is all right," I said. "I don't trust her anymore and maybe never will. It makes me terribly sad."

"You don't have to like her," said Rachell. "All you have to do is be civil. There are a whole lot of things you don't have to be so you can save your own heart from being broken again."

"I'm just so sad," I said. "It's not the relationship I want to have with her, but it is out of my hands."

"My children are married," said Rachell. "I have one son who isn't married yet. I hope he will be soon."

"Wait a minute now, isn't that the same as some man asking Jennifer how come she doesn't have a husband or a boyfriend yet?" I asked.

"What?" said Rachell, faking innocence as we all laughed.

"I think you just got caught," teased Kitty.

"All I really want is for my children to find someone who makes them happy," said Rachell, continuing as if she didn't know what we meant. "My kids say they are very happy with their mates, so I try to be a good mother-in-law. Their happiness is all that's important. The bottom line for me around marriage—if it's my kids' or my nieces' or nephews'—is that they are happy. I do judge who they bring home, but ultimately being in the relationship is up to them. I trust that if it's not a good match, they will do what I did, and they will get out of it.

"When I decided to divorce the kids' dad, I decided to chill out and take it easy. It was three years I was still in the relationship knowing that I was going to be out. It was another two years before we got divorced. I paid all of the bills and took care of all the finances that could've been a problem. We talked about visitation. By the time he actually moved out, we had a pretty good understanding about how it was gonna be. The reason we stayed married but not living together was so the kids could get adjusted to the back and forth, living at both houses. By the time we went to court, there wasn't anything to our divorce. We were already living that way. The youngest child was ten and the oldest was fourteen. It was hard to be there, but it would have been harder to just up and move. I think part of both of us hoped that we could somehow work it out."

"It's too bad the adults' problems becomes their children's problems," said Gloria, leaning back up to the table and resting on her elbows, "but it happens sometimes. I think I did the same thing. I stayed there a couple years knowing it was gonna end. Somebody needs to step forward and be honest about what is going on instead of tryin' to live day by day knowing that this thing is not working. The main thing is that I always put the kids first. You try to make the adjustment as easy as possible. All children want mother and father to be together. And that's not going to happen in all situations."

"When Ayrn's dad and I split up, we were not married," said Kitty. "It was important to not put him in a bad light. Our split wasn't about her at all. I didn't want her to ever feel like it was. She has a relationship with both me and her dad. I've seen relationships where the kids are torn between the two and bad things are said about the other. What an impact that has on the kids."

"Why is it you can love somebody so much and you can't live with him?" asked Gloria loudly. "What's so terrible you can't work through to stay with somebody that you love so much?"

"Love is not enough," said Rachell.

"It ends up being not enough," said Jennifer. "It will not solve all of our problems."

"The thing that got to me," said Rachell, "is we were both in the helping professions. We'd sit down and talk about things. We'd go through this whole dialoging thing and work it out. If it was something that I was upset with him about, it would be beautiful for three or four days, and then it would be back to where it was."

"I know that one," I said, pointing at Rachell.

"I'd be sick with disappointment," said Rachell. "We were doing all of the things you are supposed to do and being respectful to one another. I began to think that he doesn't care about this relationship or he doesn't respect me enough."

"Then I'd resent the fact that I'd have to bring it up again," I said leaning forward.

"Yes," they all said in unison.

"Over and over," said Gloria banging her hand on the table.

"Then there's the comment, 'When are you going to get off of this?'" I added.

"Then it got so I'd be waiting for it to change back," said Rachell. "I couldn't trust the three or four days when it was really good."

"That's part of betrayal," said Kitty.

"I guess it is," said Rachell. "In subsequent relationships, I've always been really clear about what I needed," said Rachell. "If I can't see evidence that it is there, then I just don't do it. We can sleep together, but that's as far as that's going to go."

"When I was in a relationship and it was time to go, I had this thing of fixin' spaghetti," said Jennifer, grinning. "I'd say, 'You want to come over for spaghetti?' I'd fix it, and he would be getting full, and I'd say, 'Have you ever heard of the last supper?' He'd say, 'Yeah.' I'd say, 'You're eatin' it.' I'd tell him this isn't going anywhere.

"I stayed in a marriage because I wanted to be married. I wanted to belong, and I worked at it. That's why it lasted. I didn't let too many of my boyfriends around my daughter. Sometimes they would try to persuade me by trying to do nice things for my daughter. I'd think, 'You know, we already got a problem there," she said, pointing her finger at an imaginary man. "You can't use my child to get to me.'"

"You know, I got so I could tell if a guy was good in bed by his conversation," said Rachell. We laughed.

"Go on, girl," prodded Kitty, and we all leaned in.

"First, I'd listen to what he said about his exes and how much consideration he saw for their end of it, for their perspective," said Rachell. "Then, I'd listen to how considerate he was on another person's feelings and concerns. If he was all about how awful that person was to him, then I'd know it was all about him. I could tell. The way a man is with one woman, he is likely to be that way with another."

"I get the ones that are quiet and don't do too much talkin'," said Jennifer with a tone of disgust, "so I can't read whether they are going to be a good person or not. I have to wait a little longer."

"Are you sure it isn't 'cause you doing all the talkin' so they just shut up?" kidded Rachell.

"Well, that's definitely part of it," said Jennifer, laughing. "I don't like empty spaces. I'm doing better at that though. I go, 'Do you have anything you want to say?' He says, 'No.' I say, 'Me neither.' I'm learning to be quiet and then see how things go. I haven't had a relationship in five years. I've been here three years and the two years before that I was focusing on my move. I call it my exodus on my journey to my promised land. I didn't want to be stopped."

"You came to Tunica for your promised land?" asked Rachell, surprised.

"I got a great imagination," said Jennifer chuckling. "It's a different lifestyle here. I'm off in the country and off to myself. I wouldn't be in the writers' group. Here I can choose to go to a party or not.

"My promised land is that I promise myself that I'm going to be whoever I want to be. Who's the real Jennifer? I promise myself that. I was born here. My grandparents raised me until I was four. My parents came and got me, and I was in St. Louis until 1954. I always said I was comin' back. My grandmother passed when I was twenty-five. It took another twenty-five years before I ended up here. I don't really know the people here. That's why I say when people start talkin' about people, I don't have the history. I don't know that person. All I know is that I met them."

"I don't really want the history," said Rachell.

"I don't either," said Jennifer. "I want to deal with that person the way they are with me. I don't want to go by what somebody else is hangin' on them because of what they did back in high school. They never let go of it. They say they have, but they haven't because it's planted in their minds. What I've learned is that when somethin' happens and if two people agree on a story, then that's the story. It doesn't mean that is the truth. Being bold enough to ask them is the only way you are really going to know the truth. What does it really matter? What difference is it going to make? I just want to know that person for who they are since I met them."

"I try to stay away from slanderous gossip," said Rachell.

"Well . . ." said Jennifer, making a face that brought us to laughter.

"Okay, Jennifer, fess up," I said.

"What you are supposed to do is not *feed* off the slander," said Jennifer. "However, there ain't a whole lot goin' on down here. When I hear the story from different people and I sit there and look blank, and they figure I don't know who they're talkin' about, sometimes I actually don't. I remember the story. Then when that person gets to talkin', a story starts formin'. I'm pullin' up the tape in my mind and then it goes '*That's* who they're talkin' about.' It really isn't important, it's just that there isn't anythin' else goin' on." We were all laughing with her.

"I find that if I listen to that, I can't let it go," said Rachell. "If I see that person, I think about that nasty story, especially if I don't have any other information about them or information to the contrary. You end up believin' the worst about a person—and it may not be true. They go and talk about you too."

"Oh, I hadn't thought about that," said Jennifer, laughing. "I don't have nothin' goin' on."

"You don't have to," said Rachell. "They will make something up."

"And they probably do because there's one guy they are always teasin' me about," said Jennifer.

Gloria looked at the clock, got fidgety, and said, "I enjoyed this, but I got to get home."

"I've enjoyed this so much too," said Jennifer, and then she offered to give Gloria a ride home because Gloria's husband had dropped her off.

Jennifer and Gloria left. Cis and Heidi headed upstairs past many family photos to the two guest bedrooms. Kitty and Rachell did the dishes, and I worked on my computer at the dining room table, which had a clear view of the kitchen. I pored over the charts and determined reasonable launching and landing options for the following week.

Rachell is a published author. After the kitchen was cleaned up, Kitty and Rachell sat at the table, and Rachell read a touching and funny story she was working on about her sister Jackie, who had died. When she was done, she put down the three-ring binder the story was in. "Jackie got sick with lupus and another degenerative disease at the same time. The doctors told her twenty years before she died to get her affairs in order," said Rachell. "I find that by writing I remember more. When I was in Illinois, I had more memories about family and being here than I do now that I'm here. I wrote stories and rhymes, and then I moved on to short stories. I can say more in a short story. I liked crafting poetry, but it's emotionally draining. I'd write and rewrite, sit it on the shelf for a while, and dream it up. I do that with stories too."

"When did you get your degree?" asked Kitty.

"I went back to school for my doctorate at forty-five," answered Rachell. Looking out the window, she said, "You know, people learn in all kinds of ways."

"It took me a long time to figure out the different ways that people learn," said Kitty. "I have to explain the same thing three or four different ways so each person in a group understands exactly what I'm saying."

"I often stop and ask, 'What do you think I was saying?'" said Rachell.

"I say that a lot," I said, putting my computer in its case and stacking the maps and charts. "Particularly to my husband."

"Well," said Rachell, "my husband would say, 'Don't use your psychology on me.'" We laughed.

"Doug has said that," I said. "I respond with, 'Too bad. I am. Now answer the question.'"

"I'll have to use that someday," said Rachell, nodding.

"We've had rough patches that brought me to being able to say, 'I don't care. You have to listen,'" I said. "He still doesn't half the time."

"Half is good," said Rachell.

Looking at one of the books Rachell wrote about parenting, Kitty said, "I needed this one twenty years ago."

"My daughter was better at parenting than I was," said Rachell. "She got it from being around me."

"My daughter is good too," I said. "I like to think she got it from me, but her degree in special education helped her define boundaries."

"My daughter's boundaries are good too," said Rachell. "She let the kids spend every summer with me. That started when they were two and three and continued until they were in their teens. It was great."

"Coming back and being on the farm with your family says a lot about how important family is to you," said Kitty.

"Yes," said Rachell. "If you look at the pictures around here, that's how I've been in my whole life, how people are in relationship to one another. My sister Julia painted a few of them."

"Do you have dresses that your sister designed for you?" asked Kitty.

Rachell took us into her room to show us Julia's creations. In her room facing her bed hung the phrase "Have the Courage to be Imperfect." She said, "It's one of the sayings that the Adlerian psychologists have. I went to the Adlerian School in Chicago." She showed us several dresses and pantsuits that Julia had designed and created for her. They were classy and comfortable with rich colors. Most were made of linen and cotton. The fabrics were marbleized, which is similar to tie-dye. Bound buttonholes were a feature Rachell appreciated. Her sister had five successful dress shops. The clothing reflected Rachell's style. "I told her what I wanted, and she created it," said Rachell.

Rachell read the following article she'd written about herself for her church.

"My name is Rachell. I'm a Church Lady. Not the kind with the big hat and gloved hands who is ready to enforce the mores of the church, but one who believes that I should develop and use my God-given talents to make this world a better place.

I became a Unitarian Universalist in the 1960s after a long search. I was married to a minister in the Lutheran Church of America. I think it's safe to say he left the ministry when he no longer believed what he was preaching. I, too, who grew up in but had abandoned the Black Baptist Church, held many doubts about the role religion (as I knew it) could play in my life. With those issues flowering our path, we visited the Unitarian Universalist Church in Rockford and knew, immediately, we had found our church home...

I served in nearly every possible capacity. I did everything that needed to be done: religious education, salad luncheons, sang in the choir, developed and delivered sermons, mopped floors and cleaned the bathroom. At one point, I was observed on the roof with the guys repairing storm damage. You see, I'm a Church Lady… For the past three years, I donated clinical hours to the Church Health Center. This is an amazing place to provide medical and psychological services to people who have jobs, but no insurance. I find that helping others helps me to improve my own sense of well-being… I've found people with the energy, vision, and intellect to help me continue to grow. It's for these reasons, the giving and getting, I'm a Church Lady…"

We went outside to enjoy the cool evening air and saw bright-green treefrogs clinging to windows and window ledges. Rachell said they were there most every night, but by morning they were always gone. In many native cultures frogs are believed to represent cleansing and honoring our tears.

October 7, Day Seventeen

I was the last one to come downstairs. Cis was busy making breakfast, Heidi was making tea, Kitty and Rachell were sitting at the table, and the conversation was lively.

"A man of quality is not threatened by a woman seeking quality," said Rachell.

"Those are words to live by," said Heidi.

"That was a bumper sticker I had on my car for years," added Rachell.

"My husband is great," said Heidi. "The first time I met his parents we were at the lake. It was lunchtime and the women automatically, on cue, recessed to the kitchen to make sandwiches for the men first and then themselves. I was offended. I looked at Matt and I said, 'If you think I'm making you a f---ing sandwich, it's time for me to leave.' I don't talk like that often. His dad still doesn't make his own sandwich. He goes out to eat if Matt's mom is gone."

"I told Doug early on that he wasn't marrying Susie Homemaker," I said, making a cup of chai. "For years he waited for me to turn into her. Now he's resigned to the fact that's not going to happen."

"I read the stories you're writing about Jackie this morning," said Heidi. "My only sibling died when she was eighteen. It was hard to fathom for a while. I was three years older. What you said about how people who are dead don't make memories, so we only have our memories left… I appreciated it."

"I'm glad you told me that because I've been trying to give back with

Jackie's stories," said Rachell.

"It was beautifully done," said Heidi.

"How long has this land been in the family?" I asked.

"Before I was born," said Rachell. "My parents built this house and moved in when I was eighteen months old. They bought forty acres at a time. Farming is big here. When I was a girl, if you drove through here, there were people along this road who had forty or sixty acres. As time went on, they sold it or their kids didn't want it. People left their land and lost it. You'll see areas with trees, but no houses."

"In North Dakota there are shelter belts, but the farm houses are no longer," said Kitty as we all took a place at the table and Cis served breakfast.

"Well, you can't make a living on this small a piece of land," said Rachell.

"I don't know farmers or ranchers who don't have other jobs," said Cis.

"My brother works for Harrah's, the casino," said Rachell. "His wife is a deputy sheriff. They have kids in college. They work ten-hour days, four days a week, and then they farm on top of that. My dad used to work into the night, and my mom would take his food out."

"Did your dad have another job?" I asked.

"Times were different then," answered Rachell. "He sent us to college on cotton crops. Education was important in our family. That's all I heard from the time I was little: 'You are going to college.' My dad got to fourth grade, and my mom finished high school. That was standard in those days. She wanted to go to college, and my dad promised her that he would let her go to college, until they got married. Then he said he needed a wife at home to be a wife. I think she felt half betrayed most of the time. My mom is an only child. They were good farmers because they did all right. We kids had jobs on the farm. We had animals when I was a kid—chickens, cows. We milked cows and cleaned stalls. My job was to milk and churn."

We began discussing the origin of the word woman, and Cis said, "Women should take 50 percent of the responsibility for giving up their power throughout history."

After an awkward silence I said, "I differ with the percentage."

"When you're born into a society that's structured in a way that promotes or enforces women being treated as second-class citizens," said Heidi, "it would be hard to even envision a different possibility, let alone create that change. It's amazing that women's situations overall continue to improve throughout the world despite the institutions that prevent that development. I think we can each take responsibility for our personal actions and working toward a better future, but I can't judge women who were born into a different set of privileges and circumstances than my own."

"Women were on their backs busy having babies," said Rachell. "I mean, what can you do? I'm not sure blame is the operative word there."

"I'm not using the word blame," said Cis. "I used responsibility."

"It felt the same to me," said Rachell.

"Did it?" said Cis.

"Yes," said Rachell. "Not that I know what women want. I know what I want."

"I took it as blame too," I said. "I thought about what it took for me to get out of an abusive relationship. Had someone come along and said I needed to take responsibility for where I was, it would have felt shaming. Actually people did say that—and it made me feel worse. The way I translated their words was, 'I'm a loser. I do deserve abuse because I should know how to do it better.' I don't think that's what you really meant."

"That helps me understand," said Kitty. "I've talked to women about bringing responsibility to their reaction to things, and my words weren't perceived in a positive light. What you said about feeling worse helps me understand what that person felt when I said that."

"When you're doing the best that you can and the crap is still hitting the fan and you can't see the light at the end of the tunnel, you're in survival mode," I said. "It doesn't matter what words are used, when you're told you need to take responsibility, something intended to be helpful becomes negative and oppressive. When those words came from another woman, I felt even worse."

"I would never say to someone, 'You need to take some of the responsibility,'" said Cis. "I'm coming from a completely internal position of men and women, two halves of a whole. I'm half of this humanity and to maintain my power I have to be fifty percent of this."

"I hear the broader picture of what you said," I said. "I think there's validity to that. It requires a higher level of thinking than a woman may be capable of if she's in survival mode."

"Women have power because without women there would be no men," said Rachell. "They owe their lives to women."

"At some point back in time, people didn't realize that sperm was fifty percent of conception, so we were truly goddesses and miracles," said Cis.

"I was listening to the radio about a Middle Eastern peace," said Rachell. "Women are still considered dirty when they have their periods. They have to move out of the house for seven days."

"In some native cultures, a woman having her period was considered to be powerful," I said. "She could disrupt ceremonies with her power."

"Has it ever been a truly equal way of being between men and women?" asked Kitty. "I'm thinking back to the beginning and the hunting-gathering society. We pulled together to provide for each other. That's lost."

"They were still role bound," said Rachell. "Men had jobs that were different from women's jobs."

"Out of the sense of survival, why would we have somebody doing a job that they're struggling to do when somebody else is good at it?" asked Cis. "Look at what you said about seeing more women barge captains pilot hazardous materials. Is it because women are given the less desirable jobs, or is it because women have more refined motor skills? I think you could argue many aspects of it."

"I guess it depends on what you believe about how society works," said Rachell. "I talked one of my nephews out of going into the military. His brother got killed in Afghanistan. While the family was going through all kinds of disruption, he was out of it. He and his mom were fighting, and he decided he was going into the military. He came over one day and I said, 'Did you decide you were going into the military because you were mad at your mama?' He said, 'Yes, but Aunt Rachell, I don't want to go.' This was three months after he signed up. I said, 'It's a voluntary military. You can rescind that.' He went the next day, and the military let him rescind those contracts that he'd signed. He got started in college, and he loves it. I'm working on my grandson because he signed up too."

"Where does that come from?" asked Kitty. "The willingness to sign up knowing they are risking their lives."

"Maybe it's because they think they're invincible," I said.

"In graduate school I took a class on the history of women," said Rachell. "It was awesome. I learned women have to struggle to get an education in the Untied States to gain equality. My daughter and I used to do the rallies in the '70s and '80s with the National Organization for Women. We have pictures of us leading the line wearing T-shirts that say 59¢. At that time that was what women earned—fifty-nine cents to every dollar a man earned."

"I think it's seventy-nine cents now," said Heidi.

"As hard as we fought?" said Rachell. "Schools were still segregated when I went to school. They didn't desegregate the schools until the '70s. There are still good historically black colleges in the South. I went to undergraduate school in Little Rock, and then I went for my two masters degrees up north in Illinois."

We finished breakfast and began clearing the table. I asked Rachell about her rolling pin collection, which was hanging at various heights near the ceiling. She said, "When I was in Illinois I had this rolling pin collection on my kitchen walls from floor to ceiling. Those ceilings were twelve feet high. I moved here and didn't have the same wall space, so I came up with this way to hang them. I didn't want to lose my collection." She changed the subject. "Have you noticed that people call you Miss So-and-so instead of calling you whatever your name is?"

"Does that have to do with discrimination?" asked Kitty.

"I think so," said Rachell. "I don't remember it being that way before. We were taught to say Miss to our elders, but not to everybody. It feels artificial to me. It feels like compensation. I noticed people are reluctant to describe people by race. They'll do it, but they pause and look for another word, you know 'the white girl down the street' or 'he's African American.' There's the long pause before they say it. They're trying to find the politically correct word. That's the way I interpret it."

"We had that discussion in the car around my writing," I said. "It was implied that I shouldn't mention race at all. I shouldn't say this is an African American woman because it doesn't matter. If I say that— "

"It loads it up," said Rachell, completing my thought.

"At the same time, that description is part of who they are, and it feels wrong to not acknowledge that," I said. "I haven't figured it out yet. There are cultural pieces to this story of our journey that I don't want lost. If I don't say them, I'm afraid they'll get lost."

"I don't think race defines culture," said Rachell. "I think Southern-ness defines culture. I think race is a tiny part of it. You give people those adjectives because you want to make another message. It leads you some-where. The words create a picture that's in the reader's head. Does that diminish the person pictured in the reader's head or does it elevate them?"

"I had not been around African Americans, and it was something that I considered when I was getting ready for the trip," said Kitty. "The not-knowing created fear. As we traveled further south, there were times those fears didn't come up the way they had before starting the trip. People became people, not white or black or whatever."

"I think the media has done a job of reporting stuff in the South that has been incongruent with reality and leans toward what they believe," said Rachell. "All the murders and the killing. It's like they're still hap-pening."

"The media does a lot of things that are incongruent," said Kitty, putting the dishes in the dishwasher.

"They had Memphis drowned in the last flood," said Rachell. "Actually, the flood was in just one small part of Memphis."

Jennifer arrived. She looked around Rachell's home and said, "Oh, her pictures are just lovely."

"They sure are," I said. "Her home is lovely."

"Seeing this art reminds me of my bucket list," said Jennifer. "No big things, just goals I want to accomplish. First, I wanted to be a substitute teacher, but they gave me the middle school and the kids drove me nuts and the schools wouldn't call me enough. Then I wanted to try being a foster mom, but they gave me too many kids, and I said, 'I'm out.' Then I said I want to learn how to sew. I do quilting and preserving. I did my preserving, so now I'm on my quilting."

"That sounds like fun exploration," said Kitty.

Soon it was time for us to leave. We said goodbye in the house, then at the van, then in Rachell's garden, and then back at the van. We teased Rachell that she had Minnesotan in her because of the long goodbye. "This is a typical Minnesota goodbye?" asked Rachell. "I thought we were doing it the Mississippi way."

On the road, the wind was intense and blew the van and trailer around. As we drove to West Helena, Arkansas, for the King Biscuit Blues Festival, Kitty and I read from the meditation book.

"Letting Go of Naiveté. Not all requests are legitimate! . . . Life may test us . . . people have been here to help us learn about what we don't want, what we won't tolerate, and how to own our power. We can thank them for what we have learned."

I felt I was dealing with a lot of letting go on the trip. I got out my journal and listed the things I had to let go:

• The van—it's my van, but Kitty or the other van support insist on doing the driving.

• My plans—a good deal of the work I did over the past year and a half was useless.

• My diet—I was doing well staying away from carbohydrates, sugar, and fried food, but eating on the road requires flexibility.

• My need for rest—the schedule dictated what I did and when.

• Paddling the river—the river was moving too slowly so it was impossible to paddle every mile.

• How I perceived things would be done—the others have different ideas that need to be considered.

• Being heard—so many people talking made it difficult to express my opinion and I'm not good at interjecting into a group of powerful women.

• Knowing directions—realizing the front-seat folks needed to find their own way.

• Being corrected—not letting being told 'no' become personal, realizing we all do it.

• My stuff—the things that were broken or lost along the way that I hadn't factored into the expense of the trip, and why was it my stuff that got broken or lost?

I reread the list and felt relief. Knowing what I had to let go of helped me feel less crazy and frustrated.

We crossed the bridge into Arkansas. The width of the river amazed me from that vantage point. The bridge seemed smaller when driving on it compared to seeing it from the river where it towered hundreds of feet above us. The wind created sizable waves that chased each other upriver. Not paddling today was a good choice.

Helena-West Helena was a thriving blues community. The King Biscuit Blues Festival's mission is to sustain the culture, the heritage, and the authenticity of the Delta Blues. The festival is held each Columbus Day weekend. We wandered Cherry Street enjoying the various performers and sampling food. The voices and heartfelt performances captured our attention, and we stood mesmerized. We ate alligator prepared two different ways—on a stick and as spicy sausage. To top off our lunch, we enjoyed deep-fried Snickers bars.

We drove to our hotel, enjoyed dinner together, and retired early. The news on the ThinkProgress website read, "Topeka, Kansas City Council Considers Decriminalizing Domestic Violence To Save Money - Faced with their worst budget crises since the Great Depression, states and cities have resorted to increasingly desperate measures to cut costs . . . the most shocking idea to save money was being debated by the City Council of Topeka, Kansas. The city could repeal an ordinance banning domestic violence because some say the cost of prosecuting those cases is just too high . . . Last month, the Shawnee County District Attorney's office, facing a 10% budget cut, announced that the county would no longer be prosecuting misdemeanors, including domestic violence cases, at the county level. Finding those cases suddenly dumped on the city and lacking resources of their own, the Topeka City Council is considering repealing the part of the city code that bans domestic battery." [By Marie Diamond on October 6, 2011, at 5:45 p.m., ThinkProgress.org] The enormity of the step backwards for women in that proposed action was mind boggling. Domestic violence is still at epidemic levels in the United States. I was restless all night.

October 8th through 13th

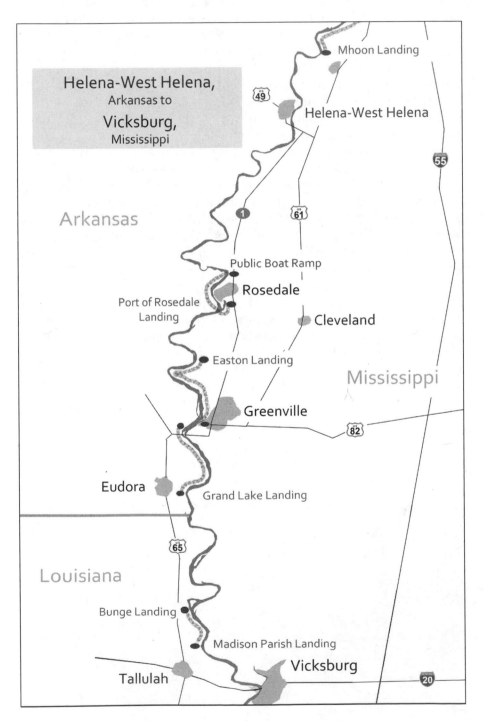

Helena-West Helena,
Arkansas to
Vicksburg,
Mississippi

Mhoon Landing

Helena-West Helena

Arkansas

Public Boat Ramp

Rosedale

Port of Rosedale
Landing

Cleveland

Easton Landing

Mississippi

Greenville

Eudora

Grand Lake Landing

Louisiana

Bunge Landing

Madison Parish Landing

Vicksburg

Tallulah

6

VICKSBURG

October 8, Day Eighteen

For the second day in a row, we found delicious fancy candies on our pillows. Cis thought she was clever, but we figured her out.

Crows followed and called to me when I ran. I had read once that crows stand for secrets, balance, personal integrity, and walking your talk, and seeing the crows now and knowing what they symbolized hit too close to home. I wasn't sure I was walking my talk. I wasn't truthfully sharing how I felt. I didn't want to paddle.

When we reached the river, the wind was strong. The churning water, the wind bending the tops of the trees, and the knot in my stomach said "Don't paddle."

Heidi was silent, but the pressure to paddle from her felt intense. She'd been waiting for and dreaming about this moment for years. Our time on the Mississippi was growing short. For safety reasons we'd be getting off the Mississippi to paddle Bayou Lafourche in a few days. I checked the charts. A landing north of Rosedale, Mississippi, offered a shorter route that required our paddling into the wind for only five miles. We decided to do the shorter paddle.

Some of the roads we took to the obscure boat ramp were not maintained.

We drove past deserted crumbling buildings, dilapidated hunting shacks, and abandoned school busses that left us feeling uneasy. The ruts were deep, and the turnaround at the top of the ramp was in tall grass. When we arrived at the landing the knot in my stomach was gone, but the wind concerned me.

The paddling was fun when we started, but I'd paddled 325 miles since St. Louis, and I felt no excitement about the accomplishment. I loved paddling and struggled to understand why I'd lost interest. I was tired on every level, and it was difficult to keep comfortable in my kayak. I had a chronic back issue that was no longer eased by constant repositioning. I was homesick. I wanted to sleep in my own bed. I needed a break from the responsibilities. I looked around at the scenery and everything appeared dull even though the sun was shining brightly.

Heidi and I paddled around Great River Road State Park, which was closed due to flooding. We stopped on the sandbar that extended from the park. Sitting on the sand, relaxing, our thoughts turned to retirement. "Kitty doesn't see herself as being able to retire one day," I said.

"That's the way my dad is," said Heidi.

"We aren't in the best position for it either, but I'm not giving up," I said. "We wouldn't be able to travel the way we would like to."

"I come from a family where retirement wasn't something that was feasible," said Heidi. "Matt comes from a family where they had the resources to plan for and enjoy retirement."

"In my family, life started when you retired," I said. "You worked hard, retired, and played."

"I figure we better enjoy life now, and if we get to have more of it later, that's great," said Heidi. "You just don't know."

A speedboat raced by. Tiny little bugs began to bite. "There's something that I can't even see that's making little pin pokes in my skin," said Heidi.

"I can't believe how lucky we've been with bugs on this trip," I said. "I've had few bites. Maybe these little guys are attracted to the sweat. It's hot today."

"No bites for you? That's saying something," said Heidi. "You usually attract them."

Heidi explored the beach that extended for more than a half mile with little vegetation. We were on the downriver end of the sandbar where the garbage tends to accumulate. A large tubular-shaped fishing net was partially buried in the sand. She tugged it loose and stared at it. She tilted her head a few times trying to figure out how she could put it on her kayak to haul it out. "With the crap that's out here, I feel like I want to get some of it out," she said, but abandoned the idea of hauling the fishing net and took smaller trash.

Unlike other parts of the river we had paddled, we didn't see much debris in the water here. What debris there was had accumulated onshore. Occasionally we saw a log floating downriver, but that tended to happen after a storm. There had not been any storms since we left Trail of Tears State Park, so there wasn't much in the water. During the second part of the journey, we'd met a few people who saw the river as a place to dump trash. We'd met a greater number of people who worked to clean up the river. On this part, it was difficult to discern how people felt about the river because there wasn't much interaction with it.

While we lunched on the sandbar, Kitty and Cis were eating at the Blue Levee in Rosedale, Mississippi. Kitty brought the recorder into the restaurant and captured their conversation. "When you get into the Deep South, you get into historic second-class citizenship where husbands are in the lead and want women to stay home and have their dinner on the table," said Cis.

"Do you think that's more prevalent in the South than up North?" asked Kitty.

"I do because you have a greater population of people who've never gotten out or moved far from home," said Cis. "They haven't given themselves permission to do things for themselves."

"Have your read the book *The Help*?" asked Kitty.

"Haven't read it," said Cis, "but I lived in that era. I was in Montgomery in '55 and '63. I remember George Wallace being inaugurated, and the KKK, and I went to a segregated school."

"At that time there was a movement to desegregate, wasn't there?" asked Kitty.

"Yes," said Cis. "Martin Luther King was getting recognized. In '63 things were starting to get rowdy and riotous. Blacks were starting to stand up for themselves. I remember it was all over the news after I left the South."

"Did you ever see the KKK?" asked Kitty.

"Yes," said Cis. "Back then they were brazen and still had power. Because my dad was in the Air Force, I lived a small life, just going back and forth to school. We didn't live on base, but I was confined."

"I would imagine that would have been difficult because you were making new friends every year, weren't you?" said Kitty.

"I was an extreme introvert, so I didn't make friends," said Cis. "Usually right when I was warming up enough to make friends, we left. My brothers made friends. The hermit is one of my archetypes, but I have a balance with that now. That came in my forties. I can feel when I need to withdraw or when I had better get myself out into the world."

"I go through that too," said Kitty. "I think about getting myself into the world, but I have no motivation to do it. I have worked a lot this year so I could take the time off to do this trip. When things were happening in town, I didn't have the energy or interest, even when I knew it would be good for me to get out. I'm alone at work, so there wasn't any balance. In my fifties I've started to be comfortable with myself and seek balance."

"Tai Chi did it for me," said Cis. "It was powerful for me to go and study something when I didn't know what I was getting into. I had to drive into the city—to me it was the city, but it was really midtown. I was terrified but had to do it anyway. Practicing Tai Chi and Qigong, I learned that energy work balances you, but you don't even know what's getting balanced. That was when I worked with Pat and was passionate about raptors. The little Girl Scouts and Boy Scouts needed somebody to talk to them. I jumped in front of five-year-olds, ten-year-olds, and fifty-year-olds. I wasn't talking to people so much as simply talking. They weren't looking at me; they were looking at the bird on my glove. I was talking about something bigger than I was. By happenstance, it coalesced. Twenty years ago, I could never be driving around here, popping in and out, talking to people, asking questions, striking up conversations. It would never have happened."

"It seems natural and comfortable for you," said Kitty.

"It is," said Cis. "Literally my parents had to force things on me without my even knowing because I would never have said yes to anything."

"I did that with my daughter," said Kitty. "I'd try different things and say, 'You can't say you don't like it if you don't know what it is.' I wanted to help her do something other than be within herself all of the time."

"There is the wisdom of other people," said Cis. "They do know better. Being an Air Force brat, I had no sense of place or family or how the norm worked. When my kids got to be of driving age, Charlie said, 'We're moving into the city.' I said, 'Over my dead body.' We moved. That was a tough spot because I liked my quiet little country no-socializing life. He was absolutely right about it being the right thing for kids at that age. When I graduated from high school, my parents literally said, 'I got you a place to live. Here's a job.' They said goodbye and left. I was eighteen and still couldn't make a phone call."

"That was your parents' way of cutting the umbilical chord," said Kitty.

"They retired within a week of my graduation from high school," said Cis. "We had never discussed their plans. Away they went. Tough love."

"How did that go for you?" asked Kitty.

"The analogy is like a fish out of water flopping around," said Cis. "They got me a place to live with a family whose daughter was a year younger than I was. I kind of knew who she was. The dad was in the Air Force and was a scary military guy—very strict. The mom was just a mom. I didn't see much of them. I was on a tennis team at the tennis club. My job was answering the phone and making reservations for court times there. That was hard. They would ask me to go and see if the hardware store was open, and I couldn't do that. I was out of balance."

"Nancy loaned me a book about Keewaydinoquay," said Kitty. "She was an ethnobotanist and worked in Michigan. She wrote the book about her early years. Her mother was a Native American and her father was 100 percent Irish. When she described her youth, there wasn't one negative thing in the whole book. I asked Nancy, 'How can someone's life be that great?' It's what you said. It's about having that experience and being able to look back and say, 'Oh, that's why that happened.' Nancy said it's the ability, with age, to reframe things. That's true, and that sticks with me. At the time things seem negative, but later they aren't."

"When you're right in the boiling of things, you can't see," said Cis. "Hopefully you're acting by spirit and doing the things you're suppose to and making the decisions you're supposed to, but it isn't until you are back on dry land and looking back saying, 'That wasn't so bad,' or "Oh, my gosh. What was that about?'"

After lunch, Heidi and I ran into headwind and barges at the same time. Heidi counted eighty-six barges parked on either side of the three-mile stretch to the Napoleon Cut-Off chute we planned to take north to Rosedale Harbor. The groups of parked barges were an odd collection of empty and loaded barges. A constant stream of tugs moved barges in and out of the chute. After one tugboat passed, we crossed the river to the chute side cutting in front of an oncoming tugboat. The current, wind, and waves kept us in the path of the tugboat longer than I wanted. I paddled hard, checking to be sure Heidi was close behind. Safe from the tugboats, we continued paddling hard due to the demanding wind until we reached the chute.

Entering Napoleon Cut-Off, we were out of the wind and paddled at a leisurely pace. Egrets lined both sides of the banks. Heidi estimated there were more than three hundred. They moved along the waterway in front of us for a couple miles before turning into their roosting area back in the trees.

It was late afternoon when we saw Kitty and Cis waving from the ramp at the Port of Rosedale. On the way to our hotel, we passed a women's correctional facility. Razor wire curled around at the top of the fence. Women in the yard wore pants and shirts with wide forest-green and white horizontal strips.

Eleven miles of paddling took more out of Heidi than she had anticipated. She napped the rest of the afternoon.

October 9, Day Nineteen

The contrast between what we saw on land and what we saw on the water was striking, and yet there were similarities. There were areas on land and water that stretched for miles with trees only in the distance. Over the land and water the sky hung like a bright blue umbrella under which butterflies and birds flitted from place to place. Looking across the quiet fields or the water everything seemed peaceful and serene. The pace of the river was relaxed and offered solitude. This was a striking difference from the land, where the commotion and audible buzz of people's activity on the roads, in the fields, and on the streets combined with a sense of danger caused by seeing businesses with bars on the windows. The resulting impression overrode a belief that serenity was possible.

We drove past cotton fields where harvest was in full swing. Bales of cotton the size of semitrailers lined the highway. One was graffitied: "We need a sweet tea party." We passed cotton gins. Rachell had told us the cotton gin was always used, but the cotton picker was invented because "the blacks left the area and it was needed to pick the cotton." I was curious why the machine was called a cotton gin when no alcohol was involved. On Wikipedia, I learned cotton gin is short for cotton engine.

At the top of a levee we turned on the road to our landing and saw a large sign with big red letters: "STOP. Private Property. '27 Break Hunting Club, Violators will be prosecuted." After driving around the road barriers at Trail of Tears, we considered going ahead, but the locked chain on the gate stopped us. Cis and Heidi looked for someone to let us in. Kitty and I sat in the van, entertained by cows in a pasture. Below the levee the cows gathered at the fence and watched us. A truck came from behind them, and they turned to watch it. Once it passed, they turned to watch us again.

"Here comes Cis—and there are two trucks following her," I said. "She's making things happen. You know you're going to have to back this rig up in front of these boys."

"I know," said Kitty, laughing.

A tall gray-haired man with a warm smile climbed from his white pickup, and the other truck drove off. The man unlocked the gate. "Hi," he said. "I'm Karl." He told us the name '27 Break referred to the levee break in 1927 during the great flood.

The road past the gate was overgrown, and the landing was washed out and no longer functioned as a landing. I wasn't paddling, and it was unsettling to watch Cis and Heidi paddle away. My sense of responsibility flared. I knew they were capable. Cis had paddled the river near St. Louis, and Heidi was a paddling guide in the Boundary Waters Canoe

Area Wilderness. They had great respect for what the river could dish out. Yet as Kitty and I sat onshore watching them round Choctaw Bar Island curve until they were tiny dots on the horizon, my body tensed.

The realization that paddling for eight hours a day wasn't helping me meet women or experience the culture in the South weighed heavily on me. The character and richness of the women's stories were on land. I hoped being on land would make a difference.

Driving toward Greenville, Mississippi, Kitty and I read from the meditation book. "Self-Disclosure. Many of us have hidden under a protective shell, a casing that prevents others from seeing or hurting us . . . We do not want others to see who we really are . . . Withholding who we are doesn't help us, the other person, or the relationship . . . to let go of our need to control others—their opinions, their feelings about us, or the course of the relationship—is the key."

I grew quiet thinking about how I hadn't been honest about my frustrations, particularly about being corrected. Being told no or getting corrected pushed old buttons that I wished to disarm. Disarm is a strong word, but I felt as if the emotions those old buttons elicited shot me down. I'd watch the shot get fired, see it hit the old tattered target, feel hurt rise, and lick my wounds in solemn amazement that I let it get to me again. I remember being told as a child that I was stupid, and those words had never been completely erased. I was told I wouldn't amount to anything, and I believed I was invisible. Even though I had a college degree and had written books, worked as a counselor changing people's lives for the better, and was now paddling the biggest river on the continent, the messages from childhood still took me down.

We stopped at Winterville Mounds, a group of ceremonial Indian mounds built about 1000 AD. At fifty-five feet, the largest mound is one of the tallest remaining mounds in the United States. The area had served as a political and ceremonial hub for Native Americans. The mounds were built by carrying dirt in baskets to the mound and stomping it down. On the top of the mounds, the Native Americans constructed buildings. We climbed the stairs to the top of the largest mound. That was strenuous and we couldn't imagine climbing the mound repeatedly with a basket of dirt. The view from the top was expansive. The Native Americans who built the mounds were the predecessors of the Choctaws, Chickasaws, and other Native American peoples.

In Greenville, Kitty and I stopped at the welcome center, which is a paddle-wheel boat in a man-made body of water located near the highway. It is called the River Road Queen Port of Mississippi. At a historical display we learned that Jim Henson, who created Kermit the Frog and the rest of the Muppets, was born near here. Greenville is home to Mississippi Slim, a blues musician known as the "quilted-suit, rainbow-haired icon." One of his suits was on display. The suit jacket was pastel green on the right and pastel peach on the left. The colors on the pants legs were the opposite.

We asked the attendant where to find good Southern cooking, and she directed us to Buck's, an African American restaurant. We pulled up to a small restaurant in a strip mall on Harvey Street with bars on the windows and doors. On the wall hung a picture of President Obama and a man we assumed was the restaurant owner. Our first mistake was not realizing it was Sunday; we were not wearing what the rest of the exquisitely dressed crowd was wearing. Heads turned and patrons' eyes watched us intently as we walked in.

The staff and patrons referred to each other as darlin', sweetie, and baby. The food was served cafeteria style. When we reached the front of the line, one of the servers said, "Okay, baby, what do you want? You get two more sides, baby." I couldn't recognize the food options, so I didn't know what to tell her. I asked about one side dish, sweet potatoes, and pointed at another that had corn in it. I ended up with fried corn, chicken-fried pork chop, sweet potatoes, a corn muffin, and banana pudding. We took our seats and ate. Everyone else in the place knew each other. The crowd acted like one big family.

The point of coming to the restaurant was to talk to people, but I couldn't bring myself to do it. I was too far out of my comfort zone. The introvert in me had me by the throat. I observed the warm boisterous interactions between people and smiled silently. A feeling that this would be a missed opportunity frustrated me.

After lunch, Kitty and I drove to Warfield Point County Park, the pick-up location for Heidi and Cis, but the park was closed. We went to a business next door on the river, and it, too, was closed. We decided to go through the park's barricade. I got out of Cis's car and moved the first barricade, and a car pulled up behind Kitty in the van. My heart raced. I thought we were in trouble for trespassing into a county park. I walked over to the car and explained to the driver that moving the barricade was the only way we could connect with our paddlers. The driver looked at me, confused. "That's fine," the man said in a smooth Southern drawl. "We were planning on doing the same thing to see the river."

In the park, the road to the boat ramp was in disrepair. While Kitty waited in the van, I drove down the ramp in Cis's car to make sure we could get the van and trailer in and out. There was enough clear passage to drive the car down, but the boat ramp was buried in mud.

The ramp was several yards up a channel into Greenville Harbor where there were many industrial sites. We made ourselves comfortable on the rubbery dry mud near the water, setting up our lawn chairs, using a large golf umbrella for shade, and waiting while the day grew warmer. We watched the tugboat, the *Amy Ross*, move barges up and down the channel. It was late afternoon when Heidi and Cis arrived looking weary after a twenty-five mile paddle. Cis was ankle deep in mud before she got

her kayak onto drier ground, but Heidi fared better. Heidi mentioned she'd seen lots of plastic milk crates alongshore. If she could attach one to her kayak safely, she'd bring it home, she said.

Before we left the park we climbed the observation tower, which had flood indicators on one corner. From the top of the tower we could see for miles up and down the river. The MV Fayettville, a river boat, was displayed in the park. It was built in 1924 and was originally steam powered. It had operated as a snag boat to pull logs out of the river.

We pulled into Lake Chicot County RV Park in Arkansas and set up camp on a site next to the lake. Randal, a railroad man who was camped across the road from us, came to talk. He said he saw our website address on the side of the trailer when we pulled in and had already looked us up online.

"I read where y'all stay in the middle of the river most of the time," said Randal. "That was interesting because you wouldn't think you'd get in the middle of that river in a kayak, especially with those river boats coming up and down. Our big river back home is the Arkansas River. We have tugs—but nothing like they have here.

"I guess you get to meet a lot of interesting people down here. Good thing you're here before it gets cold. I like it when people are doing something different."

"This is the halfway point," said Heidi. "Nancy has fifteen hundred miles under her belt, and Kitty has eight hundred."

"Well, hats off to that," said Randal. "A lot of times there's a big headwind too."

"We have been lucky with little headwind and glorious days," I said.

"The weather is supposed to be nice for the next few weeks," said Randal. "We have been going through a dry spell. We hope to get rain before there are fires. When we do, there's supposed to be a lot of tornados."

"That water will run off that dry land then, won't it?" I asked.

"Yes," said Randal. "Where I work, our railroads go through a lot of bottomland and sloughs. In seventeen years I've never seen those sloughs bone dry like they are. The wildlife—muskrats, alligators and such—aren't there anymore. When the water starts dropping, they will go find other water. We'll lose wildlife. Alligators bury up in the mud until a certain time. Animals can detect when it's time to move before we do. It was nice meeting you. Y'all have a great journey."

Setting up my tent, I encountered fire ants that bit me. Cis said, "No, they don't actually bite. They spray formic acid on you, so you're getting burned. The acid is in such a small concentration that it won't do damage. Formic acid is one of the most powerful acids known."

After dinner, Cis announced she was doing van support the following day. "I don't want to paddle," I said. The words flew out of my mouth without thinking. I inadvertently put Kitty in the position of having to paddle, and frustration showed on her face.

"I need time to process that," she said. We let the subject drop and walked to the fishing pier to watch the sunset over the lake through the cypress tress.

We slept with the tent flies off to stay cool. Without a tent fly, I had a full view of the lake. Each time I woke through the night, I was treated to a glowing full moon.

October 10, Day Twenty

I ran onto the pier for a better view of the sunrise and stopped dead in my tracks. A rusty orange and yellow sun peeked through glowing clouds of the same colors. It glistened off the water between the cypress trees. I felt engulfed in peace. I was brought out of my trance by a kissing sound. I looked around the deserted pier and peered over the edge expecting to see someone in a boat, but no boat. The surface of the water around the pier was disturbed by fish that nibbled the surface for bugs. Their nibbles made a delightful kissing sound and sent little ripples across the surface. The ripples intersected with each other and dissipated. I lingered to enjoy the fish's company and the sun's spectacular show.

During breakfast we watched egrets land in the trees near camp and great blue herons fish along the shore. Kitty decided paddling another day worked for her. We drove to the river on the Arkansas side upriver from the new Highway 82 bridge. Directly across from us construction workers were in the process of tearing down the old bridge.

We stood in the river in our sandals, and the slightly cloudy water lapped gently over the tops of our feet. The sandy bottom had bits of gravel mixed in that had been washed down the boat launch from the road above it. Farther into the water the bottom was clouded by silt stirred up by the motion of the water.

Two men pulled up in a silver pickup and watched us. As Heidi and Kitty passed the bridge, they looked like bugs on the water. When Cis and I headed for our vehicles, the men started a conversation. Billy and Emit both had gray hair and wore glasses. Emit climbed out of the truck and leaned against it using a cane to steady himself. "That bridge is only a couple years old," said Billy. "It took them ten years to build it. We been keepin' up with them."

"We saw them blow up the other side," said Emit. "Two guys got killed building the new bridge. One fell forty feet onto a barge below. One guy made a misstep and fell into the river and they never did find him. He didn't have a life jacket on, but he had a bunch of tools on his belt, so you know he went to the bottom. It's treacherous."

"Do you get on the river?" asked Cis.

"No," said Emit.

"I've been on that river once," said Billy. "A guy who was dredging invited me out there. I didn't stay long. There are a lot of folks that brave it. Most of the time the people that get in trouble are the ones that drink. They don't respect the river. That river scares me."

"Emit and I are retired policemen," said Billy. "That's how we met. When he first came to Greenville, you couldn't hardly walk because there were so many people. There's a bunch of vacant buildings now. They try to do things to get people back up there, but the crime rate is high so nobody will go there. My wife wouldn't go up there for nothin'. We were cops back in the days when it was kind of rough to be a cop. I started out on the beat and you work your way up to a car."

"I ended up in the detective division," said Emit. "Twenty-two years. Then I was a court clerk for fourteen after that. I liked being a policeman better, being outside."

"We tell the same old stories over and over," Billy laughed. "Mostly we talk about when we nearly froze to death. When it gets cold down here, we aren't used to it. We aren't like Minnesota folks, and we don't have the clothes to wear. The coldest I ever got, we had a red light go out and the guy had to come and work on it. They had me directing traffic. I wasn't prepared to stand in twenty-five degrees. The wind was blowing twenty-five miles an hour. I don't know much about Minnesota, but I sure like Garrison Keillor's 'A Prairie Home Companion.'"

"He keeps the radio alive," said Cis.

"When I was with the police department, people would jump off the bridge and try to kill themselves," said Billy. "They did a good job most of the time. We had one ol' boy that got drunk and another one bet him twenty dollars he wouldn't jump off the bridge. His daddy caught him before he got there." Billy pointed out to the bridge and said, "That cement pylon they are working on has been hit several times by barges. It's moved two and a half feet south. When you crossed the bridge, you saw it. It was wider on one side than the other. A lead barge hit that thing years ago, and it went down. Lead is expensive."

"Billion dollars worth of lead," said Emit making his way back into the truck. He sat in the seat and kept the door open.

"Several salvage companies have tried to get it up, but they haven't had any luck," said Billy.

"They knew exactly where it went down," said Emit. "The company come in, and they went out there on a big boat with a lift on it. The divers went down and hooked to it. They started to try to pull it up, and the thing flipped over."

"The water's twenty-one foot now," said Billy. "This last spring when the river flooded, it got to sixty-four foot deep. It's the highest it has been since 1927 when they had the big flood. The levees did a good job. They held everything." [When discussing the depth of the river there is a locally defined reference level in which elevation is part of the equation. In Greenville the Army Corps of Engineers has determined the flood stage is at forty-seven feet.]

We said goodbye, and Cis asked me to stand near a highway sign for a photo. Her sense of humor showed when she told me to rub my shoulders. The sign read "Shoulder Work."

Cis and I planned to drive to Grand Lake landing, where we'd pick up Heidi and Kitty, and then relax in a nearby restaurant to collect a story or two. I couldn't believe my eyes when the road to Grand Lake landing was washed away. We attempted to walk down to the landing to see how far we'd have to carry the kayaks, but we only went fifty feet until we came to water that was impassable.

Back at the vehicles I looked at the charts and maps. Cis got her iPhone out to research the area. I found a boat ramp we could use on our side of the river, but it was thirty miles downriver. While I looked for roads close to the river that we might be able to use to connect with Kitty and Heidi, Cis came over to show me what she had found. She moved the iPhone in front of me. I could barely make out a map on the nearly black screen. My polarized sunglasses caused all digital screens to appear black, which rendered the images useless to me. Cis kept insisting I look at the screen. I took off my prescription sunglasses attempting to see what she was trying to show me, but it was a blur.

The scenario of technology trumping the use of traditional maps had happened several times along the journey. The first week Laurel's iPhone was often being consulted even though we had all the maps we needed. At times, when we needed to compare motels or locate restaurants, the phones were invaluable. Other times, when it was river charts we needed that were not accessible on the phones, they didn't help. From the perspective of an iPhone owner, the information the phone provided was

The Way—as if technology had become the Holy Grail of finding your way in the world. In this case, locations of boat ramps along the Mississippi River were not part of the MapQuest information, nor were all of the back roads.

Tension rose between Cis and me as we attempted to talk about the options we had found. No matter how many times she put the iPhone in front of me, I still couldn't see anything on it.

The original landing we'd chosen was up a slough a mile and a half long, so the charts didn't help. We decided to drive to the levee to see what options we could find in the area, and the search was on. Before we made it to the levee we saw two men sitting outside a building, and we pulled over. Billy and Roger were repairing their fishing shack and wanted us to know it was "only for fishing, not hunting." They'd been working on it for three months, ever since the levee blew out and took the original one. They were using new construction materials, so the next time it flooded they would be able to hose it off, they said. The walls were being constructed with interlocking four-by-eight-foot sections that were waterproof. I had never seen anything like it.

The area along the levee used to be a fish farm, Roger said. "It was beyond a sense of reason to keep farmin' them fish," Billy added. "They got too expensive at five dollars per pound."

They recommended a couple of locations to pick up Kitty and Heidi, and they described where we could find them using hand gestures and local landmarks. My confusion showed on my face, so Billy said he'd show us. He got in his truck, gesturing that we should follow him, and then leaned out the window and said, "You need to know that once you get to Louisiana, it's against the law to drive on the levees." We followed him and drove on top of the levee where the fish farm ponds, with egrets fishing in them, were clearly visible.

Billy pulled over, pointed down a road, and said, "It's a private fishing camp. There's a gate—just crawl under it. They won't care."

We walked the road to assess the situation. I said, "I find it fascinating that the longer we're with people who have decided to help, the more they need to help us."

"No, it's not a need," said Cis.

"Okay, it's a want," I replied, feeling annoyed. "What I've been aware of during planning and on the pretrip is that people want to participate."

"You don't need anything," said Cis. "We want to do this because this is cool. I think this comes from want and not need."

Taking a moment to consider a thoughtful response I said, "In this country, I think the meanings of need and want are confused. I'm guilty of it. We use words inappropriately."

After walking a fifth of a mile we arrived at a point where the road crossed a slough. There was a small embankment next to a muddy area and large culvert that could work for a landing, but it meant hauling the kayaks a long way, and Kitty and Heidi would land in the mud. We walked back to the vehicles and got into Cis's car to look for another option. I told Cis how grateful I was that we could use her car as our official off-road vehicle. It could go places the van and trailer could not, allowing us to explore more options.

We drove the slough's levee toward the river. On one side of the levee were natural lush green wetlands and trees intermingled with the abandoned man-made ponds for the fish hatchery. The vegetation and water were full of life—including egrets, ducks, and geese—in harmonious disarray. On the other side were harvested and tilled cotton fields stretching into the distance, with bales of cotton dotting the edges. It was dry, controlled, and barren—a sharp contrast to the levee side.

We followed a road to an inviting pecan grove that stood at the edge of the river, and we drove close to the edge of the embankment. As we got out of the car into the tall grass, Cis explained that I needed to stomp my feet as I walked to scare the snakes away. After hearing that, I hesitated before each step. It was difficult to relax enough to enjoy the picturesque scenery. I looked across the river at a sandbar, fascinated by the new perspective.

We discussed the pros and cons of the two locations. The pecan grove could work, but it meant we'd have to haul the kayaks up the steep rocky embankment. The slough required Kitty and Heidi to paddle more than a mile farther than planned, and they'd end in mud; but we'd be able to portage the kayaks down a road, and Cis had portage wheels in her car we could use. We called Kitty and Heidi and let them decide. They chose the slough and I was delighted. "Should we have told them about the mud?" I asked Cis, stomping my feet as I talked. The longer I stayed in the tall grass, the more nervous I felt about the snakes.

Before we went back to the van we had a picnic at a spot in the pecan grove where the grass was short. I was on alert for snakes the entire time.

At the chosen landing we left the van and Cis's car, grabbed our folding chairs, and walked up the road. The road cut across the slough, which gave us a great vantage point to watch for our friends. Looking down the slough, I saw dozens of turtle heads peeking up from the water. On the muddy shore, eight turtles lay basking in the sun. We dubbed the spot Turtle Landing. The temperature was eighty-two, which felt hot and humid for a Northern girl, and I had no energy to move. I got comfortable in the shade with my journal. Cis took her camera and went exploring.

When Cis returned about thirty minutes later, Kitty and Heidi were dots in the distance. We carried our lawn chairs down the road and sat above the culvert with the slough on both sides of us. Startled by splashes behind us, we turned too late to see anything but ripples. It looked as if Kitty and Heidi had action around them too. It took a moment to recognize the flying Asian carp stirred up by their paddles. More jumped behind us. The fish were huge and, completely lacking symmetry or grace, hurled themselves into the air and belly flopped back in, making us laugh.

As Kitty and Heidi approached some small dead trees that stretched across the slough, the fish stopped jumping. "A little carp action out there?" I asked as Kitty and Heidi landed onshore.

"Yes," said Heidi. "How did you know?"

"We could see them clearly from here," I answered. "I can't believe how big they are."

"Could you see them? Really?" asked Heidi. "We heard you laughing. We turned into the slough and Asian carp hit my paddle blade. I nearly jumped out of my kayak from surprise, and then I nearly fell out from laughing."

"They sounded like they were skipping rocks," said Kitty. "Several jumped at the same time. I didn't dare turn around to look at them. Once I didn't put my paddle in because one was swimming right along the edge of my kayak. I said, 'Whoa! That was a big one.' It was such a surprise to see them. It was like they were saying it was time to have a little fun with us."

"We started singing our own version of 'The Twelve Days of Christmas,'" said Heidi. "Four carp a leapin', two kayakers a dodgin', multiple turtle heads." We all laughed.

"It was a good day," said Kitty. "Even though it's only been two weeks since I paddled last, I felt like I was starting over. I looked around for the dangers and where I could find my peace. The herons were everywhere, and I felt comfort in that."

"We aren't sure what the problem was at the boat landing," teased Heidi. "It looked great. We took photos for you. We passed the landing a good long while ago. The slough was beautiful. The colors and the trees and the closeness of everything in the slough were different from the main river. And the beaver! She ducked under water without slapping her tail and then came close enough to easily touch with my paddle. I saw her little nostrils moving. She made a little snorty noise. I moved away before she did. We saw several deer along the side of the slough. They were young, but then I saw a buck with a good rack."

"That's amazing," I said.

"We were hitting mud," said Kitty. "We were hoping we weren't gonna end up walking through the mud to get here."

"I could see us neck-deep in mud . . ." said Heidi.

"The barges were coming upstream today," said Kitty. "And the churning of the water—oh, my gosh. The waves rolled for a long time. I couldn't see Heidi when I was in the trough of the wave. At one point we were coming around a bend and a barge was coming. As we paddled

Using portage wheels at a muddy landing

toward the shore, it was aimed right at us. It was an eerie feeling to have something that big, that close."

We were checked into our motel in Eudora, Arkansas, by a beautiful East Indian woman garbed in traditional clothing. The décor of our rooms reflected the East Indian influence. The rooms were painted a light pink and splatter-painted with teal and magenta. Three sconces over the beds had colored lights. Kitty was overcome with laughter when she opened the pink bathroom door and saw pink tile accented with bright teal walls.

After we showered we drove to a drive-in diner next to the busy highway—the only place in town we found serving food. We placed our orders for hamburgers at the walk-up window and took a seat outside. When the server brought out the food, we had to wait to eat it. They served the hottest food I've had from a restaurant. The gentleman who'd been cooking came outside and sat quietly at a table near us. As we got ready to leave, he turned out the lights and then got into a waiting car. We hadn't realized he was done for the evening and was patiently waiting for us.

"Sorry!" I called out.

Through his rolled down window he said, "I didn't want y'all to eat in the dark."

October 11, Day Twenty-one

We drove to the Bunge Goodrich Terminal to ask directions to the boat ramp, and received them from a man who reminded me of Morgan Freeman.

When Kitty and I carried my kayak down to the river, a heron was sitting on the shore thirty feet downriver. We set the kayak down and watched her for a moment. I said, "Good morning, Kee." She squawked and flew downriver.

While we were preparing for the day's paddle, the same gentle-natured man who had given us directions walked up to us. His name was Easy and he had questions. He shook his head in disbelief that we were on the river "in those bitty boats." Easy told us he'd lost his job in West Monroe, Louisiana, where he made forty thousand dollars a year with paid vacation and benefits. "I feel fortunate to have gotten on with this group," he said, referring to the Bunge Goodrich Terminal where he made fifteen thousand a year. He'd been married for thirty-four years and had four children and nine grandchildren. Joy beamed in his face when he said he was looking forward to great-grandchildren. His grandchildren lived with him. "The boy plays basketball and he can keep playing as long as he does his chores and his homework. Those things come first before basketball," said Easy. "I told the boy if he wants to do anything else, he could bring his case to me and we'd discuss it."

He wanted to know how we got so brave to go down the river and then asked if we'd seen alligators. "My boss talks about alligators on the river." A look of doubt crossed his face as he paused, looked at us, and said, "I've never seen one."

Easy went back to work. With kayaks ready on the landing, Kitty read from the meditation book. "Recovery. How easy it is to blame our problems on others . . . The solution to our pain and frustration, however valid, is to acknowledge our own feelings . . . We know our happiness isn't controlled by another person, even though we may have convinced ourselves it is. We call this acceptance."

Heidi and I paddled away from shore, and I was thinking I had accepted a lot of the things in my life, but there were holdouts—things I grasped tightly. I was resigned to acceptance being a lifetime project.

A short distance from the ramp we paddled into a slough that curved around Cottonwood Bar and into the main river. It was a quiet and peaceful morning paddle. The weather continued to treat us to calm water and a breeze to keep us cool.

We stopped on a sandbar created by Willow Cut-Off dikes for lunch. Today was Heidi's last day paddling the Mississippi. "I've been pleasantly surprised by how beautiful the river is," she said. "I had imagined a continuous industrial area. Instead we're surrounded by big trees, and the river is edged with sandbars."

We heard heavy equipment in the distance and planes flew overhead. We sat in what others considered a dangerous wilderness, yet our experience was one of peacefulness.

"It's an odd contrast. The river is so pretty, yet in many ways too remote for people to access," said Heidi. "Fewer people will come here than any spot in the Boundary Waters. Look. There's a house that was clearly built with great expense, but there's no path down to the river. It doesn't look like the people who live there interact with the river."

"It occurred to me that we may be the first people to actually sit or walk on this particular sand due to the nature of the river," I said. "These sandbars are constantly changing; the river is constantly turning and moving things. Mark Twain said that sandbars are never at rest. The river creates her own history, and we merely brush against her. We can't contain or control her any more than we can contain or control what happens in our lives."

"That's cool," said Heidi. "That's a lot to think about. It's hard to imagine this part of the river as the same river we paddled in 2004."

She was right. The river was dramatically different from the creek we had started in—and I was different from the woman who had paddled that creek. I had witnessed the river change, and the river had witnessed and facilitated my change. An interaction with the Mississippi River alters you in ways you can't imagine or understand until you experience her. I couldn't put words to the ways the river had transformed me so far, and time would reveal even more transformations. The river never dished out more than we could handle.

"How do you feel about the trip being half over?" asked Heidi.

"I'm not sure how I feel." I answered. "At this point, we've been gone from home for more than three weeks. I long for my own bed, the feel of Doug's arms around me, and the laughter we share each evening. I miss Carly and Mavis [our dog and cat]. I haven't had time to think about it ending because each day is packed."

Teary eyed, Heidi said, "This is my last day on the river, and I'm having a hard time leaving. I didn't expect to like paddling the river as much as I do. I'd like to come back and camp on the banks."

Having Heidi along added a different dimension. She was in the stage of life where home and family were the primary focus. Sam, her five-year-old son, got daily phone calls, text messages, and emails with photos. Her calls were filled with lively detailed descriptions of what she had experienced. Sam's questions were priceless and connected us to a child's way of seeing our adventure. Time, like the river, had given me a broader perspective. The farther we traveled, the broader and more encompassing life was.

We saw two pelicans on shore and paddled closer. Their mighty wings lifted them from the shore and they took flight upriver. Heidi had her last chance at getting a milk crate, and the temptation was great, but the mud she would have had to muck through stopped her.

As we approached Terrell River Service Inc. site, our landing, Asian carp jumped and swirled in the water. The workmen fixing a barge stopped to watch. The landing was muddy, and Cis and Kitty and the workmen thoroughly enjoyed watching Heidi and me step ankle-deep into it.

On our way to Tallulah, Louisiana, for the evening, Cis and Kitty told us about their day. They had pulled into Doug's IGA and scarcely got into the parking lot when Doug, the owner, came out, full of curiosity. When they went into the grocery store, he told them that in the last two censuses Tallulah's population had dropped 23 percent. It was ranked seventh on the list for being below poverty level, he said, and its population was 75 percent black. The town's only hope was education, he said. Tallulah was a rural farming area. Doug was grateful the government allowed the city to use the prison population in the census. He said the only industry left in that area was the prison industry. A barge company was coming to town. They would build and refurbish barges and employ four hundred people, Doug told them as our groceries were bagged. Then Doug generously paid for our groceries.

One of the grocery store employees, Betty, said her husband had worked for the Corps of Engineers for thirty years. She shared a story he told her about a kayaker getting sucked under a barge. They pulled him out all right, and they got his kayak out all right, but he lost his gear. They put him back together, and he got back in the water again. "Can you believe that?" she asked.

That evening at the hotel, Cis shared an email she had received from her sister-in-law after she had written her about our journey down the river.

> *Cis—This looks wonderful! It's important that we do share our stories, our experiences, and be heard, and listen to others share the stories of their lives and hear what's said. I personally believe that this is one of the greatest avenues for healing—that until at least one person hears our pain, we will hold onto it more tightly. Once we feel heard, we can let go more easily. At least this has been my personal experience and seems to be that of many I know well. What a gift that you are doing this with other women in nature, with the wonders of water, fire, air, and earth. Enjoy!*
> *Blessings, Libby*

October 12, Day Twenty-two

We got word from Gwyn that she had a family emergency and would be unable to return to paddle. Our heads were spinning, for Gwyn's news hit the same week we learned that our extra van support person was unable to come. We'd need to dramatically revamp the schedule. Kitty and I would be alone for a week, which meant no paddling. We decided to take time to think about the changes and deal with them. My heart was with Gwyn. It's hard enough when a difficult event in our lives hits, but when the difficult event denies you of something you've been looking forward to for years, it adds insult to injury.

"Being Gentle with Ourselves During Times of Grief" was the topic in our meditation book: "The process of adapting to change and loss takes energy. Grief is draining, sometimes exhausting . . . We do not have to expect more from ourselves than we can deliver during this time. We do not even have to expect as much from ourselves as we would normally and reasonably expect." I used to think grief was only connected to death. When I was introduced to the concept that grief applied to any loss, I felt liberated. Not having Gwyn return was a big loss for me personally, and I was grieving. It was deeply disappointing that her energy and smile would not be with us. I was mad at the individuals who played a role in Gwyn's not being with us, whether they meant to or not.

I went out the hotel door to run and dissipate my disappointment but stopped in my tracks. Directly across from our room sat an Army tank. That wasn't how I expected to start the day. Then I noticed the tank was in transit, sitting on a trailer. Where I run makes a difference in how the run affects my mental attitude. I tried running down a country road, but the narrow lanes and fog made it dangerous. I settled for running a figure eight around a motel and a fast food restaurant.

While we were packing the van, curiosity got the better of a man named Jack. "I saw your rig over here, and I had to know what you were up to. I considered traveling the river on a boat, but I never thought about something that small," he said, looking at our kayaks.

"Paddling in a kayak gives you a different perspective," I said.

"I grew up on the river," said Jack nostalgically. "I live on the other side of the state now. I work for the Louisiana Natural Rural Water Association. I'm in the wastewater part, the dirty water. I go around to different cities and districts and help them when they have environmental problems. We don't charge anybody because our work is funded through the federal and state government."

"The water here tastes different than it does up North," said Kitty.

"Well," Jack said with a grin, "we take y'all's bad stuff and clean it up. We're trying to get the municipalities to understand they need to get quality people to run their programs to get the programs up to where they're supposed to be. The cities want to pay minimum wage because nobody wants to hear about wastewater. As long as the water coming out of the faucet isn't brown, everybody is okay. Folks holler when it's brown.

"We have a management training program and put on training sessions for the operators to get certified. They only need a high school education or GED to take the class. We can't get the districts to understand that you got to pay people to get quality people in there to do your work. It's hard to get a young fella with a family to live on minimum wage. They can go to McDonald's and make more. A lot of retired people are doing the work."

"We all live downstream," said Cis.

"Well, us down here get it all," said Jack. "We have programs that teach the kids about how groundwater works. Once they see it, they get it. Before we can even start on a community's problems, we got to get their trust. We aren't there to tell the enforcement people that they messed up. The governing bodies care about the water until you say you need to raise your rates to pay for the repairs, and then they know they'll lose votes."

"That sounds like a challenging juggling act," said Heidi.

"Down here they used to drill oil," said Jack, "but they haven't had much to do with the fracking part of it. The problem with fracking is the water they bring back out. Where they putting it? I got to run to a meeting. It sure was nice meeting you ladies."

The change in plans with Gwyn had unhinged me, and things I thought I had let go of bubbled back up. I struggled silently for a while as Kitty and I were driving the van to Vicksburg, and I decided to be vulnerable and talk about it. I said how frustrated I was with being corrected and that I thought I had let go of it. "I feel like I have to be careful about my choice of words. I'm even doing it right now with you because I don't want to hear you tell me I'm wrong, or the other things I hear when I try to speak up like, 'That's not what I meant' or 'That's not what I said' or 'You shouldn't feel that way.' Everyone is invested in her perception of reality. I get that. I am too. What I'm struggling with is the push for everyone to adopt or accept her position as the only correct perspective. I've been shutting up because hearing 'no' pushes old buttons. Maybe I'm sensitive because I didn't have a lot of girlfriends. If this is how women communicate, it's foreign to me."

"I think a part of it is how women communicate," said Kitty. "The part that's missing is the listening piece. It takes a lot longer when everybody is trying to get her own perspective out, yet it's respectful to allow that."

"I need a response I can practice that is respectful to me and whomever I'm talking to," I said. "I can let it roll off, but then I hit a saturation point."

"Do you need a response?" asked Kitty. "Why do you need a response if you're listening?"

"It is not when I'm listening that it happens," I said. "It's when I'm speaking. I make a statement, and I hear 'no,' which is followed by someone's perspective, like a recent conversation with Cis about the difference between want and need. Sometimes I get cut off and corrected before I have even finished what I'm saying. I'm not saying people shouldn't have their perspective, but let me have mine. When it happens repeatedly, old buttons get pushed and I feel stupid and dismissed. I feel like I'm being talked to like a child and invalidated. It takes a lot of energy for me to keep my power when it happens repeatedly, particularly in a group of powerful women like this. I'm not used to being told no this much."

"Am I doing that?" asked Kitty.

"We're all doing it," I said.

"What comes up for me is it's okay if somebody else says no," said Kitty. "That's her reality. It's about holding your own truth."

"That's my point," I said. "I need a response that lets me hold my own truth in the situation."

"I don't understand," said Kitty.

"This is how I'm experiencing this," I said. "I've been getting corrected a lot. I don't feel I can kid around anymore because my kidding gets corrected. Intended or not, the message is sent that my reality is not okay. In some cases it comes with intensity and repetition that continues until there's consensus."

"We have a rule that says we must state our preferences," said Kitty. "Maybe we need a rule that says there's no saying no. It's about finding a different way to say it that makes people think about what they're saying instead of saying no. Actually, saying no is way too easy."

"That's an option," I said. "I'd rather find a response so I can take responsibility for standing up for myself in those situations. I'm afraid a rule won't make me take responsibility. When it happens I think, 'Wait a minute. Don't get upset. What happened is okay because this is my reality and that's theirs.' Then I hear the 'no' again and feel shut down. That's what it is! When we start our response to someone with no, it shuts them down. I grew up being shut down intentionally and unintentionally. Because I've been sensitive, I've been watching, and I find it fascinating how we tell each other no and need our perspective to be accepted. I don't know if I'm ready to have this as an open discussion."

"I'm hearing a lot of resolution of old issues as you talk," said Kitty. "I experience my stuff like this: What is before me is 90 percent of what's going on. It's the 10 percent of stuff that's been buried long enough to become an automatic trigger for me that causes the big reaction, no matter what the situation is. I'm lucky when I recognize that my reaction is about something I haven't resolved within myself yet. I'll never run out of things to work on."

"Me neither," I said and smiled. "There's a 'no' that works."

"And a 'never' that works," said Kitty. We laughed. "There aren't as many old issues to resolve. I can recognize the big ones readily now. The number of buttons has lessened too. As those lessen, what's left fills in the space and the buttons are getting bigger. It's like four buttons turned into one big one."

"Do you think it's possible it was that big all along, but the little ones obscured it?" I asked.

"That could be," said Kitty. "I think back to my environmental economics class when we talked about the economics of getting rid of pollution in the environment. The first 80 percent is easy. Those are the little periphery pollutants that can be taken care of. As we narrow the issue down to the last 20 percent, it's the bigger ones that are harder to resolve. Incorporating that into my life had a huge impact on me. It's that way in the environment and in my personal life too. I got rid of the drinking, and it was huge. I got rid of the smoking, and it was huge. Then these little issues that were obscured popped up. It's like finding a path through a minefield. My use of relationships was gone; then food and sugar popped up as issues that need attention. To deal with them requires me to find my voice and explain myself in ways I never had to before. I have to explain me to me. If I have a hard time explaining me to me, I can't describe me to anybody else."

"That's why I'm better at expressing myself in writing than speaking," I said. "I am sensitive to perceived rejection. After I've written something, I'm not there when people read it. They can reject it all they want, and I don't have to hear it or see it. I don't let it alter my truth. My goal is to get to the point where it doesn't matter if I write it or say it, it's still my truth and it's valid."

"I understand that," said Kitty.

"After you read the last book, you said you didn't know that I was getting tired of you until you read it in the book," I said. "I couldn't say it. A few days ago I told Doug that this trip is perfect. He asked what I meant, and I said by the time I start getting frustrated or irritated with someone, she goes away."

"Except me," Kitty laughed.

"Even that's different," I said. "We aren't with each other 24/7. You aren't always paddling with me. We've been alternating roles this time. I've been watching conversations down here between women. They banter back and forth and get after each other, and no one takes it personally. I've never experienced that and don't know how to do it. I want to learn."

"I haven't experienced that either," said Kitty. "Mom usually had the final word, and there wasn't discussion. Growing older is fascinating. Even five years ago I wouldn't have thought about having a discussion like this."

After checking in at the motel, all four of us set out to explore Vicksburg. The city is proud of the eighteen-hundred-acre Vicksburg National Military Park and the Vicksburg National Cemetery, where the remains of seventeen thousand Civil War Union soldiers are buried. Soldiers' Rest is a plot in the city's Cedar Hill Cemetery for an estimated five thousand Confederate soldiers. Historic Vicksburg was located on the shore of the Yazoo River. Along Levee Street, the floodwall has thirty murals depicting the town's history.

Kitty, Heidi, Cis, and I climbed the stairs to the Attic Art Gallery, the oldest continuously operating single-owner art gallery in the state of Mississippi. Soft jazz played in the background. When we first walked in, we saw a barrage of color. Every inch of space displayed artwork, pottery, or jewelry. Artwork was stacked, allowing visitors to sort through to find a

treasure. Every style of work, from impressionism to contemporary to traditional, was represented. Lesley, the owner, a soft-spoken and refreshingly honest woman, sat at a large table covered in artwork. Lucile, a tall, striking silver-haired woman who worked with Lesley, stood near her.

"My husband says I'm not a Southerner even though I've been here since I was six years old," said Lesley.

"You weren't born with roux in your veins," said Lucile.

"Roux?" I asked.

"A little bit of flour and a little bit of oil cooked together," said Lesley.

"It used to be lard instead of oil," said Lucile. "Roux's a staple of Southern cooking."

"Is the art hanging in here yours?" asked Kitty.

"Some of it," said Lesley. "I get pleasure from other people's artwork. I have a hard time showing mine. It's easier to talk about somebody else's. You can dig through those pictures on the counter there."

"You're saying it's a hands-on place?" I asked.

"Yes," said Lesley. "I've gotten thrown out of too many places because I touched the artwork."

"I usually have a security guard watching me closely," I said.

"I've been there," said Lesley. "It's nice. You get your own private escort."

"But you can't appreciate the detail from twenty feet away," I said, smiling.

While Lesley went to help a customer, Lucile said, "With having her own gallery, she doesn't promote her own stuff." She showed us a recent article from the *Vicksburg Post* featuring Lesley. Her shop was forty years old, the article stated. The gallery started when she and her husband put art to sell in their home. When they ran out of room, they created the Attic Art Gallery. The article read, "Her mother was a working artist, her aunt a sculptor, and her grandfather painted." The article quoted Lesley as saying, "You're born with some of the love of art... I think there's a propensity or something that ends up in you and maybe goes down into your very being, because I feel you need art to breathe." The article went on to say that Lesley avoided art because her mom was so good. "If you don't have an art background," Lesley was quoted, "you're given permission to do anything because you don't know what is right and what is wrong ... if you wait until the mood strikes you before you start painting, you're copping out. Life is so limited, so one should utilize each moment."

Lesley returned and I said, "I like your work."

"I don't like promoting myself," said Lesley.

"I know people like that," I said.

Heidi laughed and pointed at me. "I'm an artist too," I said. "I don't promote myself."

We asked if Lesley was coming to the Gathering later and she said, "It's not tonight, is it?" The flyers I had mailed her promoted the Gathering for the following night, as did the ad in the newspaper. "We told a woman at the motel it was tonight," I said, "so I guess we will have two Gatherings." Lesley said she would be there the next night, and she would promote it.

We wandered the shops along Washington Street and spent time in the Corner Drug Store, a modern, operational pharmacy with a Civil War museum displaying medical artifacts. The medical equipment was horrifying to see. The hypodermic needle was as big around as the inside of a pen. The instruments looked like they belonged in a garage, not a medical bag. Bottles that once held "medicine"—arsenic, LSD, cocaine, opium, and a variety of tinctures and herbs—lined the shelves.

We walked down Washington Street and stepped into Rusty's Riverfront Grill. The place was buzzing with activity. At the table next to us was a loud group of men. We overheard their conversation comparing the temperance movement to current drug issues our country faced. One boisterous man said passionately, "The women who signed up then didn't know what they were doing. What we need is for the women of today to do the same thing for the drug situation. They could do something about it." He seemed to think women could make a difference, but the other men at that table didn't have a high opinion of women.

We placed our order and while we waited Cis said, "In 1977, the relatives came to St. Louis for Easter. My son Brian was small, and I was nursing him. We went to an aunt and uncle's house where there were lots of cousins in their twenties and lots of young children running around. I excused myself from the family room where everybody was gathered to go to another room to nurse. In wandered a little girl. She was five years old. She couldn't tell what was going on, so she wandered over to see, and I told her I was feeding the baby. She asked where the bottles were, and I said, 'I'm breast-feeding him.' This five-year-old girl in her Easter outfit started beating on me. I was occupied with my new baby and trying to fend off a little girl. She ran out screaming and crying. I had to finish what I was doing. Many minutes later, I went back to the family room and approached the mother of this little child and I said, 'I'm terribly sorry.' I explained what happened, and that young woman, who was around my age—this happened in the late '70s—blurted out, 'Well, every time I think of that, I think of n----r gals sitting on the front stoop hanging their titties out.' She said that in front of the children. I was speechless. This was in a time when you'd think change had happened, when it hadn't. Voiced loud and clear that way, with that inflection and in front of the children . . . that wasn't the first time it was talked about. The little girl didn't know how to react. She reacted by striking out, screaming, and running. She is older than my son, now nearly forty. This cycle is going to go on."

After lunch, we toured the Cedar Grove Mansion Inn, an 1840 Greek Revival mansion overlooking the Yazoo River. The house was a wedding gift from John Alexander Klein to his bride, Elizabeth, "Libby." She was sixteen when she married him; he was thirty. After they were married, they went to Europe for a year-long honeymoon and purchased the antique furnishings and gaslit chandeliers. In the smoking parlor, a cannonball from the Civil War was lodged in the wall. The ladies' parlor had a petticoat mirror. There, ladies used to check their petticoats to be sure they weren't showing. If one's petticoat was exposed, another lady would let her know by telling her, 'It is snowing down south.' After age thirteen, a woman's petticoat was not to show. Libby and John had ten children. Six lived to be adults. The house remained intact during the war because it was used as a Union headquarters. It had manicured formal gardens, a gazebo that had been part of the original buildings, fountains, and courtyards.

We made our way back to Riverfront Park for the Gathering. The park was located high on a bluff between two riverboat casinos. The day was warm and sunny. We opted for setting our circle under the trees rather than under the pavilion. The view from the bluff was expansive. The bend in the river appeared gentle. The river reflected the soft blue of the sky. Waves, gently stirred by the breeze, danced across the surface. Flotillas of black birds were strung in a long line in the middle of the river. A light, muddy stripe in the water stretched alongshore below me, the effect from the confluence with the Yazoo River.

After we set up, the waiting began. A slightly cool breeze played with our hair. An older couple walked the trail along the bluff's edge. They'd been holding hands, laughing, and having a good time. She had a great laugh that brought a smile to my face. Children played on the equipment near us. The Peace Fire burned strong in the Smokey Joe grill. Cars passed through the parking lot. With each approaching car, our excitement rose and then was dashed as it passed us by, a repeat of our experience from the previous Gathering.

"Do you think those people we saw earlier today when we were walking around town were gypsies?" asked Kitty.

"Maybe they were simply nomadic," Cis said.

"What the gypsy does is nomadic," Kitty said. "The term nomadic brings up a different feel."

"The nomadic surely is in me," Cis added. "I can't name the number of times we moved from place to place when I was a child. I got married and stopped, but the nomadic gene lives on."

"I wonder who in my background gave me the wandering gene," Kitty said. "I'm the only one in my family who has it to the degree that I do, but where did it come from? It wasn't from my parents."

"My mother was one of six children born in six different towns in West Texas," Cis said. "My grandfather was a wildcat oil driller. They moved all the time. If anyone's family is not nomadic, it's my husband's family. Their roots are deep and solid, but I managed to whittle on his." She turned to Kitty and me. "Look at how you pick up camp, the way you're so organized with Ripples of Wisdom boxes. You can easily set up camp or a Gathering. You've developed a rhythm to traveling down the river."

"Yeah, it wouldn't appeal to everybody," Kitty said.

A half hour passed. It was now the scheduled time of the Gathering. We pulled our chairs in a tighter circle, accepting that no one else was coming. "I think we need a new approach," said Kitty.

"The South does have a different mindset," said Cis. "Maybe there'll be a shift when you go by land this next week. Maybe that's what has been needed all along."

"I had a sense of that when we were paddling," I said. "We'd paddle on the water with little interaction with others, but you guys on land would have fabulous interactions with people. A voice in my head said, 'Get off the water. Get off the water.' I got off the water and found myself with Cis trekking through the backwoods searching for boat launches. I thought, 'I'm off the water, and now I'm sitting in a pecan grove having lunch with Cis, which is awesome, but where are the women?'" We laughed.

"They weren't near that culvert you were sitting on either," laughed Kitty. She poked a stick at the Peace Fire. "How do you think poverty fits into this?"

"With poverty comes a degree of fear, don't you think?" asked Heidi. "It's harder to welcome the unknown or get excited about it if you're just surviving. It's harder to see possibilities, accept them, or imagine them. It makes me wonder if the women are working hard to hold it together as hotel desk workers and cleaners and waitstaff. Those are the places where we're actually going to get to talk to women."

"While they're on the job," added Cis.

"God knows when they leave their jobs they've probably got more than they can shake a stick at to take care of," Heidi said. "What we're doing is an incredible privilege."

"We're going to have to do Gatherings one-on-one," I said. "The lady in the clothing shop would've talked to us and shared her story, but she couldn't come due to work. One of the problems with the way Gatherings are set up is that we have to schedule them so early that working women can't come. We have to be finished before dark, and it gets dark early."

Someone suggested we go to beauty shops.

"We'd be there awhile, which would give us an opportunity to talk with women," I said. "Maybe that's one of the reasons I feel such a strong desire to get my hair fixed. We could go to one shop to take care of the color, and another to cut it, then another for a shampoo."

"Kitty, you have to take pictures and document this," said Cis.

"I will," Kitty said. "It seems like a lot of opportunities for something to go wrong and someone to end up with a bad style."

"The last time my hair was short was when we first opened the Front Porch," I said. "Things were extremely stressful, and I felt out of control. I found myself going into the bathroom on a regular basis and cutting my hair shorter and shorter. I realized it was the one thing that I had control of. By the time things leveled out and I didn't need to do that anymore, my hair was only about an inch and a half long. That realization helped me not freak out every time I had the compulsion to cut more off. Doug was convinced I'd be bald before things calmed down."

"I think each of us should have a tape recorder and set a goal to have a significant moment with everyone we meet," said Heidi. "What a neat practice—to practice engaging on a deeper level with people."

"Maybe when they say they've got a meeting, we ask if we can come," Kitty said.

We fell silent and stared off over the river for several moments. "It's too lovely an evening to go sit in a motel room," I said breaking the silence. "I noticed today that we were not where the local people are. We need to find restaurants that are serving local folks.

"Look! Here comes Lesley. Look at that girl's car."

Lesley drove a gray station wagon with a red stripe on the hood. A hand-painted hubcap and tin boxes decorated in a wide variety of ways adorned the hood. Brightly colored bottle caps lined the wheel wells. The roof and doors were decorated with tin boxes, a remote control, flowers, and various toys. On the passenger door, a light switch to no apparent source had been installed.

Lesley noticed us staring at her car. "I have a lot more to put on," she said, "but the summer was brutal. I'll start putting more on soon."

"Does it make you smile every time you have to go somewhere?" asked Heidi.

"The worst part is I forget that there's something on the outside," Lesley said, grinning. "Sometimes I wonder why people are staring at me."

Lesley carried herself with an air of self-confidence as she moved into the group.

"The smell of the smoke from the fire is nice when you drive up," said Lesley.

"Oh, good," I said.

"We went to New Mexico and came back through Texas last summer," Lesley said. "There were fires on both sides of I-20. That was a lot of smoke and a lot of damage."

"Nature is talking to us all over the world with weather," said Cis.

"Yes, she has a lot to say," Lesley commented. "We sort of screwed up."

"There's a question you can help us with," Kitty said. "The Gatherings we did up North were well attended, but that's not been the case in the South. We're trying to figure out how to change that so it fits for the South. The women aren't coming to meet us. How do we meet them?"

"Southern women don't take chances," Lesley said. "You're asking them to get in their car and go to a place that they don't always go. What you need to do is get them to come to a place that they're comfortable with."

"We were thinking about beauty shops," Heidi said.

Lesley made a sour face and said, "I don't go very often, but in the African American community the beauty shop is the center. In 1971 I went to St. Louis and to a beauty shop on Euclid Avenue. They cut my hair only an inch away from my scalp."

"Is that what they thought you needed?" asked Cis.

"My first cousin Marcia had her hair cut like that," Lesley answered. "She had the right face for short hair. My husband thought the style would be great for me, so I went."

"Hair grows out," said Cis.

"Yes," Lesley said, "but I've never forgotten how that felt, and that was four years ago. I think we need you more than you need us, so we need to reach women. If you were to do this again, I'd be happy to have people in the gallery or out back on the patio."

"So it's about women not feeling emotionally safe?" Heidi asked.

"Yes, I think so," said Lesley. "Where are you going next?"

"We're going to Natchez and Baton Rouge," I answered. "In both places, we have good connections with people who are doing promotion for us."

"Oh, that's good," said Lesley. "You're right about Southern women."

"They're private and reserved, aren't they?" I said.

"More reserved?" Lesley shook her head.

"No?"

"In the South you grow up a certain way," Lesley said. "There's church and family. Then you go to college and there's sorority, church, and home. The women are still cooking dinner. Their lives are very much like the traditional ways you have heard about. The new thing that has entered into this tradition is now women are going to the gym."

"What did you mean when you said the women down here need us more than we need them?" asked Heidi.

"I said that because of the opening you're creating and because of your vision," Lesley said. "You see, I grew up in the South and have always lived here. My parents are from New York. My mother had a great influence on me." She paused for a moment. "I think many women have a lot of meetings."

"We were thinking that was a polite way to blow us off," I said, laughing. "Every woman we talked to today had a meeting tonight."

"Is it a way of being very polite and not saying no outright?" asked Cis.

"That's exactly right," said Lesley. "I'd like to gather a few people, and we could meet on our back patio tomorrow night, if that would work for you."

"That would be amazing," said Kitty. "We'll call you in the morning about details."

"Great," said Lesley. She turned to me. "How does your husband feel about your being gone? Does he have a problem with this?"

"No," I said. "He is very supportive of this—surprisingly so. He's pretty amazing. He's very sensitive to women's issues and is connected to his feminine side. He feels at a loss sometimes about how women are treated and doesn't feel like there's much he can do about it. Supporting me is his way of doing something, his quiet way of holding us up."

Lesley nodded her head, understanding. "Well, I'd better go now," she said.

We drove back to our motel feeling hopeful about connecting with women. We weren't in our room long and there was a knock on the door. We were delighted to find Josephine, whom we had met earlier in the lobby. She had come to talk with us. She took a seat at the table in our room.

"I worked for twenty-five years as a lab technician," she said. "A lab technician is a glorified name for a lab helper. We worked on new products and did a lot of testing. It was a great place to work. I've watched the older people start in the factory, go to school, and climb the ladder. The kids coming out of school today have no common sense. They have book learning and that's all. If it doesn't work on the computer, then it's no good. They don't understand the value of working your way up in a company.

"My mom lived to be ninety-six. During the last five years dementia came, and then Alzheimer's. It wasn't good. I said I'd rather die from cancer because the pain is there and then it's done. How horrible to die and not even know you're dying. We went two or three times a week to see her. Once in a blue moon she would remember us. On good days we'd put her in her little chair and take her for walks. I told my husband that if it ever happens to me, I'm going to take care of myself so the kids won't have to. He looked at me and said, 'But you'd have to remember you said that.'" We all laughed. "Well, ladies," she said, standing up, "I got to call it a night. Thanks for listening to this old lady."

Cis's journal entry:

> *"The days turned into daze:*
> *One glorious day after another.*
> *The ebb and flow of mud and*
> *laughter mingled in the*
> *air amongst mockingbird*
> *and the hum and buzz*
> *of bug song.*
>
> *Moon bright nights and*
> *sun lit days to paddle*
> *or drive the levee road*
> *and always with a friend,*
> *and sister of the River.*
>
> *And men have been the*
> *'balance of things'*
> *along the edge(s) of*
> *the water."*

October 13, Day Twenty-three

After a three-month reprieve, night sweats and hot flashes returned to my daily life, decreasing the amount of sleep I got. The temperature outside was too warm for my internal furnace to keep kicking on.

I had not been able to get the decriminalizing-domestic-violence-to-save-money debate in Topeka out of my head. I looked online for an update and was relieved to read on the Reuters website: "A county official in the capital city of Kansas, who had refused to prosecute some domestic abuse cases because of budget cuts, resumed enforcing the law on Wednesday after an angry public outcry."

My email inbox was full of heartache. A friend had a motorcycle accident and would have a long recovery. A fire in Babbitt, a town south of Ely, destroyed the only grocery store and pharmacy and a couple other businesses. A friend's battle with depression worsened. Another friend's husband started drinking again; she was devastated, and he was clueless how his choices hurt her. And my sister-in-law had a stroke last spring and didn't tell Doug or me. As I read the email about my sister-in-law, I felt I'd let her down. I had been busy getting ready for the trip and hadn't noticed we hadn't talked in a while.

There was good news too. A friend who'd served in Vietnam and had a debilitating case of Parkinson's due to exposure to Agent Orange had gotten help. An implant was put into his brain that immediately reduced the tremors. He's more mobile now. The disease wasn't going away, but he had a chance for a richer life again.

Kitty and I went to the lobby to start planning. Our plans were up in the air, and we had to switch gears. We studied the charts and maps. Heidi joined us and said, "Tailgating in the parking lot in ten minutes. Don't forget Cis is making her magic pancakes this morning." Parking lot meals had become the norm. We had everything we needed to cook, so we would set our kitchen up near the trailer, get our chairs, and enjoy a great meal together. Parking lot meals were also a way to connect with people.

Carolyn from North Carolina passed by, walking her dog. She and her husband had traveled to Vicksburg to pick up an RV, and she was excited about that. After hearing about our trip she said, "You guys are gutsier than I am. The people of Louisiana where the Mississippi spills out are clannish, but if they let you in they're very fun people. When we lived there, we had an in because my sister-in-law was married to a Cajun. The people in the bayou were only twenty-five minutes out of New Orleans, but many had never been to the city. They stayed in the bayous and bartered and ate what they could catch. They made little houses along the river. Well, girls, I got to go. Y'all are doin' a once-in-a-lifetime special adventure. Watch for the snakes falling out of the trees. Y'all be safe now."

During breakfast we decided Kitty and I would spend the morning developing our itinerary. We wouldn't try to paddle the following week, which relieved our need for a van support person. Instead we would go to beauty shops or other locations to find women to talk to. Cis and Heidi got on their cell phones and started changing reservations. Afterward, they decided to dress our mascots, Polly and Ariel. They gathered doilies, duct tape, and markers and headed to our room. Kitty and I went back to the lobby.

"We might get makeovers if we go to beauty shops," I said. "Maybe that's the reason my hair needs professional attention."

We viewed the changes that needed to be made in our plans as an opportunity. We weren't clear what that opportunity was, but we knew it would reveal itself.

A while later Heidi came by and said, "If you're interested in all of us paddling tomorrow, Cis and I could search out the boat launches now and we could shuttle a vehicle to a take-out spot for tomorrow."

"Yes," said Kitty. "I like the idea of four of us paddling the nine-mile stretch we saw."

"We'll check it out and let you know," I said. Heidi disappeared down the hall.

Kitty and I again scoured the charts and discussed driving time, vehicle shuttle time, and paddling time. We factored in the airport travel and considered that paddling part of the Yazoo River meant the water would be moving slower than the Mississippi. Then we realized we would have to be driving away from the motel at five thirty in the morning. It was dark outside at that time, and we hadn't factored in breakfast. I said, "The details make the idea of paddling together cumbersome, and my preference is not to do it."

"My preference would be not to do it too," said Kitty. "But it did sound like fun to paddle together."

"Heidi suggested we stay at bed and breakfasts instead of motels or camping," I said. "What do you think of that idea?"

After a long pause Kitty said, "I think we should. It doesn't cost much more compared to motel rooms. A B&B would be a good place to get stories."

"I don't want to give up the camping, though. I think we can connect with women there," I said.

Cis and Heidi joined us with our dressed-up river mascots. Other than the doilies and GoGirl funnel one of them wore as a hat, they were created completely from found objects from the river. Polly's hot-pink

duct tape made her outfit.

Heidi said, "I was thinking that if the two of you want one last paddling day on the Mississippi, we should make that happen. The way things are turning out, Nancy's and my day together on the river was Nancy's last day on the river." .

"You're right," I said. "I just realized that myself."

"I know you have a

thing with this river," said Heidi.

"I appreciate your concern about that, but my thing with this river has changed," I said. "I honestly don't have to be floating on her to finish this journey. Kitty and I've decided we'll focus on putting ourselves in places where we can connect with women. The more we work out the details, the more excited I am about this new opportunity."

"I wouldn't say I'm excited," said Kitty. "It's a change."

"We've been frustrated because we haven't been able to connect with people," I said. "Now what I see is a week where that obstacle has been removed and there's an opportunity to make those connections happen, and I'm excited. The trip is more about connecting with women than paddling. Gwyn's not being able to come back has provided an opportunity for us."

"I get that," said Cis.

After finalizing details, we went to the historic district again for lunch. Our waiter, Dean, was entertaining and funny. Looking at the menu, we Northern girls were confused about local cuisine. Cis helped. "Basically, jambalaya will be served over rice, and gumbo is a soup with seafood, okra, and meats." We ordered salad, burgers, and hush puppies.

We discussed the book *The Help*. "My mother-in-law grew up with black help in Memphis," said Cis. "Even now, in her eighties, she will be talking about somebody and she has to tell me if she is black when it would be fine to leave that detail out and just tell me the story. To point out that someone is black or white is kind of like . . . I can't even find the word."

"It feels like a subtle form of racism," I said.

"Yes," said Cis. "For her it is. We're here because we want their stories from their perspective. Whatever they decide to tell us, it's important that we not color the story one way or another with our own interpretations."

"I find that when I'm writing about someone, I don't mention it if he or she is white, but if a person is of another race, I tend to mention it as part of his or her description," I said. "In telling these stories, am I missing an important piece of the story if I leave that detail out, or am I sharing a piece of information that creates an unintentional stereotype? If I come from a perspective that we are human, that detail shouldn't need to be pointed out."

"For the story's purpose," said Heidi, 'unless the woman says something about her race within her story, including that detail would be relevant if it was relevant to her."

"What color a person is down here has been an important piece of the stories and people's lives," said Kitty.

"The reason I feel I'm conscious of it is that we have the choice to ignore it," said Heidi. "We have that privilege because of the color of our skin."

"When a woman is speaking within a group, she wouldn't necessarily mention her ethnic background because it would be evident," I said.

"Their heritage is another piece of it," said Kitty. "Do they go into the 'white' grocery stores and say 'eeeww' when they look at what we eat, like we do when we see chicken feet?"

"When I worked for the Girl Scouts in the Twin Cities, the staff were given tickets to see an interactive play called Tina and Tony's Wedding," said Heidi. "At different points in the play, when the actors portrayed people doing what people do at weddings, the African American women in our group said, 'Where do they get this crap?' For example, the women couldn't believe anyone would do the chicken dance at a wedding. One of the women said, 'Where did they dream up this stupid play?' The white people in the group told them the play was based on things that are common at white people's weddings. I think there are other things we do that African American women wonder about."

"I'm sure there are," I said.

We spent the afternoon wandering in the shops and made our way to Lesley's patio for the Gathering. Five of Lesley's friends joined us. After meeting everyone, we were seated in a circle. Linda, age seventy-one, was the elder for the evening. I handed her the basket with the tape recorder in it.

Sitting comfortably back in her chair, Linda had an air of confidence about her. She began. "I've always valued myself. I was the first born after my parents were married for six years. My father was thrilled to death to get a little girl and was always thrilled with me. I think that has been a huge influence in my life. I have a tendency to think I haven't done anything specifically wonderful. I have no art talent—but I'm good at clothes. I can pick clothes that match.

"I raised a bunch of children, and just recently I've been able to realize what wonderful kids I have. I was married, had three children, and divorced—not because I wanted to. That was a big time of adversity for me. I always just did things that I had to do. I thought I could, so I did. I also thought that I had three children to take care of, so I didn't have a choice but to handle it.

"My present husband is quite different from the first. He had two little girls. His wife had died. I and two other friends were the bridesmaids in her wedding when they got married. Several years went by before he and I got in touch with each other. We saw each other in February and got married in April. It was frightening to my friends, but not to my parents. I was in Texas, and they were here. I think they were delighted that they didn't have to worry about what they were going to do with me if things didn't work out. They knew him for years, so that felt safe.

"I've had very good women friends. I can remember when I was younger thinking that boys and men were so much more interesting than women. I don't remember when that changed, but at some point I found women far more interesting and easier because you can relate. You don't have to explain everything and then not have it gotten straight. I told my friends in Texas I was getting married, but I wasn't going to tell my parents until we went to California to meet his children. I remember Abby saying, 'I think that's a good idea because, after all, by then you will have seen him twice.' That pretty much is what it amounted to. We have been married now for thirty-three years.

"I must have done a good job in this process of raising my kids. My husband had two girls. One is perfect, and one has got real big problems. Four years ago we ended up with her two young children. My kids took over. That was a real revelation about what fine human beings they were because they were willing to take care of all of this. The first month my daughter said to everybody, 'We are going to have to do something about these children. It's a choice. We either institutionalize these children or their mother. Which will cost us less and be easier?'

"We sent the kids to a boarding school in northern Mississippi. It's a great place, not like your typical boarding school. That was four years ago. Now the older one is out in California with my son, and the younger one is in college. Things seem to be working out.

"I like being here. I was away from Vicksburg. I grew up here until I went to college. It was twenty-five years before I came back. Lesley said that I'm different and that I had only become interesting in the last thirty-something years—after I got rid of my first husband. I love Lesley. She is very honest about what she thinks. That's why we get along. I tried to be like my mother. She was a very lovely, practical, and calm lady. I'm not that—probably why my first marriage didn't work. I'm more like my dad.

"We shouldn't start talking about Daddy. He was brilliant and had personality plus. I had a psychologist friend in Texas who came over to do some work in Vicksburg, and she said that she was really frightened to meet my daddy because she knew my younger brother and me. She said, 'I don't think I really need to be exposed to the personality that I've heard about.' After she thought about it she said, 'I'm just going to put a glass frame around me so I will be protected from this man.' She said later that when she walked into the house and he reached out his hand and smiled, she heard glass shattering. That's how he was.

"For years, I was Daddy's daughter." She smiled fondly. "Then I became my brother's sister. Now I'm my nephew's aunt. I have a lot of strong lovely men in my life. They are lovely, and I'm thrilled to be in that position. That does not make me feel inferior in any way."

Lucile took the basket next. She spoke in a soft confident voice. "I grew up in a fairytale childhood in the country outside of Natchez on part of an old plantation. It was land that had been in the family since the Spanish came in and gave land grants. I grew up with women who always told stories. My grandmother told me wonderful stories. She told me about having to go from Natchez to New Orleans by horse carriage and how they crossed the rivers—the kind of things I wish I had paid more attention to. I just loved them because they were stories.

"We also had wonderful help. I hate to use that word after *The Help* just came out, but they enriched my life. We had a cook, and we used to walk her home and pick cotton with her or drag water up from the well.

"Thinking about communication and how often we get blocked because we don't communicate in the same ways, I think we are afraid. We are afraid that people won't hear what we are trying to say the way we are trying to say it, or they will misinterpret things. You have so much to offer and share—and it doesn't have to be in words.

"My father was a doctor. His father was a doctor, too, and had been in the New Orleans Symphony and played the violin. Papa was very interested in music. From the time I was little we always had music playing, whether it was classical or whatever. My mother would find wonderful things. She found a record about the piano and the harpsichord and their different voices. That's where this whole idea started with me about different voices and how they come together. We heard glorious symphonies of voices and ideas and different ways to communicate or make art, like Lesley does.

"I write. It means the world to me to play with words. I think when we reach this age communication is within reach of all of our fingertips one way or the other. It may not be words. It might be eyes. I think we pay attention better the older we get.

"I was kind of a feral little girl because they turned me loose and let me run through the woods and the pastures. I had a hard time becoming part of town life. The town kids knew each other. I had grown up in the country with my sister, for God's sake. She once told me I was her shadow side. That tells you something about me. Being a child who wasn't from town—and later moving to town—I learned how important it was to express myself. At home everybody knew who I was and what I wanted. They knew what I was afraid of and what my hopes were. Suddenly nobody knew. 'Oh, my God. I have to tell them all about myself.' Then I realized I didn't—they'd figure it out anyway. We communicate whether we mean to or not, and I think that's great."

Lesley took the tape recorder and jumped right in. "I was born in the North, and that's a hard thing to do when you live in the South because of the way people view you. We lived in New York until I was in first grade, and then my parents moved to Alabama. I had a difficult time because I didn't know exactly where I belonged. My parents didn't cook like Southerners. My mother was Hungarian, so she cooked with a lot of paprika, and we didn't eat vegetables that were overcooked. We had a different culture in our house. I remember in first and second grade not feeling a part of the North or the South and having a hard time.

When I got into the fifth grade, somehow something lifted from me, and I felt more a part of it. I found out later that my parents never did. They never liked Birmingham. It was a good thing I didn't know that because I ended up loving it and having a really good childhood. I participated in everything that children do and was a part of what you are supposed to be while growing older.

"I remember in Birmingham you dressed a certain way and acted a certain way. You felt the limitations of the people around you. You really weren't free. The freedom didn't come until Vicksburg. I know we have different cores of people around us, but I feel the freedom to be whoever I want to be. I feel free in Vicksburg. I don't have an answer to why that is because here we are in a small Southern town. It's given me the doors to open to be creative and explore who I am.

"The shop gave me freedom. I was a Southerner who went to college and got married. I always assumed before I went to college that this is how my life would unfold: I would go to college, graduate, marry someone in the North and live in the North. I was wrong on every account. I thought he would wear glasses. I never knew what I was going to do.

"My mother was an artist—and she was a really good artist—so I avoided art because I couldn't compete with her. Of course she would have loved for me to participate in art—and it was inside me—but I didn't. I moved away from it. Then I went to Hawaii. I had married a young naval officer. I took a class at the University of Hawaii and then didn't do anything again. Then I came back to Vicksburg and had children.

"My turning point was when Mike said, 'What if I send five hundred dollars to this woman in California and we put art in our living room?' Eventually the living room got too small, and we went up into the attic. I never planned on having a gallery. I never planned on doing art. I had to because it was in me and around me. It's a force stronger than I am. Over the years the gallery has led me to where I am now, and it has led me to find some pretty wonderful women. People who come into an art gallery are different from those who go into a beauty shop."

"I am so grateful for your gallery, Lesley," began Carol Z. as she took the basket that Lesley handed to her. "I came here two years ago from east Tennessee. My husband and I had a bakery and a restaurant together, and we lost everything. We were in the process of adopting an infant before it was born. We lost our business and our baby within two months of each other.

"My husband got a job here in Vicksburg, and I refused to move for three years. I was so angry at him for the loss of our business because he didn't have the guts to tell me how bad it was. I let him live here, and I stayed in Tennessee. It was two years before I even visited.

"I always had a feeling of not living up to my potential. I was the oldest out of a lot of kids. We were poor, and it was my responsibility to take care of the younger kids. In high school I had to help financially. So I was always feeling inadequate, like I could have done more with my life.

"When I came here, all of a sudden the possibilities of living up to my potential were in front of me. I had no old baggage here. I met lovely people here in Vicksburg who are not judgmental. They are friendly and accepting and willing to let you be who you are without reproach. That's amazing! I had not done anything creative outside of baking and running the restaurant for about thirty years. All of a sudden, I'm painting again, doing all my handcrafts, and doing all kinds of things. I feel free for the first time in many years. I feel the possibility of becoming this person that I thought maybe I could be and wasn't allowed to be.

"I don't have a great relationship with my mother. She is who she is, and I accept her. I also had a wonderful father. Totally different. My mother wasn't Southern. My father was Southern. He was an east Tennessean who was a big ol' teddy bear. He loved all his kids and hugged and kissed us and babied us to death. My mother was standoffish and didn't like any racket. With five kids, that is pretty hard to do. She is trying to be a better person, and I give her credit for that.

"We lost my dad when I was in my middle thirties. I felt like somebody had ripped my guts out. Outside of my father, my husband has loved me the most of anybody in my life. He is a very gentle, wonderful man. He moved me to Vicksburg and left." We laughed. "He is working in Kentucky right now. I'm so grateful to have so many good friends here.

"Maybe it's the group I'm choosing to hang out with. The great thing about being over fifty is you don't really care about those people who don't like you. That was a very freeing thing. I pick out creative, wonderful people. As my niece puts it, she doesn't like beige people. That's what she calls my sister. 'You are just too beige, Mom.' So I pick colorful people who are interesting and fun, and I've been very pleased here.

"I went to the Lebanese church to help with a dinner, and the ladies were all yelling at me. 'How can you do this? Who told you how to do this? I don't know how you know how to do this.' And Miriam was like, 'Carol, I'm so sorry they are yelling at you. I'm so sorry. Poor thing. Poor thing.' I was laughing because I liked it. They are big characters. They criticized me, and I had so much fun."

Carol Z. passed the basket to Amy.

Amy pulled her long dark, graying hair to the side and said, "I've been through a lot for my age. I've been through marriages and have had a lot of heartache through that. One day I was feeling like I didn't want to be around. I thought about my parents. Then I thought about God giving up his son for us. To me that was real special.

"I started to relate it to my parents. I said, 'How did they put up with me?' I thought about how it would affect them if I didn't go on. This was while I was younger. My dad was typical for his generation. He was a lovely man. My mom is very special to me. She said things to me like, 'Just don't worry about what everybody else thinks.' I'm still working on that because I'm very critical of myself.

"I was twenty-nine when I had my first daughter and almost thirty-three when I had my second one. When y'all were talking about your children, it made think of something that made me feel real good. I always feel guilty when I do certain things, and my youngest daughter said, 'Mama, I like that you still try to do things that interest you because a lot of my friends' moms lose themselves when they are mamas.' She knows I like to come and look at the art and do things, and she knows how much I love rock music, which sounds crazy to her friends. She said, 'I want to be like that. I want to be able to be a wife and a mom one day, but I don't want to let go of the things I love.' That meant a lot to me because I was feeling bad until she told me that. I think for her age she is a deep, wise thinker.

"It's like things were meant to happen. I think God puts something in my path, be it a person or an event. I might be flipping through the stations on the TV late at night and something will come on that is not really meant to be inspirational, but something in that particular show is. For instance, I knew I was going to tell my daughters about my past. I wanted them to learn, but I didn't want to do it at an inappropriate time. Well, we were watching the series *Seventh Heaven* about a situation where the kids didn't know something about a past event. I took that as an opportunity that was given to me, and I told them. I used it as a learning experience.

"I said to them, 'I want you to know you don't have to get married if you don't want to. Society says that you have to get married. There are some things I want you to think about. You have to respect the person and have him respect you. You have to be involved with somebody who has the same level of intelligence. I think if you are with someone you can't relate to, it makes marriage difficult.'

"Art and being here have brought a lot to my life. I told Lesley that to me, art is joyful—even if it's a dark piece of art. I used the word joy because I think it's wonderful people can express themselves. I love music and art, and I love to read all the time. I think about how complex I am inside—and how complex all of us are. I thank goodness that we make relationships with other people! If you take all that's inside of you, it's so unbelievable that you can make a relationship or a marriage or whatever with others. That is pretty amazing.

"I think a lot. I think maybe that is why I get critical of myself. I want to be a better person. There are so many things to do and be."

By the time Amy finished speaking, it was very dark. She said she needed to leave, and so did Lucile. We said our goodbyes and continued to enjoy the cool evening out on Lesley's patio. The basket with the tape recorder was set on a table between us. Our conversation turned to Lesley's art gallery as the recorder stayed on.

"I know when I first moved here from Kentucky, I got kind of depressed," said Carol Z. "I'd come up and sit in the gallery because there was color. The color was exhilarating, and it lifted my spirits."

"It's the total confusion of that place that makes everything release, and you just stare," said Linda.

"I don't consider it confusion," said Carol Z. "I am kind of like Lesley. I like all of the stuff."

"You begin to see the layers in the artwork," said Lesley.

"I love it in this place," said Linda, waving her hands around. "In my own home, I wouldn't be crazy like that." Her hands drifted to her lap in a calm manner, like a conductor quieting an orchestra. "I like to leave it to go home to the calm.

"People walk into my house and they see my art. Most of it came from Lesley, except for a few pieces that I got from friends. That's the comment we get, and we have a very unusual house. 'Wow, the artwork.'"

"I am doing something really terrific," said Carol Z. moving toward the edge of her chair and looking directly at Lesley. "I started a new piece of my grandfather, and in thirty minutes it was gorgeous. I am leaving all of the brush strokes in. It is mixed media. I am going to put his poem in the painting. I am real excited about it because it's probably the best thing I have done in a long time."

"Well, you have worked for it," said Lesley.

"When I started my bakery, it was great joy," said Carol Z. "I was a nurse before that. Then my husband turned me into a factory. It was not all wonderful. I spent eighty to one hundred hours a week working, on my feet. I got real heavy and my joints got bad. I cook here for events and things because that's fun. I love it, but I don't want to do it for a living because the bakery took the fun out of cooking."

"Starting art has brought joy to you," said Lesley.

"My mother is a fabulous artist, but she doesn't do it anymore," said Carol Z. "My grandmother and my aunt were artists. It is something I grew up doing, but I put it on the back burner because life was in the way. It's like I didn't think I deserved it."

"You gave yourself permission," said Lesley. "First of all, her husband isn't here now, and she has the freedom."

"My husband is my biggest supporter," said Carol Z. "He doesn't want me to work full time. I work for a lady now part time, but I work there because she's my friend and she's very creative. She is hysterical."

"Linda, where do you find your passion?" asked Kitty.

"I don't know that I do," said Linda, and then she paused for a moment, thinking. "I write. I write really good letters and email. I don't consider myself creative. Communication is a passion for me. It's something I'm thinking about with this little gathering. Every time somebody said something, I thought of something I could have added or responded to. That is where I fit. I get energized by being around people. I'm married to a man who is fabulous around people, but it wears him out. I get home from being around people, and I am recharged."

"You used to say you weren't a people person, but you're a few-people person," said Lesley.

"I'm not a crowd person. I don't like crowds," said Linda. "I can't say what I want to say, and I can't get to people. It's a different atmosphere when you are in a large group than a small one. It is a responding thing, which is where I feel excitement. I don't consider myself artistic."

"I want to challenge that belief system," I said. "If you write amazing letters, that's a lost art that I'd like to see come back around. You are an artist."

Linda giggled and said, "I do write good letters. If someone was in the market for a really good letter writer I'd surely get the job."

"Have you tried poetry or short stories?" asked Kitty.

"I've done some memoir writing because my sister-in-law called me ten years ago," said Linda. "She lives in Louisiana and is a character. She said, 'Do you want to go with me to a writers' workshop?' I said, 'Oh, yeah, that sounds great.' I told my husband that Joann wanted me to go to a writers' workshop in Ireland. He thought that was fabulous because his family was willing to pay for it, so we went. In the process, I became connected to the instructor. We emailed before we went.

"I got there, and the instructor sat us all around a table with a bunch of colors in the middle and a journal. I thought, 'I don't color.' Everybody there was younger than I was. I thought, 'I don't have to say anything here. I am old enough that I can say what I want or not.' Well, this woman was such a fabulous teacher that she made it easy to write. Everybody else was Irish there except my sister-in-law, me, and one other girl from Boston. There were about ten people. She had us write about something, and then she'd say, 'Please read it.' One girl said, 'I am not reading anything, I am not sharing.' Within two hours she was telling everybody everything. She's really a wonderful teacher. We had such a wonderful time we had her come here two years in a row for a writing workshop. I have taken about four workshops from her."

"You are good at keeping lines of communication open," said Lesley.

"That is an art form too," I said, and Linda laughed. "I think people who collect art or hang out at galleries begin to see themselves as not having any creativity because creativity becomes narrowly focused.

There's a whole lot of creativity out there that has nothing to do with picking up a paint brush or drawing anything."

"I have a brother that is off the wall," said Linda.

"Yes you do, Linda," said Lesley and we laughed.

"He has charisma too," said Linda. "He has the same smile as my daddy. We had a family reunion in Texas a few years ago, and he had a friend that read palms. He read my palm and he said, 'You're an artist.' I said, 'No, I am not.' He said, 'Well, yes, you are.' I said, 'No, really, I don't do anything artistic. I'm really good at picking out color for clothes.' He said, 'Well, there you go.'

"I had a friend that always looked wonderful. She had fabulous hair. It didn't matter what she had on, she always looked good. She was attractive, but she wasn't gorgeous or anything. One time I said, 'What? How come?' And she said, 'I know color. I was in California, newly married, but from Maryland. I was miserable, and I didn't have anything to do. I took a Color Me Beautiful class.' She said she went to one class and went home to her closet and everything in there wasn't right. It was a color her mother should be wearing. She had collected all of those colors because she missed her mother who was far away from her. She got rid of all of that and got the right colors and it made all the difference. It's not that you can't wear certain colors, it's that you can wear certain shades of colors."

"The first time I met you, Linda, you walked into the shop and you told Lesley, 'You need to make a sale. I am here to buy a pair of earrings, so don't waste my time,'" said Carol Z. "You looked at me and said, 'I'm not artistic, but I do know how to do accessories.' I started laughing as soon as you left and asked Lesley, 'Who was that beautiful woman with the short hair who always wears earrings?'"

"I think my daddy is why," said Linda. "I don't particularly think of myself as real secure or self-confident, but I was given that."

"Well, you certainly are," insisted Lesley.

"I have a daughter who is also able to speak out," said Linda. "Sometimes you get criticized for that. I've tried to realize where I am and tone it down when it is needed. It's a happy virtue to be able speak."

"Linda is pretty honest," said Lesley.

"I like being honest," said Linda. "That's why Lesley and I get along. Especially after you said I was quite boring until I got a divorce. Good. I felt that way. We've known each other since '63."

"Mike and I were stationed in Hawaii, and my husband was so excited because his friends were coming in," said Lesley.

"Her first husband and I knew each other, since we were boring," said Linda.

"We went to the airport to get Linda and her husband," said Lesley. "After that I told my husband, 'I don't want to spend any time with her ever again.'"

"I had two children and the younger one was five months old and the other one was two," said Linda. "My first child was lovely from the time he was born, easy and so cooperative. All you needed to do was tell him something. The second one was a nightmare. On the trip out, we stopped in California, and my friend wanted to take my oldest child out. I don't know what all she gave him to eat, but by the time we left the next morning he was throwing up all over everything. It was the first time my husband and I argued about who got to keep the baby. By the time we got to Hawaii, he was bordering on dehydration. We had to get something done about it right away. I was a good mother. I think it is a job."

"It's a serious job," I said.

"I did a good job and took care of things like that," said Linda. "It wasn't always as much fun as my children are now. I don't think I particularly liked children. I thought it was a job. I have a really good time with my wonderful kids now. This was fun."

We said goodbye to everyone and went back to our motel. Appetizers were being served in the lobby, so we went down. Carolyn was there talking to two men whom she introduced before she disappeared. Kitty and I sat down with Jerry, a large older man wearing blue-jean coveralls, glasses, and short-cropped hair. He had a big eager smile. Heidi sat down with Jerry's friend, Gordon, known as Rambo. A loud and showy character from Louisiana, Rambo had a ruddy complexion and wore a rolled scarf tied around his forehead along with a wide-brim camouflage hat. Dressed all in black, he had long graying hair that fell below his shoulders.

Jerry was a Civil War enthusiast. He had worked on the oil rigs for twenty-five years and was a liver transplant patient. "I'm in Vicksburg on an adventure to do family genealogy research," he said. "When my aunt died, my sister inherited a Bible with genealogy information in it. The women have laid claim to that Bible. My great-uncle was presented the Bible by his company commander when he was at Camp Moore, Louisiana, where they organized Confederate regiments. He had that Bible on him at the Battle of Chickamauga, and the Bible still has a mini ball in it today where it stopped a bullet and saved his life. I've been able to trace back six branches on my mama's side and my daddy's side. In my family there were four Allen brothers, and all four went to serve. Two came home and two didn't. The two weren't killed. They died of illness. The one that came back with the bullet in the Bible was minus a leg."

"While you do this research are you learning about the women's roles back then?" I asked.

"Some women went with the men," said Jerry. "'Camp followers' they called them. I read about one woman from the South and one from the North that disguised themselves as men and fought next to them in battle. Nobody knew they were women until they were killed in battle and they laid them out to fix them up for burial. One of them was married to a soldier that she was serving with. The Southern woman just wanted to fight."

"Did the camp followers cook for the troops?" asked Kitty.

"Yes, they cooked for the group that their husbands were in," said Jerry. "I didn't read nothin' about kids traveling with them. Most women stayed home and took care of the farm and raised the kids like they would today. We got to run, ladies. It was nice talking with you."

Heidi joined us at our table and said, "I saw Rambo and decided we best stay on his good side." Rambo told Heidi he was French and that his mother could speak good English, but chose not to. He was writing a book and was knowledgeable about the Civil War. His wife, Rose, was murdered five years earlier. "You don't ever want to get a call like that," said Rambo. "She was beautiful like her name. I'm okay with it now, but for six months I had to be led around by the hand."

The appetizers of chips and cheese weren't enough. We went back to our room, ordered pizza, watched TV, and kicked back.

October 14th through 18th

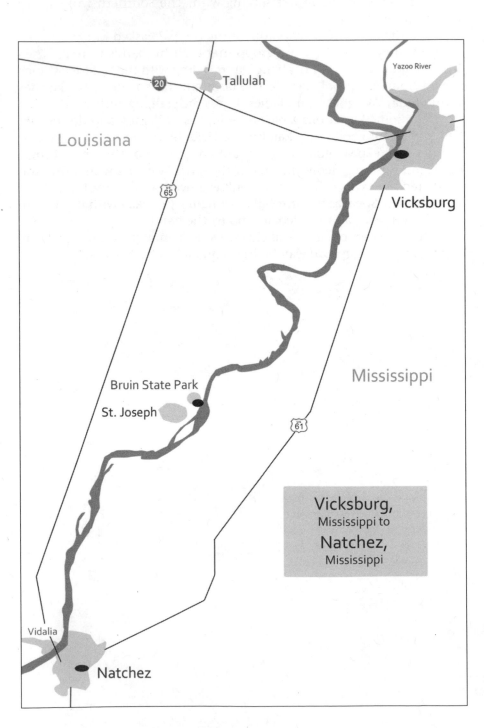

7

NATCHEZ

October 14, Day Twenty-four

Is this how people will feel after reading about our paddling trip: inspired, scared, and confused? I wondered.

I woke up early to update Facebook and catch up on email, and I stumbled upon an article on the Internet about Michele Baldwin, age forty-five, who was embarking on a stand-up-paddleboard expedition in India. Michele had terminal cervical cancer. Her story was inspiring (taking on seven hundred miles of the Ganges River), scary (paddling in a foreign country—the Mississippi is in my back yard), and confusing (to me, at least, because I don't think that's how I'd want to spend my last days, although honestly I don't know what I'd do in her situation). Our missions were similar, but reading Michele's story allowed me to experience undertaking a journey as a reader, not a participant.

I understand the urge that becomes a driving force that brought her to do it; it's a voice that grows louder with time. The web page stated, "She hopes to raise $100,000 for the Global Initiative Against HPV and Cervical Cancer and to inspire others to live to the end." [Back in Minnesota I learned that Michele completed her paddle and returned home November 26, 2011. "I felt the best when I was paddling," said Michele. "When I was paddling, I wouldn't feel pain . . . Every day on the river was certain; not like life with cancer . . ." Her final message was simple: a wish for all women to prevent themselves from fighting the painful battle she was slowly losing. "If you are moved by my story, go get a pap."]

Kitty returned from a walk through the Vicksburg National Military Park. "I felt heartbroken walking in there," she said. "I think I have an understanding of why young men go to war with exuberance. They get caught up in the war fever, the camaraderie. They're excited to go off and prove themselves. Then they get to the battlefield, like that one in the park, and the horrible reality sinks in—but it's too late. There are so many headstones over there it's overwhelming. There are monuments for each of the states with the names of those who died.

"Yesterday when we drove around Vicksburg, I had a sense of oppression and the city's being connected to something in history. The Civil War was pivotal, but it was war. It's hard on everybody and everything. It makes no sense. It's sad. There's a huge arch in the park, and across the top it states the arch is a monument to the National Reunion of the Union and Confederate soldiers. It's dated October 1917, which was during World War I. The city put up a monument to a war while our country participated in another one. It doesn't make sense to me."

Kitty and I went to the lobby for breakfast and met Mike, a fellow Minnesotan. He was riding the length of the Mississippi on his bicycle. He had started in September at Lake Bemidji in Minnesota without an itinerary. He liked the freedom of stopping when he was drawn to. He observed people he saw along the way who didn't have much, but they had positive attitudes.

"Their friendships are tight and long lasting, and family is important," he said, describing the people he had met. "Parties are spontaneous and you don't need an invitation." Mike told us he rode sixty to seventy miles each day.

At breakfast we read Heidi's journal entry:

Preparing to leave my first leg of this journey (unless you count the sixteen months of planning as a leg) there are a lot of themes swirling:

  • I'm fortunate to be in a position to do this. I can dream and reach for anything no matter how far-fetched, but I'm aware there are many privileges in my life that make it easier than if I'd been born into some of the communities we are passing through.

  • The River is beautiful. Paddling the River was a means to an end—meeting women and hearing their stories. That's not as true in the South as up North. It's a conversation starter that helps form connections.

  • I have seen fewer people paddling—especially Sunday when we only saw two or three barges—than I do most days in the Boundary Waters. Yet the sounds and signs of people are present. The woods are beautiful; the birds sing all the time; the water is full of life.

  • Everyone has a story to tell, if you give them opportunity and are open. I need to make myself more open. When I sit and listen many people share a lot in a short amount of time. I want to practice being attentive to folks who are less likely to open up.

  • I feel fortunate to have amazing women, opportunities, and role models in my life.

  Heidi

Carolyn came to say goodbye. "Here's wisdom to share," she said. "Never cook good because you'll be expected to do that all the time. If you cook poorly, you'll say, 'Honey, do you want me to make dinner for you tonight?' and he'll say, 'Oh no, honey, let's go out.' Luckily, I got a husband who's smart. He lets me do the finances; he just brings in the money. He makes the money, and I make him happy. If men are unhappy, believe me, you're unhappy too."

The four of us went to the coffee shop before Cis and Heidi left for the airport. Cis came out of the bookstore next door and handed me an early birthday present, a copy of *Rising Tide*, a book about the flood of 1927. It felt odd to say goodbye to Cis and Heidi. Kitty and I took a seat at an outdoor table with our tea. Grif pulled in and joined us briefly. Cis had met Grif in the bookstore the day before. He was riding his motorcycle on a personal journey along the river. Inspired by our trip, he gave us a copy of *The Final Summit*. "My trip is going in an amazing way," he said. "Everything keeps falling into place. I know you'll like this book. It's motivational and thought provoking without tying its message to any religion. It hones in on what we were taught by our parents about doing the right thing and being accountable. That's weaved into a story that makes you laugh I stumbled across it. It reminds me of *Ishmael* and books by the guy who wrote *The Seven Habits*. Read it and pass it on. Have a safe trip."

"When it comes to meeting interesting people, this has been a magical trip," I said to Kitty. My comment captured the attention of a silver-haired woman with a Canadian accent sitting at the next table. She asked if she could join us. Her name was Camille, she said. I gave her one of our brochures.

"'Now is the time for the feminine to come forward,'" she read from the front of our brochure. "What does that mean?"

"Do you know about the thirteen grandmothers?" I asked. She shook her head no. "There has been a prophecy in cultures the world over for centuries that thirteen grandmothers would come together and mark the beginning of the healing of the world by women. Those thirteen met in 2004. What they determined after meeting was that they were representative grandmothers. Grandmothers the world over in different capacities were coming together to heal the world in ways that aren't indicative of how men think the world ought to be healed. The Dalai Lama recently made a statement that it will be Western women who step forward to heal the mess we're in. Western women are privileged, and they have time and opportunities that women elsewhere don't."

"I might be totally off," said Camille, sitting back in her chair, "but that's too far out for me. We create our own worlds. It's our mind that creates suffering. It's our need to control that creates pain and suffering, which are a part of life. This is not a feminine culture thing."

"The concept is that men have had a lot of opportunities, and things aren't getting better," I said. "Perhaps it's time for us to step up."

"I'm on board with women stepping up," said Camille. "The other day I was flipping through the channels and noticing how few female voices we have. Okay, you got Rachel Maddow on MSNBC, but that is one voice.

"The reason we have wars and why we have to continue wars, practically speaking, is our dependency on oil. That is the only darn reason we're in the Middle East. It's not to bring democracy. Forget that. We were there and got kicked out in the '70s because they said, 'Hold it! We can make our own money.' There are European countries that are totally independent of oil. They push for that and put their resources in it. Here, one company failed with solar. So what? Think about flying. Before the first flight took off, there were a lot of failures."

"Just think of the destruction we're doing with our own exploration here with the fracking," said Kitty, reaching for her tea.

"Oh, the fracking," said Camille. "That awful natural gas thing. People are uninformed here, maybe here more than elsewhere. In Minnesota, you have public radio. That's a different culture with fresh ideas."

"You know what the first question is that we get from everybody?" asked Kitty. "'What do your husbands think about this?' I think we are scary to people down here."

"Yes," Camille said confidently. "A—you are white. B—you are women. And C—you are walking outside of the box. If you were a Baptist from Minnesota, that would be a different story. Who cares? When I came here, if you were twenty-five and not married that was the worst. You're an old maid already. It's traditional here.

"Talk about feminism! When we go to vote next in this state, 'personhood' will be on the ballots. In other words, when does life become life? That is on the ballot! They call it personhood. As it is, some pharmacists have trouble giving out birth control. If we are going to protect life, they say, you shouldn't take birth control. If this takes precedence, I'm scared about what will happen. They're attacking abortion. It's interesting that you feel that tension down here.

"If we want to change the world, we need to have our own businesses. We got to start taking control—not be in the victim role. Speaking of business, I got to get back to work."

After Camille left, Kitty and I headed to Bruin State Park near St. Joseph, Louisiana, where we would camp for two days of rest. In the van Kitty said, "I think we need to not be so noticeable and different."

"Well, we do stand out," I said. "We've got kayaks hanging all over and funny-looking dolls in the front window."

"That's it," said Kitty, reaching for Polly and Ariel. "They're going in the back so they're less visible."

"Hey, there's a beauty shop," I said. "What do you think?"

"Why not?"

"I'm excited and anxious about this."

"Why?"

"I don't have the best experiences in beauty shops, and the introvert in me is anxious about collecting stories," I said. "This takes me out of my comfort zone."

We walked into the beauty shop and met two hairdressers, Hannah May and Loretta. The shop was busy, but they had time to do my hair, Loretta said. I told them I had a temporary color in it that needed to come out. They indicated that would not be a problem, but they were confused about why I would ever want to go back to having my gray show. Hannah May was curious about where we were from. "I can tell y'all aren't from here."

I took a seat in her chair, explained our trip, and told them we were interested in their stories. I asked if we could record our conversation.

"It's too bad Anita isn't here," said Hannah May. "That girl has a story and can weave quite a yarn too. She's suffered a lot of loss in the past two years. She lost her mother and her husband. Would you believe they both had cancer? Then she lost her favorite aunt two weeks after her husband died. Then her dog got hit by the mailman. Have you ever heard such a sad story?"

"That's overwhelming," I said, wondering if she was paying attention to what she was doing to my hair.

"Overwhelmin'," agreed Hannah May. "That's what it is." Studying my head with a confused look, she paused a moment and ran her fingers through my hair. Then she began putting some goop on it. "Her husband had liver cancer," she continued. "They told him twelve months because there wasn't much they could do. He wasn't a candidate for a transplant. I think Anita held out hope her husband would get a liver when he got bad enough. It was sad. He was diagnosed with hepatitis C and went through treatment for that, but it didn't work. That's why he got cancer."

"Why don't you tell them about you?" said Loretta.

"What do I have to talk about?" said Hannah May.

"Your kids," said Loretta. "You always talkin' about how to raise up our kids."

Hannah May put me under the dryer and said, "I think it's good to make life easier for your children than the way we had it, but we make life too easy. Kids today don't know what it's like to get their hands dirty, unless they grew up on a farm or if their mama or daddy liked gardenin'. I think that's why we have a lot of immigrants in the U.S. Kids today won't pick vegetables, and the vegetables have to be picked. Where's the happy medium of lettin' them get dirty and lettin' them know computer? I don't know.

"Bein' a parent is a hard thing. There's no darn book that goes with it. What's good for one kid isn't always what's good for the other kid. One of my girls is my lady, and one is my tomboy. One has always messed with my hair and doin' the makeup thing, like her mama. The other is like my sister. Give her blue jeans, soap, and water, and she's fine. I like gettin' dressed up whenever I get a chance. Those two are always in blue jeans. The bad part is you get too comfortable in those clothes, and when they do get dressed up, they feel more awkward.

"You have to let children fall down and brush them off. Sooner or later, you have to say no more brushin' off."

"You want your hair done, sweetie?" Loretta asked Kitty. "I got time."

Kitty had been watching Hannah May work on my hair. She looked at me, paused, and said, "No, I think I'm fine."

"Nowadays, grandparents aren't as close as they used to be," said Loretta. "Now they have to go where the job is, and Grandma and Grandpa stay until they retire, and then they move if they can. You don't have family involvement like we used to, even way back in the frontier days."

"One thing you can quote me about is what I used to say to my children," said Hannah May. "I'd say, 'That's okay. You can be mad at me, but I'll always love ya, no matter what you do. I'll always love ya. Right now you don't like Mama, and Mama don't like you.'

"Loretta here is big into her church," Hannah May said.

"Yes, I'm one of the team leaders," said Loretta proudly.

"What kind of team?" I asked.

"We set up for funerals and weddins and such," said Loretta. "I like to be there and do it right. I like to be sure people get the best possible treatment. I started doin' it to honor my mom. She was big into helpin' at the church before she died. I feel I'm makin' a difference in a small way. People need other people to hold them up at a funeral. Oh, heck, sometimes I think the family at a weddin' needs more holdin' up." Everyone laughed.

Hannah May took me in the back and rinsed out my hair, and then she led me back to her chair. "I thought of somethin' to share," said Hannah May, holding the hair dryer pointed above my head, lost in her thoughts. "This is fun. We gonna be in a book! Oh, yeah. What I wanted to say: I'm a grandma, and it's the best. The funny thing is that when you're at their house or havin' them at your house, you'll hear your kids sayin' somethin' to their kids that you said to them and you go, 'I know I've heard that somewhere before.'" We laughed.

Hannah May looked at my hair and I was unable to determine exactly what was going through her mind, but she looked concerned and slightly alarmed. She said with a reassuring tone I wasn't sure I believed, "That looks just like your natural color, but I think we better trim the edges."

We were at the beauty shop longer than anticipated, and my hair was no longer red. I was concerned about my hair because it felt extremely dry. Hannah May had stripped all of the color out of it, including my normal gray. It wasn't until I was in the car and saw the color in the light of day that I realized how severe the change was. I would need time to adjust to the new color, which was a sickly shade of blonde. It was not at all what I had in mind, but we planned to go to another beauty shop, so there was hope for correcting it. We stopped at K-Mart, and I bought a black knit hat to wear that sat low on my head and covered most of my hair.

Back on the road, we saw several churches in a row, and I became fully aware we were in the Bible Belt. We stopped for a quick bite to eat at Burger King. I said, "I think what happens when someone like me is raised Christian and has a bad experience is that the church gets pushed away. I know when I pushed the church away, I pushed away valuable things too. When I try to go back, I get stuck in the dogma that goes against my grain. What I did take away with me was the wisdom that's at the core of what Jesus taught and how he led his life."

"I understand what you're saying," said Kitty. "I believe every religion has the same beliefs at the core. There's that saying, 'Take what fits and leave the rest.' There are pieces of each religion that make sense to me. There are pieces that don't. The cross is a powerful symbol, and it's a symbol of something that I embrace less. I find it fascinating that African Americans, taken from their homes in Africa and brought here, have such a strong faith in Jesus Christ. When they were in Africa, I can't imagine Jesus Christ was their savior."

"Well, you're in the Bible Belt, honey," said a woman with a thick southern drawl from the next table. "We have over two hundred churches in this dinky town and no independent newspaper. What does that tell you? I would say the Bible Belt is like this: You have a belt, and what does a belt do? It holds everything in place, right? Nothing goes in and nothing comes out. We hold on to the status quo. People are entrenched in their religion. It's part of their identity here. Sorry to butt in, but there are things I can't keep my big mouth shut about. My name is Virginia."

"I never put religion in that context before," said Kitty.

"It is a lifestyle," said Virginia, standing up. "I'm not religious. I'm drawn to Buddhist principles. To me Mother Nature is as close as I can get to defining God. How can you put this life force into these compartments and put our human proscriptions on it? That is powerful. There are a lot of churches, but you won't find many women preachers—not down here in the South anyway. I sure wish I could stay and talk with you girls more. Y'all got my blood goin'. Y'all have a good day."

"I wish she could have stayed," said Kitty. "I bet she had a lot more to say." Kitty took a drink of water. "I think men are afraid of a woman doing something that they wouldn't want them to do. I don't know if it's universal or what, but they're afraid of what we represent."

"What do you think we represent?" I asked.

"Somebody they might not be able to control," said Kitty. "Somebody with a mind of her own. That concept has popped up a few times in conversations down here. Lesley implied it when she asked you what your husband thought."

"There are roles that we're supposed to be following," I said. "Doing something like this trip means we are not in our roles. Do they think we'll shatter their worlds?"

"We do shatter them by being around them," Kitty said. "We put a little chink in it and they think, 'Oh, the possibilities.' We might rub off on their women."

"There certainly is something to that," I said. "However, we have met a lot of men who indicated they don't think that way."

We drove to Bruin State Park on the edge of Bruin Lake. The lake was an oxbow of the Mississippi. When we checked in, the attendant told us we could swim and kayak. When she said swim, our eyebrows went up. Kitty and I looked at each other and whispered, "Alligators." Our camp was nestled among tall cypress trees at the edge of the lake next to a boardwalk that went over the lake. Some of the cypress trees in the lake had stood there since before the Spaniard Hernando de Soto traveled through the region in the 1540s. The park was established in 1928 as a fish hatchery. The terrain of the park clearly showed the abandoned fish ponds.

"I'm going to have to get over it regarding alligators," said Kitty.

"What do you mean?" I asked.

"I've been nervous," Kitty said. "I agree with what I've heard that if we leave them alone, they will leave us alone unless we surprise them. Where are we going to surprise them? I don't think we will, unless we pull up in some swamp somewhere, which I'm not inclined to do."

"You mean like going into the swamp and bayou with our friend Leonard after the trip is over?" I asked. "I am looking forward to our little alligator hunt."

"I forgot about that on the agenda," laughed Kitty. "I don't think I'll be going swimming here though."

It was a picture perfect evening. We heard our neighbors having a good time and watched a heron across the water. We looked forward to our first real rest day since we left home.

October 15, Day Twenty-five

I was drawn to the pier after watching a woman intently fishing from it. She wore a gray sweatshirt and had short gray hair. She was engrossed in her fishing and didn't realize I had walked up. She dropped her little jig into the water and moved it around looking for the fish. I startled her by saying hello.

"I'm sorry," I said. "I was trying not to scare you and send you flying into the water." A big friendly smile crossed her face. "What are you fishing for?"

"White perch," she said with a thick Cajun accent. "Looky here! Do you know what a white perch is?" She showed me a bucket with several large fish in it.

"We don't have anything I know of as white perch in Minnesota," I said. "These look like crappies."

"Crappies is the right name for it," she said. "I use a jig. They aren't biting too good this morning. That's one good eatin' fish. I love to catch the crappie."

"They don't come that size up North," I said. "Where are you from?"

"About 150 miles from here, west of Baton Rouge."

"My name is Nancy. What is yours?"

"Lucy," she said. "Usually when they bite they get hooked. They got a tender mouth and it can tear out. If you can hook 'em just right, you get 'em. That bait's like a little minnow."

"You got enough to make us a good meal?" A lanky older gentleman joined us on the pier. "They got a fishin' tournament on this lake today. Where you from?" he asked.

"Minnesota," I said.

"Oh, I knew you wasn't a coony," said the man, using a slang word for someone from Cajun country. They both laughed.

"You can look at her and tell she ain't no coony," said Lucy.

"Just listen to her," he said, chuckling.

"When we go north, they want me to talk so they can listen to my accent," said Lucy. "We went into the Smoky Mountains and this lady that was traveling too said, 'I love the way you talk.' I said I was from way down south, and then she asked me, 'What nationality are you?' I said, 'You hear me talk and you can't tell?' She said, 'Not exactly.' I said, 'Cajun.' She said, 'I wanted to say that, but I didn't want to offend you.' Now why would I be offended by somethin' like that?"

"I was born and raised south of here and spent my life working in west Texas," said the man. "I retired and moved to a big lake south of here at the Toledo Bend Reservoir. It's the best fishing lake in the world."

"Toledo Bend," Lucy said. "Yeah, you done some fishin' there."

"I got pictures," he said. "I still hold the lake record for a white perch. It was four and a half pounds."

"I think the state record is five pounds and something," said Lucy, grinning. "I'd like to catch one that weighs about ten pounds. I remember years ago my daddy caught a yellow-head catfish on a taut line."

"Do you know what a taut line is?" he asked me.

"No."

"You string a line from here to them trees down yonder," he said. "You can have fifty hooks per line." He looked around the campground. "Where's your old man? Is he in bed?"

"My old man ain't with me," I answered. "I'm traveling with a friend."

"Damn," he said. "With another lady?"

"Yep," I said.

"Oh, hell. Look out, Louisiana," he exclaimed loudly. "Look out!"

"Why look out Louisiana?" I asked, laughing.

"What are you traveling in?" he asked.

"We're the ones in the van with the kayaks," I said.

"That y'all right here in the tents?" he asked pointing.

"Yeah," I said.

"Which way are you next?" asked Lucy.

"We've been paddling the Mississippi," I said. "We're taking a week off from paddling, and then we're going to paddle Bayou Lafourche."

Lucy stopped jiggin' to turn and look at me and asked, "Are you familiar with the Mississippi River?"

"Yes ma'am," I said. "I paddled it from the headwaters to Greenville."

"That's a dangerous river," said Lucy, sizing me up with her eyes. "I'm from around the Atchafalaya, and I wouldn't go on that either." She turned back to jiggin' and turned right back. "How do you like Cajun food?"

"I don't think we've had real Cajun food yet," I said. "What should we order?"

"I bet you never ate a frog leg," said Lucy.

"No, I haven't," I said.

"Oh, we got good ones down here," said Lucy nodding her head. "A lot of people don't eat that because it's a frog."

"Do you know what a crawfish is?" he asked.

"Yes, I do," I said. "I haven't eaten one though."

"I could eat a seafood platter right now," said Lucy, licking her lips.

"Frog legs, stuffed crabs, stuffed shrimp, crawfish—with a good beer," he said.

"Frog legs look like a little chicken leg," said Lucy. "They're delicious. In season they have the soft-shell crabs. Have you ever heard Cajun music?"

"Yes, I have," I said. "My husband and I like to dance to it."

"I love it," said Lucy.

"I didn't catch your name," I said to the man.

"I didn't throw it," he said, smirking.

"Aw, his name is Gene," said Lucy.

"All around me was Cajuns," said Gene. "My favorite one was Miss Brusard. That woman could cook. Her husband was a piano player and he died. Boy, everybody dies. When you get around old people, they die.

When you get old, you die. That's what I come to conclusion."

"Is that what you come to conclusion?" I kidded.

"I made seventy in August," said Lucy. "I'm enjoyin' life as long as I can."

"Where is your partner?" Gene shouted toward our camp. "She still sleepin'?"

"Yes. Well, she was," I said.

"We ought to go over and kick her butt," said Gene. "I could help. How come your husband didn't come with you? He really let you two girls hit the road, huh?"

"Yep," I said.

Gene headed back to camp hollering at the guys a couple of campsites down to get the coffee ready 'cause he was on his way.

"That man can talk," said Lucy. "Can't shut him up, oh Lord."

Gene returned with a large stack of photos and said, "Get over here and look at these." They were of fish, his kids and grandkids, and his garden. While he told me about his pictures—mostly about the fish and his pride and joy, the ninety-pound catfish he caught—Lucy quietly gathered her fish and headed back to her camp. A stack of photos later I said, "I'm going to see if my roommate is stirring yet," and left him standing on the pier.

At breakfast, Kitty and I decided not to drink the water from the park. It tasted and smelled like mold. The air had a moldy odor too. We quietly looked out over the lake. Gene walked up and told us a story about an alligator that used to be in the lake that was a "big'un" and said, "I sure am glad to see y'all enjoyin' yourself. What problems me is how the hell you got away from your ol' man by yourselves."

"I just asked him," I said.

"You tell him?" said Gene.

"I didn't tell him," I said. Kitty was laughing. "Maybe he wants me gone for a little while. You never know."

"It don't hurt when a pair breaks up," Gene said. "Do you ever turn over in those things?" he asked, indicating the kayaks.

"On purpose, yes," I said. "We do it to learn how to get back in. I haven't turned over when I didn't mean to."

"They will turn over," Gene said. "You know that? I seen 'em comin' out of the water lookin' like a drenched rabbit turnin' one of those over. I was raised on the Tensaw River. Back when I was raised, you never heard of a boat motor. We paddled boats then." Like a hyper child who can't stay in one place for long, Gene headed to another campsite.

Cypress knees grew high enough to trip us around the concrete pad the picnic table sat on. The shore was lined with what they called lilies. Stems rose three to four feet from the base. A single V-shaped leaf stretched more than a foot across. The cypress towered above us on land and in the lake. The squirrels ate in the trees and pelted us with debris.

I went for a run. On my way back into the park, not twenty feet from me, a falcon dropped out of the sky and grabbed a large squirrel. They tussled at the base of a cypress tree. The falcon repeatedly attempted to take off while the squirrel hung on to the tree and bit at the falcon. The squirrel was either too heavy or too feisty. The falcon let go and flew away. The squirrel leapt onto the trunk of the tree and shook like a dog shaking off water and then disappeared up the tree.

We spent the day relaxing. Out of respect for those in the Bible Belt, we decided it might be helpful to neutralize some of the symbolic items we typically used at Gatherings. Here, we wouldn't use the fan; instead, we'd use a basket with the tape recorder. We would call our fire a Peace Fire and drop the word sacred. We decided we'd also go out to get women's stories instead of hoping the women would come to us. The beauty shop experience was helpful for getting stories, but my hair had taken a beating.

A couple came over to our site and the man said, "Yesterday when y'all came in, I told my wife I need to talk to you." He introduced himself as James. "I been working on her about getting a kayak. I want to get a good one." The woman shook her head no.

"These are Current Designs, and they work great for us," I said.

"Y'all paddlin' to New Orleans?" asked James's wife.

"To Grand Isle," I said.

"Not much left of Grand Isle after Katrina," she said. "How'd you get here?"

"We've been paddling the Mississippi and this seemed like a nice place to spend a couple of nights," I said.

"We live across the lake and like to camp here," said James. "I don't know if you've seen the sandbags over there. I worked with the Corps and other groups for four weeks. I was finding sand boils and they were baggin' them. We had four teams. It was bad. We had sand boils that blew up in here that was as big as y'all's van."

"What's a sand boil?" I asked.

"The river was up on the levee," said James. "Where the river comes from the north, and especially where there's a bend, there's unrelenting pressure. The river channels water underneath the levee and it erupts on the other side like a mini volcano. When the sand boils first start, they look like ants built a hill, then water boils out. They continually get bigger and bigger and bigger. Some of them will get away from you if you don't watch out. There were over forty sand boils in that small area of the park that we bagged. We bag around them until we can get enough height to put back pressure on it."

James showed us a video on his phone of the erupting boils that they had contained with sand bags. "You don't want to see sand or clay. If you see clay coming out of there you might as well pack up and get out. It's eroding the core of the levee and channeling another river path. It did that north of here in Lake Providence and took out twelve thousand acres. They think the river changed its course there. When the USGS checked the water level in the agricultural fields where the river broke the old levee and came around, it was 110 feet deep. We're so close to the river that if we lose it here, all of this," he indicated the land between the river and the lake, "will be taken out."

"The river could channel back into this?" asked Kitty, indicating Lake Bruin.

"It could if it wanted to," said James. "Because of the way the levee is structured, it [the water] would follow the river down until it found another way back in. The river will spread out like it did before the levee was here. Sand boils are scary. We worked fourteen and sixteen hours a day. We had two major ones in this parish. One of them north of here pumped over three hundred yards of sand underground."

"It's like an underground river," said Kitty.

"Yeah," said James.

"So the channels the boils create undermine the levee, and the levee could drop away?" I asked.

"When the river is high and the water level over here is low, water is going to seek its level," said James. "It will start saturation below the levee. The soils here are layered, and there are natural levees formed of sand by the river's movement. When it gets saturated underneath, you have water that channels like an aquifer. It starts pumping sand out. The more pressure it channels underneath, the greater the chance the levee will collapse because you got an opening underneath. That's what happened north of Lake Providence."

"So what happens to the main channel of the river?" asked Kitty.

"Eventually it will be something like this," he said, indicating the oxbow that created Bruin Lake. "I do environmental water work for LSU."

James' son interrupted our conversation and pulled James back to their camp. Kitty grabbed her journal and I my sketchbook, and we sat in the shade on the fishing pier. Boats cruised the lake and floated a few feet from us as anglers competed in a bass tournament. The pier ran parallel to the shoreline through tall cypress trees growing from the water. The water was calm and reflected the blues of the sky and greens of the trees across the lake.

Cypress knees encircle the trees like children around their mother. Knees and trees alike bear the same gray-brown stringy-textured bark. The knees are aerial roots that enable the tree to breathe. The trunks are wide where they emerge from the water. Vertical crevices start at the base, rising up and flattening back into a smooth trunk a few feet above the water. The cypress leaves reminded me of cedars up North. Their coloring showed tinges of fall's oranges and golds. The sweet sound of birds drifted in the air.

At the base of one cypress trunk was an unusual formation that looked like a child peeking out from the tree with one arm extended. A frog disappeared into a miniature grotto by the child's legs. I expected a magical water fairy or wood gnome to pop out and perch on the child's extended arm. Kitty was reading *The Final Summit*, which Grif had given us, and she shared a quote with me. "Together you will convene with the opportunity to examine the accumulated wisdom of the past in order to determine your future." Those words summed up our trip—an amazing opportunity few would have. We were convening with women and accumulating wisdom. Ultimately our futures would be determined by the wisdom or lack of wisdom we acquired and how that wisdom was applied. I stared out at the water and felt grounded. I hadn't felt this grounded in a while.

I went back to camp, and Lucy came to our site to ask about our kayaks. I explained our trip and asked if she would let me interview her. She hesitated for a moment and then agreed to sit with me for fifteen minutes. We took a seat and Lucy began. "I was born in south Louisiana. Not all the South is swampland. I grew up near Ramah. We was poor people. The boat my daddy had was a little one-room houseboat, and that was all we had until later years when we moved off the water. I remember this one place where I was born. It's in the Grand River flats. We had nothing when we lived on the houseboat. That's why I thank God today for what I have. I can sit here right now and laugh about those times. It wasn't comical then, but it is now to think of how we was brought up.

"We played with the other kids in their boats. We didn't have nothin' for play. We didn't know what readin' was—and you know I love to read now. We fished—and you know I love to fish. Fishin' is a gift for me. Ain't nobody that can fish like I do. Everybody tells me I can catch fish where there ain't no water, but that's impossible.

"The first day of school, we went in a speedboat, like a crew boat. For a whole bunch of kids that was the school bus—the school boat. The school had one big long desk, and we sat at the same seat bench. Sometimes we had lunch to bring, sometimes we didn't, but we had to go to school. That was the good days and good times. All the family was together.

"When we lived on the houseboat, we took a bath in the river. I'm scared of snakes. I believe if I had a gun and somebody put one on me, I'd shoot him, that's how scared I am of snakes. How I survived back then I'll never know. They're everywheres.

"When we'd be cleanin' house—this will freak you out when I tell you this—when we get ready to mop the floor, we take the mop, and we walk out on the back of the porch and stick it in the water and go back and mop the floor. It was clean. Everythin' was clean. I have people ask me, 'Could you go back and live like that today, Lucy?' I could if I had electricity, runnin' water, and a bathtub. Today they have houseboats that have all the good stuff. I probably still be livin' back there if I had them conveniences. That's the way it was with the people raised on the bayou.

"My daddy was a commercial fisherman. My oldest brother fished for a livin' and he made a great livin', he did. He raised six kids. He bought him a home and land, all from fishin'. It was in his blood. He knew how to do it. My daddy fished all his life; that I can remember.

"When we lived on the houseboat, a fish boat would come and bring the groceries and pick up the fish. Everybody was fishin', and this big ol' boat would come and buy the people's fish. He'd bring groceries like lard, flour, cornmeal, potatoes—the main stuff that you have to have, like beans. I don't know how I could eat a bean today." She smiled mischievously. "Oh, I love beans. It'd be ten days sometimes before he'd come back again. If you runned out of somethin', you go bum off the neighbors.

"My daddy had what we called a putt-putt boat. The motor in the boat is inboard. That's what my daddy moved the houseboat with. The houseboat didn't have a motor. This is funny now: You couldn't move the houseboat goin' downstream because the houseboat would run over you. The boat pullin' it couldn't go fast enough to stay ahead of the houseboat." She laughed.

"I was small, but I can remember this well. The people would move to one spot because that's where the fish were bitin'. Everybody—all the houseboats—would gang up right there. First thing you know, fish wasn't bitin' no more, and everybody would gang up in another place, tie up the houseboats, and everybody start fishin' 'cause that's where the fish were bitin'. We did that so many times. I'd get mad. I'd get tired and aggravated because we moved so much. Most of the time where they tied the houseboats there was no land.

"I can just see me as a grown woman livin' on one of those houseboats with three or four kids. I'd be pullin' my hair right out of my head with those kids. No land for 'em to get out and play. I don't know how the kids didn't fall in the river and drown, to tell you the truth. It's still a mystery to me. There was six of us, three boys and three girls. I remember Mama would nail little boards across the door to keep the little ones from crawlin' out. All the folks that lived on houseboats had a bunch of kids. You get busy doin' somethin' and one of 'em kids'd be in the river before you knew it, and the parents would never know it. You got four or five runnin' around makin' noise—and people had dogs. None of 'em drowned. God was with 'em.

"They had so many houseboats in there it looked like a city at night." She leaned forward with excitement in her eyes. "There was so many lights, kerosene lamps. It was a big lake, and we were sittin' in the middle of it.

"There used to be this old black lady named Mattie. She was a midwife. As far back as I can remember, she was the onlyest black person in that whole country. They come up missin' if any showed up. They just wasn't there. This old black lady would live with the white people. She had to live with the white people 'cause there weren't no more n----rs. She'd live with one family until their baby was born, and she'd deliver their baby. When the mama got well enough to do for herself, she'd move to the next white family where there was a woman that was pregnant. She moved to my mama's, and she delivered me. I remember that old lady. You know how long ago that was? I can still remember her in my mind. I don't know what ever happened to her. I can close my eyes and see that old lady. She was good. She was old back then. She probably lived her time out.

"When we moved off the water, that's when me moved to Ramah. We moved in a house, but we still didn't have runnin' water and didn't have no electricity. We managed because we had love there. If it hadn't been for that, we wouldn't have survived.

"That was when my mother and daddy split up. That was the bottom line. We didn't have nothin'. Where we moved to was a lot of our people. We finally got electricity. We didn't have no bathrooms, and we had to carry water to bathe. There was four kids at home. We had this #3 washtub we took a bath in. You was lucky if you got to take a bath first. I wasn't always the first, but I tried to be.

"When my daddy and mother separated, my little brother was just three years old. We seen my daddy all the time, but he never did help us. He never gave us anythin'. Course he never did have anythin' to give us, either.

"My mother remarried, and he was good. He loved us too. He didn't have a whole lot either, but he took care of my mom and my little brother, who was the baby. When my mama married my step-daddy, most of us were big enough to take care of ourselves.

"Most of my people lived right close to the water like this," she said, indicating the lake a few yards away. "It was Grand River. I was still young. Our people were there, my mama's sister and brother, the onlyest whole sister and brother that she had. She had a half sister that lived there and lots of friends that live in what I call one-room huts. They weren't houses. They was all lined up. We lived in one and my grandmother and mother's mother lived in one and right on down.

"When we'd visit, we'd walk the levee. The kids would go play, and we had a little school there. We'd walk to school. My first husband's mother was the cook at school. I know now it was the good times. We didn't have no telephones, so we didn't have no phone bills to pay, and we didn't have light bills to pay. We didn't have gas bills to pay because we used wood burnin' heat. Most of the time we cooked on a wood burnin' stove.

"I can remember real good the first time I went into an outhouse and it had a toilet seat on it. Man, nobody gonna use that seat." She wagged her finger. "That was my seat. It fit my butt." She laughed.

"I'll never forget the first time we went to town. I thought I was in the White House." We laughed. "I went right down there to Plaquemine, a little bitty town. That's where my little sister was born. I thought we were really gettin' uptown. Now I can go through Plaquemine with my eyes shut.

"Me and my brother used to fight all the time. We didn't get along, but I loved him to death. Mama had had one piece of Sheetrock put up in the kitchen. One piece mind you. I'm standin' against the Sheetrock by the door, and we had a stack of wood by the heater. My brother was standin' over there. He's good size. He told me somethin' about his blue jeans, and I said, 'I'm tired of bein' your maid. You get your own blue jeans.' He picked up a stick of that wood and he slung it. It pinned me to the wall. My hair was in that Sheetrock. Mama like to beat him to death. He didn't throw no more wood.

"Do you mind if I have a smoke?" She lit up a cigarette and was careful to blow the smoke away from me, checking to be sure she was downwind.

"My brother had a cottonmouth bite him," Lucy continued. "It bit him close to his spine, and the only thing that saved him was the snake bit him under the water. The snake couldn't throw his poison like if he struck him. I guess it was meant for the water to take my brother's life because years later he died swimmin'. Anyway, they got him out of there and took him to the doctor. They stopped along the way because my mama was at the grocery store and she had a big ol' basket full of groceries. They run in that store and told Mama that they was takin' Donalee to the doctor 'cause he got snake bit. She pushed the buggy aside and run and jumped in the car and took off.

"They stopped at the doctor's office on the way to the hospital. Good thing. The doctor lanced it and pumped it. They rushed him on to the hospital and they started puttin' that snake medicine in him. His arm started blowin' up. He was allergic to the snake medicine. The doctor said, 'Don't ever let nobody give him that snake medicine or a lockjaw shot. He got a fifty-fifty chance. If the snakebite don't kill him, this medicine might. We're goin' to take our chances, him survivin' this bite.' He survived.

"After that, I saw him jig an ol' snake with a paddle in the boat. They was poppin' at him, the poison ones. He wasn't scared, knowin' he couldn't take the medicine. I can't take the medicine or a lockjaw shot. Me and him was allergic to everythin' in the book. I've never been hospitalized in my whole life. I guess when I do it'll be rock bottom. That's the way it usually happens. Never really been sick, either.

"One of the houses that we lived in we could count the chickens through the floor. The chickens were under the house. We could count the stars at night. That's how bad the cracks were in the floor and roof. In the wintertime, we'd nearly freeze to death. Oh, God, it was cold. Evidently I didn't know about snakes like I do now or I'd never of slept in there. I'd have slept on top of the house. My sisters and my mother are deathly scared of spiders.

"I can swim like a duck. I learned to swim in eighty feet of water. I didn't know how to swim, but I swim then. I was twelve years old and I was livin' with my aunt and uncle. I was there for a short time. He owned a towing company. They had a son, and he was the meanest old bastard there was in the world. I wanted to kill him so many times. He threw me off the back of a speedboat. I was standin' close to the edge, and he went 'jup' and off I went. Swim or drown. If I could've grabbed him when I was goin', I'd have taken him with me. I couldn't catch him. I swum to the bank. You can learn to swim in an instant. It's just like dancin', and that's somethin' you never forget.

"Did you ever see that show on TV, *Swamp People*? Willie and Junior is related [to me]. They're cousins. It's been years since I been around 'em. I went to school with Willie's wife, Theresa. I known 'em all they life, but I wasn't around Willie and Junior that much because I moved away when I was young.

"I left from back there when I was sixteen and went to work. I worked as a waitress slingin' burgers. When I made eighteen, I went to work in a barroom. I worked in a barroom until I got married, like a nut. Twenty-four years and five months—I guess that wasn't such a nut, was it? I acted like a nut and got married again. Best thing that ever happened to me in my whole life is the one I got now. He treats me good. I plan on keepin' him too, if I can.

"When I first got married, I worked drag races for eleven years and then he passed away. Then I went to work at a grocery store. I didn't have to work then, but I wanted to. It was a grocery store, bait shop, and gas station, and I was the only employee. That's when I met Paul. We call him Danny. His name is Paul Daniel. I was still workin' when we got married, and he made me quit. After I met him, he said, 'You don't need to work.' Boy, was I ever glad. But you know what? After I quit, I wished I hadn't quit 'cause I missed it. You know when you get up in the mornin' and you do the work you got to do? Now, I work all day long and I could still find somethin' to do.

"When I went to work at sixteen, I was makin' twenty-five dollars a week, and I'd buy my cigarettes, which I shouldn't have been smokin' at that age. I shouldn't be smokin' now, either. I'd buy my cigarettes, I had a room to sleep, and I was catchin' a bus home everyday—that was with twenty-five dollars. What can you buy with twenty-five dollars today? Gallon of milk and loaf of bread maybe? One week I'd try to buy me a skirt, a piece of clothes. The next week I'd buy the blouse. Sometimes it didn't work, though, because I didn't have it. I'd try to get me a piece of clothes at least once a week until I got enough. I wasn't worried about it. If I get it, I get it. I was workin', and I had a roof over my head, and I had a good job. It didn't bother me.

"I used to make my kids clothes without a pattern out of burlap bags. I remember my mama used to make our drawers with Martha White on the front and Red Ball [brand names printed on burlap bags] on the back." She laughed. "When we get a new pair of drawers, we was uptown. They'd be stiff 'cause you could never get all of the starch out of them. My poor mama. No washin' machine—she had a scrub board and a scrub brush. We'd fill that tub with water, put that board in, and get that brush. We used that scrub brush to clean the floor too, with Octagon soap—you can still buy it today. Comes in a bar. It's good soap. I can remember takin' that bar of soap and stickin' it down in that water, puttin' it on them blue jeans, and doin' the scrubbin'. I scrubbed so much.

"I used to be straight up like this." She raised her hand above her head. "I weighed 106 pounds and was six feet tall. You know what I looked like? A twig. I went to church and I said, 'Brother Walls, will you please pray for me to gain some weight?' I loved the ol' pastor. He did, and I started to gain some weight. I went to 172 pounds. I should have said how much weight I wanted to gain. I went back and before I could ask him, he said, 'No, ma'am. I'm not throwin' my prayer back.' He knew what I was fixin' to ask him. I said, 'You got to pray for me to lose some weight.' He said, 'Nope. When you ask God for somethin', you take what he gives you.'

"All the hard times that I been through, of everythin', hardest thing was losin' my people—my mom and dad and my brothers. You get stronger through the years and accept it and go on, but it gets awful hard sometimes. My oldest sister and my oldest brother . . . well, my oldest brother just passed away in June from brain cancer. One of my brothers died when he was eighteen from bronchial pneumonia. The baby brother died when he was swimmin' in the Mississippi River. He dove and broke his neck. I got the two sisters left and that's all of us. The rest of 'em are gone. I made seventy years old, and I'm the oldest. My dad died when he was sixty-five, my momma died when she was sixty-three. I outlived both of 'em.

"My ol' daddy, he was a Christian. His brother was a Christian. Both died prayin'. The last words his brother said was, 'Praise the Lord' and he quit breathin'. I was with my grandmother when she died. She used to pray all the time for God. She'd put her hand up like this," she said, holding her right hand to the sky, "and she asked God to let her take a long breath. I was lookin' at her like I'm lookin' at you and she went." Lucy demonstrated a long breath. "She never breathed again.

"It's like my brother that passed away. Everybody that you ever talk to that ever had brain cancer suffers terrible. He didn't suffer at all, we prayed so much. That was the onlyest thing that I asked was, 'Please don't let him suffer. Take him before he suffers.' He never suffered. I see miracles all of the time. Two years before he got sick and died, he got close to God. He got close! That's a peace for me. I'd go see him and say, 'How you feel?' He said, 'I feel good.' You could tell the way he said it he wasn't hurtin'. The last week he lived, he couldn't eat at all, and we couldn't wake him up. I went the day before he died and spent most of the day with him. His wife was standin' close to him talkin' to him in his ear. They knew he was dying because of his vital signs. She was talkin' to him, and he smiled and took a long breath, and it was over. I didn't want to be there."

There was a ruckus coming from the men gathered in Lucy's campsite. She paused and looked over in that direction, and then she waved her hand in the air as if brushing it off and continued. "I thank God I'm where I'm at today because when you're raised like that, when you have it that hard, it makes you appreciate what you have so much more. I see people that they have plenty, just plenty. I'm happy for 'em, but they have no value of money. They just go out and buy stuff, buy stuff, buy stuff that they don't need and can't use. If you're livin', there's gonna be another tomorrow. I always try to basically think of that. What're you gonna do tomorrow? I see young people today. They go out and make a paycheck, but if it's a good little paycheck, they quit. When that money is gone, what are they gonna do for money? They don't think about nothin' like that.

"The way I handle adversity is to give it to Jesus and let him handle it. Without him, we'd be in a big bind. I got a friend of mine who's a firm believer in askin' God for what you want. She's a Christian, and she needed a place to live because her and her husband had split up. He was runnin' around with her sister. She just left. She prayed for God to give her a trailer and a place to put it. She wanted a twelve-by-fifty foot. She hadn't no more than prayed that prayer and the woman that was sittin' by her told her, 'I know where they got a house for sale right now.' She went and bought the house trailer, and it was two weeks and she got the land to put it on.

"What bothers me today is my little sister is sixty-five. Her husband left her for another woman and moved right across the street. He married this other woman. I wanted to kill him and her too. I'm glad I didn't 'cause I wouldn't be sittin' here. My sister's one good person. She never one time ran around on him. She had no income whatsoever when he left. She raised her three daughters. She retired from school. She was a part-time worker. That was twenty-some years ago. She can only draw 480 dollars a month retirement. That's all she gets. She'll make seventy years old and that's what hurts my heart today—for what he did to her. The way she has it today is hard. She had it hard enough when she was a kid, and she still has it hard.

"We gonna see more hard times, but you know what I say? We're the ones that are gonna be able to survive. Our kids and grandkids? They aren't gonna be able to survive what's comin'. When the times get tough, we'll be able to survive because we know how. The people that has plenty of money, what are they gonna do if they don't have any money? They can't go out and buy steaks and this and that. You gonna have to grow it, catch it, kill it, or make it. Poor people, with the way we were raised, we will survive that. We know how to make somethin' out of nothin'.

"It was the good times because it was all we knew. If we hadn't had love in the house, if my mother hadn't loved us as much as she did, I don't know what would've happened. She kept us together when my dad left. The main thing then was everybody loved everybody. That was a bond you couldn't break there, buddy. Can't nothin' break that bond.

"I thank God that he brought us to where we are. I'd like to read a book on the people that was raised back there on 'em houseboats and see what kind of stories that they have. You're hearin' my story. I'd like to hear some of 'em other stories from the people back there that was raised on houseboats. How did life turn out? There was people that I knew back then that I hadn't heard of in years. I don't even know if they're still livin'. I'd like to know through the years what happened to 'em.

"Basically, that's the story of my life. I never told this story to nobody. I bet you never got a story like that! It's a true story."

A tall woman with short brown hair was walking past, and Lucy yelled to her, "Come on over here, woman."

"Hey, girl," she said.

"I'm tellin' her my life story," said Lucy.

"Don't let me interrupt," she said.

"She's got a story too," said Lucy, looking directly at me.

"Lucy is more interesting," she said.

"I don't know about that," I said. "We think all women are impressive and have great stories that people aren't hearing."

"You're probably right," she said, moving closer to us.

"My name is Nancy," I said as Kitty joined us. "This is Kitty, and we're from Minnesota. The South is a whole new experience."

"Oh, yeah. The deeper you get, the more it's gonna be, isn't it, Lucy?" she said, laughing. "My name is Ernie."

"We'd love to hear your story too," I said.

"I done told her about me," said Lucy. "Now it's your turn. We gonna be in a book."

"Well, all right," said Ernie, taking a seat in a lawn chair Kitty had put out for her. "We had our family reunion last year and decided to have people write somethin' down about themselves and have everybody guess who wrote it. Mine said I was born in Holly Springs, Arkansas, and I grew up with my brother and sister in half a house. These were people I've known my whole life that grew up there too, and they started pickin' names of everybody that was there."

Ernie had been surprised that no one at the reunion knew about their half a house. "Finally Earlene says, 'Well, it looked like a whole house to me!'" We laughed along with Ernie.

"My dad was killed in World War II. We lived on the farm with my grandparents. Then my mother remarried and had two children. The marriage didn't last long. We moved back to Holly Springs and the farm. My grandpapa gave Mama one acre right there on the corner, but no house. My uncle, who married my mother's older sister, wanted a house too. They'd been livin' in a log cabin. He had two boys and was fixin' to have another child. He'd bought land. So he and Mama found this eight-room house thirty miles from where we lived, and they cut it in half. He took four rooms, and we took four rooms. We enclosed the front and built a front porch on our side. He built a back porch. He had two porches; we only had one. We didn't have a bathroom. We had an outdoor toilet.

"When they went to get water for a well, an ol' black guy come out there and took a stick to witch for water. That's how we got our well. He took his Y-shaped stick, and he held it like this," she said, holding two ends of an imaginary stick in her hands with the third end out, "and he walked around, and the point went down. That's where they dug with the shovel. At thirty feet, we got water. He'd found a natural spring of water.

"We had a refrigerator and electricity—not when I was a little kid, but later. Aunt May used to keep their milk and butter and stuff down in the well because they didn't have refrigeration. When the iceman come, he brought a block of ice. Me and Charlotte used to fight over who was gonna sit on it. Can you imagine lettin' your kids sit on your ice?" We laughed.

"My first cousin that died last year was four years older than me. I told 'em at the reunion when we was talkin' that she taught me all the good things and most of the bad. We would go to the toilet at Papa's—a two-holer attached to the chicken house. You didn't sit on it; you squatted so you could see down through the hole. Them tumble bugs would be down in there and rollin' little balls up. They kinda look like Junebugs. They ball the crap up, and they roll it. We'd get up there—this is kids in the country that don't have money and nothin' better to do than find somethin'—and we'd pick us out a tumble bug, and we'd have tumble bug races and say, 'I bet my bug can roll his ball before yours does.'" We all laughed.

"The only gym we had was the chicken roost. We used to play under the porch after Mother had that front porch built. She had concrete poured, and it was hollow underneath there. That'd be perfect for snakes and spiders and bugs." She shook her head in disbelief that she went under there. "At my house there was three of us, and the dirtiest one got the last bath. That was always my brother David.

"Back when we were kids, on Sunday's everybody came to my grandmother's for dinner. It'd be nothin' to have fifty people there for dinner every Sunday. I was talkin' about how poor we were, but they raised everything we ate. My grandma would cook cornbread and biscuits. She'd have chicken, pork, and beef, peas, beans, and fried taters. The table would be full of food, and then she'd have cake, pie, milk, buttermilk, and iced tea. We ate good. We didn't know we was poor.

"I'd come home from school, and we'd have the Sears and Roebuck catalog, and I'd say to my mama, 'I want a dress like that.' I'd go down to Marvin Ramsey's store, and me and Charlotte would go through the flour sacks until we found the print we wanted. Back then they came printed. We'd pick out which print we wanted our dress made out of so we could tell Mama to get those, however many it took to make that dress. She'd look at that picture in that catalog, go buy the flour in those sacks, and she'd cut out that dress; and the next day I'd have it. She had an old treadle sewin' machine.

"My first cousin was born the same day I was born, and ol' doctor Taylor come twelve miles to deliver Freddie Joe. He didn't even get back to Sparkman before he come another twelve miles to deliver me. Freddie Joe and I went to the same school. When we were in eighth grade, a boy from town was makin' fun of the dress I was wearin' bein' made out of a flour sack. We was on the merry-go-round, and Freddie Joe kicked him off. I'll never forget it. He kicked him off and jumped on top of him and pounded him. 'Don't you never ever say something like that again.' I'll never forget that."

We were interrupted by Ernie's husband, Jim, who said to Lucy in a serious, authoritative tone, "Hey, get yourself over there and cook Danny some cornbread to go with that meat." Then he smiled at Kitty and me as if he were kidding.

Annoyed, Lucy looked at Jim and said she had made cornbread and Danny knew where it was.

"You go and be nice, Jim," said Ernie sounding irritated. The women stayed on with us awhile.

"I want the book that you gonna write about me," said Lucy.

"You'll have to wait until I write it," I said.

"Well, I hope I'm still around," laughed Lucy.

"I'll write as fast as I can," I said.

"You do that," said Lucy. "I plan on bein' here, but you never know."

"You don't," I said, "but you're feisty enough. I bet you will be."

"I'm a firm believer that when it's your time, it don't make a difference," said Ernie. "When God calls you, you're gone."

"I made my husband laugh," said Lucy, leaning in closer. "My husband said, 'Why are you so scared to go on an airplane and fly nowheres?' I told him, 'If God would've wanted me to fly, he would have put two wings back there.' He said, 'You aren't gonna die until it's your time.' I said, 'I agree with that, but suppose I'm ten thousand jillion feet up in that big ol' jet and it's the pilot's time? Then what am I supposed to do if God calls the pilot? Somebody got to fly the plane. It sure isn't gonna be me.'" We were all laughing.

"Lucy, I think I gotta go fix some supper for Jim," said Ernie.

I asked Ernie for her email address, and she said, "I used to have email, but I had a disagreement with Ma Bell. They went up on my bill and didn't ask me. Good night, girls."

"Y'all be watchin' for snakes now," Lucy said to us. "They can't git in them tents now, can they?"

"No, they can't if we keep them zipped tight," I said.

"That's good," said Lucy. "We found one in the camper one time in a compartment. Little bitty one. When I went to get a chair, I saw somethin' move. I thought it was a mouse, so I got in there so I could see. I started hollerin'. I told my husband, and he got mad. I told him, 'You can hook that thing up and take it home. I ain't never sleepin' in it again.' He did. We got home and he said, 'Now what do you want me to do with it?' I said, 'You can take it back where you bought it. I ain't sleepin' in it no more.' He traded it in and said, 'I sure hope you don't find no more snakes.'" She stood up. "Y'all have a safe trip and a good evenin'."

"Goodnight, Lucy," we said.

During dinner Harveen from Baton Rouge, who was camped near us, brought us fried fish they'd caught off the pier. Harveen wanted us to taste fish cooked with the Tony Chachere's Creole seasoning she had told

Kitty about earlier in the day. Then she brought us a container of the seasoning to take with us. The fish was spicy but fabulous.

I lay in my tent missing family, but feeling excited after talking with Lucy and Ernie. I got a card in the mail from Doug, but it wasn't enough of a connection to ease the homesickness. I was counting down the days. Seventeen days until we headed home. Eleven days until Doug joined us. Six days until my daughter, Sara Jo, arrived.

October 16, Day Twenty-six

Kitty and I packed up camp and drove to the campground boat launch to paddle Bruin Lake. It was relaxing and enjoyable to paddle water with no dangers to be wary of—except alligators. The lake was lined with homes and large docks, many with boatlifts and decks built into them. The decks were large and designed for entertaining. Cypress trees grew along the shore between the docks, and one dock incorporated a tree.

Kitty watched for alligators. She was disappointed but relieved that we didn't see one. In a lofty cypress we saw a great horned owl. It let us get only a few yards away and sat there for several minutes before flying off. I thought the cypress knees near camp were big, but the ones along the shore were amazing. They were like a fortress of little soldiers around the trees. Turtles dotted the ground nearby.

After our paddle we said goodbye to Lucy and Ernie and headed to Natchez, Mississippi. On the way we read from the meditation book: "Being Honest with Ourselves: Our relationship with ourselves is the most important relationship we need to maintain. The quality of that relationship will determine the quality of our other relationships . . ."

Some days when I would read a positive message in the book, I wouldn't want to hear it. This was one of those days. My relationship with myself the past couple of weeks hadn't been good. I resented that the reading pointed that out. Our day off had helped, but I was still not completely honest with myself about the pressure I felt from the team, from the constant adapting to changes, and the self-imposed pressure to find solutions. The solutions were unfolding in front of me, but the annoying whining in

my head wasn't allowing me to relax into them. The Gatherings weren't working according to plan, but we were meeting women and talking with them, although not as many as I had hoped. I sensed that Kitty felt my internal struggle. I was concerned about my attitude dampening the others' enthusiasm for the trip when they returned.

My hair situation was no help. I wasn't getting used to its color—a color Hannah May said was natural. My hair grew drier and more brittle each day. After washing, it needed unusually large amounts of conditioner for me to get a comb through it. I had gone from one bad hair issue to another, and it bothered me.

We stopped for lunch when we arrived in Natchez. I had deep-fried chicken fingers, deep-fried hush puppies, french fries, and coleslaw served in Styrofoam containers with a plastic fork. We were dine-in customers. The food was tasty, but it was difficult to find food that wasn't fried or tea that wasn't sweetened.

We joined a deep discussion between two women at the next table. Henrietta said, "I think there is a human tendency to stick with your own kind of people because we have a common lineage—common food and culture. I would feel strange in another neighborhood. I don't think it's always racism. Why are we so attached to our heritage? If you came from a repressed area, I say take your stuff and go and don't look back.

"When you free yourself from it, you can move free, and there's nothing better or worse. Once we quit labeling and putting things into categories, we are given a way of being without attachment. My mind has a tendency to do that all the time. It's great for problem solving.

"I tell people to quit calling themselves black. I don't call myself white. I'm Henrietta. Period. Roots are important for the children and their upbringing, but for living, how important are our roots? I don't care what culture it is, labels give you something like blinders."

"Quit identifying yourself as your skin color?" said Wanda. "People here still refer to themselves as their skin color when they talk to each other—the black guy, the white guy—because it's entrenched here."

"Yes, I know," said Henrietta. "If they would give that up—and they could take life in without their ego running the show. Self has become too important."

"I can see we need to remove labels," said Kitty. "We need to not think about ourselves as being separate."

"We're just here—or wherever we are—like everyone else," said Henrietta.

"I don't think of myself as prejudiced, but I know I have work to do in that area," I said. "Something I learned as a child—I'm not sure how; no one told me—but I learned that white men were more dangerous than black men."

"Because they are," said Henrietta. "Let's put it like this: If a black guy violates a white woman, he's going to get a stiffer sentence than a white guy, who might get off. That's the statistics. I'm not saying become totally naive to your environment."

"Particularly you two," said Wanda, "because you're traveling by yourselves, and you're women."

"This challenged me before we even left," said Kitty. "Growing up in North Dakota, I lived totally in a white culture. I've come forward with a dichotomy of the white and the black, and now it's time to challenge myself to lose it."

"Look at 'we is' you know?" said Henrietta. "We just *is*. When you look at your mind and it starts putting labels on, that's your mind making comments."

"And making up a story about what you see that might not have any basis in reality," I added.

"Our friend Cis said, 'We're part of the human race,'" said Kitty. "I'm thinking my work is cut out for me." She laughed.

"It is for all of us," said Wanda.

"Yeah," said Henrietta. "It's part of recognizing people within the culture. At least it's an awareness for you. I have educated friends who don't have that awareness yet."

Henrietta and Wanda left for an appointment, and we went to our motel.

As the dark of night fell and car lights illuminated the U.S. Highway 84 bridge stretching across the Mississippi, it became magical against the starlit sky. The bridge glowed silver. Cars traveling across it looked like fireflies.

October 17, Day Twenty-seven

We drove to Natchez Under-the-Hill to go to the landing to sing and say a prayer for the Gathering that evening. Standing on the shore of the river in the cool morning air, we felt full of peace. The sky was bright blue, and the morning haze hung on the horizon. I took off my shoes and put my feet in the water, feeling a need to connect with the river. We quietly sat with her for several minutes before turning back to the van.

At the visitor center, we learned Natchez Under-the-Hill was home to river people and was notorious for bars, brothels, and gambling halls. The red brick saloon across from the landing was rich with history. Walking on the well-worn floor, I felt as if I were stepping back in time. I imagined colorful gamblers and ladies of the evening hanging out on the wrought iron balcony out front. The wooden walkway was patched with license plates. A narrow blue building with a pair of equally narrow doors said "Mark Twain Guest House—Inquire in Saloon."

Under-the-Hill was an important port for shipping. Thousands of slaves had been bought and sold there. The river provided an opportunity for some slaves to escape by hiding on steamboats traveling the river.

According to the visitor center brochure, Natchez was originally "inhabited by the powerful Natchez Indians, discovered by LaSalle, settled by the English, developed by the Spanish, and capitalized by antebellum cotton barons, enriched by enslaved and free African Americans, and handled with kid gloves by Union forces . . . Once home to half of America's millionaires and two hundred free people of color, Natchez was one of the most prestigious and powerful cities in the South. It boasts more antebellum mansions than any other city in the South as well as some of the South's most diverse historical sites." Natchez's antebellum architecture had remained intact during the Civil War.

Antebellum means "before war" in Latin. Antebellum is not a particular house style. The term refers to the elegant plantation homes built in the South prior to the Civil War. Grand structures ranging from pillared Greek Revival mansions to Federal-style estates, antebellum architecture reflects the power and idealism of the wealthy landowners.

The Natchez Indians lived along the shores of the Mississippi. When the Spanish explorers came in 1542, the Natchez fought successfully to fend them off. But the Natchez had no resistance to the European diseases, and their population decreased. Eventually the French explorers set up trading posts that displaced the Natchez.

One of the residents of whom Natchez is proud is Judith Sargent Murray. Murray wrote essays in the 1700s that focused on women and girls, and she is considered one of America's first feminists. As a girl, Murray was painfully aware of how society restricted women. She believed women's success was dependent on two things: getting an education and being raised to revere oneself. She was self-taught and had radical ideas about educating women. One of her more notable essays was written in 1784 under the pen name Constantia and titled "Desultory Thoughts upon the Utility of Encouraging a Degree of Self-Complacency, Especially in Female Bosoms."

Kitty and I saw a royal-blue hot-air balloon drifting above a shopping mall. We'd arrived in Natchez at the tail end of the annual Natchez Great Mississippi River Balloon Race, a colorful event where gorgeous hot-air balloons float in the skies over the river and town. More than one hundred balloonists had participated in the recent event because the weather was conducive to flying.

We walked in the Natchez City Cemetery. Thousands of headstones stretched as far as we could see. There were family plots, most dating back to the early 1800s, and many children's graves. The family plots were surrounded by ornate wrought iron fences or cement walls. An enormous live oak had trunk-sized branches that arched down toward the ground, providing shade for several family plots.

That afternoon we checked into the Devereaux Shields House, a B&B,

and met one of the owners, Ron, who gave us the history of the home. "We love old homes, gardening, and woodworking. We bought this house in 2004 and were talked into making it a bed and breakfast by neighbor friends. In 2006, we bought the cottage where you'll be staying.

"This house dates to 1893. We have pictures of former Natchez residents, events, and buildings. Natchez surrendered during the Civil War, which is why the old homes survived. We have four hundred antebellum homes, two hundred Victorian, and a dozen Spanish homes still surviving.

"Natchez vied with New York for being the wealthiest city in the country. We had more millionaires per capita because of cotton. In the early '30s the boll weevil came in and wiped out the cotton two years in a row. That zeroed out the industry. It affected Natchez worse than the Depression.

"The good thing that came out of that low period was it prompted the ladies in the garden club to look around for other ways to bring money into town. One way was to put the old houses on tour. The tours go back eighty years. This house is not on tour. The people who own the houses that are on tour work hard to ensure you have an authentic experience.

"Eleanor and I favor Victorians. We feel that era was a little more flamboyant than the antebellum. Antebellums are wonderful, and we enjoy them, but for us they seem to be a little stark in terms of color and décor."

We walked down the street to the cottage as Ron continued narrating. "This is Aunt Clara's cottage. It dates to 1873 and was built as a dependency for the Burn staff and family, who lived next door in the big house. This has been a bed and breakfast for thirty years.

"Natchez was a logical place for boats to tie up. It was a safe harbor. That's changed over the past hundred years or so. The current is swift now and it's a mile wide here. It's deceiving. The shore on the other side doesn't look that far away. Being a novice to the Mississippi River when we first moved here, I thought water was for recreational sports. But folks don't do that on the river. Within the first six months that we were here, we heard of two or three accidents of youngsters out there running into logs in the river at a high speed." Ron showed us our room and handed us the key. "Let me know if you need anything."

I moved the van closer to our cottage where the lush trees hung over the road, and I nearly pruned them with the kayaks on top. We stayed in a bright, cheery room called Louise. Antique suitcases were stacked to create an end table next to a Victorian-era chair. The sweet garden out back included a waterfall and mums ready to burst. I was struck by the size of shrubs and flowers Ron said they'd planted only two years prior. Plants grow faster in the South's longer growing season than I am used to.

Kitty and I went to the mall to find a beauty shop to collect more stories. When we arrived we met one hairdresser, but she was busy, so we walked the mall handing out Gathering flyers. I was drawn to a tall blonde woman in the shoe department at J.C. Penney and offered her a flyer. She said she was excited about the Gathering but couldn't come. I asked if she had a few moments, and we sat down on a brown leather couch between racks of shoes and talked.

A soft-spoken, gentle-natured woman, Helen said, "My husband's family has lived on the Forest plantation all of their lives. It's been passed down from generation to generation. William Dunbar came to Natchez from Scotland, and he surveyed. For his services, he was given land grants. He drew out the layout of the city of Natchez. That's where I live and have roots now."

Her voice grew quieter and thoughtful. "I lost my children and my husband in an accident in 1982. I had two little girls, ages six and three. I wished I'd die at the time. I'd pray I wouldn't wake up. I prayed, 'God, why did you leave me?' I floated around. I couldn't find a place, and I couldn't find a home. I talked about my family to strangers, and I'd show them pictures." She sighed.

"I started dating a friend of my husband's, and we married in December of 1984. At the same time, his thirteen-year-old son came to live with us. He had been living in Jackson with his mother at the time. His mother worked, and he was kind of getting into a little trouble. She said, 'He needs to come live with you.' Three strangers meshed into one family. It wasn't easy." She laughed.

"I went to church every Sunday, and I'd say, 'Jody, do you want to go to church?' He would say, 'Naa.' I kept on every week. One day he said, 'Yes,' and he started going. His friends went to Parkway Baptist in Natchez. I was going to First Baptist. I could see he wanted to go to Parkway, so I moved my membership there. He got involved in church and decided before he graduated that he wanted to be a minister. So he is. He's forty now.

"I have one grandbaby." She beamed. "Jody and his wife were married for twelve years before they had a child. I didn't think I'd have a grandchild. My husband has one other daughter. She's divorced, and I don't think she will ever marry again. Jody has a five-year-old and one on the way.

"God put me in a place where I have roots. We built a house the year we married. We have been there twenty-seven years. I had the house plan when I had my first family near Utica.

"I grew up in Gloster, forty miles from here. I have one half-sister, but actually she's my sister in my heart. She's older than me. I lost my dad when I was eighteen to an accidental gunshot wound. Everything I've had is tragedy. I didn't go through the processes of knowing and grieving it until now. Everything was sudden. My mother has Alzheimer's.

"When my dad died, he was my stone, my rock. I thought I'd lose it then, which was in 1967. Then in 1982 I lost my family, and I thought, 'Oh, God, please tell me what you want me to do. Why am I here?' I see miracles all the time of why he left me and of things that have happened that wouldn't have. I guess he left me for a purpose. I've had many things that showed me I needed to keep livin'—my husband being one of them. He's my best friend. He loved my husband. He was best friends with him, and he listened to me cry. He couldn't really know what I was going through. He had seen my children, thank God, so he could understand. He could picture them.

"After my dad died, I lost faith, and I gained it back after I had my children. I'd say to younger folks, 'Don't lose faith. It's going to work out.' In fact, on the headstones—I had four, mine and theirs put together with a picture and a cross—on mine it says, 'I have kept the faith.' That's what I'd tell younger women: Keep the faith. God will get you through it.

"My mom grew up in a family of six. My dad was a farmer and had bad vision. When he was forty, his sisters sent him to a clinic in Birmingham. He drove himself there. I can't remember the name of the disease he had, but he went blind during surgery. Totally blind! He became one of the old time preachers. He went to church where Jimmy Swaggart went, in Ferriday, with Jerry Lee Lewis and Mickey Gilley. They were from that area. One time, Jimmy Swaggart in his sermon said that there used to be an ol' blind man that used to irritate him and then he understood him. That was my dad. I was eleven when he died.

"Daddy was blind and was amazing; he could tell a penny from a dime. He could work on things mechanically. He taught my sister how to drive. She was his eyes. He told her what to do, and she did it. He taught my mother how to drive too. I remember going to church with him, and I was in the backseat and felt safe. My sister was driving, and he was telling her what to do. He was awesome. His name was Ellis.

"My mom's name was Elgie. That's two aunts' names put together. She's eighty-three. She got me through so much. She was my best friend and a great adviser to me. When she started losing her memory, we could tell. A year ago, we had to put her in the nursing home. I have a stepfather whose name is Roger. He's awesome. He took care of her for three years and did everything. She'd fallen and broken her hip. When she came home, he wouldn't let anyone else take care of her. Nurses came in to check on her. He did it himself as long as he could. We kept saying, 'Pop, when it's too bad let us know.' It got too bad, and he couldn't do it. He had a nervous breakdown.

"My sister had twins that were both born with cerebral palsy," Helen continued. "The Kennedys have nothing on my family." She laughed. "The twins were in wheelchairs all their lives. Sandy died at the age of twenty-three, and Candy died last year the day after Thanksgiving.

"I think my mom would be most proud of her girls. I ask her what she wants for her birthday, and she says, 'You.' She still remembers us, although she might get us confused. She might say, 'How many children do I have?' or she might call me Betty Grace—that's my sister. When I walk in, she says, 'I thought that was you.' I can see the Alzheimer's is getting progressively worse. It feels like a gift to be able to be there."

We were momentarily distracted by a woman trying on shoes next to us, but Helen quickly got back to her story. "When I moved back and married after the accident, God placed me one-half mile from her. My husband lived one-half mile from where she lived. Isn't that awesome? That was a miracle too.

"I moved to Baton Rouge and lived with twin cousins and another cousin when I graduated from Gloster. We got an apartment together. We had a good time, you know? We were young and playin'. We were livin' right at LSU. I got a job workin' for the state, and I didn't take classes. I thought I knew everything. I worked at LSU. Then after my dad died, I moved back to Gloster with my mom, and I stayed there and went to work at Georgia Pacific, a lumber manufacturing company. Then Mom remarried—trying to replace my dad I think—and she wound up in Natchez.

"I worked at an insurance company and an oil company. I didn't work when my husband and children were livin'. I helped him. He farmed fifteen hundred acres. I was the gopher going after parts. He farmed soybeans and wheat. He had so many pieces of equipment. He had a trucking company when he died. He did custom cutting. He'd cut his crops, and then he'd go cut other people's crops in other states. He had four combines. He was gone a lot. I kept the books, thank God, because I had to take care of everything after the accident. That saved me because I knew the books and what was going on. That kept me busy for seven years. I moved to Natchez and worked as a secretary to the administrator of the Natchez hospital. It was a big job, but it was wonderful. I loved it.

"My husband's insurance agent came to see me after the accident and said, 'Come on, we're going to Jackson. I think you need to be enrolled in real estate.' He'd been through our home, and I've always loved homes. My mother's first cousin lived in one of the antebellum homes in Natchez, and we used to go over and see her. I was in awe of the homes. I'd had the house plan for the house that I live in for seven years. I ordered it before we built our home in Utica, and it had fifty-eight hundred square feet. My first husband said, 'Helen, get real.' I scaled it down a little bit and found one at three thousand." She laughed.

"I've enjoyed doing real estate. I've met many people from all over the world. Then the economy got bad in 2007, and I said, 'I think I'll give it up and stay at home.' I garden and have my little dogs.

"When my current husband and I married, he saw the plan. I'd thrown it in a closet. We talked about marriage, and he had a home and I had a home. I had to have my tubes tied. I couldn't have children. I didn't want to go through that again. I built a shell around myself and said I couldn't do that again. I focused on the house, and we started that home in October. He had the land, and I had the plan."

Her eyes began to sparkle, and she continued talking while she dug for her phone. "I have pictures of my family—all of them—on my cell phone. There were ten on my mother's side, and I used to wish that we had so many in our family. They always had someone to play with. My mother has one grandchild left. He was a year younger than the twins. She's proud of him. When we have a family reunion, it's ten.

"Here's my mother and my stepfather." She showed me pictures. "Oh, he cares about her. He hasn't missed one day visiting her. They've been married thirty-three years. They're always doing things at the nursing home. I'm impressed. We go there all of the time. I've met many of the patients that I love. It takes me thirty minutes to get in to see my mom because I'm saying hello to everybody. They're in their eighties and nineties, and they look forward to that. I try to take time with all of them.

"We have pictures of the family on the walls in my living room. Here's a picture of Katie, who was three, and Tracy, who was six." Tracy was dressed in a tutu. "She took dancing from the time she was three. This is Katie. She was the mischievous one. Oh, yes, Katie was into things all the time. Tracy had strawberry-blond hair. My husband, Charlie, was reddish haired. The girls liked each other a lot, and they were my pride and joy in my heart. Still are. That's something that never goes away.

"That's my sister. She's the serious one, but she has mischief in her. I'm the impulsive one. A month ago, my hair was long, to my shoulders. I went in for a trim, and I came out with short hair.

"Here are my two little dogs." Her face lit up. "Here is a picture of my husband. Here's my mom playing the piano. She still plays, and it makes her happy. She's happy when we're with her. She's most proud of her husband. She loves him so much. She'll say, 'I wonder when Roger is coming.' He asked her what she wanted for Christmas, and she said, 'You.' Her children and her husband are everything. She has nothing that she needs.

"Here's a picture of my home. There are a lot of live oaks and azaleas down the driveway, like a lot of old homes. I love gardening. My present husband was a farmer. My dad was a farmer. Farming is in my blood. I used to drive the tractor. I wanted to learn to see if I could, and I did. I planted when I was married to my deceased husband. I've done most everything that you could do. If there was someone working for me, I worked with him. I don't like to tell anyone to do anything that I wouldn't do myself.

"Here's my husband and me. He's good to me. He said he feels like he's raising another child. I'm still young at heart, I guess. I didn't get to go through the teenage years with my children. I feel like they're still six and three, and they'll always be. I'm in touch with some of their friends on Facebook now, and they remember me. They say such sweet things to me like, 'I could talk forever to you.' They still call my home Miss Helen's house. Facebook is great for that because I never would've found them.

"I have a best friend from grammar school I've not seen since 1963. She found me on Facebook. Next Tuesday my cousin and my best friend—we played together like we were the three musketeers—are coming to my house to spend the night. We're having a slumber party.

"We could talk forever. This has been fun. It's time I get over to the nursing home to see Mom. It was good to meet you. You be careful."

Kitty and I went to Duncan Park early to set up for the Gathering. I fought discouragement as we put chairs out, wondering if anyone would be sitting in them. Cars cruised past; some slowed as if taunting us. Then a car pulled in, but the woman was hesitant to get out. She kept looking in our direction. I walked over and spoke with her. Her name was Carolyn, she said. She had been waiting for other cars to pull in. She'd come to listen and didn't want to be the only one there. I encouraged her and she joined our circle.

We were interrupted by Ben, a reporter from the *Natchez Democrat*, who wanted to stay and listen. While he took photos I said, "One of the things that we know is women don't talk the same when there's a man present. That has remained true from the beginning of this trip in 2004 to today."

"What do you do if a man comes?" he asked.

"There was a man in Prairie du Chien who walked about as close as those kids' toys out there, and everybody stopped talking until he moved away. They didn't realize that they'd stopped talking. A man's presence changes what women say and how they say it. It's not necessarily negative; it is what it is. We want women to be able to speak out without hesitation. For the record, in all of these Gatherings there's been no man-bashing. Women may share about things that they would like to see changed, but their words have never been stated in a spiteful or hurtful manner. Men are different than we are. We have heard wisdom from every woman we talked to. You can't live as long as we have without learning something."

Ben conceded and gracefully departed.

We honored Carolyn for being our elder and, with encouragement, she agreed to speak. Her discomfort with being the center of attention was clear in her body language. She leaned away from us and hesitated to take the tape recorder when I handed it to her. Once she accepted it, she stared at it for a few moments, smiled, and shared.

"My life is centered around my family. I raised a big family. I had six children. I lost three. I had two sets of twins in thirteen months, two boys and a boy and girl. The little girl only lived two days. Then I had another boy two years later and a girl three years after that. Basically I had six babies in six years. One of them was accidentally killed when he was seventeen, and one died with cancer four years ago. It's a very hard thing. I lost my husband thirteen years ago. I have six grandchildren and six great-grandchildren. Three of our grandchildren and two of our children live in Arizona. I'll be going back Christmas. I go a couple times a year. I have a son in Louisiana.

"I've had a lot of good things happen to me. It's not all just sad. What gets me through adversity is God, of course. I have a strong faith. I don't know how you can get through something like that without God in your life. We have to rise above. That's the reason I'm here. I go to different functions and just keep going.

"I go to book club, and I go to a humanities club that has events like concerts and operas every other month. We had an operafest in May. There aren't as many operas going on right now. It's more jazz and different music. Our opera director died several years ago, and it made a big difference. There's a literary conference. There are a lot of things going on in Natchez if you pay attention. Most are free.

"I worked off and on with my husband in his business. After he died, I ran it for four years. It was a home improvement company. When he got so he couldn't walk, he taught me how to measure and give estimates for siding, carports, and that sort of thing. We had work crews do the installation. My son was head of the installation crews. After four years, my son and I decided we'd had enough and sold it. My son went on to do something different.

"My family makes my life rich, just by being with them and having memories. It's hard to get together, but we did last Thanksgiving. We met in Arizona. My son who lives in Louisiana has a daughter in Ohio who's twelve. He usually tries to go up there. I go to Arizona and stay about three weeks. I do a bit of traveling around."

Carolyn paused and smiled sweetly. "My greatest memories are about my children—when my children were born, when they married. I've always lived in Mississippi, but my husband and I traveled. Many years ago we got to go to the Holy Land. It wasn't safe even then. That's been thirty years ago.

"I think we should live life to the fullest. I married a juvenile diabetic, and before I did my mother and other family members sat me down and gave me a detailed description of what could happen. Sure enough, it did. I went into marriage expecting that it might be short, but it wasn't. We had forty-four wonderful years together. We traveled and enjoyed life. He was the type of man who liked to have fun. His name was Carlton. I have friends who never traveled, never did anything until they got ready to retire. Well, he died before retirement age. If we hadn't done those things all along, I'd have been doing them alone.

"I love to read. My favorite book right now is *Unbroken* by Laura Hillenbrand. She wrote *Seabiscuit* too. Those are the only two books she wrote. It took twelve years to write each one. She writes from bed and documents every word. She has something like fibromyalgia—only more severe. I'm interested in any kind of book, but I don't particularly care for mysteries. I like biographies. I just finished a series by Larson, who uses the term bio-history. It's a fairly new term for a biographical, historical novel in which the author takes an obscure person and writes a biography. This one, *Isaac's Storm*, was during the hurricane in 1900 in Galveston. It follows the weather forecaster's life story. It was one of the saddest things I've ever read. There were between six and twelve thousand people killed, and the book was graphic. This hurricane nearly wiped Galveston off the map.

"I've belonged to my book club for ten years. We meet once a month. To determine what book to read next, we have a feast at Christmas. We have quite a party, and hopefully people volunteer to pick a book for each month. We meet at a local bookstore. We have a great group and a diverse selection of books—things that you might not normally read. Sometimes I go to a meeting and say I didn't particularly like that book, but after the discussion, I like it.

"I love the river. The Mississippi River is very beautiful. We're high and dry here and don't suffer from floods. If Natchez floods, the rest of the world better look out. We have a lumber mill that's made a valiant effort to avoid a flood. They built their own levee, and they're still building it higher at their own expense, maybe $700,000. They're working to save their lumber mill that's been in the family. This is their one-hundredth year in operation. They should be celebrating instead of building that levee, but they saved it.

"The building at the end of Silver Street was in danger, and they built HESCO bastions, an instant levee system. It's the greatest thing. In Vidalia [across the river from Natchez], all of the areas along the riverfront flooded, but they built a levee around each one of those buildings. HESCO bastions are metal containers that come folded flat. They open them up and fill them with sand. They build the levees with them. It was the most marvelous thing. I saw them when they first started and then watched it on the news. They showed men in their shirtsleeves after they got off work working next to their office buildings, and prisoners from the prison working with the city crews. They saved all of the buildings.

"HESCO bastions are reusable." She showed us pictures on her phone. "It took months to clean up after them. All of that sand had to be carted off. They go up faster than sandbags—in a day's time.

"It's flat on that side of the river. They have a levee, but all of those buildings were built outside the levee because it was on a one-hundred-year flood plain, and the Corps of Engineers assured them that it would never flood there, but it did. There was a welcome center, a hospital, and a hotel—all kinds of stuff was built on the riverfront, all within the last twenty years. People were evacuating from Vidalia because they were afraid. They packed up their stuff and put it in storage—probably here.

"The communities north of us, south of us, and on the other side of the river get flooded out. Once the whole town of Vidalia had to be moved when the river changed course. This was in the early '40s. They picked up and moved the downtown—big houses and buildings. They went back a mile or so, several blocks anyway. They keep building the levees higher. They say that channels the water faster—but that only does more harm.

"The Yazoo River at Vicksburg flows backwards during the floods. People in the Yazoo area get flooded out. That's happened the past couple of years. Have you seen the mouth of the Mississippi? I thought it would be a big ol' swishing thing coming out over a large area. I've seen it flying over it. It's a mess—untidy looking, spread out all over with its fingers. They say that the coastal area is disappearing down there. The marshes and the land are in danger.

"A good book is *Rising Tide: The Great Mississippi Flood of 1927 and How It Changed America*. I got the author's signature quite a while back. That was when I quit eating pork—it's bad. The book is very well written. That flood changed the course of history. I lived in Greenville for eleven years and was born in the Yazoo delta. I know a good many of the families that were mentioned in the book. Greenville was one of the harder hit areas. I remember my mom telling me about it. She lived in

Rolling Fork, which is in the delta—not terribly far from Greenville or the river. They traveled in a boat from Rolling Fork to Vicksburg to get away from the flood and the high water. Most of Vicksburg is in the hills and at a higher elevation. She was about thirteen at that time. I wish I had asked her more details.

"I was awfully close to my grandmother. Two years ago, I lost my favorite great-aunt, Gladys, at the age of 105. The amazing thing about it was she kept her wits about her. She remembered everything. I was an only child, and I had nobody. She had been close to me since I was born. I'd ask her about something, and she'd say, 'Give me a minute and let the wheels start turning.' Then she'd tell me exactly what happened. She was my best friend, even when I was little. Up to the time she died, it felt like she was my age.

"I don't feel like I'm seventy-seven. I feel fifty-eight, middle age. Some days I feel seventy-something, but most days I'm in good shape. I'm independent."

The sun began to set, and we said goodbye to Carolyn and thanked her for coming. I watched her walk to her car and was surprised that having even one woman from the area come made a positive difference in how successful I thought the Gathering was.

Back at our B&B the owners, Ron and Eleanor, were sitting on the porch with two other couples enjoying wine and cheese. When Ron explained what we were doing and they heard only one woman came to our Gathering, they became determined to get stories about Natchez women in the book. They said they'd make calls and we could have an impromptu Gathering in the morning before we left town. We left to walk to dinner while they continued talking about the women they would call.

We had dinner at King's Tavern in one of the oldest buildings in town, known as Bledsoe House. In its lifetime it had housed a tavern, stage stop, and mail station. After ordering dinner we went to the two upper floors where a female ghost was often seen. We were disappointed she didn't come out and greet us.

Over dinner Kitty said, "This is like a Boundary Waters trip where you keep changing location every night. It's an interesting process, this travel. I remember I put out to the universe that I wanted to travel, and I got the job out on the Great Lakes in a boat for a month, and I have done that for a couple of years now. I forgot to say I wanted to go other places. Then this trip happened, which takes me to all different places.

"Because I've moved so much, I think I've lost out on what a sense of home is. It feels like something I'm gaining as I get older. Traveling was important to me when I was young, but I didn't do much of it. Now that I have the ability to travel, I like being home. That's strange to me.

"When this is over, we still have a four-day drive home."

For dessert, hot pecan pie was served with lemon on top. It tasted divine.

We read the meditation book before we retired for the evening. "Feelings and Surrender: Surrendering is a highly personal *and* spiritual experience . . . It is not something we can force or control by willpower. It is something we experience . . . Surrender sets the wheels in motion. Our fear and anxiety about the future are released when we surrender. We are protected. We are guided."

October 18, Day Twenty-eight

Surrounded by lush greenery and flowers, Kitty and I drank hot tea while we sat in wicker chairs on the porch. We could hear the buzz of women talking in the parlor. Across the street were stunning historic homes painted with accent colors that highlighted their character and charm. Most homes had welcoming porches and entryways, Greek columns, or Victorian gingerbread trim. The sun peeking over the treetops warmed the crisp cool air.

An energetic woman bounced up the stairs and sat opposite us, introducing herself as Teri. She had been on the porch enjoying wine and cheese with Ron and Eleanor the night before and was eager to share her story. "I've had many turning points in my life. I've been lucky enough to reinvent myself over and over. It's fun. I started off as a professional dancer and then, by accident, worked in media, which brought me to doing radio and television for twenty-five years. When I started in radio, it wasn't a career that women went into. I worked at a rock station, which was different for a woman. By the time I was in television, there were plenty of women in media. They needed a certain amount of women to get women viewers.

"Being a radio DJ helped me define myself. I was married at the age of nineteen and had children at twenty-two and twenty-three. I went to college before that, but being married at nineteen, you go from your dad's house to your husband's house. I raised two of the most incredible human beings that ever lived.

"Then I realized I hadn't marry the wrong man, but I had married before I was ready to be married. I got courage and explained to my husband that I didn't want to be married anymore and should probably do something on my own. I wasn't ready financially to do that. We had an agreement for the last two years of our marriage that I'd start to build something and ultimately move. It made sense at the time. It was a way for me to get to a point where I could live on my own with my children.

"With years of dance instruction, I decided I'd start my own dance studio. I'd been dancing my whole life. I'd danced the whole time I was married and raising children. I became a dance instructor with my own studio and a troop of dancers that were competitive. I'm originally from San Diego and a surfer girl. We're sort of free spirits, so it was fun for me to teach them to express themselves.

"I used a radio station DJ to mix the music for my competitions. Once, our troop was on the way out of town to a competition in Atlanta. I ran by the radio station to get the music for the competition. It happened to be five o'clock on a Friday—when the station did the big 'weekend begins' sort of thing. The DJ on the air was the one who mixed my music for me. He waved me in. Not knowing anything about radio, I didn't know the microphones were on. He said, 'If it isn't my favorite little dance instructor . . .' His words bothered me to no end. I said, 'Well, that makes that thirteen years of intensive training seem trivial. I'm sure your parents are very proud you went to DJ school.'

"Then he said something that made me laugh. The owner of the radio station was listening. He picked up the phone and called the hotline and said, 'Offer that girl a job. She has the best laugh I've ever heard.' I said, 'No, I have a job. I'm a dance instructor. I didn't go to DJ school.' They continually called me because evidently the owner was quite insistent. I said, 'I can't do that full time,' so they asked if I'd be interested in doing voice work. Once you get behind the microphone, you're instantly important. At that point in my life, it was important to feel important. I thought I'd failed at my marriage when I hadn't.

"Then they came to the table with an offer to be the second on a morning show with a male partner. You have to have a man in the studio to run the equipment." She grinned. "They got my attention. The morning show was about sports, and I'm a sports fanatic. He'd be play-by-play, and I'd be color. He'd do the nuts and bolts, and I'd do the background stories. They brought to the table the amount of money that would make it possible for me to be on my own. The great thing about it was I was done every day at eleven a.m.

"I found two college girls to move in rent-free if they would keep up with the housework. I hate housework. Until I got home at eleven, they were in charge of the kids. They would get the kids to school, and before the kids got home I was home. The only time of day that the kids were not with me was that horrible harried forty-five minutes in the morning. It was wonderful.

"My children grew up around the radio station. Anytime the station needed a child in a commercial, the kids were there. We were the three musketeers—and to this day it's still that way. We're very close. I'm not one of these moms who thinks that her children should be her best friends. I believe 'I'm the mom—you're the kids.' Instantly, I was the coolest mom ever because I was a DJ at a rock radio station.

"Ultimately that job morphed into helicopter reporting for television, which truly was fantastic. I did traffic reports and breaking stories that required a helicopter. The very first time I did something other than traffic reporting, we were doing a traffic report and I heard over the scanner, 'We have a hostage situation at the hotel. Are you ready?' A man in a hotel had three hostages, and I got to do the report live while watching the whole thing unfold. I considered going into television full time, and then I remembered they tell you how to wear your hair and makeup. So I stayed in radio. I got to do reports from the helicopter and watch the sunrise on a regular basis.

"When my children no longer needed me because they were teenagers and off doing their own thing, I circled back to art. I started my own design firm while I was still in radio. I've been an artist my whole life. My mother was convinced I was the most talented artist. When I was four, she took me to private art lessons. I learned color theory before going to kindergarten. People have asked me to help design spaces in their home because they liked what I'd done with mine. I'm one of those people who, if I don't know how to do it right, I don't do it, so I got the interior design education.

"The age of radio quickly declined. It became computerized, and satellite radio started. I could see it was no longer going to be a creative outlet for me. I decided to get out. I'm a finisher by trade now. I shipped myself to Europe, and I found artisans that were instructing faux bois. It was fascinating to learn the history behind these [techniques]. We had to learn about the trees and diseases to incorporate that into grain.

"That morphed into restoration, so Natchez makes perfect sense. Now I'm a full-time interior designer with a successful firm that specializes in restoration and decorative painted finishes. I'm teaching decorative paint finishes in my own studio, and people come from all over the country and discover this tiny jewel of a quirky little strange town. We tell stories, drink wine, and make food.

"I think everyone has incredible stories. I think how you feel about your story has to do with your mother and your father. I 'got' my mom. She never had a career. She married a Navy pilot and had children. She created her own life and there was always something happening— Oh! There's Anne."

A tall woman wearing a straw cowboy hat adorned with ribbon and beads was coming our way. "She's a fabulous character," said Teri. "I'll go inside so you can talk with her."

Anne took a seat in the wicker chair. "I'm glad to meet you and delighted you came to share your story with us," I said.

"It sounded like fun what you are doing, so when Eleanor called I had to come," said Anne. She took off her hat, set it on the end table next to her, and went right into telling her story. "I was born and raised in Natchez. I lived in a few different places, like New Orleans and Dallas. My parents became ill, so my husband and I decided to come home. My father died and my mother has Alzheimer's.

"We opened a business fifteen years ago, got divorced, and still run the business together. It's a restaurant—the Pig Out Inn Barbecue, right on Canal Street. We started our business from scratch. We were gonna open a flower shop or a barbecue restaurant. He won. I never thought I'd be slinging hash at sixty-five, but it's been a blessing and a good thing for both of us.

"I still have a good relationship with my ex-husband. We have no children. We opened another restaurant in Jackson, Mississippi, but we got divorced when it opened. He was up there for a couple of years and it didn't make it, so he moved back home. He's been back for a couple of years and helps me run the restaurant. I don't think you can be married to someone for twenty-three years—at least for me—and not have that ongoing relationship. I think we raised each other. You know people change and things change. People grow. It's working out quite nicely.

"I believe most people in Natchez feel it's our job to open our homes to people and make them feel wanted and part of the community. That's the way we were raised—to be hospitable. It's a Southern thing. I'm helping do a bus tour right now—a culinary, cultural bus tour—and they asked me to do a little presentation. People love to have other people come into town and show them what it's all about. I believe you should open yourself up to the universe—and people.

"I'm here to serve. I've always felt that way, although I might not have been in touch with it. I'm here to serve in many senses of the word. I have a lot of people who come into the restaurant and need money or help or a job. I hire young kids who need positive feedback—just life lessons they never got before. I don't like being in that role all the time. It's hard sometimes. Somebody said, 'The only way to change anything is to try to make an example of yourself.' I try." Anne reached up and pulled a few strands of hair away from her face.

"Since I turned fifty, I've gotten in touch with myself in a deeper way. Now I love being in my sixties. It brings a certain knowledge and wisdom you can't deny. It's fabulous! I used to go to therapy and my therapist said, 'Wait until you're in your fifties.' I said, 'Whoa. I think I'll wait. I'm not pushing the clock.' But you get better with age.

"A friend of mine says that whatever you do, do it with love. I don't like firing people, and I don't like confrontation. That's a problem for

Southern women. I remember the first time I had a confrontation at work. There was a pushy man, and I held my ground. I said, 'Man, we're going to have to come to a compromise. This isn't fair.' We did. I try to handle everything with love. Confrontation isn't pleasant. I say what I have to say, but I do it in a kind way with love. They say you can't catch a fly with vinegar—and you can't. I try to own my power as far as my serenity goes and not let people get me totally-out-there upset or take my power away. I try to pay attention and realize I have a choice. That's the biggest thing for me today, that I have a choice—in everything.

"I'm a recovering alcoholic. I've not had a drink in thirteen years. One of the things that I learned in AA is that there's a difference between fun and joy. Joy is a deeper sense of the word. Helping others is one thing that makes my life rich and nurtures my creative self. I love to create. I have a lot different interests. I decorate. I do flowers. I cater. I quilt. I scrapbook. I make cards. I garden. I'm an animal advocate—I love animals. I had a vintage car store, and I restored three aluminum trailers. I find a lot of joy in life. There are a lot of different things I like to do. I love nature and being outside.

"My quest in life would be to find that perfect soul mate, to have a passionate relationship that lasts a lifetime. That would be nice. I have a fabulous relationship with God, and I have a lot of friends. I'm taking it one day at a time as it comes, and if that happens—fabulous. Otherwise, that's fine.

"I believe you bring things to yourself and things manifest. I question illness—you know, why people get sick. I wonder about the underlying issues, not the physical issues. I have a saying: 'You can feed your dreams, or you can feed your nightmares. You can live in the solution or live in the problem.' You have to pay attention every day and every minute to where your mind is taking you—what you're doing and what you're saying, who's listening, and what she's picking up on. You have to have an awareness of what's before you. It's hard staying in the now. It's all about future.

"To be courageous is to face life with a positive attitude, knowing that whatever happens is for the greater good and that there's a lesson in it. I don't have a lot of fear. I don't have a fear of death, and I don't have a fear of getting sick. It doesn't stop me. If something bad happens, I know that for every door that shuts, another one opens. It's going to be okay. You have to keep on keeping on. I'm not saying I'm not human. I do get afraid. I'd be afraid on the river if it became super turbulent or if there was a log. We have lost a lot of people—friends—on that river over the years. I've been put in fearful situations, but to me it's about paying attention."

Anne looked past me as if she were miles away, and a sweet smile crossed her face as she said, "I was devoted to my parents. The thing that I remember the most—and what I'd choose if I could go back to any point in my life—would be my childhood. I had a wonderful childhood with a lot of cousins. We were raised downtown in a little secluded area at the end of the road.

"We used to go to a camp in the middle of the woods. We rode horses, woke up listening to roosters, swam, and fished. The most cherished moments of my life were with my family and my parents out in the country. We were living on nature, catching gar fish, making clover necklaces—just to be a child.

"We rolled down our windows when we crossed the bridge because it was rickety, and if the bridge fell down we could get out fast. We had an old phonograph that you had to crank. We'd dance around the table. Gnats would get into our milk, and adults would say, 'Drink it. They're good for you.' Those are my most cherished moments. I have a younger brother and an older sister. I have another older sister who died in her thirties.

"The other day I was coming into the restaurant from my Pilates class. I saw this older man with a crutch sitting outside, and I thought, 'That old codger—he's watching me.' I told the girls, 'There's this old man out there craning his neck to look at me.' I went home to change, and when I came back he was still there. Finally I walked on out, and I recognized him. I went over and spoke to him. He's eighty-five and deaf as a post. He looked at me, and I was who he thought I was. I sat down to talk to him. He couldn't hear me, so he did most of the talking. One of the things he said was, 'You know, you don't learn anything by talking all the time. You have to learn to listen.' I thought, 'He's right—I talk too much! I have to learn to listen.' That was funny. I love older people.

"AA has been the best thing in my life. I love the program and the twelve steps. It's the way to live regardless of alcoholism. It's brought me into a whole new world.

"I'm big into women for women. We're getting ready to have a fashion show and spa. I got a group of women together. I believe that women are strong. I'm not a women's libber. I don't like that term or when women are called 'ball busters.' I hate those terms, but some of them are over the top.

"I had plastic surgery ten years ago. I wanted to look like I felt. I did talks after that. I invited a bunch of women, and the doctor came to town. I stood up and said how I felt about it. I'm not embarrassed or afraid to say it. I think we should be our best selves. It made a difference for me, and I'm glad I did it.

"I brought this little poem I found. I didn't write it, but I like it. This is what the poem says:

> The challenge is not to create a completely new identity.
> It's to find new ways to express your whole rich, complex self.
> You won't find the answers just sitting in your living room,
> but out in the world,

interacting with people who can reflect back to you,
who you are and
where your light shines brightest.

"I picked it up from some magazine. I think it's interesting, and it encourages women to be themselves. I was married and I was happy, but I didn't want to be married. I'm not saying anything against marriage. I wanted to be myself, and since I'm in my fifties, I don't want to be controlled by anybody else. I want a partner who accepts me for who I am and encourages me.

"It's a different world. I have three girls who work for me right now who are all pregnant. None of them is married and all are under twenty-five. I'm flabbergasted. They don't have any clue. You can only teach them so much. You can lead a horse to water, but you can't make it drink. It's a different world today. Morality has gone out the window."

She shifted in her chair. "I think it's frightening with all this talk of 2012 and what's going to happen. [She was referring to the Mayan calendar predicting the end of the world.] It's going to be a mind-change thing. That's what I'm hoping for. I'm a new-thought thinker and a member of the Church of Religious Science Spiritual Center, a unity-based church. I think we all need to come together.

"Sitting around and resting are hard things for me. I need to work on that. It's a busy life. I neglect myself because I keep going, going, going. I work like a man. Y'all paddle, but I haul logs, cut trees, and work on cars. I installed five hundred pounds of tile in my trailer two weeks ago. I almost hurt myself overdoing it. I'm like a horse with blinders on. I can't see past what I'm doing. I like instant gratification.

"This has been truly great, but I have to go to Pilates class now. I haven't been there in a week."

As Anne was walking down the front porch stairs, Joan arrived and we went inside with her where a group of women had gathered and were deep in conversation. Nine of us gathered around a large table in the dining parlor: Joan, Teri, Beverly, Nancy H., Eleanor, Sandra A., Joan, Kitty, and me. Eleanor had tea and coffee for us.

"The trouble with river trips is you give up many things," said Beverly.

"I've taken four Mississippi River trips, and they're wonderful," said Joan. "On the river I can see the shore, and I know I could swim that far. Well, actually I couldn't swim to the Mississippi shore—but I could try."

"My grandson, Courtney, likes to be as far out on the water as he can be," said Beverly. "I like to sit onshore and watch the boats going by."

"We're getting off the water south of Baton Rouge and getting on Bayou Lafourche," I said. "I don't want to paddle with the ocean liners."

"But you don't mind alligators?" asked Beverly.

"It's not the alligators," I said. "It's the snakes I'm worried about."

"The alligators were a presence last spring because of the floods," said Joan, who spoke with a soft, confident voice. "They've been in people's yards. My son has a friend who catches them. The state pays him, and he was getting calls all hours of the day and night from people saying, 'There's an alligator in my yard!'"

"Listen, I've been as close as I am to you to those huge ones," said Beverly emphatically. "I didn't get too excited about that. One was trying to turn our boat over. Oh, yeah, they'll come up in the boat. You wait until you get to Lafourche."

"Driving is sounding better and better," remarked Kitty. We all laughed.

"We were in the Sabine National Wildlife Refuge," said Beverly. "The guide took us in the boat with my three little children and my husband. All of a sudden I hear this 'whomp.' After it happened three times I said, 'What's that?' The guide said, 'It's just alligators. They like to turn the boat over. This is dinner in the boat.'"

"White meat," joked Joan.

"I'm not wild about alligators," said Beverly, shaking her head. "That was close enough."

"I went paddling in the Okefenokee National Wildlife Refuge in a canoe with my sister-in-law to find out what it was like to paddle with them," I said. "Whenever we came upon an alligator, it went away from us, usually disappearing under the surface."

"Oh, no," said Beverly. "These wanted closer companionship."

"With whales and dolphins, that's an affectionate thing," said Teri. "They come up and bump the boat. Do you think it was really an aggressive thing?"

"Well, that's what the guide said," said Beverly. "Maybe he was trying to give me a scare. I asked, 'How big are these alligators?' I saw them, but I'm not very good with measurements. He said, 'I'd think that one was about thirteen feet.' They were all big.

"I'll tell you something I saw in Alaska that I couldn't get over. Have you ever seen whales bubble fishing? Collectively bubble fishing? This was half a dozen whales. They said it wasn't a pod, but they gather together to do this. They go under the water and blow bubbles. As the bubbles rise to the top, it attracts fish. Then the whales come up in a circle and eat the fish. We saw that six or seven times. Our guide said that you almost never see that."

Beverly paused and looked around the room and a nostalgic look crossed her face. "I was raised in this house," she said. "May I look around a little bit? I'd love to see the house again."

"Yes," replied Eleanor. "In fact, I'd like to look around with you and get the scoop."

"I don't know how much scoop I got," said Beverly, and the two of them went deeper into the house.

"Another house of great interest on this street is called the Bird's Nest," said Joan. "It was the home of Dr. Cartwright, who was the surgeon general during the War Between the States. Right next to the Burn house is Chatawa Cottage. His great-granddaughter, Alice Walworth Graham, an author, lived there. Alice Walworth Graham wrote a series of critical literary books—*Twentieth Century Literary Criticism*, by Gale Publishing Company. She wrote novels. *Vows of the Peacock* captured the essence of the medieval better than any author before or since. She was a little lady."

"Well, she wasn't just little," said Beverly from the other room.

"That was a loving euphemism," said Joan.

Conversation ensued regarding a local house and the histories of other houses in the area. The women around the table became very animated as they spoke about the houses and talked about the families that lived there and their connections to each other.

"I don't know if these are interesting stories for you or not," said Teri.

"We're all going to be related within fifteen minutes if we keep talking," said Nancy H., and we all laughed.

"Nancy has been here long enough to know," said Joan. "She's related to a lot of people. Nancy works at the Natchez Children's Home, which used to be called the Protestant Orphanage. It was begun about 1816 by Eliza Lowe Little. In about 1815, a group of Methodist women met in Washington, D.C. There were fifteen women there, and three were from Natchez. One was Eliza Lowe Little and one was Mrs. Tichenor. They lived on a houseboat down on the river. Did you know that Tichenor's is an antiseptic you drink if you—"

"Oh, no! You don't do that," said Beverly, earnestly. She and Eleanor had returned to the table.

"Well, my husband's uncle did," said Joan.

"But he wasn't supposed to," said Teri.

"Tichenor's antiseptic is 97 percent alcohol," said Joan. "Dr. Tichenor made millions off it. It's a very fine antiseptic, and it's still used in the South. I don't know about the rest of the world."

"Don't leave the South without picking some up," insisted Beverly.

"Is it good for mosquito bites?" I asked.

"Yes," said Beverly. "It's medicinal to put on your skin. It'll take the itch out."

"Holder's Drug Store on Franklin Street will have it," said Joan.

"You should go there anyway because it's an experience," said Teri.

"Nancy, I'm curious about the Children's Home," Kitty said.

"It was founded by a group of Christian women who saw a need in the territory," said Nancy H. with a gentle Southern accent. He words were smooth like honey. "We were not granted statehood until 1817. Our early minutes suggest that Indian wars and yellow fever outbreaks left children orphans. And there were wars . . ."

"Well, the War of 1812," said Joan.

"Yes," continued Nancy H., "wars of all sorts. This was a female Christian response to the orphans in the territory who had no education, opportunities, or places to live after their parents were killed. It was founded as the Female Charitable Society and continues to be in operation today. There aren't a lot of orphanages left in the United States today. Most have closed their doors. The buildings we are in now were built in the 1950s by a board of just women who represented·the churches in Natchez. Today we let men in. We're trying to diversify. I tell you, they were strong women with a tremendous amount of insight."

"Their husbands were bankers," said Joan.

"That probably helped," said Beverly.

"I've been there 'bout thirty years," said Nancy H. "It's considered a Christian ministry, nondenominational. Now representatives on our board are male and female, black and white, and they represent different congregations in the area. We're privately funded. We don't write grants to the federal government to pay for it. Our ancestors would be happy about that. I'm certainly happy about it.

"Our services today have diversified in the face of change that comes to any organization. Today they include foster families for children who are referred to us through the Department of Human Services because of abuse and neglect. We have foster families scattered around southwest Mississippi. When we get a call, the children go there instead of being housed in the orphanage or group home, which is not the conventional wisdom as the best way to serve children anymore. Today the national model is to try to keep them in their families—sometimes at all cost— and to provide services to those families so they won't be disrupted.

"We also have a children's advocacy center, which is something new. A young victim of crime can come and testify in front of a trained team. It's filmed and used as evidence. The child doesn't have to repeat that story over and over, basically being retraumatized."

The tone of Nancy H.'s voice was strong and confident. The more she talked the clearer it became that she was proud of the impact she and her staff were having. Her tone indicated that she was honored to carry on the legacy begun so many years before. She leaned forward and continued. "We have a preschool learning center that takes three, four, and five year olds who are totally off the chain, as I call them. We have them because of difficult issues at home, turnover, and no parenting. These youngsters aren't contained enough to operate in a regular classroom. We provide transportation, breakfast, lunch, and dinner. We teach both behavioral- and academic-related matters focused on what those children face with the hope that they'll get back into a regular classroom.

"We do a lot of advocacy and education. We're working on a case now that'll probably produce new case law about children being reunited with a parent who shouldn't have them. The father is a sex offender with a rap sheet a mile long, and the state wants to return the two little boys to him. It's not about teddy bears and ice cream for the children. It's about their lives, their souls, and their futures. I do it because it's all I've done, and I don't know how to do anything else. I also do it because it's incredibly important."

"Are you a sociologist?" asked Joan.

"No, I'm an English and education major," said Nancy H.

"Thank you for the work that you do," said Kitty. "I don't know if there's another term to use other than orphanage, but there aren't those environments any more in our country."

"The fact is that it was called an asylum—and it does provide asylum," said Joan.

"It did, and that wasn't a pejorative term," said Nancy H. "It was a safe harbor. We changed the name a couple of times. It was the National Protestant Home when I came here. There had been two Catholic orphanages that closed. We're out of the orphanage business and into helping disadvantaged children and their families."

"A wise old lady told me that with the advent of birth control, St. Mary's Orphanage for girls and Devereaux Hall for boys would close," said Joan.

"And they did shut down," added Nancy H.

"I hear a lot of pride in your voices when you talk about it," said Kitty. "It's something that makes your life rich."

"It does," said Nancy H. "It's exhausting and it's exhilarating. Parenting and dealing with children are anyway."

"I'd like to hear from the rest of you about what makes your life rich," said Kitty.

Sandra A. had been sitting quietly taking everything in. The women at the table knew each other, but she was a shy newcomer. She worked part time for Eleanor doing housekeeping. Eleanor had asked her to join us. After some encouragement, Sandra A. said, "I've been working at the Isle of Capri, a casino, for about the last eight years. I'm a supervisor in housekeeping on the boat. I grew up in Natchez and went to Roosevelt, but it was an elementary school at that time. I left here in '67 and went to Detroit because I wanted to get away from here. I've been in Detroit most of my life.

"In Detroit I had two boys, and I spent most of my young life in the hospital with them, trying to be there for them. I had a son who had sickle-cell anemia, and one who had muscular dystrophy. God blessed me. I had one until he was twenty-eight and one until he was thirteen. That's a lot of pain, but I think about God and His family, and other people who have tragedies, and that's what gets me through. I have family here.

"Now that I moved back, I'm experiencing a lot of things that I didn't when I was younger. I was gone sixteen years. Well, actually, before that because I lost my mother in 1980. At that point, I took care of business and went right back. The thing about being young is that as a child you're not paying that much attention. To me, it's been a lot different since I came back. It's gotten beautiful. Now that I'm back in Mississippi, I can experience a lot of things. I'd been praying to the good Lord that He would bring me back before I reached the age of fifty. I'm back at forty-six years old. I wanted to come home."

Beverly asked, "Did you go to the church down on—?"

"I go to China Grove," replied Sandra A.

"I don't know if y'all know this," Joan said to Kitty and me, "but the church is an important part of all cultures in the South. It's the home and the church. In Charleston they'll say, 'What'll you have to drink?' In Atlanta they'll say, 'Who was your mama?' But in Natchez they'll say, 'What church do you go to?'"

"I've often been asked who my mother was, and my response was, 'Well, who's your daddy?" said Eleanor.

"I just tell them, 'You don't know my mama and you don't know my daddy,'" said Teri. "When I was in one of the garden clubs, it was hysterical that they could get me in a hoop skirt—I was a California girl who never wore anything but flip-flops. I did it because of the restoration aspect of receiving people. Receiving means that when people come from all over the world to visit the houses here, you receive them. You tell them the history of the house. They put you in a hoop skirt and the whole deal. I asked if I could wear black pants and a white shirt and they said, 'No, you'll wear a hoop skirt.'

"I'd get the buses of people from Europe and the first thing out of their mouths was, 'You're not from the South, are you? What are you doing here?' I'd say, 'How many of you have ever been to Natchez before? How many of you have been here more than once? If this is your first trip to Natchez, I can promise you'll be back. If this is your second trip to Natchez, you're already thinking about your next trip back. After your third trip here, you will be owning real estate.' That was the progression with us. I came. I saw. I loved. I have a Southern accent. It just happens to be a southern California accent. When I have to I can say, 'My lands, it's hot in here!' They get a kick out of that."

"Did you hear about the English man who came here on a cold March day and said to the woman who was receiving at Richmond, "I say, isn't it a wee bit drafty under there?"' joked Joan.

"It's a free air conditioner," said Teri. "If you wiggle your hips, the skirt swooshes around. What's fun is trying to drive."

"Well, you don't drive with one of those on," remarked Joan.

"Well, I didn't know that!" said Teri. "I have a little Mercedes B class, a tiny little car. I gathered the hoop skirt all up and climbed in. It must have been hysterical to see a little bit of me trying to look above all the hoops while I was driving. My husband tells me that you can loosen it at the waist and it drops down and becomes real flat."

"Did you ever watch Scarlet undress?" asked Joan.

"I've never seen *Gone with the Wind*," said Teri.

"What you can do is take the hoops and pull them up behind you," instructed Beverly. "That way the other hoops stay down so you can drive. I don't do that anymore. My hoops go with other people to other places."

"I've heard a lot about the garden club, and it's very interesting to me," said Sandra A.

"Well, you should get in the garden club," insisted Teri.

"I don't know about gardening," replied Sandra A.

"I belong to two garden clubs," said Joan looking at Sandra A. "In 1952, I planted caladium bulbs around the trees in my yard, and they never came up. My husband said they came up in China because I'd planted them upside down.

"The garden clubs are about preservation of historical homes—and conservation, fellowship, and education. Beverly and I belong to the Rose Craft Garden Club. It was established before I was born. They've already celebrated their seventy-fifth anniversary, which was about eight years ago. The club was composed of twenty-four farm and rural women. They dressed in their hats and gloves and went to the meeting once a month. They don't do hats and gloves anymore, but you tell them what's growing in your garden, and there are plant exchanges. Some ladies are professionals. I'm not. The nice thing about it is when you're having a problem with one of your flowers, you can take it to the next meeting, and they'll come up with good ideas. It's a nice garden club to belong to."

"I heard some of the garden clubs own properties in town," said Kitty.

"Yes," said Joan. "It's about preservation. I read that the first preservation project was begun by the Natchez Garden Club in the '30s. They acquired the house on Ellicott Hill, which at that time they called Connerlly's Tavern.

"There was a lady here who was a historian. What she didn't know, she made up. We have wonderful stories that they've spent a long time correcting. She did record a lot of important stuff too. Anyway, the house on Ellicott Hill is the site of the first raising of the flag of the United States in the lower Mississippi Valley. The club owns that house, and they own Magnolia Hall. The Pilgrimage Garden Club owns Longwood, which is the largest octagonal-shaped structure in America."

"It was women who started the garden clubs to save their homes," said Teri. "Basically their homes were in disrepair after the Civil War, and they couldn't afford to fix them. They found out people were interested in these structures and would pay money to come in and see them. They dressed up in their finery and opened their homes."

"That actually occurred like a phoenix rising out of the ashes," added Nancy H. "The state garden clubs in 1932 were scheduled to come to Natchez to view gardens. There was a late freeze in March, and all of the gardens froze. There wasn't anything to see but dead gardens. The ladies, being a little verclempt, were concerned about what they were going to do with their garden show. They decided at the last minute that the ones who had homes would dust off their furniture and let people come in. That was a huge hit. After that first quickly-put-together spring pilgrimage, they decided that besides focusing on gardens, they would make houses available to make money to continue restoring them."

"When you were all talking about that, I thought about my family," said Beverly reaching for her coffee cup. "I grew up with aunts and my mother in this house. Even back in the 1920s, my aunts were professional people. One was a teacher at the elementary school, and one was a nurse and had been the head of the charity hospital. She did other nursing overseas and had wonderful trips. She joined as an Army Corps nurse. She was MacArthur's mother's nurse and lived in Hawaii with them and was in typhoons and all kinds of exciting stuff. They were professional women at a rather early date, when women didn't go out and work or do anything like that."

"What I'm gleaning from listening to you," I said, "is that you talk differently about your lives than the people in the North. There doesn't seem to be a separation of your life and history that came before."

"No, there can't be," said Joan and Beverly together.

"Well, that's not true in the North," I said. "We don't have that same sense of history. It's fascinating to listen to how incorporated that is and how it's a core value for you."

"One of the reasons is this architecture," said Joan. "You had to sit on the front porch to cool off because the houses were hot. They sat there and told stories."

"People would walk by and come up on the porch and visit," said Beverly. "It was a way of life, especially in warm weather."

"People would come for Sunday dinner, but then they stayed for three months," said Joan.

"I went out to my in-laws house before I married," said Beverly. "They lived out in the country. He was a farmer. There were twenty people at Sunday dinner, and I didn't know any of them except my husband and his parents. One was a Methodist minister, and the one sitting next to me had the strangest accent I've ever heard. I don't know where he came from. The one on the other side was deaf as a post. I had to try to be sociable and impress my future in-laws. It was very hard to do. I'll never forget that night.

"I spent many weekends at that house. They had twins who were my age. Ann would ask seven girls to come home with her, and Joe would ask the same number of boys. Mrs. Greer didn't know how many people were going to be there for supper until they arrived at the supper table. This was during World War II when my mama had ration stamps, and we didn't get but a little piece of meat once a week because meat was being rationed. They'd come in with a tray of pork chops. There were up to twenty-four pork chops on that plate, plenty for everybody. It was the most incredible thing I've ever seen. They were in the country so they could kill their own.

"They were wonderful, and we enjoyed the most cultured conversations. He was a horticulturist, and she was a history major. They were very intelligent and raised all of these children, none of them theirs. They had seven children in that house before it was all over with."

"Mr. Greer came here," said Joan. "He was the person who established the experimental station of Mississippi State University. It was the first one in the state. I think that was in the '20s. Mrs. Greer was teaching. He was dating a different schoolteacher who went home for the summer. The schoolteacher asked Annie Ruth—Mrs. Greer—to watch out for S. J.—Mr. Greer—while she was gone. S. J. and Annie Ruth were married while the schoolteacher-girlfriend was gone. That was a story that they loved to tell."

"I grew up in North Carolina," said Nancy H., "but I've been here all my adult life. I'm a true Southerner. I appreciate and am fed by the connections that we find important in the South. Every day that I work in the field of broken families and children who are lacking a sense of bond to important people, I value it even more.

"I had a wonderful family. My parents stayed together until one died, and I lost my mother a few months ago. They were not people of great means. They were educated people. My father was a professor in the math department at the university. They provided for me a good childhood, a sense of family, and a love of generations prior to me. I took that for granted. I thought that was the way everybody lived. I didn't know that people didn't take care of their children. I was as green as you can be about that. Praise God, I was.

"My father has informed what I've done in raising my own three children. It's what I long for, more than anything, for these children who are separated, disconnected, unbonded, and chaotic. They're dying. We're hardwired to want family and a sense of place, and they don't have either. I see how damaging it is. I think that's one of the underlying factors that keeps me there—to teach them by how we live and operate in front of them, who they have experiences with, and what their memories are. Through our work at the Children's Home, we can at least show them another way."

"My husband's family lost their mother and their father when the children were very young," said Beverly. "That's how they ended up coming to Natchez to live with a cousin. When he first came, he was seven years old. No mother, no father, and he was living with any relative who'd take him in at the moment. They took him to Jefferson Street Sunday school where there used to be a big picture of Jesus on the wall. Jesus was reaching down to hold a little boy's hand. It was his 'Suffer not, little children, come unto me' picture. My husband said that's when he decided to join the church, because that picture touched him. He had nobody, so that was a connection for him."

"I think what you're doing is very interesting, and it makes me think of my work," said Joan. "I was the director at the library in a community college. That was a career change for me when I was sixty. I found that we don't know who we're influencing. Young women would come there—and this was a second chance for some. They could get a Pell Grant. I've had them say, 'You mean so much to me.' I wasn't aware of what I was doing. I encouraged them to have a career and make their lives better. That's one reason I'll never use slang. I tried to set an example. I wouldn't do things that I'd want to if I didn't think they were appropriate. They didn't see me drinking a can of beer."

A mischievous grin lit up Joan's face. "I'm going to share one little story with you. We, as educators, try to speak clearly and specifically not use slang. One day a teacher said to a little girl, 'I want you to make me a sentence using the word red.' The little girl said, 'I gots a red dress.' The teacher said, 'Wonderful. Now make me a sentence using the word nachos.' The little girl said, 'I gots a red dress dat's nachos.' The teacher said, 'Although that was wonderful, how about making me a sentence with the word fascinate.' The little girl said, 'I gots a red dress dat's nachos, but it's got buttons that I can fascinate.' The teacher said, 'That was good. Now make me one more sentence using the word hotel.' And the little girl said, 'I gots a red dress dat's nachos, but it's got buttons that I can fascinate, and every time I bend over my hotel sticks out.' And that's the way it goes."

Joan's joke had us laughing and marked the end of the Gathering. The women began to leave, but Joan lingered to share more information with Kitty and me. Standing at the end of the table, she said, "Here we have a climate that lends itself to visiting, Think about those people in Illinois and Indiana. They were becoming states about the same time, but their summers were short. You see, up in the North, the climate was such they had to eke out a living from the soil where they could. You've read about the sod houses. Down here, they didn't live in no sod house in the summertime. They could live in a shack—even in the winter—and not suffer from the cold."

"It's about a different culture and the difference between being able to live outside instead of inside," said Kitty. "In the South, there's a lot more living outside—the analogy of being outside the walls."

"Thomas Jefferson, George Washington, and John Adams—the Founding Fathers—while they were writing the Constitution in July in Philadelphia, had to get outside," said Joan. "It was hot, but they had to keep the windows closed because they didn't want people to know what they were doing. They crossed the river and went to Bartram's garden. These were cultured people. They released their tension in the garden by being around something that was growing, like the flowers, magnolias, which were growing under those great canopies of trees.

This has been most interesting."

"You know, we didn't hear a word from Eleanor," I said. "We're going to have to hear from her."

"We wouldn't give her a chance to speak," kidded Joan. "Y'all have a good trip."

Joan left, and Kitty and I got another cup of tea and sat down with Eleanor who said she didn't really have much to say. Leaning forward with her elbows resting on the table she began. "I grew up in Baltimore, so my sense of history is different from most in Natchez. My mom is from upstate New York and my dad from Delaware. My father was a civil engineer for the Federal Bureau of Highways. Being in a big city was an advantage because of situations in the family.

"A lot has to do with cold up north. People are indoors or in the bars. In Baltimore, people turn their basements into pubs. There were a lot of those in our neighborhood, which was strange as I look back. We never went to one. There were neighborhood groceries where the store was in front and the owners lived in back. One was called Hannah's. With a couple pennies, you could buy candy. It wasn't hard to convince one of us to go buy a loaf of bread when my mother ran out.

"There were five public high schools in Baltimore. Two schools were for males, two of them for females, and one was coed. As I look back, it seems strange that they weren't all coed, but that was normal.

"When I met Ron, we got married and moved to a small town in Virginia. It took me the longest time to call Natchez a city because it's small to me. We love old homes, so when we decided to retire, Ron said, 'Let's move south because of the warmer winters.' I thought he was talking about Florida, and I didn't want to go to Florida because there are too many people there.

"Mississippi was the first state out to send us information. We visited Natchez and Vicksburg. Vicksburg was thumbs down mainly because it was devastated during the Civil War. Here the residents waved the white flag. The Burns' home next door was used as a hospital. They have pictures of the Union Army soldiers there. We wanted an older home.

"I need a good pair of glasses so I can take up knitting and crocheting again—something to do with my hands. With a B&B, you're held captive for the most part. It's great work because you get to meet people. You can hire people, but it's a 24/7 job, and that's hard. We've started to turn our phones off at night, but beyond that we're always on call. We've been here for six years.

"To vacation, we take rooms out of service. We have a couple that has been coming here since the get-go because we're pet friendly. They have two Norfolk terriers that I call my niece and nephew. We ask them to come because it's a win-win situation. We get to go out of town and keep the business going, and they get a vacation. They come back next month. When you close up the house, you never know what's going to happen. This is my hobby.

"What I love about the B&B is breakfast. It's when you have a large crowd of strangers coming together and listening to the laughter. The characters that come! Everyone has a different story. It's a rich environment compared to hotels.

"I'm always getting new recipes. I don't do much baking. I like the challenge too, as far as cooking for people with celiac and gluten intolerance. It's not that hard because now you can buy gluten-free bread. I can work with that and make little stratas, French toast, and stuff like that.

"The hardest ones to feed are the vegans. All I can give them is oatmeal. Some of them are so rigid about it that they won't eat. People get funny. I'm thinking about telling the staff to tell them that the mad Russian—like in *Seinfeld*—is in the kitchen and nothing is to come back. It has to be eaten or it's 'No soup for you!' Maybe that would make them not so picky. What I like is when people say they aren't picky."

Eleanor sat back in her chair and continued, "I was working in the city of Baltimore at a construction company for a while before we came here. It was an office job and was kind of fun. It was no challenge as far as using your noggin. It was nice to sit in the front window and take calls and do things for the boss.

"Here, maintaining two houses is constant. Some days I tell Ron I have to sit down. You get burned out. In fact, today I thought we wouldn't have a guest, and then we had you and this Gathering. Oh, don't feel bad. Ron has this competition thing going. Last year we had X number of rooms booked for this month, and we're almost there—and this month's only half over. The quiet time is in late summer down here. The

kids go back to school in August. With the heat, people don't go anywhere. The tempo picks up again in January after Super Bowl Sunday.

"People are rabid about football, from high school football to pro.
We get LSU fans. We get Mississippi fans. I told Ron we should root for a
team or we should go with whoever is here. We had one guest who's a
lawyer and went to LSU. Apparently he has a lot of bucks because he follows LSU everywhere. He's forty and has only missed a couple of games
since he graduated. The sports page here is all about what the high
school kids did in sports.

"I support Ron. That's a big thing for me. That's the way it is in my
family. My mother doted on my father. I doted on my father. Ron would
say, 'Well, you're not doting on me,' but I do. It makes my eyes roll when
he says something to me like I have to put down everything and do it.
He'll say, 'I don't mean right now.' It's in my head that I've got to do it.

"I have a lot of brothers and sisters. My mom just passed in June, so
it's been four months. I think about her a lot. I think, 'She's finally come
to visit Mississippi.' It's hard. My mother was something of yesteryear.
When I went up there, she was laid out in the house. She didn't want to
be embalmed—and no viewing. She wanted to be cremated. She lay
there for two days before they came and took her.

"I'd never touched a dead person. When I was a kid, I touched a dead
cat with a stick, and it was hard. People get like that too. However, I
know that after a certain point, the rigor mortis goes away. I touched my
mom, and her hand felt like mine does now. She looked like she was
sleeping. She had emphysema, so she did a lot of sleeping. We had a little service in the house. A deacon from her church came in. It was a little
strange, but it was nice in a way. My whole family was there. I couldn't
watch when they put her in the bag and took her. My sister and brother-
in-law stayed and watched. He broke down after they took my mother
away.

"There are eight of us—five girls and three boys. After my sister died,
I was the oldest girl. I don't remember her at all. There are pictures of her
holding me.

"Of course, you're very critical of yourself, but I look back at how I
treated my mother when I was a kid . . . You know how you know it all?
You can't turn the clock back. I regret that. Gosh, she was strong. I probably would've beaten me up. That's why I don't have children—after
being the oldest girl. My older brother had cerebral palsy. I had to deal
with him as far as taking care of him at times. I was changing my
youngest siblings' diapers and babysitting. My next sister down had
complications where she had to go in for a lot of surgery. Mom was at
the hospital with her, and I was doing the cooking.

"I remember when I was married to my first husband. When I came
home and visited, I never once brought him home with me. My father
would say, 'When are you going to have children?' I'd say, 'I don't know,

Dad.'

"I sure would love to have grandchildren. A—they're fun. B—they aren't your responsibility. C—they go home when you're done. We don't have little ones around. Neither of Ron's children is married."

Eleanor paused as if lost for what to say next, so I asked, "What would you have wanted to know when you were younger?"

"What I'd tell my younger self would probably be about my parents and about having more respect," said Eleanor. "I've not walked a mile in my mother's shoes—I haven't even walked a block. I never had that urge to give birth. It was never a craving for me. It was the fear factor for me after seeing what could go wrong—like with my older sister and my brother. Having children could possibly mean I had someone to take care of me in my old age. I remember a fellow I worked with a while ago who said that was a reason to have children. I thought that was an awful thing to say, but you know, in some cultures that's true. The young take care of their elders. He just had a crass way of putting it—and that's how I feel now even repeating it. I'm sure I'd have loved the child. It just wasn't a need.

"I remember my ex-husband. We went to counseling, and the counselor said to him, 'You're in your coffin and you're thinking about what you could've done. What would it be?' He was pragmatic. To get him to do anything was hard. He would lift his feet for me to vacuum under them, but if there was a tiddlywinks marathon going on television, he'd be watching it. He loved to watch sports. I thought it was interesting that he couldn't answer the question. Then I realized it would be my week in the barrel at the next meeting, and I wouldn't have an answer either.

"I'm tied to water, and yet I don't want to be in it. My older sister drowned. My mother wouldn't tell us how she died, but during my swimming lessons one of my neighbors told me how she died. Well, that was it for me being in water—deep water anyway. I had dreams of drowning. I couldn't figure out what it was about. Finally I realized it was that I was in an over-my-head situation. I've not had one since.

"Our parents weren't big on affection. We weren't big huggers, but we would kiss our parents good night. We never said I love you, so—being away from my family—I decided I'm going to start saying I love you. Oddly enough, as my mom got older, she would say it. I guess she realized her frailties." Eleanor looked out the door to the hallway and said, "Well, ladies, I have got to get to work. I have a couple coming in this afternoon."

Kitty and I gathered our things, put them in the van, and walked to Natchez Children's Home Services that Nancy H. ran. Its motto is "Saving lives, one child at a time, since 1816." We were welcomed the minute we stepped in the door. Children's artwork hung on the walls. Justin gave us a tour of the facility, housed in the original children's home. They served eight counties in Mississippi and, because they are on the border, two parishes in Louisiana. The staff was delightful and spoke of the children with high regard and great fondness. They were excited to work with that challenging population of children who came to them in pain. There was an overriding sense that the staff knew the importance of the role modeling they provided the children.

Before we left Natchez we wandered the downtown area and purchased Dr. Tichenor's Peppermint Mouthwash Concentrate and First Aid Antiseptic from Holder's Drug Store. I'm always looking for mosquito bite remedies. Then we went into St. Mary's Cathedral, built in 1842. It's the only church in Mississippi built as a cathedral. It has high arching ceilings, ornate statues, and colorful detailed stained glass. I stood in the aisle and was flooded with childhood memories of going to church at St. Helena's and Holy Rosary Churches in Minneapolis. I looked up at the statues and remembered sitting in church not paying attention to the service because I was enthralled with the many beautiful statues and wondered how they were created.

We took our time driving to St. Francisville, Louisiana, enjoying the lush green scenery. I opened mail we had picked up from general delivery at the Natchez post office. In the letter we received from Katie in Lakeville, Minnesota, she described her morning: "I walked into the dining room and there again was another majestic sunrise of pinks, mauves, gold, blue, and silver hues breaking through the light fog; as the fog dispersed, a ball of golden blinding light quietly rose above the horizon and radiated across the sky . . . God really put on a glorious show this year. The tress and shrubs are gorgeous in the many magnificent fall colors. This is his fall splendor splash. Praise God." I missed the colors of fall back home. Katie's letter was a gift. I closed my eyes, and I was there.

Katie sent a special note to the paddlers on our journey. The cover of the card had two laughing little girls floating in a bright orange inner tube. The inside read, 'Do unto others as you would have them do unto you or dunk them if they get too obnoxious."

We checked into the Printer's Cottage, part of the Barrow House Bed and Breakfast, a sweet building with a white picket fence, a porch running across the front, and a cozy back yard. Shirley, the owner, spoke with a slight Canadian accent. Shirley sat us down amongst several teddy bears in a small room leading to the kitchen, gave us a map of the area, and pointed out several local highlights, including a shop called Grandmother's Buttons. Shirley said, "We're sitting on a ridge that's between the river and Bayou Sarah. It's about a quarter mile down to the river back behind this building. We're called the town that's two miles long and two hundred yards wide. There's no usable land on either side. It's one of the higher spots in Louisiana. We don't have to worry about the river here.

"The town of Bayou Sarah used to be down towards the river. It was the biggest fort between Memphis and New Orleans before the war. That was where the sugar, cotton, and indigo from the plantations were shipped around the world. Indigo is the dye that's used in clothes. It wasn't a tremendous crop, but they did grow some. Processing and picking cotton wasn't anything compared to the labor required for indigo. Every year it flooded in Bayou Sarah. I say this town was founded in 1807 because the merchants looked up here to build nice houses that didn't flood." Shirley told us the town was named St. Francisville because in the late 1700s there was a monastery of Carthusian monks across the river.

She left and we settled in. We were the only ones in the cottage. We looked at the other rooms, each decorated with beautifully cared for antiques and teddy bears. The attic had another sleeping area that was rustic with the rafters exposed. There were holes in the rafters where cannon balls had gone through during the war. We felt nervous and unsettled in the attic and were glad it wasn't our sleeping space.

We walked the narrow street to Grandmother's Buttons, a gift shop and button museum in a historic refurbished bank building owned by Susan Davis. The button museum was in the old bank vault. The museum displayed thousands of antique buttons from the 1760s through the 1940s. The case that I enjoyed the most held her mother's and grandmother's buttons. It reminded me of all the buttons my mother had in a box with drawers that was nearly as large as a breadbox. Susan created a variety of unique, colorful jewelry from her vintage buttons in her studio on the second floor of the bank.

For dinner, Kitty and I went to an upscale restaurant with low lighting and a fancy bar at the back. People were enjoying their meals and laughing. Our waiter was pleasant and humorous. We enjoyed our salads and talked with the tape recorder on the table between us. Then a man stepped into the doorway. He was tall and thin, and his three-piece navy suit was impeccable. His white hair and distinguished features made him attractive, but he was intimidating. Everything about him seemed controlled and controlling. He wasn't waiting to be seated; without saying a word, he demanded acknowledgment and service. The servers jumped to attention and rushed to him calling him "Sir" repeatedly. The bartender looked nervous as he greeted him, "Good evening, Sir. The usual?" Customers fidgeted anxiously. Some turned away pretending not to see him. We dubbed him Menacing Man.

Around his neck hung a phone with a wire running to his ear. It glowed in the dark atmosphere of the restaurant. With a thick Southern accent he spoke loudly into the phone with no regard for disturbing the quiet atmosphere around him. Menacing Man sat at a table two down from us and continued to talk loudly to the person at the other end of the phone repeatedly calling him "son." His tone was condescending and demanding. Then Menacing Man said, "We've known each other for over forty years, son. I don't care if it's illegal, son. Fix it." I felt a shudder of fear move through my body. I covered the tape recorder and slid it into my purse hoping he hadn't seen it. Kitty and I looked at each other in disbelief. Our waiter came to see how we were doing, but his pleasant demeanor had changed. He was nervous. We made jokes with him and got him to smile briefly.

We were considering dessert when Menacing Man said, "Don't worry about that, son. I can fix anything." Our interest in dessert disappeared. We paid our bill and left. On the drive back to the B&B, we conjured scenarios about Menacing Man. He was mafia; he was crooked law enforcement; he was rich, powerful, and the law didn't apply to him; he was evil. We decided he was dangerous and we needed to steer clear of him.

It may have been the influence of Menacing Man, but when we returned to our rooms the unsettling feeling we had in the attic permeated the house. We didn't feel alone, nor did we feel safe. There was no reason for either feeling. Every bump and creak the house made intensified the feeling. The wind howled and made a rocking chair on the front porch intermittently bang against the wall, spooking us each time. The house felt haunted. We couldn't get comfortable enough to sleep. We watched *Sleepless in Seattle*, *Steel Magnolias*, and other movies into the morning hours. Fatigue finally overcame us, and we restlessly drifted off to sleep.

October 19th through 20th

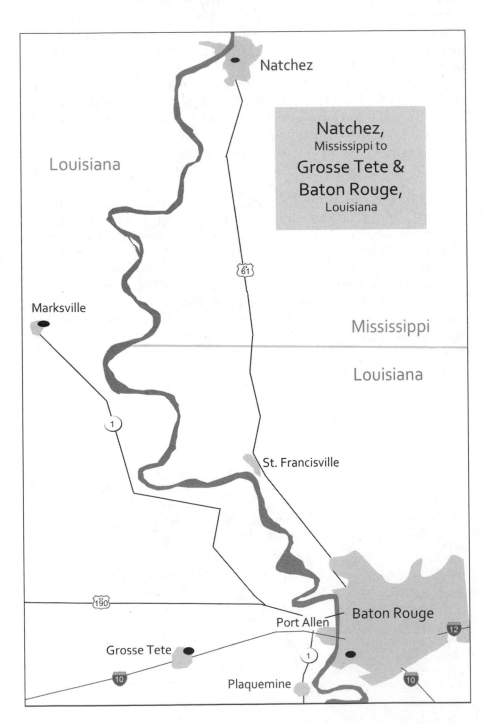

Natchez

Natchez,
Mississippi to
Grosse Tete &
Baton Rouge,
Louisiana

Louisiana

Marksville

Mississippi

Louisiana

St. Francisville

Baton Rouge

Port Allen

Grosse Tete

Plaquemine

8

GROSSE TETE

October 19, Day Twenty-nine

Before we left our room, Kitty read from a three-ring binder that Shirley had put together about the house. "Old houses and old towns spawn legends, and the Printer's Cottage is no exception. It's called the Printer's Cottage because of its long association with men and women who edited and printed the town's newspapers, and many of them were indeed the stuff of legends . . . The legend is that long before there were newspapers, long before there was much of a town, this house existed and was used as the house of the dead. In the eighteenth century . . . settlements of Point Coup across the Mississippi from St. Francisville were served by Spanish Carthusian friars, who named their parish church after the founder of their order, St. Francis of Assisi. Unwilling to bury their dead in grounds subject to flooding, the friars hallowed a burying ground on the high bluffs, now St. Francisville. The grave diggers, priests, and mourners needed sustenance, so in the natural order of things, purveyors of food stuffs, grog, shop keepers, and draymen arrived to earn a meager living meeting these needs, throwing up dwellings, business, and houses with materials closest at hand and following concepts brought along in memory. One such building was a plain post and beam structure of four rooms, and in one of them, according to legend, the bodies of the dead were kept prior to the burial. All during the years, the friars ferried earthly remains across the river . . ."

She finished reading it, and we looked at each other wide-eyed. We were convinced one of the rooms we were in was where the bodies had been kept. That spooked us more than the rocking chair hitting the wall throughout the night.

We crossed the street to the main house where Shirley had fixed us a breakfast of eggs, fruit, Danish pastries, and tea. In the dining room, a punkah hung from the ceiling over the table. A punkah is a large swinging fan, originally made from a large leaf, fixed to the ceiling. This one was a board on a hinge. It was activated by pulling a rope on a pulley system. Shirley said, "Wherever the English went they took punkahs, but they don't do a whole lot. It was run by the punkawallah. In India anybody that does something is a wallah. It means the worker of whatever. In the plantation homes they call punkah a shoofly because it keeps the flies off the table."

We told Shirley we'd love to hear her story, and she settled into a chair across the table from us and willingly began. "One day you're twenty-five and then next day you're sixty-five, and you say, 'Where did it go?' A whole lifetime has gone by. The older I get, the more I become satisfied with who and what I am, which is the definition of humility. When I was young, I thought I was going to go out and burn the world up. I think many young people think that—however, some don't have any ambition to do anything. The older you get, the more you realize and appreciate a lot of things in life. You can have a regular life. You don't have to be a Marie Curie or a Hillary Clinton or somebody that's famous that's going to leave an indelible mark on the world.

"I was brought up to believe education is everything. There are two parts to education. One is what you're taught in school during a traditional education. The other is through experience and life. Both are important.

"I went to college in 1961, before Women's Lib, which was important in shaping women's lives. My father sat me down and said, 'What do you like most of all?' I said, 'History.' He said, 'Well, you know if you like history, you can be a teacher.' I said, 'I don't like that.' He said, 'What do you like after that?' I said, 'Maybe science and biology.' He said, 'Well, there's a number of things you can do with that, but you have to have some kind of a job wherever your husband might be.' I thought, 'Man!' My dad said, 'It doesn't matter because you go to school to learn. If I look back, what I learned in school was out the door as soon as I graduated from college. That's what you do, and then you go on.'

"At Penn State, I got into the life science school. It was the first week of orientation, and we had to go to the big gym. There were several hundred kids in there, and they looked like they were all boys except for a half dozen girls. A lot of the life sciences were agriculture and stuff like that. They began to divide us by our respective disciplines into smaller groups. They called out horticulture, agriculture, and farming. All these guys were going to their corners. I'd sat next to the women because I didn't want to be the only one with all these guys. Then they called medical technology and microbiology, and the women got up and went to a corner of the room. I thought, 'My gosh, I'm the only one. I'll be the only one sitting here, everybody else will be gone, and what'll I do?' I went with them. They started talking about medical technology and microbiology, and I thought, 'If I don't like it, I can change to something else.' I graduated in that, and that's what I did for twenty years until I hit forty.

"Things have upped themselves. Now people have life crises at fifty instead of forty. I was forty twenty-seven years ago. That's when I drove along here, saw this place, and decided to completely change what I was doing. I've been here ever since.

"I was a medical technologist for twenty years and worked as a microbiologist most of that time. For two years after I graduated from Penn State, I stayed there and put my first husband through his PhD. Then I worked at various hospitals on and off. We moved back to Texas, and I worked in hospital labs. The last eight years that I was in Houston, I was in charge of a lab that served doctors' offices. I had a small staff. I liked it.

"All my life I've been very fortunate. I was discussing this with people the other day. I liked what I did. Some people were dissatisfied and saying, 'I don't like what I did. I don't like the direction of my life.' I said, 'If you don't, change it.' A lot of people think they aren't satisfied with being who and what they are. They think they have to do something else or strive for something more. If you're happy in your job, that means a lot. I hear that 50 percent of the people hate their jobs and hate their bosses. How awful.

"Being satisfied with everyday life and being who and what I am makes my life rich. I was telling one of my friends that climbing into bed, pulling the sheets up, and turning on the TV for fifteen minutes before I fall asleep is good. Just lying there I get that warm, fuzzy feeling and think, 'This is nice!'

"Not every day is great for anybody, but things are good. I'm sure there are other things that I'd want, but they say you get what you need. If you don't want too much, maybe that's a good thing. People get carried away with their wants. I think that's what's happened to this country the last twenty-five years. I can't believe the debt that people have. It goes against my grain from how I learned as a child.

"My parents had a nice house and car, but we weren't buying everything. My father didn't have a credit card until about 1970. They paid cash for everything. This was common back then. My father wasn't by any means wealthy. I had everything, but I didn't do what many people do today where they spend money on useless things and get themselves into horrible debt. People have overextended themselves. Somehow in the '80s and '90s everybody got this business where if you wanted something you went and bought it and put it on a credit card and paid it later. Later catches people.

"I'm a Canadian citizen. I've been here since I was fifteen. My parents were Canadian born. I guess my grandmother was the only Canadian born of my grandparents. My grandfather was English, and my mother's parents were from Poland.

"My father was the chief engineer of the last Canadian jet fighter." She sat taller in her chair as she spoke of her father. "In 1959, he was recruited by NASA as the chief engineer on Project Mercury. That was the first—well, I call it the John Glenn deal. We moved to Houston in 1962. They moved everybody there to build the Space Center. At that time he had conceived the Gemini Space Program and was manager of it. He received the NASA gold medal for his concept and design of the program. That medal is in the case out there." She pointed toward the living room. "In other words, he created the second American manned space program. There's also a Royal Canadian Mint coin from 1996 with a picture of him and his plane on it. He was a genius in his field.

"My mother was what they called a practical nurse, like an LPN now. She met my father in Halifax during the war, and she never worked after that. She was a housewife. They married in Montreal, which is where I was born. They moved to Toronto because that's where the job was. I have one brother, and he's in Houston. My parents are dead.

"After having worked in the medical profession for a good number of years, I see the main way to curtail costs in the long run is by preventive medicine. You aren't going to get preventive medicine if everybody doesn't go to the doctor. That's how they do it in other countries like Canada, England, and France. The head of the doctors' organization in England was on TV. He said every person is given a primary care doctor who manages their care and keeps them healthy. If there is a problem, they get sent on so they don't get to the point where we have with the extreme conditions. It prevents tremendous expense later on.

"They don't see that with our kind of system. Obamacare! Hillary Clinton couldn't get through what she wanted. They did the best they could, which is having everybody have health insurance. Who knows if that's going to hold up. The older you get, the more you need health care. I remember in the '60s when Medicare came into the hospitals and the doctors fought it. After that, they acted like they invented it because they got paid for stuff that they used to do for free. They don't get paid as much for Medicare, but they get paid a good amount. They didn't fight this time. The AMA was for this last plan.

"For fifteen years, I did dinners at night for guests. That's as close as I ever want to get to the restaurant business. That's a lot of hard work and not a lot of money. I think people can understand the restaurant business because they see people working hard. They don't understand the bed-and-breakfast business. It's amazing the number of people who come and say they want to do this. Now my response is, 'You know, that's a good idea, but you do realize that you can make more money at almost anything else you will do?' They look at me like I'm nuts. I tell people, 'Sitting here talking to you is as good as it gets in this business. This is the highlight of the deal. This is why you do it.' All they see is me sitting here talking to interesting people floating down the river in their kayaks. I don't know how anybody makes money at this.

"At about fifty, I decided to slow down. I was going, going, going, and then I looked back on that and asked, 'What does that get you?' So many people do that. What's the end result of that? Often it's not a whole lot. I don't think it did me a lot of good. It doesn't matter how hard you work, there are outside forces that go against that, like Katrina. She killed tourism in Louisiana for three years. Then when it started coming back, the recession hit.

"The best thing to do is to accept every phase of your life and to accept the things that happen and to go with the flow. I think a lot of things are meant to be—and I'm not a religious person. I think spiritually that things happen for a reason. It may not be the reason we like or want, but if we accept it, it'll be easier for us. I get worked up about things, and they don't change. We do what we can."

Shirley poured more coffee for Kitty and brought us a Danish. Then she continued. "They say that the girls today don't have any concept about what the Women's Lib fight was about. They take it for granted. I've been prowoman because of that. We have to be on an equal par with men, and that's beginning to happen. More women are graduating from college and taking over things. It may happen in our lifetime. Eventually we may get paid equally too.

"We have to be prepared for what comes with age and accept it. We don't want to have regrets about what we didn't do—like I didn't go down the river. It's like a bucket list. When I was younger, I had a bucket list of places I wanted to go. I realize now there are places that I'm never going to see. That's okay. I enjoy the places I got to, and I like to spend time there. I maintain you can relax anywhere. I like to meet the people and experience the culture. I'm the type of person that needs a vacation from my vacation."

Shirley went to the kitchen briefly to get us more tea. When she returned she said, "There are two stories I want to share with you about people coming down the river. These happened two or three years ago. One was a group of ten Germans doing a documentary on Mark Twain. They came down the river on a boat trip like Mark Twain went on, and I said, 'What are you doing that for?' They want this documentary to be shown in Germany because Germans love Mark Twain. Last week I had

Austrians here, and they said, 'Oh, yes. We read *Huckleberry Finn* and *Tom Sawyer.*' They're enamored by Mark Twain. It blew me away that would be the case.

"For the Lincoln bicentennial in 2009, a man in Kentucky decided he was going to re-create the flat boat that Lincoln rode down the river to New Orleans. That's when Lincoln first encountered blacks and the slave deal. This guy was stopping at places like you are. At every place he stopped, he had people come see him. My son read in the newspaper that he'd be stopping at the St. Francisville Ferry boat landing. I'm reading this story, and it says this man's name was Robin Cherry. That's a common name, and I didn't think too much of it. Then I looked closely at the picture of the captain of the boat, and I said, 'Oh, my God! That's my old boyfriend from thirty years ago.'" We laughed.

"He'd become a tugboat captain. My son, Chris, was a little kid then. We went down and met the boat. He came and stayed the night. It was the funniest deal. A lot of the boat was Styrofoam to keep it floating. You're the third experience I've had with people coming down the river. It's not something that most people do."

"One of the things we are asking women about is what courage means to them," said Kitty.

"I think courage is doing something you're afraid to do. They say that people who have courage have fear. Courage is overcoming it and pushing through the obstacles. I can't say that I'm a courageous person. I guess you could have courage when you take a stand on something you believe in when other people don't. We don't all have the opportunity to do big things. Like you girls coming down the river—that takes a lot of courage. To people who are courageous, they don't feel that way. They're just doing it."

Shirley glanced at a clock and was surprised how late it was and surprised she had so much to say. She had to get to her duties, so we said goodbye.

Our destination was Marksville, Louisiana. Heidi, Cis, Pat, and Kitty had found a special bed and breakfast for my birthday. The Lazy Rabbit Cottage on the Bayou had a Jacuzzi and was located away from town. As we drove down Highway 61, I was not surprised to see a heron fly over the road. Even off the water, Kee's presence was felt.

Kitty read from the meditation book while I drove. "Our Good Points: We don't need to limit an inventory of ourselves to the negatives . . . Honestly, fearlessly ask: 'What's right with me? What are my good points? . . . Am I a loving, caring, nurturing person?' We may have neglected to love ourselves in the process of caring for others, but nurturing is an asset . . . Today I will focus on what's right about me. I will give myself some of the caring I've extended to the world."

Kitty and I looked at each other and laughed. "That's a good one."

"That's always been hard for me," I said. "Saying something good about myself, embracing my good points, gets tied up in being afraid of being judged as having too much pride."

"Yeah," said Kitty. "We get judged for not embracing our power and judged for owning it."

Lost in our thoughts, we fell silent as we continued down the road. For lunch we pulled into a diner that had '50s décor. The staff was boisterous and laughed often. They served the standard deep-fried everything. We opted for burgers.

"Unlike from the headwaters down to St. Louis, this trip has required the most adjustment," said Kitty.

"In regards to adapting to changes in the terrain, the culture, the people who are with us, the people we meet . . ." I added.

"For me it's about taking this knowledge home," said Kitty. "I guess I'm curious about how to incorporate what I've gained into my daily life. I haven't put as much time into the planning and doing of the Ripples of Wisdom project as you have, and yet it's been a huge part of my life. After the 2007 trip, it took me at least a year to process everything. Getting ready for this trip has been a two-year process. Last time, going home felt like I was crawling back into a box. I don't want to lose in my regular life the openness and the fluidity that this trip has produced."

"I can see the challenges given the job you have," I said. "It's confining. In a lab things need to be precise and there are timelines. You're literally in a box with one little window. Do you have any idea what life would look like if you didn't lose the openness and fluidity when you got home? What if you incorporated this into your life back home?"

"That's what I'm asking," said Kitty. She paused thoughtfully, holding a French fry halfway to her mouth.

"I'm asking you to play with possible answers," I said.

"I don't know," said Kitty.

"If you were to know?" I asked.

"It wouldn't be continuing to do the work that I do," said Kitty, biting decisively into the French fry.

"You've got to stop going on these trips," I kidded. "You change jobs every time."

"I didn't think that would happen this time," said Kitty.

"I'm not surprised," I said. "The confinement has been worse this last year because you worked to build hours for this trip. There's something about being confined and not being outside that doesn't work for you."

"Next year will be different because I'll have vacation and comp time," said Kitty.

"Let's assume you have preconceived notions that limit your seeing options," I said. "What if you let those preconceived notions go, particularly the one that says it's not feasible to incorporate. Decide you can incorporate this, and you can see how. What does that look like?"

"It feels like you're turning it around and asking me," said Kitty, looking at me confused.

"Because I am," I said. "The answer is inside you."

"I don't want to go home to confinement," said Kitty. "We talked about the openness and the adventure this trip has allowed. When I get back, I don't want to feel the confines of other people's notions of me, let alone the ones I put up for myself."

"It's the ones you have for yourself that are getting in the way," I said. "Maybe it's time to redefine adventure. That sense of adventure can be found everywhere and anywhere. Does openness have to be big adventure like this? Is there adventure right there within your own life?"

"I get that," said Kitty. "I'll go back with new eyes and see things that I didn't before with new knowledge gained on this trip. There's something about keeping it right in front of me so I don't forget."

"You could create a program for your life," I said. "Like AA. Something with systems, daily tools, readings—those kinds of things. Create your own—or take what you already do and make it broader."

"That sounds like fun," said Kitty. "I like that idea. At the beginning of this trip, I had the journal with the pages of words to live by. I want to live by those words no matter where my life takes me. They're universal words on how to be and how to walk in this world."

"You've already created the basis for your adventure," I said. "Each day, take one of those words in the morning and attach the word's meaning to adventure. Put it on a card and make your intention for the day. For example, 'I'm going to have an adventure around serenity.' Or say, 'I can't wait to see what the adventure around serenity is today.'"

"I could get a fish bowl and put in slips of paper with those concepts written on them, and I could dig into the bowl and see what comes out," said Kitty.

"It has to come from you," I said. "There's something important about leaning into what you know and reducing the amount of looking outside of yourself."

"This isn't for anybody else to fix," said Kitty. "It's for me to walk in the shoes of those words."

"The word embrace came up while you were talking," I said.

"Embrace the words and the knowledge," said Kitty. "That's something I can lean into."

We pulled in to Marksville and stopped at a nail salon to pamper ourselves. We intended to only have a manicure, but to celebrate my birthday and to heed the words of the daily meditation—"give myself some of the caring I've extended to the world"—we opted for a manicure and a pedicure. We'd hoped to gather a story while we were there, but the women doing our nails spoke little English, and the other customers were in their teens. The woman doing Kitty's nails was funny and teased her often. After having our feet in and out of the river, it felt wonderful to have them massaged. The pampering helped us feel less like river rats.

I love a good cup of Chai made with steamed milk, and we hadn't found one for more than a week. The ladies at the nail salon directed us to the Gator Coffee Shop at Paragon Casino. We walked into a spacious lobby with an enormous pond. We walked a bridge that crossed the pond and stopped to look at the lifelike statues of alligators on the rocks and floating in the pond. There were more than a dozen of various sizes. We discussed how they looked so real, and one of them moved. I looked at Kitty. "Here are your alligators," I said. "You don't need to be afraid of these." She laughed. We savored our Chai as we gazed at the alligators.

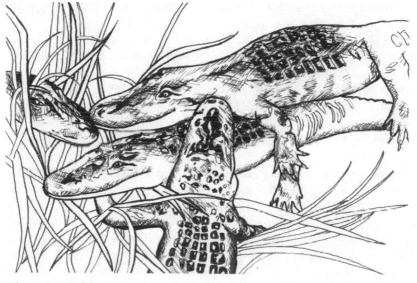

The Lazy Rabbit Cottage was more than we expected. Stunning gardens with many sitting areas surrounded it. The view beyond the garden was a picturesque bayou. The setting was quiet—no barges, trains, traffic, or hustle and bustle of civilization. We settled in, made tea, and sat in the swinging chair at the end of the dock, watching an egret and a heron fishing in the reeds on the far shore. It was peaceful and pleasant to be among the lush greenery. Doug's email indicated there was snow back home. The setting sun cast an orange hue on the bayou thick with large cypress trees. It reminded me of photos I'd seen of the deep bayou. Staring down the bayou, I forgot about my messed up hair, stress, fatigue, and my responsibilities. I could have sat there all night, but the air grew cool quickly.

While Kitty pampered me by making dinner in our big kitchen with the leftovers from our cooler, I checked email, the Facebook page, and voicemail. They were full of delightful birthday wishes. I connected with Doug. As I relaxed during the evening the fatigue that had been building over the past weeks of travel caught up to me, which made the gentle massage of the Jacuzzi particularly delightful. I slept like a baby.

October 20, Day Thirty

Bill, the owner of the Lazy Rabbit Cottage, didn't mind that their grandson's new puppy chewed at his shoelace while we talked. In his British accent he explained that his wife, Carol, who was from the area, had been creating her gardens for ten years. Carol joined us and they asked what winter was like in Ely. We told them about cross-country skiing on the lakes (a concept they had trouble wrapping their minds around), and that I was a snow carver at the annual Ely Winterfest. Bill was fascinated by the idea of turning an eight-foot cube of snow into a work of art that we knew would melt.

Bill and Carol's home was at forty-seven feet in elevation. The flood last spring reached forty-six feet. The smelly water, full of manure and farm runoff, had lapped at their door.

Bill asked if we'd be paddling the Atchafalaya River. He said that river was more dangerous than the Mississippi. It was the deepest and shortest river in the United States with whirlpools that took big boats down. We explained we'd be paddling Bayou Lafourche, which was dramatically smaller.

The current path the Mississippi River takes to the Gulf of Mexico is its third route over its lifetime. The first was the Atchafalaya River; the second, Bayou Lafourche. The current route has been stabilized by the levee system. The Atchafalaya River is the furthest west route and a major waterway in the delta. Bayou Lafourche is located between the two. When the levee system went in, the Army Corps of Engineers cut Bayou Lafourche off from the Mississippi River. The amount of water flowing from the Mississippi into Lafourche is controlled and generally only increased during floods. Bayou Lafourche is stagnant in Donaldsonville where it originates. As it moves south, it grows in size and in current with other water sources joining it. By the time Bayou Lafourche reaches the Gulf, it's large enough for small barges and commercial shrimp and fishing boats to use.

Our next stop was for an appointment at a beauty shop that was highly recommended to us. The beauty shop was in a tiny building. Inside was bright and cheery with pale-yellow walls and a black-and-white-checkered floor. Lou Anna sat me down, and I told her I wanted the color to be more natural and anything they could do to fix the color would be appreciated. Lou Anna was very animated and spoke while she fixed my hair. I told her about the book I was writing and wanted to know about her and the ladies in the shop. She jumped right in.

"I'm from Louisiana. I was a foster child, and my husband's aunt took care of me. I was married for thirty-seven years. I have three sons and am soon to have a third grandchild. I've been a hairdresser for forty-two years." She stopped talking, put her hand on her hip and looked at the chair I was sitting in. "I've been standin' behind this chair in the same corner in the same building for forty-two years. Mary Kay over here was my teacher in Baton Rouge. I finished high school in 1969. I went to beauty school in 1969. I got married in 1969. Sixty-nine was a very big year." She pointed to a woman sitting under a dryer. "Judy over there was my classmate. We rode to beauty school together."

"They were very good students," said Mary Kay.

"The best," said Lou Anna. We all laughed. "My beauty shop was moved from, as we say, 'the back of town,' a residential area. We moved uptown. You ever see that commercial with the beauty shop going down the road? That's what we were doing. We moved the whole little shop. That was in 1989. I added on since. Mary Kay came to work, and we remodeled and changed things. When you've been here for forty-two years, you gotta change the appearance every now and then to motivate you a little bit.

"My husband died five years ago from pulmonary fibrosis. I recently found someone else. I'm happy. I met him dancing. I love to dance. We do swamp-pop music and jitterbuggin'." She stopped what she was doing for a moment and looked at us. "Do y'all know jitterbuggin'? It's fun. I love to travel. I love to play with my little grandkids. They're the light of my life.

"My husband was a sugar cane farmer, and my three sons are still farming. We farm two thousand acres of sugar cane. I'm sayin' 'we,' but it's my children. I feel like I still do it. I cook supper for 'em.

"My three boys are married. My husband's generation had nothin' but boys. My granddaughter that's five years old is the first in forty years that was a girl. You think she's spoiled?" We laughed. "It doesn't matter. We spoil 'em all. I love cookin' and bakin'. You're writing a book about women. You got to ask me questions."

"What does it mean to be courageous?" I asked.

"I don't know," Lou Anna said and she looked over at Mary Kay. "What does it mean?"

"It means goin' through what you did with your husband and the illness," said Mary Kay. She turned to us. "She was courageous."

Lou Anna stopped what she was doing for a moment and stared ahead. "It was bad. What I went through with my husband was bad," she said. "Thank God for the LSU Tigers. When I got off on a Saturday afternoon, that was when me and my husband did things. It was like, 'I have to find somethin' to do with my life. I can't go home and mope.' I started watchin' the LSU games on Saturday afternoon. Thank God for good friends that you could call. It helped me a lot. If you didn't have friends and God in your life, you wouldn't get through those kinda things. God helps you."

Two women entered the shop. One assisted the more elderly across the room to a chair. "Hey," said Lou Anna. "You look like you doin' good, Miss Lillie.

"It's been so many years doin' this. I've lost a lot of customers. You love 'em all. We had that conversation yesterday about what would you do if you retired. I can't imagine not havin' people in my life. It's been so much of my life."

Lou Anna had a brief conversation with the woman accompanying Miss Lillie. "We'll take care of Miss Lillie," Lou Anna said with a big smile. "If you aren't back, I'll have to take her home with me."

While Lou Anna helped Miss Lillie get comfortable in a chair, she continued. "We're never gonna retire, Mary Kay and I. We redid the beauty shop, and we intend on workin' for the rest of our lives. One time, when I first got this beauty shop, I had four hairdressers in here. As the years went on, I felt like all I was doin' was managing people. They come for a while—then they open their own shop. I felt like, dern, all I'm doin' is puttin' everybody else in business. When Mary Kay came over here, I said, 'What you need? You need your hair done?' She said, 'No, I need a job.' I said, 'A job?' Well, it didn't take me long to hire her. I said, 'You're hired.' She was in here and I said, 'The thing is, if you come work for me you have to work here until I die. I have to go first.' When people work for me, I get too attached; and when they leave, it's horrible. I had someone workin' for me for ten years. When she left, I thought I was gonna have a breakdown.

"I didn't have to break Mary Kay in a bit. She came with her own business. It wasn't like some people. She was in the town of White Castle workin', and she wanted to move. That's where I went to high school. It's a cute little town. There's not a lot of people there. It's goin' down a lot. I'm not sayin' anythin' about 'em, but the town has run down. Everythin' goes down—schools and everythin'. We had a cute little Catholic school there, but there's no students who can pay to go to school.

"Nothin' stays the same, and that's good because I love change. People say, 'You're doin' it again?' I say, 'Why not?' Paint is cheap. Fresh paint is clean, and it makes everythin' smell good. That's enough about me." She spun around and looked at Mary Kay. "Okay, Mary Kay. It's your turn."

Mary Kay smiled and continued styling the hair of the woman who was in her chair as she began. "I was born in 1947. I'm goin' on sixty-three years old. I've been married since 1966. I've been a hairdresser since 1965. I taught in a beauty school and managed it for twenty-one years. Then I opened my own shop in White Castle and worked there since 1986.

"I had a good business and came down with breast cancer, survived that, and it's been fifteen years. Took radiation and chemo. I had to let go of some of my clientele. Then I started workin' three days a week. A year ago February I came over here because I wanted a little excitement at the beauty shop."

"Girl, do we have excitement," said Lou Anna.

"We always have fun," said Mary Kay. "I also do artwork. And I love animals to a fault."

"Tell 'em how many you have," said Lou Anna.

"Wait, let me see," said Mary Kay. We all laughed. "Marty, Brock, Midnight, Tee Cat, Popo, Kitty Kitty, Oralee, Sweety Pie, Bunny, One Dot, Two Dot, and Gray Boy. I think that's it. Three of 'em are in the house. The others are in the garage.

"The people across the street from us were elderly, and they died. They had a dog and a cat. The family took the dog and left the mama cat. She came over to our house and had two batches of kittens. I had them fixed. I don't believe in lettin' animals run around without bein' fixed. This lady right here," she said indicating the woman whose hair she was doing, "has a daughter that's as cuckoo as I am with cats.

"I got to show you a picture of Tinkerbelle. She got lymphoma, and she died. She had birthday parties and a real big social life." She passed around a photo of a dog dressed for a party. "She stayed in my beauty shop with me. She had her own little chair, but most of the customers would pick her up and walk with her. Tinkerbelle was a papillon. Then we had a big black stray dog that got arthritis really bad. He was fifteen, and we had to put him to sleep. His back wasn't able to move around. I've had many more animals, but those are my most recent episodes. We had a little worm named Joseph."

"There's a story behind that," said Kitty. "What's the rest of it?"

"He was cute and fuzzy," said Mary Kay. "He was a caterpillar, but not a stingin' one. He lived a good long while."

"I don't know what animal we haven't had," said Lou Anna. "I love frogs and lizards. I don't pick 'em up. Tell 'em the lizard story."

"My husband found a drowning lizard in our fountain," said Mary Kay. "We're talkin' a green thing. He gave it to me, and the lizard was almost dead. I gave it CPR, and the lizard came back to life. It was cute."

"She gave it CPR," said Lou Anna, astounded.

"I'm trying to picture it," I said, giggling.

"Well, watch," Mary Kay said and walked over to us. "I turned him over, and I went ee-ee-ee." She demonstrated pressing one finger down repeatedly. "The water went spurt, spurt, spurt. I unhinged his little mouth, and I blew in a little bit. I turned him over again, and the water went spurt. Finally he opened his eyes, and he was lookin' around, like that." She looked to the left and right. "And he bit me." Everyone was laughing. "He was cute with a white dot on his head. I put him on our back porch in some hedges. About two weeks later, I saw that same lizard 'cause he had that little white dot on his head. My little buddy. You can revive a lizard with CPR. I want y'all to know.

"We didn't have any children. My husband, Bruce's, sister and my brother were married, and they had three children, two daughters and a son. They were like our kids. They lived right next door to us from infants to when they was grown up. They was our rent-a-kids. We took 'em on vacation and everywhere.

"When my nephew was thirty-two years old, he came down with testicular cancer. It spread throughout his body and went to his brain and everythin'. He was the healthiest kid. He never did drugs or drank excessively. John worked out, played hockey, and was a good kid. He died after he fought it for two years. We have an apartment in back of our place, and after his bone marrow transplant they stayed with us. He'd been married for six months when he found out.

"We'd been prayin' for a miracle of course. When he was dyin' in the hospital, I was prayin' to Jesus, Mary, and Joseph to come and get him. We're Catholic. He was holdin' this little rosary and right before he died, he opened his eyes wide, and I know he saw 'em. He made this huge sign of the cross and turned his head and told Alisha goodbye. That was a miracle. I know where he is." She showed us a picture of her nephew. "He was strong. John had all different kinds of friends. One of his friends said John was one of the strongest people he ever met—spiritually, physically, and morally." She turned to the woman in the chair. "This is my friend Judy, and she lost her son tragically."

"We have been hearing a lot of stories about women losing their kids," I said.

"We all have something, but we have to go on," said Mary Kay. "Miss Brown lost a son tragically. He drowned."

"It's a pain that never goes away," said Miss Brown.

"This picture is my artwork," said Mary Kay, pointing to a picture hanging on the wall near her hair-cutting station. "I had an exhibit in Port Allen. It started as a hobby. I've sold some of them. It's funny. The ones that I start painting because I like them is hard for me to sell. I get attached to them. If somebody commissions me, I can paint 'em and don't get attached. I give some away. Painting, my husband, and my religion—my spirituality—make my life rich. And all of my friends."

While she helped Miss Lillie across the room and into her chair, Lou Anna said, "This is Miss Lillie. How old are you, Miss Lillie?"

"I'll be ninety-nine in March," said Miss Lillie.

"Oh, my word," said Kitty.

"Miss Lillie broke her hip not quite a year ago," said Lou Anna. "She's still a go-getter. She still lives in her own home."

"I'm old, and my hip's not gonna heal like it would heal on you," said Miss Lillie. "It takes longer to heal, like everything else when you get old. You have to be patient. Sometimes I lose it though. The doctor said he can't get over how good it's healing. I said, 'You just telling me that.'

"I grew up in Bayou Goula, which is before you get to White Castle on River Road. It's about ten miles. I think I'm right. There were twenty-one years, and then I got married and lived in Plaquemine the rest of my life. I had the hard times and the good times like everybody else. I was married seventy-five years."

One of the ladies leaned over and said, "She was married for forty-five years when her husband died. She counts the years like he is still with her."

"It seems long to you, but it didn't seem long to me. I have two children, and my oldest is gonna be seventy-four. No, wait. He's sixty-nine. I think that's right . . . I got to get a pencil. My mind's no good anymore. It's terrible."

"I think it's good for ninety-nine," said Lou Anna.

"I don't remember well. I used to be like that," Miss Lillie said snapping her fingers, "and get it right. Now I get it confused. They tell me I should be glad I have a memory much less remembering things. I keep quiet. Sometimes I'm like this, and sometimes I'm good. It all depends on what I been doing all day."

"What's your favorite memory?" I asked.

"I got a few favorite memories," answered Miss Lillie. "When I had my baby son and daughters, I was thrilled to death. By the way, Little Jeanie, that's my granddaughter, is pregnant, and the baby weighs about seven pounds and something. She still has to wait about two more weeks. She's carrying that baby, and she didn't think she could have one after the other two. She has two boys and she's waiting. This is gonna be three boys. The oldest one is gonna be six. I wanted a little girl."

"Tell us about where you went to school, Miss Lillie," said Lou Anna.

"I went to school in Bayou Goula," said Miss Lillie. "The postmistress was our teacher. The post office was downstairs. She was teaching upstairs. She taught twentieth-century classes. She taught quite a few ladies of Plaquemine and men that are working. Course a lot of them are gone. I'm still here, and she taught me. That was a good memory.

"Our teacher was a register pharmacist too, and when her brother got sick she took over the drugstore, and she put me in the post office. I was a postmistress. I loved it. I didn't want to go back to school and finish my high school, but I had to. I loved to watch people get mail because it's a small community. You know everybody and everything. I enjoyed my life there. My favorite food is pasta."

"You guess what nationality she is?" asked Lou Anna.

"Oh, yes, they can guess I'm Italian," boasted Miss Lillie. "Did you know you can fix pasta with cauliflower and sweet pea? It's delicious! I like it a lot. I didn't know about it."

"We talk to Miss Lillie about what we cook with pasta," said Lou Anna. "My husband was Italian, and I was raised with the Italians. I learned to cook Italian."

"She knows exactly what went on with the pasta," said Miss Lillie. "You would be surprised when you go to the doctor's office how many ladies have fallen. They're younger than I am too."

"I guess when you're ninety-nine everybody's younger, huh?" kidded Lou Anna.

"Everybody should be," said Miss Lillie, smiling broadly.

"It's time to get under the dryer, Miss Lillie," said Lou Anna.

Reaching for her walker, Miss Lillie said, "This is what scares me. I could fall with this thing. It's not solid. You got to hold me from the back." Mary Kay and Lou Anna helped her.

"What's your favorite holiday?" asked Lou Anna.

"Mine's been Thanksgiving," I answered. "Everybody gets together, enjoys a big meal, and we actually talk. It's not about presents."

"I love Christmas," said Lou Anna. "You're right about Thanksgiving. We need to get rid of all that presents. I like the hustle and bustle and to go shoppin', but at some point you got to stop. My children expect so much."

"That's how we trained them," said Miss Brown. "That's the problem."

We were about to leave, and so was Miss Lillie. She nearly fell, and every woman jumped to help her. Heartwarming looks of love and concern were exchanged between the women.

We drove towards Grosse Tete, and I wondered if I had further damaged my hair by letting them try to make it look more natural. I reached up, and my hair was drier than I had remembered before I went in. I tried to run my fingers through it. It felt like straw. I assumed the stiffness was the product Lou Anna had put in to style it. I'd wash my hair later and see what I could do with it. In the meantime, it distracted me and left me self-conscious.

We arrived at the Iberville Parish visitor's center, the site of our next Gathering, and checked in with the staff before setting up.

Kitty and I made a circle of chairs on the lawn of the visitor's center, but no one came. We discussed options for making the last couple of Gatherings work. We talked about finding contacts in each location who could help bring people together, over coffee or something. We decided to make sure our releases were getting in the local newspapers. We agreed to hand out more flyers. My frustration welled up as we talked. I stood up. "I'm going into the visitor's center to talk those ladies into coming out when they close. Then we will at least have two."

Nan and Kathy S. joined us without hesitation. After we honored Nan for being the elder and gave her a mug, she and Kathy S. started laughing. Shaking her head, Nan said, "Wow. I'm the oldest! I'm not good at sharing at things like this because I don't read and I don't hardly watch TV. We're on the go all the time. I'm not good at all this stuff. I'm being honest."

"Can you tell us what makes your life rich?" asked Kitty.

"Family together makes my life rich," said Nan. "I have three grand-children, and that's what it's all about in my house. I have two children, and they are my life. Outside of being with my family, I go to Grand Isle and saltwater fish on a boat. My favorite fish to catch is speckled trout.

"My daughters keep me on my toes. I was born in Grosse Tete. I worked at a pharmacy as the pharmacy tech until four years ago when I got this job. My husband and I were best friends with the pharmacist. It was fun. She owned it. We did what we wanted to.

"I've been here a year and a half. It is a lot of fun. I love it here. We meet all kinds of interesting people from around the world. I got a good boss." She looked over at Kathy S. and smiled. "Kathy is the director and the youngest one in the bunch."

She looked confused as to what to say next, so I asked, "What would you tell younger women that you would have wanted to know when you were younger?"

"What I would tell younger girls is to obey your parents. I lost mine at a young age. Honor your parents while you can because you don't know how long you're going to have them. I was twelve when my father passed away and nineteen when my mother passed away. That's young. There's that saying, 'If I knew then what I know now.' When you try to pinpoint what that is, you don'' know what you wish you knew then. I would tell them to be independent too.

"Education needs to be a high priority. I didn't go to college. What little I know I got from working on the job. The first ten years I worked, there was no such thing as a pharmacy tech. I worked as a pharmacy clerk. Then I went and took my test and got my license. Now you have to go to school for it. I was in so long ago that I just had to take a test to be certified. That's why I keep my license up. Every year you have to have ten hours of CE [continuing education] and turn the money in to renew your license. It's only fifty dollars. You never know when you might need it again.

"I would like to travel more. I would like to go to Hawaii, but any-where would be good. There was times when I said I would like to go to Germany because my father went there in the service. Germany seems interesting, but I don't know if that will happen. I'm wary of traveling outside of the United States.

"My grandchildren were a turning point in my life. My oldest one is almost nine. I believe it when they say there's nothing like it. We take them out in the boat. We go camp in the woods and all that with them. They love it. They like to travel. We do basic stuff.

"Now it's your turn," she said, looking at Kathy S. and handing her the tape recorder. "Kathy is better at this than I am."

"No, I'm not," said Kathy S. "I'm dying for grandchildren. I'm not saying that my life isn't rich now because I've got two boys. They have a tendency not to interact with their mother unless they absolutely, totally, positively need something. They're all grown up.

"My life is tolerable. Let me put it like that: my life is tolerable. I lost my husband and son in one year. It's been seven years. I know it sounds like a long time, but there are things you don't get over. All my friends are still married, which is very unusual. You'll find that a lot in the South. People have longer marriages than other places in the country. We're at that stage where Harold and I could have been doing fun things with other couples, but I can't because I feel like I'm the third wheel. Everybody likes to include me, but I don't feel comfortable. I pretty much retired from life. I come to work and then go home. That's my life until I get grandchildren, and then my life will be centered around them. The pain of loss just doesn't go away. You have to get up because life does go on. Grandchildren represent hope. I'm waiting for them. Until then, I'm just here.

"It takes courage to be able to get up every morning and continue on with life. When people are sick, they have to overcome whatever is involved in that illness. I guess it depends on whatever your base is and whatever life hands you. You have to be able to overcome that adversity. For me, it's getting out and carrying on with life. Now that I'm working here with women, life seems a lot lighter, and it's easier to get up in the morning." She giggled a little.

"The visitor center has only been open for a year and a half. I worked in a chemical plant in Plaquemine for twenty-one years before this. I trained the men in the unit—regulatory training and that type of thing. I didn't enjoy my job, but I enjoyed the people I worked with. This is a wonderful change. When I worked there, I worked with nothing but men. Now I get to work with ladies, and it's very refreshing—very, very refreshing! You know how the men have the typical clichés about women in the workforce—that they're difficult and they're picky? Men are ten times worse.

"We have the most wonderful working relationship. None of the ladies who are here knew each other before we started working here. We come from different backgrounds, different areas—and we're the closest group of ladies you'd ever find. The thing we hate most about it is we're open seven days a week, so somebody is always working. We don't get to socialize away from the office all together. We would love to be able to do that. That's our biggest regret. Somebody is always missing.

"I love to work in my garden, and I love to read. With this job I don't have as much vacation as I normally would. I like to travel, but I haven't been able to since I switched jobs. I went from five weeks of vacation to one week this year. Everything all comes out in the wash. There were benefits to switching the job, but it's still a big adjustment. I traveled in the states with my family. We're very close even though we're extended around in different areas. We traveled together a lot.

"Nan has the cutest daughters." Her face lit up. "My closest friend's daughter is going to be like the daughter I've never had. She lets me do everything from planning the wedding—you know, you don't get to plan the wedding when you have boys—everything that the mother and daughter would get to do, I get to do with them. My boys aren't married. They aren't even serious. It's funny because they were both in serious relationships for a while, and then all of a sudden—boom—they're both done.

"My oldest boy got his nursing degree. What's going to happen now is he is going to move to California and he is going to marry a kooky New Age California girl and stay in California. I will have to like to California to see my grandchildren." She laughed. "I don't think I could live in California. If I move, I'm going somewhere where it's warm all year long. I don't ever want to have to be cold. I'm from here. I was born and raised in Plaquemine."

She paused and looked at me as if to ask, "What else?"

"What would you want younger women to know that you didn't know?" I asked.

"There are a lot of things I would tell younger girls today," said Kathy S. "In this day and age, I want to tell them education, education, education! You don't know when you might be on your own. Education is a high priority down here for certain segments of the population. Living on the dole has become a lifestyle for a large section of the population. I don't know if it's like that all over the country. We want to focus on having our children get a good education, but for many people life on the dole has become normal. They're working on third and fourth generations of that, and they don't know any different. They start having children at fourteen or fifteen and quit school. I don't know that at this point in time there's any way to correct that because it has become ingrained in certain populations. I don't see any way that you can change that mentality. I can't even imagine how you can broach the subject to switch the brain to understand that there's more to life than what they have become accustomed to. It's very sad.

"I have a degree in anthropology. I haven't gotten to use it, but it was fun getting it. Education down here has been equal for both men and ladies, and it has been for a long time. I would like to learn Spanish with my boys.

"What are you going to do when this project is done?"

"I want to find my studio again," I answered. "I'm an artist, and I have not had time to do any artwork. I'm looking forward to that—and having a garden."

"We're going to be paddling Bayou Lafourche," said Kitty. "It appears to run through people's backyards. We have researched the Internet and asked our connections in the area without luck. Without the information we're not sure how we'll complete the trip as planned. Do you know how we can get information about boat ramps?"

"You're right," said Kathy S. "The river's banks are primarily private homes or businesses. I don't know about boat ramps, but my son for his undergrad—he has a degree in microbiology—did an *E. coli* study on Bayou Lafourche."

"Don't go swimming in it," laughed Nan.

"Wash your hands," instructed Kathy S. laughing loudly. "I don't see how y'all do it."

Nan and Kathy S. went to close the visitor's center while we packed our things in the van. Then Kitty and I drove to our motel in Port Allen.

"We've heard about a lot of death on this trip," I said.

"It's part of getting older," said Kitty. "We're getting closer to an age when death happens more often."

"I mean we're hearing about death more on this trip than on previous trips," I said. "We're still talking to the same age group."

"Yes, we are," said Kitty. "I'm more aware of what it means having lost my dad. I wasn't putting death in the same perspective as I do today. We have four more years of experience since our first trip, and death is more of a reality for us. Look who's been lost in Ely."

"I get that part," I said. "The point I'm trying to make is on the other two legs of the trip the talk of death wasn't like this. At almost every Gathering, somebody has lost a child, or a spouse, or parent. That wasn't the case before. In the beauty shop, three of them had lost a child. Death wasn't a major theme of the women's lives we talked to up North. I'm fascinated that it's such a recurring subject on this leg of the river. We've heard stories about cancer, drownings, heart attacks, accidents . . ."

"I wonder if it means anything," said Kitty.

"We have been doing a lot of letting go on this trip," I said. "Death is the ultimate letting go."

We pulled into our motel and right away felt uncomfortable. The motel was in an industrial area near Interstate 10. We got our key and went to our room. The doors to the rooms opened into a main courtyard. The door next to our room was propped opened, and we saw several men drinking beer inside. They and other groups of men across the courtyard watched us closely as we walked back and forth to our room, unpacking the van, and we grew more uncomfortable. We said hello to them when we passed by—but that didn't ease our discomfort.

We hadn't had dinner, and our cooler was empty, so we walked next door to a truck stop with a Burger King attached. We ate quickly and went back to the motel. Walking into the dark courtyard, we realized the second floor of the motel wasn't in use and was in disrepair.

We quickly locked the door to our room, but we didn't feel safe. No one had made any advances or indicated they intended to do any harm, so we stayed for the night, but we decided not to stay for the second night of our reservation, a decision validated by the dirty condition of the room. We didn't want to walk around barefoot.

I took a shower and washed my hair. Its texture was worse. I tried to comb it, but the comb moved less than an inch before it got stuck. My hair needed a lot of cream rinse for the comb to move through it. The color, a pasty gray-blonde, wasn't any better—and certainly not my natural color. The beautician's best efforts had failed. I was very upset but tried to make it okay. I called Doug for moral support. When I told him about my hair, he joked and laughed. I didn't find his joke the least bit humorous and was devastated by his reaction.

Then I got a call from my brother Bruce that one of my other brothers, Gary, was in the hospital. He'd been in an accident, and his hand was injured. The initial injury wasn't a big deal, but he had a serious staph infection and would be going into surgery the following day. Bruce told me the doctors might have to remove Gary's hand. I couldn't imagine what that change would mean to Gary's life. My heart ached for him.

My brother's issue was enormous compared to mine, but I felt broken. I was convinced all of my hair would have to be cut off after two trips to a beauty shop. I let the roots showing and the color bug me to a point that I turned my hair over to beauticians knowing that never works for me. It had taken years to grow my hair long. I couldn't trust yet another beautician to fix it. Trusting one beautician months ago had gotten me into this. I hadn't wanted to color it, but my insecurity buttons had been pushed. I wanted to look young. I wanted to be noticed. I gave away my power about something very dear to me, and now I was paying the wretched price.

And I wasn't yet ready for the stress of Pat, Cis, and Heidi coming back to join us. I resented that the wonderful feelings I'd had the night before had dissipated quickly to a mood that was nastier than the motel room.

I wrote in my journal:

> *"I feel broken and alone. I want to go home, but instead I*
> *have to gear up for a presentation about this trip tomorrow.*
> *Everyone is coming back in the next couple days. They'll be*
> *expecting me to have the details figured out for the rest of the*
> *trip, and I don't. They'll be making suggestions about how I*
> *should handle things and expecting that I want to paddle,*

when I don't. I'll have more to be responsible for again. It's four o'clock in the morning, and I'm still not asleep. I'm crying quietly. I don't want to wake Kitty. I feel trapped. I can't go outside because it's not safe. Everything feels out of control. I don't want to tough my way through the rest of the trip. That's old behavior. I have to finish this trip, but there's so much that's not working the way I had hoped it would or had envisioned. I need a second wind—no, I need a gale force wind.

I don't know how to explain this, but I need to be heard. Explaining how I feel means taking a risk, being vulnerable. That's scary when I feel this broken. If I speak up maybe I can pull from within and see what's next—see why this happened. I don't want the trip to be something I look back on with regret or as something I didn't like. That's where I'm quickly headed.

Everything got out of control because I was looking outside of myself for answers. I fell prey to cultural pressure—pressure from people about how I should be. That's such a worn out old tune. I dance to it to be accepted. Apparently I still haven't accepted myself yet. I want to go home. I need to be where I can allow myself to feel, be relieved of expectations, but there are expectations at home too. This has become other people's trip, and that's fine, but they want me to lead.

I got my laptop and pulled the sheets over my head so the light wouldn't wake Kitty, and I wrote an email to Kitty, Heidi, Pat, Cis, Sara Jo, and Doug, all of whom would be joining us the next week, and copied it to Gwyn and Becky. "Before you rejoin us I need to share some things I've been struggling with on this trip. I'm out of gas. There have been many challenges and they have chipped away at me. Much of the work that I did to get ready has had to be redone on the road—I expected some redoing, but not to the degree it has been. There have been losses, like the stuff that fell off the trailer and the issues with the van in the beginning, and others that in the moment were not big, but together have made an impact.

"As you know, paddling has not gone as anticipated either. The mileage was wrong due to current conditions. Now we have issues that are greater than I had anticipated regarding locations to get on and off the water. I don't have answers about how to go about this next section and don't anticipate having much figured out by the time you get here. To be honest, right now I would be fine with not getting on the water again, or just get in at the Gulf from the beach at the state park. That doesn't seem fair to you who are coming to paddle. You need to decide what it is you want to do and what's important to you and not look to me for solutions right now.

"The repeated Gatherings where no one came are a source of discouragement. I can brush it off and say it's as it's supposed to be, but women are the reason for doing this. To deal with the low turnout, we took a new and creative approach—go to them—which I was excited about and will continue to try to do, but I'm an introvert and this new tactic requires a great deal from me. I'm constantly thinking I should be walking up to a woman and talking to her and can't bring myself to do it as often as I think I 'should.' I sense I'm missing opportunities because my introversion makes me hesitate. Reaching out to strangers drains my personal resources.

"I saw the beauty shop approach as a good one to connect with women and as an opportunity to correct the hair color issue that has been bugging me. Last spring after I let myself get talked into the 'temporary' color, I knew I had made a big mistake, but I tried to embrace the new color and enjoy it, and for a while I did. The reason coloring my hair was a mistake is because, whether I like it or not, it's connected to some deep feminine identity issues for me that I have yet to work through. We've been to a couple of beauty shops where we have collected a number of women's stories and experienced beauty shop culture like none I've known, but I now have bleached-out hair that feels like straw. This has hit me hard, and all the self-talk I can muster isn't helping—yet. I'm looking at an extremely short haircut in my near future. Yes, I know hair grows back, it's not about that—this is an old issue for me that has no quick fix.

"I know myself well enough to know that I'll rise above this, but right now I'm feeling sensitive. As for what I need—I don't know. Writing this to all of you is a break in what I usually do—I usually don't tell anyone when I get like this. I hide. I know the mission of the trip will keep me putting one foot in front of the other because my sense of responsibility is strong, and I'm good at looking like all is well. No one we encounter will know anything is wrong.

"In addition to that, I got a call that my brother Gary is in a hospital struggling to save his hand after an accident. Everything I mentioned is nothing in comparison, and yet I'm messed up."

OCTOBER 21ST THROUGH 24TH

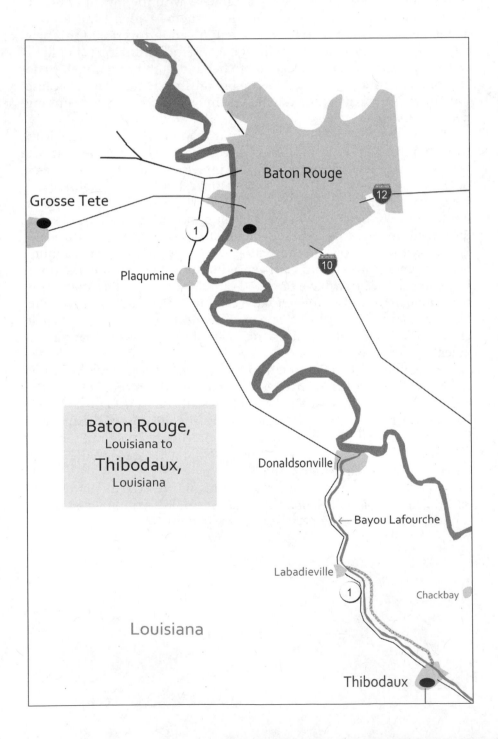

Baton Rouge

Grosse Tete

1

Plaqumine

Baton Rouge,
Louisiana to
Thibodaux,
Louisiana

Donaldsonville

← Bayou Lafourche

Labadieville

1

Chackbay

Louisiana

Thibodaux

9

THIBODAUX

October 21, Day Thirty-one

Kitty read my email and said it was a departure from how I usually handle things. It felt good to have that acknowledged. We packed up and got out of the motel quickly. The men we had seen the night before at the motel were gone. We found out they were work crews who lived at the motel. They had cleaned out the continental breakfast long before we got to it.

We didn't talk much through breakfast or while we drove the fifteen minutes to our hotel in Baton Rouge. After we checked in, we took long naps. When I woke, I stood in the bathroom staring at my hair. Kitty peeked around the corner at me. "Don't do anything rash until Sara Jo gets here," she said with concern and encouragement. I styled my hair as best as could be done with a pile of straw.

My phone rang and I looked at the caller ID. It was Pat. I wasn't ready to talk to anyone about my email, so I let the call go to voicemail. Seconds later Kitty's phone rang and it was Pat again. Kitty took the call. Pat had a lot of questions about our plans for the rest of the trip: Were we going to finish it? How was it going to work? Was I okay? What could she do to help? What was the plan? As I listened to Kitty respond to the questions I felt overwhelmed. I was glad I didn't take the call.

We left for the Carver Library presentation. The library is situated next door to a Head Start school. The school's programming is integrated with library programming, and the preschool kids come to the library on a regular basis for story time. Cynthia, the branch manager, had advertised the presentation in the paper and on local TV. She got us situated and we waited. People slowly filtered in: a couple, a young woman who was interested in our project and doing a paper on it for school, and another woman. Cynthia had anticipated thirty people. We had four.

I told the audience about our journey downriver and the Ripples of Wisdom mission, and I showed slides of the previous two trips. After the presentation Kitty and I answered a few questions, and the gentleman in the audience began to leave. He turned around, looked at the woman he had come in with, and said, "This is Nancy. Listen to her. She's got lots of wisdom." Nancy A. blushed.

The young woman writing the paper for school asked a couple of quick questions about when our trip would be over and if she could follow us on the Internet. After I answered her questions, she flew out the door to school. Four of us—Mary Ann, Nancy A., Kitty, and I—sat in an intimate circle. I had left the fan in the car, so I handed Mary Ann the tape recorder and asked her to begin.

"I'm jealous of what y'all are doing," said Mary Ann. "I'm a longtime freelance author. I do nonfiction. I do a lot of Louisiana history and culture. I love the natural history, and I get out as much as I can, which isn't very much. I write about things that I want to know about. I want to write about them in a way that other people will be interested in them too. The idea of empowering women and doing it through an activity like this is terrific.

"Working with history and nonfiction has turned me into a preservationist and a conservationist. The more I learn, the more I realize how rich our history and our natural history are. There are many people who don't appreciate either. That motivates me to write about things beyond the mainstream or beyond the celebrity kind of things. It's all pretty selfish, frankly. I don't think there's anything or anybody in the world that's not interesting at least once. I can get a good story out of anybody by just talking to him or her for a little while.

"I'm writing a book right now. I had previously done a book on the river road between here and New Orleans. It's about what's along the river on both sides, but not in the river. I've gone back, and instead of the book being an overview history-guide kind of thing, I'm picking out places that I think are, if not unique, very unusual. The book is in essay form. I'm having a hell of a struggle with it. I want to finish it. I've already missed one deadline, but it's what keeps me going."

"What part are you struggling with?" asked Kitty.

"The writing," said Mary Ann. "I struggle with the writing. It's just a matter of organizing it in a way that other people will think is interesting." She looked off to the side for a moment in thought and then handed the tape recorder to Nancy A.

"I'm not originally from here," said Nancy A., shifting uncomfortably in her chair. "I'm from Virginia. I've been here for twenty years now. When I first moved here, I hated it. All I did for several years was try to get back to Virginia. I couldn't afford it. Every place I go, I try to act the tourist and see everything there is to see. I started doing that here and eventually Baton Rouge grew on me." A few tears formed in her eyes. "I like it here now. I still miss Virginia.

"I don't have kids. Never wanted any. God, with His sense of humor, has brought many of them into my life that I've had to take care of against my will. With Mark [her longtime good friend with whom she had come to the presentation] I might as well have a four-year-old." We laughed. Her body relaxed into her chair and a smile lingered on her face. "God got His vengeance. I met Mark down here at church. He was born here and lived in Oklahoma, Texas, Alberta, and a lot of different places before he came back here. We keep each other out of trouble.

"I was in my fifties before I figured out what I wanted to be when I grew up. It was one of the times that I came out of my shell. I wanted to drive trucks. I went and practiced, I took the test, and I made it. I got my CDL license and drove for a few years. I was a truck driver and I loved it. Then seven or eight years ago, I was rear-ended by an eighteen-wheeler. I lost my job. I loved the job very much, and I miss it to this day.

"I have herniated discs and all kinds of problems with my back. I had a bad concussion and went to therapy for years. I'm doing better now. I can't do a lot of the physical things that I used to do. I've read books about people who've paddled the entire Mississippi and books on different sections of the river. Paddling it has been a lifelong desire," she said tearfully, "but at this point I'll never be able to do it. Not even a section. I'm living vicariously through you.

"I don't like water, but I like boating. I don't swim. I haven't been out on anything since the accident. Physically I couldn't do anything for so long, and then I lost all of my savings. I haven't had the money to do a thing. I haven't been able to take vacations or do anything for years. I've got my disability pension, and I'm getting out of debt. I think I can do the Nantahala, one of those whitewater rivers in North Carolina. There are three or four whitewater rivers there, and you can pick your difficulty level one to five. I can still do one of those. I might even be able to go to St. Louis and take a bigger boat down the Mississippi. At least I'd get to see part of the river. We got a few boats down in New Orleans that go all the way up to St. Louis.

"Besides reading, I get excited about traveling, photography, antiques, architecture, and animals of all kinds. I don't have any right now, but I have raccoons that come out of the woods behind my house. I feed them and play with them."

"What does playing with a raccoon look like?" I asked.

"Handing them food and their taking it out of my hand," said Nancy A. The delight she gained from interacting with the raccoons was evident in her smile. "When they have babies, I sit down and the babies crawl back and forth over my legs. I'm careful because they're wild, and I never know if they might fight or if they have rabies. I enjoy them. I'll get a dog again soon, but I've wanted to travel.

"When I was younger, I'd have liked to have known about everything. That's why I enjoyed my thirties. I was beginning to gain a little bit of wisdom by that time, and I still had my face and figure. It was the best of both worlds. The older I get, the more I realize I haven't learned anything. I feel like the older I get, the less I know and the less I'll ever know. I feel like I'm back at square one again." She laughed.

"The Lord makes my life rich, and I have a couple of genuine true friends. A genuine true friend is somebody who's put up with me for decades, who's there for me and I'm there for her. I'd like to share a quote by William Hazlitt: 'To be capable of steady friendship or lasting love are the two greatest proofs, not only of goodness of heart, but of strength of mind.' That's how I feel about my true friends."

"I went back to college when I was in my midthirties," said Kitty. "I realized that there was so much that I didn't know. For me, that's part of the definition of wisdom: finding out how much I don't know and being curious to learn more. As I got older, I found out that I have limitations. There's wisdom in that. Finding out what I'm capable of and what I'm not capable of."

"I'm coming out of a depression after the wreck," said Nancy A. "I'm trying to do what I can and not worry about what I can't do. There's still plenty that I can do, so I'll concentrate on that."

"Coming out of depression takes courage," I said, taking the recorder and setting it down between us. "I struggled with depression for years. I was on and off medication."

"I've refused the medication," said Nancy A. quietly. "Maybe I shouldn't have."

"Were you doing kayaking when you were depressed?" Mary Ann asked me.

"No," I said.

"Do you think that would have helped?" asked Mary Ann.

"Yes," I said. "I find any kind of exercise outside helps. I heard once that a Native American remedy for depression is a cucumber a day and a fifteen-minute walk outside. I did that for a while, and it helped. I don't know why the cucumber, but the walking got me up and moving."

"Exercise releases endorphins in your body," said Nancy A.

"The most adversity I've experienced was when my husband

dropped dead when we were out taking a walk," said Mary Ann sadly, and then she paused. "Leaning on family and friends helped. I tried to exercise so I didn't feel like nothing was happening. I toughed my way through it and let time go by. Time is very healing.

"I've spent a lot of time making a point of visiting with women who have lost their husbands. Mine died when I was forty-six. I was young, and I didn't know anybody my age who had been widowed. I know there are plenty of people who are, I just didn't happen to know any of them. I made a point of reaching out to other people. I read books. Some of them were very helpful. I didn't join a support group. That's not my style. At that point I was too raw to be able to share with other people anyway. I was lucky enough to be able to come out of it. I won't forget and will always be influenced and affected by it. I was able to come out more or less a whole person at the other end. I want to be able to help other people do that.

"I haven't written about that. Two years ago I treated myself to a writing workshop that was in Guatemala. I'd never been to Guatemala, and I respected the woman who was leading it. She's a national leader. I decided that it had been long enough, that I could write something about my experience. We wrote on site. That was the first time I'd written about it, and I probably won't write about it again. I'd rather talk to people. I think one-on-one is more effective anyway. I'm fairly introspective, but I don't write that stuff down.

"This book that I'm doing now is not entirely first person, but it's me in the stories, my experiences. This is the first big piece I've written in first person other than a couple of essays that were in first person that were published. It's taken me a long time to want to put me out there. Third person is easier."

"I used to journal a lot, but I stopped," I said. "I realized the only time I was journaling was when I felt my life was in the tank. I stop journaling when life gets good because I don't want to stop having fun long enough to write it down. Then I realized that when I die and my kids read my journals, they're going to think I had a horrible life and nothing good ever happened."

"I agree with you," said Mary Ann. "It's like the people who take their camera on every trip. They see everything through the camera instead of experiencing the trip. I feel that way about journaling. If I have to process it, I'm not going to be doing it. I know some people do a very good job of it."

Nancy A. pitched in. "There was a dead tree in the middle of New Orleans that had two branches that looked like an ice skater doing one of those lean-back spins. I loved that tree. Katrina knocked it down. I waited too long to take a picture of it."

"You still have the tree in your heart, and it still makes you smile," said Kitty.

"I lost my one and only," said Nancy A. downhearted. "He just left. He walked away, and it changed me. I didn't try to change or go to any support groups. I changed for the better. I'm not as needy as I used to be. It wasn't my choice to change. It just happened, and I noticed it.

"I persevered in times of adversity by choosing not to kill myself but instead going with whatever comes next, and I get through it. I usually choose by not choosing. I let life happen to me. I don't do well with choices. I can't make up my mind."

"I'm diametrically opposite," said Mary Ann. "I may make the wrong choice, but I make it, and I go ahead. If it's wrong, I'll know it soon."

"That's how I live my life," said Kitty. "It's hard for me to be in a place of indecision, so I make a decision. If it's the wrong choice, I'll be able to change course. To just spin is difficult."

"It takes me half an hour to decide what I want to order at a restaurant," said Nancy A. "Once I do a lot of study and finally make a decision, I stick with it. I might not remember a week later why I made that decision, but I made it with a lot of effort and study at the time, so I can trust it."

"Unless it's something that's earthshaking or life-threateningly deep and heavy, I'm not making the wrong decision," said Mary Ann. "I've learned in my older age, making the wrong decision doesn't make any difference. There are many things that you think are important when you're younger, and then you get older and realize that in the scheme of things, those things aren't. That's extremely liberating.

"I'd love to go back to being thirty again knowing what I know now. I'm sure I'd do things a whole lot differently and do it better. I'd know what to take seriously and what not to. I don't know that I'd make particularly better choices about big things because so far I don't have regrets about the choices that I've made. I've been lucky.

"I have three grown kids, and they're all good people. Parenting is a challenge. You never know when you're starting out—no matter how serious you are—how they're going to turn out. I like knowing that I can go try a canoe trip or a kayak trip like the one in Bayou Lafourche and it's not a stain on my escutcheon if I have to quit. It's not going to affect how people see me. If it does, I don't care. I'm sorry that they do. That feels good. It took a long time to get here."

"I have a peace now because God can take all my mistakes and turn them for good," said Nancy A. "He makes something good come out of them, and He can redeem all that wasted time."

"Was it wasted?" I asked.

Nancy A. looked at me and smiled. "Probably not."

"We're often hard on ourselves," I said.

"Oh, yeah," exclaimed Nancy A. "Like Mary Ann, I don't care what people think anymore. I only care what God says. I'm not worried about it, and too bad if they are."

"On big things, I'm more serious," said Mary Ann. "I think when we're younger, we tend to fret about way too much. I haven't had enough courage. That's why I like seeing what you're doing. It's an inspiration."

"I've no idea how to answer the question about courage," said. Nancy A. "I don't feel like I've had courage. I went with the flow and did the best I could at the time."

"It depends on how you define courage," I said. "We tend to look at courage as conquering a great feat out in the world, but courage can be as simple as getting up in the morning when your life stinks."

"Yep," said Nancy A. introspectively.

"I no longer see traveling the river as courageous, but I hope it's inspiring," I said. "I admit that when I climbed into the kayak for the first time on the river back in 2004, I was scared. Once you move through whatever it is that you're afraid of, you're no longer afraid of it anymore. One thing I'm terrified of is deep water, and yet I go out there. As long as I'm in my boat, I feel safe. When we practice rolling over our kayaks to learn how to get back in, the whole time I'm out in the lake in the deep water I'm freaking out."

"I've wanted to bike the C&O Canal the whole way—it's along the Chesapeake and Potomac River," said Nancy A. "I never did."

"Well, you aren't asking for my opinion," said Mary Ann, "but my opinion on that would be you aren't dead yet; you can still try to do it."

"I can still ride a bike," said Nancy A. "I'm wobbly, but I can do it. I wanted to hike the Appalachian Trail from Maine all the way down."

"You have a lot on your bucket list, "I said. "You had better get going, girl."

"I have a huge bucket list," said Nancy A.

"Me too," said Mary Ann. "It gets longer and longer instead of shorter and shorter."

Mary Ann and Nancy A. said goodbye and left. We packed up our things and went out to the library to thank Cynthia again for sponsoring the event, and we met Miss Betty. She wore a sheriff's uniform, and her face was framed by short curly gray hair. She looked stern, not someone I wanted upset with me. After meeting her, a sweet welcoming smile crossed her face, and she was irresistible. She agreed to speak with us briefly but made it clear that her duties at the library were a priority.

"What makes my life rich is I'm a Bible believin' person," said Miss Betty. "I grew up to be a Christian. I obey Christ's word and read it because His word is not going to come back void. He says He'll be whatever I need Him to be. I want to be Christlike. He showed compassion. When I'm blessed that means, for me, to look back to the fellow people I passed on the way. We have a tendency of forgetting how we got somewhere and don't look back.

"Everything for me goes back to being a Bible believin' person. I got

to pray about things and let God take control. That's how I handle adversity. You can't change people. You have to be able to deal with them on their level. We try to make people be what we want them to be, but we can't. We have to accept them for who they are and work around them. We all got faults. We aren't perfect, but some people think we are." We laughed.

Miss Betty continued. "The turning point in my life that changed me is when my mother died. Her name was Ikie. She was named after her father, Isaac. I don't have a sister or a brother. It was just me and her. Then I realized that I had no other place to get help but from the Lord. I was thirty-eight when she died. I'd just had my baby—she was five. First, it was me and my mother in my life; then it was me and my daughter in my life.

"Kimberly [her daughter] for the first time has got her baby. She is twenty-nine. She's got a little boy. I told her that I hope her child brings her as much joy as she gives me. She wasn't no trouble. I like being a grandmother. Oh, yes, I really do . . .

"I was a sheriff for thirty years, and then I retired. I've been on reserve for six years. I've been working for the sheriff's office for thirty-six years. I got into it because I was unemployed and looking for a job. Once I got there, it was on-the-job training. It's not something that you can just walk out there to do. I guess that's why I got a lot of strength and a lot of compassion. Everybody's got a story.

"I lived in North Baton Rouge by Southern University all my life. I never lived down here in what they call the bottom of Baton Rouge.

"The most challenging part of my job is that you have to be a peo-ple's person. The whole career is different. You see different people from all walks of life. There's no one level. You learn that no matter where you come from, trouble is easy to get into, but it's hard to get out of.

"This younger generation—if they could see that everybody is not your friend. When you get in trouble, that's it. You're on your own. Your friends disappear. This younger generation, they don't want anybody saying anything to them. They want to be controlled by themselves and their peers. It's hard times for them. I'm worried about them.

"I did thirty-one years in the jail, and I hated to see the young boys waste their lives. They can't read. They drop out of school at sixth grade. You got to know what you're doing. When are we going to turn this thing around? Education is important, but they don't think so. Every-body's got to get an education. It's not something that you see every day. What I do—you wouldn't want to see some of it—it makes a difference.

"It wasn't hard being a single mom, I guess because I was thirty-three when I had Kimberly. It wasn't like I was a youngster having a kid. I was ready to come in and be a mom. These young girls having babies, they still want to go and do. They're tied down and that makes a difference.

"At the library, I do security. I walk around trying to keep peace and keep the order. Some days there's trouble. The kids are restless, and they come in here and want to take over, be in control. You would be surprised how they'll argue with me.

"I better get back to work." We walked with her out into the main library and said goodbye. We got in the van and drove to a coffee shop Cynthia had recommended, and then we headed for the airport.

We picked up Sara Jo, who had flown in from California. She had been warned about my hair, but the pain was evident on her face when she saw it. She tried to make jokes about it, but the condition of my hair wasn't funny to her, either. Having her positive energy in the van helped lift my spirits. We went out to dinner at Applebee's. Sara Jo kept feeling my hair trying to figure out what it reminded her of. "It looks and feels like dry Barbie doll hair," she concluded.

"Some of this has to go," I said. "Chunks are falling off in my lap. We have to cut my hair tomorrow. Let's find a beauty supply store and get scissors and some real wash out color. I'm so self-conscious about this I can't enjoy anything. Last night my hair crunched every time I moved my head."

"Who is going to cut it?" asked Kitty.

"Sara Jo," I said.

Sara Jo's head spun around. "I am?"

"You don't think I'm going into another beauty shop do you?" I said. "Besides, it's not like you can wreck my hair any more than it already is. Let's look at the hair cut as tomorrow's adventure."

The hotel was buzzing with people when we returned. It was located close to the university, and there was an LSU game the next day. The people in the hotel were parents of players and coaches from the other team. They were jazzed.

Back in our room, I read supportive emails. Doug apologized for laughing at me about my hair: "It sounds hard. Just know that I love you no matter what happens or how it turns out, and so does everyone else. It's okay to say enough is enough, too."

Becky's first email read, "Wow! And Yeah! Maybe the mission for this trip wasn't about helping other women to find their voice, but for you to find yours! I don't know how to say this except to say your voice now matches with you. LOVE IT!" Her second email read, "I hope my last email didn't come across as insensitive. I'm sorry you are having so many challenges. I was so excited that you put it all out there—and about the hair—maybe it is time for the Sinead O'Connor look?!?!" She attached a picture of Sinead O'Connor looking fabulous with her head shaved. I appreciated her response and particularly the humor.

I talked to my brother Gary, and he was going home from the hospital. The surgeon looked at his hand and put him on high doses of antibiotics in an attempt to avoid surgery. It worked. Amazingly, he would be going back to work in a couple of days. I was elated for him.

Doug called to follow up on his email. It was especially reassuring to hear his voice.

October 22, Day Thirty-two

We spent the morning working to figure out how to get on Bayou Lafourche. Generally, a bayou is a sluggish stream that meanders through lowlands and marshes. Bayou Lafourche starts out sluggish and grows in size to a main waterway. We looked at our maps and looked at Google Earth. The images were not clear, but we found options we could check out. We decided the rest of the day was for playing in downtown Baton Rouge. The hotel lobby was still buzzing with football game fans when we left.

Our first stop in downtown Baton Rouge was at a department store so I could get a hat. Kitty read the meditation book. "Holding Your Own: Trust yourself . . . Sometimes, it is hard to stand in our own truth and trust what we know, especially when others would try to convince us otherwise . . . They may have their own agenda. When we discount that important part of ourselves that knew what is the truth, we cut ourselves off from our center. We feel crazy . . . Trust what you know."

Sara Jo looked at me and grinned. "With that email you sent out, it sounds like you're on top of that one, Mom."

We located a beauty supply store and purchased everything we needed to have our own haircut shop. I purchased hair color rinse and verified with the staff at the store that the color would wash out with normal shampoo.

We wandered the streets of downtown Baton Rouge. The city's name originated from the first impressions of French-Canadian explorers traveling the Mississippi. They saw a bloody cypress pole on the bluff that demarcated hunting territories between Native tribes. Baton Rouge means "red stick." There is a sculpture of a red stick in Riverfront Plaza.

We sat on a wall near the red stick sculpture in a park overlooking the river, quietly absorbing her beauty and reconnecting with her. Parked onshore was the *USS Kidd*, a World War II Fletcher Class Destroyer restored to 1945 configuration as a floating museum and national landmark. She's one of the last ships of her era. We were approached by a member of the Tin Can Sailors, a group that annually visits the *USS Kidd* to restore it to "all its working glory." He informed us they'd be firing the gun as a reward for their work and to celebrate the end of their annual gathering.

We watched the activity around the gun. The Tin Can Sailors spun the gun toward downtown and then spun the gun back toward the river. We waited with great anticipation, braced for the sound. Then they fired. We jumped and laughed. We were talking about how fun it was when they fired again, and we jumped even higher because we didn't expect it. After the third time, our hearts raced.

Another Tin Can Sailor came by. "We only used a tenth of the powder that was used during the war, so the gunshot would have been louder then," he said. "The first time we fired the gun, we used a lot more powder, and we didn't tell the local authorities. We shook windows all over town and scared a few folks. We warn them now.

"There's a lot of old wiring and electrical work to be done," he explained. "We sometimes just paint things. There are half a dozen of this kind of boat at museums around the country—and bigger battle ships. This one gets the prize every year for the most completely restored. We had Cub Scouts aboard last night. They and other groups, like Girl Scouts and schools, have sleepovers in the berthing areas. We are living aboard the ship now.

"The ship was made in '42 and was the most prevalent design of the destroyers, which are the smallest of warships for WWII. The volunteers come from a group of veteran sailors called Tin Can Sailors. They called those ships tin cans because they're made of very thin steel. Battleships have a side on them that is thick so torpedoes won't hurt them, supposedly. These ships could travel faster and were cheaper to make. They were dispensable. A bunch of these guarded other ships—they're out there as a fleet. Aircraft carriers had these around for protection.

"One of the jobs of the *USS Kidd* was to follow an aircraft carrier when it was launching planes. It's called plane guarding. They picked up anybody that went into the drink if they ditched their plane or the plane missed the carrier and that sort of thing. That happened more than you want to believe. Usually the pilot survived."

We thanked him for the information and walked past beautiful fountains to the Old State Capitol. We climbed the stairs between two lion statues, one sleeping and the other relaxing, to the stately building with its Gothic Revival architecture. The center hall of the capitol had an immense spiral staircase rising from the center of the room. Directly above the staircase was a stained glass dome made of red, blue, and yellow glass. The pillar in the center fanned out like an umbrella. We felt as if we were standing in a kaleidoscope.

The Old State Capitol housed a museum in which hung a photo of Sarah Morgan Dawson. The Civil War broke out when she was nineteen, and her family suffered many losses. The diary she kept during the war, *A Confederate Girl's Diary*, is still in print. The museum has her handwritten pages on display. She never intended for her diary to be printed and had originally requested the six volumes be destroyed when she died. In her later years, she used her diary to resolve a dispute about one of the accounts of a Civil War battle.

In the museum we learned Baton Rouge has an area called Catfish Town near the Freight Station warehouses. It was named for the times when neighborhood residents caught catfish from their front porches during the annual spring flooding of the Mississippi River. That ended after the levee system was put in place.

Back at our hotel we had pizza in our room and watched movies. We set up our haircut shop by spreading a sheet down on the floor. I cut Kitty and Sara Jo's hair first. Then Sara Jo reluctantly cut mine—after we gooped a lot of cream rinse on it to get a comb through it. Her scrunched face revealed her discomfort each time she touched my hair. She cut three inches off, leaving my hair long enough to go back into a tiny ponytail. Then I put the color rinse in, which darkened my hair to a color that was closer to something one might find in the natural hair-color spectrum. After the hassle of putting the color in, and because the color made my head itch like it was dirty, I decided I wouldn't wash it often.

Once my hair air dried, it was so stiff it wouldn't move—not even in the wind. Whatever style my hair was wet, it stayed that way when it dried. There was no getting a brush or comb through it. I felt like I had a helmet on. I convinced myself my hair was better shorter and more naturally colored.

To make myself feel a little more feminine, I touched up my nail polish. Then I took our mascot Polly and used the polish to give her rosy cheeks and bright red lips, which made us smile.

October 23, Day Thirty-three

Through the night, the crunching sound my hair made when I moved on my pillow was louder than before, but my hair looked exactly the same in the morning as it had when I went to bed. I decided that could be handy.

In the van on the way to Bayou Lafourche to check for boat launches, Sara Jo shared her frustration regarding the opinions of some people in California. She said, "They think God is going to save us, so it doesn't matter if the world falls apart because we aren't going to be here."

"So God gave us this world so we could trash it?" I asked.

"Essentially that's the view that they hold," said Sara Jo. "It's hard being an environmentalist there because we try to educate people that these are our resources—and I don't care if you think God is going to come to save people. We say, 'You don't know when God is coming. Wouldn't it be great to know that your grandchildren or their children aren't living in a cesspool waiting to be saved? You don't have a date, so don't trash your children's children's future.' That's the only argument I've been able to find."

"That you need that kind of an argument and perspective so you can stem the tide of damage to our earth is crazy," said Kitty. "How do you keep up your motivation for the environment or humanity in the face of all that?"

"Humanity?" said Sara Jo. "That's a whole different thing. That's harder. I struggle. So does my husband. That's part of why we need to get out of California. We look at the way people treat each other. They don't value each other or their environment—they value things. It's hard for us to see that all the time, and it weighs on us.

"As far as the environment goes, that's easy for me. I'm not happy unless I'm in a place where I can get to nature. When I'm surrounded by everything that's falling apart, it makes me want more than anything to save it. When I see kids playing in fields of garbage and breathing bad air, or playing in streams with signs that say people shouldn't be in the water because of pollution or the bacteria that's there now because the water runs through sewer systems, I get fired up. The parents don't have anywhere else for the children to play. I look at that and see it isn't right. It doesn't matter how many people don't understand that we have to take care of our environment, don't get it, don't want to get it—you have to keep pushing.

"That wasn't my childhood. I can't imagine not having experienced the wilderness. It's a part of who I am and what fulfills me. Seeing wilderness experiences being torn from people and their experiencing what it's like to exist without interacting with the wilderness motivate me all of the time. It gets frustrating because it's a thankless effort.

"We can't make people value the environment until we tell them what it costs. When we link wasting our resources to their pocketbook, they perk up. We have gotten people to change their yards to gravel and succulents by telling them how many gallons of water they save and what that means at the end of the year to their pocketbook. If that's how we can do it, that's what we'll do. Get this car and this is how much money you're going to save. Little do they know they're burning less gas and putting fewer fumes in the air. They don't care about that part; it's about the money. You have to pick your battles and celebrate them quietly so they don't know that you won.

"Spiritually, you have to escape once in a while and get renewed. It's the only way, or you feel yourself disappearing."

"That's the value of living in Ely," said Kitty. "We have so much area to escape to and become connected spiritually to life. That's a bonus. I think that's what has kept me out of the cities. I need to be able to touch the ground and look at the stars."

"That's why you go climbing and camping so often, isn't it?" I said to Sara Jo.

"Yes, but we don't have time to do that anymore," said Sara Jo. "It's like an abusive relationship—how an abused woman gets comfortable in her discomfort. It's work to get anywhere—an hour and a half to two hours, and then back. Once you get there, it will be so crowded you can't really get away. Then add the cost of gas. You almost stop going anywhere. When summer comes, you want to go anywhere else, but it's so hot to get anywhere that you stay where you are. In winter, southern California people get active, but it's frozen everywhere we want to go.

"Ten years ago we'd go to Joshua Tree—arrive on Friday night and find camping. You could share camping, especially with the climbers and hikers. The families don't want to share, and they'll take up two or three sites. They've taken over, and now there's nowhere to camp. There are generators everywhere and pop-up tents. Volleyball courts are hung between Joshua trees. People are trashing the place. You want to say, 'Why don't you go to a park with a lawn that's fertilized and irrigated? Why come here and destroy plants that take hundreds of years to grow? You're trashing them. When you are done, there's no janitor who comes and fluffs everything back up. They don't come and water all of this and fix what you just did.' We don't get the escape we are looking for out there because we're ecologically minded. It's painful to see it happening. We're better off not going, so we get on our bikes and ride closer into town, save our money, and hope that one of us gets a job so we can get the heck out of town."

Traveling Highways 1 and 308 on either side of Bayou Lafourche, we found two possible locations to put in the water the next morning. Neither of them was perfect, but getting to the water was the goal. When a heron appeared near one of the landings, I knew we'd find what we needed for the rest of the trip regarding getting on and off the water. "Thank you, Kee," I said aloud.

Just before lunch, we checked into the Naquin's Bed and Breakfast in Thibodaux. While we were standing outside talking with Frank and Joyce, they pointed out a United States flag bunched up at the top of a tree. They had watched a squirrel chew the flag off the pole, pull the flag up the tree, and tuck the flag into its nest. Frank was installing a new flag. "I hope the squirrel won't decide he needs that one too," he joked.

Over lunch at Burger King, we continued the conversation we had started in the van. Kitty asked, "Is there a correlation between thinking there's climate change taking place and religious beliefs?"

"I think that's regional, and it's changing," said Sara Jo. "The evidence of climate change is being more and more accepted in all groups."

"There are still those who flat out deny that there's anything like that taking place," said Kitty. "It's incredible to me."

"In some areas that belief could be slightly tied to religion," said Sara Jo. "As far as I know the trashing-the-earth mentality is not true for most religions in southern California. I wonder how much of that stems from our society's fear of change. Some people don't want to have to accept the reality because that means they'll have to accept the responsibility and alter the way they live. Nobody really wants to do that. It's easy to fall back on faith if you have fallen back on faith for everything else."

"I've seen that in the politics of our nation," said Kitty. "It's easier to be the sheep than it is to promote any kind of change or believe there's something to take responsibility for."

"It's not about religions not accepting global change," said Sara Jo. "It's individuals needing to step up and take responsibility, whether they're saying 'God is going to save us' or whatever it is they fall back on to justify their decisions. There's a shift happening, and it's centered on individually based decisions. The shift requires such a big change for so many people—it's hard to do. For people like us who already try to live in a more responsible manner, we don't understand how big a shock the required change is for some people.

"The degree of change required for people in southern California is amazing. I try to remind myself of that. When you talk to people who were wealthy and suddenly find themselves with less, but you are far less wealthy, and then they say, 'Oh, my God. I'm so poor,' you say, 'No, you aren't. It's your perspective on how much you have to give up.' For them to have to accept global change is a far greater challenge. Some of us have been working towards that goal and are halfway there. We don't have to give up as much.

"Some of those people grew up in cities and still live there. They aren't as attached to the environment. They don't understand what the environment is doing for them. 'I don't go to the parks, so I don't care' is their attitude."

"For their health alone, I'd like to believe that people would take more responsibility," said Kitty. "Living with the pollution in the environment is ruining their health."

"I was thinking about what Lucy from Bruin State Park said about poverty and how those who have money and things are going to have it harder," I said. "She said her family didn't know they were poor because they didn't know any differently. I'm wondering if it's harder for folks on land than those in the bayou. People on land see what they don't have."

"It can be right across the street . . ." said Sara Jo.

"I can go without thinking I need stuff until I get to the city and see all of the advertising, glitz, and fancy cars, and it seduces me," I said.

"Walking into any discount store does that," said Kitty. "It's the variety of choices."

"You have to be mindful when you walk into those places and ask, 'Do I need this?'" said Sara Jo. "'Is this really going to make me happier? Is this an impulse buy?'"

"It's neat to be mindful and know where I'm finding my happiness," said Kitty, "to know it's not resting in something to buy. Another thing I want to be mindful of is the word 'just.' I want to remove that word from my vocabulary."

"Why?" I asked.

"It's limiting and devalues whatever is being talked about," said Kitty. "She's 'just' van support. It seems like I'm trying to belittle her role."

"You mean using 'just' makes the van support less important than those paddling?" I asked.

"Yes, something like that," said Kitty.

"That's not your intention," said Sara Jo. "It just comes out as part of the sentence. It's habitual. Like I just did 'just'—twice."

"It defines things negatively," I said.

"Right," said Kitty. "I was saying it about myself, which was when I first caught it. I said, 'I'm just van support.' Well, no. No matter what role anyone is playing on this trip, it's all important."

"That's true in life," I said. "People say, 'Oh, she just works at McDonald's.' People count on McDonald's."

"I want to stop using the word and stop putting a value judgment on whatever the topic is," said Kitty.

We pulled into the airport and Heidi, weary from traveling but healthy, was waiting for us. On the way back to Thibodaux, we went to the Louisiana Gumbo Fest at the Chackbay-Choupic Fair Grounds. Gumbo is the African word for okra. It was brought from Africa in seed form in the Africans' hair. The festival featured two of History Channel's *Swamp People* stars, Trapper Joe and Trigger Tommy, who are local celebrities. I had watched several episodes of *Swamp People* as preparation for the trip. The place was crowded with people playing games, listening and dancing to Cajun music, and eating gumbo.

When we got back to the B&B, Joyce asked, "How did you like the Gumbo Festival?"

"The music was great," I said, settling in around the table with the others. "It was fun to see a couple of the *Swamp People* stars up close. They clean up nice."

"Yeah," said Joyce. "If you go alligator hunting, it's a messy thing."

"Have you been alligator hunting?" asked Heidi.

"Yes," said Joyce. "On a Labor Day weekend, we happened to be at my son-in-law's on a houseboat. Frank and them were going to go fishin'. Two of his friends drove up and asked Bruce, Frank, and Jacob if they wanted to go alligator huntin'. Frank said he didn't want to go, and I said I'd like to go. The next day when they showed up and I was ready to go, they was like, 'She really is comin'?' Bruce, my son, said, 'You said she could.'

"They have a path the boat makes, and it's muddy, and one of Frank's friends is going real slow. Bruce says, 'What are you doing?' Referring to me, the friend says, 'I don't want to . . .' Bruce said, 'Go fast. That doesn't bother her.'

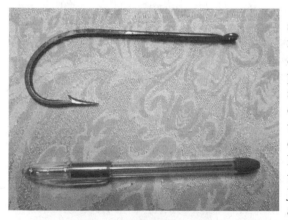

"My grandson, Jacob, says, 'Don't you tell my mama that I'm shooting alligators.' He wasn't supposed to handle a gun. He shot four and Bruce shot one. Jacob was twelve or thirteen. He was old enough. You know how Mama is. It was fun. You use that hook up here." Joyce pulled a hook down and handed it to Heidi.

"Oh, that's a big fishing hook!" exclaimed Heidi, looking at it closely and then passing it around the table.

"They put out chickens for a couple of days in the sun so they smell," said Joyce, sitting down with us. "Then they hook that to a cane rod and string. The higher you have the line with the chicken, the bigger the alligator. The alligators lunge after it. That's why it's dangerous to feed them. The swamp tours feed them. It's bad. We have a fishing camp, and we takes friends down to see the alligators. You throw a piece of bread down in the water and you get them to walk on the land. Those are the ones that aren't afraid of people. Those are dangerous. They swallow the whole chicken and the hook and it goes in their stomach. If the alligator is not big enough and you don't want it, you cut the line and let him go."

"Can he survive that?" asked Heidi.

"He will digest the hook in no time," said Frank, who came in from watching a football game in the den. He wanted to be part of the conversation, but he kept getting drawn back to the game. He popped in and out.

"Like fish do?" I asked.

"They don't chew their food," said Frank. "They swallow it and it digests. When they eat a rat, all that comes out is the fur. All the rest digests. You don't want to get bit by an alligator."

"You will lose your arm or your leg or die," said Joyce.

"If you don't have Clorox or alcohol to pour on the bite right away, you gonna get infected," said Frank. Cheering sounds from the TV pulled him back into the den.

"They have the bacteria in their mouth," said Joyce. "When they started *Swamp People* I said, 'Here we go again, makin' fun of us.' Then the show was really good. It was very educational to see how they hunt. They play it up some.

"The alligators fight when you pull them in. They're rollin' all over the place. You have to hold them at a certain place because you have to shoot them right between the eyes. That's the only place and it's a tiny soft spot."

"And your grandson was able to do that?" remarked Heidi.

"Here everybody goes huntin'," said Joyce. "They have safety classes the kids have to take. Everybody hunts. They have a lot of huntin' around here."

Joyce reached into a bowl that was in the center of the table and picked up an orange fruit and asked, "Anyone like a satsuma? It's like a mandarin orange, but they don't have any seeds in them. This is a persimmon." She held up a dark red-orange fruit that resembled a tomato. "You can try that tomorrow. They grow here. We have okra, all kinda vegetables—and we have muscadine." Muscadine is a grape-size berry.

"Frank is from a family of seventeen children and lived on a farm. They raised everything. Seven boys and ten girls. Frank's mama in twenty-four years had seventeen children. He has eleven siblings older than him still alive. There are still fourteen of them alive. Frank will be seventy-three in January."

"He doesn't look it," said Heidi.

"To have eleven siblings older than you at that age is amazing," Kitty said.

"The oldest one has either made ninety or she's gonna be ninety," said Joyce. "She lives in Colorado. My daughter says she's going to live to two hundred because my mother died at ninety-one and a half and all Frank's family lived to be old. I said, 'Girl, watch what you wish for.'"

"How many in your family?" I asked.

"Seven," said Joyce. "I'm in between two boys. I'm the third child. We have a sister that's nine years older than me.

"When we got married, his daddy had eighteen hundred rabbits. He had retired, and that was his hobby. He sold them to the laboratories. In those days that's how they did pregnancy tests. We ate more rabbit when we first got married than we did chicken. You cook rabbit like you do fried chicken. It was good.

"I was born right here on the Lafourche plantation. In first grade we moved to Jefferson, and my mama and daddy built a house there. The oldest sister got married at sixteen because she said if she had to help with the others she'd just as soon start her life. Most kids did that in those days. I was born on a plantation, married in a warehouse, lived in a corncrib." We all laughed.

"My mother's family is Spanish. Here we have the Spanish, the French, and the Germans. The Spanish came first. There was a land grant from the Spanish. The Naquins come from St. Malo in France. They came on the St. Reme. My daddy's family came from Strasbourg—part German, part French. When Mama would get mad, she would say in French that the German was coming out." We laughed some more.

"My daddy worked on the plantation. He was a boiler. He boiled the sugar cane and the syrup to make the sugar. They have to boil it down and take the pulp out and then they have to take the molasses out. Then they make the raw sugar, the brown sugar, and they send it off. You will smell it right here. They're harvesting right now. When they weren't boiling, they worked in the field and fixed the equipment.

"We speak French, and they say we speak the Cajun French, but what we speak is the old French. It's from hearin' it. My mother never learned to read or write. We had a guy here, and I was talking to him in French, and he would stop and shake his head. I said, 'Did I say something?' He said, 'No, keep talking. It sounds like it's my grandmother talking to me.'

"The first time I went to France in 1985, it was real Frenchy. Then I went in 1991, and I could see the change from Americans. I went in 2000, and it was totally changed. It's Americanized."

"That's too bad," said Heidi.

"In such a short period," said Kitty.

"They have the big eighteen-wheelers, the wider streets, and most of them are getting fat like we did," said Joyce. "They're eating a lot of fat food. They don't blame it on us. They blame it on McDonald's." Joyce got up and offered us all iced tea.

"Did you feel any effects from Katrina here?" asked Kitty.

"You have the wind, but you get used to it. At our fishin' camp, it got water 'cause we're right there," Joyce said referring to the Gulf. "We bought the fishin' camp nineteen years ago after Hurricane Andrew. The roof had blown off, but we still had plenty of land. We had a freshwater pond, and now it's salt water. You see the trees all dyin'. We have the swamps and the marsh here. The marsh is salt water, and the swamp is fresh water.

"By our fishing camp, we have alligators, so the water isn't as salty as out in the Gulf. Alligators couldn't live in that much salt. It's what we call brackish water. In Bayou Lafourche, it's the same thing. We used to have shrimp in there. A couple of years ago, after one of the hurricanes, there was so much fresh water we had crawfish galore in the bayou. It was like one of those hundred-year things."

"Crawfish is a freshwater animal?" asked Heidi.

"Yes," said Joyce, sitting down again. "Shrimp is salt. Then we have a choupic, which is a prehistorical freshwater fish. It's a Native American name. A long time ago the choupic lived on land and had legs. It has to come up to breathe. When we grew up, that was all that we had. They started hunting them a couple of years ago and taking the eggs out and selling them as caviar. Now the season during the months she has her eggs you can't catch them. Paul Prudhomme, the chef, started cookin' blackened choupic and made it popular. Everybody was fishin' them too much. We have a limit on all our fish down here and on our shrimp, fresh oysters, and crabs."

"How do you catch crabs?" asked Heidi.

"When the tide's down, Frank goes under the sand with his hands and pulls them up," said Joyce. "They go froggin' at night in the bayou. You have to make sure you catch a frog and not a snake or an alligator."

"How do they go froggin'?" asked Kitty.

"One drives the boat, and one stays in the front and gets on his stomach and shines the headlight," said Joyce. "If it's an alligator, the eyes are bright red. They blind the frogs, but sometimes the snakes are there to get them too, so you have to watch. You grab them with your hands and put them in the basket. We eat the body and everythin'.

"Ya ever seen catfishin' by hand?" asked Joyce.

"No," we said collectively.

"The man holds his breath and goes underwater, and they go lookin' and feelin' for the catfish holes. They grab and don't know if it's a snapping turtle or what."

"Those people are crazy," said Sara Jo. "That's terrifying—'I might have a hand when I'm done tonight.' They had it on TV and some of those fish that they get are big."

"Catfish, if it stings you, you better have had a tetanus," said Joyce. "People get blood poisoning from them. They have whiskers that are stingers. They worry more about the snapping turtles than the alligator."

"We got three kinds of snakes," said Frank, popping back in again. "The rattler, the cottonmouth, and copperhead. We got a snake that looks like a coral snake, but it's not poisonous. We got a king snake too."

"It can make you sick if you get bit by a king snake, but it won't kill you," said Joyce. "Sometimes when you are fishing, they fall in your boat out of a tree. If it's a snake, I—"

"If it's a snake, it could be that long," said Frank, cutting in and indicating about six inches with his hands, "and she gonna run." We laughed.

"I had two brothers, so you can tell what they did to me," said Joyce. "They'd put them over the doors. When I'd walk in the house, some kinda way, they would make them fall on me. They'd throw them at me all the time."

"I was like a brother and did that to my sister," said Sara Jo. "Mostly with frogs, but we did it with garter snakes too."

"When my daddy would go huntin' or fishin', he would put what he got in the kitchen and my mama would have to clean it," said Joyce. "First thing I told Frank when we got married was, 'You hunt, you fish, whatever—you kill it, you clean it, and I'll cook it.'"

Through the door window, I thought I saw something small move across the far wall of the outside patio area. "I want to go see your geckos outside on the house," I said. We went to the backyard. There were several geckos on the walls. A few scurried behind the window shutters.

"You got to look fast, and they go under," said Joyce. "You can try to catch them if you want. Look how clear they are. Sometimes they come in the house."

"They're so thin-skinned you can see through their bodies," said Sara Jo. "I can see their organs, and their eyes are light colored."

A mist of light rain fell while we enjoyed Joyce's backyard—swings, statues, flowers, ponds with fish, and beautiful plants that included ginger. Walking back into the house, Joyce said, "Toothpaste is what we use to take the itch out of any kinda bite."

"I never heard of that," I said. "I've got to try it."

Later I found in my room a Ziploc bag full of small toothpaste tubes for when I would need them.

October 24, Day Thirty-four

Frank and Joyce served fresh biscuits, maple sausage, eggs, dulce de leche (a thick, creamy caramel-like milk-based spread), fruit, and orange juice for breakfast. Kitty and I tried the persimmon. Mine was sweet and juicy; hers was hard and extremely bitter. Frank hadn't realized the persimmon he sliced for Kitty wasn't ripe when he served it to her.

"If you eat them and they're not ripe, they lock your mouth," said Frank.

"That's what it felt like," said Kitty.

"How do you unlock your mouth?" asked Sara Jo.

"You take water and you rinse it out," answered Frank mischievously.

"So if you are at a get-together and someone offers you a hard persimmon, you should take the hint?" joked Heidi.

"Yeah," said Frank, grinning. We laughed.

"I might eat that whole basket of biscuits," said Sara Jo.

"You can have them," said Frank.

"I'll take some on the boat with me," said Sara Jo.

"When you get farther down Bayou Lafourche, it gets wider and wider and you start to have the shipyards," said Joyce. "Then you get to the end and you have Port Fourchon where the oil is. That's why you have fifteen hundred eighteen-wheelers that travel Highway 1 and 308 everyday."

Frank gave us information about locations between Thibodaux and the Gulf to put in and take out of the bayou.

"You never gonna hear somebody say 'north' or 'south' here," said Joyce. "You are going to hear them say 'up the bayou' or 'down the bayou.' That's how we do direction here."

"What elevation are you here?" asked Kitty.

"About seven and a half feet," said Frank.

"Thibodaux is the highest around," said Joyce, beginning to clear the breakfast dishes.

After breakfast we drove north to Labadieville to a boat launch next to a bridge over Bayou Lafourche. The murky bayou was narrow, about fifty feet across, and thick with vegetation. It had very little current where Sara Jo, Heidi, and I put in and started paddling. We waved goodbye to Kitty and headed downriver. The banks were lined with houses and tall trees. Running parallel to both sides of the bayou were the highways, one busier than the other. The sounds of nature were there, but hearing them required staying attuned to them. Herons and egrets flew ahead each time we neared them. We felt anxious about paddling with alligators, and Bayou Lafourche was home to both alligators and snakes. We kept a close watch for them.

A large pile of debris—plastic and household items—burned onshore behind a home. The fire popped like fireworks. The black smoke smelled toxic. A couple doors down, a woman came out her back door with a large bowl. She carried it to the shore and tossed its contents into the water. We were surprised the bayou was used for dumping garbage.

Mullet, small fish about nine inches long, jumped a few inches above the water surface during our eleven-mile paddle to Thibodaux. Several large Muscovy, a domestic duck, appeared along our route. Most had white chests; the rest of their bodies were mottled black and white or gray and white. There were no feathers on a portion of their face, making it look like they wore red masks. They had bright-orange webbed feet.

Two men wandered onto their dock and greeted us with thick southern accents. "Howdy, ladies. Great day for a paddle." One used a cane

and wore a floppy hat. The other carried a can of beer. The man with the cane put his arm around the other one and said they were longtime friends. They asked if we'd seen the ten-foot alligator they were trying to get rid of. The man with the beer said alligators have a two-mile territory, and the one they were after was so big he left a wake when he swam. The alligator had been crawling onto the docks and eating the ducks. Their greatest concern was that because this alligator didn't have any fear of people, it could go after their grandchildren who played in the yard and on the dock. Our anxiety rose, and we became even more vigilant.

We heard a voice from shore calling to us. It was Frank. He was visiting a friend's house and had been watching for us. He pointed out a satsuma tree and a sassafras tree growing in a yard alongshore.

Down the bayou there was a dark-brown lump that rose from the vegetation floating near shore. We were convinced the lump was an alligator and studied it closely as we approached with caution. I was disappointed when we realized the lump was a log. Sara Jo and Heidi were both disappointed and relieved.

The bayou vegetation grew thick in spots, making it a challenge to paddle. Ahead of us the vegetation appeared to close off the bayou, and we thought we were going to have to portage. Portaging brought up my fear of snakes, and I thought the area might be a good place for a ten-foot alligator to hide. I grew tense as we approached the thick lush green vegetation. Luckily we made our way through narrow passages. Then we came to two aquatic weed harvesters removing the vegetation from the bayou. They pulled off to the side to let us pass safely. After we passed them, paddling was easier.

A peregrine falcon swooped down and flew off with something in its talons. The falcon perched on the top of a dead tree to eat its catch. We were close enough to see markings on its face that looked like heavy black sideburns, its sharp downward-curved beak, and its white-spotted chest.

We saw another dark-brown spot floating in the green vegetation alongshore. We hesitated to think it was an alligator after mistaking a log for an alligator last time. As we paddled past, the spot slowly sank below the surface and disappeared. We surmised it was a small alligator. "That's spooky," said Sara Jo.

"We could be paddling right over alligators and not know it," said Heidi.

We approached a bridge where Cis and Pat waited for us. They were rejoining us and stopped there on the chance we'd be coming that way. We paused for a quick break and then continued.

Heidi rescued an inflatable ball from the water to take home to her son, Sam. "Perhaps I'll have to put a face on this and make it another mascot," she said.

Toward the end of our paddle, we were joined by Leonard, who paddled his solo canoe. Leonard and I had connected several months back. As I planned the trip, he was a great resource and generously shared his knowledge. He talked about his canoe club. I told him that Diane from the Carrot Patch had spilled the beans about him not being fond of kayaks and I teased him about it. He smiled, blushed, and confessed he had considered getting one, but his allegiance was to canoes.

With our destination in sight, we paddled past a man sitting in the shade in his backyard. He was playing guitar and singing along. He paused briefly to greet us and continued singing. We paddled up to the park behind the Jean Lafitte National Historical Park and Preserve in Thibodaux where Kitty, Cis, and Pat waited. The water teemed with large catfish. The bank was a mixture of mud and clamshells. Onshore, Pat gave me an extra-long hug. I knew it was her way of showing her support for me regarding the email I'd sent.

Kitty, Cis, and Pat had been in the Jean Lafitte National Historical Park and Preserve building and learned about a common boat used in Louisiana, particularly by Cajuns, called a pirogue. It's a small flat-bottomed boat that's been in use for hundreds of years in the shallow backwaters of the marshes. The pirogue was originally made by digging out cypress logs.

Leonard joined us for lunch at Bubba's Restaurant. "Where are you going from here?" he asked.

"We're heading home," I said.

"That's going to be a rough paddle," joked Leonard.

"I know," I said. "We were thinking we would run really fast and hit the water and slide for a while. Seriously, we're driving."

"Are you going to do the Phatwater Challenge next year?" asked Leonard.

"It's on the list of possibilities, but don't be holding your breath," I said.

"What is that?" asked Cis.

"A forty-two-and-a-half-mile race from Port Grand Gulf to Natchez on the Mississippi," said Leonard. "Most of them are in racing kayaks, but there are some canoes. Some people in our canoe club do it."

"We heard the wind was so bad this year that 50 percent of the paddlers pulled off half way," I said.

"I've never done it," said Leonard. "They say when you come around the last curve, you can see the flags of Natchez on the bluff in the distance. With a headwind, it's like a mirage, and you never get there."

As lunch continued, the others at the table talked boisterously, catching up after not being together for more than a week. The normally animated Leonard was subdued. He had a lot of competition with all the talking, but he jumped into the conversation when he could.

We went back to Joyce and Frank's B&B to clean up. We couldn't find our ad in the paper, and no one we spoke with had heard about the Gathering. It appeared we would have another Gathering with no local women. Joyce said she had called friends to get them to come. We went to Peltier Park Pavilion in Thibodaux and set up for the Gathering. We were joined by Joyce and her friends, Frances and Irene, who called themselves the three musketeers. With these three dynamic ladies, who all have owned bed-and-breakfasts, we began.

"One of the things we do is honor the elder in each group," I said. "Who might that be here?"

"I turned eighty in October," Frances said proudly.

I gave Frances a mug, handed her the basket that held the tape recorder, and asked her to speak first. She began without hesitation. "I thank my Lord every day that I can do the things that I want to do. It's not just that I do the things I want to do, but that I have the guts to do them. That's my philosophy in everything I do. I see many people who don't have the guts to do what they want to. If you don't get up and do it, it doesn't happen. You learn so much—and you're never too old to learn—but to learn you have to be open.

"Being alive is my big thing. I get up in the morning and move this leg, and I move that leg, and then I move this arm, and then I move that arm up and down. Then I say, 'Okay, body, we got it evened out a bit.' I'm not being a Pollyanna about it. I'm being thankful. Every day is a new beginning.

"One thing I've learned is that you should never just stay with old people. Try to balance your life and be with as many young people as old people. If you always take the same kind, you're going to end up knowing nothing new. You know how old you are. At a certain point in life, age is just a number. When you hear people from different generations, listen close. A lot of times you think that you're right, but then you realize it's not that you're right. When you listen to other people's thoughts and feelings, you open up to feelings that change your life. Heck, I've made men blush. I'm not ashamed of anything." We all laughed.

Frances looked at the logo on my shirt and said, "I love your logo." Then she reached over and picked up a photo and showed it to me and continued. "The photo reminds me of the Southwest. I love the Southwest. My daughter lives in Colorado Springs, and I go to visit her three times a year. When I go, I go lie in the warmth of the Garden of the Gods. My daughter, who is a teacher, said every time she went to work at the candy shop, she drove through the Garden of the Gods. 'Mom, the one thing that I wish from the years that I live here is that I don't forget how beautiful the Garden of the Gods is. I don't want to take it for granted, you know, like we take our city for granted, our homes, our towns, our families, and our friends. I hope I never get like that.'

"I went to Costa Rica in 2007, and in 2008 I went to China. I walked the Great Wall, and I just spent a month in France. I came home, and my daughter asked, 'Mom what did you do?' I said, 'I had so much fun!

I went hiking for twenty miles. The thing that was the most fun was the zip line.' She said, 'I can't believe you did that.' I'm not a could-have, should-have, would-have kind of person.

"I have been working at the food bank since we started it twenty-five years ago. If I can help someone, I will go to every inch of the earth to do it. I will do everything I can. If I can't, it doesn't bother me. I give to the Lord.

"I grew up and, at the time, I thought we were poor. Then I got older, and I found out that wasn't true. We might have been poor in terms of material things, but there was a lot of extra stuff hanging around. We had a lot of food because my mom and my dad were hard workers. My mom was a seamstress. We were the best-dressed kids for the money we had. The thing is, we had a big Christian mom and dad, and family came first.

"I got turned on to bed-and-breakfasts by somebody. Then I heard how much fun Joyce was having and I can't let her have all the fun.

"My first husband died when I was twenty-three. He was twenty-four, and my daughter was a year and a half. I had parents I was able to hang with—and younger siblings. It's a matter of what you do with your life. I keep men on the side. Joyce has learned a lot from me." She smiled mischievously and we laughed.

"When my daughter was three years old, I met my second husband. We were married thirty-two years, and then he died. He has been gone thirteen years now. I feel blessed because my first husband was wonderful, and my second husband was wonderful. Some women go all through their lives getting bummers. Gosh, I got two good ones. If you're friendly and you're happy and you know yourself, it can work out—but you have to know yourself.

"My first husband and I, we were married four years and four months before he died. Prior to that, he was in the military, and we decided that we wanted children. We were in Oklahoma when he started to deal with the headache, and it developed that it was a malignant tumor. The fact that I didn't have any children bothered me. He had his surgery, and I went to be with him. In the meantime, I got pregnant. I was happy because the doctor said he would have six months to live. I wanted his child.

"We didn't have two pennies to rub together. There was this wonderful lady who worked with the wives of the men who had been in the war or were hurt. When I got to be three months pregnant, she let me live in her house with the other army wives.

"One morning I was going downstairs to go to the base to visit my husband at the hospital. My shoe got stuck on the carpet, and I fell three flights of stairs and lost my baby. It would have been a little boy. They drove me to the hospital, and I got the D&C. I will never forget that doctor. I had not been well since the conception of my pregnancy. He said,

'Little Mama, you must remember it isn't because you fell that you lost the baby. It's because you didn't have a healthy pregnancy that you lost the baby.' It makes me think that the Lord works in mysterious ways. This could have been a crippled child. That was His way of doing something. I accepted what happened without question. We came back home, and three weeks after my D&C I got pregnant with my daughter. She was born and was a year and a half when my husband died. She doesn't remember him. Then I met my second husband. I got pregnant and miscarried. I never had any other children.

"My second husband had lost his wife the same time I had lost my husband. We didn't know each other. We met on a blind date. He came to pick me up, and I met him at the door. I'm five eight and he was five seven. I wore spiked heels, so I looked down at him. He said, 'Are you ready to go?' I said, 'Yeah. What have you got planned?' He said, 'We're going dancing.' We went dancing. The next day I went and bought two pairs of flat shoes. A couple of months later he said, 'Boy, I guess you were sure of yourself.' We met in August on my daddy's birthday, and we were married December twenty-ninth. He was always saying, 'I know you can do it.' He was a picker-upper.

"One day my daughter started playing the piano. She ended up being a music major at the University of Lafayette in voice and piano. She minored in business. She practiced all the time, and we wouldn't hear her. Then she'd hit a bad note, and our ears would perk up. We learned not to say anything. When she would come back home from school, he'd look at something she was doing. One day I caught him saying, 'Oh, honey, that's real good . . .' and then he threw in that word 'but.' I didn't tell him anything in front of Mira, but later I said, 'You can't give a compliment and take it away. Anything you want to tell her to help her, you do that later—or the next day or two days after.' He learned to do that, and for him that was an enrichment.

"I have had my ups and downs. I had a brother who died a year ago March and a sister who died in July. Then I had another one die not two months later. She was in a nursing home here. I would come every day and visit her and do things I knew she liked. Then she was in hospice. She was five years younger than me, and that's what hurts. My other sister was a baby sister. She was sixty-eight and on her deathbed, and I was seventy-five and still going strong.

"On that Friday, I found out that her grandson was killed in Maryland. My niece had to go home and couldn't take care of her mother. I was leaving on Tuesday for a trip to Colorado. I canceled my trip. Every day, I would drive to New Orleans. My brother's wife came and stayed at the house. We drove to New Orleans every day, and my brother would come from Baton Rouge. We didn't do anything physically with her, but we were there. Whether she heard us or not, we don't know.

"She loved to sing—and, oh, she had a beautiful voice. Her favorite song was 'In the Garden.' While I went to get some food, my brother sang the song to my sister. When I came back, they said she had made faces while they were singing. I looked at her and said, 'May, was it that bad?' She gave me that half smile because she couldn't talk.

"That Sunday I brought my sheet music with me. My brother was there—and my sister-in-law—and I said, 'You know the choruses. You sing that.' I sang the verses, and they came in with the choruses. During the second verse my brother pointed at my sister. She had been there since the day before with her mouth wide open and one eye open, the other one closed. She had not been showing anything, and all at once she closed her mouth and started mouthing the words to the song. She had tears coming out." Frances was teary-eyed herself as she recalled this.

"After I got through singing, I said, 'May, the tears? Was it because I was so bad—or because you were so happy?' And she gave me that little half smile.

"What I'm coming to is that someone said it was good that I did that for my sister. I did it for her in a sense, but I did it for myself. That was my way of grieving. After she died I felt lost because I had lost two siblings in two months. We do things we have to do. It's difficult to know that I have lost these girls because we were close, but they aren't suffering anymore.

"My niece was able to come back to be with her mom the last couple of days. My niece said, 'I'm sorry about your trip.' I said, 'My body would have been over there, but my mind would have been here. We do what we have to do.' That's the important part.

"My daughter is fifty-eight years old. She was married seven years before her first child came because they were both in law school. They wanted to go riding off into the sunset and didn't want anything holding them back. Then all at once she decided she was getting ready to finish law school and needed to start thinking about the family. She had Jack and then Shelley and then Erin. Once she got the machine running, she didn't know how to shut the switch off.

"I have grandchildren, and I'm telling you it's wonderful to Skype. They live out there in Colorado. I love all these new things that we can enjoy. I can see them, and they can see me. They can feel like they have a relationship with me. They call me Momo. In between, I send them boxes of stuff that I get at the thrift store. It's a joy to have these little ones.

"Mira said something the other day that almost made me cry. It was about how important grandparents are. Grandparents and great-grandparents offer something that parents never could because they look at things differently when they're with the children.

"I was allergic to birds, and Mira had two parakeets. My mom lived only six houses from my house. Guess who had parakeets at her house? My mom. Every day Mira would go over there to feed the birds, change the cage, and do everything for them. It allowed her to have her pets when she couldn't have them at my house. Grandparents are there for teaching children things sometimes the parents are too busy to do.

"You teach them different generational things. One of the great-grandparents was teaching my granddaughter how to drink coffee.

"My son-in-law never knew his grandparents. When he was born, his two older brothers were twenty and nineteen years older than him. He looked at them as uncles instead of brothers.

"There are magical things that happen as you grow older. You get to be a teenager mentally. You can be with your teenage granddaughter, and you're just as young as she is.

"We're a kissy-kissy family. You will learn that down here. The minute you walk in, you get the kiss whether you want it or not. You either grit your teeth or you enjoy it. I enjoy it when it's a nice-looking man. When my son-in-law first came to meet our family, I said, 'All I can tell you is you can let it all loose because I'm not changing.' He is a wonderful son-in-law. Sometimes I call over there to talk to my daughter, and I spend all my time on the phone with him. It used to be he would say, 'Oh, hi Mom. Here's Mira.' Now he has many things to say. I think it's because he felt the love that we had for him.

"I spent a month in France at a bed-and-breakfast with people I had made friends with over the years. It's an exchange, so when I go over there or they come here, it doesn't cost any money. I enjoy it. It's not that the bed-and-breakfast is going to make me rich or that it's going to make me poor. It's the friendships that I make. I go all over France. We don't get paid from the people who come to our house; we get paid from the lady who does the booking. That leaves a different feeling because there's no money that transpires.

"You get out of life what you give. Sometimes you have to be the aggressor. I never dreamed that the Lord would give me this. I started my bed-and-breakfast in '94, and my husband died in '98. Just think, if I hadn't started this adventure, I would not have done all of the things that I have done. I would probably be getting up in the morning at ten o'clock looking like an old hag just draggin' along. It's fun. I mean, who could be so lucky to have all of these things happen?"

Frances handed the basket to Irene, who nervously accepted it. "I'd like to say that Joyce and Frances are older, and I'm the youngest of us three friends. They're lucky to have good health. They're in very good health, and you have to be to do all of that walking on tours and running a B&B. I have health problems. I can't physically do as they can. For fifteen years I've had diabetes, high blood pressure, and thyroid issues. I had surgery this year.

"I've been to Europe quite a few times. I know a lot of French people that I've hosted through my bed-and-breakfast. I don't do it anymore. My husband was a French teacher. He enjoyed and entertained the people while I did the cooking and whatever. We had some real good times, and we traveled together.

"I have two children, a girl and then a boy, and now three grandchildren. The grandchildren belong to my son and his wife. They wanted another child very badly, but were unable to have a child. With good insurance, they were able to do the in-vitro program. That failed the first time. The second time, my daughter-in-law got pregnant and had twins, a little boy and a little girl.

"Abby is the little girl's name—my husband's name. In his family Abby was a popular name. The little boy they named Alexander because that's my daughter-in-law's maiden name. They were born in April of last year, and it just so happened that my daughter-in-law's father had an accident and died in July. We have Alex, who represents that grandfather, and we have Abby, who represents the other one. We think that's a nice thing that happened after losing both grandfathers. They have their two grandmothers. The grandchildren are the joy in my life."

Irene gazed off into the distance for a couple of moments and said, "Life goes on.

"I started out teaching in 1965. There was a time when everyone took home economics. It was a wonderful thing as you would learn practical things and then teach them to others. If you got married and decided not to teach, you could still use this education. I did marry and had children and taught too. I stopped teaching while the children were very young, and when I returned to teaching I taught biology. I enjoyed every aspect of this subject and tried to make it interesting and fun for my students.

"Retirement brought us time for travel and then the interest in a bed-and-breakfast business. We made some great new friends with some other B&B people in our area and, of course, with the guests. Joyce and Frances are two of those new friends. We have a lot of fun with new experiences. Life continues to change, and we adapt. My husband passed away six years ago of cancer, and I'm learning to do things on my own. Sometimes it's not as pleasurable as if I had a husband, but I'm adapting."

Pat took the basket and said, "My life is changing too. This trip has in a way been a life-changing experience. The fact that I know I'm being responsible for myself—I don't have to be responsible for anybody but me—and these gals are open about everything that happens makes it that way. It's nice to be involved in the attitude they have about the trip or about whatever comes. When things go amiss, they figure it out and go on to the next one. It's not like, 'Oh, my God. We have to go get something.' There's nothing negative about it. If something happens, it gets worked out. I need to adopt that in my life because I don't necessarily do that. This has been very good for me.

"I don't have any children. That was a choice I made when I first got married. I feel as if I have children. I feel I am a grandmother for people I've worked with in the past—my nieces, nephews, great-nieces and great-nephews, and children who are around. I don't feel upset that I didn't have any children. How can they say that because you didn't have any children you should feel guilty?

"I come from a German-Irish Catholic family. The two collided in many ways. The last couple of years I've been doing genealogy work. My mom died when she was sixty-four. When we were growing up, we had this amazing other family—brothers and sisters and cousins. We were always getting together. Almost every weekend there was a gathering. As I got to be a teenager—it wasn't that I resented it; it got to be routine. Almost all of the first cousins were boys, and I was the only girl. I never had any girl my age I could bond with. As a teenager, I was a mother figure to the younger ones, and I took offense and resented that. I threw that all out of the window and said, 'I'm leaving. I'm going away.' I had one girl cousin my age, but we never saw each other very often.

"I left home at twenty-one and moved to Kentucky with a girlfriend. Eventually I met my husband there. Now that I have come back around and I'm doing genealogy work, it is interesting. We had a family reunion in the summer of 2011, and my first cousins all got together. It was like we never separated. We started where we left off. It was fabulous to feel that way with all of those people down there—and to see their children. To see that whole thing starting all over again is amazing."

Cis spoke next. "Well, I grew up as an Air Force brat. All of the trips down here talking to people with close families and large families that are in touch with their families have been interesting. That wasn't how I was raised. We moved every year all over the world. Your family is where you make it and who you make it. I have many families, and I think that's great.

"I guess whatever your normal is, is your normal. I married the exact opposite of what I grew up in. I married an enormous family. Very late in life I learned what that was all about.

"I have a son in Wyoming and a daughter in St. Louis, and I live in Montana. In that respect, the nomad gene that Dad had is in my children. They don't know it yet. I'm not one to say, 'When are you getting married? When are you going to have kids?' That's all up to them. If they should, then I will do whatever it takes to be there for those children, and for my children. That's something that I didn't have in my normal. I'm anxious to close that little gap when or if that ever happens. It is a joy, a true joy."

Joyce accepted the basket and spoke with confidence. "I believe age is just a number. As long as you can get up, you're healthy, and you can move around, it is a good day. My daughter, when she was turning thirty, was upset. She said, 'I'm turning thirty.' I said, 'It's just a number. Be thankful you're still alive.' I don't consider my age. My body is healthy, and my mind is well." She paused and made a funny face indicating some doubt, and we laughed. "I guess that's debatable.

"I like to have fun. I worked all my life. Now I'm enjoying my life. I have children and a lot of grand-kids. We try to get together with the children and grandchildren as often as we can.

"What I taught each of my girls is that you have to be independent. You never know what life is going to bring you. The first thing you need to do is to learn to be independent so you don't have to depend on anybody else.

"I have been blessed. I never lost a child. I had a big family with lots of children and lots of in-laws. My husband is number fifteen out of seventeen children. He is going to be seventy-three. He has eleven siblings older than him. Ten girls are still alive. When we get together, it's like 150 people. I've been blessed."

Accepting the basket, I said, "That made me think about my family. Mom died when I was eleven, and there were eight of us. We didn't have much adult supervision, and we're all still alive. That's amazing! It became clear to me that one of a mother's jobs is to keep the family together. Dad did a good job of that, but there were pieces missing. We didn't know how to interact very well, and we didn't have anybody to help us learn that stuff.

"As we get older, we realize how special our family really is. It has become a priority to get together. We do it a minimum of once a year, sometimes twice. My brother Bruce is the first one to get information out.

"Last week, I got a phone call that my brother Gary had had an accident on a firing range. His hand got caught in a kickback and pinched. It didn't seem like a big deal at first, but then it turned into a severe staph infection. It looked for a while like doctors might have to remove his hand. He is fine now. With different antibiotics, it completely cleared up within two or three days. He went back to work today.

"In the process of all of that happening, I called him twice. Each time he mentioned that he had heard from Mike or Mark or one of the others. I listened to how important that was. Everybody either called or came to the hospital. It didn't used to be like that, and I'm very grateful.

"I'm amazed how this family has transitioned over time. When Mom died, we went our own ways to survive. We've come back around. When I think about the stupid stuff we did, I continue to be amazed we're all still here. One brother crashed an airplane, and there were car accidents."

I put the basket down in the middle of the circle, and Joyce spoke again. "As your children get older, they focus on their children. They have their lives, and you don't get to see them quite as much. It is a cycle, but as their kids go off, they start coming back because they have more time. Sometimes it depends on how far away you live. It happens in all families. It is one big circle of life that goes around.

"My oldest daughter told me about an article in the newspaper where this guy wrote about how his mother was a horrible mother. She wouldn't let him do this and she wouldn't let him do that. He wrote that he was very thankful that he had the worst mother in the world. He was thankful because it made him a better person. He sees now why she didn't say he could go. She was protecting him. So my daughter said, 'Thank you to the meanest mother in the world.'" We laughed.

"Children are good, grandchildren are better, but great-grandchildren are even better because you play with them and send them back home to Mama. We were a good family. At the supper table every night, you took your turn and brought up whatever you wanted. Some things weren't so nice that were brought up.

"Once my daughter came back from school. They were studying about genes and different color hair. She said, 'Why don't I look like y'all?' She had blue eyes and my mother's complexion, very fair. Frank is dark, and I'm dark. Well, Frank and I've been together so long that we think together. We both came out and said, 'We adopted you.' She says to this day that was the meanest thing we ever did. That's how bad I was." We all laughed again.

The Gathering ended, but we stood around and continued talking with each other for another twenty minutes. Being in the presence of Frances, Irene, and Joyce felt nurturing and fun. We didn't want to leave each other's company.

Hunger won over, and we drove to a steak house for dinner. Crossing Bayou Lafourche, we saw along the shore that hundreds of egrets had roosted in the trees for the night. Their white feathers glowed in the light of the slivered moon above.

After dinner we enjoyed time at the B&B with Joyce sitting around the table before retiring for the evening. We talked about parenting.

"Parents holler at you because they love you," said Joyce. "If they didn't love you, they'd let you do what you want."

"You never hollered at me that much," Sara Jo said to me.

"Not holler at you, but tell you no," said Joyce.

"I don't think you had to do that much," said Sara Jo. "Did you really have to tell me no?"

"When you first got back," I said.

"There was that readjustment period," said Sara Jo.

"At a certain age, all kids are very rebellious," said Joyce. "Probably adults are at the same time because the kids get on their last nerve."

"I got very wise advice from a guy I was working with who didn't have any kids but who worked with teens," I said. "He said, 'Pick something to argue with your kids about that you don't care about. They need something to rebel against you about so they can claim their individuality and independence.' I don't remember what I picked for Sara Jo or Naomi, but with Wade it was his hair. I didn't care what he did with is hair. He had green hair for a long time."

"I can't imagine that looking good on him," said Heidi.

"What color hair does he have?" asked Joyce.

"He has brownish-reddish hair," said Heidi. "It's very handsome."

"We were having a family reunion once," I said. "My husband's dad had died in the winter, and he was cremated and was to be buried that summer. The whole family was coming, and Wade was in his long-green-hair phase. The green had faded, and I knew he was about to color his hair again. I said, 'You can do the green hair if you want to, but I want you to think about one thing. This is the only time some of your relatives are ever going to see you. They're going to take pictures, and that's how they will remember you.' He didn't make his hair green again until they left."

"I had to use reverse psychology on my kids," said Joyce. "You have to sometimes to get them to listen. What does Wade do for a living?"

"He is a carpenter and a potter," I said. "He's very good at both."

"Do you have four children?" Heidi asked Joyce.

"Two girls and two boys," said Joyce. "I have nine grandchildren and one great grandchild."

"Tell us about the cemeteries here," said Heidi. "Are people cremated?"

"We are just starting to cremate the Catholics," said Joyce. "For a long time, you couldn't."

"The larger tombs are the ones that have more bodies," said Frank, walking into the room.

"We saw some that had six names on them," said Heidi. "It didn't look like there was room for six."

"You can get six in there," said Frank. "Matter of fact, you can probably put more 'cause after a while you can drop them in the hole and put another one in."

"We bought one, and we're on the bottom," said Joyce.

"We're in a mausoleum," said Frank.

"Those are done like that because we have so much water," said Joyce. "By our fishin' camp after the hurricane, they popped out of the ground and floated all over the place. They are in sealed concrete."

"It's a concrete box with a top on it," said Frank. "The concrete is watertight. If you look at them in the front and they have window, that's a tomb. That window is an opening, which you take the screws out of to take the cover off. A coffin will slide in there."

"You will see they're all cleaned up now," said Joyce. "We're having All Souls Day."

"Did you know people are dying to get in there?" joked Frank, grinning and looking rather proud of himself.

"Your and my husband's humor have a lot in common," I said, laughing.

"Yeah," said Sara Jo. "I was kind of waiting for that comment."

"After I die, I don't care where I'm buried," said Frank. "Just don't bury me in a cow pasture."

"One of his brothers raised pigs," said Joyce. "You know the hard candy that you get, you know, those wafers? Well, they used to make them over here in Thibodaux. His brother would get the broken pieces, and he'd feed them to the pigs."

"When we killed the pigs, they tasted sweet," said Frank. "I told him pick all the different kinda flavors, and give one vanilla or cherry. He had to quit because he was giving them too much at a time. Boy, they gobbled that stuff up."

"I want to taste a vanilla pig," Heidi said, laughing.

Joyce got her photos. "When I traveled for home health, I didn't like to drive," said Joyce. "I always had my camera with me so I could take pictures, and then I'd paint them. Now I'm retired. I don't have time to paint.

"Do y'all know what a shotgun house is? Look. There's one there." She pointed at a photo of a rather plain house on stilts with a door in the center of the front. "You can stand in your front door, and you can shoot a gun straight out the back door. It's elevated off the ground. You open all your doors and windows and the air circulated. These were for the lowest paid working on the plantation. The one with the two doors in the front, they were the higher rank. The bigger house was the overseer. They say they had slaves. Well, they had the white slaves down here.

"Like the song says, 'You owe your soul to the country store.' My daddy on the ranch—he didn't have to pay rent for the house, but the plantation owned the house. You could only live in it if you worked. If you quit working, you had to leave. They paid you once a year in December, so you had to pay all your money to the grocery store. It was a big circle. December's when the plantation owners make the money, when they sell the sugar cane.

"Mama never drove and never went to the store. There was a country store on the bayou side that had material, anything that you need to sew with—lace and all. The owner would come, and Mama would make a list of the things that she needed for the next week. He'd deliver what she'd ordered the week before. He'd bring bolts of material so we could pick out what we wanted for a dress or anything. We could cut the material then, or he'd bring it back."

"Do you still sew?" asked Kitty.

"I do," said Joyce. "I don't have my sewing machine right now. The girls from India that I know are making cloth diapers and pads with it.

"Mama used to bake bread every day, and you had the flour sacks. I made my girls' clothes with flour sacks. In fact, I kept some of the dresses."

"That's a definition of recycling," said Kitty.

"That's not new," said Joyce. "We recycled everything. The way we were taught, you didn't throw food away. If you had a little bit of beans or vegetables, we put them in the container and froze it. When the container was full, then you made vegetable soup. The jambalaya is made the same. That's how it got started. You add a little chicken, pork, and beef. They chop the meat and sausage together, and you threw rice in it and make it jambalaya."

"And a lot of spices right?" asked Kitty.

"It depend what restaurant you go to," said Joyce. "We don't spice it up. The seafood, they gonna put plenty spices, and you can't even eat 'em. They sell a lot of alcohol and beer, and they make a lot of money off of it. When I make vegetable soup now, one of my kids will joke, 'Mama cleaned out the refrigerator.'"

"Isn't that what goulash is for?" asked Sara Jo.

"Yeah," I said. "I'd clean out the refrigerator and add noodles and tomato sauce."

"I worked hard, but I played hard," said Joyce. "In the summertime as teenagers, we had dancing. You went to the dance hall with your parents. You learned to dance, and at weddings you danced on the foot of your parents so you could learn how to dance. I was working at eleven, and I was dancing before that. During high school, Tuesday and Monday nights were the only nights we didn't have dancing. We danced, and we didn't drink."

"Do you still go out and dance?" asked Kitty.

"If I have a partner, yes," said Joyce.

"Frank doesn't dance?" asked Kitty.

"He did," said Joyce. "I have to put my foot down, let's put it that way. It was fifty years a couple of years ago that we graduated from high school. We still have class reunions. Anything to have a party. The party started at eight at night until midnight. Frank says, 'Nobody's gonna stay that late.' Well, the band was so good nobody left, and they had to kick us out at midnight.

"This year everybody was turning seventy in our class, so they threw us a seventieth birthday party in August. Same thing—eight to midnight. I told him he didn't have to dance. I was up there all night, and towards the end he was up there just as much. We used to go dancing at least once a month; then it was hard to find a place to go dancing. You can dance at all of the festivals."

I made the first move toward bed by standing up and saying good night. Everyone else was right behind me. Before I went to sleep, I read the mediation book. "Opening Ourselves to Love: We do not have to limit our sources of love. God and the Universe have an unlimited supply of what we need . . . there is plenty of good love available—love that heals our heart, meets our needs, and makes our spirit sing."

I smiled. Being on the water had connected me to spirit and healed some of the pain of self-doubt and the sense of isolation I had been struggling with. No one, other than Sara Jo, had mentioned my email, which was fine with me. I had a ways to go to feel grounded and confident. I felt nurtured in Joyce and Frank's home. They demonstrated warmth and love for each other,

Left to right: Frances, Joyce, Heidi, Nancy, Sara Jo, Kitty, Pat, Irene, Cis

October 25th through 28th

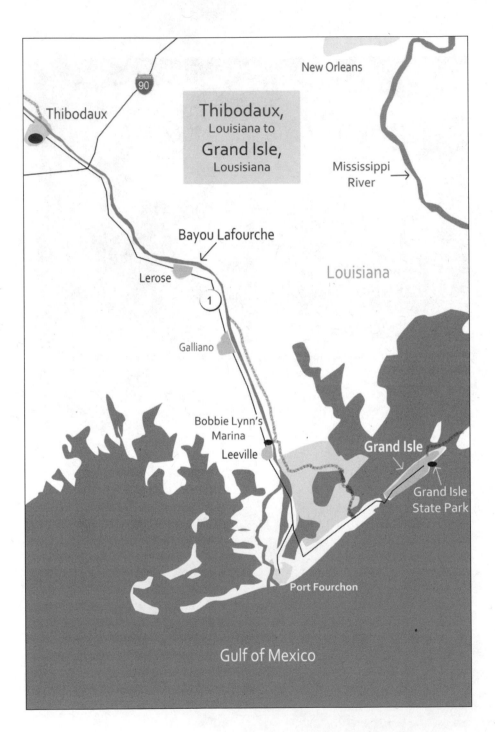

10

GRAND ISLE

October 25, Day Thirty-five

I snickered when I opened the meditation book to the day's passage and read "Letting Go of the Past: Whatever our philosophy, our interpretation can be similar: Our past is neither an accident nor a mistake. We have been where we needed to be, with the necessary people. We can embrace our history, with its pain, its imperfections, its mistakes, even its tragedies . . . Today we are right where we need to be . . ." The women traveling with me, and those we'd met, had been teachers. Some lessons were challenging and others sweet.

Over a breakfast of eggs, maple sausage, and homemade biscuits, Frank and Joyce talked about the local sugar production. "There's brown sugar, white sugar, cane sugar, molasses, and sorghum," said Frank, standing next to the table.

"When we were growing up and the brown sugar got separated out, it was in a giant silver dome building," said Joyce, bringing more food in from the kitchen. "They didn't even sell the brown sugar. The workers could take it home for free. That's what I have in my kitchen. My mama baked with brown sugar. When we got married, I couldn't tell why my cookies didn't taste right until Mama told me to go get the brown sugar."

"What you get in the grocery store now isn't the same as the brown sugar that we had," said Frank. "They refine it further now. There are three different levels of syrup. The molasses is what got spun out and the thing at the bottom was the dregs. It was thick goo with crystals in it."

"The thick cane syrup is what nursing mothers used," said Joyce. "It has lots of iron and it helped them make milk. The light syrup doesn't have as many nutrients."

Before we left, Frank proudly showed us his fishpond with fish called brim in it. The fishpond was covered with screens to keep the birds from eating the fish.

We left Joyce and Frank's and drove to Thibodaux. At the Carrot Patch, a health food store, we bought granola bars and healthful snacks.

Diane, a blonde muscular woman, cheerfully greeted us. She was excited about our trip and phoned her boss, Deb, to come join us. Diane and Deb were kayakers. In between waiting on customers, Diane shared her story.

"I was born and raised in this town. I have some Cajun, maybe in my little toe. My dad's family came from Italy. We were raised with Italian cuisine. I married a Cajun, and I had to learn how to cook that. I started eatin' it, and I started gettin' sick. All the fried food and the roux, the burnt flour with the oils. The vegetables were cooked down with oil until they were mush. I ended up at age twenty-five sayin' this wasn't going to do.

"I'd heard the Carrot Patch had opened in 1976. My digestive system was shot. I weighed ninety pounds, and nothin' was agreein'. I decided I was goin' to try this out. I walked in and I thought, 'What's this? A voodoo place or what? Is there a witch in here or something?' The original owner guided me. [Deb is the third owner.] She said, 'The first thing I want you to do is start drinkin' aloe vera juice.' At that time, there was no juice. It was gel, and you had to mix it in water and try to get them lumps down. I said, 'I feel so bad that I'll do anything.' You tell me to drink deer pee, I'd a done it.

"I went to see the nutritionist that used to be here. We worked on systems first. The digestive system, nervous system—I never had to go into the hospital. When you start feelin' better and start eatin' fresh foods, it's wonderful. I haven't had medicine in thirty-somethin' years. It saved my life. I drank so much aloe juice. I don't have to drink it since fifteen years ago. You don't put all that junk back in.

"I started trainin' in the gym. The chiropractor that was workin' on me was an older man, and he believed in weight and strength trainin'. He said, 'You don't need to strengthen your back. What you need to do is strengthen your abdominal muscles.' There were only men's gyms here then. I said, 'Ladies don't do that.' He said, 'You're goin' to the department store, and you're goin' to get a set of bar bells.' My husband thought I went crazy. I'm doin' leg lifts in the bedroom and all these things he showed me to do. I got much stronger. I started workin' in the gym and the health food store 'cause it saved my life.

"I'm a grandmother of two and I have an eighteen-month-old great-grandson. I made sixty-three in August. I feel great. Every day I wake up and I think, 'Am I supposed to feel this good?' It works. Exercise and keepin' busy. I did marathons. We were trainin' for a triathlon when Katrina started comin' this way. We did weeks and weeks of trainin', swimmin', runnin', and bikin'. The Saturday that we were goin' to get our packets, we went to New Orleans and they said it's cancelled cause it's comin' this way. We never got to do our triathlon. I couldn't believe we trained all that time and had it cancel. The triathlon was called Girl Power. All ladies. It didn't come back until maybe two years ago. I stopped runnin' because I got to a point when I realized I had to tone it down a notch. I still get out and do cardio, biking, and power walkin'—but not runnin'. Before it falls apart, we bought the kayaks."

A tall woman with dark hair walked in. Diane introduced her as Deb, the owner.

"So you have a mission?" asked Deb with a New York accent.

"Yes," I said, "We're collecting stories of women over fifty."

"Fifty is too young," said Deb. "That's the new thirty." She leaned against the counter facing us. Kitty, Pat, and I had taken a seat on a bench. "I'm a misfit. I'm a Yankee, and I've been here thirty-five or more years. I'm from Yonkers, New York, and ended up here.

"My husband got a job here, and he told me it's just like Florida. 'You're going to love it.' That's when I said that man lies. He said, 'Oh, yeah, they have water there.' He took me to Grand Isle. I put a white bikini on the first time we went swimming, and I threw my bathing suit away because it was gray when I came out. 'This is not like Florida,' I said. 'What kind of water is that?' Well, you know you have the oil rigs out there and other things going on in the Gulf. I was used to the Atlantic.

"I've been here a long time. I'm still here because it's a safe area. We don't have a lot of crime issues like New Orleans. Everybody in this town knows everybody. I have people that run into the store and say, 'Just put this on my tab. I forgot my purse.' We still have that service. Mostly we're very trusting in this area.

"Have you seen any alligators yet?"

"We saw a little one yesterday," I said.

"I hate goin' past them," said Deb. "I say, 'You go first.' I know it doesn't even see me. They aren't supposed to be aggressive. The eleven and twelve footers are a little more aggressive, and they get rid of them. Now they're talking that we have bull sharks in the bayou. You got to be careful.

"We have Northerners come for the bayou clean up. They're in the water up to here," she indicated her waist, "picking up trash. They must not be aware. We're all aware. There are water moccasins in the water. They splash and play around. The trash is not worth that. When they clean the bayou, they're getting big tires out of the water. I'm thinking a snake could be wrapped around in there. They're brave. You have to realize that this bayou has some sewage thing goin' on. Don't wash your face in the bayou. Don't take a little bath." She scrunched up her face as if to say, "Ick."

"You have to ask me a question," Deb said.

"What would you say have been turning points in your life?" I asked.

"I've had a great life. I don't think people have one turning point," Deb said. "Turning point—coming here. Turning point—going to Florida. Those are major points in my life. I have four children—turning points. This business was a big turning point. People say, 'How did you get into this?' I say, 'I'm repenting.' Seriously. For all of my sins that I've done in the past. It's like waking up one day like an alcoholic and doin' something about it. That's how I look at it. It was a turnaround that has done a lot in my life—the lifestyle, not just the Carrot Patch. It opened a lot of doors that led into a lot of areas spiritually and physically.

"The Carrot Patch was down the road. It was a little hole in the wall and was about ready to go under."

"Has she told you her story yet?" asked Diane, who had been waiting on customers in the back of the store. "She still has that New York thing."

"Yeah," said Deb. "When I get mad, I fight New York. Just ask my husband."

"That's what I'd expect," I said. "I haven't met a New Yorker yet that doesn't go there when they're riled up." The others laughed.

"The bad thing is I go up there and I'm a misfit," said Deb. "I'll say something, and they turn around and say, 'Where you from?' I say, 'I'm from here.'"

"That Cajun gets in ya," said Deb, shaking her head.

"I'm curious," said Kitty. "Diane was talking about when she first started going to the gym and how that was mostly male and how that's changed over the years. Are there more women-friendly gyms around here?

"We have just-women gyms," answered Deb. "You have to realize the area. It's the South where the woman is home and cooks and takes care of the kids. It's changed now because you have both people that have to work. They get pushed into that. You still carry over—your parents stayed home and cooked. The man was more chauvinistic, and they still have the last say here. We need more women in politics down here.

"It was strange when I first came here. When you go out with a young couple, the two guys sit in the front and the women sit in the back. If you go to somebody's house, the men are in one room and the women are in the other. You remember that, Diane, back when you were young? Even now. It's kind of strange. That was different from where I was raised, the separate thing. I remember being told to get out of the front seat so the man could sit next to my husband who was the driver. I sit with my husband.

"Goin' to my first crawfish boil, that was a trip. I didn't know anything about it. You been to one?"

"I have," said Pat. "What's weird is they bring them out in these mesh bags, and they're alive, so they're crawling around."

"You watch them do it," said Deb. "You dump them in there with your seasoning, and they're trying to get out, but you put the lid on. They take a picnic table, and you're outside, and they dump it out in a pile. You have corn, potatoes, and the beer. Now they throw sausage in there.

"I never knew about any of this when I first came here. We got invited to a crawfish boil, and I'm from the North, so I wore my skirt and white blouse. I'm going to somebody's house, so I brought a bottle of wine. My mother taught me that when you go to somebody's house you bring a bottle of wine. These people were in their cutoffs and T-shirts—I mean dirty-out stuff. In New York, you never go to somebody's house dressed like that. They dump all this on the table. I thought they were crazy.

"What about your first taste of crawfish? I told my husband we need to get out of this town; there's something wrong with these people. My lips from the salt or the seasonings were four times their size. They blew up. We used to catch those things in the creeks, and we never thought about eating them. We never used spice or salt. We boiled everything to death. I thought, 'What are we going to eat if we stay in this town?' That was a rude awakening. We never fried anything."

I looked out at the bayou, just across the street from the shop, and said, "The bayou water looks gross to us. We're spoiled. In Minnesota, we have crystal-clear water. You can see the bottom. You can see the fish. I can't even see my paddle blade here."

"When I've been out there, I'm washin' my boat down," said Deb. "I got the bottle of vinegar out, you know, an antiseptic." A smile crossed her face and she said, "When you get to Grand Isle, you need to put your kayaks in early in the morning in the bay area. Sometimes the dolphins are there and you can see them. Don't go to the beach side, go on the bay side."

"I'm looking forward to that," I said. "Thanks for the information. We've got to get moving. We have twenty miles to paddle today."

We drove on a highway that ran parallel to the bayou, which wasn't used by boat traffic for a few miles south of Thibodaux except for an occasional personal fishing boat. Areas of the bayou were completely overgrown with vegetation. At Larose, the Gulf Intracoastal Waterway crossed Bayou Lafourche, and the boat traffic increased dramatically. The Gulf Intracoastal Waterway is part of a three-thousand-mile intracoastal waterway along the Atlantic and Gulf coasts and runs from Carrabelle, Florida, to Brownsville, Texas. It provides a navigational route for shipping traffic that crosses dozens of other navigable rivers and waterways. It's a safe haven free from the shipping hazards inherent in traveling the open waters of the Gulf. The Gulf Intracoastal Waterway has a lot of commercial activity and is used by recreational boaters too. South of the Gulf Intracoastal Waterway, the fish and shrimp boats were parked alongshore.

We watched for a place to put in the water and drove as far as Galliano before we found one twenty feet from the road with nothing but grass between us and the water. Our day's paddle would be twenty miles. It was already in the seventies, and growing warmer. Sara Jo, Heidi, and

I were on the water quickly with the help of Kitty, Cis, and Pat. The light breeze pushed waves up the bayou. There wasn't any current. The bayou was a no-wake zone, so boats moved slowly and were easy to maneuver around.

photo by Heidi Favet

The section of the bayou we paddled was distinctive from other sections we had paddled. It was narrow, and the paralleling highways were close to the water. In some sections there were no buildings between the water and the highway. Parked alongshore were a variety of watercraft—fishing boats, shrimp boats, and houseboats. We paddled past a well-maintained cemetery that was, as Joyce said, "all cleaned up" for All Saints' Day. The mausoleums and grave markers were bright white, and the grounds were well manicured. The cemetery seemed out of place, and then I remembered dry land is scarce here. The bayou travels down a narrow strip of land that is less than four miles wide. From Golden Meadow south, the strip of land averages less than a half-mile across.

A large houseboat was being towed up the bayou. We pulled over to let it pass. In one of the windows, a rubber witch's face peered out, an indication Halloween was near. We were curious about the purpose of a boat with no engine. We passed an identical houseboat parked onshore with men working on it. They came to the ornate iron railing to talk with us. This houseboat was a party boat, and it could be rented and moved to where the party was. The boat was thirty feet wide and eighty feet long. The walls of the two-story boat were windows that looked out on a walkway around both levels.

We passed two blue-and-white tugboats parked nose to nose. The names painted on their bows were Squeegee and Sponge. Fish and shrimp boats passed on their way out to the Gulf. Some of the boats were large—forty feet in length; others were barely longer than our sixteen-foot kayaks. I was fascinated by the nets that hung from all of them and curious how they worked. Other boats looked like miniature ocean liners. They carried supplies to the oil rigs in the Gulf.

We felt like we were paddling against a slight current and then realized it was high tide. We were paddling against water coming in from the

Gulf, which was twenty miles away!

The two highways along the bayou were connected by lift bridges. The headroom was tight as we passed under. On the east side of the bayou, the number of structures diminished until there were only trees beyond the highway; eventually even the highway ended. A few people fished from shore or from a bridge.

Frequently we heard cars honking. Looking toward the highway, we'd see people waving at us from car windows. Kayaks on that part of the bayou were a novelty, especially with women in them.

I thought about my daughter Naomi who couldn't join us due to work commitments and her dedication to my grandson, Tony. She desperately wanted to join us, but at nearly two years of age, Tony was rightfully her first priority. I was proud of the mother she had become.

Sara Jo and Heidi paddled near each other, talking. I was elated that Sara Jo was able to share the last week with me. Heidi and I had known each other for nearly eight years, and I thought about all she had in common with Sara Jo. They had wisdom beyond their years, and at times they were my best friends and others cherished daughters. They shared values about the environment and cared deeply about people.

We reached the Leon Theriot Lock located a couple miles south of Golden Meadow. It had an elevation of thirteen feet, and the water was fourteen feet deep. The lock allows marine traffic to reach safety during approaching hurricanes. At nonhurricane times, the lock ensures water access to Port Fourchon from the intracoastal waterway. The lock stood open when we passed through, with no sign of a lock attendant.

South of the lock a man in blue jeans and a bright-blue T-shirt crouched over his pirogue, checking his catch for the day. We paddled over. It was hard to miss the tattoo of the backside of a naked woman wearing thigh-high boots standing in front of a large bird whose wings wrapped around his arm. The fish he showed us was a sheepshead. It was silvery in color and had five distinct wide vertical black stripes on its sides and prominent sharp spines on its fins. The man's pinky finger was bleeding; he said the fish bit him.

Heading south, we paddled into a slight headwind. I had become uncomfortable from sitting so long without a break. My back ached and my legs were stiff. There was only marsh on both sides of the bayou, and the bayou was twice as wide as where we had put in. Skeletons of trees stood out in the marsh, reminders of a time when the water had been fresh there. The marshes were brackish—a mixture of fresh and salt water. On each tree a single heron or cormorant perched on an outermost branch. Channels through the grass and shrubs wandered out into the marsh. Fishing boats and industrial places were spaced further apart. There were a few dry docks, which are also called boatyards, with large boats on hoists getting their hulls repaired or getting a fresh coat of paint on their bottoms and sides.

The closer we got to the Gulf, the more boats there were. The captains often greeted us as they passed. Some wanted to know where we'd started. I told them Minnesota, and their replies varied from disbelief to cheers. One captain said, "Well then, you must be tired. How about I give you a tow?"

A large, severely rusted boat was anchored onshore. A hatch door hung precariously by its lower hinge, ready to drop into the water. Doors and windows were missing. A railing in front was crushed inward. Its name was still clearly visible on the back, *Lucky XII*. The next boat we passed wasn't as lucky; it had sunk. All we saw was the wheelhouse.

There were no opportunities to pull over for a bathroom break, and the day was growing painfully long. I stopped drinking water for fear I would make my discomfort worse. I kept thinking we were close and I could make it, but each time we reached a building onshore, it wasn't our destination; and the next building was so far away that it appeared to be a bump on the horizon. Finally we paddled to shore where à couple and another gentleman fished. They were on top of a three-foot-high retaining wall that ran several yards along the edge of the bayou. Camper trailers were parked behind them. We asked if they knew where we could find a restroom, and they said there wasn't one around. Then the man sitting with the woman said we could use the one in their trailer. I was glad to hear that; however, there was no landing or dock.

Heidi paddled to the end of the wall. With enviable balance, she managed to get out of the kayak onto the narrow board. Then she walked along that board plus another before reaching solid ground. She made it look easy. "You just need a little balance," she said. I crawled up next and then Sara Jo. Heidi was already in and out of the trailer by the time I got there. I was grateful I didn't have to wait for her. The bathroom in the trailer was one of the most beautiful things I had seen all day. I thanked the woman, who had come in the trailer to start dinner.

We talked with the fishermen for a while and reversed our climb to get back into our kayaks. Getting in was easier than getting out. We pulled away from shore, and the people wished us well. They assured us Bobbie Lynn's Marina wasn't much farther. But the bayou seemed endless. Highway 1 was just a few yards narrower than the strip of land that supported it, running for miles with water and marsh on both sides.

Getting back into my kayak, I splashed the cool water on my face. It trickled down my cheek and onto my mouth. I licked my lips and tasted salt. I realized why my hands had felt gritty—a layer of salt had formed on them.

We paddled past a row of wooden pylons, remnants of a dock. Gulls perched on top of the pylons. We paddled close before they took off squawking. From a foot above to far below the water line, the pylons were covered with barnacles. A barnacle is a type of arthropod—a crustacean that is related to crabs and lobsters. Barnacles tend to live in shallow and tidal waters, and they attach themselves permanently to a hard surface—to the surface's detriment. They often attach themselves to the bottoms of boats and ships. I reached over to touch them. They were hard like a clam shell. Some were attached deep in holes in the wood pylon.

The barnacles were a momentary distraction from fatigue. For motivation, I thought back to the Thibodaux Gathering and Frances's attitude about life. Her bubbling energy was inspiring. It had a delightful childlike quality combined with matter-of-fact common sense. Unconditionally caring for others was natural for her. She saw the world as family. I smiled thinking about how much fun the three of them—Frances, Joyce, and Irene: the three musketeers—must have celebrating life together.

Finally Bobby Lynn's Marina was in the distance. Kitty stood on the dock waiting for us, and then Pat and Cis joined her. Several brown pelicans floated near the marina. Some took flight when we approached; most seemed adapted to people. Pelicans have large bodies covered with feathers that range in color from silver to gray to brown. Their heads and long necks are bright white. A pelican's tannish-yellow bill is long and flat with a tinge of orange on the tip of the lower bill. Its large throat pouch is solid gray and folded close to its neck. The brown pelican is considered one of the smallest pelicans, but it can still have a wingspan of six feet.

When we stepped out of the kayaks, I was stiffer than I'd ever been before on the trip. I walked around to loosen my legs. The marina had one large building with the office and store on the main level and two bunkhouses upstairs. There were several individual rental units elevated ten feet off the ground next to the water. Picnic tables and a fish-cleaning station were under them.

Smelly, tired, and hungry, I was introduced to a tall, thin, handsome man in his late thirties who worked at Bobby Lynn's. His name was Jean, which he pronounced "zheen" in a blend of French and English. Each time he spoke to me he called me "Miss Nancy" with a soft southern accent and a charming tone that made me melt. Jean was enthralled with our kayaks and our adventure. Bobby Lynn's rents sit-on kayaks that are peddled, not paddled. I mentioned to Jean that I still didn't know what route to take to the Gulf the next day, and he said he had a map that could help. "Let's get together after dinner," he suggested. We put the kayaks near our van in the parking lot and went into the bunkhouse to shower before dinner.

The bunkhouse was a long, narrow room with three bunk beds, a table and chairs, refrigerator, microwave, TV, and couch. It had the basics and was comfortable. The walls were royal blue, and the room had one small window. It felt a bit like a cave. We thought it was designed for men who came to fish.

A few moments to lie down and a shower were heaven. I came out of the bathroom after my shower and said something about how frustrated I was with my hair. It seemed to get worse each time I washed it.

"It's only hair," Cis said. As I tried to run my fingers through it, she repeated, "It's only hair" a few more times and reminded me it would grow out. I heard an internal voice telling me I was overreacting to my hair, and I should let it go.

"You're right—," I began.

Then she said it again. "It's only hair."

That was it. Her words pushed my hot button. I turned to face her. "No, it's not only hair. My hair is connected to some old hurts that I have yet to heal." Once the words started to trickle out, they flowed out in a steady stream. "I'm surprised at how upset I've been about my hair. I've always been a tomboy, and when I was little I did what my brothers did—often ignoring the dolls I was given. My mother had let my curly red hair grow, and it was down to my butt. In a house with five boys, my hair was what set me apart. My long hair made me feel like a pretty little girl, and it got me attention. Then when I was five, my mother put my hair in a ponytail and cut it off. She said it would be easier to take care of. I remember being confused and sad. When she was done cutting, my hair was only a few inches long. Because my hair was curly, it looked even shorter.

"In the following months, I seemed to disappear among the boys. Mom had become pregnant again, and a couple months after my sixth birthday, she went to the hospital to have the baby. I was at a neighbors' playing when Dad came home from the hospital. Mrs. Smith and I leaned out the side door of the house, and she called to my dad, "What did you have?" Dad smiled proudly and said, "We finally got a girl." I remember thinking, 'What am I?' I was deeply disturbed by what I heard. As an adult, I understand that he was excited to get another girl after five boys, but at age six I didn't understand his true meaning. That experience started a long struggle with my understanding of femininity and self-acceptance."

"It'll grow out again," Cis said with a smile.

"I know that." I looked at her in disbelief. "That's not the point. This hair," I said, tugging at my hair, "has touched off some core issues that I'm upset about."

After that, no more words were spoken. Everyone finished what she needed to do before dinner in silence.

We headed to the Starlite Grille for dinner. On the way, we saw that the trees in the marsh were specked with hundreds of white birds. Pat and Cis were avid birders and were engrossed in identifying them. There were egrets and ibises roosting for the night. Pat and Cis pointed out great white egrets, little blue herons, and Louisiana herons.

At dinner we enjoyed fresh seafood. Heidi took a risk and ordered the soft-shell crab. When it came to the table, Heidi stared at the crab's body and legs not knowing how to eat it. She started by trying to pick the meat out, but it was tender and stuck to her fingers. She made a mess and wasn't getting much to eat. Pat told Heidi to bite it, shell and all. The whole body of the soft-shell crab could be eaten. Her eyebrows rose in disbelief. She stared down at the crab for few moments, picked it up, and took a bite. She said, "It's tasty, but this texture is going to take some relaxation to enjoy. I thought this would be like regular crab." As part of a crab's growth cycle, it

outgrows its shell and sheds it. The new shell underneath is soft for two to three hours before it turns hard again. When Heidi was done eating, she said she was glad she tried soft-shell crab, but she was not sure she would again.

Back at Bobby Lynn's, Cis mixed a clay facemask for us that she'd purchased at the Carrot Patch. Cis felt we could use some pampering after our long trek and the clay would remove toxins from our skin. We waited to put it on until after Jean came with the maps to show me the route he'd suggest. When Jean arrived, it took me a moment to focus on the map and not him when he started with "Miss Nancy . . ." After six weeks of feeling grubby and unladylike, it felt good to hear my name said so sweetly.

I explained that we were planning to parallel the road so we wouldn't get lost, but I wanted to go through the marsh if it was safe. Jean showed me a laminated map of the entire marsh area and said we could get one at the gas station down the road. He was excited to show me the channels and canals that the shrimp boats used to enter the Gulf near Grand Isle, our destination. I studied the map. The channels, canals, lakes, and bays looked like a large maze. I noted carefully the route he suggested, absorbing every detail. I was ecstatic we'd be able to cross the marsh and wanted to be sure I understood where we were going so we wouldn't get lost out there. I was glad that I had years of experience navigating the Boundary Waters and that reading shorelines was second nature to me. My experience would be valuable in the marsh. Jean said his brother had been considering offering kayak tours out in the marsh so he was looking forward to hearing about our experience.

We asked Jean if he'd always worked at Bobby Lynn's, and he said he was a tugboat captain on the rivers. He started on boats with his grandfather, who had trawlers. His father worked docking ships in the Bahamas and hauled limestone cargo in Mexico. "It's in my blood. I've always done it. I didn't want to, but here I am. I loved being on the river at sunset," he said with a tear in his eye. He talked about not wanting to do that work because of all that he missed while he was gone from home, like family birthdays. He said he always seemed to get home the day after. "It's hard on relationships."

Jean left, and we each smoothed the green clay mask on our faces. Our faces looked particularly eerie with the blue light reflecting off the walls. Waiting for the masks to dry, we talked and took care of Internet responsibilities like replying to email and posting on Facebook. Then we heard a knock. We were close-lipped and wide-eyed as our heads spun toward the door. Sara Jo got down from her bunk and hesitantly opened the door. Jean started in, holding a bag. He glanced around the room at us, stopped dead in his tracks, paused, and said, "I thought you ladies might like some satsumas. I'm sorry if I disturbed you." He quickly put them on one of the beds and left. Sara Jo closed the door, and we cracked up. "I bet that's not something he sees at fish camp every day," laughed Heidi.

Cis was right. A little pampering and a good laugh was what I needed. After I removed the mask from my face, my skin felt smooth and soft.

October 26, Day Thirty-six

The rising sun cast a brilliant orange hue on everything. The horizon was a rusty orange that melded into yellowish pale blue, which transformed to brilliant blue above us. Wispy clouds drifted by. The lower edge of the clouds reflected the yellows and oranges, and the trailing edges were deep grays. A pair of dolphins skirted the opposite shore and disappeared into a channel.

I was more excited about our sixteen-mile paddle through the salt marsh than I had been about any other paddle we had done. The weather would hit the eighties, and we'd have a light cool breeze. If there had been high wind we'd have canceled the paddle. There would be no shade on the water, so it could get uncomfortable, but I was too thrilled to care.

Sara Jo, Heidi, Cis, and I paddled out of the marina and down the bayou. The greatest challenge in reading the map was judging distance. Some objects—like the Leeville Bridge, an elevated expressway that curved and stretched miles across the marsh—appeared closer than they actually were. Other objects—like the canal that was our destination—appeared farther. We were headed to the Southwest Louisiana Canal, which ran east-west for seven miles. It was one of the main routes used by commercial fishing and shrimp boats to access the Gulf. The Southwest Louisiana Canal had no bends, so it would look endless.

The closer we got to the canal, the more fishing and shrimp boats were parked alongshore; and the closer we got to the Gulf, the larger the size of the boats became. I studied the way the boats were put together, and my curiosity grew about how they worked. Nets were attached to long arms that stretched out to the sides of the boats.

I was surprised when Cis and Heidi turned into a channel. Not even a quarter mile down the channel were shrubs and grass. Cis was using her iPhone and Google Maps for directions. To me, it seemed we hadn't paddled far enough to be at the canal we were looking for, and the Leeville Bridge wasn't where I had anticipated it should be. Influenced by Cis's confidence, I ignored my sense that we were headed the wrong way and anxiously followed them in.

The tide was low, and scattered alongshore were discarded wire cages about the size of small trunks. The cages were bent and tangled. They had become oyster habitats. Oysters grew inside and clung to the outside of the wire mesh.

A lone heron stood atop a tree stump in the tall marsh grass. The herons here were taller than those in northern Minnesota. It warmed my heart to see Kee. I greeted her and thanked her for being such a dependable guide and consistent companion on the journey downriver.

It wasn't long before I was convinced we were not in the right canal. My anxiety rose as I studied the marsh map and saw several options where we could have turned in. The area looked like a maze, and I became concerned that we could become lost. The water grew shallow, and we were intermittently grounded. I attempted to say I thought we were in the wrong channel, but before I got all the words out Cis referred to the information her iPhone provided. Each time she did, I grew angrier. My resentment flared. I felt as if this special day of paddling were being ruined.

Sara Jo paddled over to me. "Are you okay?"

I didn't answer and looked at her knowing she could read the frustration on my face.

"Do you know where we are?"

When I didn't answer again, Sara Jo sighed. "I'm frustrated that Cis is leading the way on your last day of paddling," she said. "This is your trip."

"I'm frustrated too," I finally said. "I'm going to be quiet for now." I wasn't exactly sure where we were, but I had become certain we'd find the right canal. It was a matter of how much time paddling this canal would add to the day.

Cis shouted directions. We rounded a couple more bends and saw big, open water. I knew we were looking at Lake Jesse. The Southwest Louisiana Canal cut through the lower part of the lake. I headed out to the opening. Cis thought we should go to the left. The water grew shallow again, and we became grounded, so we had to lunge our bodies forward to move the kayaks out of the mud. Because of the low tide, oysters were near the surface, and they gouged into the bottoms of the kayaks when we paddled over them. I continued toward the open water and chose not to respond to Cis's directions to turn. I was in a position I dreaded. I disagreed with the information Cis was getting from her iPhone and wasn't willing to follow it. My anger and resentment could easily generate a big argument that wasn't worth the negativity it would create. I wanted to do what I thought was best for the group.

The tension had grown to a point that Heidi was compelled to say something. She called us together, but like a couple of children with their heels dug in, neither Cis nor I would join her. Heidi paddled to me and looked at my map. I showed her where I thought we were and where we were headed. Then she paddled over to Cis and looked at the iPhone. After a minute Heidi said, "You're both where you think you are, but you aren't going to the same place. We need to follow Nancy because she's taking us to the route that Jean showed us." That was when it occurred to me that Cis hadn't been part of Jean's full map orientation.

Heidi said later that evening, "I felt like I had to figure out where we were right then because I knew I could still get us back. I was nervous that if we kept going forward, we could easily get lost in the immense maze of the salt marsh, and I wasn't going to let that happen."

I continued to paddle toward the open water and was frustrated because the canal wasn't appearing. Everyone followed me. We lunged ourselves over the last of the muddy spots and eventually came around a corner of the marsh where we saw a canal that went on forever. I relaxed knowing we were where we needed to be.

It took a while for me to let go of my anger and frustration. I knew the others felt the tension. Being confident about where we were, I was more determined to keep it that way and not mistrust myself again.

photo by Sara Jo Dickens

We passed small oil platforms with pipelines running in several directions under the surface, which created many of the channels and routes through the marsh. Many people believe the pipelines are one of the factors causing the deterioration of the marsh. The pipes, which have several valves, rise out of the water; pelicans perch on the pylons around them.

We watched for the fishing camps we had been told were out in the marsh and saw a couple in the distance. Fishing camps are large one-story buildings perched above the water on pylons. Each has a stairway underneath that leads to a small boat dock. The fish camps are owned by families or groups of friends for easier access to fishing in the marsh.

There were no more trees, just miles of water and grassland with occasional areas of shrubs. We paddled the canal, which was an eighth-mile wide. A fin sliced through the water, and previous talks of sharks came to the forefront of my mind. I yelled, "Shark!" Everyone came to attention and focused in the area where I had seen the fin a few yards away. Then we saw a spurt of water blown several feet into the air and knew, to our relief and delight, it was a dolphin. It blew water again and

photo by Sara Jo Dickens

came a little closer, checking us out. It was exciting. The dolphin leapt into the air, dove under, and disappeared.

Commercial boats passed us from both directions. Those returning from the Gulf had their nets stretched out to dry. The outstretched nets made the boats look like large bugs. Larger shrimp boats spend a few days out in the Gulf; smaller boats spend one night.

There was nowhere to pull off for a break. The shoreline was soft smelly mud. Eventually we found a narrow piece of ground thick with oyster shells. It provided a stable area to walk and access to the reeds for a private bathroom break. I didn't pull in far enough to be able to step onto the oyster beach and sunk to my ankles in the soft oozy mud. I had to clasp my hands around my lower calf and yank to pull my foot free. My foot came out with a thick coat of smelly mud. I washed most of it off before joining the others. I didn't want the smell to detract from our rest stop.

We sat in the warm sun and enjoyed granola bars and water. Sara Jo ate the remaining biscuits she'd acquired from Joyce and Frank. The only thing breaking the horizon was an occasional shrub that rose a foot or two above the grass. In the distance were power line poles that looked like toothpicks.

In the shallow water a couple of hermit crabs scurried across the mud. When we moved close, they disappeared into their shells. Looking carefully, I saw tracks left by the crabs running in every direction.

Paddling again, I remained watchful of our location. I carefully tracked each opening, bay, or channel branching out from the canal we paddled. We needed to turn south, and I want to be sure we turned into the right canal. My focus was directed far ahead as I scrutinized the shapes along the shore. Suddenly my paddle hit something—whomp! A huge fish flipped its body to swim away, making a big splash, and buckets of water poured on me. I screamed.

My mouth was open when the splash hit. I spit out the water and burst into laughter as salt water ran down my face and into my eyes. I was drenched. I shook off the water like a dog coming out of the lake.

"You got a face full," said Cis, laughing. "You got christened."

"I didn't get to see enough of it to tell what kind of fish it was," I said, still spitting salt water. The humor dissipated the last of the tension.

"Two guesses on the fish would be tarpon or barracuda," said Cis. "They bask on the surface—or perhaps it's a habit of sleeping on the surface—and you snuck up on her. You scared the bejesus out of her."

"She scared the bejesus out of me," I said. "That was the longest fish

I've ever seen. A barracuda sounds dramatic—let's say that's what it was. I never saw its head. It disappeared too fast."

Alongshore a pair of long-billed, long-legged brown birds was feeding. They stuck their long, thin bills down into the mud. Cis identified them as godwits. They were probing for worms and mollusks.

We had been paddling against the tide, but when we turned down the channel, we didn't feel the strain as much. We paddled into a little cove and pulled our kayaks together for a floating lunch. At this point in the trip, we were eating whatever was left in the cooler: lunch meat, hard-boiled eggs, cheese sticks, and veggies.

As the heat of the sun beat down, we watched oysters spurt water into the air. Little geysers rose from the surface of the water all around us. Then a roseate spoonbill flew overhead, and we were ecstatic because it is rarely seen. Its white neck was extended. The underside of the belly and wings was deep pink. It beat its wings a few times and then glided for a while. The sun made the pink feathers glow. Then it disappeared quickly. As the day progressed, we were treated to more sightings of roseate spoonbills.

During the excitement about the spoonbill, something dropped into the water from either Cis's or my kayak. We looked down into the water at the mud below. I didn't want to dig around to retrieve whatever fell. Cis reached in. As soon as her hand submerged into the mud, her facial expression was that of disgust. She played it up and had us cracking up. Then she said, "This feels like pudding." Her hand went deeper into the muck, but she couldn't locate whatever had fallen in. We couldn't believe she kept digging deeper and deeper.

The salt collected on our paddles, hands, and faces. Sara Jo developed blisters on one of her hands. I got the pink duct tape from my deck bag, and we wrapped it around her hand, which relieved the discomfort.

In addition to the birds mentioned, we saw wood storks, egrets, lady fish, needle fish, jumping fish, osprey, vultures, terns, and numerous oyster beds. The channel we paddled wound its way south and came out at Bay Ronfleur. Through an opening into Caminada Bay, we saw three-foot rolling waves. Heidi was drawn to see what was beyond the marsh and paddled out. She came back and said, "I saw Grand Isle to the right, but straight ahead was water, water, and more water."

With fewer than two miles to the end of our paddling, we paddled into Bayou Laurier. I was glad the paddle for the day was almost over, but I struggled to grasp these were the final moments of the paddle to the Gulf and that tomorrow we would paddle in the Gulf. After eight years of planning and traveling, the journey was coming to an end.

We saw Kitty and Pat pull alongshore in the van near Caminada, the last tiny town before the bridge crossed over to the island of Grand Isle. Caminada sits on the north side of a narrow strip of land dividing the bayou from the Gulf.

My excitement drove me to paddle quickly, and my desire for the trip not to end made me pause to float and savor the last moments. I paddled and paused repeatedly, torn by the mix of emotions. When I landed I got out slowly, as if in slow motion, noticing the details of this final landing; the transitions of color from the mud to the roadside gravel, the way the water lapped onto shore, how my foot sank slightly into the mud, the way the sun felt on my skin, the smell of salt air, the soft gritty texture of the salt on my hands, and the smiles of excitement and amazement in the faces of my companions. I stood at my kayak clutching my paddle tightly, as if holding it would delay the end. I couldn't comprehend all of the emotions that surfaced, and I felt disoriented. I stared across the road, past the marsh on the other side, at the calm soft blue water of the Gulf as I grappled with the reality of the journey's end.

Heidi bounced out of her kayak, ran over, and hugged me. "Congratulations, you did it!" She had tears in her eyes. Kitty walked up with a broad grin, and we shared a long heartfelt hug. Sara Jo bounded over and hugged me, and then Pat, Cis, and I hugged. We shared a giggly group hug and stared at each other in amazement.

We did it!

While they loaded the gear with the efficiency created from weeks of practice, I stood and watched, still grappling to get grounded in the moment. As we drove off I kept staring out at the Gulf. The loud ruckus in the van brought me out of my daze. Stories of the day were being shared with Pat and Kitty. Then fatigue hit, and we quieted down. As we crossed the Leeville Bridge, our energy levels rose again. The bridge rose high above the water, and we could see for miles. We saw the Southwest Louisiana Canal that we had paddled and more open water than we expected after paddling the narrow channels through the marsh. The landscape was a vast expanse of blue and green. The bridge had been built to facilitate evacuations in the event of a hurricane in the cities of Grand Isle and Port Fourchon, which were vulnerable to flooding regardless of the strength of a storm.

When we got back to Bobby Lynn's, Jean said he was glad to see us. He'd seen us turn down the wrong channel.

Heidi and I took Jean out in our kayaks to thank him for providing us with a route we thoroughly enjoyed. After a quick how-to session from Cis and Kitty, he climbed in as if he'd paddled a kayak all his life. We paddled down toward the Gulf for a mile or so and returned. From the smile on Jean's face I knew he was hooked.

"We might have to get some of these," he said.

When we paddled back to the marina, I saw my husband, Doug, onshore walking with his sister, Kathy, to the edge of the water. I was so excited to see him I wanted to race to the landing, but I didn't want to be rude to Jean. Doug met me at the landing. Being in his arms, I felt enveloped in unconditional love. "I'm proud of you," he said, looking me deeply in the eyes. I was giddy. He leaned back to look at my hair. "It's not that bad," he said.

Kathy, standing next to us, scrunched her eyebrows. "I thought your hair was different," she said. "What's wrong with it?" I greeted Kathy with a long hug and then told her my hair story. I don't get to see Kathy often, and it meant a great deal to me that she had come to the Gulf to meet me.

Kathy is sixty-nine and lives in Jacksonville, Florida. She has been married to Brian for forty-two years and has three children. She and Brian are now raising two of their grandchildren. Kathy's passion has always been family and friends.

For Sara Jo, Kathy is more than an aunt; she is also her mother-in-law. My husband, Doug, is Sara Jo's stepfather. Sara Jo married Kathy's son, who is also named Doug. (Kathy named her son after her brother, my husband, Doug.) The arrangement has made for rich and occasionally challenging family experiences. We deeply care about each other and work to keep communication open.

Kitty gave me the key to the room Doug and I would share for the evening. She said that she, Pat, Cis, and Heidi went in there with the intention of creating a romantic setting for Doug and me, but they weren't able to do much. When Doug and I walked in, we understood. The tiny bedroom had four bunk beds. Doug and I enjoyed a few moments alone to catch up, but I was hungry and knew the others were too. I went to the bunkhouse to let the others know they could come over. The evening's dinner would be cooked in our room because it had a kitchen.

While Cis and Pat cooked, the rest of us relaxed with tea and coffee on the deck overlooking the bayou and marsh. Checking email, I read that Rocky, the brother of my sister-in-law, had died. I sent a condolence email back, but sending an email felt impersonal. I wanted to go to the funeral to be there for her, but that wasn't an option. I quietly told Sara Jo and Doug. It was hard to be so far away at a time like that.

I glanced over and saw Kitty had taken an immediate liking to Kathy. They were lost in conversation. I put the computer away, and Cis said, "I hear you cut hair."

"Really?" I said. "You want *me* to cut your hair?"

"Why not?" Cis said. "It grows back."

I got my scissors and gave her a haircut on the deck. I was particularly concerned about making a mistake, or perhaps I had fleeting thoughts of intentionally making a mistake. Her hair came out fine.

The sun set after a delicious celebratory dinner of traditional Louisiana red beans and rice that Cis made. When we were done eating, the colors of the setting sun and the sight of flocking birds drew us back outside. Hundreds of white birds flocked to the trees across the marsh to roost for the evening. They were the same species we'd seen earlier.

The sky became a spectacle of vibrant pinks and oranges as the piercing yellow sun moved toward the horizon. Around the sun, the sky was gleaming yellow. The clouds took on deep shades of color with brilliant white and silver edges. The sun turned pinkish as it disappeared below the horizon. There was a pink cast on the water and trees. Birds flew across the majestic scene, heading to their roost in the trees. Slowly the colors softened as the blues of night set in.

Doug and I headed for our room. I was eager for time alone with him. We tried taking a mattress off the bunk bed and putting it on the floor, but it didn't fit between the beds. We considered dragging two of the mattresses into the larger room, but they had rigid edges and wouldn't have been comfortable. We cuddled in one bed for a while but eventually ended up in separate beds.

So much for romance.

October 27, Day Thirty-seven

We started our day with Cis's magic pancakes, the same tasty treat we had enjoyed in the motel parking lot back in Vicksburg. Then Jean gave us an opportunity to test-drive the sit-on kayaks he rented to customers. With a sit-on kayak, the kayaker's entire body is on top of the boat. The ones we were trying were leg powered. They had pedals, like those on a child's pedal car, that moved the kayak forward or backward. The rudder was hand controlled. They were more stable than our sea kayaks, but I found them bulky and felt like I was too far above the water. I preferred paddling to pedaling. Doug looked like a little kid joyfully playing with a new toy as he pedaled all over the marina and the bayou. He was exploring a channel on the other side of the bayou before the rest of us—Jean, Sara Jo, Kitty, and Jean's brother, who was testing one of our kayaks—could catch up to him. Grinning, Doug shouted, "This would be a great kayak for fishing."

Back on land we loaded up and drove across the Leeville Bridge toward Grand Isle, the final Gathering stop on the journey. Had we paddled farther on Bayou Lafourche, we would have paddled past Port Fourchon, a major petroleum seaport. We would have seen a steady stream of oil tankers and other ocean-going ships along that section of the bayou. According to Wikipedia and Port Fourchon's website, the city exists to serve domestic deepwater oil and gas exploration, drilling, and production in the Gulf of Mexico. More than six hundred oil platforms within a forty-mile radius of Port Fourchon furnish about 17 percent of the U.S. oil supply.

We followed the road as it skirted the Gulf for nine miles before crossing another bridge connecting Grand Isle to the mainland. The island was originally a sandbar formed by the Mississippi River and connected to the mainland. When the river changed course six hundred years ago, part of the sandbar and marsh eroded away, creating the island. The town of Grand Isle encompasses the entire island except for Grand Isle State Park on the southeast end. Inhabited since the early 1700s, its population is less than two thousand in off-season and swells to twelve thousand during the tourist season. The primary industries for the island are tourism, the seafood industry, and oil-field-related professions. Hurricane Katrina ripped through Grand Isle en route to New Orleans in 2005, but we saw no signs of remaining damage.

The island of Grand Isle is a breakwater between the Gulf and the many canals, channels, and bays that connect to Bayou Lafourche and other waterways to the Mississippi River. Most of the buildings on the island are on stilts—high enough to park cars and to house patios underneath. Buildings such as the grocery store and restaurants were on ground level.

Before setting up our tents at Grand Isle State Park, we walked over the shrub- and grass-covered sand dune to the beach. We were at the

photo by Cis Hagar

Gulf of Mexico. We kicked off our sandals and left them scattered across the beach as we walked to the water. On the way, I found a tar ball from the oil spill in the Gulf in April 2010. It was a flat four-inch blob that was squishy and reminded me of the tar used to fill cracks in roads. I could squish it like clay, but it rebounded. The tar ball broke apart easily; the inside was shiny jet black. There were no other signs of the oil spill anywhere on the beach.

While the others studied the tar ball, I walked into the water. I stood ankle deep, feeling the waves gently splash against me. Under the surface, hermit crabs scurried away. With each receding wave the sand slowly washed away from under my feet. The smell of the salty air was refreshing, and the sun was warm and sparkled off the waves. In the distance we could see six oil rigs.

The Gulf was vast. We had come all the way from the Mississippi's headwaters and watched the water grow from a little stream ten steps wide to a broad river that carried ocean liners. The river had looked big and daunting; now the Gulf dwarfed it. The river had ended, but the Gulf was a new beginning. I wondered what new beginning was coming in my life. I became lost in the sounds, sights, and smells of the water.

Kitty stood next to me staring over the water with a look of peaceful awe. Farther down the shore, the others did the same. After a few minutes Doug, Sara Jo, and I wandered the beach to the east toward a pier and large flocks of birds. We stopped and collected shells and sand dollars. The shells were a variety of shapes and ranged in color from white to chocolate brown. Thousands of tiny shells, some so small you'd have thought they were merely lighter colored sand, collected in groups. The waves cut grooves in the sand creating patterns. Flocks of sandpipers ran alongshore playing tag with the waves. Jellyfish washed up onshore, looking like clear blobs. We assumed the holes in the sand were where crabs had buried themselves. Small beautiful pink jellyfish swam in the shallow water.

I relished these moments with Sara Jo and Doug. Because Sara Jo lives in California, we see her only once every couple of years. We jogged to the pier where large flocks of common terns sat near the water's edge. The birds rose and squawked as they flew farther down shore. We took our time getting back down the beach and to camp.

After setting up camp, we spent the afternoon relaxing. I completed the final Internet posting I needed to do for the trip:

"Today was our last day paddling with the Gulf as our destination. Tomorrow we are at Grand Isle and will paddle for fun in the Gulf and in the bay around the back of the island where they tell us we will see more dolphins. I am amazed that we have completed this journey—it feels a little surreal."

It felt odd making the final entry.

A conversation started about a woman that Sara Jo, Heidi, Kitty, and Cis had met earlier. "I think the important part of her story is that she stepped into the mother-grandmother shoes," said Cis. "She uses storytelling because she wants her children to know where they came from."

"She wants them to be proud that they are the women in the family," said Sara Jo. "She said her mom told her that as long as you can make a bed and scrub a toilet, you got a job and you can take care of yourself. I thought that said a lot about how committed and determined she is—and probably how that whole line of women is."

"Her mother and grandmother died by the time they were in their early fifties," said Kitty. "She plans to live to 127. She wants to be the storyteller and tell the family's history to her children, grandchildren, and great-grandchildren. One of the kids was disabled."

"This is the real South," said Kathy, who lived in Jacksonville. "Even on the East Coast, it's not South. Jacksonville is more of a melting pot. Anybody read *The Help*?"

"That book and movie have come up more than once on this trip," I said. "I saw the movie and loved it."

"I loved it too," said Kathy "I remember going to Atlanta in the '50s and riding a bus with my cousin. I asked, 'How come that drinking fountain says for coloreds?' 'That's because the colored people have to drink out of that fountain,' she answered with a whisper. 'Come to the front of the bus, Kathy.' I said, 'But I want to sit in the back.' She said, 'No, you can't. Colored people sit in the back. White people sit in the front.' I said, 'But I want to sit in the back.' Kids like to sit in the back of the bus, you know? I said, 'That's not fair.' She said, 'Well, that's the way it is.'

"After I saw that movie, I wanted to go to work and hug the little black girls that work there and say, 'I'm so sorry I did that to your family.' We have the sweetest little girls working there." Her eyes caught sight of the large bag of satsumas that Jean had given us. "My gosh. Do you think we'll get through these by the end of the week?"

"Even if we do, we'll probably get more," said Heidi. "Everybody keeps giving them to us."

"Anybody hungry for dinner?" I asked. "Diane and Deb from the Carrot Patch recommended Sarah's Restaurant."

"I would trust them," said Cis. "All we've had has been fried, fried, fried food."

"Don't forget deep fried," joked Pat.

"Would you like that deep fried, deeper fried, or deepest fried?" kidded Heidi.

"And then, 'Would you like a vat of butter with that?'" said Cis, and we broke into laughter. "At the restaurant in Thibodaux, the baked potatoes were served with a portion of butter the size of an orange, and at the buffet you could get more."

"I haven't yet met a butter I didn't like," Doug joked. "I would like to try the Starfish Restaurant before we go. The guys at our coffee shop said I'm supposed to have crawdaddies before I go back. I'm not that convinced about them."

"It's not the season for boils," said Cis.

"They taught me to pronounce that 'ball,' like the word you use if you are going to a fancy dance," I said.

"That's right," said Cis. "It's a 'crawdaddy ball.'"

We drove to Sarah's Restaurant and walked in. We were the only customers in the place. A short older woman came out of the back and seated us. In a soft-spoken voice she told us she was alone. She had sent her helper for groceries, but she hadn't come back. We asked her what her name was and she said Miss Sarah. She brought drinks out and took our food order. Most everything on the menu was fried. We ordered BLTs, soup, and appetizers.

Before Miss Sarah headed back to the kitchen, Kathy asked, "You gonna cook this up by yourself?"

"Yes, ma'am, I am," said Miss Sarah.

"Can I help you in the kitchen?" asked Kathy.

"No, you don't have to do that," said Miss Sarah.

"I know my way around a kitchen," said Kathy. "Back home I cook for 150 preschool kids. I would love to help you."

"She's a good cook," said Sara Jo.

"Well, all right," Miss Sarah said hesitantly. She and Kathy disappeared into the kitchen.

Doug went exploring the restaurant and came back excited. "That's all kitchen back there—the whole length of the building! Miss Sarah is seventy-six. She handles the place by herself. She said she did well until her husband died two and a half years ago."

Kathy brought Doug's soup and an order of hushpuppies and disappeared back into the kitchen.

Miss Sarah came to make sure we were doing well. She looked at Doug and said, "Sir, you eatin' with a little spoon? You wouldn't rather have a soup spoon?"

"That's all the waitress brought me," kidded Doug, and we laughed. "It's okay. The waitress is my sister."

Miss Sarah went into the kitchen again, and I followed her to see what Kathy was up to. She was working on our sandwiches and told me there weren't any tomatoes. That was one of the things the helper was supposed to have brought back. She and Miss Sarah got creative and used the tomatoes from the salad bar. Miss Sarah was deep-frying the bacon, French fries, and another order of hushpuppies.

A few minutes later Miss Sarah and Kathy brought the rest of our meal, and Kathy sat down with us to eat while Miss Sarah stood at the end of the table.

"Doug was telling us you've had this place a long time," said Heidi.

"Yes, I have," said Miss Sarah. "It'll be thirty-seven years the first of the year. I'm not originally from here, but my mom and dad lived here. My dad worked with the oil fields. I came here and was workin' at another restaurant and met my husband. My husband was born and raised here on Grand Isle. He was a trawler, and I'd trawl with him. Growin' up, I was raised in a restaurant because my mother owned one. I said, 'I think it's time that we get us a little side business,' you know? So we bought this property. I started out with that front part, and it was just a trailer. The business was so great we started addin' on. We got four different sections here. It grew as we went along over the years."

"What was it like being on a trawler?" asked Heidi.

"I loved it," Miss Sarah answered. "He owned a boat. I don't even know how to swim, and I was surrounded by water. He would make me put on a life jacket every mornin'. He said, 'Until you learn the ways of the boat—how it's goin' to rock—you gonna wear that life jacket.' I did that for a few months, and after that, I said, 'Well, I know what the boat is gonna do. Now I'm gonna see what I'm gonna do.' I just started goin' without my life jacket, and it worked out fine. I never did fall overboard." We laughed.

"How long did you work on the trawler with him?" asked Kitty.

"Two or three years," said Miss Sarah. "He became a deputy sheriff for the parish and trawled on his days off. He got tired of doin' that, so he started helping me, and we wound up together here. He was a great cook. We were married for fifty-five years. It was a long life together. It's been awfully depressing without him sometimes."

"Do you have children?" asked Kathy.

"I've got a boy and a girl," said Miss Sarah. "There are pictures of my family hangin' up over there," she said, pointing to an area next to the salad bar where there were several family pictures displayed. "The girl has lived with me since her dad passed away and since she and her husband separated. She's supposed to be working with me tonight, but Mama can handle everything. Wait until I tell her the great help I got when she wasn't here."

"Maybe you'll hire me if I lose my job," said Kathy.

"Okay," said Miss Sarah. "That would be great. I don't think you would like Grand Isle. I was born and raised in Florida in the northwest part in a little town called Defuniak Springs. I stayed there until I was seventeen years old. I only go back about every six months to visit and see about my mama's and daddy's graves an' take care of that. I'm always on the go."

"These ladies have been on a kayak trip down the Mississippi," said Doug.

"Down the river?" said Miss Sarah. "Holy mackerel!"

"And they ended up here at your restaurant," said Doug.

"Oh, my goodness," said Miss Sarah putting her hand to her mouth. "I'm glad you did. How you gonna get home?"

"They're going to swim upriver," joked Doug. Miss Sarah tilted her head down, raised her eyebrows, and smiled in disbelief.

"We have a van," I said. "We'll drive."

"This lady paddled from the headwaters," said Cis, motioning to me.

"You paddled all the way down and you're not exhausted?" said Miss Sarah. We laughed.

"Not tonight," I said. "But there have been days . . . "

'Y'all have family back home?" asked Miss Sarah. "And they let you leave for that long a time?"

"I had to run our restaurant by myself," whined Doug.

"Oh, my goodness. You poor thing," said Miss Sarah with a wink. "I'm so glad that y'all made it here. I'm so excited to meet y'all." Miss Sarah filled our water glasses. "When school starts, we lose 75 percent of our business. Our last two summers have been a disaster because of the oil spill."

"Were you busy in here with the workers who came down to help?" asked Kitty.

"No," said Miss Sarah. "They brought in a big catering company and had them down at the end of the island. We lost a lot of business. People weren't coming down because the oil was on the beach. Then the workers that were here were taken care of, so we didn't get their business either."

"Wow." We felt her disappointment.

"The way I looked at it," said Miss Sarah, "there was so many of them that they didn't think that we would be able to handle it."

"There's another hushpuppie on my plate I'm not going to have room for," said Doug. "Here," he said as he held it out to the group. "You want to try it?"

"I'll try one," said Kathy.

"You hadn't had one yet?" asked Miss Sarah.

"I was in the kitchen having fun with you," said Kathy.

"That was so sweet of you," said Miss Sarah.

"That's my sister!" said Doug proudly.

"She raised him from a pup," said Heidi.

"That I did," said Kathy.

"Is she the one that taught you how to cook?" Miss Sarah asked, pointing at me.

"She didn't teach me that," said Doug.

"Mom didn't teach him that," said Sara Jo. "But she likes to bake."

"I think I learned to cook by watching my mom from a distance," Doug said.

"Most of the recipes at the restaurant are mine," I boasted. "But he makes them."

"We're a good team like that," said Doug. "She's the brains, and I'm the brawn."

"My husband was like that," said Miss Sarah. "He was a great cook. He liked to make jambalaya and big-dish things—like the gumbos. The recipes might have started out as his, but they got changed over the years."

"How did you cook on the boat?" asked Heidi.

"We had a little two-burner stove that we cooked on if we had to stay out late," said Miss Sarah. "We came home every night because we had two children."

"Your kitchen back there's a lot bigger than the kitchen I work in," said Kathy. "Mine is the size of this table."

"For 150 kids," Sara Jo pointed out.

"I don't have a stovetop," said Kathy. "I have an oven and a microwave. I went out and bought an electric pan to do my vegetables in."

"You make magic," said Sara Jo.

"How many days a week do you cook here?" asked Heidi.

"Seven," said Miss Sarah. "I'm not supposed to, but our employees decided they wanted to leave Grand Isle. They've been gone three weeks, and I haven't hired anyone yet."

"Do you get the oil-platform workers in here?" asked Kitty.

"Not too often," said Miss Sarah. "They usually stay on the rigs 'til they're ready to go home. When they comin' down, they go to the airport and catch a helicopter out to the rigs. If they work on base down here, we get them most of the time."

"Are there still a lot of trawlers that fish from Grand Isle?" asked Kitty.

"Yes," said Miss Sarah. "They claim that the seafood is safe to eat now. The Wildlife and Fishery has made them test it so many times. I feel confident about it because I've tried it. There's no smell or taste of oil. It's the regular taste that you usually get. I wouldn't serve it if I wasn't sure of it."

"What's the best thing about living on Grand Isle?" asked Heidi.

"I don't know, baby," said Miss Sarah, pouring more water for us. "I don't go on the beach at all. I was down there when my children were small, but since they've all grown and had children of their own, I haven't been on the beach in twenty years." She gathered plates and paused. "My husband's family was French. I don't know if y'all heard about Jean Lafitte, the pirate?"

Doug perked up. "He was a pirate?"

"Some of my husband's ancestors were," said Miss Sarah. "They hooked up with Jean Lafitte when they got down here. They were robbin' everybody. They would rob the people that was goin' to New Orleans. They were all fancy and rich back at that time. They would bring stuff down here to people that didn't have it. They'd hide out in the marshes in the back. The little island across the big bayou at the end of this island is where they had their fort."

"Have you ever had to be evacuated from the island because of the weather?" asked Kitty.

"Oh, yes, ma'am," said Miss Sarah. "Lots of times. In fact, in Hurricane Betsy in '65, we lost our home. We got back an' we didn't have nothin' but the property. There was a lot of the houses that were washed out. The ones that weren't were so damaged; it took a long time to get everybody back to normal. For Hurricane Juan—I think that was eight years ago—we had water in the restaurant up to where that wood was put in. We had to cut the paneling out and put the new wall in.

"My house is so high—it's eight feet high—so I didn't get water in my house, which is good. When we rebuilt, we had it put up high enough so we wouldn't have to worry about the house."

"When the weather gets bad, do you always leave?" asked Kitty.

"We all leave, honey," said Miss Sarah. "Ain't nobody stayin' here. Now that I've got grandchildren in Thibodaux, that's where we go. It's far enough to get away from the water. If the wind gets bad here, it calms down by the time it gets there. If it's one hundred miles an hour here, it would be like sixty over there, so it's not that bad."

"Sixty?" we asked, shocked.

"Sixty is a lot to us," Heidi said.

"Since my husband's gone, we have people from the city come help us board up," said Miss Sarah. "My husband and my son used to do all of that. My son doesn't live here anymore. He moved to Mississippi 'cause that's where his wife was from." Miss Sarah saw we were done eating. "Can I get you anything else?"

"No," said Doug. "And we're going to bus the dishes, Miss Sarah."

"Y'all don't have to do that." She smiled appreciatively. "My goodness."

"Can we help with the dishes?" Doug asked.

"No, I'm savin' them for the mornin'," said Miss Sarah. "How sweet of you."

"We'll be back for breakfast before we leave the island," said Doug, and we left for camp.

It was well after dark when we arrived at camp. Doug, Kathy, Sara Jo, and I went out on the boardwalk to look at the water. Heidi joined us as she was coming back from the beach. In the darkness, the lights out in the Gulf made many oil rigs visible. They looked like stars in the night sky. We walked back to camp, said our good nights, and went to bed.

October 28, Day Thirty-eight

I rose before the sun so I could go to the beach and watch the sun rise over the Gulf. Kitty was already at the beach. Pelicans flew past. We walked down and put our feet in the gently rolling waves. The sky was pale rusty peach and the clouds stretched thinly across the horizon, reflecting the bright-yellow light of the sun, which wasn't yet visible. The sun peeked above the horizon, and the rusty peach intensified. The clouds were on fire. Rusty peach gave way to brilliant oranges that reflected off the surface of the water. The crests of the waves were deep blue shadows rolling toward us. We watched the sandpipers play tag with the waves and dig their tiny beaks into the sand. Their white feathers were tinted orange by the sun. As the sun rose above the horizon, the colors became muted and the sky turned to pale blues.

Kitty and I sang for the last time on this journey the sacred Anishinabe song I had sung each morning of the trip, and a tear rolled down my cheek. I made an offering of kinnikinnick for the Gathering that would be held later. It would be the final Gathering. We lingered on the beach not wanting the moment, or the trip, to end. We hugged each other, smiled, and silently headed back to camp.

A steady stream of helicopters passed overhead taking oil workers to and from the oil platforms. Their activity continued the entire time we were on Grand Isle. We spent the morning reorganizing the van, sorting borrowed gear so it could be returned to its owners, and doing laundry. We were interrupted by Abby, a photographer for the *Daily Comet* out of Thibodaux. He was there for a paddling photo. Kitty and I got our kayaks down from the van, and Sara Jo and Doug helped us carry them over the dune to the Gulf. We hadn't planned on paddling the Gulf side of the island; it was a treat. Abby snapped photos of us getting in, paddling out, and paddling back.

I was attempting to move closer to Kitty so Abby could get a good photo when a wave caught my kayak and turned it directly toward Kitty. I yelled to warn her that we were about to crash, and I tried to make a diversionary maneuver with my rudder and paddle strokes. I felt the wave pick me up and thrust me at Kitty, who grabbed the nose of my kayak and deflected it. I lost control and the wave spun me sideways, filling the cockpit. I was going over and thought briefly about how much I disliked water up my nose. I began to roll. I took a deep breath and mentally psyched myself for being underwater. Rolling to the right, I felt my elbow land on the sandy bottom. I was astonished that my head didn't go under. I was in only a foot of water. The next wave washed me out of the kayak, and the next one knocked me down when I tried to stand.

Finally standing, I laughed and waded after the kayak, but it was gliding quickly across the water. I broke into a run to catch it. My kayak caught up to Kitty, who grabbed it. I hauled it to shore and dumped the water out. I thought it was comical. We'd paddled the length of the Mississippi River, and no one had tipped over. Our last day playing in the Gulf, the water played a practical joke on me.

Not ready to get off the water just yet, we went out once more. We paddled toward the breakwater, a long rock wall built parallel to the shoreline to protect the beaches, and we saw dolphins. We paddled toward them and saw more. A game of tag ensued that we had no chance of winning, but the play was enthralling. Every time we moved close, the dolphins disappeared under the surface.

photo by Sara Jo Dickens

Reluctantly we headed to shore. Doug and Sara Jo were still waiting. Abby had left. I was so excited. I raised my paddle in the air as I rode the crest of another wave. Then I felt the same thrust that put me over before, and I shifted my focus to paddling. When we got to shore, Kitty and I hugged. I was elated that Doug and Sara Jo witnessed that special paddle. They grinned broadly with pride in their eyes. Sara Jo bounced over to me and hugged me with exuberance. Doug's hug was solid, nurturing, and grounding.

For a few minutes we watched the dolphins, which had moved closer to shore. Then we carried our kayaks back to camp. When we got there, everything was out of the van and organized in piles by owner. Heidi had been busy. Our next task was to put our things back inside in an organized way. While we did, the perfect weather we'd been experiencing changed. A big storm moved in. We quickly finished packing gear and drove to the bay side of the island to the Sand Dollar Marina. Sara Jo, Heidi, Kitty, and I prepared for our final paddle in Bay Andre.

The clouds parted and the sun began to shine again as we waved goodbye to Pat, Cis, Kathy, and Doug. Their excitement showed in their smiles. We paddled around a small island and headed along the shoreline toward the east end of the island. As promised there were dolphins—lots of them—only about a kayak's length away. They played in groups of two, three, and four, swimming slowly and leaping into the air. We floated, pausing to admire the dolphins, more than we paddled.

The bad weather we had seen from camp stayed to the north. The temperature was in the low seventies. We came to the end of Grand Isle Island and saw bright white pillars across the water on the northwest end of Grand Terre Island. A cloud that looked like a pepper storm rose around them and disappeared. Curiosity drove us across the Barataria Pass to see what the white pillars and the clouds were.

Approaching the island, we noticed the pillars moving in a familiar waddle. They were white pelicans. Their reflection in the water had made them appear three times their height. The cloud rose again. It was hundreds of smaller birds taking off, swirling around, and landing.

The pelicans kept a close watch on us as we approached the island.

photo by Sara Jo Dickens

They made an unhurried departure, swimming off in single file. We landed a distance from the birds and got out of our kayaks to watch them. The white pelicans towered above the brown pelicans and common terns that rested with them on that small strip of sand.

We stepped onto the sand and the last of the white pelicans flew away, while the brown ones took to the water and leisurely moved away. The white pelican's impressive wingspans can reach nine feet. Their wings were brilliant white with deep-black wing tips accented by the blue-green water of Barataria Bay behind them. They gracefully landed a hundred yards away on the water.

The terns were gathered in a large group near the water. When we neared them, they put on a show. They rose in a synchronized fashion, swirled out over the water, dipped down, and curved upward, circling back and landing on the other side of the narrow sandbar in a tight pack. The sounds from a gentle breeze and soft crashing waves were drowned out by a chorus of flapping wings and squawking birds that crescendoed as more birds joined in and then faded as the birds landed again, leaving only sounds of the breeze and the waves. Interacting with the birds was joyful and spellbinding.

Every inch of the sandbar was covered in bird tracks. Part of the sandbar was submerged in ankle-deep water. We waded through it, focused on the birds. Then Heidi saw a jellyfish in the water. Once she noticed the jellyfish, we saw a lot of them and waded more carefully to avoid their painful stings. The jellyfish were a translucent mushroom shape. Their clear outside edge had deep magenta specks on it; their centers were a cloudy pale pink. Thin pink tentacles trailed below. Most of the jellyfish we saw were less than three inches wide with nine-inch tentacles.

Sara Jo pointed out the many hermit crabs in the water. They scurried across the bottom, leaving trails in the sand that made it look as if they had five feet. Their shells created deep groves in the sand.

Farther south on the island, we saw tall tan walls adjacent to the water, the ruins of Fort Livingston, which was Jean Lafitte's headquarters that Miss Sarah had told us about. With more time we'd have explored the fort, but the sky began to cloud over again and the wind was picking up.

We got back into our kayaks as the waves crashed onshore. Getting on the water in waves required agility and speed. The kayak had to remain pointed into the waves during entry. Timing our entry between waves was key. Once in, we had to paddle quickly into an oncoming wave so our kayaks didn't turn. If a kayak turned, it could take on water, and the paddler would easily roll over.

Fishing boats passed us headed for Leeville. Dozens of dolphins played in the bay. Nearing shore I thought, "I need to create another adventure. I don't want this to end." Then I remembered the work involved and how doing an adventure such as this had taken over my life. I smiled as I thought about having more time with family and friends, having a garden, painting in my studio, or doing more writing. The simple things.

Sara Jo paddled over. I turned to her and said, "Paddling the lakes back home is going to be boring after this."

"I don't think you'll have any trouble finding fun and beauty up there," she answered.

Before responding, I saw a dolphin closer than the others. I pointed it out to Sara Jo as it disappeared under the surface. I watched for it to resurface and felt a bump on the bottom of my kayak. I didn't know what to think. Sara Jo beamed and said, "That was a dolphin." As she finished saying that, it happened again. "That's its way of greeting you," she said. "Dolphins do that to us sometimes when we're out surfing. I think she's congratulating you and welcoming you to the Gulf."

I was so excited I could barely contain myself. I called out, "Thank you. That was a gift."

On the final stretch, the wind and the waves were building. We paddled through many areas of jellyfish. They were larger than the jellyfish we had seen on the sandbar and were many colors: pink, pale white, blue, yellow, green, and orange. I thought about how nasty it would be if one of us tipped among all those jellyfish.

photo by Kathy Dickens

When we landed, the others were waiting. Doug and Kathy bought pizza for lunch, and we sat at a picnic table near the landing and ate. A shrimp boat passed, headed to shore with its nets hung out to dry. The gulls and terns swarmed it like bees around a hive.

By the time we were done eating, the wind was cold and more intense. Kitty said, "Can you believe it?" referring to the change in temperature and wind. "The weather was totally with us all the way down the river." We headed back to camp for the Gathering that evening. Heidi and Kathy walked through the campground and talked with the women, encouraging them to come to the Gathering.

When we created a circle of chairs for the Gathering, Doug took his book and went to the pier to read. We sat down and waited for a few minutes, hoping someone else would join us. While we waited, the weather continued to get windier and colder.

No one came.

Kitty picked up the fan that was sitting on the table and began. "This being the last Gathering of this journey down the Mississippi River, it seems there's finality going on because this is the last day by the water. The trip isn't over yet because there's another week of getting home, but when we were out paddling today, there was a sense of finality around being on the water and paddling with the dolphins. Imagine paddling in the Gulf of Mexico with dolphins! Who would have thought? It's a piece of what this whole journey has meant to me.

"When I started out, I was only going to paddle a couple of weeks with Nancy on the last leg. To be there for the whole of this trip and to do all of it was inconceivable. 'Wow. What would that look like?' I wondered. When I said yes, I knew it was the right thing. I thought, 'Go into the planning and keep on moving with it.'

"When I was done at the end of the last trip, I knew that I wasn't going to be paddling on this trip. I had this absolutely wonderful opportunity to paddle on the Mississippi River and hear all the women's stories at the Gatherings. What an honor that was. I knew it was time for somebody else to paddle and have that same experience. The thought of doing car support—knowing that I'd be able to do it for the whole of the trip—felt very right too.

"Right now it feels confusing. The journey continues on from here, and yet it's ending. I'm looking forward to having down time to process what this has all meant. I had some insights into how I can keep the momentum going when I get back to Ely. It feels like I'm going back to a confinement because all of this has felt expansive and incredible. I never would've guessed five years ago that I'd be partaking in something like this. Wow. It's really amazing. To be here sharing it with all of you is so cool. I've learned from everybody. That doesn't happen when I'm not open or not willing to keep moving on in this journey of life. Let the adventure flow." Kitty smiled warmly as she handed the fan to Pat.

"I'm sad that it's ending," said Pat. "The whole experience that I've had with all of you and the other women who have come and gone and all of the people we've met—it's hard to describe. Rewarding is one word that comes to mind. I feel more alive now that I've had this experience. I wonder, 'What is the next experience?' I'm looking forward to whatever that may be. I've no idea what it may be, but there must be one out there somewhere.

"Experiencing it all with women has been special. Young or old, it doesn't matter—the men as well. The men who have helped with this leg of the trip need to be recognized. They were an inspiration, and they taught us that there are a lot of good guys out there. Some people think that there aren't. They were willing to come—and not necessarily help us, but be there—in a moment of distress. I didn't experience that on the other trip.

"Spending the week with Gwyn was probably the highlight for me because I don't see her very often. I feel like she is with us tonight. I feel like she has been with us this whole week." Cis pulled a very small chair into the circle to represent those who were not physically with us, but were with us in spirit. "That's the perfect Gwyn-size chair," Pat added and we all laughed.

Kathy took the fan next and gently ran her fingers down the length of the feathers. "I'm happy to be here. I'm sorry I didn't make it before because you gals are fantastic. Knowing these two," she pointed at Sara Jo and me, "for a number of years, I know they're fantastic. Meeting their friends is super.

"What brings joy to my life are moments like this that make me feel fulfilled. Family. Happy moments. Things that you can share—but not material things. Talking to people. We have so few of those moments because we're so busy rushing here and there. I'm grateful I can be here. You make me feel rich. I have been blessed with a wonderful family." She began to tear up. "I cry like I laugh—easily." She quickly passed the fan to me.

"I can't put into words what the last couple of days have been like," I said. "This morning was magnificent, riding the surf in—and crashing. I think it's a riot that I fell out of the boat on the last day. I'm glad the photographer came or we wouldn't have paddled on that side of the island.

"On the phone I explained to Cara Bayles, a reporter from the *Thibodaux Daily Comet* who called during lunch, how I felt about all of this. I told her it wasn't real yet. Part of the reason for that is the role I had to be engaged in all of the time we were on the road. There were so many things to pay attention to that I'd forget that I was paddling the biggest river on the continent. Those things disappeared while I focused on what I had today. I'd think, 'I'm doing this today and doing it the best I can.' Now what do I do with all of that energy? This trip could not have had a more amazing ending with that paddle out in the Gulf and getting bumped by the dolphins. I won't forget getting christened the other day by that big fish. That was funny.

"I don't feel like I have wisdom today." The others laughed. "I have to catch up with myself after this. I don't know what the next thing is. There was a moment when we were paddling out there today when I realized this adventure was over, and I thought, 'Now what? This is way too fun!' I remember saying to Sara Jo, 'Paddling on flat water in Minnesota is going to be boring after this.'

"I've been truly amazed at watching you all work hard to make this happen. You jump up and do what needs to be done. I'm deeply amazed that I put it out to the universe that I wanted to come home without owing money on this trip, and it looks like that might happen. It's astounding. We did it with garage sales. We did it the way women do it: we sold chocolate!

"The men have impressed me as well, their wanting to help us—like Doug at Devil's Backbone Campground. After he threw his beer on the fire, he didn't think he had been helpful until he gave the car a jump when the battery was dead. And Darriel, with all of the food—hearing we only had a bagel and an apple, he said, 'Well, I got to do something about that.' And I think of the guys who helped with the vehicle, and the guys at Current Design who quickly and cheerfully crawled under the trailer to cut off the metal bars. Women stepped forward too. It's been an amazing journey since I left Itasca and the headwaters in 2004.

"It will be interesting to get home to the next phase. The journey is over, but not for me, because when I get home I'm going to write it. I get to do this again—about eight times before the publisher says it's a go." We all laughed.

"I didn't paddle today because I wanted to watch you from a distance," said Cis. "It was wonderful to be where Pat and I were, watching you fine ladies out there. I've paddled the Gulf, and it's very special.

"A lot of things are bubbling around for me. I think they'll come out in a very interesting series of poetry. Some of the things that have been flying around in my head have to do with the fact that from the birth of the river to the Gulf is like a woman pregnant [and the baby] traveling down this birth canal. To be born is really the end of the river, and yet it's the beginning of the whole mother ocean. I want to find a voice to that in some way.

"You all speak the things I know, I think, and I feel. It's special to have joined together like a sisterhood, a nomadic caravan traveling around, learning the rhythms of one another. It's a little bit harder when you jump in and out of the trip than when you can be with the whole fluid motion, ebb and flow, and the tenor of the river and the people who live along her. I can't put words to it, but it has been a wonderful experience. I want to thank you all."

"Writing about this through poetry is such a cool idea," said Kitty. "This is amazing for me to say, but we're all creative women. I've not felt that way most of my life. To think of it coming through in poetry—we all have that ability. I want to thank all of you for sharing your days with me. It has been pretty darn special." Because the fan had made its way around the circle, we began to pass it to whomever wanted to speak next.

"I like your metaphor of the river, being born into the ocean, and being a better part of the world," said Kathy. "I respect the courage it has taken all of you to do this. I'm not sure I'd have had the courage to do it. It's wonderful.

"I don't think we know where we get our courage. We just do—and you did. Think of all the people you've met along the way. Look how much you have stirred up. You have inspired other women and shaken the men a little bit, you know?" We laughed. "You really have! To take this up and be gone six weeks takes a lot of courage. I don't think you even know how much courage it takes because you have so much courage. For someone who doesn't have that much courage, I admire you all for having done it. Thank you for putting it into words and pictures and sharing your books—and for allowing your thoughts and feelings to be published. That's wonderful."

Everyone wanted a chance at the fan to speak to Kathy.

"Me first," I said. "Yes, it takes courage to do this, but I've seen women along the way with just as much courage. They compare themselves to us in regards to this trip and come up short. I know from my history that some of the things I've done prior to this took way more courage than this has. They aren't the things our culture acknowledges as courageous. Fighting to get my kids back took a lot of courage. Leaving my ex-husband took a lot of courage.

"Raising your grandchildren, Kathy, takes a lot of courage on a daily basis. Coming into a group of women who have been traveling together for six weeks takes courage—I can't do that. Well, maybe if you were already there. My point is, Kathy, you have an enormous amount of courage. I needed to say that to you aloud, in front of other people, in the hope that you would hear it.

"I've heard a lot of other women say they don't have courage. Then I hear their stories and listen to what they have gone through. I hear how they get up in the morning, and they go through the day. I know what they do takes courage." The wind, blowing the tent so much that it occasionally twisted around us, was demanding more and more attention. "Like the courage it takes to sit under a tent that's bending and folding around you.

"My definition of courage has changed dramatically since the beginning of this trip. I flash back to the picture Sara Jo took of me in the beginning when it was my first time paddling in the kayak under a tree that had fallen across the river, and the current was strong. I didn't know what I was doing. She snapped pictures like crazy because she was convinced I was going over, and she wanted to catch it on film. I remember how scared I was that I was going to tip over, and now I think, 'Yeah! There's a barge and the waves are going to be great!' or 'Oh, look! We're going over a wing dam. Woo hoo!' Courage changes over time. The stories that I've heard women share have dramatically altered my description of courage. They have validated the need for something like this project and journey for all the women out there who think they don't have anything to offer—and they do!"

"It has to do with our perception of courage," said Cis. "Everybody's walking one step in front of the other, experiencing her own life and her own life's story. The things that we all do in our own life stories—while they're uniquely ours—are bigger than us. Some things that people think are hard when they say, 'I can't believe you're doing that'—like taking care of aging family or disabled family—you do it for no other reason than it is in front of you to do.

"In a circle of women, the circle gets bigger and bigger and bigger, and it has spiraled down the river like all of the eddy pools, sinkholes, and all the terminology the local folk color the river with. That's what our lives are. Our lives are full of whirlpools and eddies and backwater and strangers we meet. We are here to provide that extra 'oomph' of courage that any of us need to do what we need to do."

We were joined by a ginger-colored cat, to which Pat said, "There's our Gwyn-spirit."

"The word that keeps coming up for me is 'imagine,'" said Kitty. "It's very exciting to think about what comes next and not have any clue and yet to remain open to whatever comes along.

"I remember turning forty and thinking, 'Oh, my God. This is the end of the world." Then fifty came along, and I'm half way through the fifties. It's true: life does keep getting better. There's not an age I'd want to go back to. It's so cool to move forward and to find out things about myself and about my perceptions of the world and how they have changed. I look forward to keeping open and gaining knowledge and discovering what that means to me and the people around me."

Pat took a few moments to gather her thoughts. Then she began. "I hope the people we've talked to will reach out to people and spread our thoughts or the things that they have shared with us. I hope that they will not feel afraid to speak to other people about the way they really feel. Sometimes that can be a hard thing. I think it's easy for all of us to think that because we grew up that way."

"We're all on a journey," said Kathy confidently. "All of our journeys are different. We're here for a reason, and your reason is different from my reason. I have known that we're here for a purpose. Our purposes change as we age due to different times in our life. I have talked to Nancy a lot of times about spirituality, how things affect you and the people who pass through your life. They may say something to you and all of a sudden it takes you from a dark spot to a wonderful spot because that person passed right through your life. There have been a number of times that has happened with my children.

"I've known there is a higher power, and I have looked to that higher power. I think that's what has gotten me through a lot of difficult moments in my life. There are a lot of times when I try to do everything myself. That's when I have to keep in mind that I have lost track of my spirituality. When I look back I see what has happened—or maybe something that didn't happen—and I think, 'How did I get through that?' I know I didn't get through it alone.

"I have to keep remembering that there is spirituality in each one of us. We have a purpose. We have a higher power—whatever that power means to everyone—that might be different for each of us. We need to reach out to that power because we are not alone. We have each other. That's what has gotten me through some tough times and some great times."

I took the fan and looked at Sara Jo and Heidi, who were under fifty, and then I chose to break protocol and offered the fan to them. Sara Jo spoke first. "I've had this message echoing since I got here. I don't remember if I read this in the grandmother's book or not, but it's the idea that this is the time of grandmothers. It's not just about grandmothers but also about recognizing the men and grandfathers and the role that they take in supporting women in stepping forward. There were men who helped us on the first two legs, but even in the short time I have been on this leg of the trip, that help has been strong. Watching the relationships with the men and women here makes it seem that women have this role in which they don't necessarily have the opportunity to speak or do all of the things independently that we feel are so important. At the same time, they have men who support them in a way that maybe we don't see as readily.

"I think it's interesting that as we come to the end of the river, we're reminded that we have become strong as women. We've gathered women together and heard their stories and reminded them to speak their wisdom, but we can't leave the men behind and not recognize their role. I find it interesting that this idea was brought up many times.

"For me, it has been weird being at the end of this trip. I started the trip, but I feel like I've missed most of it. I'm kind of bummed out that I didn't get to be along on more of the journey. As Cis said, jumping in makes it a little bit harder to get into the swing of everything, but it has certainly shaken up a place in me that had become comfortable.

"I think that comes from being in the city and separating myself from nature—not intentionally—by being so far from it and being so far from other people who are like-minded. In big cities, especially in areas of California where many people are all about owning things, people have lost the sense of family. It's easy when you're surrounded by that culture to forget who you are and what is important while you try to survive each day. This has been a good shaking to break that habit. It happened at a good time because I'm looking to move on. This experience has been a kick to get me out of there, not so I can go play, but to save who Doug and I are and to keep growing. So thank you."

"There's a feather that keeps coming loose on the fan," I said. "It won't stay in place. Kathy, it wants to go home with you. Perhaps it's to remind you of your courage." I handed Kathy the feather, and her face lit up.

I turned to Pat and said, "I want to say something to Pat. When you joined us on the last trip, you were so quiet. You'd take the fan and you'd say, 'I'm not talking,' and pass it on." We laughed. "If you said even a little at one of the Gatherings, I got so excited. This time you've talked every time. It's been magnificent to witness the growth and change in you. It's been a gift that you've shared some of who you are and not just listened to what everyone else has said."

"That's a hard thing for me to do," said Pat.

"I know it took courage," I continued.

"I feel comfortable, and that is a big part of it for me," said Pat. "I was feeling the comfort that you all give. Now it seems like there's more camaraderie, comfort, and friendship."

"I like the thought that my Taoist priest teacher talks about," said Cis, "which is this: in meditating is stillness.

"The style of Taoist meditation that I'm studying and practicing says that what we do in our meditations affects not only the future generations but also the past generations of the matriarchal line. That gives me a wonderful lot to think about because we all know that there are things in our mothers'—and our mothers' mothers'—pasts that were never shared, and we can gain a sense of whatever their struggles were.

"I've no idea who said it, but it's a true statement, that you're only as happy as your unhappiest child. For whatever reason, when your children struggle, you also struggle. To think that my meditation practice can effect energetically good changes for my daughter and—should she ever choose to have children—her daughters; it can affect my mother, and grandmother, and great-grandmother. I find that a very positive thing for me to be able to put out there."

"I'm wearing my mother's engagement ring." I said looking down at it, appreciating its sparkle even in the dim light. "Somebody said, 'You're not going to wear that on the trip are you?' I said, 'Yes, I have to because that's how I keep her with me.' There were several times paddling on this trip when I wasn't paying attention to it and the ring sparkled in a way that I had not seen it sparkle before. It was very clear to me she was with me. Maybe it was the sun catching it, but it didn't feel like that. Your comment about what we're doing might help us heal previous generations—it's very hopeful. Because I've not had a mother since I was eleven, it's been uplifting and heartwarming to feel her on this trip. I felt her on the other trips, but there's something about this one. I've felt her close to me."

We looked at Heidi, who had not spoken yet, and the fan was handed to her. "I don't know what to say." She paused. "I came to listen."

"What has it meant to you to be a part of this?" I asked. "You've been a part of this for over, well . . ."

"Eight years," said Heidi.

"After eight years, you can't just listen," said Cis.

"When Nancy started, it was about supporting a good friend in doing something that was important to her," said Heidi. She turned to me. "I was impressed with what you were doing. I wanted to do the little things that I could to help make it work. It was fun to be there on days three through six on the first leg, to be part of that and see you in it. I didn't feel like I was in it; I was excited to see you in it.

"I don't know if I was joking when you came back and I said that if you were going to do the whole thing, I was going to paddle into the Gulf with you. Then it kind of snuck up fast, and all of a sudden it was time to get ready to paddle in the Gulf.

"It was a strange change about a year and a half ago to think about switching from just supporting you to actually feeling like I was a part of it. It took me a long time to figure out how to be part of it when it was still your baby.

"It was strange to do all the work leading up to the trip and then have you drive away in September. I would do all my normal work stuff and home stuff and check the Facebook page at night. Then to show up and be ready—it was hard to relax and say, 'It's okay' and not get caught up in 'I have worked hard for this and here I'm lying on a sofa wishing I was dead.'" We laughed. "I knew there was so much going on, but you guys were taking care of me instead. I was grateful because I really needed that.

"I was surprised at how beautiful the river is. Getting to paddle with each person for one day was totally unexpected and great. Then I went home and rushed around and did my work stuff again. When I came back for this leg, it felt entirely different.

"The experience has been a lot of things. I tried to focus on not making it something big because I felt like the entire process—from planning to the river to wrapping up—is the journey, not just the paddling.

"I'm a big-picture thinker, and I can see everything that's going on around me. This has been good practice for getting to be in the moment right now, whatever 'right now' is. I'm practicing letting go of expectations and being amazed with what the results are. Every day of paddling has been great. Every day of meeting people or being with this group of people has been beautiful. I feel very fortunate and grateful."

"Listening to Heidi brought up what that means in my life," said Kitty. "I've learned a lot. I've learned how to state my preference. We made it a rule early on to state your preference. Sometimes that's hard. To be able to do that seems small in the moment, yet the impact that it has on my life and my interactions with my fellow travelers is huge. It's about taking care of myself. It's about letting others get to know me because I'm sharing with them. That has been cool.

"When Pat and I came out of the store the other day, there were some rough-looking characters around. I walked by them like they were not there. Pat said, 'Good morning.' They nodded and said, 'Good morning.' It's such a simple thing—acknowledging other people in my space. I'm getting better at doing that. What an awesome lesson to learn. Thank you for being my teachers."

"I guess I have to say something again," said Pat reaching for the fan. "I've enjoyed being at bed-and-breakfasts and the motels, but the most comfortable experience I've had is camping. In times of rain, cold, wind—whatever the conditions were—it didn't matter. It was the whole experience of the togetherness of the group, which you don't necessarily get at a hotel. However, we did have that at a couple of places where we had adjoining rooms—oh, and in the bunkhouse. That was a very together moment. That's something I don't always experience with a group.

"I know I have a lot of courage. It's hard for me to throw it out there. I acknowledge that I have it. I don't have fears of being with different kinds of people—male, female, or different races. It doesn't matter. When I talk to different women and I hear their different stories about things that have happened to them in their lives, my mouth just drops. I feel guilty because I haven't had those kinds of experiences. I've had very fortunate experiences with people, family, and friends.

"I have such a network of people out there. This is a new network here, and it has been here throughout this whole trip. It's part of that whole network of people that I have in the world. I thank you from the bottom of my heart for the experience."

"I don't think I have a lot of wisdom," said Kathy. "I sometimes feel like I'm flying by the seat of my pants, you know? What is wisdom? Is it making a good choice? What is a good choice? If something turns out good, is that a good choice? Is it luck? I look to other people for a wise comment. From them, I take little pieces. I've had a few experiences in life that have made me do things differently. I'm not sure those experiences made me really wise. I never thought of myself as being a wise person like some people I know who are wise people. They know what to say at the right moment to give you encouragement.

"I'm not sure what experience has given me a lot of wisdom. Maybe raising children helped me gain a little wisdom. You do grow a little wiser from the first one to the second one to the third one. Maybe raising the first three helped with the next two.

"I look to others for wisdom and not just to myself. I call my sister-in-law. She has given me a lot of wisdom. I call my daughter-in-law. She's got more wisdom than any other young person I know. I look to ladies like you. We get it from each other, and we each take little pieces from each other. You take a little bit at a time from everyone for when you need it. It's when you're listening that you find it. You have to stop and listen and be quiet for your wisdom to come."

"Kathy, what would you want younger women know?" I asked.

"Oh, goodness, that's a good question," said Kathy. "First of all, there are a lot of good choices. I think young people are always looking for the right person, the right one to marry. If you are right with yourself and you know yourself, then the right person for you will come along.

"Second, it's not always an easy road. You don't give up. You keep at it. Your life is not promised to be an easy road, but you won't go it alone. You need to know yourself first. You need to love yourself because if you don't love yourself, you can't love anybody else. That's what I'd like young people to know."

"Those of you who have been at Gatherings before have seen this," I said, holding up a talking stick that had been at each Gathering. The talking stick was wooden with a straight handle that spiraled at the end. Some of the bark was carved away, leaving the surface smooth; some of the bark remained. White, pink, and purple yarn was wrapped along sections, and feathers and beads hung from the top end. "This was the original talking stick. I bought it at a conference in Chicago. It's made of kudzu. The gentleman who makes these feels that kudzu needs to find a new purpose. I put the feathers and beads on it. When the new fan arrived from White Buffalo Man, I gave this to Kitty. It's been at the Gatherings like a silent witness. It's never been acknowledged before, so I want to pass it around our circle so we can put some energy into it and acknowledge that it's been listening and serving its purpose. Please say something and pass it on."

"I have always been aware of its presence," said Cis. She stroked the talking stick thoughtfully. "They are very different, talking sticks." As she examined the stick from different angles, she continued. "There are a lot of turns in our lives, aren't there? I don't think we can ever predict, nor should we ever try to predict, what our lives would be like 'if this' or 'if that.' All we can do is make the best choices in the moment that feel right. If we will only stop and be still enough to hear the right answer to our deepest questions, and then go with the flow through its twist and turns. Our life gets whittled away through time, but we sometimes have to get a tough cover to make it through. It's only the hardships that help us to get tough. Life is tactile. Life is messy.

"I never in my wildest dreams would've ever thought I'd have the life that I've had. I never planned for anything. Every day is an adventure. This has been a wonderful adventure. Wow. To have the opportunity and privilege to be a part of it . . .

"I think of your trip as trimesters of pregnancy." We all laughed. "We're the helpful doulas and midwives helping things along the way. Heidi said it last time: 'Oh, my God. Is it time? We're at the Gulf. It's like my water broke.'" We laughed some more. "That's it exactly. Life is like that, and you go with it. You can only gain wisdom because you have been going down the river—your own river—getting caught in eddies and the whirlpools of your own life. You deal with the stagnation and the pollution that gets poured into your own life, the shit and the chemicals. What are you going to do with it? It's what you can do with it. In hindsight, all you can do is learn from your past and act in the now so that you're ready for whatever comes your way."

"It's interesting to think about this, having been the observer," said Heidi. "I feel like when I first met you, Kitty, that you had a backseat role. I've loved getting to know you and having you come out and getting to work with you. Now, travel with you has been a fortunate thing for me. It feels like you embody a peacefulness that I admire. It's fun that this stick has been fully sitting by, but it has its own little power to go with it."

For most of our trip, the talking stick had been stored in a pocket behind the driver's seat, sticking out where all could see it. After Heidi gave the stick the attention it didn't get earlier in the trip, it was handed to Kitty, who said, "I knew it needed to come along. I had to go back into the house to grab it because I started to leave without it. I had to find a place where it was going to be safe. I was going to get a mailing tube because I didn't know where I was going to put it so that it wouldn't get crunched. It's a good analogy for me that no matter what happens, I will be safe. That's why the stick was out there.

"I felt that out on the water today. I was pausing and hesitating and I thought, 'This is how I've lived a lot of my life, being a witness.' I do feel a lot like this stick. I'm a witness. I don't come forward. I watch and let others test the water so I can figure out what I want to do from there. Now I get to state my preference. How cool is that! I was counting on this stick to come along and absorb all of the energy and wisdom that the women have said. I know that it has. To take it home is special."

"I look at the colors, and I see Kitty for sure," said Pat, touching the part of the talking stick with the multicolored yarn. "They're the colors that I'll always associate with you, along with the sturdiness yet the light-heartedness of it. What a perfect night for your stick to come out and be a part of the evening."

"This is interesting," said Kathy. "I love the beauty and the twists and turns of it, like the twists and turns of our lives and the rough spots we have. It also has color—and we have color—and alikeness and happiness, along with rough spots. That's how it happens in life. It's like it is supposed to hold us and talk to us, rather than for us to hold it and talk to it. Kitty, I have enjoyed getting to know you. It's beautiful that you have a lot of color in you, a lot of beauty in you, and calmness. You are tranquil, and I look at your talking stick and think of that."

"I find it interesting that Kitty said she needed to find a safe place for the talking stick in the car," said Sara Jo. "When you said safe, I thought it's about when we find something in our lives, like an object that we need to find a safe place for, that represents something that is a part of us. In keeping it safe, we're deciding to respect ourselves. In protecting this very simple but powerful object that represents a part of you, you have decided also to express who you are and to grow and respect all that is and all that you will become. I think this was a good group, a good place, and a good journey to feel safe enough to do that. I think that's very cool.

"As a botanist, I think it is very interesting that I'm holding a weed." We laughed with her. "I'm cherishing a very invasive weed right now," she said with amazement. "I have admired how simple it is. I'm sure everybody gets lost in the complexity and noise we're surrounded with in life. I have talked about not noticing the noise that you're noticing because I'm surrounded by noise all of the time. Being at the marina, to me, was very peaceful and quiet. It allowed me to strip back some of that complexity.

"You look at this stick and its complexity is gone. Everything that was attached to it—like its leaves and everything that made it a complex being—was stripped down to the core. It reminds me that every once in a while you need to strip back down to the core and remember who you are and what it is that you want to be. Start listening within.

"I've been very lucky. I was raised knowing that wisdom was within if I would listen. It's hard to listen when you have all that noise and all those little things that are oh so important and complicating. To be able to look at this and see how simple it is, to choose to see the colors, to choose to realize that maybe I need to be a little coarser, to choose to quiet down and not to hear those voices and to know that we all have the ability to reach our wisdom—it's there for us if we can accept and acknowledge; to choose to honor ourselves enough and give ourselves enough permission to accept that we are deserving of that wisdom and to know that wisdom doesn't separate us or make us better than anyone else.

"It's okay to be wise. It doesn't make us weird or crazy. It's not something that should be rejected. It's something that comes to you and is to be cherished. Sometimes it takes looking at something beautiful and simple and natural—and maybe less wise and maybe a little twisted—to see it."

"I want to talk about kudzu," said Cis. "We drove down here through the South not knowing that this wonderful talking stick was kudzu. If you look at kudzu, it envelops everything. It weaves itself around everything. It smothers and kills everything. Yet, why can't we mother and love and nourish in a web of growth of humanity and the other side of kudzu? I will end by quoting an artist from St. Louis: 'Life is too mysterious. Don't take it serious.'"

"I want to do a stick and throw it off the pier in the morning," said Heidi.

"Oh, what a wonderful idea," we said collectively.

We created our aspirations sticks and ended quickly to take down the screen tent so it wouldn't blow away when we left for dinner. It had taken as much wind as it could stand.

We were cold and hungry. We called Doug, and he came back to camp. Then we went into town for dinner at the Starfish. When we walked in, the place was bustling. We sat at a long table, and a waitress in her sixties with her hair streaked deep purple came to take our order. Cis asked her about her purple hair. She stopped, smiled coyly, and said, "It's Halloween. Besides that, who gives a damn? I don't." We cracked up.

We ordered hamburgers, as did Doug, who had been seriously considering getting the crawfish. Cis and Pat asked the staff to turn the TV to the station that had the St. Louis Cardinals baseball game on. Our conversation was periodically interrupted by "Oh, baby. Oh, baby. Oh, baby!" shouted by Cis and Pat when an exciting play happened. The rest of us were quiet and too tired to get rowdy.

A man who was eating dinner at a table across the room paid his bill and walked up to Doug. "I have to say to you, I've been sitting here all evening, and I've been curious and filled with admiration for you," he said. "How did you manage to be sitting here with these beautiful women?"

"Just lucky I guess," answered Doug. Then Doug started to tell him why we were there, but the man didn't really want to know—he walked out of the restaurant. We went back to our conversation, and the man came back in with a knowing look on his face.

He walked to our table, looked at Doug, and asked, "Montana?"

Cis, the only one from Montana, raised her hand to indicate she lived there. The man nodded and smiled like the cat that ate the canary. "I thought so," he said. He turned and walked away again without further conversation. It took us a moment to figure out his behavior. Then we realized there are a lot of Mormons in Montana who believe in polygamy. We laughed, realizing the guy thought Doug was married to all seven of us.

When we reached camp, we noticed some of the stakes on the tents had been pulled free by the wind. We tied things down and put away everything that could possibly blow away. The cold drove us quickly to our tents.

During the night, the wind was relentless. It averaged fourteen miles an hour with gusts to thirty. The stake on one of the corners of Doug's and my tent repeatedly pulled out. The sandy ground didn't provide a solid anchor. Each time the wind's howl grew loud, the tent bent down over me and I felt like meat in a sandwich. We didn't sleep much, and we heard the others outside of their tents making adjustments. It became a night of waiting for daylight to come so it would be over.

photo by Sara Jo Dickens

October 29th through October 31st

11

NEW ORLEANS

October 29, Day Thirty-nine

I sat up in the tent and reached for the meditation book, hoping it would soften my weary attitude after the tumultuous night. I read "Clarity. When we are in the midst of an experience, it is easy to forget that there is a Plan. Sometimes, all we can see is today. If we were to watch only two minutes of the middle of a television program, it would make little sense . . . How often we use that same, limited perspective to look at our life—especially when we are going through a difficult time . . . When we are being pelted by events that make us feel, think, and question, we are in the midst of learning something important. We can trust something valuable is being worked out in us . . . Faith is like a muscle. It must be exercised to grow strong . . . "

This journey had pelted me—and not just during the traveling. This journey was eight years of testing myself, pushing through perceived barriers, reflecting on how I interact with people, considering my priorities, coming face-to-face with my beliefs and stereotypes, and repeatedly leaning into my faith that everything would work out the way it was supposed to. And it did. I was clearly not the same woman who started the journey. I knew and trusted myself on a deeper level than I had dreamed was possible. I had grown to accept my humanness, and self-laughter came quickly. My bouts with depression had diminished, which I related to accepting myself and releasing other people's judgments. I began to own my wisdom and acknowledge my value.

I thought about what Kathy had said at the Gathering—that we are all here for different reasons and as we age our purposes change. The gift of time brought me to see the truth in her words. There was no one purpose for our lives.

Kathy had said she realized that when she was trying to do everything herself it was an indicator that she had lost track of her spirituality. When she looked back she could see that she didn't get through difficulties alone. I knew I wasn't alone, certainly not during any part of this adventure. I hadn't named my spirituality. Spirits traveled with us and guided us, and neither they nor my higher power cared if I put my hodgepodge of spiritual beliefs under one name. My beliefs brought me serenity, and they were solid enough for me to lean on heavily.

By the time I was out of the tent, the others were well on their way to having camp packed up because they wanted to get to the pier before sunrise. Doug and I quickly caught up with them, and we all drove to the pier.

The sun was already rising, and it cast an orange hue on everything. The cold wind blowing off the Gulf turned the sand on the beach below into a dust storm. We stood on the pier looking over the water. Each of us quietly threw our sticks into the Gulf with prayers of gratitude. Waves claimed each one as it landed.

I silently said to the Gulf, "You are such a broad expanse of water, and so beautiful. Goodbye and thank you for such a warm welcome with the dolphins." The eight-year-old in me who started all this by wanting to see how that tiny creek at the headwaters turned into the big Mississippi River was bursting with joy. Her dream had manifested in a much bigger way than she could ever have imagined.

I started back down the pier with Kathy. I smiled at her, and she playfully put her arm around me. "This is really something," she said proudly. I looked in her smiling eyes and put my arm around her and pulled her close.

In the car Kathy, Doug, Sara Jo, and I were chatting as we pulled out of the pier's parking lot. While the others continued to talk, I fell silent when I saw a great blue heron take off from a tree. It flew north toward the marsh. Even on the last day, Kee greeted us. I grinned and silently thanked her for her companionship and guidance. I would miss her. Long after the trip, my spirits would be lifted every time I saw a heron.

For breakfast we went to Sarah's Restaurant, where a couple of other groups were already seated. Miss Sarah had help. She greeted us warmly and sat us at the same table we'd had before.

We placed our breakfast order, and Heidi turned to Kathy. "Tell us how you met your husband, Brian," Heidi requested.

"I tease him because I tell everybody that he picked me up off the street corner—which he did" said Kathy. "I had a girlfriend whose name was also Kathy, and we were airline hostesses. There's that old cliché that airline hostesses meet a lot of people. Well, we didn't. She went in on a time-share at a ski lodge in Vermont one winter, and we were supposed to ride a Greyhound bus to it on the first of the year. She had a blind date for New Year's—Brian.

"On New Year's morning, she called and said, 'Forget the bus. My blind date is taking us to Vermont. Meet us on the corner.' I lived in

Manhattan on Sixty-Second and York. He pulled up in a little BMW, and I got in. We drove to his parents' to get something he needed. We went in and said hello to them. Brian went to get his stuff. His mother followed him and said, 'Which one was your blind date last night?' He said, 'The one on the left.' His mother said, 'That's not the one you need to be with. You need to be with the one on the right.' He said, 'I already know that.' That was after a forty-minute ride to his parents'."

"What did you say during those forty minutes?" asked Heidi.

"I have no idea," said Kathy. "I sat in the back seat. The story gets even funnier. We went to the ski house for five days. He had never skied before, but Kathy and I loved skiing. Kathy and I would go up the mountain and go down the hill and have hot chocolate, go up the mountain and go down the hill and have hot chocolate, and so on. Brian decided that we two women were crazy, and he took lessons.

"When we came off the slopes we'd go to the grocery store. Back at the time-share Brian would fix the fire, and Kathy and I would cook. Then she would go to bed, and Brian and I would sit up in front of the fireplace and visit. On the way home I stayed in the back seat of the car because I didn't know if Kathy liked him or not. When we came back from that trip, Brian asked me out and I said no. I called Kathy and said, 'Kathy, Brian asked me out. I'm not going out with him because I don't know what you think about him.' She said, 'Oh, I thought he was a real nice guy, but he's not my type. If he asks again, go.' He asked me again.

"After that he used to take us—both Kathys—to a ski house. Once I couldn't go because I had a bad neck. On that trip he fell and cut himself, and she fell and broke her leg. Same trip, different slopes. They ended up in the emergency room together. The staff in the ER said, 'Didn't you come here with Kathy?' He said, 'Yes, I did.' 'Well, she's in the next room getting her leg plastered.' A storm was coming, and he realized he had to get her back to Manhattan before the storm. She was in a cast up to her hip; it was a bad break. He put the back seat down and laid her in the back.

"They got to the Tapency Bridge, but it was shut down because of the snowstorm. He pulled into a truck stop and said he needed a couple of rooms. They said, 'No rooms around here, buddy.' Well, they found him a room. Brian got a couple of truck drivers to help her out of his car. He and Kathy were in one room. We had started dating by this time. He called into work because he couldn't make it and said, 'I'm stuck on the other side of the Tapency Bridge with Kathy.' They laughed and said, 'Yeah, right, you're stuck.' He said, 'No, you don't understand—it's the other Kathy.'

"Brian and Kathy were stuck for three days. She needed help with everything—the bathroom and everything. That was our winter. It was fun."

"What took you to Manhattan?" asked Heidi.

"I flew international for TWA and chose to fly out of New York," said Kathy. "I loved living in the city. It was quiet, believe it or not. We didn't meet a lot of people. And I took another job. I had a job with the airline and one helping to start a temp agency when they needed those early keypunch operators. Remember computer keypunch in the '60s?

"When we got married, I could still work at TWA, but back then flight attendants couldn't have children. Early on you couldn't be married and work there. Flight attendants had to maintain a certain weight. We had checks. We'd go in, and they'd check our nails, and they'd check that our hose had straight seams, our white gloves were clean, our high heels were polished, our hats were straight, and our white shirt was starched."

Breakfast came. Sara Jo's hotcakes were enormous and had us shrieking. "Miss Sarah, you should have warned me," said Sara Jo.

"You didn't ask me," Miss Sarah chirped back. We all laughed

"It's yellow margarine—oleo," said Doug, looking at the generous helping of margarine on top of the hotcakes.

"Remember how we used to fight over that?" said Kathy. "It came in a package and had a little orange dot in the middle. You'd squeeze it and knead it back and forth in the plastic. It was when margarine first came out."

"It was fun to mix it up," said Doug.

"Why would you buy it?" asked Heidi.

"It was cheaper," said Kathy. "Mom and Dad saved a penny whenever they could."

"We used to get whole milk in the bottle," said Kitty. "There were eight of us in the family. The milkman made rounds at the farm, and we got two gallons twice a week. Then we'd mix it half with powdered milk to make it last. I can't do powdered milk now. That stuff is nasty unless it's very cold."

After breakfast, we split up. Cis and Pat headed to New Orleans to connect with Pat's husband, Dave. The rest of us drove to Joyce and Frank's to drop off the trailer so we wouldn't have to tow it through New Orleans.

While the others unloaded the trailer, Kathy, Sara Jo, and I sat down with Joyce in the front room. "I'm seventy years old, and I'm very blessed," Joyce said. "I shouldn't be alive today. Angels have been around me for so many years. When I was sixteen, my appendix ruptured on a Tuesday night, and I didn't get to surgery until Friday. I was so sick my daddy had to carry me in. They took me and did an exploratory, and they found out it had been ruptured all that time. They didn't know. They didn't have all the tests then. I didn't come back to consciousness until Monday. High fever and all."

"That's scary stuff," said Kathy.

"They kept taking pints of fluid and puss out of me," said Joyce. "I was all rotten inside.

"Another time, when we were doing the fish camp, I fell off a ladder. I was on the balcony on a seven-and-a-half-foot stepladder. I fell, and somebody just sat my butt on the rail. It wasn't me. I'd have fallen fifteen or sixteen feet back."

"You were on a ladder and fell, but you found yourself sitting on the railing instead of falling?" I asked.

"Right," said Joyce. "I was going backwards, and somehow I just sat on the hand rail. I would've been crippled the rest of my life.

"One time, I got in a car accident. This lady hit me on the side and threw me into oncoming traffic. I saw it coming and braced myself. When my car stopped, I was going into the bayou. The impact threw my driver's door open. My glasses flew out. My syringes flew all over, and all I could think was, 'They're going to think I'm a drug addict.' The car was still running. My keys were on the dashboard. And I walked away."

"You walked away?" I said. "Yeah, you got angels."

"They had to throw my car away," said Joyce. "They couldn't even put it on the rack because it was still running and the wheels were locked. Frank wouldn't believe it. The car-wrecker guy told him, 'It's a miracle that she's alive. We usually have to cut people out like this. I've never seen anybody walk away.'"

"No bruises or anything?" I asked.

"Nothing," said Joyce, shaking her head. "I'm blessed. I wanted to be a nun, but my father said I couldn't. I had to help support the family. He pulled me out of school. I decided it wasn't meant to be. God wants me to do something else.

"Another time, after 9/11, we were going to bring my grandson to Raceland—that's where I was gonna meet his mama. They had gone shopping. We'd gotten to the caution light by the bypass road in St. Charles, and I slowed down. A car stopped and then all at once pulled in front of me. There was traffic coming and a bridge. She pulled out right when I got to her. I saw everybody in the car. I was going forty-five miles an hour or more. My car just did this, and this," she said, demonstrating the motions of her car swerving. "I just kept on after we got clear. Then I got the shakes. My little grandson was in seventh or eighth grade. He says, 'Mama, do you think that was a suicide bomber that did it?' I said, 'No, baby. Something happened to that car.' I do have angels that are protecting me. That's why I live a happy life. I do the best every day and am thankful for what I have."

"You wanted to be a nun?" I asked. "Was there something from inside driving that direction?"

"I was at school then," said Joyce. "We had the Way of the Cross after school. They let you off on Friday early enough so you could walk to church; the whole school wanted to go. Then we walked back to school and took the bus home. I did that every day. When I was old enough to walk, I'd walk to church in the morning. I just wanted to be a nun. Daddy said, 'No, I need you to help support the family.' That's what I did. Then I went into nursing.

"Early in the morning, I used to sit on my patio. That's where I pray before I start my day. If I'm too busy, I sit on the toilet. That's the only time I have peace and quiet. He doesn't care where you pray, just so you pray.

"My mother was sickly. She was the baby in the family, and I think she was pampered. I don't know what it was. Every time we wanted to do something, she was sick. She was one of those. My daddy didn't say much, but when he did say something you'd better listen, you know? Mama is the one that spoke most of the time. I just couldn't disobey him."

"How many were in your family?" asked Kathy.

"We were seven," said Joyce. "I started work before age eleven. I got my Social Security number and started selling clothes in the clothing store, like on the weekend or whenever we had off. I worked at the five-and-ten-cent store. When I turned fifteen I went and worked at the hospital, bathing patients. I stayed there until I went into nursing. I saved a little bit of money, and I had enough for my tuition. I didn't have much for food, so I ate peanut butter and jelly sandwiches every day through nursing.

"I'm blessed and have a lot great in my life. We have our health. We started with nothing and worked ourselves up. We never bought anything if we didn't have the money for it—and we still don't. Now I got money I don't know what to do with. I just give it to my grandkids. Their college is all paid for.

"For my family, I went to the thrift store to buy used clothing. I used to make their clothes too. They couldn't stand the clothes from the dollar store. The clothes that they'd buy with the labels—I'd keep the labels and put them on their dollar store clothes. Once they looked at the tag and saw it was from this other store, it was fine. It's just in the mind. They wanted to be like their friends. Now the kids wear uniforms. Do y'all have to wear uniforms at school?"

"No," I said. "I had to wear uniforms until sixth grade, and then I went from a Catholic school to a public school. That was an awful transition."

"Here, since the shooting in Colorado," said Joyce, "the public school and your Catholic school in Louisiana have to wear uniforms. Every school. Each school has a different color shirt with the school logo on it. That way if a child from another school goes in that school, they can spot them right away."

"They're starting to do that in California," said Sara Jo.

"My daughter said it's easier for teaching," said Joyce. "You can see how they dress, and you don't mean to, but you know which are the rich kids and which are the poor. They have to wear the same kind of shoes and everything so you can't tell one child from another. The boys can't wear their pants down around their butt either.

"What made you go with your mama paddling?" Joyce asked Sara Jo.

"I'm not a kayaker," answered Sara Jo. "I prefer canoes. All of us kids were raised going camping in the Boundary Waters, and all three of us love it. We love the water. In Minnesota we're surrounded by water. I think to some degree Wade and Naomi and I need to be near water. It calms us. It allows us to recharge and heal and then face whatever it is we've got to face in life.

"This was something that seemed important to Mom. There are few things that I've seen my mom do for just her. In the beginning she woke up and said, 'There's something I want to do. I'm turning fifty, and this is important to me.' While she's done things that were important to her, this seemed like one of those that was attached to something happier. Not like, 'This is important because I think I have to or should.' This is a childhood dream that reoccurred to her. It felt like it needed to be supported. I couldn't not support it.

"Of course, in my mom's style, nothing is ever just simply paddling down a river." Hearing Sarah Jo say that, Kathy laughed knowingly. "It turned into something bigger than that. Knowing that she was going to create something where I'd be able to experience not just the wilderness, not just time with the family or friends, but really experience other people—and grow. It was an opportunity for me to step into something she was doing where I could learn and grow. After the first time, you get hooked. You experience one Gathering, like you did, and hear what the women are saying—a lot of things that I've heard in one way or another from my mom. Only now I'm hearing it from other women.

"I don't think I hear it differently from other women, but having grown up with my background—I experienced a lot of trauma as a child that most people my age can't even fathom. They've had easier childhoods, so I've always been different. I think everyone, to some degree, feels this way. Because I had to grow up faster than everyone else, I felt isolated. I thought no one else could understand what I was thinking. I hung out with people that were older than me. I felt more comfortable with the adults. It became easy for me to believe I'm the only one that thinks and feels this way.

"While I don't have the same level of wisdom these women have, I have inklings of things that are being said. I've heard it before, but to hear so many other women say it—you become a part of something that's greater than you. For me that's powerful. It's not about hearing it different, but it's an invitation to be a part of something. That's all I got."

"That's all you got?" I kidded.

"How old are you?" Joyce asked me.

"Fifty-seven," I answered.

"How old are you?" Joyce asked Kathy.

"I'll be seventy in June," answered Kathy. "I'm grateful. My mother died at fifty-six, and every year after I reached that age I was grateful. Then, five years ago, I had heart failure. When I went in to see the doctor after I found out I said to her, 'What's that going to mean?' She said, 'You're going to have to have a new heart.' I wanted to slap her.

"I had a checkup two weeks ago. After the treadmill test she said, 'Man, you're in great shape. Your heart is perfect. You've come a long way.' I said, 'Yes. Do you remember what you said to me the first day I met you?' She said, 'I remember. You were in bad shape.' I'm grateful for every day I get."

"They told my mother she was in congestive heart failure and had a bad heart," said Joyce. "It was twenty years later, and she just kept going. She died at ninety-one and a half. If you keep exercising . . .

"My daddy died at sixty-two. He got up that morning, got dressed, and fell at the foot of my mom's bed and died right there. We'd gone to see Frank's mom and daddy the night before, but I hadn't seen my daddy that day. He wanted to see the kids every day. They lived right there, so I went to see my daddy. When we'd come in, he would lie on the floor, and the kids would climb all over and play with him. He hadn't seen them that Sunday, so I said, 'We got to go see Daddy and Mama.' Good thing because the next morning at seven o'clock, he got up and died right there.

"That's one thing they can't tell about is the heart—how long you have. This couple was leaving to go on vacation; she insisted that he go to the doctor. She didn't want to go on the road without getting him checked. She stayed home, and he got a checkup. We were doing the EKG, and he was doing fine. The last part where he was holding his breath and let it out, he never let it out. Five doctors were working on him.

"She was upset when I had to call her. I got her to come in, and I talked to her for a long time. The next day we talked to her again. She blamed herself. I told her she could have gotten killed too. It was God's way of telling him. That is one thing you can't predict, and you can't live in fear. I just thank God for giving me another day when I go to bed and thank Him for getting me out of bed in the morning. You just have to take it like that. You can't worry about it."

"Live every day," said Kathy.

"And live it crazy," said Joyce with a big grin. "Crazy like you want. I'm an old lady. I can do anything crazy that I want and blame it on the crazy lady inside of me. I'm goin' on seventy-one next month.

"We have one of the ladies, Miss Rodgreus, she's eighty-five or more, and she goes to the nursing home and does the old people's hair. She's not a beautician; she just volunteers. Our best friend lived next door to her. When we had the hurricanes, Freddy heard the chainsaw going so he looks out the door. She has the big oak trees. She climbed in the back of her husband's pickup truck on a chair, climbed on top of the roof of the truck with a chainsaw, and cut the branches. When she couldn't reach, she would get down and move the truck so she could reach until she did all of her trees. Then she went and got the husband, who is way older, and lookin' bad right now. They loaded all of that and hauled it. She still plants her garden and everything."

"Our Auntie Joyce was a volunteer firefighter until she was at least eighty-two," I said. "They told her she couldn't drive the fire truck any-more—"

"—because her feet didn't reach the pedals," added Kathy, laughing.

"The kids are spoiled," said Joyce. "We didn't have cars. My daddy had a car. We had to walk everywhere. You worked harder; you hung up clothes and washed with a washboard. Now you don't even have to cook. Go to one of the supermarkets, and your food is cookin'. Just pretend. Put it in a pot and pretend that you cooked it, and your husband would never know. Rouse's—one of the supermarkets in town—his wife didn't know how to cook. She'd buy it and put it in the pot. He never knew she never cooked it. He found out after they got divorced. Maybe one of the boys told him. I wouldn't have bothered dirtying my pots.

"Frank's mama never had leftovers. His mama cooked breakfast, lunch, and supper. With all the kids, there never was anything left over. At our house, when Mama cooked something, if you ate it at noon, you ate it at night, and if you had more, you ate it the next day. Most of the time she cooked so she didn't have enough for the next day.

"Frank was always complaining that he didn't want leftovers. Then one night I came home from work, and I'd had a bad day. His famous words were, 'It doesn't taste like Mama's.' That night he said it, and the kids started complaining, and I said, 'Oh. Okay.' I didn't say anything. I got up and picked up the garbage, brought it to the table, took their plates, and threw the food in the garbage, and I took the food out of the pots and threw it in the garbage and said, 'Go eat at your Mama's.' She was dead." We laughed.

"You don't take any crap, do you?" I asked.

"Nope," Joyce said smiling. "Never heard it again.

"I make my menu for the week. The kids were in high school and college, and they knew how to cook. I'd get back from work, and they'd be sittin' there watchin' TV and say, 'What's for supper?' I said, 'The menu is all there.' The nights that I had to work late, I put something on the menu that anybody could fix easy. One day I'd just had enough. I said, 'You know what? I'm not hungry.' I sat down and watched TV with them. Nobody said anything, but they got the hint. Next time, some-body took over and cooked."

"I could have taken lessons from you," I said.

"I should have been in her class," said Kathy.

"When I was young and we didn't have a mom, I did a lot of the cooking," I said. "My brothers never liked anything that I made. I kept trying to make it better. That's why I don't like cooking now. I'll bake. They liked the cookies and stuff, but they never liked the food I made. Those would have been good tactics to use on them."

"Fine. Don't like it? Don't eat it," said Kathy.

"I just kept trying harder," I said.

"You still work?" Joyce asked Kathy.

"I work in a day-care center," said Kathy. "I make lunch for 150 kids. The work is not fun, but the joy that I get from those children is tremendous. They are precious. I have kids that have to come in and say good morning every day. I get hugs and kisses. I take lunch in, and I get swarmed. They grab me around the leg and give me a hug. I guess that's what keeps me going back. Not the work. It's the kids. We take them from six weeks old to pre-K."

Doug came in to say he and Heidi were eager to get to New Orleans, so we headed out. In the French Quarter we connected with Pat, Dave, and Cis and began to wander the streets. I was so engrossed in looking at the architecture that reflected French influence that I didn't notice a piece of iron sticking out of the sidewalk and I kicked it. I kicked it so hard my ankle ached. My foot was in a lot of pain, particularly my big toe. I didn't want to take my shoe off to see how bad it was. I took a moment to let the worst of the pain pass while Doug rubbed my ankle. Then we pushed on. I walked with a bit of a limp.

The streets dated back to the 1700s and were narrow, having been designed for horses. Balconies with ornate black wrought-iron railings ran the length of most of the second floors. Many balconies had a variety of colorful flowers flowing down from them. Private hallways led to interior courtyards where the people who lived there got away from the crowds. Down the hallways we saw inviting lush plants, fountains, and tables and chairs. Long ago, the courtyard was where livestock was kept.

Street performers were on every corner. Each had a bucket for tips. One man was dressed in pink feathers with a headdress that rose four feet above his head. His outfit had a breastplate with red and blue gems encased in silver. Silver earrings hung to the middle of his chest. It looked as though he were wearing a dress that was thick with the pink feathers. When he raised his arms, the feathers spread into enormous wings. His eyes were visible, and we saw only the skin on his hands and nose.

It was Halloween weekend, and the city was dressed up. It was one of the busiest weekends of the year, second only to Mardi Gras. Skeletons, witches, and spider webs hung everywhere.

We walked the outside edge of Jackson Square, where local artists worked. Their artwork hung on the iron fence encompassing the square. We crossed Decatur Street to Café Du Monde for beignets and coffee with chicory. While we waited in line, we watched the horses and buggies pass, listened to street musicians, and watched a street performer in a trench coat. He was painted silver from head to toe and acted like a robot as he performed to music from his boom box.

While we were seated in Café Du Monde's outdoor area, our order of beignets was served. Beignets, pronounced ben-yays, were brought to Louisiana by the Acadians. A beignet is a square pastry made from deep-fried dough and sprinkled with a generous dusting of powdered sugar. If we hadn't been headed to dinner, we would have ordered another round.

We walked up the stairs to the footbridge over the levee to say hello to the river. The size of the ocean liners parked upriver was impressive. There were signs of commercial traffic—tugboats, barges, and docks. The tugboats were dwarfed by the expansiveness of the river.

The streets were full of people in costume: witches, cartoon characters, vampires, and characters we could only guess at. We wondered if the outfits some people were wearing might be their normal attire. One man stood in the middle of an intersection directing traffic with a whistle. The nails on both his hands and feet were impeccably painted hot pink; he wore makeup with ruby-red lipstick. A black curly wig framed his face, and he wore black-and-white leg warmers that went from his ankles to just above the knee, flip-flops with big flowers on them, a skin-tight black miniskirt, and a black-and-white top with flowing fishnet sleeves. I had never seen a traffic cop with such flair.

The shops had everything from fine furniture and jewelry to T-shirts and plastic souvenirs. We stopped to watch a magician's show. Pat and Dave became part of his act. The magician was a comedian too. He did card tricks and made a game of telling people information about themselves, such as the names of their boyfriends. He was right every time.

Bourbon Street was the busiest and had the most bars. Loud music poured from nearly every door. The costumes—and in some cases, lack of clothing—made it evident that on Bourbon Street the rules were different from what we were used to.

Doug talked to a woman picking up trash along the street and asked if it was busy every weekend. She smiled at him and said, "Pretty much. Occasionally we have a slow weekend. I don't like those weekends because then I don't have much of a job."

"So it's about job security then," said Doug, teasing.

"Yeah," she said, lifting one eyebrow. "So give me your trash."

We came to the corner of Royal and St. Ann where a waiter from the Pere Antoine approached us and talked us into going inside. The walls were painted with a variety of murals of scenery. The waiter who talked us inside served us. His name was Shine. He had a smile that lit up the room. Gregarious, he laughed easily and genuinely enjoyed people.

Doug had his crawdaddies in a meal called Gaige's Crawfish Chicken. It was fabulous. The rest of us had blackened catfish, gumbo, shrimp creole, and more. We tried each other's meals so we could each get a taste of New Orleans. Dave generously paid for the dinner to congratulate us on the conclusion of our adventure.

It was dark by the time we finished dinner, and we made our way back to our cars. The area was coming more alive. More people were streaming in than were leaving. We passed a one-man band. His instruments—pan lids, cowbells, harmonicas, and horns—were attached to a wheelchair that he pushed. His decorations included large plastic eyeballs, skele-

Photo by Kathy Dickens

tons, photos of flying saucers and friends, a thermometer, black-and-white zebra-patterned fabric, a boat propeller, a Mardi Gras mask with beads, sunglasses, space aliens, and lots of little spot lights. The man wore a wire-mesh vegetable strainer on his head with a light on it. A restaurant owner paid him to play. A man following him wore a washboard on his chest and metal clips on his fingers. He played along, running his fingers across the washboard. I couldn't make out the tune, but it was lively.

We drove to our hotel, where we spent a few moments with Cis. She'd be going home first thing in the morning. Cis's journal entry:

> *Long River, you are running into the sea, pregnant from beginning to beginning . . . with tears of laughter and pain. Thank you for allowing me to bear witness to the ebb and flow of this remarkable journey. May your journey continue from your beginning to your next beginning.*
> *Miss Cis*

Our rooms were on the eleventh floor and had a view of Lake Pontchartrain and the city. We couldn't see the lake in the dark, but the lights over the city were marvelous. My foot was tender. Dried blood was crusted on my big toe and my nail was split all the way down the center. I cleaned it and carefully put a Band-Aid on it to hold the nail in place. Then we retired for the evening.

October 30, Day Forty

After a wonderful night's sleep, I woke to the sun in the window. I looked over Lake Pontchartrain and watched the waves crash against shore. It was the second-largest inland saltwater lake in the United States, Great Salt Lake in Utah being the largest. Its oval shape stretched forty miles from east to west and twenty-four miles north to south. Because its average depth was fourteen feet, the wind easily stirred up waves.

Doug, Sara Jo, Heidi, Kitty, and I gathered in the hotel restaurant for breakfast. After reviewing the trip budget and remaining funds, Kitty and I were delighted and surprised to determine that financially we were much better off than we had expected. There was enough left to get us home, and we treated everyone to breakfast.

We planned to drive to the mouth of the Mississippi River but chose instead to go back to the French Quarter. Doug's first stop was Café Du Monde's for beignets. Pat and Dave wandered the streets for a while with us and then went off alone. Doug, Sara Jo, Kitty, Heidi, and I continued on. I found Shirley, a psychic reader I'd met the previous spring when I was in the French Quarter. I was drawn to her because she'd been doing readings for over sixty years, and I wanted to connect with her again.

Before my first reading with Shirley, all my stereotypes surfaced about how a psychic in New Orleans might act and dress. I expected a crystal ball, maybe a candle, and a woman dressed like a gypsy. I walked through the beaded curtain, came around the corner, and saw a woman with short white hair who looked like her next stop was church. There were no tarot cards—she used playing cards. The room was cramped and used for storage. There were boxes piled along the walls and a poster above the tiny table. Shirley had a big welcoming smile and was all business. She wanted to bypass small talk so she could give a client as much information in the allotted time as she could. I asked her why she had done readings for so long, and she said, "It's my hope that I am helping people heal. People come to me with so much pain. My work is to help them heal."

Shirley worked at Rev. Zombies House of Voodoo where there was an eclectic collection of T-shirts, voodoo dolls, beads, charms, and masks. Kitty, Sara Jo, and I had readings done. She read my palm and told me I would have a long life and then described accurately my relationship with Doug.

While we waited for everyone to see Shirley, we hung out on the street and watched the street performers. A beautiful woman with a powerful voice sang and played the clarinet. With her were a guitarist, a tubaist, and a trumpeter—a young boy about five who played skillfully. They drew a big crowd that closed down the street. The woman was belting blues songs.

Doug wandered into a shop down the street while the rest of us were drawn into a tiny clothing store called The Royal Boutique. Brightly colored clothes hung on the walls and lay in piles. Country and '60s music played in the background. The owner, an energetic woman with long salt-and-pepper hair, was named Zarina. She helped Kathy pick a lavender dress to wear for her seventieth birthday in June. As Kathy paid for her dress, she asked, "How long have you had this store?"

"The store I have twenty-five years," said Zarina. "I used to be across the street and sell my country's stuff. Indian stuff. I'm from India. I've been here for thirty years."

"The school I work at has a lot of Indian children," said Kathy. "On special holidays, they come dressed in these beautiful outfits. They're so gorgeous. Their mothers come to get them all dressed up. I've always admired them."

"Thank you," said Zarina. "I'm proud of my country stuff."

"What brought you to New Orleans?" asked Heidi.

"My in-laws were living here," said Zarina. "They were from my country also. We have arranged marriages. I marry over there, but my husband brought me here. I've been married exactly thirty years. I have three daughters. One of them married already last year."

"Are they arranged marriages as well?" I asked.

"Yes," Zarina said with enthusiasm. "We show them this is the people you can meet and if you like. It's not a blind date. We match the families and let them meet each other, the girls and the boys. If they think it can work, they can meet one or two times and exchange their views. If they like it, we do it."

"We have some families in our school whose children are pre-K," said Kathy, "and they've already arranged for them to be married."

"My daughter got married a little later," said Zarina. "She was twenty-six. I was married twenty-two years old. We try to do it a little early instead of the kids going out with the boys and girls. Better make the marriage and study, whatever they want to do. They can focus on studies. We say this is yours, and you're going to have to stay with them and not to fool anywhere. I'm not saying hundred percent goody-goody when we marry like this, but it's successful. If sometime we aren't happy, the elderly person come between and try to counsel, and it work out.

"We like one roof for the children grow up. Not a mom have a child, dad have a child, supporting each other. That's not good. Kids need both parents. You can see the difference when any child have both parents. He's more happy; he's more focused. Otherwise, they're looking all the time, 'Who is my dad? Who is my mom?'

"Very easy to leave the person. It's hard to keep it like this. I got a lot of hard times, but thank God. I pray all the time and it work out. Whenever I have a problem, I have a focus on God. Ask, 'Help me.' God always help. You have to just talk and it work out."

"And listen," added Kathy.

"Oh, yes, and listen," said Zarina, folding a scarf that was on the counter. "Nobody's happy in this world all of the time. If we try our best, do something good around us, sometime you get hurt, but believe me the end is going to be good because you're doing good. You know in your heart you didn't do anything wrong, so this bad time will go away soon. That's my belief, and I'm working on it, and it's good for me."

"That's beautiful," said Kathy.

"Thank you," said Zarina. "My daughter that got married, every single day I talk to her and tell her do this, this, this. It's respect. You're living with your in-laws over there, and you can make it stick. It's a big family. The boy have two brothers and three sisters. A sister is married, but the brothers live under the one roof, and one brother already have children.

"My daughter's mother-in-law is very happy. She cook by herself. My daughter clean the kitchen and make the dessert. She like American stuff to make. Her mother-in-law get happy. She treats them on the weekend and do everything. They come with mother-in-law, go shopping, get massage. She says, 'I'm happy more than what my daughter did with me. My daughter-in-law is the best.' Her friends—everybody not good. Some of them said, 'You're lying with us. You aren't that much happy.' She said, 'You can come in my house anytime you like to visit. Ask anybody in my house how much I'm happy.' It make me proud of myself. I raise my child like this. Husband sometime get jealous. He said, 'I pick you and now you taking care of my whole family.' His mother said, 'I'm happy more than anything else. This is my daughter-in-law.'

"This is the thing I want to go generation to generation in the families. People ask—even my in-law's family where we're living—they ask my daughter when she come over to visit, 'Let's gossip.' She said, 'Everybody is fine.' They said, 'You're lying.' She said, 'I don't lie. I spent twenty-six years over here, and you know I like to work with everybody.' I said, 'This life is little. Don't make enemies; make friends.' Sometimes you have hard times from the people, but it's okay. They're going to turn around and love you.

"I said, 'When you have a baby, I'm going to leave everything alone, and I'm going to raise your child. These days kids don't have time to raise them. When he talk, I want to start teaching good things so that when he grows up, and I'm not living, I know my generation is good. Then I don't have any regrets what I do with my life. I raised my generation and it's going to be fine. That's the way I feel.

"I'm not open from ten to five. I'm open late. People looking for me, and they come back. Sometimes several years, sometime two years. It makes me happy. Money is not everything, but when you meet somebody, a good person, that's the most important. I make a lot, a lot of friends in twenty-five years.

"I try to do a little bit of work. If somebody's life change, that make me happy. It has happen. One girl—was a black girl—I don't know why she came. I think God sent her. She's American girl, forty years old, skinny, and she's crying. She said, 'I don't have food. I don't have a boyfriend.' I said, 'I understand the food. I bring the food with me, and I'll share with you right now. You don't have a place to live. You're on the street, and you're crying for the boyfriend. Honey, you need to work first to stand on your feet. Get yourself a job. Be a powerful woman. Men will fall in line.' She's working in the movies now, and whenever she have rough time, she calls me. She said, 'I'm coming. You give me hug and I feel better.' She bring her friends, and she said, 'This is my mom. Meet this lady. I'm proud of her because she make me stand on my feet.' These little things."

"That's a big thing," Kathy said with tears in her eyes.

"She have a daughter after a time," said Zarina, "I said, 'Take care of your children like a mom because they need you. Don't ever pick up a boy on the street. Watch, everybody is going to come now.' She's not a big shot in the movies, but whatever she's doing is earning the good money.

"One more girl, she used to help me in the store when I was across the street. She and boyfriend have a fight a couple of times, and they leave each other. I pray for them. These days they're finally together, and they have a child five years old. I'm gonna yell at the boyfriend because I love the girl. 'She's so sweet,' I said. 'You not gonna find a beautiful girl like this. Nobody is perfect. Give her a chance.' She's a little hyper—she's on medicine. I said, 'With good people, everybody can work out. When the person have a little disability, if you help, God going to give you credit in this world and the other world also.' They're together. He's an artist, and he appreciate because they have a daughter. She always running to me, 'Auntie Zarina, Auntie Zarina.' I'm here. It make me happy, and I say, 'Thanks, God.'"I feel if you do a little bit with someone, God gives you good credit, and that's my victory in this life. I say to God, 'When you give me more years to live, let me do something good, but will stay in this world.' A lot of time I don't make anything at my shop, but still sitting here making some stuff, sitting praying and talking to friends, it make me happy."

"You've made us happy and given us a lot," said Kathy. "Thank you for sharing with us. That was beautiful."

"Thank you," said Zarina. "Have beautiful birthday."

We left Zarina's shop and walked back to our car for the drive to Joyce and Frank's for our final evening of this adventure. On the ride, I read Kathy's journal entry:

To be able to spend a week with my brother, sister-in-law, and daughter-in-law (niece) was a real special time. Especially since it was during and about such a great adventure.

I'm so proud of Nancy and what she has accomplished. I can see how she has grown so confident because of it. But then, I'm sure the mighty Mississippi makes strong people even stronger.

This entire week, I have lamented over the fact that I was unable to join until the end, but so delighted that this time I could be here.

From the first sunset to the wild winds of the Grand Isle and no tomatoes at 'Sarah's', the fancy hotel and now the last night after a beautiful paddle in the Bayou and a game of cards. Wow. I don't want to miss the mention of the French Quarter and especially listening to the stories of the few women that I heard. Zarina (the lady in the dress store), who gave us such a beautiful gift of her Indian (Hindu) belief. And then Joyce.

I love the experiences, the laughter, fun and food—especially when I got to paddle in the canoe.

Thanks for the memories—I will hold them dear.
Kathy

After the thrill and wonder of paddling with the dolphins, I thought the best part of the journey was over, but Shirley and Zarina reminded me that true sustaining joy is found in sharing our truth and wisdom. If I kept my eye only on the big prizes, like paddling with dolphins, I'd miss touching life-giving experiences. Women's wisdom was all around us and would be shared in subtle and touching ways. We need only to pay attention.

October 31, Day Forty-one

I smelled bacon cooking and heard my traveling companions chatting in the kitchen, but before I headed down to join them I read Sara Jo's journal entry:

The Navajo people used to take their children early in the morning, long before sunrise, to the top of a nearby hill. As the sun would rise, they would tell their children 'This sun has but one day of life. Today it will rise and once it sets, it will never rise again. In honor of this day in which the sun burns, live this day to its fullest that you do not waste this precious life.'

That is paraphrased, but I feel it says so much of what we have heard along this journey and what I have known in my heart. Each day is a gift to be cherished. Living it true to ourselves respects who we are, the gift of this life, and all that lives alongside us.

I began this journey seven years ago with the initial intention of supporting what was the first major adventure my mom did just for her, making a childhood dream come true. I now know, so many years later, that this journey is for more than just that small girl who grew up in Minneapolis near the Mississippi. In true Mom style, her adventure became the journey of self-discovery for a community of women now bonded by her dream and the waters of the Mississippi. What began as a journey for one drew in the support, wisdom, and power of many. I'm grateful to be among that community that physically and emotionally participated in this adventure, and honored to be a part of the even greater community of women whose honesty, courage, creativity, compassion, and perseverance have inspired me to live true to myself as a result of their wise words.

Thank you for this opportunity to open, reconnect, and unite with myself in something greater than myself.

This journey is only the beginning for us all. May your journey ahead be full of joy, love, compassion, and adventure.

Love to you all, Sara Jo

Sara Jo's words spoke of the sense of fullness and completion that surrounded me, yet I knew that what had been put into motion on this journey would continue. Like the water of the Mississippi, healing energy was blending into the Gulf, those ripples would blend into the oceans, and the waves would caress distant shores. In my vision—my dream—the fluidity and power of the Grandmothers' messages was rippling out from the women who touched this journey, creating waves of healing that would join forces with other like-minded women around the globe.

I took my place at the kitchen table where Joyce and Frank served a hearty meal for our journeys home, complete with homemade biscuits for Sara Jo. Then, after long hugs, Doug, Sara Jo, Kathy, and Heidi drove to the airport.

Kitty and I grinned broadly and spontaneously shook our heads in amazement.

"Wow," I said. "We did it."

"Yeah, wow," said Kitty. "Ready?"

"Ready." I smiled as we climbed in the van. We turned north on Highway 1.

We were heading home.

June 12, 2011

12

MORE WOMEN'S STORIES

Ely, Minnesota, is where the Ripples of Wisdom idea was born. With the final section of the journey only three months away, I became hungry to hear stories and wisdom from the women in my hometown. The entire community had offered immense support since the beginning of this project in 2004. I scheduled a Gathering, inviting Ely area women, and held it outside on a beautiful evening near the Kawishiwi River. Twenty-six women took advantage of the opportunity. Some, under age fifty, had come to listen. These are the stories told that evening.

Sue S.'s Story

"My name is Sue and I'm seventy-nine years old. I'm going to be eighty in October, and I can't believe it. I just can't believe it. I don't know how I got here. Somewhere inside there's a part of me that's still about fourteen or maybe nineteen. When I was that age, eighty seemed so far away, but all of sudden—here it is.

"I'm honored to be the first one to speak. I don't think I've ever been the oldest person who actually admitted to being the oldest. All of my life, I've been in groups where people talk about their age, but I typically don't say my age because I don't think that it's that important.

"The single most life-changing event for me was the death of my daughter. This happened in May, on Mother's Day, in 2004. Mercifully she wasn't ill with brain cancer for more than sixty days after she was diagnosed. Watching her suffer, I was ready to let her go, but it's been hard, very hard. This year, for some reason, it's particularly hard. This is year number seven.

"What I've gotten out of that experience that has affected my behavior and my feelings is that when I meet another mother who has lost a child, something in me just opens up. I either call her or I go to her. I try to spend time listening to her because I've been there. There's nothing quite like losing a child because it's not supposed to happen. Well, maybe it's not supposed to happen, but life happens—and that happens.

"The first six months after she died . . . People always talked about being depressed, but being this kind of depressed was different. I had been depressed from time to time in my life. I don't think I know too many women who haven't been depressed at some point. Just look at how hard life is. But this depression was different, and I felt it all through that first year of grieving.

"I feel I was blessed because I had parents who were elastic sorts of people. Things may have been tough for them, but they came out of the bad times. They had tools—a toughness—and they had grace and charm. Somehow or another, I guess I got enough of that toughness that I was able to persevere.

"I worked in mental health for years, and I worked with a lot of depressed people. One of the things I know is that when people are depressed, they can't get out of bed in the morning. I had mornings after Joann died when I thought I couldn't get out of bed. But I had this quality that I think I got from my dad where something in me said, 'If you stay in bed today, you aren't going to get up tomorrow either. So here's what you do: Get out of bed. Go in the kitchen. Make some coffee. When it's done brewing, drink it. This will take about twenty minutes. If you still want to go back to bed, that's okay. But if you can stay up for another twenty minutes after that, you'll be okay.' That's what I did and that's what worked for me—that and the grace of God, which is the most important thing in my life. I never did have a morning when I couldn't get up—when I didn't get up.

"I like to share that story with people, with mothers who have had losses. I've had grief groups for people like that because the other thing I learned from Joann's death is that it gave me a purpose that I didn't even know was out there. I could do for others in some way. I was doing mental health—but not for money. I did mental health for money for thirty years, and boy was I glad when I stopped doing it for money. This way, I could do it for real.

Today what makes my life rich is getting to come to Ely, being retired, and having a very devoted husband, a beautiful place to live, and enough resources that I don't have to worry about working.

"One of the things I like most about being here in Ely is I love trees. I love seeing the birds. I live in St. Louis on a very fast stretch of the Mississippi, although I don't live where I can see it. I live in an area where two major highways come together, and so police cars, ambulances, and fire engines—with sirens—come by about every thirty minutes. It's so wonderful to sleep here with all of the shades open. I can see the stars and the water. I don't hear any sirens and cars and trucks. It's so quiet. I think about that in January. I really start thinking about that because there aren't any leaves on the trees so everything is louder. I just can't wait to get back to peace on the lake with the trees and the quiet and the people I love here."

Lydia's Story

"Four years ago, my husband and I were diagnosed with cancer within five days of each other. It's just good to be here."

Carol O.'s Story

"When I first heard the poem 'Imagine a Woman,' my mother came to mind because she wasn't able to be that woman; and for a really long time, I wasn't either. As I look back, I think that most of my life I was reacting to life rather than being an actor in my own life, and that affected how I raised my children and how I did everything, really. I don't think I had much courage. I blamed circumstances. I blamed my ex-husband. I blamed my mother. And then I found Co-Dependents Anonymous. It took a lot of courage to examine my soul and my deepest feelings. I didn't really know what I was feeling when I was feeling. I was probably fifty by the time I started figuring out who I really was. I thank the Twelve Step program for that.

About the same time, I became involved in Sufism, my spiritual path. The Twelve Step program and Sufism coincided perfectly. Both enabled me to have true relationships with my children. I honestly didn't know how to be with them. I was so controlling, and it always blew up in my face. I was controlling with men—way too many men—and with friends, although less so with friends. Today I feel so much more able to be true to myself and to the people I'm with. I am very, very grateful for what I now have in my life and for the people I now have in my life."

Kitty's Story

"When I was reading the 'Imagine a Woman' poem, what surfaced for me was the word imagine. I moved to Ely in 1997 with my daughter. I moved with the intention of getting married. That didn't happen, and I told my daughter we were going to stay here anyway. I told her that she was going to graduate from high school here. She did, and I'm still here.

"In Ely, imagine has become a part of life. I never imagined my life to be what it is today. I never had the ability to think big enough. The things that take place in my life today are not things I was able to dream.

They come from my spirituality, which has happened since moving to Ely too. They come from being in groups like this. They come from sitting and sharing with other people. There is so much out there, but I really never paid attention to it before. I never really listened. I get a chance to do that today, and it's really wonderful.

"Spirituality is a huge part of life. It allows me to be open to life. I kept myself pretty closed off when things would take place in my life that I didn't like. Instead of going outward with things, I stuffed them inside each time. I didn't share with anybody. I never had friends close enough to be able to share feelings that came up and not have them think I was a monster. Then things would become big within me.

"This is part of what is huge for me—being able to speak. It had not been a part of my life, but I find that it gets easier each time I do it. Life gets easier when I do it, when I'm able to share what is going on with me and inside of me and to hear what other people have to say. There are a lot of guides out there in life, and when I share, I get to listen to them.

"Thanks for being here tonight. I'm going to listen."

Martha's Story

"I lived in Ely from 1985 to 1997, so I know some of the people in this circle. I've been away and now I am back for the summer. I discovered in my wisdom that being an Outward Bound instructor based in Ely, Minnesota, was the best job I ever had. Pushing sixty now, I decided to come back and do one more summer as an Outward Bound instructor. So far, I've been here for five weeks, and it's fabulous—totally fabulous. There's a lot of wisdom and a lot of connecting with youth.

"The Outward Bound that I left fourteen years ago and the Outward Bound that I've come back to are quite different. This new one is kinder and gentler. The students treat each other with more respect than I remember. The students and the organization seem to follow what evolves in the good parts of our society, in the multiple ways that our society moves.

"I am very happy to be back in the north woods based in Ely and working for Outward Bound. The ropes course at Outward Bound is my power space, and it's just two miles away from where I am sitting tonight. Can anyone else feel the power?"

Betty F.'s Story

"One of the things at the heart of what makes my life rich is faith. I was aware of it as a child. Sometimes it's gotten rather thin through life, but I never totally let go of it. There's something beyond us—whether you call it God or universal consciousness or a hundred other names—according to Sufism. I've been practicing Sufism the last couple of years.

I've visited witches and synagogues and all different kinds of alternative forms of seeking spirituality and meaning. I found the Quakers. When I was there, I knew that I was home. The other places I went? I might last one Sunday and then I'd be gone.

"For me, a significant group other than spiritually was a group of women. When I was thirty-three, I moved to Minneapolis. I got connected with a women's group that invited me to join them. I was with them, the same women, for fourteen years. We got very close. It was the first time I had that sense of sisterhood. I only had one brother, and I didn't have friendships in my adult life that appeared to be close, so these friendships were quite a revelation. After fourteen years I left that group, which was very difficult, because they were not willing to go beyond the group, to really go for intimacy and deeper levels of being together.

"Some significant events in my life were that I had a number of deaths when I was very young. One was a girl who was about as close to a sister as I've ever had. Her family and mine did a lot together. She died at twenty-one the night before she was going to be released from a mental hospital. It never was determined if her death was caused by suicide or if she had been given drugs or what. That was pretty difficult to deal with, especially because her family didn't want to even look at it. My mom died when I was twenty-five. She was terminally ill, but I didn't know that when she committed suicide. Another close friend died of a brain tumor when I was thirty-one. My dad died when I was thirty.

"I was a pretty serious kid with a deep faith that carried me through. I was always questioning and introspective. I've been writing since I was a kid, and now I'm writing a lot more with a focused intention. Those things that were most difficult are also the things that gave me the most courage. I think in life there's always that two-sided coin, the yin and yang.

"I was married for ten years and separated for two when I was thirty-one. I've lived alone with short periods of having roommates since then. Because I've been single, I've been able to make choices a lot of people couldn't if they were in a committed relationship or marriage that would keep them physically in one place. When I decided to move to Ely, one of the Quakers told me, 'You are very brave.' What is brave about leaving the city and going to Ely? I realize, in retrospect, that for many people moving to Ely would seem like a courageous thing to do. I had done it before in my life—leave a community and start a life in some place new. All of that has contributed to the richness in my life.

"I've suffered depression a lot in my life too. Depression has been described by Thomas Moore in *Care of the Soul* and in another source, a Sufi source actually, this way: If you are willing to go—and it may not feel like you are willing—into depression and experience that, if you choose not to obliterate your consciousness with alcohol or drugs or whatever other means, you are diving down into your deep stuff. You are diving down into the muck and the darkness, which can be very rich.

"My connections with people are probably the most important thing next to my connection with God consciousness. I don't see them as different. One of the things Quakers and Sufis say is that there's part of God in every person. When I feel like I'm doing my best and I'm really centered, alive, and present in the world, that's how I connect with people. That's reflected back. That makes for a very rich life."

Debbie H.'s Story

"I turned fifty on Monday. I haven't gathered much wisdom since Monday though." The group laughed. "I feel really happy to be here tonight. I woke up this morning, and I went to church. I went to a graduation party. I rode my bike. I spent time with some friends and my daughter. And I'm sitting out here with all of you on such a beautiful night, so I have a lot of gratitude tonight.

"I was born in Los Angeles to teenage parents. My mom died when I was young. I remember being in my early twenties and just not knowing how to do all of this. I didn't have any role models, and then I came into the Twelve Step program in 1984. I've been active for quite a number of years.

"I remember living in Ely and having a young daughter and not knowing how to be the woman that I wanted to be. I woke up one day and decided to look towards people I wanted to be like—some of you guys are here—towards people who were a step ahead of me. I wanted what you had in parenting or the way that you went around and did things. I've used some of you women to learn how to do things.

"I went to a retreat at Alice's house many years ago, and I looked on her refrigerator and read a note that said, 'God has no grandchildren.' I've used that a lot with my own kid and my friends. I'm just realizing that I don't have a lot of control over other people. When I get centered in that, I'm so much happier than when I'm trying to be God."

Ella's Story

"The big plan was to move here and become a hermit in the woods, but Ely is such a rich place to live. It's full of people who are just rich, true selves. I'm so inspired by people like Nancy who just said 'I'm going to do this' and did it. I wanted to be here to support her. It reaffirms how interesting Ely is and how special it is to be among all of these true, authentic people. They all have wonderful stories."

Leone's Story

"I want to speak to what makes my life rich. I've been up here for about twenty-two years. What I've found, but only realized a few years ago, is that what I really enjoy the most is meeting people who have a passion for doing what they're doing. You can always tell when people start talking about what they're doing if they have an absolute passion for it. First off, they can't stop talking about it because they care about it so much.

"One example that comes to mind is a woman in Duluth who has taken over a family operation on dog agility training. She has the most remarkable relationship with animals. How she teaches is so different from how I've seen other people teach. She is just totally into it. It's how she talks or the way she teaches a simple little thing. She is 100 percent into what she is doing.

"Another example is a gentleman I did some monument conservation work with about eight years ago. He is so passionate about old cemetery monuments, some of which might be 150 or 200 years old. He says—concerning the repair—that you have to look at it not in terms of if it's gonna last five or ten years, which is what most people think about for their repairs, but if the monument will last seventy-five or a hundred years, just as the original did. In his case, his passion is stones that have been worked by other people years ago.

"Every time I find people who have a passion for what they do, I see the same thing. It's in their eyes. It's in their whole being when they walk around. I've started to look for people who have a passion for something. I don't care what it is. It's cool to find these people because they are so alive."

Consie's Story

"As I've been listening to everybody talk, I've had scenarios running through my head about sharing this story or that story, so I'm not quite sure which one is going to come out of my head. What comes to mind right now is my daughter.

"My daughter turned thirty this year. I never had another person as close to me as she is, you know, genetically. She is closer to me genetically than my husband is. It's a neat thing to think about.

"When I think in retrospect about her younger years, I remember she was a really easy, fun, interesting little girl. And then she hit adolescence, and all hell broke loose. It threw both my husband and me for a phenomenal loop. Both of us had been easygoing adolescents, and we figured that was the way she would be too. I don't know if we thought that because she was smart or because she was our child or what, but she was awful. She was just awful. There were periods when I cried in the shower. There were times when I'd think, 'Why did I ever want to have a child? Why did I think I wanted to do this?' There were times we were scared she would do something and end up dead. And there were times I thought—and this is so awful—if she died, then this would be over. In retrospect, I think what an awful thing to think. But, really, she was awful.

"She came through, and I can look back and laugh about it because she survived. About every six months or so, she apologizes for giving us such a hard time. The thing that amazes me now is that she is the most amazing young woman. I just love her to pieces. It's a really nice thing to see what a neat woman she's become.

"When she was sixteen, she dropped out of high school, and it knocked my husband and me out of the we-can-quietly-handle-this-by-ourselves state. At that point we realized, 'Whoa, something is going on here.' We went to a parenting group that was kind of a tough-love group. There we realized that there were a lot of people who had it a lot worse than we did.

"One of the things we learned from the parenting group was about her list and our list. We learned if something was happening, to ask ourselves, 'Is that on her list or is it on my list?' If it's going to affect me, it's on my list, and then I interact with it. But if it's not, then it's on her list, and I need to let it go. That was a really good thing to learn. My husband and I still use this technique.

"We are in Ely all the time now, retired even though my husband does a zillion things. It's like people talk about: When somebody is retired, he is around more. I was used to having a fair bit of space to myself, and I have to adjust to his being around. Even today I find myself asking myself, 'Okay, is this on his list or my list?' If it's on his list, I can just let it go if it's not something that really matters to me.

"I like where I am going. It's a nice place to be."

Gail's Story

"I always say I'm Heidi's mother. For a long time, that was pretty much my identity. She was a wonderful student and well known in the community.

"I can definitely relate to loss. Heidi and her sister were no more alike than the stars and the moon. Heidi loved the out-of-doors. Our other daughter was the princess. She died just before she was nineteen. This last year was seventeen years since she died. Friday was her birthday. At first, her birthdays and the anniversary were really hard for us. Now it doesn't matter if I don't think about it all day long because I remember her, and that's the important thing. I do. I remember her all of the time.

"The rich thing in my life now is my grandson, Heidi's son. He is the light of our lives. I can tell you lots of stories and you would say, 'Oh, she's got another one.' There are lots and lots of stories because he has lots of ideas.

"We came up here four years ago after my husband lost a job he'd had for twenty-three years. We thought we were going to be at that job until he couldn't go to work anymore. It was a big change. It was an okay change for me because I could be closer to Heidi, but my husband has struggled with it a lot. That has been my big challenge, trying to get him to understand that we have so much to be grateful for. We don't have to worry about what we had. We have to enjoy what we have.

"I've met so many people here. I need to work harder on making friends. I never really had close friends. I had a couple in high school, but then we moved to Chicago. I had some good friends who are still good friends. It's hard to be so far away from them. It seems like every time you make a good friend, you are moving on, and you leave them behind. I'm making new friends, and I think I'm too old to move on."

Johnnie's Story

"Yesterday I celebrated my fortieth anniversary of moving to Ely. The weekend has been a little cosmos of what Ely means to me. Maybe it's been because so much of my life has been in Ely—and it's been the subtext for so long—that Ely means so much to me. I don't see myself going anywhere else. Something could happen, but I think I'm here for the duration.

"One thing that reminded me of the richness of our community and the many ways I'm privileged to participate in it happened yesterday morning. I got up and met Steve, who is one of our expert birders, at four fifteen in the morning. We did five hours of breeding-bird surveys, which was wonderful. Right after that I joined up with the first-responder group that I'm a part of to do training in water rescue. I got to spend a bunch of time with them. Then I went out to dinner with someone who shared the best job in the whole world with me, being an Outward Bound instructor. Then I talked to most of my children. As a hippie who was all for zero population growth, I still feel embarrassed to say that I have five kids. It wasn't that I didn't know where they came from, but nothing seemed to work for me. I have great kids—four daughters and one son, who said, 'I grew up with four menstruating females; of course I'm in touch with my feminine self.'

"Another part of the story that seems to come from age is this wonderful circle that happened to me. It's a gift of living long enough to have things circle back. When I was eighteen, I had a child I gave up for adoption. I'm starting to learn there were thousands and thousands of us. Thousands of children were given up or given away or taken away. I was seriously impacted by giving up my child. It was an expectation that it wouldn't bother you at all. You just give up this baby and you go on with your life. Nobody talked about it being a loss or something to grieve, but it impacted me pretty hard for many years. I came to accept it, and I came to accept that I'd never meet her. I hoped that she knew that I loved her and that I didn't give her up because I didn't want her or that I didn't love her. It was because I hoped she would have a better life than the one I could give her.

"It's been over a year now since I got an email that read 'I think you are my birth mother.' And I was. We got together last August, and she is coming with her family—two sons and husband—in August. All of my children will be here together in Ely. They have not met each other. They Facebook and stuff but haven't actually met.

"I'm so glad that I live here and have this rich community of so many people—including most of you—who I know and love casually or in-depth or in my most spiritual places, my Twelve Step meetings. I feel so gifted. My life is so special for having you in it and for having such wonderful women as daughters and friends. I'm so grateful."

Judy's Story

"The life experience that generated the most wisdom? Well, I've got to go back to when I first experienced depression. I had no idea that's what it was. Not knowing can be part of depression. I lost a lot of weight and wasn't eating much. I finally went to the doctor because I was drinking too much water. I thought I had diabetes.

"I walked in the door—he knew me quite well—and he took one look at me and said, 'Judy, you are clinically depressed.' He just knew it right off. I ended up on medication, but he was a very wise doctor, and he said, 'You go find somebody to work out your life with.' He basically let me know this isn't just a chemical thing. I got myself a counselor, and that experience started generating wisdom for me because from that point on, I started taking responsibility for my own life. I had to start really learning. It's been a long journey not to blame anybody else for any of my sadness or anxieties, to learn that I could respond in a different way to whatever was going on around me. That was just the seed of the beginning of my growth and development, what I think has been a wonderful new way of life.

"Today was a great day and was about what makes my life rich. One of my kids is here with his wife. My son and his father finished a new dock today. It was mostly my son who did the work, and my husband helped him in the way that he could. It was wonderful seeing them work together because they've had an uneasy relationship their whole lives. I was worried. How were they going to work together for two days? I kept out of it because that's part of the wisdom that I've learned. It's their relationship, not mine. They worked beautifully for two days, working together for ten to twelve hours. I went down and watched them for a little bit, and I could have cried. I'm teary right now talking about it because it was that meaningful to me to see that kind of companionship that they had working together. I used to always want to jump in and fix their relationship, but I can't do that anymore. Life works so much better when you don't try to fix other people—oh, my gosh—so much better.

"I decided this morning to enjoy this day. With the kids coming up, I used to think I had to do it all, you know, cooking and preparation. I'm working constantly at letting go of more and more. I decided that I didn't want to cook so I could enjoy this beautiful day. I told my son it would be fun to go out in the boat today, and that I'd like to do that. I suggested I get Subways for everybody so we could spend as much time as possible together after they finished the dock. He thought that was a great idea. That's exactly what I did. I bought everything and didn't make a thing. I sat there listening to their conversation, and I thought about all of that prep and all of that work that I used to think I had to do. That's not what makes life rich.

"I'm seventy-six and I just loved every minute of today."

Mary's Story

"I recently came back from Hawaii. I'm a travel nurse. In Hawaii, they do what is called talk story. It's a very revered thing to listen to the older women. Working in a nursing home and a hospital, I learned residents there are called Auntie or Uncle. They call people by those names because the whole concept of the Hawaiian culture is 'ohana,' which means family.

"I was a little afraid to go to Hawaii at first, but my vibrational self knew that I really wanted to go. I got a call, 'Would you like to go to Hawaii?' and I said, 'Okay.' I went and I walked in spirit. I learned so much from the culture and how they are connected. I went to goddess celebrations and met a lot of Filipino women who were very hard working. They worked from the time they were seven years old. They never really had a childhood. I learned to be very good friends with these women, and I learned their work ethic. They work until they are into their nineties. They listen to their elders and what they have to say.

"The women there reminded me of my mother. I grew up in a family where my mother was a single parent raising six children. I come from a long lineage of women who were single parents. My grandmother came over from Yugoslavia, alone, and met my grandfather. My mother was born and raised here in Ely and then moved to Duluth. I took care of my mother in her later years when she had dementia. She lived with me. My mother was my mother, my sister, my friend, and my companion. In the end, I was her mother. She used to call me Mother. I took care of my grandmother and my aunt, who lived to be in their nineties. I learned a lot about what it took and how hard it was back then and how easy it's become.

"One of the things I've learned now at the age of fifty-six is that there's a vibrational connection that I need to stay in. Being here and moving to Hawaii and having those roles there have made me more prepared to work with my daughter now. I came back from Hawaii to a long struggle with a child with addiction, and the connection that comes out of that is this.

"She was singing a song to me today called 'I Had the Best Day with You Today.' It was really beautiful." Choked up, she passed the fan on.

Pat L.'s Story

"It's an honor to be here. I've read Nancy's books, and I can't believe that I'm holding this fan. It's a real honor.

"Moving to Ely changed my life. It opened me up to nature and actually made me realize that this is my church. As we sit here with the birds and the smells and the trees and the rocks, I feel a part of it. It's enabled me to find out who I really am. I never really knew who I was. I was always searching, searching, searching and holding myself hostage, never giving myself permission to do what I wanted.

"I taught first grade, and I found great pleasure in teaching at-risk children to read. Slowly through the years, I started loosening up, not having to control or be controlled. Coming to Ely has opened me and freed me. Instead of railing against the injustices of the world and whining and crying, I have learned to be more proactive.

"I went back to school a couple of years ago and got my nursing diploma because I was railing against the injustices of those without insurance and wondered, 'What can I do?' So now I volunteer in free clinics. That's been one of the greatest things I've ever done, finding the courage and strength just to get out there and do something about it. I look at the patients that come in and think it's a great place to be. I absolutely love it.

"This is probably the best time of my life. I've had wonderful moments. I've had ups and downs and endings and a lot of scary beginnings. I think each time has given me more courage and more strength.

"I love the time in my life right now. Being sixty-one has its pros and its cons. I still can't believe it. I think my parents should be in their sixties, not me.

"I'm thrilled to be here tonight and hear the stories. I can feel a part of each one of you inside of me. It's really touched me."

Mitch's Story

"I've come a long way. I've been struggling with depression since my middle thirties. Somebody told me I was clinically depressed and put me on an antidepressant, and off I went. About two months ago, I said, 'I don't like this. I don't feel good.' So I went off the antidepressant and realized that it was making me depressed, which was very odd.

"In my sixties, I feel like I'm thirteen and learning how to deal with myself emotionally all over again. It's horrific. I'm all over the map. I'm weepy. I'm happy. I'm pissed off. I'm all of it. I'm learning how to be an emotional being and deal with emotion—as an adult. It's very hard. I don't much like it," she said humorously like a defiant child.

"I had what I thought was a great life as a kid, and then my memories came back. I realized that I had a delusional life as a child, although parts of my childhood were really great. There was a lot of abuse, a lot of alcoholism, and insanity. But it got me where I am today, and I'm okay with that. My mom was incredibly difficult. Her gift to us was dying. That was a gift she gave my siblings and me because it finally freed us from that unhappy and unhealthy family system. When I was twenty-one, my dad committed suicide due to his depression and alcoholism. So that life was my normal. People live with crap like that—and even worse—all the time.

"I got lucky. I found a Twelve Step program. It gave me a moral code and some boundaries. It taught me about being a human being and being respectful and kind. It gave me answers to things I didn't have answers for. I was really, really grateful for that—until I got mad and I started to drink again.

"I had a lot of fun though. I remember a friend of mine asked, 'What are you doing? Are you insane?' I said, 'I just want to have fun.' And I did. If I had known how hard it would be to get back into the program, I don't know that I'd have done that. It was very difficult to come back to sobriety the second time. I don't even know how old I was. I'm really glad I'm back in the program and that I have a sense of life again.

"Moving up here four years ago was the best thing I ever did. This is a wonderful place to live. I have a little apartment that's about as big as this circle, and I love it. I just go do my thing. I love that I get to work two days a week at Ace Hardware. Isn't that a hoot? I can survive that way. It's amazing.

"Life is good at sixty. Life is good."

Barb's Story

"It's an honor to be here and hear these stories, these lessons, and hard truths. The stories that I'm hearing take my breath away. The Ojibwa do this. This is common.

"When I came here tonight, Nancy gave me this—a little tobacco—for one of the elders who happens to have a little Anishinabe in her, which is me. I really have a strong connection to Spirit. It's a little overwhelming to have this much Spirit in one place. That's what is happening here tonight.

"One of the life-changing events for me was getting to sit in a circle like this just below La Crosse, Wisconsin. That was part of Nancy's journey awhile back. When I got this tobacco, I was overwhelmed.

"It feels good to be here, and I'm blessed every day that I rise and see the sun. I'm blessed to breathe another breath."

Becca's Story

"I am thinking about the adversity in my life. Six months after my twenty-fifth wedding anniversary and my fiftieth birthday, my husband, Mike, died. He was my best friend, my lover, and coparent of my kids. He was all that and so much more. I didn't know how I was going to survive.

"I was lucky in so many ways. It wasn't much, but I had enough from Mike's death to keep my house, and I had a good job. Friends came and supported me. My daughter was just about to leave home, and my son had left home. But suddenly I was alone, and I really had never wanted to be there.

"I was lucky because I had Al-Anon and had been practicing it for a long time. Al-Anon is for the family and friends of alcoholics. I don't think there's anybody in our culture who doesn't fit that criterion. It's about not interfering in other people's lives and being too controlling. Fortunately, I had many years of practice in all of that. I was also fortunate in having had practice with feeling my feelings. I knew how to cry and how to rage. It was okay to make noises. I was lucky I lived in the middle of my thirteen acres. If my neighbors heard me, at least they never came over and asked, 'Who are you killing in there?'

"Writing helped. I kept a journal. I've always written. All of those things are doors to my higher power, and that's what sustains me. My definition of a higher power changes almost every day, and that's okay. I think that what is out there is so indescribable that it can't be encompassed by any one definition.

"I recently picked up the journal I had written the year after Mike died. I'm making that into a manuscript. What came to me as I was rereading the journal was this fantasy: I'd get in bed and pull the covers over my head. I'd wait until one of my friends would figure out that I was missing. She would come and fix tea and toast for me and provide solace. Then, at some point, she would get sick of me and she would say, 'Go get in the shower and get back into your life.' I never actually did stay in bed because I was afraid if I did that one day, I'd never be able to get out the next day. I never gave myself that gift.

"The whole time I've been working on this journal these past few months, it's been my intention to carry tea, toast, and solace to someone else. That's how I survive adversity."

Thea's Story

"I was in my forties, and I had spent three years in a very interesting form of therapy. At the end of the time, I looked at Bob, my therapist, and said, 'It's about my name.' He said, 'Yeah?' I said, 'It's time for me to change it.' He said, 'Oh, you finally know that.' He wasn't surprised at all.

"My daughter was fourteen at the time. I went home and told her I was going to change my name, and she got very angry. Martha doesn't stay angry very long. That afternoon she went to the library to study. I picked her up three hours later, and she came out with a book that was very thick and said to me, 'If you are going to change your name, I want you to consider all of them.' She called my bluff.

"I have this interesting habit, especially with magazines. I start at the back and work my way to the front. So I started with the z's and worked my way all the way to the front and the a's. The one thing I knew about myself was that I was on the earth to heal and be a healer of other people. When I found the name Althea, I knew that was my name. I read that Althea was the Greek goddess of healing; however, I had a name that had three syllables, and I didn't like it. I decided that I'd nickname myself Thea. Because I was born just before Christmas—which has always been very special to me—I took a middle name of Noel. I kept my family name as my last name. I wasn't willing to give that up.

"Being the person I am—very steeped in spiritual life and especially ritual—I asked my friend Kaia, who is a ritualist, if she would help me create a ceremony. She was very honored, and we began the preparations for my naming ceremony.

"I lived in St. Paul at the time. I was going to meet with Kaia that afternoon, and it was maybe thirty minutes before the meeting. I went into the bookstore at the Women's Press and immediately went to a book that was about Thea. It described the meaning of the name Thea. Some of you might be on to me by now: Thea is the feminine name for God. I saw that in the book and had not been aware of it. So I went to the meeting with Kaia and said, 'I looked at this book at the Women's Press bookstore, and it says that Thea is the feminine name of God. How dare I name myself that? I think the naming ceremony is off.' She looked at me and said, 'Oh, no. You have taken that name, and it's yours.'

"We went through with a fabulous naming ceremony, and I assumed the name. It was, on the one hand, the most natural thing to do, as if it had been my name all of my life. On the other hand, it was very scary.

"So we fast-forward, and I move to Ely. This was fifteen years ago. I met the love of my life and began some spiritual exploration with a teacher from another part of the country. Her name is Barbara, my old name. I told her the naming story and said, 'It's this funny thing that your name is Barbara and you are my spiritual teacher. I went through all of that to name myself a new name . . .'

"She laughed and said, 'From the Egyptian, Barbara is Ba, Ba Ra, the name of God in three ways. So you had to change your name, and it still means God.'

"When I was four years old, I knew there was something about my life that I needed to accomplish. I like to hold it lightly at times but at the same time remind myself—and remind all of you—that we are standing on holy ground. The sacredness that has been brought together in this circle tonight is life giving, it is source connecting, it is spirit filled. I'm so honored to have listened to the stories of each one of you tonight. Nancy has caught on that her job is to collect the stories. I appreciate, Nancy, that you took it on and stayed with it.

"The only thing I'd say beyond what has been said tonight is that I take a stand for every woman's voice being heard. That's the work that I do. I have a difficult time getting some of the segments of the world to understand when I tell them that I'm the True Voice coach. They don't always catch on to what the True Voice means. Each of you tonight has spoken with your True Voice. You have the story in you, which is the story you stand on and your reason for being. For you to be silent is simply wrong. It's not okay. I encourage you to continue to tell your stories. They are beautiful."

Winnie's Story

"It's the diversity of everybody who has come to Ely that makes it such a fascinating and rich place. There are people from all backgrounds. I grew up on a farm in south-central Minnesota. The only people around were farmers. That's all you knew. It was a little community of five hundred people, and everything was centered around the farm. I came to Ely and—my goodness—there's everybody and everything here. It makes it a rich community. That's probably why we like it. How can you beat this?" She gestured to the forest around us. "It's really wonderful.

"I worked with special-needs preschoolers for twenty-three years. I became very close to the families. We think of ourselves as having adversity—everybody has adversity at some point in life—but when we think globally, we realize most of our adversity is pretty negligible.

"I worked with families that had a child who wasn't the child they were expecting. They were expecting a beautiful child. Sometimes that doesn't happen. Sometimes the children have some very significant problems. Then families go through the grieving process. Sometimes they grieve for the whole life of that child because the child they were expecting died, and they were given something else. They have to live with that adversity a long time and to go through many battles. In the '60s when I was working with special-needs children, the battles were with the medical people, the social-work people, the schools, and the list goes on and on as the child gets older and becomes an adult.

"At seventy-five I understand we all have adversity in our lives, but once you really get to know some of these families and can understand them, our adversity seems kind of trivial."

Sandra L.'s Story

"This is my third summer in Ely. I'm here because of the Boy Scouts. In 1987, I became a Cub Scout leader. I've been working with the Boy Scouts ever since. My husband started working for the Charles L. Sommers canoe base after he retired. I thank the Boy Scouts for lots of opportunities in the life of my family. The opportunities changed all our lives. My younger son joined the Peace Corps and went to Bolivia. He laughed when they asked if he could survive by only taking eighty pounds of stuff with him. He had worked at the canoe base in the summer and probably didn't take twenty pounds of gear with him.

"It's odder for me to be in a group of women than to be the only woman in a group of men. I went to school at Mississippi State, and the year I started there were five hundred girls and forty-five hundred boys. It was usual to be the only woman in the class, which is also true with the Boy Scouts.

"I've met and gotten to know a wonderful group of people here in Ely. I didn't come up here until 1999. The reason I didn't come up earlier is I had grown up with mosquitoes. I knew I wanted to come, but the bugs kept me away. Finally my younger son said, 'Oh, Mom.' Finally I came.

"We used to do canoe trips every year until my husband started working for the Boy Scouts. Now we don't do trips anymore." We broke into a laughter of recognition that making a living in the north woods can mean you don't get to enjoy it the way you thought you would before you moved there. "But I still love canoeing."

Janet's Story

"I've been in Ely ten months. I have my good days, and I have my bad days. It's been an adjustment. I left my job, my children, and a lot of friends. The flip side is I'm learning to live life on life's terms. I don't have to have an agenda. I'm learning to let go. I don't have to control all of life's minutia. My relationships with my kids are actually more meaningful. Time is more precious with them.

"It's been a tremendous change. I'm surviving, and I've made some wonderful friends. I'm doing things that I've never done before. I'm becoming less fearful and willing to take more risks.

"I've really screwed up in life sometimes. I'm learning to let go of the past and what cannot be changed, to have compassion for myself, and to stay out of yesterday. I think probably one of the best things I've done is to really get out of yesterday. It took a physical, geographical move to do that. I don't know what to do with the rest of my life, but I know what I don't want to do—so that's good. I want to find and make my own path.

"I had a wonderful day today. It wasn't planned, it just happened, and it was great. I went kayaking and learned some new skills. The one I have to practice is getting out of the kayak so I don't end up in the water.

"Today I feel a sense of peace. I feel a connection with life, and I'm grateful. I need to make a conscious decision daily to be grateful, to not take life for granted, and to stay in the present. Coming here has afforded me the opportunity to think about those kinds of things. In my old life it was go, go, go, go and high pressure, a be-on-my-toes type of life. I had a routine, but I never took the time to look at whether or not the routine was really beneficial. It was comfortable. It took my getting uncomfortable in order to slow down and reassess who I am and where I want to go."

Gloria's Story

Gloria began tearfully. "I'm choked up because I don't know what to say because I get wrapped up in what else has been said. I can't do it." She began to pass the fan on, but didn't. "I'll try this."

"One of the biggest things I'm learning is gratitude. I realize I took a lot of things for granted in my past—family, husband, and things I had. Listening to Janet talking about not living in yesterday is something that I really took to heart too. I'm pretty darn stubborn and headstrong, but that's what got me here.

"A lot of people say it's courageous to move to Ely. When I moved to Ely, it wasn't an act of courage. It was something I had to do. People say, 'Ely is paradise,' and in a lot of ways, it is. Ely has made life fuller for me. It's not that I didn't have a full life before, because I did. It's good here too. It's just different.

"I made choices that I'm not too proud of, but I also made choices that I am proud of.

"I had a period of six months when six people died. Two of them were my grandmothers, who I was very close to. That period was probably the biggest factor that made me look at what was happening in my life. I said, 'You know, this life is not quite working. I need to change.'

"I have a great ex-husband who gave me the space I needed. He knew me well enough to know there was no choice. I had to do what I had to do. He was supportive. In doing that, though, we lost each other." She became tearful again. "He is still there and still my friend, so I'm very grateful. I'm not like some of my friends whose husbands have died. Those women didn't have a choice. I had a choice.

"I don't regret coming here. I've done some pretty incredible things that I never thought I'd do. Do I second-guess myself? All the time.

"I have a dream place right now. It's what I dreamed about and fought so hard for. But I sit there alone and think, 'Let's see . . . my family is not here, my husband is not here, I'm here by myself.' I got this place, and I'm on my own. A lot of my friends say, 'You go, girl! You did it!' But I'm in a place right now where I'm questioning that. I wonder, 'Why was I so damn pigheaded, and why did I have to do it my way? This way—was this the only way?'

"I know this will pass because when I'm out swimming, or when I wake up in the middle of the night and I look out at the stars, or when I'm in my kayak then it's right. I find my peace. I just have to find the peace that gives me permission to be happy and to say, 'You know, you do deserve this' because a lot of times I don't think I do. Most of the time I don't think I do. That's what I'm working on. I feel very gifted and grateful for being here in this moment. This is frickin' paradise. But it cost me a lot to get here.

"I'm fifty-two, and every time I hit one of those ten-year markers, I always seem to have to reinvent myself. For two years, I've been figuring out how I'm reinventing myself. I quit my job three years ago here in Ely and have been struggling as to where to go next. I work, but I do a lot of things. I'm not proud. If anyone has a job from cleaning to cooking, I will do it. That kind of spirit is what keeps me here and keeps food on my table, even though sometimes I wonder if food is going to be on the table or not. Somehow things just seem to work out. I worry about how I'm going to pay a bill—and it all works out. I step back and ask myself, 'So why do you keep worrying?'

"Those are the things I have to keep reminding myself about, the gratefulness. I don't have to worry because things are going to work out."

Patti Jo's Story

"I've unplugged from media and technology, and I take each day as it comes along my path. I have a job Monday through Friday. I'm a nanny in the Duluth area for a young professional couple, both doctors. I nanny for a nine-month-old bright and beautiful boy. I've been working with this family as a personal assistant for two years. Even before conception, I had been a part of this family's life.

"Each day I wake, I'm grateful for breathing the air and for the sparkles on the lake. I have an apartment on Park Point in Duluth and an apartment here in Ely. Ely is my place to come for grounding, balance, to let it all go, rejuvenation, and spirituality. I do a lot of reading and meditation. The people I've met over the last five years or so in Ely have been so awesome.

"I don't have any grandchildren. I have a daughter who is twenty-eight and a son who is twenty-four. I'm finding in my job as a nanny that compassion and working from the heart are really strong in my life right now. I find everything in life has been a stepping-stone that brought me to this. I watch things now almost as if someone is illustrating a movie for me of what to expect or what to think about. As I think and wonder spiritually about everything, I find life illustrating some of these wonders for me.

"This child I nanny, I was told, may have developmental issues. It creates a fluttering in my heart now to think about him. He is so sweet. Being doctors, his parents are researching, analyzing, and looking far into the future. I prefer to live in the moment. That little baby is such a beautiful light and energy. I feel this tremendous heart love and spiritual connection to him.

"My daughter came to school up here and stayed for four years because she loved Ely so much. Now she has one more year at Stevens Point, Wisconsin, in hydrogeology. She works for the Forest Service and is out in Wyoming this summer riding horses in the backcountry. I'm enjoying her. She is remaining single. I told my children to remain single through their twenties, if possible, because the twenties are so much fun. Enjoy your life and get your feet under you. That's precisely what she is doing.

"My son grew up in Duluth and was sailing young. He announced, 'Don't waste money on school, Mom. I know exactly what I want to be. It will probably have something to do with aerodynamics or flying or something like that.' Right now he is a tall-ship sailor and has been sailing the West Coast on a 1794 sailing ship. How perfect this is for him. I'm so happy, and I smile from ear to ear when I think of him. As a child he was fearless. I could tell he was going to take on some type of adventurous life, and that's precisely what he's doing. He is looking forward to getting on a transatlantic tall ship as crew, and he talks of European tall ships and mariner school.

"Spiritually, I've just completed two years at St. Scholastica in its Shalom Spiritual Direction program. It's a two-year program, and I'm in the second class that's graduated. I enrolled because I wanted to fulfill my own spiritual growth and interests. The spiritual-direction certificate at the end is a great benefit. I'm happy to perhaps help others as a spiritual companion in their life. It's a wonderful program. We were led to understanding and provided with books to read. I wrote a lot of reflection papers.

"I was raised Lutheran, but in the '80s I found myself gravitating more and more to Unitarian. In Duluth we have the Interfaith Church. I've gone there a few times. I just find myself more interested in the Oneness of all. I don't even like to bring up the word 'religion' because to me it's all Oneness. I'm relishing that with studies I've had over the last twenty years. My own path has provided many perfect lessons.

"I sea kayaked on Lake Superior. I've led groups, guided, and instructed. I had the best day today instructing someone here in this group. It was just a lovely, peaceful, tranquil day."

At the end of the Gathering, with gratitude in my heart, I looked around at the amazing women who were deep in conversation with each other. I was brimming with anticipation regarding what would unfold during the final paddle. I carefully wrapped the aspiration sticks they had created during the closing ritual in a silk scarf. I took the sticks home. Then they traveled with us to our starting point in St. Louis, where they were released into the river on the first day.

13

KNOCKOUT HAIR

We often hear it said, "You'll laugh about this later." When possible, I like to laugh about personal tragedies sooner rather than later. Enjoy!

Round One—Gray Is Not Okay
My hair is well past my shoulders. I've embraced the gray, but they say,
"It makes you look old."
I'm not ready for that! I want to be irresistible.
"You can change it easily."
Why's everybody so interested in my hair? Heck, it's none of their business. But what if they're right?
"It would be fun. It's only hair."
Why not? It will wash out—it's temporary. It would be different, and it could be fun . . . Let's do it.
Back to the red I miss!

Round Two—The Color
We're on a road trip. My head sticks out of a garbage bag in a motel. Friends smear blackish goop in my hair. They're so excited. My hair is so long I need two boxes of color.
What was I thinking? I don't want to maintain this . . .
"It's okay. It'll wash out."
They're sure having fun, but I'm not sure I am. What's wrong with this picture?
"Oh, just enjoy it."
What am I doing?
"It'll wash out."
Holy crap! That's not what I expected. Can I wash it out now? Years of growth . . .
"You'll get used to it."
Oh, God, I hope so. I look ten years younger? It feels phony. What's that you said?
"You're a knockout."

Round Three—The Transition
My husband loves it.
Really?
Others love it.
Maybe it's worth the bother?
There are those roots again!
Attention and praise. Is that my ego inflating? "What did you do?" she accuses.
She caught me; I'm a fraud. It cuts to the core.
But everybody likes it.
Why did I do this? I had such beautiful hair.
Why's everybody so invested in my hair? Why do I care what they think?
Those damn roots grow like dandelions!
I have to get it out . . .
It's not only hair!

Round Four—It's Got To Go!
It's not fading. The products don't work.
"Try vinegar."
It's not coming out. The roots are neon.
"Try Dawn dish soap."
It's still not fading. I'm so done. Maybe I should just keep coloring it . . .
No! It's got to go.
What's that? You can color hair any color but gray? How do they do it in the movies?
What? It has to be stripped? What does that mean? What happened to temporary?
I've been duped.

Round Five—The Solution
What's that?
"We're going to the beauty shop."
Yes! They can fix this!
We walk in.
The colors . . . Did we fall into a vat of spumoni? The fumes and floor pattern are dizzying. Posters of women with beautiful hair cover the walls. Hustling and bustling—that must be good.
"Hey!" the beauticians say. The names on their smocks are Thelma and Runs with Scissors.
I relax. I'm getting my hair back. Country music plays. Ladies sit under dryers, getting cuts and styles. Are Thelma and Runs with Scissors stretched too thin? They're professionals. I'm fine.
My hair is inspected. *"What is it you want? Go back to gray? Are you sure?"*

I thought I was. Yes, I am! No more roots!
Eyebrows raise; heads tilt.
Am I in the best place for this? They're professionals . . . right?
I'm in the chair. My friend leaves. The cape is cinched tightly around my neck. The room spins.
Where did my friend go?
"It'll be just fine . . . "
I can't wait to get back to my natural color.

Round Six—The Process

More thick goop that stinks gets smeared on my head. Runs with Scissors looks confident. There's a bag on my head. I'm under the dryer. My eyes water. My nose hairs curl. Everybody shares stories—or wait—that's gossip. I've been under here a long time. I'm having trouble breathing. An industrial fan is turned on me. Air is good. I'm woozy, and the floor is moving. Should I say something? They're cutting, perming, rolling, and styling. I'm about to lose consciousness.

My friend returns. Our eyes connect. Her eyes widen; her eyebrows go up. Did I see *"Oh, my!"* in her expression? No, everything's fine. They're professionals.

My friend asks, *"Are you done?"* and throws me a look. What did that mean? She leaves again. She wouldn't leave if it was bad, right?

Please bring me some fresh air.

Is that smoke coming out from under the hair dryer?

My throat burns. Maybe I'm invisible. Thelma and Runs with Scissors throw each other a look. Silent words blare between them: *"Oh, my God, we've got to get that off."* It can't be that bad. They understood what I wanted, right? They're professionals!

I'm rushed like I'm in an ambulance to the back room rinsing station. Was it too risky to walk into a beauty shop where I'll never be a return customer? Was the Runs with Scissors name tag a clue I should have paid attention to?

Wait . . . They're professionals.

It's only hair. It's only hair. It's only hair.

Round Seven—The Knockout

Another hair inspection. Silent words ricochet off the walls: *"Holy shit. What are we going to do now?"* Backs turned. Whispering.
Do they have a clue? How bad could it be?
They have a plan. I'm fine. Back in the chair.
Why isn't she letting me see the mirror?
Is the comb stuck?
My hair grows bigger as she dries it. Her fingers are stuck; the strands

won't separate. She tugs her fingers until the hair surrenders them.
Was that a crunch?
Let me see it.
She steps away. I spin around to the mirror. My hair knocks bottles off
the counter.
What bizarre color is that? Paste? It's a noncolor.
I reach up. My hair is bristly. It's a joke; this isn't real.
"I'm ready for Halloween. Just give me a witch's hat," I mumble.
She hears me. *"Oh, we're not done yet."*
They're not done yet?
Escape while you can—escape.
Wait. She's a professional. Maybe it's not that bad . . .

Round Eight—A Little Damage?

I'm in the twilight zone. I search the mirror for a caution sign. "Objects
in the mirror are not as bizarre as they appear." It must be there. Pictures
of glamorous women stare back at me. Did I just see their eyebrows go
up? One has a bouffant. How old are these pictures?
"The ends are a little damaged. They need to come off," she says.
Three inches fall to the floor. Is that what you call ends? I don't see her
license hanging on the wall, but she has a plan.

Round Nine—The Fix

Ladders come out. The solution hides in the topmost cupboard. How old
is that stuff? Crusty colored tubs are dug through. A combination is dis-
cussed and mixed.
"This'll match your natural color."
Which natural color?
The back and front of my hair are different colors. Speak up, Nancy!
It's too late.
They goop it on thick. It's baby-poop gray.
My hair is as dry as the Sahara desert and sucks up the goop like a dehy-
drated camel at an oasis. They run out. Will the new batch match? Does
it matter at this point? Why do I trust these people? It's gone too far. I
don't have a choice.
It's only hair. It's only hair. It's only hair.
Back under the dryer. Minutes feel like hours. I feel invisible. Am I an
experiment? Have they forgotten me again? Her head pops up. Careful,
you'll get whiplash. She darts over. I'm finally out from under that heat.
We sprint to the back room for the rinse. The beauticians convene to
inspect my hair. Shoulders shrug.
"It's not red anymore," they say.
Getting the red out is what I had asked for.

Round Ten—The Escape

Back in the chair . . .

That's my natural color? Do they need new prescriptions for their glasses? They're not wearing glasses. It won't comb. Ouch, my neck is only so strong, lady! After oceans of conditioner, she wrestles the comb through. Blow dry it? I don't think so. I've got to get out of here. My friend returns. I see a look of shock and then sadness.

"You'll love this," the professional says. *"It matches your natural color."*

There's nothing natural about this color that I can identify. I need to escape before they have another solution.

I pay her.

What am I doing? Posting bail?

I thank her.

Why in creation am I thanking her?

"Be sure to condition it. It's a little dry."

A little dry?

I'm out the door.

Thank God for fresh air.

Round Eleven—Desperate Measures

I need chocolate.

I touch my hair and it crunches like someone stepping on a bag of potato chips. Pieces lie in my lap. It's breaking off.

I'm a fire hazard.

My friend warns, *"Don't do anything rash. Wait until your daughter gets here."*

I'm way past rash.

Another piece lands in my lap. Years of growth. They certainly took care of the roots. It's all gonna have to come off.

I need a hat!

What was I thinking?

My daughter arrives. She recoils. *"It's wiry. It's worse than bad Barbie doll hair."*

We get scissors.

Give me chocolate!

With each cut, a crunching sound echoes through my head. Three inches hits a sheet laid out on the motel room floor. Paste-colored tumbleweeds of my hair blow across the parking lot. I need a color cover-up to be seen in public.

"It's a true wash-out rinse, right?" I had asked the saleslady and then thought, "Why does that matter now?"

"It has to be put it in each time I wash my hair?" Fine. I won't wash it. Why bother? The color makes my hair stiff. I could sell strands for hinge springs.

I share how distraught I am with a traveling companion.
"It's only hair," she says.
It's—only—hair?
"It's only hair," she says again.
I might have to slug her if she repeats those words again. It's not only hair; it's my self-esteem. Oh, man. That's so shallow . . . Maybe if it's shorter, it'll be okay . . .
Another three inches hits the floor.
What was I thinking?
Shorter?
Another two inches hits the floor.
No, you can't take my scissors away! I need them!
Where's the chocolate?

Round Twelve—Surrender

There's pain in my husband's eyes. He strokes my hair. Let me help pull those porcupine quills out of your hand, honey, I want to say.
"It'll be fine," he assures.
This started with me listening to them. What do they know?
Another two inches hits the floor.
Years of growth, gone.
I said take the color out. Three hours later they had—all of it. I got a special that day: buy one, get three free.
They removed the color, softness, life, and luster. It's going to take years to correct this.
Maybe if it's shorter?
Another two inches hits the floor.
My hair is brittle. I can't afford the vats of conditioner required to comb it. It's ALL got to go. I can't cut it myself anymore—but go to a beauty shop again?
I need more chocolate.
My friend comes along with a promise not to abandon me this time. She thought they were professionals.
Three more inches hits the floor, making the total loss eighteen. At best, my hair is a half-inch long. I look like my brothers.
At last. Yea! There's my natural color.
"Soon I'll see the curl again," I said.
"I wouldn't count on it," this professional says. *"Damaged follicles."*
What? That's not possible!
Oh, great. I have two cowlicks.
"It's cute," they say.

Why should I believe them?

It doesn't matter. I didn't speak my truth: It's not only hair. My hair is part of the identity I orchestrate to present to the world about who I am; yet I gave it away so easily.

I rub my fuzzy head, wrap a scarf around my neck where my hair once kept me warm, and hope this lesson needs to come around only once.

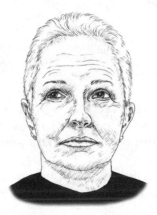

Round Thirteen—It Sure Grows Slowly . . .

14

WHO ARE YOU

AND WHAT DID YOU DO WITH MY FACE?

I recognize her when she looks back at me quizzically. I see her every day, sometimes several times a day. I trust this trickster and rely on her information to start my day, for a quick security check later on, and for that last validation before retiring for the evening. She keeps things familiar—yet inconsistent. Has something changed again? Is it the light? The angles? The background colors? How could it have changed so quickly? Did I overlook important developments, fine details? Did I focus only on what I wanted to see? Her information must be flawed . . .

Who are you and what have you done with my face?

I never trusted photographs. They rarely match the image of myself I cling to. In photographs I'm heavier, or my hair is out of control or a different color, or my legs are scrawny. There is always a detail that's incorrect. In recent photographs, my eyebrows appear to be in the same place, yet below them sacks gently fold down over my eyes. What is up with that? When did these jowls form? My lips turn down at the edges. When did that happen? Do I always look sad or angry now? Who is the old lady in the picture? She's not me—inside or out.

Wearing glasses doesn't help, but wearing them has become a constant. I remove them for photographs—when I remember. It no longer changes the outcome: I'm still the old lady in the picture. Not wearing my glasses, I run the risk of making my image worse. My eyes seem to disappear in the photo. It was easier when I could blame the glasses.

The trickster doesn't show me these things like photographs do. The trickster tells me I am ten years younger than the photographs. At least, she used to.

The trickster and I have done a face plant right into each other. Wait . . . that explains it. It's an oily smudge that has caused the altered image. I look—there's no smudge. I look closer—the image only gets worse. Those tiny lines are road maps to undetermined destinations. I could store nuts in those pores. What have I been eating that makes those hairs on my chin grow a half inch overnight? The trickster hides those hairs when I try to pluck them. I certainly can't trust her to tell me if hair starts growing in my ears.

The lighting has to be just right to get the desired information—one candle in the far corner creates the best results. I twist my head, contort my neck and body, hoping the information changes in my favor. I suck it in, prop it up, twist just so, look only out of the corner of my eye, but the sought-after result is attained less and less often.

She betrays me daily! My reality is shaken. Am I really one of *them*? Am I really one of the old ones now? I don't consider myself old. If I am old, what does that mean? Do I need to dress differently? Behave differently? Wear my hair in a bun? I refuse!

I mourn my friend. My confidante lost her magical transformative power. Our relationship has changed forever.

My mirror—the trickster—got real.

Who are you and what have you done with my face?
And why does it bother me . . . so much?

15

HUNTING FOR ALLIGATORS

Before leaving Louisiana, Kitty, Sara Jo, Heidi, Doug, Kathy, Pat, and I enjoyed a wilderness paddle in the Lac des Allemands Bayou. We hoped to see more nature than we had on Bayou Lafourche.

We wanted to see alligators.

Leonard, who had paddled with us on Bayou Lafourche coming into Thibodaux, would be our guide. While asking about paddling on Bayou Lafourche, I had been referred to Leonard and met with him during my reconnaissance trip. He guides canoeing trips in the Thibodaux area. He was extremely helpful in providing necessary planning information. He arrived at Joyce and Frank's, where Pat and Dave joined us. Leonard and Doug drove in his truck, Pat and Dave followed in their truck, and Kitty, Kathy, Sara Jo, Heidi, and I followed in the van. I took advantage of the time in the van to tape my broken toenail with pink duct tape. A Band-Aid wouldn't stay secure with my feet going in and out of the water. It looked like there was a hot-pink splint on my big toe.

We drove to Edwina's Cookin' Cajun restaurant, which is also the site of Zam's Swamp Tours, in Kreamer, Louisiana. Leonard arranged for us to use their docks to put in the water. The sky was clear with a slight breeze; temperatures were in the low seventies.

Kitty, Sara Jo, Heidi, and I were in kayaks; Doug and Kathy were in one canoe and Leonard and Pat in another canoe. Dave waited onshore. With Leonard in the lead, we paddled Lac des Allemands Bayou. The trees hung low over the edges of the water with Spanish moss that draped from every tree branch waving in the breeze. Cypress knees grew out of the water at the base of the trees, reaching for the dangling moss. Rich green vegetation grew in the water alongshore.

After a half mile the bayou dumped into Lac des Allemands and we turned left, skirting the south shore for a third of a mile. It was an adventure for Leonard, who hadn't found the bayou that was our destination in two previous attempts. Paddling across the lake, we searched for the mouth of the bayou. At the west end of the lake we found the opening and turned in. Our hunt for alligators began in earnest.

Not far down the bayou we saw a six-foot alligator at the edge. Its nose, a thin strip of its snout, its eyes, and a section of its back were above the surface. It floated motionless, watching us for a long time before slowly submerging. Kitty was unnerved. "It hadn't occurred to me that we were paddling over alligators this whole time," she said. "That's just spooky."

We paddled on, hearing and spotting many small black birds in the air and seeing trees that we could not identify. After three quarters of a mile we stopped for lunch, gathering our boats together on the edge of the bayou. Floating, we ate crackers, meat, cheese, and Famous Amos cookies. Doug took the opportunity to lie back in the canoe and put his feet up. The sun beating down on us felt good but became too warm.

After lunch we headed back. We saw a smaller alligator briefly. It submerged when we approached. Paddling back across the lake, Doug and Kathy took the lead. A strong headwind came up, creating substantial waves.

On the way back down Lac des Allemands Bayou we took our time, hoping for another alligator sighting. As I paddled under an enormous cypress, I looked up into the tree's maze of branches where Spanish moss hung in bunches. The moss had alternating thin, curved leaves, similar to short pine needles, that grew in a chain-like fashion and draped down in soft clumps as much as five feet long. Their pale-gray and silver lacy appearance had a greenish hue. Spanish moss, also known as "air plant," absorbs nutrients and water from the air and rain. Looking up through the tree, I was enjoying the colors of the moss against the greens of the tree and the bright blue sky, but then I remembered Spanish moss was home to snakes and spiders and that we had been warned that snakes fall out of the trees. I quickly paddled on.

We arrived back at Zam's with our alligator count at a disappointing two.

"We probably didn't see many because the weather has been so cool," Leonard said. "The alligators move down in the mud when it gets cool." For us Minnesotans, the weather didn't feel cool. Alligators or not, we had enjoyed a peaceful paddle in a spectacular area.

We went into the restaurant for an ice cold drink before lashing the boats to the vehicles. The restaurant had a fenced-in patio out back that nestled against water thick with vegetation and home to boisterous ducks. In a back room were cages with snakes—two large pythons. One was an albino; it was white with yellow spots and red eyes. Doug joked that the snakes and ducks might be on tomorrow's menu.

We all climbed into our respective vehicles, drove back to Thibodaux, and stopped at the Carrot Patch for smoothies. Soaking in the warm afternoon sun drinking our smoothies, we thanked Leonard for a great taste of Louisiana.

Epilogue

"Each life becomes a part of the landscape. It becomes someone's landmark." – Douglas Wood, *The Things Trees Know*

Majestic landscapes don't rely solely on large, impressive subjects, like a mountain or a river, to captivate us. They rely on rocks, a smattering of shrubs, a clump of grass, or a single leaf drifting past to create inspiration. Each person I encountered on this journey has become part of my internal landscape. They are the rocks, shrubs, grass, and drifting leaves. Even the briefest encounters became significant components of the greater landscape. My belief that we are all extraordinary was reinforced.

Most of the time we think we understand our roles in life; however, the roles we play create a web of silky, sticky strands that are woven into every area of our lives. I become aware of the web when something— an event or person—pulls on one of the strands, and I find my world shaking. How the shaking is perceived depends on where I stand, my focus, my wants, my previous experiences. The pull may be experienced as joy and validation. It may be experienced as pain and elicit the need to reassess my values, beliefs, and priorities. The inspirational women's stories I heard on this journey are examples of those strands being tugged, broken, and rewoven.

What had the most impact on me was looking into the eyes of so many strong, resilient women who found ways to honor, trust, and respect themselves—Grandmothers who own their pasts in ways that increase their capacity for accepting our humanness, Grandmothers whose hearts yearn for healing for all.

The women were mirrors. I saw a piece of myself in each of them. They were teachers with life-giving gifts. I am particularly grateful for those who pushed my buttons and made me uncomfortable enough to search my soul and own both the dark and light sides of myself. I am grateful for the women who portrayed some of the things I already knew in my heart, but that hadn't taken hold in my everyday consciousness: that we are adaptive beings, that what we do in stressful situations shows us who we are, that we are capable of more than we think, and that our resources—family, friends, and faith—give us strength.

We think we know what our dreams and life are about, but life defies our beliefs and unfolds like a mystery. Developing a dream happens within the arena of relationships—an arena where we learn about our inner selves, our boundaries, values, and truths; an arena where we face conflict with grace and awkwardness and where we have the opportunity to rise above our limitations.

During this adventure I stepped into the Grandmother role, stepped back out, observed it, stepped back in, stepped back out, and observed it—repeatedly. This is how transformation works. I had glimpses of clarity. Owning the Grandmother role brought fear of restructuring my life, of losing my identity. In reality this last part of the journey was about losing the inaccurate identity I'd clung to. It was time to get over myself and acknowledge that I was the woman I had been striving to become. This was my "Grandmother Journey."

I believe dreams are divinely inspired. Traveling the river, we knew we were being watched over by Spirit. There were many examples, such as Kee guiding us the entire way, and other more practical events. One such event happened while Kitty and I drove home. A loud knock came from the engine. I recognized the sound and knew we were in trouble. The check-engine light came on, and the hand on the oil gauge was bouncing. We were dangerously low on oil. Only two blocks later we came to a Quick Lube. Cory, the mechanic, got us right in and drained less than a cup of oil from the pan. With eyebrows raised he said, "You were seconds away from needing a new engine." I knew that and thanked Spirit for helping me hear the noise and for the convenient Quick Lube.

Dreams, particularly transformative ones, take a toll on the body. For most of the first three months after I returned home I was sick with high fevers. I had planned to lie low while transitioning back—but not that low. After being in nature and being physical every day, it was challenging to spend my day sitting or sleeping. In retrospect, I believe I was burning off toxins from the river, and my body was forcing me to catch up on needed rest.

Loss was a recurring theme on this section of the journey, and many people shared stories of the death of loved ones: husbands, children, siblings. Death is not a stranger in my life, but you are never really ready when it visits. My sister, Diane, died suddenly two weeks after I was home. She was the second youngest of my seven siblings. I was devastated.

Driving to the hospital after the call, I searched my mind for regrets or unfinished business I had with her. I found peace and cried with relief. We had not been close the past few years, but I knew that she knew I loved her dearly. I wondered if there were others in my life for whom I would have a different answer. Discovering the answer to that question would have to wait.

My life at home stopped for a few weeks while I stayed in the Twin Cities and helped my nephews, Jason and Jonathan, get Diane's affairs in order. My brothers, their wives—our entire family—demonstrated our family's strong connection by being there for each other every step of the way. I was proud to be a member of the Grout family and sensed Dad and Mom smiling down on us.

The hole Diane left in my heart was huge. Her death created a stopping point in my life. I stopped to reflect on what and who was important to me. I made a commitment to myself to slow down so I would have time to interact more with and show my appreciation of the people in my life.

Then a dear friend who had struggled with severe depression for more than thirty years attempted suicide. Others close to her and I became focused on helping her put the broken pieces of her spirit back together. She came out of it fighting for herself unlike she ever had. It seemed a piece of her did die—the part of her that resisted inner healing and believed she had no value. She let go of old beliefs that she didn't have a family that cared about her. She had family—they just weren't blood relatives. She learned that she could lean on her chosen family and that there were no hidden agendas. She has a lot of work to do to heal fully, but she approaches it with hope and enthusiasm.

Death knocked on my door again five months after I returned home. A close friend's husband committed suicide. It's nearly more than I can bear when the people I love are in so much pain. Being there for them never seems like enough. Knowing that time is the only remedy is a blessing and a curse.

Six months after returning home, my sweet, funny Uncle Dick died. He was ninety-four and ready to go. He reminded me of my dad, who had died sixteen years earlier. Uncle Dick had a rich, full life and deeply missed his cherished wife, Louise, who had died six years before. His passing was painful for those left behind, yet a blessing for him. He was the last of the elders on my father's side of the family. His passing marked the end of an era.

These moments of life and death become stopping points providing time for necessary reflection. Then trivial things wiggle their way back into my consciousness, like the issue with my hair. Each time I looked in the mirror my hair needled at me, and I thought, "Let it go. It is so small and insignificant."

But then there would be that reflection in the mirror again.

On the drive home from Louisiana, Kitty and I stopped in St. Louis for dinner with Becky and Kit. Becky touched my hair and with a look of disgust on her face said laughing, "That's one of the nastiest things I have ever touched."

"I'm afraid it's all going to have to go," I said.

"I'm telling you, shave your head like Sinead O'Connor," Becky said, laughing.

"I can't go there," I said, laughing along with her. "But there will be a funny short story that'll come out of this."

The question of what to do with my hair loomed for longer than two months after I returned home. I waited impatiently for it to grow so I could cut the damaged ends off without looking like Sinead O'Connor. Friends tried to console me. "It's an opportunity to see yourself from a new perspective," one said. I certainly was doing that already. "Our hair represents our thoughts," I was told by another friend. My hair had become a symbol of the shift in my self-identity. I had come home feeling and looking different. It would take time to unravel what the new feeling was that I held about myself. It took another trip to the beauty shop to begin embracing the different look.

Kitty accompanied me to the beauty shop where all the damaged hair was cut off, leaving it less than a half-inch long. When I look in the mirror, the image reminds me I am not the woman who started this journey down the river. The new image has been overwhelming, sad, adventurous, daring, unsettling—and a relief. I've been released from the image I was so attached to and have a new-found freedom from what others think.

I was recently asked what I would have done differently if I had the journey to do over again. I pondered that question for some time and realized the only things I'd change would be trusting my inner knowing faster and speaking my truth faster. That said, I did the journey the best that I could, the way it was meant to be. It took the experiences of the trip to transform the person I was into a person who can consider there are different ways of doing things.

What's Next?

I find myself in the midst of a paradox. I have no idea what is next, but I am a heartbeat away from knowing.

I feel called to model the Grandmother's Journey—walking in her footsteps; and I feel daunted by the task. I hang judgments on it, and I make up stories in my head that create turmoil and jubilation. I dance between acceptance and doubt. Am I really up for this? When it comes down to it, I still have more to learn about what it means to model the Grandmother's Journey. Learning, growing, and gaining wisdom won't stop until I die.

I have come to understand that the Grandmother celebrates an intimate connection to intuition. My intuition has developed into a powerful tool. I've used it to aid others in finding their direction, peace, and healing. I used it often throughout the journey down the river, and I quietly own it without boasting. It's not really something to boast about; we all have an intuition we can lean into. Mine is based in my spirituality, so leaning into it is like leaning into Spirit. Living from my intuition is far from linear and not where the general population is most comfortable. I admit at times during this journey I lost sight of my intuition's validity under the barrage of questions, distractions, and other people's strong opinions.

Since my return home, the question people ask most often is "What is next?" They mean which river do I plan to paddle next. I tell them I want to paint, write, garden, and play with my grandson. There doesn't need to be another river for me. All I need to do is live my life the best that I can, true to what I believe. The journey downriver has opened untold doors creating unknown opportunities. I anticipate those opportunities showing themselves as I move forward. And as I move forward, I will remember the advice of Joyce from Thibodaux:

"Live it crazy. Crazy like you want."

photo by Heidi Favet

PICTURES FROM THE RIVER

The Mississippi River starts at Itasca Lake.
It is narrow and intimate there.

We paddled canoes the first week.

Well-behaved women rarely make history.

Bumper sticker on Nancy's deck bag.

We had spirit- and music- filled send offs.

The first Gathering was held at
Cass Lake Reservation in Minnesota, 2004.

We passed through 24 of the 27 Locks.

2007

2007

2007 & 2011

We were packed tight.

2004

2004, 2007, 2011

2011

Fashions ranged from thick mud to leopard boots to scarves for bug and sun protection to the feathers we saw in New Orleans.

2011

Cis—Scarf cover-up.

2011

New Orleans Bird Costume.

Sometimes we had to wade due to shallow water.

2004

We clowned around often.

Sara Jo pretended to eat clams left by an otter.

2007

2007

Nancy stopped traffic.

2007

2011

Buoys were our constant Companions.

St. Louis Arch

2007

2004, 2007, 2011

Sandy beaches offered serene moments.

Heidi, 2011

2004

We enjoyed the strength we acquired.

2007

2007

2004

Car support greetings included Naomi bringing her fresh-picked strawberries and Karen, Cis, Pat, and Gwyn doing jumping jacks.

2004

2007

2011

We paddled, danced, and
splashed in the rain.

Kitty - 2011

2004

Technology evolved from
land lines and walkie talkies
to cell phones, laptop computers, and GPS locators.

2011

Dolphin   2011

2011

I often carried my
camera in my mouth to
be ready for surprise photo opportunities.

INVITE
NANCY SCHEIBE
TO YOUR AREA

Learn how ordinary
people can do
extraordinary things.

Hear the wisdom of the
women she met.

Enjoy a first-hand
account of her
adventures.

Nancy's presentations are down-to-earth, heart-warming, and honest. Her sense of humor is refreshing, and she is gifted at tailoring the subject matter to the audience.

To contact Nancy or learn more about her events and appearances go to:

www.NancyScheibe.com

To purchase a copy of this book or of
Water Women Wisdom, Voices from the Upper Mississippi
or *Ripples of Wisdom, A Journey Through Mud and Truth*
go to the Ripples Of Wisdom web site:

www.RipplesOfWisdom.com